D1807264

Valeria Lingua • Verena Balz
Editors

Shaping Regional Futures

Designing and Visioning in Governance Rescaling

 Springer

Editors
Valeria Lingua
Department of Architecture (DIDA)
Regional Design Lab
University of Florence
Florence, Italy

Verena Balz
Department of Urbanism
Delft University of Technology
Delft, Zuid-Holland, The Netherlands

ISBN 978-3-030-23572-7   ISBN 978-3-030-23573-4   (eBook)
https://doi.org/10.1007/978-3-030-23573-4

© Springer Nature Switzerland AG 2020
This work is subject to copyright. All rights are reserved by the Publisher, whether the whole or part of the material is concerned, specifically the rights of translation, reprinting, reuse of illustrations, recitation, broadcasting, reproduction on microfilms or in any other physical way, and transmission or information storage and retrieval, electronic adaptation, computer software, or by similar or dissimilar methodology now known or hereafter developed.
The use of general descriptive names, registered names, trademarks, service marks, etc. in this publication does not imply, even in the absence of a specific statement, that such names are exempt from the relevant protective laws and regulations and therefore free for general use.
The publisher, the authors and the editors are safe to assume that the advice and information in this book are believed to be true and accurate at the date of publication. Neither the publisher nor the authors or the editors give a warranty, expressed or implied, with respect to the material contained herein or for any errors or omissions that may have been made. The publisher remains neutral with regard to jurisdictional claims in published maps and institutional affiliations.

This Springer imprint is published by the registered company Springer Nature Switzerland AG
The registered company address is: Gewerbestrasse 11, 6330 Cham, Switzerland

Contents

Part III Envisioning Metropolitan Futures

Introduction

Verena Balz and Valeria Lingua

Abstract

The book *Shaping Regional Futures: Designing and Visioning in Governance Rescaling* discusses the roles of regional designing and visioning in the formation of regional territorial governance. It aims to increase our understanding of (1) how the recognition of spatial dynamics and the imagination of spatial futures inform and are informed by planning frameworks and (2) how such design processes influence cooperation and collaboration on planning in metropolitan regions. The book gathers theoretical reflections on these topics and illustrates them through practical experiences in several European countries. The book appeals to a community of readers with an interest in experimental strategic spatial planning. It is innovative in the way it associates this interest with knowledge from the design field.

Keywords

Strategic spatial planning • Governance • Regional design • Visioning

1.1 Contextual Remarks: The Multiple Objectives of Strategic Spatial Planning

Since the 1980s, planning approaches in European regions have shifted as a result of the influence of increasing spatial patterns of interaction and movement on regional levels of scale, and alongside 'a relative decline of the role of the state, a growing involvement of nongovernmental actors in a range of state functions, the emergence of new forms of multi-agency partnerships and more flexible forms of networking at various spatial scales' (Davoudi 2008, p. 63). Subsequent approaches, often called 'strategic spatial planning', focused on regional and supra-regional spatial development. They switched the attention from the planning of predefined, contained territories to the planning of spatial networks, stretching across multiple and multi-scalar administrative boundaries. Planning that relied on generally applicable regulation and authoritative planning power was challenged by planning that relied on an understanding of the specificities of regions, political consent for their desirable futures, and the dedication of actors to those visions (Albrechts 2004). New decision-making approaches emerged that typically involved coalitions of governments at multiple levels as well as the market and civil actors (Hooghe and Marks 2003; Rhodes 1996). In an 'institutional void' (Hajer 2003, p. 175)—almost absent of statutory regional planning guidance —collaboration sought to generate agreement on strategic planning interventions and to operationalize them by pooling institutional capacities (Faludi 2012). Collaboration in governance arrangements also aimed to legitimize planning. The inclusion of many figures in decision-making—'good governance'—became a normative goal of planning in itself (Mayntz 2004).

Strategic spatial planning is commonly described as a planning approach that pays more attention to the specificities of the built environment than statutory planning does (Albrechts et al. 2003; Allmendinger and Haughton 2010; Healey 2006;

V. Balz (✉)
Department of Urbanism, Delft University of Technology, Delft, The Netherlands
e-mail: v.e.balz@tudelft.nl

V. Lingua
Regional Design Lab, Department of Architecture, University of Florence, Florence, Italy
e-mail: valeria.lingua@unifi.it

© Springer Nature Switzerland AG 2020
V. Lingua and V. Balz (eds.), *Shaping Regional Futures*,
https://doi.org/10.1007/978-3-030-23573-4_1

Nadin 2007; Schön 2005). Its objective, 'to articulate a more coherent spatial logic for land use regulation, resource protection, and investments in regeneration and infrastructure' (Albrechts et al. 2003, p. 113), is broadly embraced by practitioners and scholars because it focuses on the resolution of evident spatial problems and thus reiterates a political argument for planning. It is also common to describe spatial planning as a collaborative endeavour that considers the multiple voices that have a stake in spatial development (Albrechts 2012; Healey 2003, 2006). Since the 1980s, a multitude of spatial planning initiatives have emerged around observed spatial interdependencies and structuring spatial elements, particularly in urbanized 'metropolitan' regions. Attempts to comply with the broad spatial planning agenda show that it is challenging to sustain both a spatial logic and a collaborative spatial planning rationale. Experimentation has made the set of barriers to such integration, outlined below, apparent.

The built environment forms a complex system. Places have various characteristics and are connected in many ways, leading to multiple, intricate interrelations. Different disciplinary knowledge on regional spatial development leads to different perceptions of what aspects of development are problematic and therefore deserve planning. Debate on what constitutes cause and effect in development is intensified by new technologies producing new (big) spatial data. Against this background, it is virtually impossible to demarcate 'the' region as an undisputed object of evidence-based planning. Dedicating planning resources to the resolution of specific spatial problems involves making political choices. Spatial planning experiments demonstrate that such choices are not only determined by a shared recognition of planning needs. Spatial selectivity, no matter how well argued for, involves competition among actors over scarce planning means. As a result, spatial planning often results not in new institutional arrangements for urgent planning tasks, but in the fragmentation of governance. Added complications arise during decision-making. Planning that addresses spatial development in formally undefined, 'soft' territories relies on the voluntary engagement of plan actors. The formation of consensus during negotiation between these actors lacks formal democratic legitimation and is often unaccountable. Governments hesitate to establish these territories. They feel that they lack the political mandate to solve problems whose causes are likely beyond the sphere of their influence. Reaching beyond this concern often leaves them with high risks. Decisions implemented in 'soft' territories are vulnerable to opposition that is established via formal democratic procedures. Experimentation has, last but not least, shown that planning that recognises the specificities of particular areas and regions accentuates the different objectives of governments at different levels. Strategic spatial planning is praised for how it considers 'place' and for how it involves local actors with stakes and expertise in the development of these areas. It is associated with creativity and planning innovation. However, custom-tailoring planning to local places is naturally at odds with generally applicable planning rules that can be applied across a variety of situations. There are no spatial planning rationales that are both abstract and detailed, and that are in effect both distributional and strategic. As several observers have noted, this dilemma between a wish for specific yet comprehensive spatial planning has triggered the emergence of overly pretentious planning agendas, hiding away incompatible political objectives behind rhetorical narratives and planning imagery (see, e.g., Allmendinger and Haughton 2009; Davoudi 2003; Markusen 1999).

1.2 Discussing the Role of Designing and Visioning in Governance Rescaling

The strategic spatial planning experience has brought tensions between spatial and collaborative planning rationales to the foreground. As a result, the approach is at times portrayed to be experimental by nature: due to the uniqueness and complexity of particular spatial and institutional situations, it can only evolve via trial and error, conjecture and refutation. However, the experience (and the observation of it) has also led to the uncovering of mechanisms that are typically involved in addressing the multiple challenges that spatial planning presents. Two of these mechanisms are the central focus of this book: governance rescaling—the reflexivity of planning collaboration—and, under the header 'designing and visioning', a reflection on desirable spatial planning outcomes during planning decision-making.

1.2.1 Governance Rescaling

The theory and practice of strategic spatial planning—as a decision-making process that concerns the use of land and that involves assessing and balancing the multiple competing societal demands that are at stake in processes—is strongly linked to governance discourses (Neuman 1998; Nuissl and Heinrichs 2011). Within these discourses, governance arrangements are commonly described as the product of social bodies that form intricate networks, composed of multiple and multi-level, horizontal and vertical relations among public, private and civil actors (e.g. in Ansell 2000; Booth 2005; Hooghe and Marks 2001; Jessop 2004). These networks form temporary political entities, which are continuously re-established while demands for planning arise from above, below or the side (Ansell 2000; Jessop 2001, 2004). The involvement of governance arrangements in spatial planning has different purposes, as outlined above. Governance may be justified by an appreciation of plurality, and aspire good, inclusive democratic decision-making (Healey 2003; Innes and Booher 2003). Another governance rationale relates to 'governing': the resolution of occurring socio-spatial problems (Mayntz 2004). According to this more politically motivated reason for involvement, governance aims to bundle the resources that actors have available to execute planning action. *Governance rescaling* in spatial planning is about the shifts in organizational planning structures resulting from the balancing out of these different governance purposes. It concerns, in a first instance, changes in cooperation among plan actors and/or a new distribution of planning responsibilities, roles and resources. In a second instance, governance rescaling concerns the redefinition of territories within which planning action takes effect. Redefinition is expressed in changes to the shape and/or the formal status of these areas. Observation shows that governance rescaling processes take place in many European countries. Obvious results are, for instance, the amalgamation of municipalities, the establishment of new metropolitan regions and the devolution of planning competencies to lower levels of government. Empirics show that the direction of rescaling processes varies. They emerge through an up-scaling of territorial cooperation from local to higher levels of government, the equivalent down-scaling, or both at the same time. The rescaling of governance has generated considerable scholarly debate. Underlying the debate is the (at times critically reviewed) assumption that these processes are an inevitable outcome of strategic spatial planning; that governance reflexivity is required to facilitate an approach that considers the substantive matters of specific geographies.

1.2.2 Designing and Visioning

A second mechanism that gained wider relevance in the realm of strategic spatial planning concerns the consideration of geographies in planning decision-making. Spatial planning has implied a 'spatial logic' since the approach first emerged in the 1980s. From the outset, it involved attention to material practices and settings. Visioning—the setting out of desirable spatial planning outcomes in spatial terms—emerged as an important approach to motivating planning action in distinct but formally undefined territories (see, e.g., Albrechts et al. 2003; Dühr 2006; Healey 2004; Zonneveld 2008). The perceived importance of visions and visioning has increased over time but received critical remarks too, in particular due to the recognition that geographies are sensitive social constructs. During an 'argumentative turn' in planning, spatial plans first came to be seen as tools that do not fully determine planning output but rather portray temporary, malleable compromises between actors: a 'drifting cloud' (Friedmann and Gross 1965, p. 39), or 'a fleeting summary of current knowledge, expectations and goals' (Faludi and Korthals Altes 1994, p. 405). Distinct from images that merely communicate, spatial representations became perceived as meaningful and purposefully employed by plan actors to inform the behaviour of other related actors (Davoudi 2012; Dühr 2004; Faludi 1996; Graham and Healey 1999; Jensen and Richardson 2003; Neuman 1996; Thierstein and Förster 2008; Van Duinen 2004). The perception that spatial representations are social constructs gave rise to new, relational concepts of space (Davoudi and Strange 2008). Strongly inspired by notions from the fields of critical and political geography (Brenner 2004; Jessop 2012; Jones 2009; Paasi 2010), a perception of geographies as discursive structures raised attention to their role in both the institutionalization of innovative planning approaches and the conservation of existing ones. A recent—at the time of writing this introduction—definition of spatial imaginaries, by Davoudi et al. (2018, p. 101), accentuates this role and summarises its multiple implications: 'Spatial imaginaries are deeply held, collective understandings of socio-spatial relations that are performed by, give sense to, make possible and change collective socio-spatial practices. They are produced through political struggles over the conceptions, perceptions and lived experiences of place. They are circulated and propagated through images, stories, texts, data, algorithms and performances. They are infused by relations of power in which contestation and resistance are ever-present'.

Albeit often in implicit ways, the above-summarised implications of using spatial imaginaries are recognised across a variety of planning fields. Seen from a critical governance perspective, emphasis is usually on the use of hegemonic geographic perceptions. Their repetitive use in planning decision-making is associated with attempts to sustain existing planning regimes. However, the recognition that geographies are deeply intertwined with the values and interests of actors implies that existing spatial planning rationales can also be challenged through alternative spatial imaginaries. This idea—

that the use of spatial representations can play a role in the transformation of planning frameworks and approaches—resides more strongly in the scholarly and practical fields of design. Over recent years, an array of design practices emerged in the realm of regional spatial planning, taking the form of design studios, design competitions and design exhibitions. These practices—in this book summarised under the header *designing and visioning*—re-iterated an interest in design-led approaches to spatial planning decision-making (Neuman and Zonneveld 2018). Design, in theory, has normative aspirations: practices are orientated towards finding good solutions for problems that occur in the built (and unbuilt) environment (Hillier and Leaman 1974; Lawson 2009; Rittel 1987; Schön 1983, 1988). It is defined to be a holistic endeavour: design is deeply engaged with the multiple elements and socio-spatial practices that shape particular spatial environments. Design practice is described to be a 'conversation with the situation' (Schön 1992, p. 4): an iterative exploration of how interventions into the built environment affect these settings and, vice versa, how settings inform interventions. Although 'regional design' has only recently become an established issue in spatial planning research, it has triggered debate. By linking the issue to the above-sketched notions concerning the use of geographies in planning decision-making, it became perceived as a practice that performs in an institutional context. A particular proposition is that the practice can, due to its reflective nature, perform in the realm of governance: that it can assist in the alignment between governance arrangements and occurring socio-spatial problems.

1.2.3 Aims and Objectives of the Book

Governance rescaling concerns changes in the scale and scope of cooperation brought about by tensions between a spatial and collaborative spatial planning rationale. Designing and visioning concern the consideration of geographies in planning decision-making. Practices make use of imaginary spatial representations to reflect on the outcomes of strategic spatial planning. This book discusses these two mechanisms in conjunction. Its central aim is an increased understanding of how practices, engaged in imagining plausible spatial futures, support the creation of institutional capacity for strategic spatial planning. Its main proposition is that interrelations exist between governance rescaling, designing and visioning: that design-led approaches to planning decision-making incite changes in governance arrangements, and that governance informs the performances of spatial imagination. From this main proposition, two more detailed questions arose (see Fig. 1.1):

- *What are performances of design and visioning in governance rescaling?* Designing and visioning practices are employed in many European regions (see, e.g., Förster et al. 2016). While in few countries they are compulsory and/or formally required, in most cases they are voluntary planning activities. An observation of these practices shows that they trigger multiple expectations. Design is supposed to increase analytical knowledge about spatial development and thus enhance the technical quality, strategic value and comprehensiveness of planning strategies and projects. Practices are expected to perform in political settings: to clarify political preferences, support the formation of political consent, and mediate in cases of conflict. Practices are supposed to perform in organisational terms: to unlock actors' capacities to implement planning. The involvement of actors in design practice is associated with legitimacy; the intense use of planning imagery is associated with accountable planning. By identifying different performances of design-led approaches, the book provides insights into the possible outcomes of these approaches. By analysing their governance settings, it highlights what has hindered or enhanced their performances in this realm.
- *Which key aspects of governance determine the performance of designing and visioning?* Governance rescaling seeks to align the territories within which planning action unfolds and areas that are affected by problems arising from autonomous spatial development. It results from tensions between a spatial and collaborative planning rationale, as noted above. Rescaling can imply the re-distribution of responsibilities, roles and resources among actors and changes in horizontal and vertical cooperation. It can also be reflected in the redefinition of territories, which cover small or large portions of land and where hard statutory regulation or softly defined planning guidance applies. By identifying processes of governance rescaling, the contributions in this book provide insights into these processes. In particular, they highlight how they have been induced by the recognition of spatial phenomena and the use of visionary geographies.

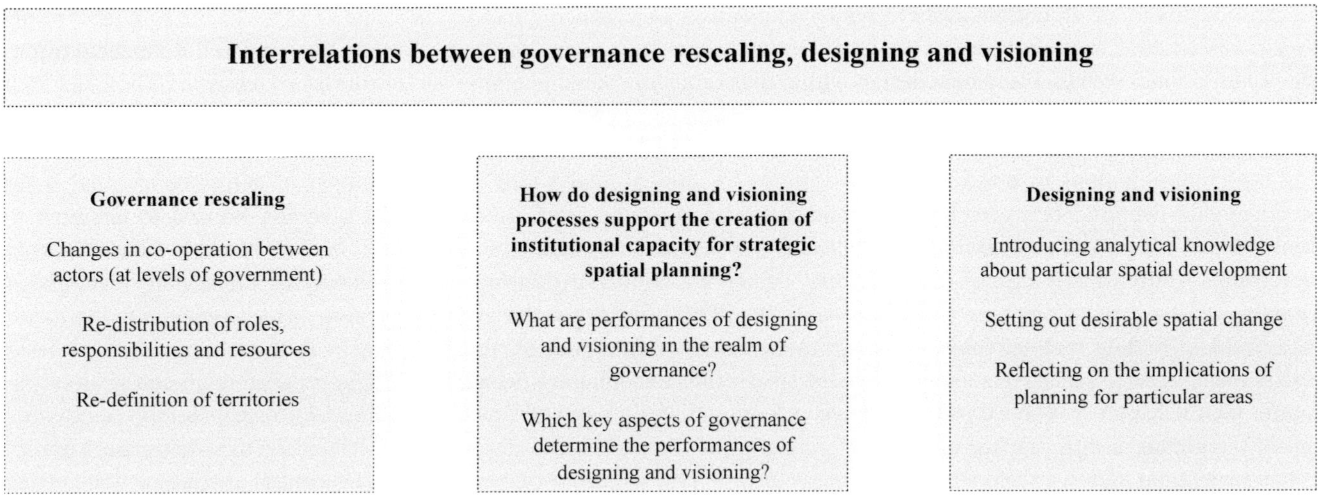

Interrelations between governance rescaling, designing and visioning

Governance rescaling

Changes in co-operation between actors (at levels of government)

Re-distribution of roles, responsibilities and resources

Re-definition of territories

How do designing and visioning processes support the creation of institutional capacity for strategic spatial planning?

What are performances of designing and visioning in the realm of governance?

Which key aspects of governance determine the performances of designing and visioning?

Designing and visioning

Introducing analytical knowledge about particular spatial development

Setting out desirable spatial change

Reflecting on the implications of planning for particular areas

Fig. 1.1 Conceptual framework

1.3 Contents of the Book

Perceiving designing, visioning and governance rescaling as intertwined practices involve a dynamic conception of strategic spatial planning in which the spatial imagination of regions and planning collaboration inform each other during iterative processes. An understanding of such reflexivity must be approached through routes that do not focus on either issue but instead on the interdependencies between them. This book is organized into three main parts, each dealing with a specific perspective on the dependencies and each dedicated to a particular purpose. Part I of the book employs a theoretical perspective and seeks to provide the reader with propositions and arguments concerning interrelations between governance rescaling, (regional) designing and visioning. Part II explores governance rescaling processes in different European countries. Its purpose is to demonstrate how these processes relate to spatial planning and, in particular, to identify actual and desirable spatial development. Part III investigates designing and visioning practices. It collects empirical material to provide an understanding of how these practices have informed or were informed by governance. The next section explains these perspectives and purposes in more detailed. A brief summary of the chapters provides the reader with further guidance.

1.3.1 The Terms of Reference

Part I develops the key concepts considered in the book. It sets out the 'rescaling of governance', 'visioning' and 'regional design' concepts in theoretical terms. The interrelations between these concepts are central. The chapters explain the interrelations from a variety of perspectives and highlight the critical aspects that determine them. In conjunction, they provide a body of notions to interpret the roles, positions and performances of regional design and visioning practices within the realm of governance. The chapters in Part I of the book respond to the questions listed below:

- What are governance rescaling processes; why and how do they come about?
- What aspects of governance are influenced by 'regional design' and 'visioning' and how is this influence conceptualized?
- What are the roles and positions of regional design and visioning in the realm of spatial planning and governance, seen theoretical notions and disciplinary knowledge?
- What are the (expected) performances of regional design and visioning in the rescaling of governance and how do they likely unfold?

In Chap. 2 'Regional Designing and Visioning in Planning Rescaling: An Interactive Governance Perspective', Valeria Lingua investigates governance rescaling processes, using the concept of interactive governance as a conceptual framework. The chapter identifies interaction in statutory planning processes and in the formation of soft planning spaces of governance. Particular focus is placed on images and visions as determining elements in these processes. The author argues that these mental constructs are important tools to render interactive governance effective. In Chap. 3 'The Institutionalisation of a Creative Practice: Changing Roles of Regional Design in Dutch National Planning', Verena Balz and Wil Zonneveld discuss the organisational setting of regional design within the realms of spatial planning and territorial governance. They first argue that regional design practices resemble discretionary action: as such they aim to improve planning decisions by proactively judging the implications of planning frameworks when applied to particular situations. On the basis of this notion, it is stated that actor constellations in practices require scrutiny. A critical analysis of the involvement of actors in regional design practices that occurred between the 1980s and 2010s in the context of Dutch national planning is used to underpin the argument. In Chap. 4 'The Transformative Capacity of Regional Design', Lukas Gilliard, Fabian Wenner, Alain Thierstein and Nadia Alaily-Mattar discuss how regional design introduces a transformative perspective on spatial development. Drawing on a review of planning paradigms since the 1920s, they argue that regional design—as a problem-solving as well as a problem-finding methodology—is at the forefront of an emerging planning approach. In their view, regional design operationalises inter-scalar, relational notions of space, thus encouraging debate rather than presenting an end solution or a master plan. Chapter 5 'The Connection between Regional Designing and Spatial Planning,' by Annet Kempenaar, focuses on how regional design practice and spatial planning are entangled and discusses the critical factors that arise from that entanglement: an iterative regional design process in which the expertise of the designer(s) is central, the interaction between involved stakeholders, and the proper embeddedness of regional design in its particular planning context. The chapter builds on notions from research into Dutch regional design practice, consisting of multiple case studies.

1.3.2 Governance Rescaling Across Europe

Part II investigates governance rescaling processes in distinct institutional and organizational circumstances. Over the past two decades, spatial planning systems in Europe have become increasingly differentiated in their attempt to influence and shape spatial development processes. Planning that addresses discrete, permanent and fixed territories, conventionally depicted by nested hierarchies (i.e. between municipal, regional and national government levels), has long conflicted with planning that involves actual spatial transformation processes. Part II of the book looks into the rescaling of governance in European regions that represent the results of this conflict. It investigates specifically how rescaling processes have accommodated an alignment between administrative jurisdictions' boundaries and the rather fluid spaces of functional regions. The chapters in Part II 'Governance Rescaling across Europe' respond to the questions listed below:

- What are governance rescaling processes in European regions?
- What are the key factors, barriers and challenges in the formation of governance?
- What role do the position and performance of (strategic) spatial planning, spatial plans, visions and spatial representation play in governance rescaling processes?
- What enhances or hinders the performance of these frameworks?

In Chap. 6 'Constrained Governance Rescaling and the Development of a New Spatial Framework for Greater Manchester', Graham Haughton examines the evolution of city–regional planning for Greater Manchester in England. The chapter draws on an analysis of how new forms of city–regional governance emerged in this city—playing a pioneering and central role in current English debates on devolution. The chapter focuses on the politics involved in the rescaling of planning. It is argued that the spatial planning framework developed since the 2010s served as a potential platform to integrate the various social, environmental and economic issues facing the region, as well as the levels of government pursuing them. The conclusion reflects on how changing degrees of softness have informed integration. Chapter 7 'Administrative Organisation and Spatial Planning in Portugal: A Push towards Soft Planning Spaces in Europe,' by Cristina Cavaco and João Pedro Costa, investigates the emergence of soft planning spaces in Portugal. Particular attention is paid to the role of the European Union as a driver of this development. The analysis presented shows how the 2014–2020 EU Cohesion Policy has interacted with the statutory Portuguese spatial planning system and points to the tensions and detachments that such interaction has caused. The conclusions discuss the importance of interaction between soft planning, evolving around shared place-based visions, and statutory planning schemes. In Chap. 8 'Governance Rescaling in Danish Spatial Planning: State Spaces between Fixity and Fluidity', Daniel Galland examines governance rescaling processes in Danish spatial planning since the 2000s. He argues that the evolution of spatial planning in this Nordic country is indicative of planning systems that have moved away from hierarchical approaches to structuring territory, towards a multifaceted, iterative and more open understanding of planning as an evolving political process. Through his analysis of interrelations between legal and spatial planning frameworks, however, he also demonstrates that development has retained a vertical spatial anchor in order to guarantee the stability and permanence of power structures. In Chap. 9 'Governance Rescaling and Regional Planning in France: Is Big Really Beautiful?', Xavier Desjardins and Anna Geppert critically discuss the series of administrative reforms that have led to the change in France's mainland administrative regions since 2015. The focus is on how reforms—aimed at adapting to new economic situations as well as modernising public action—have influenced the capacity of France's regional authorities to act in view of regional and spatial development. The chapter concludes that the rescaling of governance in France has left regions with more comprehensive planning tasks but insufficient political and financial strength to meet aspirations. In Chap. 10 'Strategic Planning in Russia: From National to Local Government Approaches', Leonid Limonov and Artur Batchaev provide insights into the origin, establishment and development of strategic planning in Russia. The chapter builds upon a brief history of strategic planning in this country since the 2000s, paying particular attention to the development of the innovative St. Petersburg strategic spatial plan. The chapter concludes by pointing to the complex problems that strategic spatial planning in Russia is confronted with, in particular with regard to consistency, firstly between strategic planning documents adopted at different levels of public authority, and secondly between the provisions and parameters of documents relating to different types of planning.

1.3.3 Envisioning Metropolitan Futures

Regional design concerns the imagination of spatial solutions to problems in particular regions and the use of these visions for planning purposes. When employed in the planning realm, processes often have territorial implications. They challenge statutory planning in predefined administrative boundaries. In this sense, they present incentives to reform current organizational planning structures and forms of governance. Part III 'Envisioning Metropolitan Futures' explores regional design practices in European regions. It investigates how an understanding of spatial dynamics and the imagination of spatial futures informs and is informed by planning frameworks, and how such design processes inform cooperation and collaboration on planning in metropolitan regions. In addition to the earlier parts of the book, this part also includes, along with scholarly writing, contributions by planning and design professionals. Their analyses contribute to an understanding of the performances of designing and visioning processes in the realm of governance. The chapters in Part III respond to the questions listed below:

- What are regional design and visioning products and processes? What are their aims and objectives, scales, and scopes? Who is involved?
- How are design-led approaches and visioning embedded in planning and governance settings? What was their role and position in processes that changed these settings?
- What are the performance of regional design and visioning in governance rescaling processes? What enhances or hinders performances?

In Chap. 11 'Belgian Design Laboratories of Post-Sprawl Urbanisation', Michiel Dehaene discusses what makes urban projects urban, and what it takes to urbanise deliberately. To answer these profound questions, he investigates design research laboratories and other regional design efforts in Flanders and Brussels, Belgium. By means of this analysis as well as theoretical reflection, he argues that designing for the urban involves articulating the various scales at which urbanisation processes play out, and that such an articulation of concrete, multi-scalar settings is required to make sense of local action. The conclusions emphasise the importance of contextualising local actions in this way, so the felt collective burden of urbanisation can be converted into collectively perceived opportunities. Chapter 12 'Metaphors, Figures of Space and the Horizontal Metropolis,' by Paola Viganò, focuses on the use of metaphors in design practice. Through a brief review of her design experiences in Paris, France, and Brussels, Belgium, she shows how metaphors—expressed in word and image— facilitate interpretation of and reflection on the state of cities and their future. Overall, the chapter argues that conceptual metaphors are needed to reframe planning discourses as well as to establish new territories within which new organizational structures can evolve. In Chap. 13 'Open and Closed Figures in Dutch Spatial Planning', Carlo Pisano and Veronica Saddi take a similar stance. The authors argue that, thanks to their strong evocative power, rhetorical expressions are an important part of an urban vocabulary that enables spatial visions and urban projects. The 'Patchwork Metropolis', by the Dutch architect Willem Jan Neutelings who in 1989 proposed a conceptualisation of the region around the Dutch cities of Rotterdam and The Hague, is investigated in depth. It is shown how this abstract model and its implicit meanings informed the transformation of the related urban territory. Chapter 14 'Concepts of Landscapes: Informing Local Plans in Albania', by Roberto Mascarucci, reviews an innovative regional design approach that was taken to achieve a more strategic planning in local areas surrounding the city of Tirana, Albania. Central to the approach is the conceptualization of different landscapes. It is shown how bringing these concepts to the foreground has contributed to ecological integration, the integration of historic and new urban settlements, and the accommodation of economic functions in environmental protection areas. Particular benefits for organisational planning matters—e.g. concerning the use of municipal budgets—are highlighted in the conclusions. In Chap. 15 'Integrating Experiences in the Palermo Mediterranean Gateway City: Identity and Innovation', Daniele Ronsivalle elaborates on how the envisioning of the city of Palermo, Italy, as a 'fluid, gateway city' has become an example inspiring the planning of similar cities in Italy and Europe. The chapter identifies key components of the vision and the visioning process and shows how each component related to particular planning processes in the Palermo region. The main conclusions summarize the development and emphasize a need for conceptual and thus policy integration. In Chap. 16 'Regional Design: S, M, L', Agnes Förster discusses the effectiveness of design interventions in metropolitan regions by presenting a set of interrelated levels for spatial transformation. She argues that categorising regional projects with these levels enhances productive interaction between the various 'users' and 'producers' of a region. Considering its multi-actor setting, she calls for attention to a product and process dimension of regional design in her conclusions. In Chap. 17 'The Zurich Metrobild', Anna Schindler explains how regional design has contributed to the consideration of the metropolitan area of Zurich as a whole functional region in planning circuits. The chapter first outlines the background of the Metrobild regional design initiative: the federal planning system in Switzerland. It then analyses the design process, including its advantages and disadvantages. In the conclusions, it is argued that, although not the basis, the process was an important source of inspiration for the following, more formal, spatial planning framework for the region. Finally, Chap. 18 'Enhancing Perception of Regions: A Vision for Florence Metropolitan City,' by Valeria Lingua, Giuseppe De Luca and Fabio Lucchesi, describes a vision-making process that responded to formally required governance rescaling in Italy. Taking a historical perspective, it is first shown how settlement patterns and functional relations in the Florence region were addressed through forms of governance and planning instruments before the reform became effective. The strategic planning process that occurred thereafter is then presented as a vision-making process. Based on regional design theories, it is explained how different metaphorical narratives and representations were explicitly used to shape the boundaries of the urban region and conceive a shared vision for its future spatial development.

This book aims to increase appreciation of (1) how the imagination of spatial futures informs and is informed by planning frameworks and (2) how such processes inform cooperation and collaboration on planning in metropolitan areas. The chapter 'Conclusions' summarises the findings of the research undertaken for the book and offers a research agenda to further elaborate on these questions. The chapter also calls for ongoing exchange between scholars and practitioners in governance and design in order to increase our understanding of planning experimentation in a post-regulatory era. It is argued that the further integration of these usually separate disciplines is essential to gain deeper insights into how tensions between a spatial and collaborative planning rationale can be explained theoretically and resolved practically.

Acknowledgements This book was produced as part of the research project "AREA VASTA 2.0 A New Form of Localism in Italy: Challenges, Risks and Opportunities for Spatial Planning Across Local Boundaries" (ref. RBSI14M63F), funded by the Italian Ministry of Education, University and Research (Ministero dell'Istruzione, dell'Università e della Ricerca — MIUR) within the framework of the "Scientific Independence of Young Researchers" programme.

References

Albrechts L (2004) Strategic (spatial) planning reexamined. Environ Plan B 31:743–758

Albrechts L (2012) Reframing strategic spatial planning by using a coproduction perspective. Plan Theory 12(1):46–63. https://doi.org/10.1177/1473095212452722

Albrechts L, Healey P, Kunzmann KR (2003) Strategic spatial planning and regional governance in Europe. J Am Plan Assoc 69(2):113–129. https://doi.org/10.1080/01944360308976301

Allmendinger P, Haughton G (2009) Critical reflections on spatial planning. Environ Plan A 41(11):2544–2549

Allmendinger P, Haughton G (2010) Spatial planning, devolution, and new planning spaces. Environ Plan C: Gov Policy 28(5):803–818

Ansell C (2000) The networked polity: regional development in Western Europe. Governance 13(2):279–291. https://doi.org/10.1111/0952-1895.00136

Booth P (2005) Partnerships and networks: the governance of urban regeneration in Britain. J Housing Built Environ 20(3):257–269. https://doi.org/10.1007/s10901-005-9009-2

Brenner N (2004) Urban governance and the production of new state spaces in Western Europe, 1960-2000. Rev Int Polit Econ 11(3):447–488

Davoudi S (2003) European briefing: polycentricity in European spatial planning—from an analytical tool to a normative agenda. Eur Plan Stud 11(8):979–999. https://doi.org/10.1080/0965431032000146169

Davoudi S (2008) Governing polycentric urban regions. In: Thierstein A, Förster A (eds) The image and the region. Making mega-city regions visible. Lars Müller Publishers, München, pp. 59–66

Davoudi S (2012) The legacy of positivism and the emergence of interpretive tradition in spatial planning. Reg Stud 46(4):429–441. https://doi.org/10.1080/00343404.2011.618120

Davoudi S, Strange I (eds) (2008) Conceptions of space and place in strategic spatial planning. Routledge, London/New York

Davoudi S, Crawford J, Raynor R, Reid B, Sykes O, Shaw D (2018) Spatial imaginaries: tyrannies or transformations? Town Plan Rev 89(2):97–124. https://doi.org/10.3828/tpr.2018.7

Dühr S (2004) The form, style, and use of cartographic visualisations in European spatial planning: examples from England and Germany. Environ Plan A 36(11):1961–1989

Dühr S (2006) The visual language of spatial planning: exploring cartographic representations for spatial planning in Europe. Routledge, London/New York

Faludi A (1996) Framing with images. Environ Plan B: Plan Des 23(1):93–108

Faludi A (2012) Multi-level (territorial) governance: three criticisms. Plan Theory Pract 13(2):197–211. https://doi.org/10.1080/14649357.2012.677578

Faludi A, Korthals Altes W (1994) Evaluating communicative planning: a revised design for performance research. Eur Plan Stud 2(4):403–418

Förster A, Balz V, Thierstein A, Zonneveld W (2016) The conference 'Shaping Regional Futures: Mapping, Designing, Transforming!' A documentation. Munich/Delft

Friedmann J, Gross BM (1965) Venezuela: from doctrine to dialogue, vol 1. Syracuse University Press Syracuse

Graham S, Healey P (1999) Relational concepts of space and place: issues for planning theory and practice. Eur Plan Stud 7(5):623–646. https://doi.org/10.1080/09654319908720542

Hajer M (2003) Policy without polity? Policy analysis and the institutional void. Policy Sci 36(2):175–195. https://doi.org/10.1023/A:1024834510939

Healey P (2003) Collaborative planning in perspective. Plan Theory 2(2):101–123. https://doi.org/10.1177/14730952030022002

Healey P (2004) The treatment of space and place in the new strategic spatial planning in Europe. Int J Urban Reg Res 28(1):45–67. https://doi.org/10.1111/j.0309-1317.2004.00502.x

Healey P (2006) Relational complexity and the imaginative power of strategic spatial planning. Eur Plan Stud 14(4):525–546. https://doi.org/10.1080/09654310500421196

Hillier B, Leaman A (1974) How is design possible? J Arch Plan Res 3(1):4–11

Hooghe L, Marks G (2001) Multi-level governance and European integration. Rowman & Littlefield Publishers

Hooghe L, Marks G (2003) Unraveling the central state, but how? Types of multi-level governance. Am Polit Sci Rev 97(02):233–243. https://doi.org/10.1017/S0003055403000649

Innes JE, Booher DE (2003) The impact of collaborative planning on governance capacity. Institute of Urban and Regional Development, UC Berkeley, Berkeley. Retrieved from http://www.escholarship.org/uc/item/98k72547

Jensen OB, Richardson T (2003) Being on the map: the new iconographies of power over European space. Int Plan Stud 8(1):9–34. https://doi.org/10.1080/13563470320000059246

Jessop B (2001) Institutional re(turns) and the strategic—relational approach. Environ Plan A 33(7):1213–1235

Jessop B (2004) Multi-level governance and multi-level metagovernance. Multi-level governance, pp 49–74

Jessop B (2012) Cultural political economy, spatial imaginaries, regional economic dynamics. Cultural Political Economy Research Centre (CPERC) Working Paper, (02), pp 1–29

Jones M (2009) Phase space: geography, relational thinking, and beyond. Prog Hum Geogr 33(4):487–506. https://doi.org/10.1177/0309132508101599

Lawson B (2009) Design expertise. Architectural Press, Oxon/New York

Markusen A (1999) Fuzzy concepts, scanty evidence, policy distance: the case for rigour and policy relevance in critical regional studies. Reg Stud 33(9):869–884. https://doi.org/10.1080/00343409950075506

Mayntz R (2004) Governance theory als fortentwickelte Steuerungstheorie? [Governance theory as a progression of political steering?]. Retrieved from MPIfG Working Paper

Nadin V (2007) The emergence of the spatial planning approach in England. Plan Pract Res 22(1):43–62. https://doi.org/10.1080/02697450701455934

Neuman M (1996) Images as institution builders: metropolitan planning in Madrid. Eur Plan Stud 4(3):293–312. https://doi.org/10.1080/09654319608720347

Neuman M (1998) Planning, governing, and the image of the city. J Plan Educ Res 18(1):61–71. https://doi.org/10.1177/0739456X9801800106

Neuman M, Zonneveld W (2018) The resurgence of regional design. Eur Plan Stud 26(7):1297–1311. https://doi.org/10.1080/09654313.2018.1464127

Nuissl H, Heinrichs D (2011) Fresh wind or hot air—Does the governance discourse have something to offer to spatial planning? J Plan Educ Res 31(1):47–59. https://doi.org/10.1177/0739456X10392354

Paasi A (2010) Commentary: regions are social constructs, but who or what 'constructs' them? Environ Plan A 42(10):2296–2301. https://doi.org/10.1068/a42232

Rhodes RAW (1996) The new governance: governing without government. Polit Stud 44(4):652–667. https://doi.org/10.1111/j.1467-9248.1996.tb01747.x

Rittel HWJ (1987) The reasoning of designers. University of California, Berkeley

Schön DA (1983) The reflective practitioner: how professionals think in action. Temple Smith, London

Schön DA (1988) Designing: rules, types and words. Des Stud 9(3):181–190. https://doi.org/10.1016/0142-694X(88)90047-6

Schön DA (1992) Designing as reflective conversation with the materials of a design situation. Res Eng Design 3(3):131–147. https://doi.org/10.1007/BF01580516

Schön P (2005) Territorial cohesion in Europe? Plan Theory Pract 6(3):389–400. https://doi.org/10.1080/14649350500209397

Thierstein A, Förster A (eds) (2008) The image and the region—making mega-city regions visible!. Lars Müller Publishers, Baden

Van Duinen L (2004) Planning imagery. The emergence and development of new planning concepts in Dutch National Spatial Policy. Doctoral thesis, University of Amsterdam, Amsterdam

Zonneveld W (2008) Visioning and vizualization. In: Thierstein A, Förster A (eds) The image and the region: making mega-city regions visible. Lars Müller Publishers, München, pp 107–125

Regional Designing and Visioning in Planning Rescaling: An Interactive Governance Perspective

Valeria Lingua

Abstract

This contribution investigates governance rescaling processes using interactive governance as the conceptual framework. It identifies interactions between statutory planning processes and the formation of the soft planning spaces of governance across local boundaries. In particular, focusing on images and visions as elements of interactive governance, it explores the interrelation between governance and planning. Scalar shift sheds light on the reciprocal influences among statutory and soft planning spaces by providing for new spatial imaginaries, making the boundaries of new regional contexts visible and shaping their futures. In this framework, the author argues that visioning practices matter both for shaping regional boundaries and conceiving shared visions of their spatial development.

Keywords

Governance rescaling · Interactive governance · Images · Spatial planning · Strategic planning

2.1 Introduction: Governance Rescaling and Changing Planning Systems and Spaces in Europe

Strong rescaling processes are occurring across many European countries, leading to the up-scaling at regional and supra-regional levels and the down-scaling at local and micro-local levels of institutional and planning powers and activities. These governance rescaling processes and institutional organisation systems have been engaged in response to the emergence of widespread neo-liberalism (Waterhout et al. 2013), which has led to State space rescaling (Brenner 2004, 2009) and a strong affirmation of localism; moreover, rescaling is seen as a way to promote efficiency and to improve the resource management of both central and local government after the 2008 financial crisis, as well as a response to the need to address climate change and connected risks. Such rescaling is expressed in different ways: it may result in the amalgamation of municipalities, the establishment of new metropolitan authorities or the increased importance of local (non-governmental) actors.

Although there are clear differences in its general impact and real effects in practice, the rescaling of institutional organisation is strictly connected with the reform of planning systems which could be associated with reducing government. Indeed, every level between national and local is now up for discussion (Waterhout et al. 2013), and planning and programming instruments are being challenged. In some cases, intermediate regional planning levels have been abolished, as occurred with the English Regional Spatial Strategies in 2011. In other cases, (i.e. Denmark, Portugal, Italy, Norway) competences are nominally shifted between governance levels, through local government reforms aimed at merging municipalities or else by increasing the development of planning practices across local boundaries (Lingua 2018a). National governments expect local planning authorities to undertake joint work on sub-regional planning issues, while at the European Union level the scale of territorial strategies eligible for future funding is under discussion.

In this context, spatial planning policies and practices, still traditionally anchored to rigid administrative boundaries, require reinventing. Rescaled planning functions, delivered through devolution, have created a range of new planning

V. Lingua (✉)
Regional Design Lab, Department of Architecture, University of Florence, via P.A. Micheli 2, 50121 Florence, Italy
e-mail: valeria.lingua@unifi.it

© Springer Nature Switzerland AG 2020
V. Lingua and V. Balz (eds.), *Shaping Regional Futures*,
https://doi.org/10.1007/978-3-030-23573-4_2

spaces, not only in the framework of formal and statutory planning, but also by defining new "soft spaces" with "fuzzy boundaries" (Allmendinger and Haughton 2010). These new planning spaces rely on strategic but nevertheless informal spatial planning approaches and are defined among soft governance networks, moving beyond administrative limits. However, these new planning spaces necessarily need to confront or rely on "the regulatory functions of hard-space forms of governance in various ways, not least financial, use of statutory powers and democratic legitimacy" (Allmendinger and Houghton 2010: 813).

The defining and redefining of sub-regional boundaries and territorial scales, through the coexistence of formal and informal (soft) governance networks and related planning spaces, call for a revival of "spatial visioning" for both institutional/formal and non-statutory/informal planning spaces. In some cases, this may even entail a resurgence of regional design (Neuman and Zonneveld 2018), i.e. of spatial visioning and design practices for shaping the boundaries of urban regions, providing proactive knowledge of their characteristics and trends and conceiving shared visions of their spatial development. This chapter elaborates upon the core interest of the book from the governance perspective by addressing the role of designing and visioning in the formation of regional governance in territorial spatial planning. It aims to increase our understanding of the role of images in enhancing the relationship between statutory and strategic spatial planning, and between planning levels and scales in governance rescaling contexts.

The framework of thinking developed in this chapter takes as its starting point the concept of interaction in governance, moving from local practices to supra-local and sub-regional ones. Ongoing institutional reforms, through the devolution of power, competencies and reference scales, call into question hierarchical forms of governance in favour of collaboration with different actors (Healey 1997, 2003) required to interact within each other. This shifts the focus from the level of planning decisions and their legitimisation to the level of *interaction* between institutions at different levels, and between institutions and public and private actors. Interaction serves to establish local planning strategies to coordinate institutions as well as the activities of public and private actors, despite their fundamental differences in values and epistemic understandings. Such a turn towards interaction challenges planning systems at diverse institutional levels and calls for new relationships with soft governance and soft planning spaces. Combining both institutional design theories and self-organisation theories, the framework draws on the "paradigm" of interactive governance (Torfing et al. 2012), borrowing from political science a vocabulary that can help to explore the nexus of hierarchical and soft forms of governance, as well as the associated changes in planning levels and instruments (Sect. 2.2).

The concept of interactive governance thus provides a theoretical framework through which to read, interpret and unravel both the interaction among actors at different institutional levels and spatial planning scales, as well as forms of soft and hard governance and connected planning spaces (Sect. 2.3).

In order to evaluate the effect of these interactions, a focus on images is provided in Sect. 2.4. By recognising spatial dynamics in particular areas, the use of images to communicate and transfer information (visualisation), create meaning (spatial representation) and define future perspectives for regional development (visioning) can improve spatial imaginaries and enhance spatial planning concepts (Balz 2018). Consequently, visioning and visualisation can play an important role in interactive governance, by defining the extent and nature of problems and possible solutions (Sect. 2.5). Whether both statutory and soft planning spaces are challenged by governance and planning rescaling, the process of interaction creates new challenges and opportunities. The concluding section thus explores the potential application of the framework for comparative planning studies and outlines a research agenda by framing a number of research questions that have been addressed during the research project, and which gave rise to this book.

2.2 The Theoretical Framework: Interactive Governance

Koimann and Jentoft (2009: 820) define *interactive governance* as "the whole of interactions instigated to solve societal problems and to create societal opportunities; including the formulation and application of principles guiding those interactions and care for institutions that enable or control them". Interaction between social and political actors with diverging interests is intended "to formulate, promote and achieve common objectives by means of mobilising, exchanging and deploying a range of ideas, rules and resources" (Torfing et al. 2012: 14).

Referring to *interactive governance* as a "paradigm" (Torfing et al. 2012; Hart 2013), and borrowing from social science some useful features to define it, could provide a valuable key to better understand the relationships and tensions between forms of soft and hard governance in the framework of governance rescaling, as well as their effects on spatial planning practices.

As a matter of fact, this concept is the basis for collaborative planning theories that approach cooperation in planning as a *complex system of interactions* (Innes and Booher 2010), in which the "power to change governance modes will come from the development of the interactive practices of collaborative partnerships of some kind. These range from consultations around a strategy articulated by government officials or by consultants, to enlisting local elite actors into involvement in analysis and policy formation and complex interactions with diverse social groups" (Healey 2006: 540). These forms of interaction, due to their "informality", challenge the traditional rigid forms, processes and instruments that inform spatial planning systems. On the one hand, these processes can slow down planning because of the extensive negotiations involved. On the other, they can contribute to the re-definition of planning spaces, bypassing administrative divisions and established institutions and referring to soft forms of governance with fuzzy borders (Allmendinger and Haughton 2010; Haughton et al. 2010) that involve both governmental and non-governmental actors. Moreover, in many spatial planning systems the final outcomes of these forms of soft governance generally have to pass through the decision-making process in use by local administrations (Zonneveld and Spaans 2014). The main governance question that affects the relationship between formal and informal control mechanisms—if and how to institutionalise soft planning spaces—is a great constraint.

This issue places two main factors in contention: the collaborative nature of governance networks (co-governance) and the higher government levels that aim to control or influence the governance process through hierarchical or meta-governance. This form of "organisation of self-organisation" (Jessop 1998: 42) implies the management and indirect control of interactive governance through the use of more or less subtle forms of control over devolved decision-making (Torfing et al. 2012). Law directives and financial incentives for cooperation are typical means of meta-governance.

The presence of diverging interests affects questions of process accountability: at one level, it is thought to be more democratic and effective because it involves affected interests in society more directly and continuously, but the representativeness of those groups with regard to the general public is an issue (Sørensen 2013; Esmark 2007). At another level, even if it usually concerns "governance without government" (Rhodes 1997; Peters and Pierre 1998), public actors generally remain important in defining and shaping the arenas within which interactions may be occurring (Torfing et al. 2012: 3).

These issues concerning accountability in interaction practices and the role of public and private actors are strictly linked to Kooiman et al.'s definition of governing modes (2008, 2009, 2013). In the context of societal governance, Kooiman and Bavinck (2013) distinguish between three types of interactions: hierarchical, self-governing and co-governing.

The first type, *hierarchical governance*, is the expression of the state's sovereign rule in interacting with citizens. In the movement from government to governance, this kind of governance has been challenged by an increasing functional differentiation and institutional fragmentation of the governing processes, leading to a great need for coordination of informal interaction through meta-governance (Sørensen 2006). Hierarchical governance has been redefined in recent decades, passing from a commanding and delivering role of the state to a regulatory and enabling one. However, a hierarchical organisation based on steering and control mechanisms is the basis of public institutions and even private actors in the market and civil society (see large organisations such as corporations, Kooiman and Jentoft 2009). The principle of hierarchy affects the state's organisation into levels and scales, as well as its instruments and interactions.

Outside the purview of government, actors can take care of themselves in the realm of *self-governance*. This second type of governance is often associated with stakeholder/interest groups, referring to social movements connecting private actors or entities involved in a public matter (Bryson 2004) and which often represent small proportions of the population (Nash 2005) engaged in particular issues (environment, sustainability, food behaviours, etc.). Self-organised forms of governance vary from spontaneous social action groups to institutionalised interest groups. They differ in organisational form, applied strategies and styles of interaction with government, ranging from opposition to proposition.

When self-organised groups or organisations and authorities start to work jointly, recognising mutual interdependencies and advantages (Huxham 1996) in sharing their governance responsibilities and conducting activities together, *co-governance* emerges as a third type. Collaborative and cooperative governance interactions rise from a common purpose around which parties join hands and stake their identity and autonomy in the process. In governance theory, public–private partnerships and networks (Castells 1996; Rhodes 1997) are manifestations of co-governance.

The interrelation between these modes is an important issue in the governance debate and has been faced principally in terms of *institutionalisation* and *governing interaction*. The term "institutionalisation" is widely used in social theory to refer to the process of embedding concepts, social roles, values or modes of behaviour within an organisation, social system or society as a whole. From an actor-centred perspective, institutionalism is "a process in which recurring patterns of the agent's behaviour lead to valued and stable organisations, procedures and beliefs" (Waterhout 2008:165). In the framework of hierarchical governance, the interrelation between different levels, as well as the application of policy approaches and instruments that refer to vertical collaboration among different levels and scales, is institutionalised through formalisation processes: the outcomes of negotiation and collaboration are conveyed through "hard" instruments such as laws, rules and regulations.

When institutions seek collaboration with citizens, stakeholders and third parties—interaction being an informal field of governance—it emphasises the role actors play in activating changes through the modification of existing institutions and even the creation of new self-organised ones. While hierarchical governance moves within the framework of formal institutions, referring to interaction in the domain of collaboration, the major concern raised is the need and opportunity to institutionalise interactive governance arenas and, at the same time, ensure their capacity for self-organisation around a specific issue, even altering the boundaries of cooperation by changing the actors and networks involved.

How to institutionalise interactive governance, in order to give it persistence, is an interesting issue in planning because soft governance spaces move within the framework of hard planning spaces. As such, they have to confront the institutionalised planning instruments by planning authorities. According to Sørensen, "although interactive governance arenas cannot be institutionalised the 'hard' way by means of strict rules and regulations, they can be meta-governed by means of 'soft' reflexive law, as well as by a whole range of 'soft' institutional features if public authorities and other polity designers should decide to do so" (Sørensen 2013: 80). This means that official actors in the public sector can frame and influence interactive governance, even though it is conceived of as the product of autonomous actions by social actors. This is why *meta-governance* is intended as the "governance of governance" (Jessop 2011).

In the framework of relationships between hierarchical governance and other forms of interaction, self-governance and co-governance actions are intended to influence hierarchical governance processes. Meanwhile, meta-governance actions aim to ensure that self- and co-governance develop and operate within a "shadow of hierarchy" (Scharpf 1994) intended to shape and legitimise their outcomes, as well as guarantee their effectiveness. In fact, there is general consensus that meta-governance is a way for any system of governance to be effective (Sørensen 2013). The structures and procedures involved "need to develop some capacity to persist in the face of challenges, and furthermore, they will function better if it is possible to develop common values, symbols and routines that support governance. The danger, however, is that the procedures will become overly institutionalised, with rigidities that prevent adaptation to changing environmental conditions" (Torfing et al. 2012: 7). This awareness is a current issue in spatial planning, where planning systems with an already high degree of formalisation are now being confronted with and challenged by flourishing co-governance planning practices.

2.3 Interactive Governance in Spatial Planning: Making Strategic Choices

The concept of interactive governance is used in this section to unravel the relationship between spatial planning systems and new soft planning practices that are derived from governance rescaling and connected with complex institutional dynamics, and which ultimately need to challenge existing planning instruments and structures.

When discussing interactive governance in relation to planning systems, the architecture of a national planning system can be referred to as what Kooiman and Bavinck (2013) call *hierarchical governance*, because of its structure in planning scales. This usually corresponds to administrative levels, each relating to diverse planning authorities and charged with specific planning instruments required to both comply with the superordinate level and to interact in the creation of the planning instrument. The institutionalisation of hierarchical governance interaction takes place through formal instruments, i.e. the spatial plans informing each planning level. At any level, the plan, despite differences in scale and degrees of prescriptivity, is both the product of and the way to formalise interaction.

Nowadays, these forms of interaction, etched in the conventional, hierarchical "cascade-shaped" ideal of policy implementation, seem to be superseded by increasingly complex societies and territories and challenged by the need to give voice to an increasing number of actors who claim to participate in the definition of spatial choices. As a matter of fact, in urban and regional planning, interaction usually refers to strategic planning and to soft planning practices in general and is described as having a collaborative nature. An institutionalist perspective (Healey 2007; Servillo and Van den Broeck 2012; Gonzalez and Healey 2005) has contributed to the consideration of co-governance as the process of dialectical interaction between actors and social institutions. From this institutionalist perspective, a planning system can be considered as a technical core embedded within an "institutional frame" (Servillo and Van den Broeck 2012; Servillo and Lingua 2014). Looking at the interdependencies between social, economic and political values, norms and laws, rather than focusing just on formal planning institutions, planning appears as an institutionalised practice guided not only by technical rationality but also by a multiplicity of social rationalities. This challenges the definition of planning spaces, the role of the planner and also the planning possibilities across local boundaries. As a form of collective action (Albrechts 2004; Healey 2007), strategic planning results in mutual adjustments by actors to engage with strategy in appropriate ways, be it in the form of a partnership, agreement policy or political compromise (Albrechts and Balducci 2013: 22).

However, the interrelation between hierarchical governance's forms of hard institutionalisation (Sørensen 2013), developed within the conventional "cascade-shaped" framework of statutory instruments that inform spatial planning systems, and collaborative governance's forms of soft institutionalisation is at stake. The nature of soft planning practices, in the form of "informal negotiation" involving different actors and their capacity to produce scenario and long-term visions (such as some of the regional design practices that are discussed in this book), makes strategic planning something "other" than statutory planning (Albrechts and Balducci 2013).

Notwithstanding its contribution to spatial innovation, creativity and political discussion on spatial priorities, strategic planning can be additional to, but not substitutive of, land-use planning (Kunzmann 2013; Mazza 2013). Due to the different goals and objectives of the two disciplines, their combination using the same approaches and instruments seems to be difficult and quite impossible (Van den Broeck 2013).

According to Mäntysalo, a possible way to solve this conundrum is to approach strategic spatial planning as essentially a *practical skill*: "the object of strategic planning should not be the production of plans themselves (not even strategic ones), but the production of insights of prospective change and encouraging public debates on them" (Mäntysalo 2013: 52). These considerations pave the way for various reflections on the legitimacy of informal strategic planning in respect to statutory planning (Mäntysalo et al. 2015) and conversely on the strategic role of spatial planning (Galland and Elinbaum 2015).

Seen from an interactive governance perspective, in the latter case strategic planning offers a contribution to planning that will be institutionalised within the hard forms of hierarchical governance (the plan and its rules), moving through defined planning levels and instruments. In the former case, soft/informal planning being a separate process from statutory planning, its institutionalisation becomes an issue to be tackled in order to avoid the detachment of informal planning into a parallel planning procedure, moving from hard to soft forms of formalisation.

If informal negotiation is not only a prerogative of soft planning, but it is also embedded at different levels of government, the concept of interactive governance can be useful to explain both the ties between planning levels and the relationships among different governance modes moving from hard to soft planning practices. In this sense, the Torfing et al. (2012) interactive governance perspective can help highlight how—at any given scale or administrative level—there is a mutual and implicit relationship between actors and their shared agreements with and within the hierarchical organisation of the planning system.

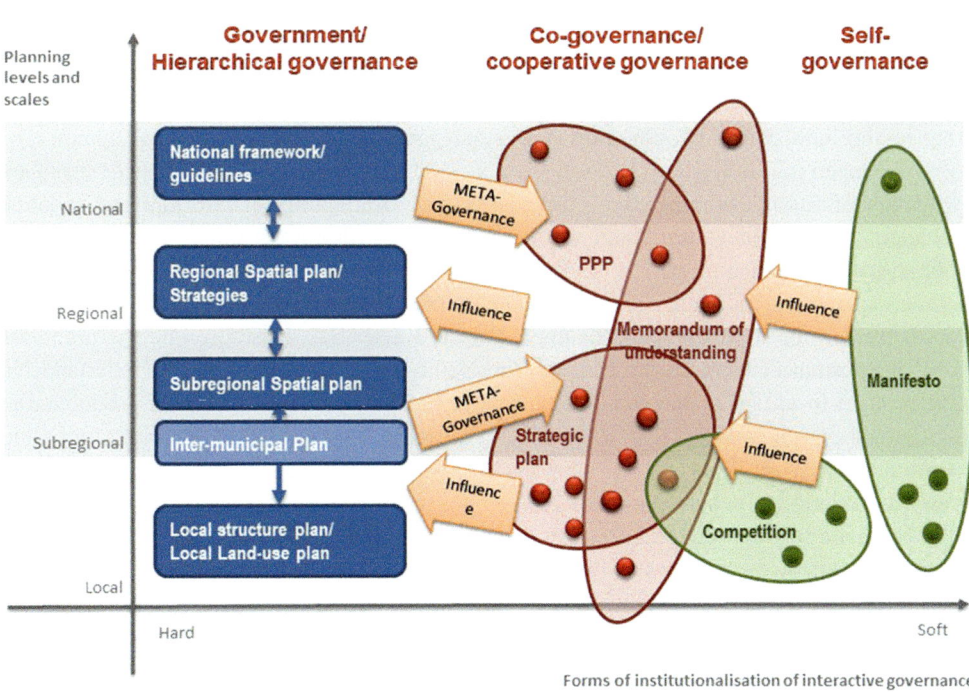

Fig. 2.1 Analytical framework: forms of interactive governance at different planning levels

Thus, the concepts unravelled in Sect. 2.2 can offer a useful framework of thinking to define the relative position of informal negotiation in relation to planning instruments at different territorial levels (or scales), and with different degrees of institutionalisation (from soft to hard forms) in relation to governance modes. For this purpose, the diagram in Fig. 2.1 sets up the governance modes with the tools to formalise interaction, using the legal instruments that inform local statutory planning as a starting point.

As we move away from the local level on the y-axis, planning tools take on names and competencies that change from country to country. Nowadays, in Europe, 32 countries have 255 types of planning instruments, most of which are statutory.[1] Figure 2.1 offers a way to match formal and informal planning, using the notion of governance modes. In this simplification, formal planning systems are considered as an expression of a hierarchical mode of interaction that relies on planning institutions or agencies and leads to formal planning instruments.[2]

The sub-regional level is the most complex to define, since it depends on national planning systems and institutional frameworks. It corresponds to "provinces" in southern European countries such as Italy, Portugal and Spain, and to the French *département*, but it also refers to the agglomeration of municipalities that are obliged or incentivised to engage in joint planning across local boundaries. This is mostly evident in Metropolitan regions. In some regions, the planning level in-between national and local levels has been revoked, as happened in England, where county-level planning was abolished in 2004 and the "vacuum" was replaced (Bianconi et al. 2006) with "regional spatial strategies" that have since also been revoked, in 2010 (Ward and Hardy 2012; Haughton et al. 2013; Pugalis and Townsend 2013). In other countries, such as France and Denmark, the regional level has changed in recent years due to governance rescaling processes tending to provide for bigger regions (Brennetot 2018; Geppert 2015; Galland 2012).

As the scale increases from local to national level, planning tools take on less binding and more flexible features: from regulatory tools at local level (municipality) to strategic frameworks or guidelines at regional and national level. The "statutory" nature of plans covers clear-cut rules set out in planning (and sectoral) legislation. Regulating form, content and planning processes guarantee legal certainty for civilians and investors (Mäntysalo 2013; Van den Broeck 2013).

At both the local and upper levels, a more "strategic" nature of plans is envisaged in order to create possibilities for discretion within the planning system, by providing strategic imagination and guidance to statutory local master plans (Mäntysalo et al. 2014, 2015). This openness to discretion changes in relation to the nature of the planning system (Nadin and Stead 2008) and seems more difficult in planning systems coming from the Urbanist tradition, such as the one in Italy (Lingua and Servillo 2014). In other countries with a comprehensive, integrated planning approach, such as the Netherlands (Zonneveld and Spaans 2014), a degree of discretion is possible and opens up flexible and creative approaches (Balz 2018).

At the same time, moving along the x-axis, the modes of governance can be visualised in terms of different degrees of institutionalised interactions, in which interactive governance develops from a hard mode (hierarchical governance) to softer forms of institutionalisation, meta-governed (co-governance) or self-determined (self-governance).

This form of visualisation also encourages reflection on the differences between forms of institutionalisation relating to hard or soft governance and their connected planning spaces and instruments. While the final outcome of hard interactive governance, which is developed within legal procedural frameworks, is a plan and its apparatus of maps and documents, the panorama of soft ways to institutionalise interactive governance in the framework of informal and collaborative planning is wider, from an exchange of letters of commitment to the definition of multilevel policy arrangements (memorandum of understanding, public–private partnership, etc.) or a joint strategy within the framework of a strategic plan/programme. In the context of self-governance interaction, engagement may result in a proposal for public authorities or collaborative arenas, as well as a manifesto on defined topics (typical examples are the activities of environmental organisations) or even to bottom-up reflections on future scenarios. In the case of The Netherlands Now as Design (Nederland Nu Als Ontwerp— NNAO), an initiative brought to life by planners and designers as individuals with the aim of producing a public exhibition on Dutch urban and regional design, held in 1987, it led to a 3-year long design process imagining four alternative futures for The Netherlands (for a summary, see Balz 2018; Salewski 2013).

Last but not least, the relationship between hard and co-governance modes has to be targeted: the contribution of co-governance in clarifying the role and interrelationship between the different planning levels and territorial scales needs to be explored. Albeit for convenience of representation, a planning system is usually depicted as a linear and incremental sequence of plans, yet it is rather a multifaceted and complex process in which informal and strategic planning can both play a key role, by giving voice to diverse actors and voices aiming to influence the legal framework. Moreover, within the framework of meta-governance, it is in the interest of governments to boost planning collaboration by encouraging hierarchical governance to embrace co-governance soft forms of institutionalisation, referring to soft spaces with fuzzy boundaries.

---

[1] Böhme (2018).

[2] Of course, reality is much more complex and some planning systems, even if used in a centralized way, do not have strong hierarchical features. Moreover, some countries engage in national planning but without much expertise (e.g. in federal systems such as Germany and Austria); in other countries, some levels are lacking (in England, the county and regional planning levels have been revoked, and in Italy, there is no national planning level).

Allmendinger et al. (2015) identify these soft spaces as social constructions—existing in conjunction with, but separated from, the corresponding spaces and scales of political–territorial boundaries—and internal divisions of the nation state in regions, sub-regions and local governments. Such a nature poses questions of accountability and legitimacy regarding the engagement of private actors and even elected politicians and government actors. In the end, the outcomes of these forms of governance, in order to be effective, need to change or at least challenge ordinary hierarchical policies and instruments. If they succeed in this task, they cannot avoid being institutionalised by passing through formal government decision-making processes: "While soft forms of governance are not directly controlled by elected councils, the final outcomes generally still have to pass through the decision-making process employed by such councils" (Zonneveld and Spaans 2014: 4). The concern of institutionalisation implies a need to focus on how to make the output of interaction effective. Again, a focus on a particular notion coming from policy analysis and administrative studies can be useful for this scope.

2.4 Making Interactive Governance Effective: The Role of Images

In previous sections, how formal forms of spatial planning (statutory, binding) relate to informal forms (strategic, visionary, designed) has been linked to different concerns which have gained emphasis in literature: separating strategic and informal planning from statutory planning (Albrecht and Balducci 2013); defining spaces for interaction and their boundaries (Allmendinger et al. 2015); ways of encouraging or enhancing soft governance (Zonneveld and Spaans 2014; Allmendinger et al. 2015); the strategic dimension of spatial and land-use planning (Mäntysalo 2013; Van den Broeck 2013; Galland and Elinbaum 2015). Emphasis was placed on the need to—at certain times—compare formal planning (i.e. the hard form of the institutionalisation of interaction in spatial planning) with informal spatial planning practices (Mäntysalo 2013; Galland and Elinbaum 2015). Here, we discuss a lateral question: how can we institutionalise and make the output of informal planning and soft governance processes effective?

An interesting suggestion for analysing ways to institutionalise interaction can be found in what Kooiman and Bavinck (2013: 18) call "governing elements": images, instruments and action. The scholars argue that "[i]n general terms, images are sets of governing ideas, instruments give these ideas substance, and action puts these instruments to work" (*idem*, p. 18). This distinction certainly sounds pertinent in the spatial planning domain. In highlighting the role of *images* on decision-making processes, politics can be seen as a process of "image formation" (Boulding 1956) that defines "visions, metaphors, models, knowledge, facts, judgements, presuppositions, hypotheses, convictions, ends and goals. They not only relate to specific issues at hand, but to fundamental social, political and ethical questions, often of a systemic nature such as in value or knowledge systems" (Kooiman and Jentoft 2009: 820). *Instruments* are the intermediate element that links images to action through a varied assortment of tool boxes (Hood 1983) consisting of rules and regulations, taxes, fines and subsidies, while more recent ones include covenants and certification. Given the number and degree of formalisation of instruments, the question of their nature and possible instrumental use arises: "contrary to what the instrumental toolkit metaphor suggests, however, instruments are not a neutral medium—in fact, their design, choice and application frequently elicit strife. It is clear that the choice of instruments is not free" (Kooiman and Jentoft 2009: 821). Finally, *action* causes instruments to become operative. "This includes the implementation of policies according to set guidelines, which is often a dry and routine affair. However, action may also consist of mobilising other actors in new and uncharted directions. In this case, actors rely on convincing and socially-penetrating images and sufficient socio-political will or support. The interactive aspect of governance thus emerges succinctly" (ibidem). Societal support and political will, more than financial resources, are key factors to avoid pertinent and relevant images and instruments remaining on paper.

The above-outlined governing elements assume the central role of images in governance, and this role is confirmed in both public administration and spatial planning studies. Taking as given the role of instruments and actions as institutions—i.e. as a formal construct of a planning process that has been built up through interaction (plans and their operative instruments in the context of hierarchical governance, agreements and memoranda of understanding and their actions in the context of co-governance)—this paragraph will therefore focus on the role of images in interactive governance therefore.

According to Kooiman and Jentoft, "images constitute the guiding lights in terms of the how and why of governance" (2009: 820). A major strand of spatial planning literature refers to "image-formation" processes in terms of strategic framing. Such acts of creating orientation, i.e. identifying critical actions by recognising strategies through a process of evocation, visualisation, naming and framing (Healey 2007: 188–189), require "intense simplification and selectivity" (Healey 2009: 449). A minor strand of literature treats this process in terms of regional design. This strand explores how spatial representations, maps and plans—by referring to different dimensions of planning concepts—can add discretionality to indicative planning frameworks (Balz and Zonneveld 2015; Balz 2018). The focus on images as spatial representation in planning is obvious. They are the means of planning the arrangement in space of material public and private elements (buildings, infrastructures and activities) through diagrammatic representations (Faludi 1996). Notwithstanding, visualisation by using images to display actual and future scenarios plays a crucial role in planning (Söderström 1996, 2000), and spatial representation in the form of maps, plans, sketches or other cartographic illustrations is acknowledged to be a powerful means of assisting decision-making processes involving complex organisational settlements at the macro-regional, inter-regional, sub-regional and metropolitan scales (Neuman 1996, 2000; Dühr 2006; Zonneveld 2008).

From a relational perspective, considering images to be socially constructed, images are the relative expressions of actors' preferences (Davoudi and Strange 2008). In planning, images are spatial representations that "are used to indicate physical change, as well as to influence the organisation of planning processes, the position and decisions of key actors in these processes, and the deliberation of political norms and values" (Balz and Zonneveld 2015: 873). Neuman underlines the role of participants' mental images in the planning process, together with the role of visual and verbal images (plans, drawings, models, rhetorical slogans and metaphors) as "the glue that bound the participants to the process and held process together" as well as the "lubricant for political accord because beneficiaries could "see" what they were getting" (Neuman 1996: 88). In order to enhance its persuasive power, durability and widespread acceptance, an image has to be flexible and open to negotiation (Neuman 1996: 91). By indicating territorial boundaries, images thus constitute power structures and may produce agreement, but they can also elicit strife (Zonneveld 2005: 41). This is probably why discourses on spatial imageries have often been associated with the domain of strategic spatial planning (Healey 2006; Davoudi et al. 2018) and regional design practices (Neuman 1996, 2000) rather than statutory planning. By intentionally drawing on repertoires of existing symbols for the purpose of politics and planning, visualisation generates meaning and—in the form of general principles or spatial images such as maps and diagrams—makes spatial strategies work as shared orientation or "reference frames" (Davoudi 2011: 438) with persuasive power (Healey 2009: 441).

A comprehensive summary of the notions above would see images as playing the role of "institution builders" (Neuman 1996: 293). From this perspective, images become integral to the evolution of an institution when they capture salient characteristics that form part of the mental images that its members use to understand and perpetuate it (Neuman 1996). This widespread dissemination of powerful arguments and metaphors imprinting strategic orientations implies that—changing the scale and the complexity of the context and authors involved—even the choice of the images and their construction becomes an important issue, as does their role in orienting governance relations within the planning process.

2.5 The Use of Images in Governance Rescaling: Regional Design Practices of Interchange

Considering governance rescaling as an interactive practice opens up interesting reflections on horizontal and vertical movement along the conceptual framework in Fig. 2.1, together with its transposition into images. This section concerns an approach to these movements, focusing on images that move or "travel" through planning levels and governance modes and relative planning spaces, in order to understand the nature and forms of interconnection among horizontal and vertical movements and to seek to enhance it.

Within the framework of interactive governance, it may be useful to look at the relationship between planning instruments and the images that define them at different levels (vertical movement) and in different governance modes (horizontal movement). Figure 2.2 depicts a reflection on such relations.

The figure first shows how the *vertical movement* among planning levels and instruments informs spatial representation changes at each level. Images have a very clear boundary between the local level (where georeferenced maps conform the usage of soils, for example, and give normative prescriptions with legal value) and the territorial level (where the change in scale results in greater imprecision in the depiction of infrastructural corridors and development areas that have more or less defined buffer zones). In scaling images up from local to "larger than local" level, the highly political nature of visions and maps has to be recognised, accepted and appreciated. In Zonneveld's (2005) analysis of the attempts to visualise European transnational space and its connected images, the choice of images can even result in avoiding maps, as in the European Spatial Development Perspective—ESDP—where pictograms without spatial dimension were produced. At regional, trans-regional and even national and transnational levels, spatial visions in the form of analytical maps are the foundation for creating visions (however, they are not visions in themselves). These visions usually come in the form of diagrams and pictograms.

The fact that images can assist in the vertical movement of governance is implied in a set of theoretical notions: since maps are a spatial construct, the product of a complex social and political process, Zonneveld conceives visioning and mapmaking as a process of "multiple visioning". This means they provide not for a single vision but for "a plurality of visions and maps with multiple strategies for one and the same territory. Instead of striving for a single vision the aim should

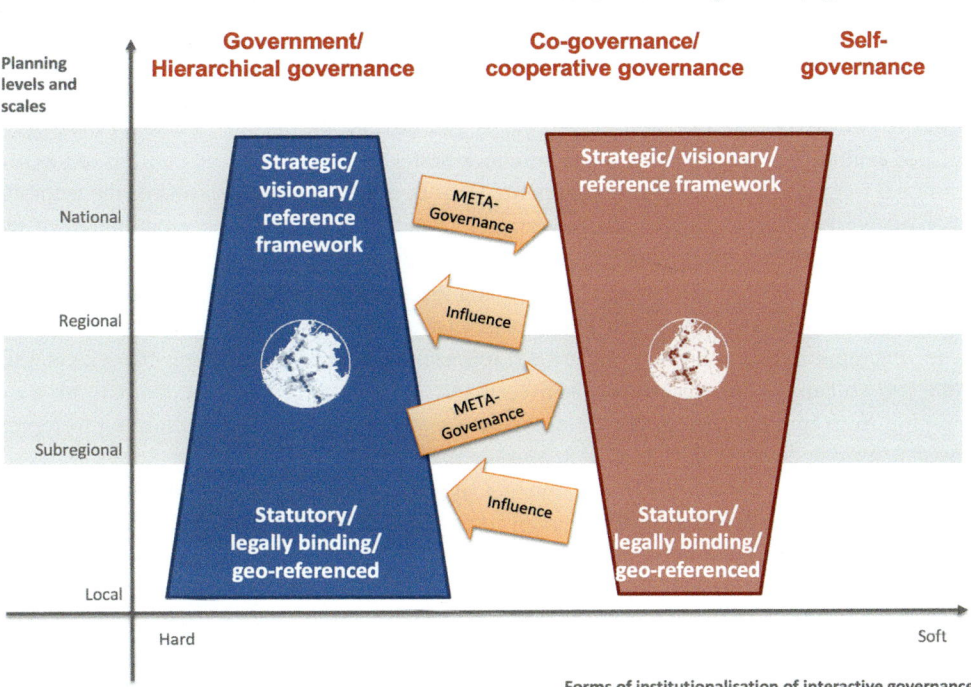

Fig. 2.2 Focus on images and visions in changing scales and governance modes

be to develop an array of visions and maps, each unveiling a 'reality' or a desired future" (Zonneveld 2005: 59). This is quite difficult at every statutory planning level because, despite the fact that "many European planning systems have undergone more or less far-reaching reforms over recent years, the cartographic representations of spatial policy appear to remain unaffected by this evolution and continue to carry forward traditional approaches" (Dühr 2006: 125). In this context, the metaphorical use of maps and ideograms is an issue: even within hierarchical planning, while moving from local to regional levels, forms of visioning emerge that are increasingly abstract, and which take on strategic characteristics.

A useful concept with which to understand vertical governance changes, both in scale and in the prescriptiveness of images that challenge the planning instrument, is that of a "bifurcation point". Mäntysalo suggests that, as strategic framing moves from historical trends and the present situation towards possible futures, it becomes possible to identify "the future 'bifurcation point' where the scenario paths start to separate from each other" (Mäntysalo et al. 2015: 177). This bifurcation point is envisaged as a departure point, which starts to frame the more immediate (short-term) realm strategically. Up to this point, the provisions of local plans followed historical paths and, by providing for certain land-use developments and related rights, lay in the realm of statutory planning. After this point, instruments and their images take on more strategic meanings and features. This gives these plans a different nature and form: "the more schematic, "higher" levels of planning (local master planning and regional planning) would be given the task of accommodating alternative longer-term development scenarios with the necessary flexibility. At the detailed planning level, we would ask what we can "fix" in the "positive" instruction of land-use development and the distribution of related development rights in the immediate horizon of existing development trends, perceived needs, goals and initiatives. In longer-range master and regional planning, we would rather take the "negative" approach of identifying the limits of longer-term flexibility required in our preparation for alternative scenarios" (Mäntysalo et al. 2015: 178).

Figure 2.2 also depicts horizontal relations: for our purposes,[3] in effect, this reading is particularly interesting also for interpreting *horizontal movements* as it provides a deeper understanding of the effects of spatial representations coming from the different modes of interactive governance. It aids our understanding how statutory and strategic/informal forms of

---

[3]Mäntysalo refers to the Finnish planning system, where even higher-level, regional planning instruments have binding contents and respond to the needs of legal clarity, definition of land property development, and legitimacy of planning information and interaction. But the complex framework characterised by the coexistence of overlapping networks and partnerships among different levels of administration, private and third-sector actors, assuming diverse geographic ranges and scales, has to be recognised and challenged.

planning interact, as expressions of hierarchical and soft forms of governance, respectively. On the one hand, indeed, strategic framing should be used in the context of hierarchical governance, in the preparation of plans at different levels (from local statutory land use to regional plans and frameworks), in order "to provide strategic imagination and guidance to these processes" (Mäntysalo et al. 2015: 179). On the other hand, this strategic imagination is also due to the horizontal interaction with softer forms of cooperation, both spontaneous and developing in the context of meta-governance. Visions and scenarios envisaged within the framework of co-governance and self-governance interactions are expected to affect and enter into the institutional framework of planning instruments. This is not only in the interest of the actors involved, but also of governors at all levels who can act through meta-governance to enhance the strategic imagination of informal networks. This is what was intended in England by the introduction, in 2010, of neighbourhood planning as a way to institutionalise parish planning at local level (Gallent and Robinson 2013). Even the institutionalisation method changes through the plan in the hierarchical governance mode and through different, soft instruments (scenarios and visions represented in different forms, from maps to diagrams to pictograms, even artistic representations) moving along the x-axis. Accordingly, while moving from statutory to soft modes of institutionalisation, maps and spatial representations assume a different degree of prescriptiveness, passing from binding cartographic representations to spatial frameworks aiming to represent one or more strategic objectives.

In brief, the theoretical framework provided by the concept of interactive governance and the focus on images allows us to read and interpret both the vertical interactions among actors at different institutional levels and concerning different spatial planning scales, and the vertical relations between forms of soft and hard governance and related planning spaces. Against this background, it is therefore of interest to gain a combined understanding of the interconnections between horizontal and vertical movements: how images from co-governance (soft governance in which visualisation acquires a certain importance) interact and/or interfere with statutory planning and, moving in the vertical direction, how images can then orient the transition from local to regional scale, where issues assume a more complex and strategic character.

In general terms, the main question in planning concerns the effectiveness of the outputs of design imagery, in particular those delivered through co-governance or soft governance planning or that provide regional planning with a strategic character. This question has raised concern in regard to the "external"[4] efficacy of visualisation (Söderström 1996) as the "capacity for certain representations to win over public opinion" (Söderström 1996: 252) and coordinate action (Dühr 2006). Efficacy is thus related to the persuasive power of visualisation, especially for communicating planning policies to the general public, outside of the professional sphere (Söderström 2000). The need to influence the images that people have of the world is recognised as a precondition for initiating change (Sørensen 2006: 110).

Healey (2009) relates this power to frame discourses and shape action through core arguments to the possibility of spatial strategy lasting over time: "If sufficient power is accumulated to give momentum to these strategic orientations, then the framing ideas may travel across significant institutional sites of urban and regional governance, to enrol others with the power to invent, invest and regulate subsequent development. In this way, strategic orientations may come to endure through time and have consequences in shaping future qualities and potentialities" (Healey 2009: 441).

This idea of travelling framing ideas, i.e. the use of images, metaphors and narratives intentionally conceived as "travelling metaphors" (Albrechts et al. 2003; Healey 2006; Hyvärinen 2013), suggests an area of research concerning the capacity of images to travel between different planning and institutional levels (from bottom to top and back) and different planning modes (from soft to hard and back) with a lasting effect over time.

In this travelling process, visioning and visualisation provide for mutual interchange between statutory and strategic planning. Focusing on images as proposed above overcomes the dichotomy between strategic and statutory planning, through a design process that acts as a reflective and argumentative practice at regional scale, centred on images.

In this sense, the concept of "regional design" seems to be a pertinent reference to understand the role of visioning and visualisation between statutory and strategic planning. It is more than simply an up-scaling of urban design, rather it is "a distinctive method of policy argumentation that makes use of spatial representations of the plausible future of regions. Such representations are intended not only to indicate physical changes, but also to stimulate debate on sharing responsibilities and resources for planning tasks among planning actors" (Balz and Zonneveld 2015: 871).

The activation of a regional design process can act as the matching point between statutory and strategic planning, as well as different planning levels, because it provides visions and a "vision is not a plan: it is, at the same time, a great deal less detailed and more complex; it does not define rights and specific duties, or construct executive procedures, but rather delineates a vanishing point, a horizon of meaning for an entire community while specifying the appropriate strategies to

---

[4]The "internal efficacy" of representation enables the translation from one complex reality to its simplified configuration.

reach it. A vision is open and flexible, but endowed with discriminating power: not every action is appropriate within a single vision. It can receive, change or refute not on a juridical basis, but on a logical basis of substantial and formal coherence" (Secchi 2003).

This process of thinking about the future by selecting and reasoning lies between the need for spatial representations to assist the analytical process of co-producing knowledge and, simultaneously, to aid policy definitions through their spatial transposition. Moreover, regional design as a form of network urbanism at regional scale can contribute to institutional design: "regional design prompts a reallocation of the capacities of governance institutions, and the rights and responsibilities of constituent institutions (levels of government) incident on the region. Regional design in this sense—as a form of informal 'interstitial' planning—becomes a matter of creating and enhancing institutional capacity" (Neuman and Zonneveld 2018: 1306).

In this form of "interstitial" planning, regional design contributes at all levels to "an extreme effort of imagination" (Velo and Pace 2018; Lingua 2018b) by providing new analytical perspectives on the region, exploring ways of spatial, functional, temporal organisation and, in the end, promising a better region (Förster et al. 2016).

2.6 Conclusion

The reading of governance rescaling processes proposed in this chapter examines the governance relationships affecting a region through the lens of interactive governance. This concept has enabled processes and tools of governance rescaling to be related to planning levels (from local to national level), governance modes (from hierarchical to co-governance) and the underlying spaces of interaction (from hard to soft). Recognising the relative position of a process and the actors involved allows a better understanding of the interrelations between the different stakeholders and the objectives they pursue. Interactive governance has been used to look at the horizontal and vertical interrelations between different governance modes (hierarchic-, co- and self-governance), in order to verify where (even explicit) situations of meta-governance emerge and where and when soft governance processes manage to influence hierarchical governance and its tools.

In the planning domain, co-governance and self-governance interactions provide for scenarios and visions with different degrees of formalisation and institutionalisation. If the institutionalisation of hard planning practices passes through the formal procedure of approval of the plan, soft planning practices are expected, with or without formalisation, to affect statutory—hardly formalised—planning practices.

This expectation, emerging both from a bottom-up perspective as well as a frame of meta-governance, emphasises the role of actors in activating changes through the modification of existing institutions and even the creation of new self-organised ones. If this process of the institutional design of regional governance is accompanied by regional design, new visual languages and narratives can emerge that change the perception of a region and the design of its future (Neuman and Zonneveld 2018). This creative practice is intended to define the region, not only in terms of physical interventions but also by helping to create institutional and organisational capacity through spatial representations (Balz and Zonneveld 2014; Kempenaar et al. 2016; Balz 2018; Neuman and Zonneveld 2018). In this sense, regional design does not replace statutory planning, nor any other strategic planning model, but represents the moment of blurring of the lines between these two dimensions, through the construction, clarification and sharing of a vision by establishing indicative frameworks, images and visualisations of the territory that are functional to the interaction between institutions and stakeholders involved in a territorial project.

Within this process, the creation of spatial representations is essential not only for creating, testing and calibrating strategies, but mostly for building the institutional basis to support and implement them. Regional design as a form of network urbanism at regional scale (Neuman and Zonneveld 2018) can contribute to institutional design: "Regional design prompts a reallocation of the capacities of governance institutions, and the rights and responsibilities of constituent institutions (levels of government) incident on the region. Regional design in this sense—as a form of informal 'interstitial' planning—becomes a matter of creating and enhancing institutional capacity" (ibidem: 1306). In this sense, images act as "institution builders" (Neuman 1996: 293) and are used in regional design to make the region visible and legible (Thierstein and Förster 2008) and to build up institutional capacity through a visioning process. In formal planning systems, this process of visualisation, passing through the "bifurcation point" (Mäntysalo et al. 2014), i.e. the point from which the planning process loses statutory contents in favour of strategic framing, leads to changes in the perception of the region and its future.

In this chapter, the images produced during interaction are assumed to be indicators of such changes, both in the form of visualisation of the region in its multiple facets and scales (from the administrative boundaries to functional dynamics, from intermediate entities between the state and the local to complex urban and metropolitan regions) and of visioning as the act of providing future scenarios for such regions. Given their capacity to influence a decision, build a bridge, help frame decision-making, plan a region, enhance innovation in plan-making, and change things or ways of thinking (Faludi 1996), the performance of images is thus a major factor in analysing interactive governance.

By analysing the visions and visualisations that have been produced during interaction among different actors, both in terms of hierarchical and soft governance, as well as the ways they have been used, it is possible to understand how these processes have mutually influenced each other, the first in a context of meta-governance and the latter with the will to influence the institutional contexts and even to create new institutions. Finally, the institutionalisation of visualisations and spatial representation passes through both hard governance instruments in processes of hierarchical governance (the plan) and softer governance instruments (memoranda of understanding, agreements, etc.) in co-governance planning practices.

In this interaction, regional design as a process of construction, clarification and vision-sharing does not replace statutory planning, nor any other strategic planning model, but represents the moment of interchange between these two dimensions, by establishing indicative frameworks, images and visualisations of the territory that are functional to the interaction between institutions and stakeholders involved in a territorial project. It is the moment in which images "travel" from one level to another, from soft to hard governance and vice versa, and this "travelling" process can change spatial imaginaries about the region and its future.

How we measure the performance, and even predict the efficacy of a regional design process is an issue (Förster et al. 2016). Consequently, interesting questions for further research concern the capacity of regional design to make governance and spatial changes visible and to make spatial imaginaries shift between scales and planning, and between governance modes and spaces.

References

Albrechts L (2004) Strategic (spatial) planning re-examined. Environ Plan 31(5):743–758

Albrechts L, Balducci A (2013) Practicing strategic planning: in search of critical features to explain the strategic character of plans. disP 49:16–27

Albrechts L, Healey P, Kunzmann K (2003) Strategic spatial planning and regional governance in Europe. J Am Plan Assoc 69(2):113–129

Allmendinger P, Haughton G (2010) Spatial planning, devolution, and new planning spaces. Environ Plan C: Gov Policy 28:803–818

Allmendinger P, Haughton G, Knieling J, Othengrafen F (eds) (2015) Soft spaces in Europe. Re-negotiating governance, boundaries and borders. Routledge, London

Balz VE (2018) Regional design: discretionary approaches to regional planning in The Netherlands. Plan Theory 17(3):332–354

Balz VE, Zonneveld WAM (2015) Regional design in the context of fragmented territorial governance: South Wing Studio. Eur Plan Stud 23(5):871–891

Bianconi M, Gallent N, Greatbatch I (2006) The changing geography of subregional planning in England. Environ Plan C: Gov Policy 24(3):317–330

Böhme K (2018) COMPASS (Comparative Analysis of Territorial Governance and Spatial Planning Systems in Europe) project, intervention at the ESPON workshop regional and national spatial planning: new challenges and new opportunities, contributions from ESPON research, 28 March, Paris

Boulding KE (1956) The image. University of Michigan Press, Ann Arbor

Brenner N (2004) New state spaces: urban governance and the rescaling of statehood. Oxford University Press, Oxford

Brenner N (2009) Open questions on state rescaling. Camb J Reg Econ Soc 2:123–139

Brennetot A (2018) A step further towards a neoliberal regionalism: creating larger regions in contemporary France. Eur Urban Reg Stud 25(2):171–186

Bryson JM (2004) What to do when stakeholders matter: stakeholder identification and analysis technique. Public Manag Rev 6:21–54

Castells M (1996) The network society. Blackwell, Oxford

Davoudi S (2011) The legacy of positivism and the emergence of interpretive tradition in spatial planning. Reg Stud 46:429–441

Davoudi S, Strange I (eds) (2008) Conceptions of space and place in strategic spatial planning. Routledge, London/New York

Davoudi S, Crawford J, Raynor R, Reid B, Sykes O, Shaw D (eds) (2018) Spatial imaginaries: tyrannies or transformations? Town Plan Rev 89(2):97–124

Dühr S (2006) The visual language of spatial planning: exploring cartographic representations for spatial planning in Europe. Routledge, London

Esmark A (2007) Democratic accountability and network governance: problems and potentials. In: Sørensen E, Torfing J (eds) Theories of democratic network governance. Palgrave Macmillan, Basingstoke, pp 247–261

Faludi A (1996) Framing with images. Environ Plan 23(1):93–108

Förster A, Balz V, Thierstein A, Zonneveld W (2016) The conference 'Shaping Regional Futures: Mapping, Designing, Transforming!' A documentation. Munich/Delft

Galland D (2012) Is regional planning dead or just coping? The transformation of a state sociospatial project into growth-oriented strategies. Environ Plan C: Gov Policy 30:536–552

Galland D, Elinbaum P (2015) Redefining territorial scales and the strategic role of spatial planning. disP 51(4):66–85

Gallent N, Robinson S (2013) Neighbourhood planning. Communities, networks and governance. Policy Press, London

Geppert A (2015) Anna Geppert—France. disP 51(1):36–37

Gonzalez S, Healey P (2005) A sociological institutionalist approach to the study of innovation in governance capacity. Urban Stud 42:2055–2069

Hart P (2013) Reviews. Public Adm 91(4):1071–1082

Haughton G, Allmendinger P, Counsell D, Vigar G (2010) The new spatial planning: territorial management with soft spaces and fuzzy boundaries. Routledge, London

Haughton G, Allmendinger P, Oosterlynck S (2013) Spatial planning and the new localism. Plan Pract Res 28(1):1–5

Healey P (1997) Collaborative planning: shaping places in fragmented societies. Macmillan, London

Healey P (2003) Collaborative planning in perspective. Plan Theory 2(2):101–123

Healey P (2006) Relational complexity and the imaginative power of strategic spatial planning. Eur Plan Stud 14:525–546

Healey P (2007) Urban complexity and spatial strategies. Towards a relational planning for our times. Routledge, London

Healey P (2009) In search of the "strategic" in spatial strategy making. Plan Theory Pract 10:439–457

Hood CC (1983) The tools of government. McMillan, London

Huxham C (1996) Creating collaborative advantage. Sage, London

Hyvärinen M (2013) Travelling metaphors, transforming concepts. In: Hatavara M, Hydén LC, Hyvärinen M (eds) The travelling concepts of narrative. Jhon Benjamins, Amsterdam, pp 13–42

Innes J, Booher D (2010) Planning with complexity: an introduction to collaborative rationality for public policy. Taylor & Francis, London

Jessop B (1998) The rise of governance and the risks of failure: the case of economic development. Int Soc Sci J 155:29–45

Jessop B (2011) Metagovernance. In: Bevir M (ed) The SAGE handbook of governance. SAGE, London, pp 106–123

Kempenaar A, Westerink J, Van Lierop M et al (2016) Design makes you understand—mapping the contributions of designing to regional planning and development. Landsc Urban Plan 149:20–30

Kooiman J, Bavinck M (2013) Theorizing governability—the interactive governance perspective. In: Bavinck M et al (eds) Governability of fisheries and aquaculture: theory and applications. Springer, Dordrecht, pp 9–30

Kooiman J, Jentoft S (2009) Meta-governance: values, norms and principles, and the making of hard choices. Public Adm 87(4):818–836

Kunzmann KR (2013) Strategic planning: a chance for spatial innovation and creativity. disP 49:28–31

Lingua V (2018a) Institutionalizing EU strategic spatial planning into domestic planning systems: trajectories of change in Italy and England. Plan Perspect 33(4):591–614

Lingua V (2018b) Regional design for strategic planning: a vision for the metropolitan city of Florence. In: Velo L, Pace M (eds) Utopia and the project for the city and territory. Officina Edizioni, Roma, pp 158–164

Lingua V, Servillo L (2014) The modernization of the Italian planning system. In: Reimer M, Getimis P, Blotevogel H (eds) Spatial planning systems and practices in Europe. Routledge, London, pp 127–148

Mäntysalo R (2013) Coping with the paradox of strategic spatial planning. disP 49(3):51–52

Mäntysalo R, Jarenko K, Nilsson KL, Saglie IL (2014) Legitimacy of informal strategic urban planning—observations from Finland, Sweden and Norway. Eur Plan Stud 23(2):349–366

Mäntysalo R, Kangasoja JK, Kanninen V (2015) The paradox of strategic spatial planning: a theoretical outline with a view on Finland. Plan Theory Pract 16(2):169–183

Mazza L (2013) If strategic "Planning Is Everything, Maybe It's Nothing". disP 49(3):40–42

Nadin V, Stead D (2008) European spatial planning systems, social models and learning. disP 44(172):35–47

Nash J (2005) Social movements: an anthropological reader. Blackwell, Oxford

Neuman M (1996) Images as institution builders: metropolitan planning in Madrid. Eur Plan Stud 4(3):293–312

Neuman M (2000) Regional design: recovering a great landscape architecture and urban planning tradition. Landsc Urban Plan 47:115–128

Neuman M, Zonneveld W (2018) The resurgence of regional design. Eur Plan Stud 26(7):1297–1311

Peters BG, Pierre J (1998) Governance without government? Rethinking public administration. J Public Adm Res Theory 8(2):223–243

Pugalis L, Townsend A (2013) Rescaling of planning and its interface with economic development. Plan Pract Res 28(1):104–121

Rhodes RAW (1997) Understanding governance: policy networks, governance, reflexivity and accountability. Open University Press, Buckingam

Salewski C (2013) Dutch new worlds. Scenarios in physical planning and design in The Netherlands, 1970–2000. NAI 010 Publishers, Rotterdam

Scharpf FW (1994) Games real actors could play: positive and negative coordination in embedded negotiations. J Theor Polit 6:27–53

Secchi B (2003) Projects, visions, scenarios. Planum. J Urban 2(7). http://www.planum.net/projects-visions-scenarios

Servillo L, Lingua V (2014) The innovation of the Italian Planning System: actors, path dependencies, cultural contradictions and a missing epilogue. Eur Plan Stud 22(2):400–417

Servillo LA, Van den Broeck P (2012) The social construction of planning systems. A strategic-relational institutionalist approach. Plan Pract Res 27(1):41–61

Söderström O (1996) Paper cities: visual thinking in urban planning. Ecumene 3(3):249–281

Söderström O (2000) Des images pour agir. Le visuel en urbanisme. Payot, Lausanne

Sørensen E (2006) Metagovernance: the changing role of politicians in processes of democratic governance. Am Rev Public Adm 36(1):98–114

Sørensen E (2013) Institutionalizing interactive governance for democracy. Crit Policy Stud 7(1):72–86

Thierstein A, Förster A (eds) (2008) The image and the region. Making mega-city regions visible. Lars Müller Publishers, München

Torfing J, Guy P, Pierre J, Sørensen E (2012) Interactive governance. Advancing the paradigm. Oxford University Press, Oxford

Van den Broeck J (2013) balancing strategic and institutional planning: the search for a pro-active planning instrument. disP 49(3):43–47

Velo L, Pace M (eds) (2018) Utopia and the project for the city and territory. Officina Edizioni, Roma

Ward M, Hardy S (eds) (2012) Changing gear. Is localism the new regionalism? The Smith Institute, London

Waterhout B (2008) The institutionalization of European spatial planning. Delf University Press

Waterhout B, Othengrafen F, Sykes O (2013) Neo-liberalization processes and spatial planning in France, Germany, and The Netherlands: an exploration. Plan Pract Res 28(1):141–159

Zonneveld W (2005) Multiple visioning: new ways of constructing transnational spatial visions. Environ Plan C: Gov Policy 23:41–62

Zonneveld W (2008) Visioning and visualization. In: Thierstein A, Förster A (eds) The image and the region. Making mega-city regions visible. Lars Müller Publishers, München, pp 107–125

Zonneveld W, Spaans M (2014) Meta-governance and developing integrated territorial strategies: the case study of MIRT territorial agendas in the Randstad (Netherlands). Plan Theory Pract 15(4):543–562

The Institutionalisation of a Creative Practice: Changing Roles of Regional Design in Dutch National Planning

Verena Balz and Wil Zonneveld

Abstract

This chapter discusses the organisational setting of regional design in the realms of spatial planning and territorial governance. As a starting point, it argues that rules on how imagined design solutions function in an abstract, simplified 'planning world' are an important regional design product. When focusing on these rules, regional design practice resembles discretionary action. As such, it aims to improve planning decisions by judging the implications of planning frameworks when applied to particular situations. This implies that the involvement of actors in design practice requires careful consideration. As in any form of legitimate rule-building, a critical distance between those who initiate practices and conduct design, and those who judge the quality and relevance of design outcomes is essential. On the basis of these considerations, the chapter investigates regional design practices that occurred between the 1980s and the 2010s in the context of Dutch national planning. It shows how they transformed from being a form of professional advocacy, criticising planning, into a practice that was pragmatically used to implement a national planning agenda. The chapter concludes by discussing this institutionalisation of a creative practice in the Netherlands, reflecting upon the implications of these outcomes for territorial governance in particular.

Keywords

Regional design • Spatial planning • Territorial governance • The Netherlands

3.1 Introduction

The 'region'—especially the metropolitan region—has become a central focus of spatial planning in recent decades. There is a range of pressing societal problems that spatial planning seeks to deal with which do not occur locally but are instead found at higher levels of scale. Functional and socio-economic relations, embodied in transport and mobility patterns, traverse the boundaries of single administrations. Recently, due to the rising societal and political importance attributed to environmental sustainability and climate change, the accommodation of flows of water, energy and waste, for instance, has become encapsulated in planning agendas. These flows, as well as the spatial developments they cause, are quintessentially regional or even multi-scalar.

The regionalisation of spatial planning has several critical consequences. One important effect lies in what Hajer (2003, p. 182) calls a loss of 'territorial synchrony', that is, an increasing mismatch between autonomous spatial development processes that produce societal problems and the scales and scopes of territorial governing. The result is what Hajer identifies as an 'institutional void' (*idem*, p. 175): a lack not just of effective and efficient politico-administrative structures but also of institutions that hold the knowledge and deeper cultural understanding required for appropriate responses. What one might call

V. Balz (✉) · W. Zonneveld
Department of Urbanism, Delft University of Technology, Delft, The Netherlands
e-mail: v.e.balz@tudelft.nl

W. Zonneveld
e-mail: W.A.M.Zonneveld@tudelft.nl

© Springer Nature Switzerland AG 2020
V. Lingua and V. Balz (eds.), *Shaping Regional Futures*,
https://doi.org/10.1007/978-3-030-23573-4_3

the 'inertia' of statutory planning further perpetuates the void. To find, promote, legitimise and formalise generally accepted, regional spatial planning rules and norms are a highly complex, often contentious and therefore time-consuming affairs. Since regions differ, such rules and norms are likely to lead to an unequal distribution of the costs and benefits of planning across areas, thus often rather accentuating mismatches between societal problems and governing structures than resolving them.

One coping strategy for the loss of territorial synchrony involves taking the geographical scope of spatial problems as the point of departure and letting this inform the creation of more provisional governing structures (De Vries and Zonneveld 2018). Such an approach (embodied for instance in the formation of non-statutory metropolitan regions) entails what Allmendinger and Haughton (2010) call 'soft spaces'. These are malleable territories with a temporary spatial fix, established by informal and often voluntary networked governance arrangements. Addressing regionalisation in this way is not unproblematic, however. Such governance does not equate to representative democracy, giving rise to legitimacy issues. Another problem lies in accountability. Network governance is often shaped by overly pragmatic behaviour, hidden political agendas and a wish to sustain the status quo of power relations (Allmendinger and Haughton 2010). Soft space planning—with all its positive connotations concerning territorial synchrony—is a fragile construct that can easily be crushed between powerful and hegemonic interests. Just like any form of planning, it requires mechanisms that expose and justify action.

This chapter takes the position that regional design in the Netherlands (and possibly also elsewhere) has emerged as an approach that seeks territorial synchrony—an alignment between the geographical scope of spatial problems and comprehensive territorial governing—through addressing the above-mentioned deficiencies of soft space planning. It does so by exploring matches and mismatches between imagined solutions to particular problems, on the one hand, and planning frameworks that are employed by governing actors on the other. Whilst planning strives to establish generally applicable rules and norms, regional design seeks to assess their spatial, political and organisational impact on the ground. In this sense, it is a critical reflection used to justify governing based on its contribution to the resolution of real problems affecting communities in particular regions and areas. Building upon this understanding of regional design as a discretionary action, we argue that design can only thrive in situations which are characterised by a certain distance between actors in design practice and the formal planning apparatus. In particular an accountable distance between those who design and those who determine the relevance of design outcomes for revising existing rules and norms is required.

The chapter explores this necessary distance, taking the use of regional design in Dutch national planning as a case. This exploration has three main sections. The first section supports the understanding of regional design as discretion, by means of concepts from the fields of design and planning theory. The second section contains an empirical analysis and discusses the organisational setting of design practices in Dutch national planning since the mid-1980s. It investigates who took design initiatives, how design briefs and commissions were related to existing planning frameworks, who engaged in making design products and who acted as a 'court of appeal'. Based on observed repetition of practices, as well as their formalisation in policies and policy-making procedures, we identify three consecutive periods in the institutionalisation of regional design in Dutch national planning. The empirical section is followed by a discussion on the implications of this analysis for Dutch national planning. The last section comes back to the starting point, reflecting on the added value of regional design in planning and governance, and how its contribution to territorial synchrony can be further enhanced.

3.2 Perceiving Regional Design as a Discretionary Planning Practice

Design activity is a daily routine, deeply rooted in human behaviour (Lawson 2009; Rittel 1987; Van Aken 2007). It decides the best possible next steps to take, by means of imagination: 'All designers intend to intervene into the expected course of events by premeditated action. All of them want to avoid mistakes through ignorance and spontaneity. They want to think before they act' (Rittel 1987, p. 1). In daily life, design draws on individual experience and intuition. When a body of expert knowledge is used, the practice turns into a professional one. Architecture, urban and regional design all involve expertise on multiple facets of the built environment and the intricate factors that determine the course of its development. The way that this professional practice evolves is most precisely articulated in the fields of architecture and urban design. In these fields, design appears to be a process of argumentation oriented towards desirable, valuable spatial change. Design thinking is said to engage with holistic wholes and complex interdependencies among parts, which turns the practice into an exploration of problems by means of imagined solutions (Caliskan 2012; Cross 1990; Hillier and Leaman 1974; Hillier et al. 1972; Moughtin 2003; Schönwandt et al. 2011). Instead of a linear problem-solution path, design argumentation follows one of 'conjecture and refutation', as Caliskan (2012) noted, referring to Popper (1957). The building of arguments involves creativity and ingenuity, luck and also doubt (Cross 2004).

To argue for change, a designer imagines design solutions whilst simultaneously imagining the world around him or her. The latter is a process of abstraction that leads to the recognition of 'types': simplifications of real, material settings sited between general, abstract categories and highly specific ones (Caliskan 2012; Hillier and Leaman 1974; Schön 1988). Such simplification is instrumental in design because it enables a designer to take account of matches and mismatches between an imagined design solution and the context within which the solution is expected to perform (Schön 1988). The sorts of conclusions drawn during iterative design processes can be threefold. Firstly, the testing of solutions against types of real-world settings (the 'design world', as it is called by Schön (1988, p. 182)) may lead to the modification of a design solution. Secondly, it may also lead to a changing appreciation of this design world: 'The transaction between familiar type and unique design situation is a metaphorical process, a form of seeing- and doing-as, in which a designer both transforms a design situation and enriches the repertoire of types available to him for further design' (idem, p. 183). Whatever conclusions there are, they rely on recognition of the interdependence between imagined solutions and perceptions of the environment. A third sort of conclusion or design product is implicit in this recognition of interdependencies—the rules that are deduced from testing the imagined solutions against the types that constitute the design world.

Compared to the literature on architecture and urban design, there is relatively little scholarly writing on *regional* design and thus few notions on communalities between practices. What literature there is, however, suggests that regional design is often situated in a context of spatial planning or, to use the above terminology, a 'spatial planning world'. Multiple theories and modes of representation from the field are used to explain concrete regional design outcomes and also their less tacit influence on decision-making. The literature shows that regional design is particularly intertwined with what Davoudi et al. (2018) call 'spatial imaginaries' (see also Van Duinen 2004). Indeed, the relevance of regional design solutions is frequently explained by references to dimensions of collective spatial concepts or 'geographic ideas', for example: the knowledge of spatial development that they imply (Klaasen 2003), the imagery that represents them (De Zwart 2015; Neuman 1996), the concepts, doctrines and discourses that rationalise them (Van Dijk 2011), the planning and governance routines that put them into practice (Balz and Zonneveld 2015; Kempenaar 2017), and the power structures that sustain them (De Jonge 2009). Regional design practices are concerned with highly diverse situations in regions and often refer to multiple dimensions of the spatial imaginaries that underlie the spatial planning frameworks in place. The multiple references that unique practices assemble hinder our understanding of them as one unified approach. However, when grasping regional design practices as a form of rule-building that evolves in the context of preconceived planning frameworks, the following generalisations about the interrelations between regional design and spatial planning become theoretically plausible.

Schön (1988, p. 183) compared design processes to legal procedures: 'As rules of law are derived from judicial precedents, … so design rules are derived from types, and may be subjected to test and criticism by reference to them … [A] designer's ability to apply a rule correctly depends on familiarity with an underlying type, by reference to which the designer judges whether the rule "fits the case" and fills the inevitable gap between the relatively abstract rule and the concrete context of its application'. This perception of design as rule-testing bears a resemblance to *discretion* that is, in popular terms, 'the art of suiting action to particular circumstances' (The Rt Hon Lord Scarman 1981, p. 103), who famously promoted legal discretion in the UK. Discretion, evolving in the context of generally accepted law or regulation, is a search for 'leeway in the interpretation of fact and the application of precedent to particular cases' (Booth 2007, p. 129). It aims to improve rules by judging their implications for particular situations. Understanding regional design as a form of discretionary action (proactive and focused on geography) has implications for the role and positioning of the practice in planning decision-making (for an elaboration of the argument, see Balz 2018), in particular its organisational setting within institutionalised decision-making routines.

In design theory, there is an emphasis on the 'epistemic freedom' of a designer, which is in the 'logical or epistemological constraints or rules which would prescribe which of the various meaningful steps to take next' (Rittel 1987, p. 5). With discretion, the 'room for interpretation' that rules provide in the first place—their flexibility—is a central issue because the choices built into rules determine the discretionary nature of local responses. When there are many choices, discretionary action will likely constitute a refinement of rules based on their application to particular situations; when there are few choices, on the other hand, such action will likely challenge rules and call for their revision (Booth 2007). Depending on the number of choices, decision-making likely evolves in the form of policy argumentation, with a strong collaborative rationale, or else in the form of more contentious dispute (Booth 2007; Tewdwr-Jones 1999). When assuming that regional design is a form of discretion, what in design theory is called 'the relative abstract-ness' of contextual geographies equally predefines the performance of design practices. The ambiguity of these geographies determines if proposed design solutions are either likely to (1) be deduced from premeditated ideas about the built environment, or (2) uncover new aspects, and thus confront the existing ideas. Scholarly literature indicates that regional design is often a collaborative effort involving experts, planners, politicians and designers (De Jonge 2009; Kempenaar 2017; Van Dijk 2011). These distinctions imply that collaboration differs in the light of given choices or degrees of freedom: it may entail pragmatism, where actors commonly work to operationalise a shared spatial imaginary, or it may be a form of advocacy where they pursue different ideas about the imaginaries that constitute the existing 'spatial planning world' and are thus divided by controversy and conflict.

An equivalence between regional design and discretion not only leads to a distinction in the collaborative rationales of regional design practice, it also brings the different roles of design actors to the foreground, as well as the relations between them. One critical implication of all this lies in the power of the regional design commissioner, the party who frames design tasks and thus provides room for interpretation (or epistemic freedom) in the first place. By formulating problem definitions, policy agendas or design briefs, the commissioner predetermines the outcomes and performance of practices as outlined above. Room for interpretation in preconceived rules also predetermines the relations between commissioners and the 'authors' of design proposals—those who engage in the making of design proposals. Whilst in a pragmatic use of regional design both are united by shared spatial imaginaries, they are divided by them in case design is used for advocacy. Last but not least, the equivalence between regional design and discretion implies a need for judgement. In discretion, there is a distinction between discretionary action—the constitution of precedent, or the interpretation of rules on the ground—and discretionary control which is in judging if discretionary action should indeed lead to rule reform. In legal and administrative practice, the quality of discretion is accommodated, like any legitimate rule-building, by transparency and accountability. In organisational terms, distance between a court of appeal and those who seek exemption is essential. Actors need to be free to define objectively whether an imaginary future is a relevant interpretation of fact or an arbitrary fantasy; a precedent to be considered in future planning decisions or a negligible incident.

Above we have explained our perception of regional design as a discretionary planning practice. Below we investigate the implications of this perception by analysing the organisational setting of regional design practices that occurred in the Netherlands between the 1980s, when regional design first appeared as a distinguished discipline in the country and the 2010s. The main focus of this analysis is the constellation of actors involved: those who initiated design practices and formulated briefs or commissions, who engaged in the making of designs and also who judged the outcomes. To provide insight into their motivation for involvement, we also pay brief attention to regional design commissions and products, as well as to the expectations that the practices raised beforehand. For the sake of consistency, this analysis focuses on practices related to Dutch national spatial planning. All the practices chosen involved the national government as a commissioner, advisory and/or court of appeal.

There is widespread recognition that the use of design-led approaches in spatial planning decision-making is relatively mature in the Netherlands (Neuman and Zonneveld 2018). This maturity, reflected in part by the frequent use of practices, allows us to take an institutional perspective on the use of regional design in Dutch national spatial planning. Institutions are 'social practices that are regularly and continuously repeated, that are linked to defined roles and social relations, that are sanctioned and maintained by social norms, and that have a major significance in the social structure' (Jessop 2001, p. 1220). Following this definition, we identify practices that gained prominence in Dutch planning discourse over time, were repeated, adopted in formal policies or else have become enshrined in dedicated organisations with distinct roles in regional design practice. This institutional perspective, in conjunction with our perception of regional design as a discretionary planning practice, has led us to identify three particular periods in the use of regional design in Dutch national planning. These are presented below in three separate subsections. Each starts with a brief description of the aspects of spatial planning frameworks that played a role in regional design practices at the time. We then identify the organisational settings of practices that, in our view, set precedents for others to follow. In the final part of each subsection, we discuss the characteristics of those practices and demonstrate institutionalisation.

3.3 Institutionalisation of Regional Design in Dutch National Planning

3.3.1 The 1980s to Late 1990s: Regional Design as Professional Advocacy

Using design-led approaches in planning was not a new phenomenon in the Netherlands in the 1980s. On the contrary, their use built upon a long tradition that can be traced back to the emergence of urban planning during the early twentieth century. When urban planning appeared as a discipline to address the explosive growth of European cities, the Dutch planner and designer Cornelis van Eesteren became a distinguished figure in a Europe-wide debate on where to take the new discipline in the future. As a member (and chairman of the fourth) Congrès Internationaux d' Architecture Moderne (CIAM), van Eesteren sought to consolidate calls for the realisation of a radical, utopian social program with calls for the consideration of the complexities and evolutionary change of existing cities in planning discourse (Van Rossem 2014). As a Dutch design practitioner, he engaged in making a series of highly influential urban plans—the most famous being the General Extension

Plan (AUP) for Amsterdam—in close collaboration with the more analytically minded Theodoor Karel van Lohuizen (Van der Valk 1990).

Their common work established design as an evidence-informed search for the essence of spatial structures and also as a practice that turns such insights into simple and persuasive guiding planning principles (Van Bergeijk 2015; Van der Valk 1990). Design, as the production of such principles, has become deeply embedded in Dutch planning practice since then. However, it was not until the 1980s that regional design appeared as a particular strand of design, in the context of broad discontent with Dutch national planning (Balz and Zonneveld 2018). The early 1980s were a period of deep economic recession. Planning, which had turned into an overly rigid system largely relying on prohibitive and restrictive land-use regulation, was accused of restricting economic development, specifically by neglecting emerging entrepreneurial, development-led initiatives on the ground. Furthermore, it was perceived to be inward-looking and locked in self-involved procedural complexity. This was because its main emphasis was on administrative reform, expanding the bureaucratic apparatus with projected high costs but unclear benefits (Den Hoed et al. 1983).

The first and most prominent example of regional design initiatives in this period was titled 'The Netherlands Now as Design' (*Nederland Nu Als Ontwerp*, NNAO). The initiative, officially launched by the dedicated NNAO Foundation in December 1984, was taken up by individual planning and design professionals. It was also supported by the Dutch town planning institute (*Bond van Nederlandse Stedebouwkundigen*, BNS), a non-governmental organisation called Architecture Museum Foundation (*Stichting Architectuur Museum*), the Netherlands Scientific Council for Government Policy (*Wetenschappelijke Raad voor het Regeringsbeleid*, WRR) and an organisation representing Dutch building industries (Van der Cammen 1987). NNAO's motivation was rooted in unrest surrounding the rigidity and introverted character of Dutch national planning, as outlined above. In particular, it was driven by dissatisfaction regarding the recurring government's neglect of regionalisation and the impact that had on the different regions and areas (Hemel 2013; Salewski 2012). The NNAO initiative was set up to organise a public exhibition to pillory neglect and was prepared using a carefully staged, three-year design process. In the first instance, robust regional spatial development trends were analysed by experts. In the second instance, these trends were associated with four major political streams (socialism, liberalism, Christian democracy and a self-invented stream developed from trends in technological innovation). The scenario technique was used to illustrate the willingness of political parties to act upon development. In the last instance, these four scenarios were turned into 'images of the future' (*toekomstbeelden*), portraying development in national and regional territories as well as 32 so-called design fragments, each imagining the local spatial interventions that the scenarios could lead to (Fig. 3.1). Together these renderings of plausible spatial outcomes, accomplished by experts and professional planners and designers, were to indicate the political weight of planning decisions (De Zwart 2015).

A second prominent regional design initiative that occurred in the 1980s was taken by the EoWijers Foundation, set up in 1985 by members of BNS and the association of Dutch garden and landscape architects (*Bond van Nederlandse Tuin- en Landschapsarchitecten*, BNT), in collaboration with national and provincial planning agencies. The organisation was named after a former director of the National Spatial Planning Agency (*Rijks planologische Dienst*, RPD) who advocated, like the NNAO initiative, the consideration of regional spatial development in planning decision-making by means of design. To develop (and maintain) professional expertise on these matters, from the outset the foundation organised frequent design competitions, generally every three years. Over time, design briefs were formulated to reflect changing tendencies in planning approaches (De Jonge 2008, 2016). The first brief asked designers to identify innovative guiding principles that enhance the characteristic spatial structures of four typologically different Dutch river landscapes whilst simultaneously adapting them to new functions and uses. Its overall aim was similar to that of the NNAO initiative. Regional designs were to bring regionally differentiated, spatial-planning approaches to the foreground by considering spatial development on the ground, and to thus inspire national spatial planning (De Jonge 2009; Eo Wijers Stichting 1986).

In terms of their organisational setting, these two early regional design practices shared a set of characteristics. Both were established by non-governmental actors and both were deliberately placed outside the formal planning apparatus. Their framing, embodied with references to prevailing planning approaches, was self-imposed. Both sought to challenge the rigidity of national planning by advocating more attention to the particularities of regions. Although appealing to different audiences (the general public in the NNAO case, and design and planning professionals in the EoWijers case), the judgement of designs was separated from the framing and conduct of design tasks. Both practices also shared a similar appreciation of design. Van der Cammen (1987, p. 10, our translation), a prominent member of the NNAO organising committee, claimed: 'Artists bring the unconscious to the conscious and in this way create meaning from the meaningless. Conscious action is … highly determined by our ability to position behaviour in a cultural-historical perspective which not only includes the past but also the future'. He saw design as a serious effort to create such consciousness, as a base for planning.

A depiction of regional design as an artistic and inspiring practice can also be found in the EoWijers initiative, albeit with a stronger (and growing) emphasis on efficiency and effectiveness in practice (De Jonge 2008).

Advisory boards and individual members of the national government participated in the first regional design initiatives. A more structured engagement of the government came about in the mid-1990s, with an expansion of the scope of its policy to stimulate architecture design. This policy was first introduced in 1991, to enhance the quality of building across the country, nurture public concern about it and enhance the competitiveness of Dutch professional designers in an international context. In 1996 urban design, landscape architecture and infrastructural design were added to the professional practices that were seen to deserve public support (Ministeries van OCW et al. 1996). More ministries became involved and a set of institutes was associated with the policy, among them the Netherlands Architecture Fund (*Stimuleringsfonds voor Architectuur*, SfA). This was founded in 1993 to set out more detailed funding calls and award funds to design proposals and initiatives. The SfA gained much freedom in facilitating the new focus on design at 'higher levels of scale' (idem, p. 14). Policy guidelines merely indicated that fundable practices had to address the 'cultural dimension' of the built environment, 'spatial quality' and stimulate a diversification of approaches on the grounds of regionalisation, decentralisation and policy-sector integration. Funding was linked to a few substantive design tasks (e.g. the integration of infrastructure, natural and urban development). Above all it was to stimulate the reflexive capacity of design, by means of exhibitions, competitions and publications. The NNAO was mentioned as an inspiration for this approach to the building of critical stances towards planning. It was noted that similar practices are difficult to forecast, due to the creative nature of the design. The policy agenda was deliberately kept broad to 'create room for new opinions and ideas' (idem, p. 18, our translation). Design was to 'mobilise thinking capacity' so 'to enhance policy-making later on' (Ministeries van OCW et al. 1996, p. 18, our translation). In a review of the impact of these early policies, the Netherlands Institute for City Innovation Studies (NICIS) noted: 'In fact, a policy of "soft institutionalism" … was used which—mostly unintentionally—has increased not only the quality, but also the competitiveness of the industry' (Stegmeijer et al. 2012, p. 55, our translation). Policies were seen to have enhanced design expertise on the 'supply side' as well as the quality of commissions and the 'demand for such expertise' (idem).

Fig. 3.1 The Netherlands Now As Design (NNAO): scenarios discussing the impact of societal trends on the spatial development of the Netherlands, from Collection Het Nieuwe Instituut/NNAO, by (from left to right) H. de Boer and T. Koolhaas (Dynamisch scenario), H. Bakker and W. Hartman (Kritisch scenario) and J. Heeling, H. Bekkering and H. Lörzing (Zorgvuldig scenario)

3.3.2 Early to Mid-2000s: Regional Design as a Governance Practice

In the late 1980s and early 1990s, planning approaches in the Netherlands, as in other European countries, shifted as a result of the increasing importance of regions in the liberalising European market economy. Upcoming approaches moved attention away from the planning of formally bounded territories towards the planning of regional spatial networks that stretched across multiple, multi-scalar administrative boundaries. As in other European countries, decentralisation became a more prominent issue in Dutch national planning, resulting in an enhanced appreciation of regional governance (Hajer and Zonneveld 2000; Salet 2006; Salet and Woltjer 2009). To facilitate change the earlier, narrowly defined spatial-planning frameworks were expanded in both their spatial and organisational scope (Balz and Zonneveld 2018). In response to these changes, subnational governments started to form partnerships, on a voluntary basis at first. As will be shown below, some of these became engaged in regional design, thus triggering the emergence of a new generation of practices.

The first Dutch regional design practice that reflected these new planning approaches emerged in the mid-1990s and was concerned about the Randstad region. It was initiated in academic circles when a group of professors at the universities in Delft and Amsterdam set up a discussion platform to denounce the neglect of regional spatial development in national spatial planning once more. The discussion, called The Metropolitan Debate (*Het Metropolitane Debat*, HMD), was led by means of design proposals, largely undertaken by students within design studios at universities (Frieling 1998). The proposals exemplified desirable futures for the region, promoting in particular the integration of urban and open land as well as internationalisation. On the HMD platform, the proposals were used to challenge the rigidity of national planning and also to discuss alternative governance-led approaches. As with earlier initiatives, the HMD sought a broad, public outreach: ideas were debated not only within academia but also in the public arena. Beyond that, planners and politicians at subnational levels became a targeted audience, in an attempt to create broader organisational support for the novel ideas about spatial development and planning. Frieling (2002, p. 494 ff), a key figure in the HDM initiative, noted retrospectively: 'The designs made … expectations visible, publicly debatable and subject to planning and decisions on investment priorities'. He emphasised that these designs were made not only to foster the consideration of spatial development in planning and politics but also to 'forge societal alliances' (Frieling 2002). In 1998, after two years of lobbying efforts, a group of local governments in the Randstad embraced one of the designs, called the Delta Metropolis (*Deltametropool*) and presented the idea to national government as a much-needed alternative for the long-lived Randstad/Green Heart doctrine (Van Duinen 2015). They used the proposal to call for more sector integration in the national planning for the Randstad region and also to advocate their greater autonomy in spatial planning.

In the same year, 1998, the co-operation that had emerged around the Delta Metropolis design was consolidated in the Delta Metropolis Association (*Vereniging Deltametropool*, VDM, an organisation still existent at the time of writing) (Vereniging Deltametropool 1998). In 2001, the Delta Metropolis was adopted by the Dutch Ministry of Housing, Spatial Planning and the Environment (*Ministerie van Volkshuisvesting, Ruimtelijke Ordeningen het Milieu*, VROM). It became one of the national 'urban network' territories that the Fifth report on spatial planning—a new national plan then in the making—had laid out in order to facilitate regionalisation and regional governance (Ministerie van VROM and Rijksplanologische Dienst 2001). Possibly inspired by this precedent, at least four practices resembling the Delta Metropolis then emerged from 2002 onwards: Studio IJmeer 2030+, conducted between 2003 and 2006 and concerned with integrated spatial development in the greater Amsterdam region (Koolhaas and Marcusse 2006); the Arnhem-Nijmegen Node project, concluded in 2003 and considering such integration around the two eastern Dutch cities of Arnhem and Nijmegen (Urban Unlimited 2003); the Design Studio Brabant City, dedicated to development around Den Bosch, Eindhoven, Breda and Tilburg (Bosch Slabbers 2007); and the Studio South Wing, conducted between 2005 and 2007 and concerned with a region approximating the highly urbanised part of the South Holland province (Fig. 3.2) (Atelier Zuidvleugel 2008).

When considering their organisational setting, these four successive regional design practices shared characteristics with their Delta Metropolis precedent. Most remarkable is the strong involvement of coalitions of subnational governments in practices. Design products were created during collaborative processes, led by one or several design professionals, and involved a broad array of experts, politicians, planners, market parties and civil organisations in 'design dialogues' (De Jonge 2009, p. 180). The 'studio' setting, facilitating communication and exchange between participating actors during workshops, excursions and panel debates, became a common format. Communalities between practices are also found in their shared main expectation. The capacity of regional design to 'forge societal alliances', to contribute to effective regional governance, became a key proposition (Balz and Zonneveld 2015). The brief to the Studio South Wing expressed this expectation in an exemplary way: 'The studio is a machine to make an inventory of the relevant projects, plans and programs on local, regional and supra-regional levels of scale; to denominate the relations among these (horizontal); to define nodes and gaps; to distil a hierarchy from this (vertical)' (Provincie Zuid-Holland 2004, p. 2, our translation).

However, an examination of their organisational set-up also highlights the differences between the Delta Metropolis regional design practice and its successors. As already mentioned, the Delta Metropolis design proposal became an 'urban network' of national importance in the fifth Dutch national spatial plan. Besides the Delta Metropolis, the plan had identified a range of other such networks across the country, calling upon local governments to develop regional project and strategy proposals to foster integrated regional spatial development. Subnational governments were expected to act in unity and to coordinate their plans and actions (Balz and Zonneveld 2018). The later regional design practices mentioned above were a response to this open call. Governance arrangements adopted the broad national urban-network agenda, as is evident from the many references to the concept in design briefs. Regional design was used to reflect on how this agenda could best be operationalised in the light of the particularities of each region. These practices thus had a different relationship with Dutch national spatial planning in comparison with the Delta Metropolis design approach. As we have seen, this approach challenged the rigid dichotomy between a (red) Randstad and a Green Heart. The later practices sought the refinement of a national spatial plan that was more flexible. Consequently, the role of the national government changed. The national government was an addressee of criticism in the Delta Metropolis regional design practice. Through framing the later design initiatives with its soft urban-network concept, it became also a commissioner in these, albeit in an indirect way. The national government's engagement in regional design practice was predominantly informal. However, as the Ministry of VROM was a co-funding body of practices and/or a member of the boards that advised and supervised them, in some cases engagement also took more formal shapes.

When comparing this new generation of regional design practices to the earlier ones, which we called 'professional advocacy', a clear shift towards pragmatism is their common characteristic. The examples show that regional design practice started to play a more important role in the implementation of Dutch national planning policies. This tendency was also reflected in revisions of the architecture policy mentioned earlier. The third version of the policy, published in 2000 and entitled 'Designing the Netherlands', had already identified ten 'large projects' that were to be explored by means of design (Ministeries van OCW et al. 2000). Among those projects with a regional scope, one was concerned with the impact of a future international rail connection, another one with increasing the aesthetics of highway infrastructure, and a third one with developing the cultural–historical landscape around the Dutch Water Line, a former military defence (for a review of this national project, see Luiten 2011). Furthermore, the Delta Metropolis had become a 'large project' that was to be explored through design. For this purpose, a coalition of ministries set up their own design studio called the Delta Metropolis Design Studio (*Ontwerpatelier Deltametropool*) (Ministerie van VROM 2003). Four well-known design professionals were invited to engage in a search for the identity of the Randstad region, its 'unity in diversity' and also to reflect on the role of regional design in spatial planning.

In the fourth revision of the architecture policies, published in 2005 (Ministeries van OCW et al. 2005), the relationship between 'fundable' design practice and national planning became even stronger and more formalised. The new policy note was published not as a stand-alone document but as an extension of the National Spatial Strategy, a 2006 revision of the Fifth report by a new government of a more centre-right political colour (Ministeries van VROM et al. 2006; see also Zonneveld and Evers 2014). Under the header 'an action program', funding for design practice was thoroughly linked to the implementation of this plan. Of the ten 'large projects' few were maintained. Projects that were added were more strongly associated with ongoing national policies, most importantly the Belvedere policy which targeted cultural heritage, and the Room for the River programme (*Ruimte voor de Rivier*) (for an analysis of this programme see Rijke et al. 2012). Fundable design was now to be engaged with 'best practice' in the application of these policies and programmes, often within clearly predefined project boundaries. The assessment of funding also became more regulated. The note criticised the way earlier design funding schemes were evaluated and judging the success of future design practices became an obligatory part of assessing national spatial planning (Stegmeijer et al. 2012). A particular trajectory, entitled 'Elaborating professional commissioning', was set up to investigate effective organisational formats in design practice. An independent board advising the national government on architecture policies was enlarged, where previously the Chief Government Architect of the Netherlands (*Rijksbouwmeester*) had fulfilled this task on his own. In 2005, the Board of Government Advisors (*College van Rijksadviseurs*, CRa) was established, adding two professionals with expertise in landscape architecture and infrastructure design, respectively. Altogether expectations regarding the contribution of design to national planning changed: whereas it was initially seen as an approach that inspires planning by means of constructive criticism, the 2005 action programme portrayed it as an approach that first and foremost enhances the efficiency of national planning.

Fig. 3.2 Studio South Wing: scenarios discussing the impact of regional planning agendas on transit-oriented development in the South of the Dutch Randstad region, from Atelier Zuidvleugel (2006)

3.3.3 The 2010s: Regional Design as a Governmental Practice

Whilst the early 2000s produced a strong emphasis on collaborative spatial planning in the Netherlands, from the mid-2000s onward, enthusiasm for involving subnational government in national planning diminished. The National Spatial Strategy published in 2006 indicated the further decentralisation of planning tasks and responsibilities, though not through greater co-operation between levels of government, but rather by minimising the involvement of national government in regional planning. The national planning agenda was slimmed down too, in particular through a diminishing interest in 'spatial quality'. Integration and simplification of national sector policies had to be facilitated by combining ministry strategies and merging their organisation. Planning instruments were also sorted out. Under the purview of this plan and its successor—the 2012 National Policy Strategy (Ministerie van I&M 2012)—direct investment into (largely infrastructure) projects became virtually the sole spatial planning tool (Needham 2015). This had a particular impact on regional design practice.

The Long-Term Program for Infrastructure, Transportation and Spatial Development (MIRT) is dedicated to the distribution of the Dutch Infrastructure fund (*Infrastructuur fonds*) and the implementation of nationally funded infrastructure projects. Since 2008, it has been revised several times (for an analysis of this process Van Geet et al. 2019). In 2008, it became compulsory to consider the spatial impact of new infrastructure, thus in fact turning MIRT projects into integrated area-development projects. In 2010, the MIRT 'rules of the game' were adjusted, with strong implications for the role and position of regional design in Dutch national planning: it became mandatory to employ the practice during early stages of decision-making (Ministerie van I&M 2010). The adoption of design in the highly regulated MIRT procedure had an efficiency rationale regarding the length and complexity of decision-making. The expectation was that design would help to identify proactively the multiple effects of infrastructure change, to identify potential conflicts early on and thus to avoid delays due to ongoing political discussions and battles in judicial courts at later implementation stages. Commenting on the new position of regional design in the MIRT procedure, the then acting Director-General for National Spatial Planning noted that 'the complicated decision-making process had run aground because certain things had been overlooked in the early stages of planning. … [If] you don't do your homework beforehand you'll have trouble through the whole planning process' (Blank et al. 2009, p. 29). Shortly after becoming an obligation, a manual for regional design practice was published by the Ministry of Infrastructure and the Environment (*Ministerie van Infrastructuur en Milieu*, I&M), successor of the former ministries of VROM and Transport and Water (*Verkeer en Waterstaat*, V&W) (Enno Zuidema Stedebouw et al. 2011). It contained detailed instructions on how to use design for different purposes during MIRT procedures. These included the refinement of problem definitions, the identification of preferred solutions as well as the investigation of their spatial and organisational implications. Prescriptions were meant to help funding applicants—usually governance arrangements in predefined so-called MIRT regions—in defining how design will be used during decision-making since it had become compulsory to indicate such use in bids.

Examples of regional design practices under the MIRT programme include Spatial Models SMASH 2040 (*Ruimtelijke Modellen SMASH 2040*), conducted in 2012 and discussing alternative infrastructure solutions for the Amsterdam-Schiphol

Airport-Haarlemmermeer region (Fig. 3.3) (Zandbelt and Van den Berg 2012) and the 2017 MIRT study Accessibility Rotterdam The Hague (*Bereikbaarheid Rotterdam Den Haag*) which elaborated preferred infrastructure change in the Metropolitan Region The Hague-Rotterdam (MRDH) (De Zwarte Hond et al. 2017). The role of the national government differed in these two practices. In the SMASH design practice, it was the sole commissioner because its corresponding territory was projected to become the subject of a national structural vision. The study into MRDH, which lacked this status, was commissioned by the Ministry of I&M in collaboration with governance arrangements in the South of the Randstad. There were similarities in their briefs that included, next to MIRT objectives, multiple references to relevant operational sector policies of both national and subnational government. The design processes also exhibited resemblances. Led by individual design professionals, they involved experts, different ministries, subnational governments, private and civil actors in workshops, expert sessions, panel discussions and also surveys. Their aim was to prepare for Administrative Consultation MIRT (*Bestuurlijk Overleg*, BO MIRT) where the Ministry of I&M, who until 2017 held the sole responsibility for the distribution of the Infrastructure Fund, was to judge the outcomes.

The Ministry of I&M thus embraced regional design as a practice that can help to speed up the implementation of national projects, formalising it under the MIRT programme in 2010. In the same period, the ministry followed a similar rationale when becoming engaged with the International Architecture Biennale Rotterdam (IABR). Since its first edition in 2003, the IABR has been funded by the SfA. The fifth edition, entitled 'Making Cities', had a particular interest in the implementation of design proposals, especially by means of collaborative and participatory planning (Brugmans and Petersen 2012). Next to projects that illustrated tacit outcomes of such approaches on 'test sites' in Brazil, Turkey and the Netherlands, its programme incorporated a distinct branch called Studio Making Projects (*Atelier Making Projects*). The studio was initiated and programmed by the Ministry of I&M, in collaboration with the IABR curators (among them the Director-General for National Spatial Planning). Seven projects were selected for elaboration, all tied in with ongoing national policies. Ministries, other actors with a stake in the projects and design studio supervisors (the latter acting on behalf of the IABR) all became co-commissioners of the professionals selected to develop design proposals for these projects (Boeijenga et al. 2013). The organisational structure around the studio was complicated and deliberately diffuse. The IABR catalogue explained that such diffusion was necessary to meet the twofold objective of the biennale: to enhance the implementation of projects and, at the same time, appeal to broader research and public interest. The explanation concluded: 'So not just double commissioners but also—deliberately—double hats. Welcome to the world of Making Projects, because this will increasingly be the way things are done. Fewer and fewer projects will exist just because they have been started; we can no longer afford to do so. Changing coalitions, connecting interests and joining forces are all part of making a project' (Brugmans and Petersen 2012, p. 42).

The aforementioned regional design practices vary, especially when considering their addressees: a formally appointed commission to judge infrastructure project proposals in the case of MIRT regional design practices, exhibition curators and a critical public audience in the case of the IABR design studios. Their main similarity is the firm position that the Ministry of I&M took as a regional design commissioner, next to its role in 'courts of appeal'. Funding for regional design practices via the architecture policy was reduced at the same time: the production of art should comply more with market mechanisms in the future it was argued (Ministerie van OCW 2011). In 2012, the SfA was merged with other public institutes in the cultural sector to form the Creative Industries Fund NL. In the same year, a new update of the architecture policy was published (Ministeries van I&M et al. 2012). Fundable design efforts were to contribute to the implementation of a national vision on the preservation of cultural heritage, the quality of decision-making in MIRT procedures and the implementation of innovative projects by means of design dialogues under the framework of IABR. A brief paragraph summarised expectations on the performance of funded regional design practices. They were associated with the creation of spatial quality and added societal and economic value as well as innovation. At the same time, they were also expected to deliver a 'better, faster and therefore cheaper process' (idem, p. 9).

Fig. 3.3 Spatial Models SMASH 2040: scenarios discussing interrelations between national infrastructure projects and policies by decentral governments in the Amsterdam-Schiphol Airport-Haarlemmermeer region, from Zandbelt and Van den Berg (2012)

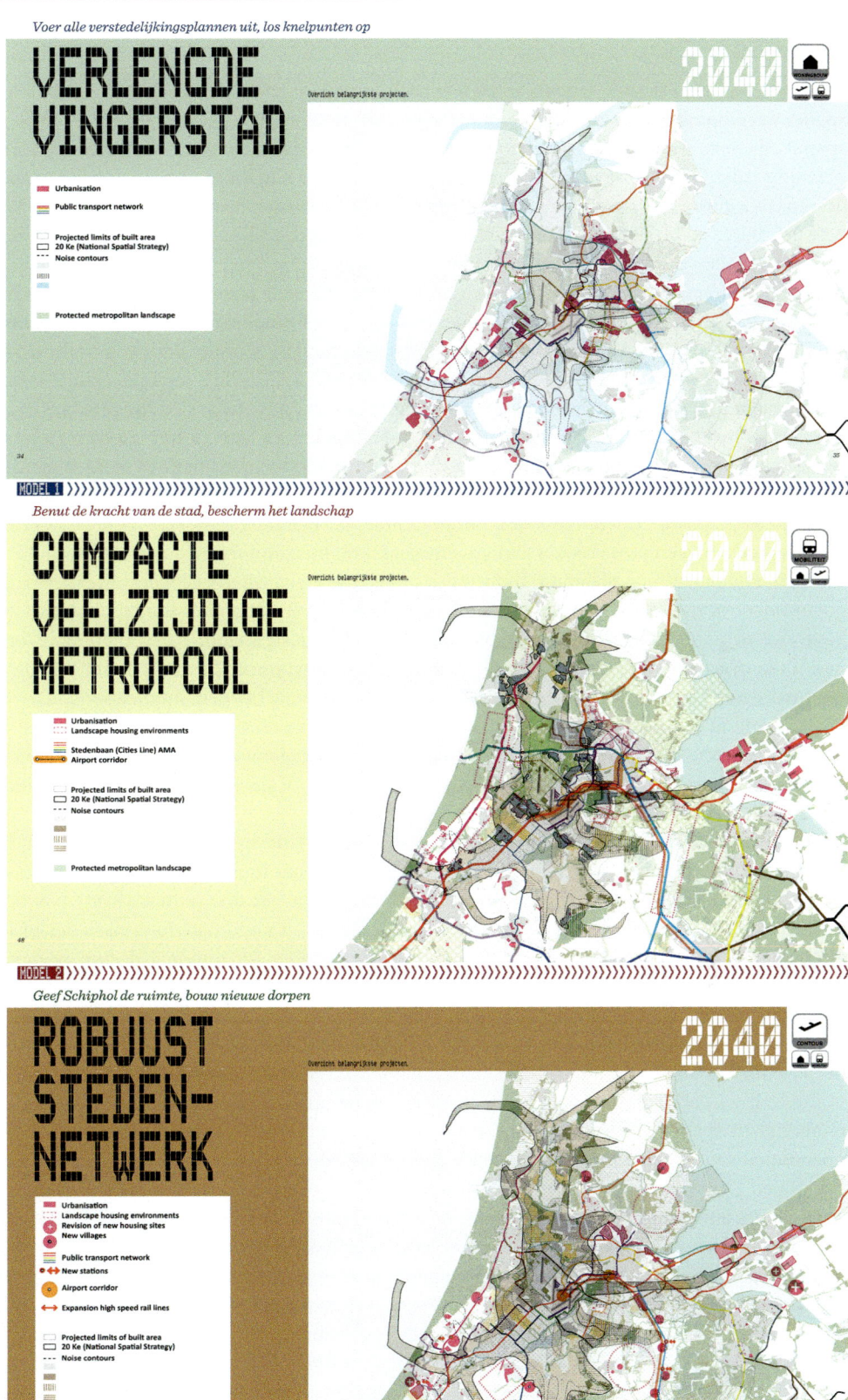

3.4 Discussion

In theory, regional design appears to be testing how imagined local solutions for problems caused by autonomous regional spatial developments can function within a world of planning that is composed of geographic ideas, spatial imaginaries and spatial concepts. Above it was argued that in this testing regional design functions as a form of discretion: it aims to improve planning rules by judging their implications for particular situations. It was further argued that, when employing regional design as a form of discretion in spatial planning, the involvement of actors requires scrutiny: a distinction and distance between those actors who initiate practices, conduct design, and judge the quality and relevance of design outcomes for the revision of rules is essential, as in any other form of legitimate and accountable rule-building. Drawing upon this argument, the organisational setting of regional design in Dutch national planning between the 1980s and the 2010s was analysed, as well as its institutionalisation through repetitive use and formalisation in policies and organisations.

The results of the analysis show that the Dutch national government has become increasingly caught up in regional design practice, during three, at times overlapping, stages. When in the 1980s regional design emerged as a distinct discipline within spatial planning, it was professional designers and planners who first used the practice to challenge Dutch national planning. Supported by their long-established professional associations and policy advisory institutes (operating on behalf of but separately from government), they called upon the public to help them express their discontent about national planning. Although the national government was criticised, it embraced the approach via its architecture policies and channelled grants towards design as a critical reflection on governmental planning.

Distance between professional and governmental realms diminished when decentralisation and governance became prime issues in Dutch national planning. In the mid-1990s, the Delta Metropolis design practice was the first to involve subnational government in the making of a regional design proposal. By adopting the practice as a precedent, the Ministry of VROM gave rise to a generation of comparable practices. The 'design studio' emerged as a format for collaboration, engaging a multitude of actors from different levels and sectors of government and civil and private organisations in the setting out of regional design tasks, the making of designs and judgement of their implications. The national government still had one distinct role in the Delta Metropolis practice, namely to act as a kind of court to which lower levels of government could appeal. From the mid-2000s onwards, it diversified its engagement with the design studios. It remained an important judge, but also started to participate in the framing and running of design practices in particular via its 'urban network concept' policy.

During a third stage, it strengthened its role as a regional design commissioner. From 2000 onwards, funding for regional design practice became ever more tied to projects of national importance, which themselves became increasingly refined in terms of their scale and scope. In 2010, regional design became a mandatory practice in the highly regulated MIRT programme. Two years later the Ministry of I&M became an important commissioner of regional design at the International Architecture Biennale Rotterdam. In the same year, funding for regional design became dedicated to these two national programmes. Subnational government remained involved in the production of designs; however, its role became largely confined to that of a co-designer.

Above, it was noted that the 'room for interpretation' that rules provide in the first place is important for discretion because the choices built into the rules determine if discretionary action is likely to be a refinement of the rules or a challenge to them. It was argued that a similar distinction can be applied to regional design practices. Depending on the ambiguity of premediated spatial imaginaries, they tend to evolve either as a form of advocacy or else play a pragmatic role in their operationalisation. Our empirical analysis based on this distinction reveals that since the early 2000s the national government developed a preference for a pragmatic, instrumental use of regional design for planning decision-making. This is reflected in attempts to unite actors under the umbrella of nationally important projects. It is also reflected in expectations about the performances of regional design. Design was first primarily understood as an artistic and inspiring practice that builds a cultural understanding of regional spatial planning and unleashes 'thinking capacity'. Implementation could come later on, it was argued. During later stages, regional design was expected to perform as a form of territorial management above all, aiming at the formation of societal alliances, the acquisition of organisational capacity, the speeding up of decision-making and, in this way, the reduction of the costs of non-coordination. To employ regional design for pragmatic reasons is certainly a legitimate choice. However, criticism regarding the institutionalisation of regional design in Dutch national planning can also be raised.

One such criticism concerns the re-occurring actor constellations in regional design practices. In any use of regional design, a distance between actors with different roles is required to enhance legitimacy and accountability. When used in the operationalisation of planning, design commissioners and designers are bound by their agreement on a preconceived design task. Discretionary control gains importance in considering, for instance, the implications of conflicts that regional design can bring to the foreground. By occupying a strong role in both the formulation of design tasks and the judgement of design outcomes, the national government has refrained from being truly open to critique.

A second criticism concerns the overly high expectations about the performance of regional design. A pragmatic use of regional design focuses on easing the implementation of national projects, as noted above. However, pre-existing performance expectations were not dropped when the use of regional design in Dutch national planning changed: in a highly pragmatic setting shaped by the commissions and actor constellations described above, design also remained to be seen as an adventurous and inventive practice that can bear unexpected and inspiring results.

A final criticism concerns public support for regional design practice, particularly as provided via the national government's architecture policy. This policy was first dedicated to the creation of a critical spatial planning audience. The nurturing of what was early on called a 'cultural-historic perspective' on planning, or a broader awareness of 'spatial qualities', has faded away into the background—a rather unfortunate development.

3.5 Conclusions

In the introduction to this chapter, it was argued that regional design, through its close resemblance to discretion, may contribute to territorial synchrony: an alignment between societal processes that produce problems and opportunities in particular situations, politico-administrative structures that effectively and efficiently address these problems and opportunities, and cultural adherences that explain the appropriateness of action through shared knowledge and understanding. The analysis presented here indicates that Dutch national government has, to some extent at least, shared our argument: that regional design practice can help to fill the institutional void that results from a lack of synchrony. It employed regional design for an enhanced understanding of its planning implications on the ground, in both cultural and practical terms. Over time, it used practices to enhance understanding of its planning—to create a conscious and critical public that appreciates it. The Dutch government also used regional design practices to accelerate efficiency and effectiveness. When assuming that regional design can indeed assist territorial synchrony, not just in the Netherlands but also elsewhere, a more sophisticated understanding of its performance in spatial planning and territorial governance is required.

Our analysis reflects a particular perspective on regional design: design forms a discretionary practice that assists planning decision-making. Taken from this perspective, two uses of regional design should be distinguished, each with different outcomes: design can be used as expertise that translates a holistic understanding of spatial development and planning into comprehensive, refined planning action on the ground, or it can be used as a more adventurous practice that challenges planning frameworks with unexpected results and surprises and thus expands existing planning frameworks. In theory, these two uses and their outcomes are highly dependent on the choices or 'room for interpretation' that are provided beforehand. Choices predefine the different uses. They also influence the type of collaboration in design practice.

The conceptualisation of regional design as discretionary action emphasises an institutional perspective on practice. This means that actor constellations come to the foreground as an important determinant of the quality of regional design. Distance between those who formulate designs (including the design commissioner, as we have argued) and those who judge the relevance of design outcomes for the revision of rules and norms is particularly required in order to create the legitimacy and accountability of rule-building. In governance and planning theory, there is a distinction between governance that follows a collaborative rationale, based on the appreciation of a broad involvement of actors ('good governance'), and governance that is oriented towards the resolution of real problems on the ground. The latter rationale requires strategic selectivity which in turn often incites conflict, overly pragmatic behaviour and political hidden agendas regarding the rules and norms on which plans are based. Regional design, providing there is distance between actors who pursue different roles in practices, can function as a powerful tool to connect these two governance domains. A precondition for its contribution to territorial synchrony is recognition of the tensions that exist between these domains.

References

Allmendinger P, Haughton G (2010) Spatial planning, devolution, and new planning spaces. Environ Plan C: Gov Policy 28(5):803–818

Atelier Zuidvleugel (2006) Ruimte en Lijn: Ruimtelijke Verkenning Stedenbaan 2010–2020 [Spatial survey city line]. Den Haag, Provincie Zuid-Holland

Atelier Zuidvleugel (2008) Netwerken in Zuidelijk Holland: 1000 Dagen Atelier Zuidvleugel [Networks in Southern Holland. 1000 days of Studio South Wing]. Den Haag, Provincie Zuid-Holland

Bakker H, Hartman W (1987) Kritisch scenario. Nationaal Ontwerp Nieuw Nederland. Onderwerp van Ontwerp [The New Netherlands. An Object of Design]. Stichting Nederland Nu als Ontwerp, Staatsuitgeverij's Gravenhage, Den Haag

Balz VE (2018) Regional design: discretionary approaches to regional planning in The Netherlands. Plan Theory 17(3):332–354. https://doi.org/10.1177/1473095217721280

Balz VE, Zonneveld WAM (2015) Regional design in the context of fragmented territorial governance: South Wing Studio. Eur Plan Stud 23(5):871–891. https://doi.org/10.1080/09654313.2014.889662

Balz V, Zonneveld W (2018) Transformations of planning rationales: changing spaces for governance in recent Dutch national planning. Plan Theory Pract 1–22. https://doi.org/10.1080/14649357.2018.1478117

Blank H, Van Boheemen Y, Bouw M, Brouwer J, Feddes Y, Van Hees J, Hendriks M, Petersen JW, Wierenga E (eds) (2009) Ontwerpen aan Randstad 2040/Designing Randstad 2040, Design and Politics #2 (vol 2). Uitgeverij 010, Rotterdam

Boeijenga J, GerretsenP, Wierenga E (eds) (2013) Nederland Projectenland/The Netherlands in Projects, Design and Politics #7. 010 Publishers, Rotterdam

Booth P (2007) The control of discretion: planning and the common-law tradition. Plan Theory 6(2):127–145. https://doi.org/10.1177/1473095207077585

Bosch Slabbers (ed) (2007) BrabantStad Mozaïek Metropool [Brabant City Mosaic Metropolis]. 's-Hertogenbosch, Programmabureau BrabantStad

Brugmans G, Petersen JW (eds) (2012) Making city. 5th IABR 2012. Catalog International Architecture Biennale Rotterdam. International Architecture Biennale Rotterdam, Rotterdam

Caliskan O (2012) Design thinking in urbanism: learning from the designers. Urban Des Int 17(4):272–296

Cross N (1990) The nature and nurture of design ability. Des Stud 11(3):127–140. https://doi.org/10.1016/0142-694X(90)90002-T

Cross N (2004) Expertise in design: an overview. Design Stud 25(5): 427–441. http://dx.doi.org/10.1016/j.destud.2004.06.002

Davoudi S, Crawford J, RaynorR Reid B, Sykes O, Shaw D (2018) Spatial imaginaries: tyrannies or transformations? Town Plan Rev 89(2):97–124. https://doi.org/10.3828/tpr.2018.7

De Boer H, Koolhaas T (1987) Dynamisch Scenario. Nationaal Ontwerp Nieuw Nederland. Onderwerp van Ontwerp [The New Netherlands. An object of design]. Stichting Nederland Nu als Ontwerp, Staatsuitgeverij's Gravenhage, Den Haag

De Jonge J (2008) Een kwart eeuw Eo Wijers-stichting. Ontwerpprijsvraag als katalysator voor gebiedsontwikkeling [A quarter century of Eo-Wijers Foundation: design competition as a catalyzer for area development]. Gouda

De Jonge J (2009) Landscape architecture between politics and science. An integrative perspective on landscape planning and design in the network society. Doctoral dissertation, Wageningen University, Wageningen

De Jonge J (2016) Ontwerpen in de regio [Designing the region]. The Hague

De Vries J, Zonneveld W (2018) Urban transformation in the Northern Randstad: how institutions structure planning practice. In: Salet W (ed) The Routledge handbook of institutions and planning in action. Routledge, Abingdon, pp 364–377

De Zwart B (2015) Republiek van Beelden. De Politieke Werkingen van het Ontwerp in Regionale Planvorming [The Rebublic of images: the political performance of design in regional planning]. Doctoral thesis, Technische Universiteit Eindhoven, Eindhoven

De Zwarte Hond, Goudappel Coffeng, Rebel, Touw (2017) Eindrapport analyse- en oplossingsrichtingenfase MIRT-onderzoek Bereikbaarheid Rotterdam Den Haag [Final report study phase MIRT-research Accessibility Rotterdam The Hague]. Ministerie van Infrastructuur en Milieu, Den Haag

Den Hoed P, Salet WGM, Van der Sluijs H (1983) Planning als Onderneming [Planning as enterprise]. Staatsuitgeverij, The Hague

Enno Zuidema Stedebouw, Studio Platz, veenenbos en bosch landschapsarchitecten, ECORYS Communicatie (2011) Ontwerpen in het MIRT [Designing in the context of MIRT]. Den Haag

Eo Wijers Stichting (1986) Nederland Rivierenland [The Netherlands - River Land]. The Hague. Retrieved from Juryrapport [1st Eo Wijers competition, report of the jury]: http://www.eowijers.nl

Frieling D (1998) Het Metropolitane Debat [The metropolitan debate]. THOTH, Bussum

Frieling D (2002) Design in strategy. In: De Jong TM, Van der Voordt DJM (eds) Ways to study and research. Urban, architectural and technical design. Delft University Press, Delft, pp 491–500

Hajer M (2003) Policy without polity? Policy analysis and the institutional void. Policy Sci 36(2):175–195. https://doi.org/10.1023/a:1024834510939

Hajer M, Zonneveld W (2000) Spatial planning in the network society: rethinking the principles of planning in The Netherlands. Eur Plan Stud 8(3):337–355. https://doi.org/10.1080/713666411

Heeling J, Bekkering H, Lörzing H (1987) Zorgvuldig scenario. Nationaal Ontwerp Nieuw Nederland. Onderwerp van Ontwerp [The New Netherlands. An object of design]. Stichting Nederland Nu als Ontwerp, Staatsuitgeverij's Gravenhage, Den Haag

Hemel Z (2013) Nederland als Ontwerp [The Netherlands as design]. In: Brouwer P, Hemel Z, Oxenaar A, Van Rossem V, Stissi V (eds) Liber Amicorum Manfred Bock. Cuypersgenootschap, Druten

Hillier B, Leaman A (1974) How is design possible? J Arch Plan Res 3(1):4–11

Hillier B, MusgroveJ, O'Sullivan P (1972) Knowledge and design. Environ Design: Res Pract 2:3–1

Jessop B (2001) Institutional re(turns) and the strategic—relational approach. Environ Plan A 33(7):1213–1235

Kempenaar A (2017) Design in the planning arena. How regional designing influences strategic spatial planning. Doctoral thesis, Wageningen University, Wageningen

Klaasen IT (2003) Knowledge-based design: developing urban & regional design into a science. Doctoral thesis, Delft University of Technology, Delft

Koolhaas T, Marcusse E (2006) Atelier Ijmeer 2030+. Amsterdam IJmeer Almere [Studio Ijmeer 2030+. Amsterdam IJmeer Almere]. Uitgeverij 010, Rotterdam

Lawson B (2009) Design expertise. Architectural Press, Oxon/New York

Luiten E (2011) Gereanimeerd erfgoed: Nationaal project Nieuwe Hollandse Waterlinie als format voor het landschapsbeleid [Reanimated heritage: the national project New Dutch Water Line as a format for landscape planning]. Bull KNOB 110(6):223–230

Ministerie van VROM (2003) Ontwerpatelier Deltametropool [Design studio delta metropolis]. Ministerie van Volkshuisvesting, Ruimtelijke Ordening en Milieubeheer (VROM), Den Haag

Ministerie van I&M (2010) Handreiking MIRT-Verkenning [Manual for decision-making in MIRT procedures]. Projectdirectie Sneller & Beter, The Hague

Ministerie van OCW (2011) Meer dan Kwaliteit: Een Nieuwe Visie op Cultuurbeleid [Vision on cultural policy]. Ministerie van Onderwijs Cultuur en Wetenschap (OCW), Den Haag

Ministerie van I&M (2012) Structuurvisie Infrastructuur en Ruimte: Nederland Concurrerend, Bereikbaar, Leefbaar en Veilig [National policy strategy for infrastructure and spatial planning]. Ministerie van Infrastructuur en Milieu (I&M), The Hague

Ministerie van VROM, Rijksplanologische Dienst (2001) Ruimte Maken, Ruimte Delen: Vijfde Nota over de Ruimtelijke Ordening 2000/2020. Vastgesteld door de Ministerraad op 15 December 2000 [Fifth report on spatial planning]. Ministerie van Volkshuisvesting Ruimtelijke Ordening en Milieubeheer (VROM), The Hague

Ministeries van I&M, OCW, BZK, EZ, Def. (2012) Werken aan Ontwerpkracht. Actieagenda Architectuur en Ruimtelijk Ontwerp 2013–2016 [Working on the power of design. Action agenda architecture and spatial design 2013–2016]. Ministeries van Infrastructuur en Milieu (I&M), Onderwijs Cultuur en Wetenschap (OCW), Binnenlandse Zaken en Koningsrelaties (BZK), Economische Zaken (EZ) en Defensie (Def), The Hague

Ministeries van OCW, VROM, LNV, V&W (1996) De Architectuur van de Ruimte. Nota over het Architectuurbeleid 1997–2000 [The architecture of the built environment. Note on the architecture policy 1997–2000]. Ministeries van Onderwijs Cultuur en Wetenschappen (OCW), Volkshuisvesting, Ruimtelijke Ordening en Milieubeheer (VROM), Landbouw Natuurbeheer en Visserij (LNV) en Verkeer en Waterstaat (V&W), Den Haag

Ministeries van OCW, VROM, V&W, LNV (2000) Ontwerpen aan Nederland. Architectuurbeleid 2001–2004 [Designing The Netherlands. Architecture policy 2001–2004]. Sdu Uitgevers, Den Haag

Ministeries van OCW, VROM, LNV, V&W, EZ, Def, BZ (2005) Actieprogramma Ruimte en Cultuur. Architectuur- en Belderebeleid 2005–2008 [Action programme the built environment and culture. Architecture and belvedere policy 2005–2008]. Ministeries van Onderwijs Cultuur en Wetenschappen (OCW), Volkshuisvesting, Ruimtelijke Ordening en Milieubeheer (VROM), Landbouw, Natuurbeheer en Visserij (LNV), Verkeer en Waterstaat (V&W), Economische Zaken (EZ), Defensie (Def) en Buitenlandse Zaken (BZ), Den Haag

Ministeries van VROM, LNV, V&W, EZ (2006) Nota Ruimte, Deel 4: Tekst naar parlamentaire instemming [National Spatial Strategy, after parliamentary approval]. Ministeries van Volkshuisvesting Ruimtelijke Ordening en Milieubeheer (VROM), Landbouw Natuur en Voedselkwaliteit (LNV), Verkeer en Waterstaat (V&W) en Economische Zaken (EZ), Den Haag

Moughtin C (2003) Urban design: method and techniques. Routledge

Needham B (2015) The National Spatial Strategy for The Netherlands. In: Knaap G-J, Nedovic-Budic Z, Carbonell A (eds) Planning for States and Nation-States in the U.S. and Europe. Lincoln Institute of Land Policy, Cambridge

Neuman M (1996) Images as institution builders: metropolitan planning in Madrid. Eur Plan Stud 4(3):293–312. https://doi.org/10.1080/09654319608720347

Neuman M, Zonneveld W (2018) The resurgence of regional design. Eur Plan Stud 26(7):1297–1311. https://doi.org/10.1080/09654313.2018.1464127

Popper K (1957) Science: conjectures and refutations. In: Mace CA (ed) British philosophy in mid-century. George Allen and Unwin, London

Provincie Zuid-Holland (2004) Ontwerpatelier Zuid-Holland/Zuidvleugel [Informal discussion note]. Provincie Zuid-Holland, Den Haag

Rijke J, Van Herk S, Zevenbergen C, Ashley R (2012) Room for the river: delivering integrated river basin management in The Netherlands. Int J River Basin Manag 10(4): 369–382. https://doi.org/10.1080/15715124.2012.739173

Rittel HWJ (1987) The reasoning of designers. University of California, Berkeley

Salet W (2006) Rescaling territorial governance in the Randstad Holland: the responsiveness of spatial and institutional strategies to changing socio-economic interactions. Eur Plan Stud 14(7):959–978. https://doi.org/10.1080/09654310500496396

Salet J, Woltjer J (2009) New concepts of strategic spatial planning: dilemmas in the Dutch Randstad region. Int J Public Sector Manag 22(3): 235–248

Salewski C (2012) Dutch New Worlds. Scenario's in de Stedenbouw en Ruimtelijke Ordening in Nederland, 1970–2000 [Dutch New Worlds: scenarios in urbanism and spatial planning in The Netherlands, 1970–2000]. 010 Publishers, Rotterdam

Schön DA (1988) Designing: rules, types and words. Des Stud 9(3):181–190. http://dx.doi.org/10.1016/0142-694X(88)90047-6

Schönwandt WL, Hemberger C, Grunau JP, Voermanek K, von der Weth R, Saifoulline R (2011) The art of problem-solving—design and evaluation of a training program in solving complex planning problems. disP—Plan Rev 47(185):14–26. https://doi.org/10.1080/02513625.2011.10557130

Stegmeijer E, Kloosterman R, Lupi T (2012) Bouwen op een Sterk Fundament: Een Tussenevaluatie van het Architectuurbeleid [Building upon a strong basis: intermediate assessment architecture policy]. N. I. P., Den Haag, p 31

Tewdwr-Jones M (1999) Discretion, flexibility, and certainty in British planning: emerging ideological conflicts and inherent political tensions. J Plan Educ Res 18(3):244–256. https://doi.org/10.1177/0739456x9901800306

The Rt Hon Lord Scarman (1981) The Scarman report: the Brixton disorders 10–12 April 1981. Retrieved from Report of an Inquiry, London

Urban Unlimited (2003) Visie Stedelijk Netwerk KAN [Vision urban network Arnhem-Nijmegen]. Nijmegen, Rotterdam

Van Aken JE (2007) Design science and organization development interventions: aligning business and humanistic values. J Appl Behav Sci 43(1):67–88. https://doi.org/10.1177/0021886306297761

Van Bergeijk H (ed) (2015) Van Lohuizen & Van Eesteren. Partners in planning and education at TH Delft. TU Delft Open, Delft

Van der Cammen H (1987) Nieuw Nederland. Onderwerp van Ontwerp [The New Netherlands. An object of design]. Stichting Nederland Nu als Ontwerp, Staatsuitgeverij's Gravenhage, Den Haag

Van der Valk A (1990) Het Levenswerk van TH.K. van Lohuizen 1890–1956. De Eenheid van het Stedenbouwkundige Werk [The livework of TH.K. van Lohuizen 1890–1956]. Delftse Universitaire Pers, Delft

Van Dijk T (2011) Imagining future places: how designs co-constitute what is, and thus influence what will be. Plan Theory 10(2):124–143. https://doi.org/10.1177/1473095210386656

Van Duinen L (2004) Planning imagery. The emergence and development of new planning concepts in Dutch National Spatial Policy. Doctoral thesis, University of Amsterdam, Amsterdam

Van Duinen L (2015) New spatial concepts between innovation and lock-in: the case of the Dutch Deltametropolis. Plan Pract Res 30(5):548–569. https://doi.org/10.1080/02697459.2015.1076155

Van Geet MT, Lenferink S, Arts J, Leendertse W (2019) Understanding the ongoing struggle for land use and transport integration: institutional incongruence in the Dutch national planning process. Transp Policy 73:84–100. https://doi.org/10.1016/j.tranpol.2018.11.001

Van Rossem V (2014) In search of a better world. Cornelis van Eesteren and the rise of urban planning. In: EFL Foundation & gta Archives (eds) Atlas of the Functional City. CIAM 4 and Comparative Urban Analysis. Uitgeverij THOTH, gta Verlag, Bussum, Zurich

Vereniging Deltametropool (1998) Deltametropolis. A declaration by the spatial planning aldermen of Amsterdam, Rotterdam, The Hague and Utrecht regarding future Urban Development in The Netherlands

Zandbelt, Van den Berg (2012) Ruimtelijke modellen SMASH 2040: Amsterdam-Schiphol-Haarlemmermeer [Spatial models SMASH 2040: Amsterdam-Schiphol-Haarlemmermeer]. Rotterdam

Zonneveld W, Evers D (2014) Dutch national spatial planning at the end of an era. In: Reimer M, Panagiotis G, Blotevogel H (eds) Spatial planning systems and practices in Europe: a comparative perspective on continuity and changes. Routledge

The Transformative Capacity of Regional Design

4

Lukas Gilliard, Fabian Wenner, Alain Thierstein,
and Nadia Alaily-Mattar

Abstract

This chapter discusses how regional design introduces a transformative perspective on spatial development. It argues that regional design complements statutory regional planning within the setting of governance processes and that it represents a new methodology emerging as a reaction to the current political inability to re-scale unfit governance structures, with the objective of more effectively steering the development of metropolises. The proposition of a design exercise at regional scale shifts the discourse from issues of formal governmental reorganisation towards methodologies for imagining alternative spatial futures. It does so by proposing a complementary method for formulating regional plans that is interdisciplinary and design-based, similar to urban design but on a wider spatial scale. Design as a process of synthesising can identify and visualise future regional development challenges and convey the need for spatial interventions. The chapter argues that regional design is, therefore, a problem-solving as well as a problem-finding methodology, which should be impact-oriented and strategic. It should operationalise the inter-scalar, relational notion of space. The product of the regional design exercise should encourage debate rather than present an end solution or a master plan. It is, however, complicated by the multiple knowledge domains involved in this process, as well as by extensive, multi-scalar actor networks, fuzzy responsibilities and complex interrelations.

Keywords

Planning education • Regional planning • Regional governance • Regional design

4.1 Introduction

This chapter proposes that regional design should complement statutory regional planning in order to give regional governance structures a greater transformative capacity. This proposition builds upon the emergence of regional design practices as a reaction to the mismatch of administrative boundaries and the extent of functionally interrelated regions. The regional governance debate is gridlocked between two contrary positions. While some argue that formal administrative boundaries need to be better aligned with functional urban areas to resolve challenges on supra-local scales, others insist on working within the given boundaries to preserve local identity and facilitate inter-municipal competition.

L. Gilliard (✉) · F. Wenner · A. Thierstein · N. Alaily-Mattar
Department of Architecture, Chair of Urban Development, Technical University of Munich, Arcisstrasse 21, 80333 Munich, Germany
e-mail: l.gilliard@tum.de

F. Wenner
e-mail: f.wenner@tum.de

A. Thierstein
e-mail: thierstein@tum.de

N. Alaily-Mattar
e-mail: n.alaily-mattar@tum.de

© Springer Nature Switzerland AG 2020
V. Lingua and V. Balz (eds.), *Shaping Regional Futures*,
https://doi.org/10.1007/978-3-030-23573-4_4

Regional design shifts the discourse from the issue of governmental reorganisation towards methodologies for imagining alternative spatial futures. A growing number of regions and cities across Europe identify a lack of imaginative capacity in regional development processes (Bruns 2011; Balz and Zonneveld 2014: 3; Balz 2017). Within this context, regional design practices are increasingly deemed a useful tool for creating both a common understanding of challenges and a shared vision for alternative futures. Regional design allows us to think strategically about the future before engaging in the legally complicated implementation of statutory regional planning. Strategic thinking has gained importance in planning because the role of the state has shifted from regulating economic growth to attracting private investments for the public good (Madanipour 2006). The emergence of urban design reflects the same shift of power on the urban scale (Gilliard and Thierstein 2016). Hence, regional design acquires a role similar to urban design, but on wider spatial scales (Lapintie 2016).

Both urban design and regional design are more than the creative and personal skills usually associated with good designers, such as architects. At its core, design represents a synthesising methodology that generates and proposes new solutions for various problems. Good design requires an intricate understanding of how design decisions will affect the overall impact of the design. Thus, designers utilise, more or less explicitly, knowledge from various relevant disciplinary fields. We therefore understand design as a knowledge-based process of 'joining-up' pieces of knowledge from fields relevant to the design topic (Carmona et al. 2003).

Regional design as a synthesising process can help to identify and visualise future spatial development challenges and convey the need for interventions that are required to achieve social, ecological and economic goals. This means that practitioners engaging in regional design activities must have a sound analytical understanding of the various regional development domains, from settlement patterns to economic change drivers. While design as a methodological approach comprises core activities across scales, the different domains require a variety of skills and knowledge that only are acquired through a combination of science-based skills and through professional experience (Jensen et al. 2007).

Working at regional scale is further complicated due to contexts characterised by extensive, multi-scalar actor networks, fuzzy responsibilities and complex interrelations of physical and functional spatial configurations (Allmendinger and Haughton 2009). Figure 4.1 shows that the planning process is part of an overarching development process involving cities and regions. Its role is to formulate development objectives based on spatial conditions and actor constellations, creating spatial proposals and implementing them with the help of plans and policies. In urban development, an investor ideally takes up the proposal and constructs various types of properties. The process at urban scale is clearly defined—at least in this simplified manner. We are aware of the manifold complications that an urban development process undergoes and that most processes follow iterative and often messy patterns. On the other hand, regional development processes seem to be even messier on a simplified, theoretical level. We identify three major knowledge gaps regarding the relationship between regional design and planning:

- The first one concerns the planning process itself. While urban design complements statutory urban planning—for instance by imagining spatial qualities and developing concrete building proposals—statutory regional plans lack complementary design methods. So, *can we transfer a design-based approach from the urban to the regional scale*?
- The second gap within the regional development process is an unclear implementation path. Regional plans are not simply executed by a single actor. Regional planning informs the action of various actors. It is therefore strategic in nature. This invites the question as to whether our proposition of transferring design methodology from the urban to the regional scale is appropriate and *how the strategic nature of regional planning alters the design methodology*?
- And lastly, if regional design and regional planning go hand in hand, *whose responsibility is the task of regional design? Which profession is adequately prepared to perform regional design*?

On the basis of regional planning and design practice observations, and a review of literature on design, planning and innovation, we propose that regional design is problem-finding and problem-solving methodology, which should be impact-oriented and strategic. It should operationalise the inter-scalar and relational notion of space. The product of the regional design exercise should encourage debate rather than present an end solution or a master plan. Regional design is therefore not a unitary discipline. Complex processes, and the multitude of affected domains require an interdisciplinary practice. Hence, there cannot be just 'one' regional designer; rather, regional design is an activity that cuts across the boundaries of multiple disciplines.

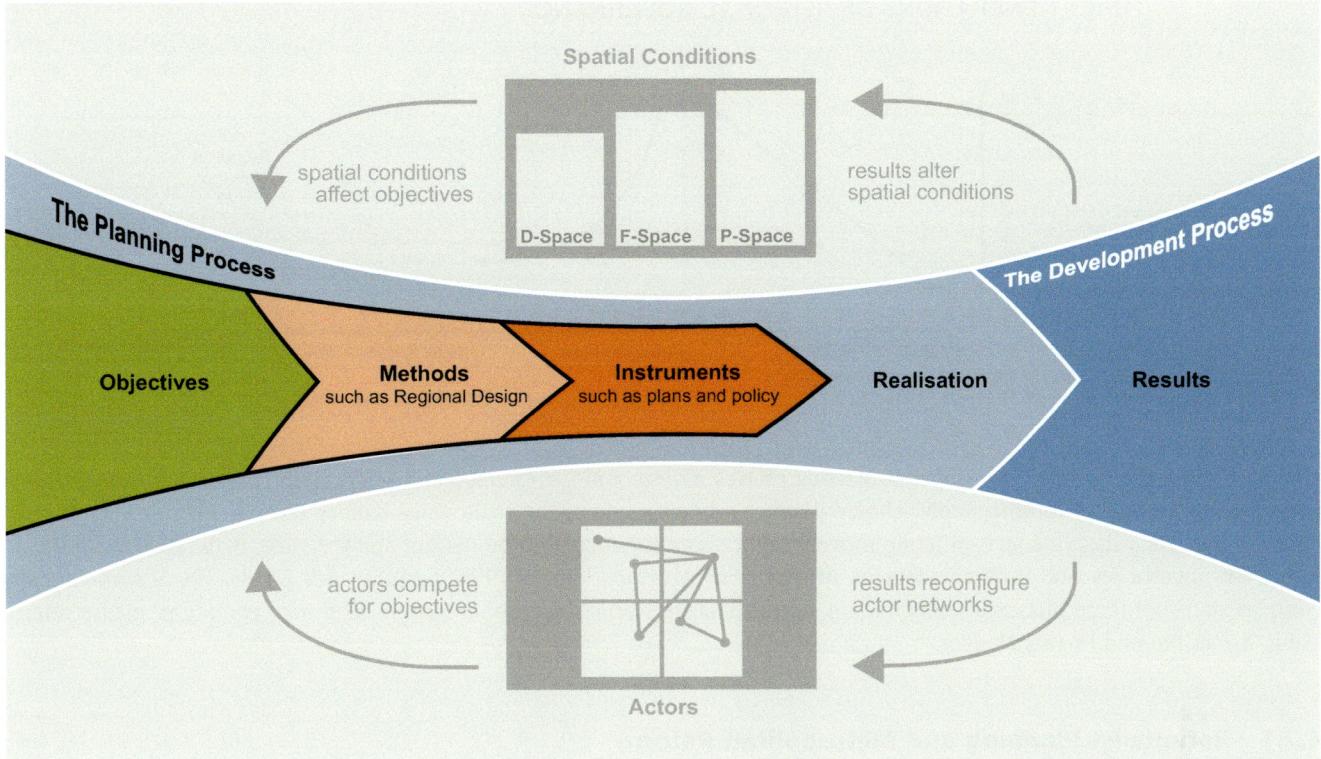

Fig. 4.1 A simplified regional planning and development process, elaborated by authors, inspired by Schönwandt (1999)

The chapter is divided into five parts. Following the introduction, the second part of the chapter briefly summarises notions on past generations of governance and planning theory and their influences on spatial development and the re-scaling of governance. Part three argues that the historical development of regional governance and planning has resulted in a lack of imaginative capacity and regional steering power and that this capacity can be introduced by design-based approaches that complement formal planning procedures. The argument is illustrated by looking briefly at two recent regional design projects across Europe. Based on observations, part four outlines a regional design methodology. The chapter concludes that regional design—if practised as outlined—can create new momentum for development. It requires an interdisciplinary approach not only involving architects and urban designers, but also other spatial experts such as urban and regional planners, regional economists and geographers, to name just a few.

4.2 The State of Regional Governance and Planning

The governance and planning set-up is an outcome of societal agreements on how a territory should be organised, whether and to what degree spatial units should be defined in accordance with principles of solidarity and who should have a say. As societal value systems shift, governance and planning are subject to recurrent change. Since planning evolved as a separate discipline about a century ago, modernist conceptions of technocratic top-down planning have been gradually supplemented or replaced by notions of planners as advocates or mediators. In some instances, even planning as an activity has been questioned altogether. The financial crisis of the late 2000s, in some cases, then led to a renewed role for stronger state control, indicating a pendular swing in planning thinking (Ellin 1996).

This observation can be made not only regarding the role of planning in general, but also sub-disciplinary discourses, such as statutory planning and urban design, which have represented diverging discourses in the planning community over the last few decades (Frank et al. 2014: 84; Gilliard and Thierstein 2016: 44). The following briefly and schematically describes three generations (Schönwandt 1999: 25–27) of thought in regional governance and spatial planning (see Fig. 4.2). Each is illustrated with mostly German cases, but reference is occasionally made to examples from the UK, Netherlands and France. We argue that the phases, which we label as rationalism, post-modernism and strategic incrementalism, should be

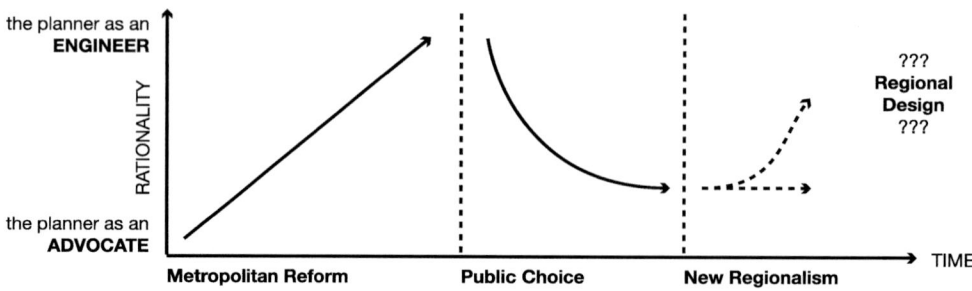

Fig. 4.2 Pendular movement of planning thinking in regional governance, elaborated by authors. Adapted from Gilliard and Thierstein (2016)

viewed in connection with the contemporaneous phases of regional governance and governance re-scaling, which can be framed as metropolitan reform, public-choice theory and new regionalism [following Kübler (2003); Pütz (2004: 42–43)], respectively. They describe an oscillating movement between the forces of the market and the state, between bottom-up and top-down approaches and different degrees of public involvement (Ellin 1996; Schönwandt 2008). For a summary and comparison of all three phases in combination with this proposition of 'regional design' as a new paradigm, please refer to Table 4.1 at the end of this chapter.

4.2.1 Rationalist Planning and Metropolitan Reform

The first approaches to regional planning are rooted within the modernist and rationalist ideals predominant until the 1970s in many parts of Europe. The rationalist view generally assumes the predictability and controllability of urban development and strives for the planned development of urban space according to defined goals; hence, it assigns an important role to planners (e.g. McLoughlin 1969). In statutory planning, the emergence of region-wide structure plans in the 1950s and 1960s perfectly exemplifies this approach. From an urban design point of view, Haussmann's redesign of Paris in the early second half of the nineteenth century provides a well-known very early example of this view on a city-wide scale. Interactions began to expand in these spaces of daily life, and thus, so did urban design and governance initiatives.

Changes to governance structures often went hand in hand with these grand spatial visions. The 'metropolitan reform' (Kübler 2003) tradition can be conceived as the first structured approach to spatial governance. Its main tenet is that to create an efficient territorial administrative structure, functional relations in space, such as commuting zones or continuously built-up areas, should be represented and not crossed by administrative boundaries (Parr 2007). The proponents of such a matching of functional and administrative spaces argue that it creates economies of scale, allows integrated planning and reduces the unfair distribution of public expenditure and revenue between centre and periphery municipalities (Priebs 2005), thereby also typically creating a socially mixed territorial entity. In addition, advantages in terms of democratic accountability are put forward (Kübler 2003: 535–536). Accordingly, measures preferred by metropolitan reformers to react to changing spatial structures and tasks encompass the incorporation of smaller towns in the vicinity of cities into the core city, the merging of neighbouring towns of equal size or the (top-down) set-up of entirely new territorial institutions on city-regional or metropolitan scales where a public service task requires it. Generally, the aim is to create territorial units whose size and endowment are sufficient to carry out the tasks that have been allocated to the respective tier of government.

In order to illustrate the effect of metropolitan reforms, the number of independent municipalities in Germany was reduced by almost 2/3 between 1960 and 1975. Similar observations can be made in other countries. The goal was always to create municipalities capable of fulfilling a growing number of newly allocated tasks and to streamline spatial governance. At the same time, regional planning was institutionalised and new regional institutions created. The 'metropolitan reform' of governance and rationalist large-scale spatial visions went hand in hand.

From the 1970s on, the metropolitan reform tradition was increasingly rejected by different sides and for several reasons. The appropriateness of its methods was questioned on the grounds of its top-down and positivist tenets. It became increasingly clear that territorial reform carried the risk of alienating citizens from their municipalities, resulting in lower democratic participation. Furthermore, theorists began to criticise the 'futility' of constant administrative reforms, since spatial structure was always in flux (Davy 2004: 40–42). In planning, the desirability and attainability of the rationalists' goals were called into question. Modernist cities were regarded as 'a blueprint of placelessness, of anonymous, impersonal spaces, massive structures and automobile throughways' (Ley 1987). The assumption that planning could optimise peoples' lives through technocratic interventions lost support in both academia and society.

4.2.2 Post-Modernism and Public Choice

As a major new approach to spatial governance, the 'public-choice' paradigm, originating in the US, gained ground. Its main proposition can be best summarised by Tiebout's notion (1956) that 'people vote with their feet'. He stressed that competition between municipalities can have desirable effects on bureaucratic efficiency; hence, small territorial units should be maintained. Different qualities of public service in the municipalities—corresponding to differing local tax levels—would allow people to choose a municipality that offers the right 'package' of costs and benefits to them or, in Tiebout's words, to 'vote with their feet'. With some delay, the model also gained acceptance in Europe, especially in research on federal governance systems (Frey and Eichenberger 1995; Kirchgässner and Pommerehne 1994; Feld and Kirchgässner 1998; Feld 1999).

Consequently, regional forms of cooperation should be reduced in favour of smaller, more autonomous local units, and spatial structure is not a criterion for boundary realignments. Additionally, the private provision of services that is not bound by territorial limits is preferred to public provision (Frey 2003). The public-choice governance model assigned a reduced role to regional planning, due to the re-communalisation of planning responsibility. Effectively, the use of planning was restricted to situations in which zoning and urban design helped a municipality become more competitive.

Rather than being an exact blueprint of how to organise space territorially, 'public choice' acts as an argumentative support against more formalised supra-local powers and is subject to compromises. Hence, there is no example for a radical 'public-choice' territorial structure. A famous example that goes far in its application is the oft-cited abolition of all metropolitan councils in the UK, including the Greater London Council in 1986, with the resulting atomisation of governance. Similar developments can also be observed in other European countries, e.g. with the communalisation of regional planning in Lower Saxony, Germany, in 2004, the end of national planning in the Netherlands in 2010, and the abolition of devolved regional functions in England in 2011. The 'public-choice' model goes hand in hand with the withdrawal of state-led planning interventions in favour of creating market conditions for inter-municipal competitions.

At this point, the debate in the planning community was somewhat split between urban design and statutory planning (Salet and Woltjer 2009: 241). The strong preference for individual architectural design projects over large-scale regional plans favoured architecturally trained professionals over other planners, while urban designers re-discovered the dense city and its traditional morphology and typologies as a playground for city improvements. Other practitioners and academics, by contrast, began to criticise the imbalances in an atomised governance landscape and the loss of regional steering and decision-making powers, especially for public services that require networked approaches, such as transport planning (Thierstein et al. 2015). A lack of accountability has been highlighted in situations where public services were shifted to private or non-governmental actors (Swyngedouw 2005). In effect, 'the discourse is largely split within the architectural urban design and the statutory planning community' (Gilliard and Thierstein 2016: 44).

The German 'international building exhibition' (IBA) in Berlin between 1979 and 1987 illustrates this divide well. Thirty years after the first IBA 'Interbau' in 1957, which was a showcase for modernist urban design and architecture, Berlin renewed its planning ambitions demonstrating new post-modernist urban design.

'One of the most notable urban design products created during the IBA was Josef Paul Kleinhues' grand city plan' (Gilliard 2013: 9), which would later become Berlin's 'Planwerk'. It was a form-based, two-dimensional plan showing the desired footprint of the city—basically a detailed figure ground (see Fig. 4.3). It was developed in parallel with legally binding zoning documents (see Fig. 4.4). The existence of the two plans—a zoning plan and a morphological plan—can be interpreted as illustrating the gap between the design and planning communities.

Fig. 4.3 Detail of Berlin land use plan (FNP Berlin)—Legally binding statutory zoning plan for Berlin, interactive updated working document, as of November 2017, from Senatsverwaltung für Stadtentwicklung und Wohnen Berlin (2017)

4.2.3   Strategic Incrementalism and New Regionalism

As a response to the shortcomings of the public-choice approach, the importance of the regional one became recognised again, often described as 'new regionalism'—but this time mainly through voluntary cooperation between municipalities and joint decision-making (Evers and de Vries 2013: 551) rather than forced reorganisation. 'Networking, cooperation, contracts, functional organisation, etc. are the instrumental recipes for this strategy of flexible response' (Salet 2006: 969). The cooperative strategy had the advantage that obvious economies of scale could be more easily exploited and the most pressing shortcomings of the public-choice approach could be tackled. In addition, this approach incorporated civil society groups and businesses into spatial governance structures (Blatter 2006).

However, voluntary cooperation is generally limited to win-win situations, and only solutions with low transaction costs will be considered due to the high coordination effort. Regional planning under the paradigm of new regionalism is hence often considered as incrementalism. Inter-municipal coordination of land-use planning is still rare. Criticism is also directed at business involvement, as it encroaches on the welfare state (Swyngedouw 2005). On a more general note, the loss of direct democratic control in increasingly fuzzy and confusing cooperative structures between municipalities is subject to debate.

The IBA 'Emscher Park', set up in the German Ruhr area in the 1990s and well known among planners, provides further insights. It was the first international building exhibition to make the region the focus of attention. The IBA, however, remained a strategic framework for a series of individual projects. An overarching strategic spatial plan did not exist, and instead, all projects had to follow only a few, deliberately open guidelines (BBR 1999), symbolising the 'strategic incrementalism' approach.

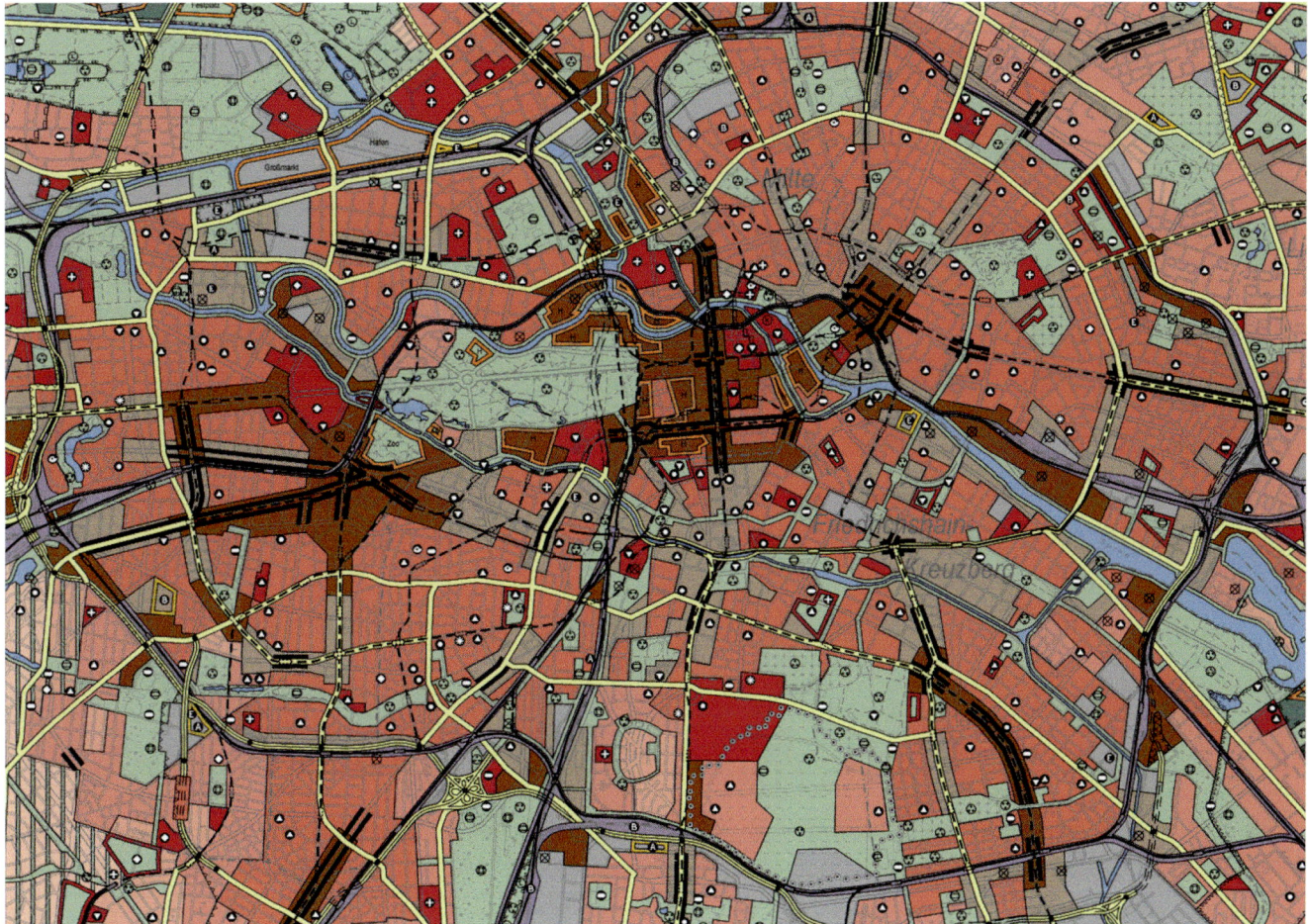

Fig. 4.4 Detail of 'Planwerk Innere Stadt 2010'—Form-based two-dimensional plan for the inner city of Berlin, from Senatsverwaltung für Stadtentwicklung und Wohnen Berlin (2010)

The short schematic overview of regional governance thought has shown that modernist ideas of the need for a constant top-down, re-matching of 'functional' and territorial spaces were followed by decades of relative territorial 'fatalism' and later renewed 'regionalism' with calls for stronger (voluntary and case-based) cooperation (cf. Table 4.1).

4.2.4   Summary: Diverging Discourses and the Lack of Imaginative Capacity

In planning, the functionalist *tabula rasa* was replaced by a phase of refraining from ambitious public spatial planning, to the benefit of individual architectural projects, and then followed by a move to reinvigorate planning, this time in a more open and flexible manner, as a strategic task. Besides these similar pendular movements in history, the discourse on regional planning has split somewhat along the sub-disciplinary lines and between theory and practice. Whereas the statutory planning community still proposes governance changes as solutions to spatial challenges, the theoretical debate in urban design has somewhat departed from this viewpoint.

Here, it is worth reflecting for a moment and acknowledging the seemingly widened gap between urban designers on the one hand—who re-discovered the dense city and its traditional morphology and typologies as a playground for city improvements—and practitioners and academics on the other hand, who criticise the above-described imbalances in an atomised governance landscape with the loss of regional steering and decision-making powers. This seems to hold true particularly for a wider range of public services that require networked approaches, such as mobility services planning. The reasons for this widened gap—and sometimes even severe misunderstandings—lie partly in the inaugural years of the planning discipline. Planning as an independent academic field, as well as institutionalised regional planning, emerged

Table 4.1 Four approaches to spatial governance and governance re-scaling

Terminology of planning paradigm	Rationalist planning	Post-modernism	Strategic incrementalism	Regional design
Terminology of governance paradigm	Metropolitan reform	Public choice	New regionalism	
	Based on analysis of Sect. 2			*Proposition outlined in the following sections*
Prevalence (time)	1920s–1970s	1970s–1990s	Since 1990s	Recent
Who plans?	Municipalities; regional planning authority	Private planning firms, municipalities as businesses	Voluntary inter-municipal cooperation	Private planning firms mandated by municipalities; civil society groups
For which territory?	For their own territory	For their own property or territory	For the territory of participating municipalities	Spatial extent is itself open for design proposals depending on case-specific evidence; not bound by given administrative structure
Territorial governance method	Incorporation, merger, realignment	Atomisation, land swaps	(Re-) Institutionalisation of cooperation	Flexible, based on case-specific evidence, covering the entire bandwidth of previous methods
Mode	Directive	Competition	Cooperation	Entrepreneurial persuasion
Role of planner	Authority	Consultant	Mediator	Systemic expert
Novelty	Plan	Product	Project	Process-led

before the turn from rationalist planning to post-modernism. The growing critique of the modernist city prompted the urban design community to abandon working on larger scales. Post-modernist urban design concentrated on re-building and improving the urban cores, alongside the re-emerging interest in cities as drivers for economic growth and prosperity (Smith 1996: 67; Madanipour 2006: 177). Planning scholars with a specialism in statutory issues remained interested in the regional scale. The split along sub-disciplinary lines seems to have led to a lack of imaginative expertise at regional scale. Regional planning practice dominated by statutory planning has hindered undesirable development but has not managed to trigger new development (Albrechts 2004: 745).

4.3 Regional Design in Practice

A new generation of thought and practice has emerged to compensate for this lack of imaginative expertise at regional scale. Cities and regions across Europe have started inviting architects and urban designers to imagine regional futures. Many European cities opted for international design competitions, thus benefiting not only from a design approach but also from a competitive environment in which multiple concepts can be discussed. An interdisciplinary composition for each team, including architects, was required in case of the Greater Helsinki Vision in 2006/2007, and the public authorities explicitly only invited big architectural firms in the case of the French Le Grand Paris competition from 2007 until 2009. Since then, many more European regions have followed suit. Some scholars even speak of a renaissance of big plans (Hutter 2006; Bruns 2011). Design competitions such as 'Metrobild Zurich' in Switzerland or 'RuhrImpulse' in Germany, as well as regional visions like the 'Metropolitan Region Amsterdam' in the Netherlands, signal new growing attention to the regional level—especially within the urban design community. This new amalgamation of regional governance and urban design is discussed as 'regional design' (Balz and Zonneveld 2014). An analysis of six European examples was undertaken in order to understand the characteristics of regional design in practice (cf. Table 4.2). Three examples in particular, which were intensively discussed during the 2015 Shaping Regional Futures Conference in Munich (Förster et al. 2016), exemplify the nature of such regional design exercises.

Regional design played a crucial role in shaping the **Amsterdam Metropolitan Region**. Within a wider context, it is worthwhile highlighting the decade-long efforts of spatial visioning initiatives for the Randstad, the western part of the Netherlands, with its large circular mega-city connecting Amsterdam in the North and Rotterdam in the South. This

Table 4.2 Key information on case studies (own research)

	Noordvleugeloverleg (North Wing Consultations)	Metrobild Zurich	Idea Competition Future Metropolis Ruhr
Date and location	2000–2006 (–2008)	June 2010–Jan 2011	Apr 2013–Apr 2014
Kind of project	Informal inter-municipal consultation	Contract work	Closed competition
Awarding authority	Later, Amsterdam Metropolitan Area	Metropolitan Conference of Zurich	Regional authority Ruhr
Designers	Employees of public authorities	Three contracted interdisciplinary design teams in the field of architecture and urban design	Five invited interdisciplinary design teams in the field of architecture and urban design
Goal	Balancing competitive advantages with sustainable and liveable spaces	Designing a discursive process to shape a common understanding of the metropolitan area	Generating ideas for the new statutory regional plan

	Greater Helsinki Vision	Le Grand Paris	Glatt! Eine Stadt im Werden
Date and Location	Dec 2006–May 2007	Dec 2007–Mar 2009	2008–2012
Kind of project	Open competition	Closed competition	Initiative
Awarding authority	City of Helsinki and other surrounding authorities, supported by the Finnish government	French government	None
Designers	86 interdisciplinary design teams with a strong focus on urban design and planning	Ten invited interdisciplinary design teams with a strong focus on architecture	Group of five architectural firms based in Zurich
Goal	Increasing inter-city competitiveness and a sound growth strategy	Modernisation of infrastructure and quality enhancement of urban and natural environments	Strategies against urban sprawl in Switzerland

dominant discourse for a spatial vision for the Randstad 2040 (Blank et al. 2009: {OECD 2007 #11890}) eventually faltered following a changed majority in central government and the aftermath of the financial crisis of 2008/09. Although governance approaches for the Randstad were among the earlier prominent examples of spatial planning in Europe, the Randstad never became a formal planning territory. Other efforts to institutionalise at least the northern wing of the Randstad as a city province also failed in the 1990s. The mismatch of functional interrelations and territorial boundaries remained in place (Janssen-Jansen 2011: 264).

Planning officers in the city of Amsterdam and the surrounding municipalities, rather independently from the longstanding Randstad activities, started a series of informal meetings on a smaller scale. With informal cooperation among 32 municipalities, two provinces and one city region, over the course of ten to fifteen years, it has become a rather intimate club—a dense social network of actors who are all familiar with each other. They gathered in response to a perceived institutional fragmentation to address problems in their area (Förster et al. 2016). In the beginning, these meetings were as unsuccessful as other efforts before them. Not until a group of officers with great enthusiasm for regional planning started to draw without formal inter-municipal consent did regional cooperation gather any initial momentum. Based on spatial qualities and the visual impressions of their designs, a dynamic arose from which no municipality around Amsterdam wanted to be excluded—although the relationship with the international airport Schiphol Amsterdam remained somewhat contradictory (Schaafsma 2010). Regional design as a methodological approach allowed the Amsterdam Metropolitan Region to just start planning. Considerable inter-municipal, inter-institutional and interdisciplinary cooperation was required to produce a convincing regional design. Years of unfruitful debates about governmental structures ended suddenly after the discourse shifted to the actual spatiality of regional issues. By coincidence, external global economic shocks and a change in government contributed to the change, and the Amsterdam region illustrates how an incomplete understanding of many key dimensions led to the failure of the decade-old Randstad vision. Although the Randstad idea is based on functional findings from an emerging polycentric metropolitan structure between Amsterdam and Rotterdam, it neglects strong differences in local identity. Joint regional governance did not succeed until Amsterdam planning officials proposed a much smaller, more sensitive regional cooperation based on local challenges and within the historic and still physically visible First World War Amsterdam Defence Line.

In the case of the **Ruhr Region**, regional design is implemented in a more hierarchical way. Although a strong regional structure was already in place, statutory planning lacked a convincing regional strategy to put into action. The Ruhr, despite being the most populous urban region in West Germany, with approximately 5.1 million inhabitants, is affected by high rates of unemployment following deindustrialisation. Despite its contingent built-up space and functional integration, the polycentric Ruhr has been partitioned into more than 50 independent and 'introvert' municipalities and several middle-tier districts, for most of its history, with few overarching regional governance structures and largely following the characteristics of the public-choice approach. This gave it a specific heterogeneous urbanity and numerous 'patchy' juxtapositions of densely built-up areas next to greenfields, affluent and poor neighbourhoods as well as industrial and residential areas, since there was almost no coordination at inter-municipal level during its growth phase. The spatial governance structure, consisting of 11 independent cities and four counties, worked as long as the Ruhr was the economic powerhouse of Western Germany. As a response to the structural change that started in the 1970s, the aforementioned 'IBA Emscher Park' tried to improve conditions with a project-oriented approach. Recently, the regional assembly, newly tasked with regional planning in 2009, started a competition to generate new ideas for urban and regional development in the Ruhr as a preparatory step for the statutory plan. Conventional regional planning was not expected to deliver these ideas. Local gridlock required external inputs to be broken up. A design competition allowed for multiple competing ideas. The four participating teams proposed plans that concentrated on creating an image, identification and citizen involvement. They aimed to strengthen societal consensus, with an emphasis on visualisations and the making visible of problems, not solutions. The focus was on regional strengths, regardless of administrative boundaries. This makes the Ruhr competition a good example of the requirements and advantages of regional design. Despite the fact that in the case study, governance powers were changed prior to the competition, and although it is too early to call for an impact assessment of the design competition, it can already be recognised that it improved mutual trust and acquaintance between planning administrations. Moreover, universities in the region are expected to cooperate more closely, strengthening knowledge as a future resource for the Ruhr.

The **Metrobild Zürich** was commissioned by the Metropolitan Conference of Zurich, a joint organisation by the Swiss cantons of the economic area around Zurich, in 2010. The conference had existed for just a year at that time. Its humble goal was to shape a common understanding of functionalities, qualities and potentialities. The metropolitan area is broken up into 500 municipalities in 8 cantons without overarching planning competencies at regional level. The challenges, however, are immense. Dynamic growth has put pressure on the environment and resulted in a sprawling regional landscape with social disparity. Cooperation among municipalities seemed necessary, but the highly federal governance landscape is dominated by competition. Three different design teams were invited to visualise how the metropolitan area is functionally and morphologically interlinked. At the same time, the Glatt initiative developed a spatial vision to concentrate development in the Glatt area. The results of the 'Metrobild Zürich' presented an in-depth analysis of spatial functionalities and proposed a process-orientated governance structure (berchtoldkrass et al. 2011).

Regional design in the case of the Metrobild can be understood against the backdrop of the Swiss tradition of direct democracy and a culture of finding consensus and agreement, including in intellectual discourse. The latter led to inviting design teams who, to begin with, applied rather spatio-analytical approaches. Later in the discourse, they shifted more to visualisations, images and narratives. It was argued during the process that it would be the visuals from these projects that would stay in the minds of actors, enhance the imagination and also inform expectations concerning a new regional design initiative (Förster et al. 2016). The Metrobild initiative was meant to provide a common ground for developing a subsequent 'strategic spatial concept' and future governance arrangements. Alexander (2006) also called this approach 'institutional design'.

In the cases analysed, the regional design exercises proposed either the shaping of new regional governance structures (e.g. in Zurich) or enabled the creation of innovative momentum for existing regional planning bodies (e.g. in Ruhr and Amsterdam). These exercises are flexible in their utilisation of methods. They can be initiated by municipal planning offices, but also by private planning firms or civil society groups. Unlike the metropolitan reform strand, regional design does not organise territorial change by decree but resorts to the power of a convincing plan that creates awareness. Thus, it has the potential to break the inertia of territorial structures and brings together spatial planning and governance. Even the governmental structure itself can be an aspect to be designed. Regional design is therefore able to increase the capacity of regional governance bodies to act.

In summary, we find that recent regional design exercises are based on the assumptions that:

- legally binding planning instruments are insufficient to generate enough innovative ideas and momentum for regional development (see Ruhr Region);
- suitable planning spaces are delimited according to functional criteria and relations, historical and sociocultural areas of common identity, and only partly according to administrative boundaries (see Amsterdam and Zurich case); and
- existing planning instruments do not place enough emphasis on graphic and visual tools to communicate planning ideas (see Ruhr and Zurich cases).

All projects feature a key map or diagram envisioning a certain understanding and/or the future of the whole area, and all projects set their own framework of desirable goals. Despite that, the content of each framework is similar, corresponding to the current zeitgeist. A regional design strategy contains physical proposals such as small- and large-scale physical interventions, but it can also focus on non-physical proposals such as the amendment of the administrative structure. The novelty of regional design is that it places a very high emphasis on graphic tools—an approach most often found in urban and architectural design, and indeed, leading practitioners in regional design in most cases have an architectural background.

4.4 Regional Designing as a Methodology

Based on our historical and current observations of previous paragraphs, it seems that regional development will benefit from the re-coupling of design and statutory planning expertise. We see an inherent close relationship between design and governance. In all three exemplary cases, regional design has either informed policy or regional governance arrangements. Regional design is not an alternative to existing regional planning efforts, but is a complementary method prior to statutory plans and policies (Lapintie 2016) (cf. Fig. 4.3). Regional design, in relation to statutory regional planning, has certain analogies to Berlin's unique arrangement of form-based 'planimetric' (Kleihues 1993), urban design and legally binding urban planning (see Figs. 4.3 and 4.4; Gilliard 2013). Design projects are well-established methods of planning at urban scale. Many larger urban development projects include an urban design competition before a decision is legally regulated as part of a zoning plan. Design competitions explore options for the content of plans and policies. They are concerned with the economic, societal, environmental and aesthetic issues themselves as well as their manifestation in space. Designing indicates the conceptualisation of various observations into one coherent picture. Regional design is, therefore, part of a longer development and planning process.

Thus, we hypothesise that regional design must play the same role in the regional development process as urban design does in the urban development process. Regional design appears to be more than just a pendular swing towards another decade of planning thinking; it might represent a major new paradigm shifting the attention from a normative debate on contesting concepts towards a methodology to overcome a stagnating discourse. Table 4.1 summarises the four generations of planning and governance of regions. The following part puts forward three propositions for the implementation of regional design as a complement to regional planning:

1. Regional designing is a process-led methodology, because it is always embedded in a long-term development and planning process.
2. Regional designers are systemic experts of regions, because the object of design in regions is not merely morphological but rather functional and organisational in nature.
3. Regional design employs the persuasive power of entrepreneurialism, because it deals with complex constellations of actors.

4.4.1 Process-Led Perspective

Regional design must be understood as part of a long-term planning and development process (cf. Fig. 4.1). Even when regional design prepares ideas for a statutory regional plan, such as in the example of the Ruhr region, pro-active concept ideas need to be taken up by various actors over time. Over the course of the past eight years, the authors of this chapter have developed a design approach that builds on the inter-scalar and relational notion of space (Droß et al. 2010, 2012; Erhard et al. 2015; Wiese et al. 2014; Alaily-Mattar et al. 2014). The process-led perspective outlined below builds on this previously developed design approach. We argue that regional design as a problem-solving/problem-finding methodology should be impact- and strategy-oriented. It should operationalise the inter-scalar, relational notion of space. The product of the regional design exercise should encourage debate rather than present an end solution or a master plan.

These five aspects of (1) inter-scalar and relational notions of space, (2) future thinking, (3) impact orientation, (4) strategic orientation and (5) debatability are hence the key aspects at the forefront of the regional design exercise process.

Adopting the inter-scalar and relational notions of space expands the definition of space beyond its physical and functional components. 'Rather than viewing space as "a container within which the world proceeds", the relational concept of space sees it as "a co-product of those proceedings"' (Khan et al. 2013: 290). The relational notion of space favours relations between places, identities, functions and so on, over the focus on the static physicality of contained space (Albrechts et al. 2003; Healey 2006). This yields an understanding of space as a 'multi-layered' (Massey 2005) site of interaction between social, cultural, political, economic and ecological processes that operate at various scales. Hence, inter-scalarity is a key attribute of the relational notion of space. 'Fluidity, openness and multiple time-space relations of "relational complexity ideas" (Healey 2006: 534) mess up the territorial concerns of the administrative apparatus and the contained borders of the various disciplines. The inter-scalar and relational notions of space defy the normative administrative restrictions and are at odds with the scalar fixation of disciplines. Adopting these notions of space can bridge gaps between the various disciplines engaged in the regional design exercise; it enables the search for solutions where they are effective rather than forcing solutions within the frontiers of individual fields of expertise or the territorial confines of defined mandates of activity.

While planning is concerned with the future, it is not necessarily future-oriented. A gap exists between 'future studies as a science that studies the future in order to understand and influence it and strategic planning as a method to use available resources so as to obtain a given result' (Cole 2001). Regional design can address this gap by bringing in a much-needed 'future'-oriented approach into the design exercise. While planners usually think about the future in form of scenarios, we use the term futures, in its plural form, very deliberately. A scenario describes the future development under certain boundary conditions. Future thinking cannot be a quest for certainty, and pretentions that it could are both naïve and dangerous (Sardar 2010: 178). When we think about the future, we must make a distinction between scientific forecasts that speak with authority and educated guesses that are based on connecting the dots between available and intrinsically consistent facts. Vester (2012) calls the latter the art of connected thinking. As cities are complex systems, with multiple inter-dependant variables whose developments are connected with positive and negative feedback loops, we must abandon the idea that a scientific truth about the future exists. Rather, we endorse the fact that well-informed judgements based on trend forecasts are a more suitable way of thinking about the future. 'The future cannot be "predicted" but alternative futures can be "forecasted" and preferred futures "envisioned" and "invented", continuously' (Sardar 2010: 178). Thinking through a number of alternative futures, rather than one, is about testing assumptions and fine-tuning the details during the thinking process. Such an approach is a shift away from rational planning models where a supposedly clear goal is set, by a government-led agency, usually after lengthy and rigorous analyses are 'completed' and interventions are proposed accordingly to achieve this goal. Rather, a future-oriented approach is a continuous intellectual back-and-forth that allows room for improvement and acknowledges the necessity of selectivity in analyses and syntheses. Such an approach can assist in identifying 'the signals amidst the noise' (Silver 2012).

The above notions of space and future thinking are necessary for analytic purposes; however, more importantly they place consideration of the impact of proposed spatial interventions at the forefront, considering the impact during the design exercise rather than at the end of it. As we take into consideration the temporal and multi-scalar aspects of the impact of spatial interventions, it becomes evident that area-based spatial interventions and their associated impacts are not necessarily congruent in temporal or spatial scales. In other words, area-based interventions might have immediate local impacts at local scale, but in the long run, they could also trigger impacts in other areas or even at larger scales. On the other hand, interventions at other spatial scales are sometimes necessary to induce impacts at local levels. For example, national policy interventions produce impacts at the local scale, although there is a time lag in which this occurs.

Interventions are only steps towards a possible desired future. Achieving desirable futures actually requires the strategic employment of, and coordination between, interventions. Designers have to weigh up between resources and short-, medium- and long-term impacts. Time therefore becomes a structuring element—a boundary artefact in itself.

The regional design exercise results in proposals that provide possible directions and incentives for regional development. These proposals intervene in various disciplines in order to achieve a desired impact through a combination of factors. Within the context of regional development, it is difficult for public authorities to assess the impact of the decisions they take. Indeed, different decisions, which at first glance seem to be consistent, are frequently counterproductive and end up pulling development in contradictory directions. This is echoed in the demands for a 'communicative turn' in planning. Regional design can serve the political process as a platform for debate, as stakeholders and experts ask: Where to? Which way forward? Regional design can also serve a useful communication purpose for stakeholders engaged in taking decisions today to prepare regions for the future tomorrow. It provides a link between plan-making and decision-making. The urban design exercise is in itself a negotiation exercise, in which the object of debate is not just a certain locality, but rather the normative values with which each participant relates to a certain locality. 'It compels [decision makers, planners, institutions and citizens] to confront their key beliefs, to challenge conventional wisdom and to look at the prospect of new ideas and consider "breaking out of the box"' (Albrechts in Oosterlynck et al. 2010: 19). Hence, the products of the regional design exercises can serve as consistent storyboards, against which public authorities can continuously check the effectiveness and consistency of their decisions. Backed up with evaluation tools, it is possible then also to identify different paths towards change that can have different rhythms, speeds and scopes and that can focus on certain elements of change rather than others.

4.4.2 Systemic perspective

Design itself is a methodology for synthesising. Designing at regional scale requires a multitude of knowledge and skills from all sub-disciplinary communities of planning, not just the morphological and architectural attributes of the built environment, but also a good understanding of economic drivers of regional development, infrastructure networks and governance arrangements, to name just a few. Historically, we observe a tendency that regional matters are limited to issues of governance (cf. Sect. 4.2). The inability of regional planning to trigger new development is, for instance, deemed to be the result of inadequate territorial structures. Regional design needs to find a balance between the physical, functional and procedural dimension of space (Boesch 1989). The interdisciplinary nature of regional design imposes major challenges for the process of designing.

Generally speaking, knowledge can be split up into four groups: factual, conceptual, procedural and meta-cognitive knowledge (Anderson et al. 2001). '"Factual' knowledge encompasses the basic elements that experts use in communicating about their disciplines, understanding it and organising it systematically" (Anderson et al. 2001: 41). 'Conceptual' knowledge is the interrelation of these basic elements including 'schemas, mental models [...] and theories' (Anderson et al. 2001: 48). 'Procedural' knowledge describes subject-specific skills, techniques and methods. Lastly, 'meta-cognitive' knowledge is the ability to reflect on self-knowledge, skills and limits.

Regional design is first of all 'procedural' knowledge, because the methodology of designing is a generic set of skills transferable to a variety of tasks. Every design task requires a combination of 'factual' knowledge and a new piece of 'conceptual' knowledge (Hocking 2010). Carmona and colleagues (Carmona et al. 2003: vii) describe the design process as a process of 'joining-up'. Design methodology, in its defined sense, is 'at the core of an interdisciplinary, creative, problem-solving discipline' (Carmona et al. 2003: vii) such as planning. The range of 'factual' knowledge in regional planning and design is broad. We further identified the physical and functional social aspects, besides the obvious organisational aspects, of regional governance. The challenge lies in considering the enormous variety and often contradictory nature of sub-discipline-specific factual knowledge and interdisciplinary concepts within the limited timeframe of a design process. The task of designing is to solve a problem, taking into account different requirements, conditions and the normative goals of various actors. We adopt from urban design 'a broader understanding of [regional] design, which sees [regional] design as an integrative (i.e. joined-up) and integrating activity' (Carmona et al. 2003: vii). Design as an activity has to be clearly differentiated from product-centred design definitions. Regional design is not the multitude of 'designs' of a region, in the way that an architectural design competition produces multiple designs for a building. Regional design is a methodology based on design thinking (Brown 2008; Luka 2014) for an interdisciplinary regional planning process.

The value of taking a design approach to regional governance issues is the integration of non-governmental issues into a debate that was only recently led by generalising and normative arguments. While regional design may also lead to a redesign of institutional structures, it only proposes it based on spatial case-specific evidence. Evidence in spatial sciences is based 'on methodological grounds' (Faludi and Waterhout 2006: 9), e.g. accountability, falsifiability or testability. In this case, design provides the necessary method. Producing this evidence base for regional planning requires more than a thorough training in public policy making. In other words, planners need to look into physical, social and organisational aspects to understand regions. What design does in addition is to embrace the fact that multiple solutions to given challenges exist and to offer a choice of concrete manifestations of these solutions to the local community and stakeholders. This means that 'regional designers' must have a good analytical understanding of various domains of regional development, from settlement patterns to economic drivers of change. While design as a methodological approach comprises core activities across scales, the different domains require a variety of skills and knowledge.

Regional design is an activity across the boundaries of multiple disciplines. The strong involvement of architects in regional design processes discloses an apparent lack of design competency in current regional planning practice. However, architects are not the regional design specialists per se or at least not exclusively. We also propose that 'regional designer' will not become a new discipline. Rather than superficially touching upon all relevant domains for regional design, regional design should be practised collaboratively by various established disciplines (Lapintie 2015a, b; Tewdwr-Jones 2015), with design as methodology bridging disciplinary boundaries.

4.4.3 Entrepreneurial Perspective

The role of interdisciplinary regional design practice varies significantly from the role of an architect in an urban design process, or a planner in a statutory planning process, if debatability becomes an integral part of the design, planning and development process of regions. Urban design is based on the idea of competition and particularly on creating attractive public spaces—waterfronts, cultural sites and squares—that render a location more visible, more legible and more attractive than other locations catering for a similar, or even the same, audience. Planning is based on the idea of the directive. Regional design requires both and positions itself within this continuum: a multitude of competing ideas but at the same time directive power of one strong shared narrative.

A stimulating approach, which helps to bridge the competition perspective of urban design with the directive perspective of planning, comes from a recent contribution to management theory. The so-called St. Gallen Management Model (SGMM) in its most recent version (Rüegg-Stürm and Grand 2015) proposes discussing the future evolution of an enterprise in quite a similar fashion to how we would today conceive a region's transformation. The SGMM understands the three dimensions of a firm—environment, organisation and management—as 'communicative streams of actions' (Rüegg-Stürm and Grand 2015: 1). Against this conceptual backdrop, we link the systemic perspective of the SGMM with regional design thinking: the future in general is open—for firms as for regions—but stakeholders in a region are still able to conceive alternative futures (Alaily-Mattar and Thierstein 2014), which simultaneously work on three perspectives: entrepreneurial, systemic and process-led.

- The firm, as well as a functionally delimited region, can be perceived as a creative practice. Designing alternative futures implies moving from ex-ante conceptualisation to real-time plausible realisation.
- Applying a systemic perspective for the designing process of alternative futures acknowledges that many elements of a relevant system, on firm level or regional level, relate to many other elements of that very system. Transforming such an entrepreneurial or regional system calls for continuous and strong communication, which negotiates and aligns elements for intended impacts. In the case of designing the transformation of a region, it will involve analysing the interrelationships of trends important to the region and identifying regional impacts, thereby supporting the management of a region more effectively.
- Designing alternative futures for firms and regions is possible. The third perspective is thus to do with transformation as a negotiation process. The identified impacts for the region are debated and negotiated, and then some of these impacts for an alternative future become more desirable to the stakeholders involved in the region. Other unwanted or less-desirable impacts also have to be negotiated in order to prevent them from happening. Such a process-led perspective will always bear in mind the contingency of any future development, be it for a firm or a region.

The SGMM thus serves as a helpful backdrop which calls for a threefold, simultaneous perspective in order to be able to transform a firm—or a region—effectively. Transformation has to be perceived and conceived as an evidence-based creative endeavour, which works entrepreneurially, systemically and is process led at the same time.

4.5 Conclusion: Regional Design as an Interdisciplinary Practice

This chapter proposes that regional design is the missing part of the overall regional development practice whose transformative capacity is based on its ability to imagine spatial futures. This argument is supported by comparing the regional scale to the urban scale and the complementary natures of urban design and urban planning. Regional planning has missed its complementary regional design practice since large-scale urban plans became a synonym for rationalist planning as part of the post-modern planning paradigm (see Sect. 4.2). Recent examples of regional design in practice (see Sect. 4.3), however, demonstrate the positive impact of design exercises for the overall regional development and planning process. Design approaches can contribute to an evidence-based debate about case-specific regional planning and governance. Nonetheless, the strategic nature of planning and designing at regional scale requires us to practice design in a different way from architectural or urban design (see Sect. 4.4).

The strategic nature of regional planning requires a design-based approach to combine the multitude of spatial facets of a region. If regional design takes into account the systemic nature, the process orientation and the entrepreneurial regime of regional development (cf. Table 4.1), then it serves as a successful methodology to trigger new dynamics for regional planning and potentially enable a re-scaling of governance arrangements. Architectural design, urban design and regional design are each concerned with a unique set of domains requiring different 'factual' and 'conceptual knowledge'. The up-scaling from a single building to a region increases the number of actors concerned and affected by the design activity. Consequently, regional design needs to be practised collaboratively to think about the future of regions, involving experts from various disciplines and local actors. Integrating design with regional governance requires an interdisciplinary approach.

If design as a methodology manages to bring people together from different disciplines, design competencies must be an integral part of all involved planning-oriented disciplines, including all kinds of planners, geographers, engineers, architects and others. A planner primarily focused on statutory tasks, for instance, does not need to become an expert designer, but he or she should be able to engage in a design process—perhaps led by an urban designer or architect—to collaboratively develop strategic ideas for the development of regions and the re-arrangement of governance structures. Basic familiarity with design thinking will be an integral competency for all disciplines that wish to engage in making strategic decisions for regional development. Thus, training more academic disciplines in design thinking must be a decisive part of a more impact-oriented and engaged regional development practice.

References

Alaily-Mattar N, Thierstein A (2014) Urban Transformation, Spatial Transformation? Developing Alternative Futures as a Planning Methodology. AESOP Annual Conference, Delft

Alaily-Mattar N, Thierstein A, Förster A (2014) "Alternative futures": A methodology for integrated sustainability considerations, the case of Nuremberg West, Germany. Local Environ Int J Justice Sustain 19:677–701

Albrechts L (2004) Strategic (spatial) planning re-examined. Environ Plan 31:743–758

Albrechts L, Healey P, Kunzmann Klaus R (2003) Strategic spatial planning and regional governance in Europe. APA J 69:113–129

Alexander ER (2006) Institutional design for sustainable development. Town Plann Rev 77:1–27

Allmendinger P, Haughton G (2009) Soft spaces, fuzzy boundaries, and metagovernance: the new spatial planning in the Thames Gateway. Environ Plann A 41:617–633

Anderson LW, Krathwohl DR, Airasian PW et al (2001) A taxonomy for learning, teaching, and assessing: a revision of Bloom's taxonomy of educational objectives. New York

Balz VE (2017) Regional design: discretionary approaches to regional planning in The Netherlands. Plann Theor 1–23

Balz VE, Zonneveld WAM (2014) Regional design in the context of fragmented territorial governance: south wing studio. Eur Plan Stud 23:871–891

BBR BfBuR (1999) Projektorientierte Planung—das Beispiel IBA Emscher Park, Informationen zur Raumentwicklung, Heft 3/4.1999. Bonn: BBR, Bundesamt für Bauwesen und Raumordnung

berchtoldkrass so, Studio UC and zürich irb (2011) METROBILD. Ein Bild für den Metroraum Zürich. Abschlussbericht. Verein Metropolitanraum Zürich, Karlsruhe, Berlin, Zürich

Blank H, van Boheemen Y, Bouw M et al (2009) Ontwerpen aan Randstad 2040—designing Randstad 2040. Design and Politics. 010 Publishers, Rotterdam

Blatter J (2006) Die Vielfalt des "New Regionalism". Communitarian, Civic und Creative Governance-Ansätze für die Steuerung und Integration von US-amerikanischen Stadtregionen. disP—Plann Rev 2008:84–92

Boesch M (1989) Engagierte Geographie. Zur Rekonstruktion der Raumwissenschaft als politik-orientierte Geographie, Franz Steiner, Stuttgart

Brown T (2008) Design thinking. Harvard Bus Rev 2008:84–92

Bruns F (2011) Renaissance großer Pläne? Stadtentwicklungsplanung und Wandel des Planungsverständins am Beispiel Hamburg. Chair of Regional Planning and Development. Hafen City University, Hamburg

Carmona M, Tiesdell S, Heath T et al (2003) Public Places. Urban Spaces. The Dimensions of Urban Design, Elsevier, Oxford

Cole S (2001) Dare to dream: bringing futures into planning. J Am Plann Assoc 67:372–383

Davy B (2004) Die neunte Stadt. Wilde Grenzen und Städteregion Ruhr 2030. Verlag Müller & Busmann, Wuppertal

Droß M, Alaily-Mattar N, Thierstein A (2012) A conceptual foundation of spatial strategy. A methodology for spatial transformation. AESOP Annual Conference, Ankara

Droß M, Thierstein A, Haag S. (2010) 'Spatial Strategy' or how to unlock the fix spatial planning. AESOP Annual Conference, Helsinki

Ellin N (1996) Postmodern urbanism. Blackwell, Cambridge

Erhard K, Dross M, Thierstein A (2015) Step-by-step design of a local spatial strategy for a mega transport infrastructure project. In: Fabbro S (ed) Mega transport infrastructure planning. European Corridors in Local-Regional Perspective. Cham, Heidelberg

Evers D, de Vries J (2013) Explaining governance in five mega-city regions: rethinking the role of hierarchy and government. Eur Plan Stud 21:536–555

Faludi A, Waterhout B (2006) Introducing evidence-based planning. disP—Plann Rev 165:4–13

Feld LP (1999) Allocative And Distributive Effects Of Tax Competition: An Empirical Analysis For Switzerland. Aussenwirtschaft 54:503–528

Feld LP, Kirchgässner G (1998) Fiskalischer Föderalismus. Wirtschaftswissenschaftliches Studium (WiSt) 2: 65–70

Förster A, Balz V, Thierstein A et al (2016) The conference 'Shaping Regional Futures: Mapping, Designing, Transforming!' A documentation. TUM, TU Delft, Munich/Delft

Frank AI, Mironowicz I, Lourenco J et al (2014) Educating planners in Europe: a review of 21st century study programmes. Elsevier, pp 30–94

Frey BS, Eichenberger R (1995) FOCJ: creating a single European Market for Governments. In: Schmidtchen D, Cooter R (eds) Constitutional law and economics of the European union. Edward Elgar Publishing, Cheltenham, pp 195–222

Frey RL (2003) Regional Governance zur Selbststeuerung territorialer Subsysteme. Informationen zur Raumentwicklung, pp 451–462

Gilliard L (2013) A critical reconstruction of Los Angeles. Cardiff School of Planning and Geography, Welsh School of Architecture. Cardiff University, Cardiff

Gilliard L, Thierstein A (2016) Competencies revisited. disP—Plann Rev 52:42–55

Healey P (2006) Relational Complexity and the Imaginative Power of Strategic Spatial Planning. Eur Plan Stud 14:525–546

Hocking V (2010) Designerly Ways of Knowing: What Does Design Have to Offer? In: Brown VA, Harris JA, Russell JY (eds) Tackling Wicked Problems - Through the Transdisciplinary Imagination. Earthscan, London, pp 242–250

Hutter G (2006) Strategische Planung. Ein wiederentdeckter Planungsansatz zur Bestandsentwicklung von Städten. RaumPlanung, p 210–214

Janssen-Jansen L (2011) From Amsterdam to Amsterdam Metropolitan Area: A Paradigm Shift. International Planning Studies 16:257–272

Jensen MB, Johnson B, Lorenz E et al (2007) Forms of knowledge and modes of innovation. Res Policy 36:680–693

Khan AZ, Moulaert F, Schreurs J (2013) Epistemology of Space: Exploring Relational Perspectives in Planning, Urbanism, and Architecture. International Planning Studies 18:287–303

Kirchgässner G, Pommerehne WW (1994) Tax harmonization and tax competition in the European Union - Lessons from Switzerland. Journal of Public Economics 60:351–371

Kleihues JP (1993) Städtebau ist Erinnerung: Anmerkungen zur kritischen Konstruktion. In: Kleihues JP (ed) Die Projekte. Gerd Hatje, Stuttgart

Kübler D (2003) "Metropolitan Governance" oder: Die unendliche Geschichte der Institutionenbildung in Stadtregionen. Informationen zur Raumentwicklung: 535–542

Lapintie K (2015a) Kimmo Lapintie—Finland. disP—Plann Rev 51:32–33

Lapintie K (2015b) Long March of Strategic Planning. disP—Plann Rev 52:4–5

Ley D (1987) Styles of the times: liberal and neo-conservative landscapes in inner Vancouver, 1968–1986. J Hist Geogr 13:40–56

Luka I (2014) Design thinking in pedagogy. J Educ Cult Soc 63–74

Madanipour A (2006) Roles and challenges of urban design. J Urban Des 11:173–193

Massey D (2005) For Space. Sage, London

McLoughlin JB (1969) Urban and regional planning, a systems approach. Faber and Faber, London

Oosterlynck S, van den Broeck J, Albrechts L et al (2010) Strategic spatial projects: catalysts for change. Routledge Taylor & Francis, New York

Parr JB (2007) On the spatial structure of administration. Environ Plann A 39:1255–1268

Priebs A (2005) Stadt-Umland-Problematik. ARL, Akademie für Raumforschung und Landesplanung, Hannover

Pütz M (2004) Regional Governance—Theoretisch-konzeptionelle Grundlagen und eine Analyse nachhaltiger Siedlungsentwicklung in der Metropolregion München. oekom verlag, München

Rüegg-Stürm J, Grand S (2015) The St. Gallen Management Model. English translation of the fourth generation of the German text. Haupt, Bern

Salet W (2006) Rescaling territorial governance in the Randstad Holland: the responsiveness of spatial and institutional strategies to changing socio-economic interactions. Eur Plan Stud 14:959–978

Salet W, Woltjer J (2009) New concepts of strategic spatial planning dilemmas in the Dutch Randstad region. Int J Public Sector Manag 22:235–248

Sardar Z (2010) The Namesake: futures; futures studies; futurology; futuristic; foresight—what's in a name? Futures 42:177–184

Schaafsma M (2010) From airport city to airport corridor. In: Knippenberger U, Wall A (eds) Airports in cities and regions. KIT Scientific Publishing, Karlsruhe, pp 173–179

Schönwandt WL (1999) Grundriss einer Planungstheorie der "dritten Generation". Plann Rev 136/137:25–35

Schönwandt WL (2008) Planning in crisis? Theoretical orientations for architecture and planning. Ashgate, Aldershot

Senatsverwaltung für Stadtentwicklung und Wohnen Berlin (2010) Planwerk Innere Stadt 2010. Available at http://www.stadtentwicklung.berlin.de/planen/planwerke/de/planwerk_innere_stadt/. Access date: 20/02/2018

Senatsverwaltung für Stadtentwicklung und Wohnen Berlin (2017) Berlin land use plan (FNP Berlin) (interactive updated working document, as of November 2017). Available at http://www.stadtentwicklung.berlin.de/planen/fnp/de/fnp/index.shtml. Access date: 20/02/2018

Silver N (2012) The signal and the noise: why most predictions fail—but some don't. Penguin, New York

Smith N (1996) The new urban frontier. Genrification and the revanchist city. Routledge, New York

Swyngedouw E (2005) Governance innovation and the citizen: the Janus face of governance-beyond-the-state. Urban Stud 42:1991–2006

Tewdwr-Jones M (2015) Mark Tewdwr-Jones—United Kingdom. disP—Plann Rev 51:84–85

Thierstein A, Wenner F, Bentlage M et al (2015) Spatial integration and administrative complexity: housing, employment, and mobility in the case of the Munich Metropolitan Region. AESOP Annual Conference, Prag

Tiebout CM (1956) A pure theory of local expenditures. J Polit Econ 64:416–424

Vester F (2012) The art of connected thinking: tools and concepts for a new approach to tackling complexity. MCB Publishing House, Munich

Wiese A, Förster A, Gilliard L et al (2014) A spatial strategy for the production of place in two German cities—Urban design interventions as a driver for spatial transformation. City, Territory Archit 1:1–9

The Connection Between Regional Designing and Spatial Planning

5

Annet Kempenaar

Abstract

Regional designing envisions and develops possible and desirable regional future scenarios, including how they can come about. It is a particular envisioning method used to draw up strategic spatial plans and, as such, is closely entwined with spatial planning. Regional designing has become a regular practice in the Netherlands, which is the context explored in this chapter. Dutch regional design practice teaches us that, like other kinds of designing, regional designing is highly contextual. It adapts and responds to the characteristics of a situation. Regional design projects build on a thorough understanding of the planning situation and the issues at hand, and they are tailor-made to fit that situation. In turn, regional designing aims to enhance the planning situation. It affects and influences the aims of planning, the planning process and/or the conditions of spatial planning. These effects arise from an iterative regional design process in which the expertise of the designer(s), the interaction with stakeholders and a proper embeddedness in its context are critical factors. Relationships and networks, as well as mutual understanding and shared concepts develop during the regional design process. They become strong assets in pressurised spatial planning situations that need to adapt and change their organisational structure.

Keywords

Regional design • Strategic spatial planning • Envisioning • Stakeholder participation • Landscape architecture

5.1 Introduction

Fortune tellers are not the only ones who make it their profession to predict the future. The majority of spatial planners and designers also have their professional focus on what will, or can, be in future. This is particularly the case in strategic spatial planning, which concentrates on long-term future perspectives for geographic regions in which the spatial situation is under pressure and needs to be adapted. Regional designing, which has its roots in landscape architecture and urban planning and design, is used in strategic spatial planning processes as a way to envision possible and desirable future situations. As such, it is closely entwined with strategic spatial planning. This chapter will explore that connection and the effects of regional designing on spatial planning.

The chapter predominantly builds on notions from research into Dutch regional design practice, consisting of multiple case studies on different aspects of regional designing (De Jonge 2009; Meijsmans and Beelen 2010; De Zwart 2015; Kempenaar 2017). The Netherlands is an inspiring case study for regional designing because it has developed a strong regional design tradition over the last few decades. In the 1980s, in response to the rational planning approach of the previous decades, various experiments explored the potential of designing, and in particular the visual and integrative

A. Kempenaar (✉)
A-scape, Heerdlaan 17, Bennekom, The Netherlands
e-mail: annet.kempenaar@a-scape.nl

Faculty of Spatial Sciences, University of Groningen, Groningen, The Netherlands

© Springer Nature Switzerland AG 2020
V. Lingua and V. Balz (eds.), *Shaping Regional Futures*,
https://doi.org/10.1007/978-3-030-23573-4_5

capacities of designing, within the realm of regional spatial planning (De Jonge 2009; Salewski and Paine 2012). These experiments were successful and fuelled the uptake and development of regional designing in the 1990s and 2000s. Today, regional designing is a widespread practice in the Netherlands, with a substantial community of regional designers and regional designs for almost every region.

In the context of this chapter, the term (regional) 'design'(s) will be used to indicate the product(s) that are the outcome of the design process, the term (regional) 'designing' to refer to the process of creating such products (Lenzholzer et al. 2013) and the term (regional) 'designer' to refer to a professional who works on regional designs and who is trained and educated in a spatial design discipline.

5.1.1 Regional Designing

Regional designing is the collaborative envisioning of the future physical form and arrangement of settlements, infrastructures, water features, nature reserves and other land uses within a region, including the relationships between them, their aesthetic appearances, and how this future could come about (Kempenaar 2017, p. 13). This section touches upon four defining aspects of regional designing: developing long-term visions and perspectives, a regional focus, the act of designing and the collaborative production of regional designs.

The core of regional designing is to envision possible and desirable future perspectives (Stremke et al. 2012; Neuman 2000; De Jonge 2009; Van Dijk 2011; Balz and Zonneveld 2015) for regions in which the existing spatial situation is under pressure from factors such as climate change, transition to renewable energy sources, economic developments or structural demographic changes. Regional designing focuses on pointing out long-term aims and interests, on developing and testing alternative perspectives, and on the ways and means of achieving these. It, therefore, not only creates visions of what regions can become, it also develops strategies towards these futures and short-term actions that set the development into motion. However, regional designs are not blueprints or fixed plans (Van Dijk 2011; De Jonge 2009), they are adaptive navigation devices that direct actions towards the uncertain future (Langner 2014). As such, their goals and objectives provide direction and aim to guide decisions and developments concerning the physical environment over the long term.

Regional designing has a supra-local or regional focus. It takes a large geographic area with all its land uses and physical characteristics into account (e.g. Neuman 2000; De Jonge 2009; Stremke 2010). Such a region can range from the size of several municipalities up to a (nation) state. A region, or the area concerned in regional designing, can be defined in various ways by institutional, functional, physical, historical or cultural borders, or a combination of these (e.g. Keating 2004). A relational perspective on regions is also present in regional designing; it actively addresses relationships, for example between stakeholders and different land uses, and seeks to attune them (Neuman 2000; Rauws and Van Dijk 2013).

Regional designing employs a design mentality, uses design-based methods and methodology, and follows the logic of design processes (De Jonge 2009; Rauws and Van Dijk 2013; Van Dijk 2011). These processes are nonlinear and iterative, have a cyclic character and are particularly suited to deal with so-called wicked problems (Rittel and Webber 1973), that is with problems that cannot be defined completely and for which the possible solution depends on how the problem is framed. Problem and solution frames develop in pairs. This co-evolution of problem and solution space (Cross 2006; Dorst and Cross 2001) is a core characteristic of designing and thus of regional designing. Another characteristic of (regional) designing is synthesis, in other words blending different kinds of information and perspectives into a comprehensive set of ideas (Lawson 2005). Furthermore, regional designing, like other spatial design disciplines, pays attention to three-dimensional form and function (Lenzholzer et al. 2017), and makes extensive use of visuals such as maps, infographics, images and sketches to represent the regional design ideas, plans and proposals (Balz and Zonneveld 2015; De Jonge 2009; Meijsmans and Beelen 2010).

Regional designs are often the result of a collaborative creative process, according to various descriptions and accounts of regional designing (e.g. Brand et al. 2014; Kempenaar 2016; Waggonner et al. 2014; Stein 2005). Regional designers collaborate with various groups of stakeholders during the design process in order to draw up a regional design. This means a regional design is created by a group, not by a single designer. Although the goal and form of the participation of stakeholders vary in different projects, the co-production or co-creation process is a key factor in regional designing (Meijsmans and Beelen 2010). This collaborative creation process is often referred to as a dialogue with and between multiple participants (De Jonge 2009; Kempenaar and Van den Brink 2018). Along with experts, who bring specific expertise to the regional design process, various stakeholder groups are generally also invited to participate and collaborate in regional designing. These include groups of 'producers', who build and develop projects and create new situations, 'regulators', who regulate land use, and 'users', who live and work in the region and use the space (Madanipour 2006).

5.1.2 Intertwinings with Strategic Spatial Planning

The field of spatial planning is broad, complex and dynamic (e.g. De Roo and Hillier 2016; De Roo and Silva 2010; Innes and Booher 2010) and encompasses multiple ambitions, activities and perspectives. Spatial planning can be both regulatory and strategic; it addresses different geographic scales; it includes long-term and short-term processes; it produces visions, policies and legal regulations; it is both an action-oriented and a communicative discipline; it is the domain of political deliberation, among other things (Carmona and Sieh 2008; Sanyal 2005; Knieling and Othengrafen 2009). This complex field can be conceptualised as a network of multiple planning arenas, both formal and informal (Rydin 2007), in which various operational and strategic planning issues take centre stage, and governmental and non-governmental stakeholders interact in different settings (Innes and Booher 2010; Healey 2006) engaging with different planning situations on various levels of scale. These planning arenas exchange information and ideas, interact with each other and together make up the complex and dynamic landscape of spatial planning.

In this complex planning landscape, strategic spatial planning gets taken up by cities and regions in response to a changing planning context, increased uncertainty and new planning issues (Albrechts and Balducci 2013; Schatz 2010). Strategic spatial planning initiatives usually coexist with traditional statutory planning systems, but where traditional planning systems are mainly focused on regulating land use and spatial initiatives, strategic spatial planning deals with pressing issues in the face of an unpredictable future and is focused on actively inducing long-term structural change (Kunzmann 2013; Sartorio 2005). Strategic spatial planning also tends to involve multiple stakeholders and takes place in an informal setting (Albrechts and Balducci 2013). Though the outcome of strategic spatial planning generally has no formal status, it aims to influence decisions, actions and activities in other (formal) spatial planning arenas and, as such, the actual spatial developments in a region.

Within strategic spatial planning processes, regional designing is employed as a particular method to develop spatial visions, long-term perspectives and strategies (Rauws and Van Dijk 2013) and as such it is closely linked with strategic spatial planning. However, regional designing and spatial planning are two distinct areas, each with its own theoretical and methodological base, history and educational traditions (Van Assche et al. 2013). While both operate in the realm of adjusting and improving spatial arrangements and layouts, designers and planners tend to have a different, albeit complementary, focus on their work. A prime concern for designers is the content, whereas planners focus on the process (De Jonge 2009). Figure 5.1 shows how this different focus works out in the Netherlands with regard to designers' and planners' aims and results, activities and competencies, and the character of their working process.

DESIGNERS	REALM OF ADJUSTING AND IMPROVING SPATIAL ARRANGEMENTS AND LAYOUT	PLANNERS
Aims and results		**Aims and results**
- Spatial quality		Democratic legitimacy and justice -
- Change, renewal		Execution of public goals -
Activities and competences		**Activities and competences**
- Develop and visualise visions for the future		Give direction, formulate goals and frameworks -
- Order information		Describe problems and solutions -
- Create coherence between components		Programme activities -
- Shape and create		Use instruments to achieve goals -
Character of the working process		**Character of the working process**
- Iterative, interactive and integrative		From goals to means, from problem to solution -
- Creative search		Difficult and full of tension -
- Visual, imaginative		Together with society and decision makers -
- Listening to stakeholders, raising awareness		Weighing interests -
- Being proactive		Looking for public support -

Fig. 5.1 Aims and results, activities, competencies and character of the working process for Dutch designers and planners in the realm of adjusting and improving spatial arrangements and layouts, elaborated by the author, based on De Jonge (2009, p. 127, 129, 130)

5.2   The Responsive Character of Regional Designing

Every regional design project is different. Regional designing responds and adjusts itself to each individual regional planning situation (De Jonge 2009; Meijsmans and Beelen 2010; Kempenaar and Van den Brink 2018). Each region is unique, with specific physical, historical, socio-economical, cultural and political conditions and its own history. Regional designing takes the existing spatial arrangement into account, including how it came about; it provides solutions to the problems that put the existing spatial arrangement under pressure; the results have to fit the economic, social, cultural and political situation in the region. Regional designing does not start with a tabula rasa, it starts with understanding the existing planning situation in order to develop an appropriate response.

Regional designing develops responses to regional situations through, as Schön (1983) described it, 'a reflective conversation with the situation'. That conversation is a process of framing the situation (a form of 'seeing as'), developing proposals for new situations and then evaluating these proposals which, in turn, can lead to new proposals or the search for a new frame. Regional designers have developed several general principles that help them respond to the specificities of a situation during this conversation (Kempenaar and Van den Brink 2018). Firstly, they perceive regions as evolving and dynamic systems in which interventions can be made to direct development towards the envisioned future. Secondly, they address multiple geographical scales and investigate the history to develop a good understanding of the region. Thirdly, they work back from the envisioned future to develop appropriate strategies and actions. Reframing the region and the issues at hand is a pivotal step in this process, one which is focused on identifying new perspectives and possible solutions. Furthermore, designers engage in a continuous dialogue with stakeholders to learn about the region and to develop appropriate responses. They sense and respond to the planning situation and to whatever comes up during the design process. Finally, they have learned to balance direction and openness during their interaction with stakeholders, in the design process itself and also in the end-product.

In most regional design processes, various stakeholder groups and experts participate alongside the designer(s). They actively take part in framing the situation, and developing and evaluating proposals, thereby turning the process into this collaborative 'conversation with the situation'. Stakeholder participation is pivotal for drawing up appropriate regional designs (Meijsmans and Beelen 2010; Kempenaar 2017) because stakeholders have detailed knowledge of the spatial, social, political, economic and cultural situation in the region. This makes them an important source of information that is needed for both a good understanding of the region and making regional designs that fit the requirements of a particular spatial planning situation. Next to bringing knowledge into the conversation, stakeholders also actively participate in discussions and exchange ideas, enabling them to respond to the spatial planning situation, help frame and reframe, and adjust the process that leads to new perspectives.

The role of the designer(s) in the conversation is to develop technically sound and comprehensive regional design outcomes. Designers bring their substantive knowledge of spatial situations and systems, their experience with designing new situations, their expertise in blending disparate ideas and information into a coherent whole, and their visualisation skills to develop and draw up the intermediate and final regional design ideas and products. In addition, designers structure, organise and facilitate the collaborative design process during which the conversation unfolds (De Jonge 2009). Designers, therefore, must have a strong ability to respond to situations, both in the creation of regional designs and in the design and facilitation of the collaborative process (Kempenaar 2017).

The collaborative conversation generally ends when the goals of the regional design endeavour are reached. Not all regional design projects lead to similar end products though. The context of the design process generally defines what an appropriate final product for regional designing should be. This means that depending on the context, regional designing may focus on, for instance, investigating the longer-term trends and developments in a region, mapping the perspectives and interests of multiple stakeholders, attuning them, drawing up an integrated strategic plan or developing an appropriate strategy. Therefore, the end products also differ and can range from a fully worked-out, integrated strategic plan to an elaborate strategy or from multiple viable options for future development to a reframed planning situation or a regional spatial development agenda.

5.3   The Effects of Regional Designing on Spatial Planning

Regional designing not only responds to (strategic) spatial planning situations, but also aims to alter these situations and enhance spatial planning processes. It has a spectrum of influences on spatial planning (De Jonge 2009; Balz and Zonneveld 2015; Kempenaar et al. 2016b, 2017), ranging from direct influences on ongoing strategic spatial planning processes and long-term impacts to influences beyond its immediate context (Kempenaar et al. 2017). However, not every regional design effort has similar effects. Overall, regional designing influences spatial planning in three important ways: it affects the aims, process and conditions of spatial planning.

5.3.1 Influencing the Aims of Spatial Planning

Developing a new or alternative perspective on the future spatial arrangement of a region lies at the heart of regional designing. This influential contribution often affects the aims of spatial planning in a region (De Jonge 2009; Meijsmans and Beelen 2010; Kempenaar et al. 2017). New perspectives open up new and innovative ideas that would otherwise never be thought of, which broaden the options and possibilities for desirable futures and, as such, influence what is strived for through spatial planning. This is a valuable contribution to spatial planning that underpins many regional design projects.

In the process of developing new perspectives, designers look at information from a spatial angle and often draw it on a map (Meijsmans and Beelen 2010; Kempenaar and Van den Brink 2018). They actively explore, map and research the regional situation, including its history and specific qualities. Furthermore, they investigate the spatial dimensions and consequences of the issues at hand. This combined mapping, researching, relating and visualising of spatial information are important in regional designing because it provides designers and stakeholders with insights into the planning situation, spatial relationships and dynamics of a region.

These spatial explorations are an important instrument in the process of reframing the spatial planning situation and its issues. Through reframing, new perspectives develop that identify possible future situations and can influence spatial planning substantially and over the long term (Kempenaar et al. 2017). For example, until the 1980s there was no MHAL Region (Maastricht, Hasselt, Aachen, Liège; a cross-border region located in Belgium, Germany and the Netherlands). National perspectives had framed the respective national parts of this region as peripheral and marginal border areas, but the MHAL Spatial Development Perspective (Internationale coordinatie-commissie 1993), for which a conceptual design for the MHAL Region was drawn up (Fig. 5.2), altered this perspective radically. This design, which visualised a polycentric urbanised region, centred around a valuable cultural landscape in the middle, represented a radically new concept for this cross-border region as one coherent region with complementary parts. It is still guiding spatial planning decisions in the region today.

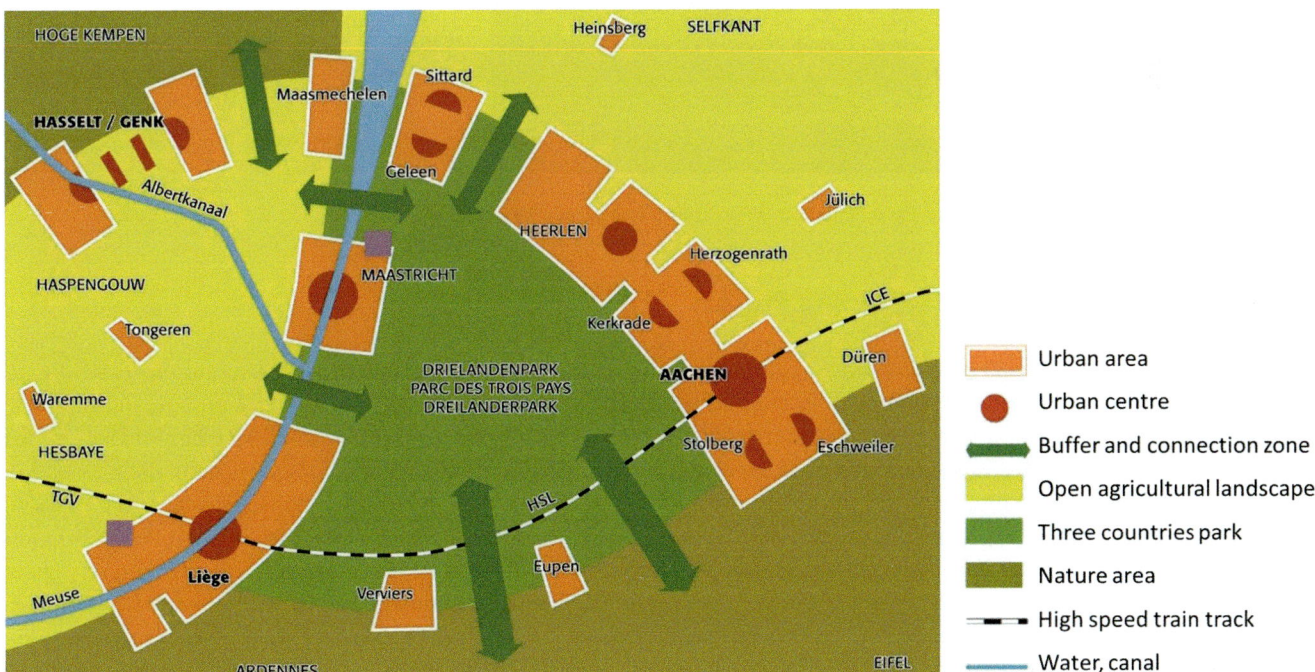

Fig. 5.2 Conceptual design for the MHAL spatial development perspective, from Internationale coordinatie-commissie (1993)

The strength and longevity of the spatial concept from the MHAL perspective are illustrated by its transference to multiple national, regional and local spatial planning arenas. Since its publication, the MHAL spatial concept has influenced regional and local spatial plans and policies, including the 'Plan Regional d'Aménagement du Territoire de Wallonie' (Internationale werkgroep MHAL 1996), the Spatial Structural Plan for the Belgian Province of Limburg (Provincie Limburg 2012) and the Provincial Environmental Plan for the Dutch Province of Limburg (Provincie Limburg 2014). Moreover, the MHAL conceptual design was used as a framework to programme EU Interreg II funding for the Euregio Meuse-Rhine (Internationale werkgroep MHAL 1996). Furthermore, it formed the basis for later regional designs that were drawn up in 2003 (Fig. 5.3) and 2014 (Fig. 5.4) (Kempenaar et al. 2016b) as part of cross-border collaboration on the development of the Three Countries Park, the cultural landscape in the middle of the MHAL Region. These subsequent regional designs also influenced spatial planning in the MHAL region and instigated various (cross-border) implementation projects.

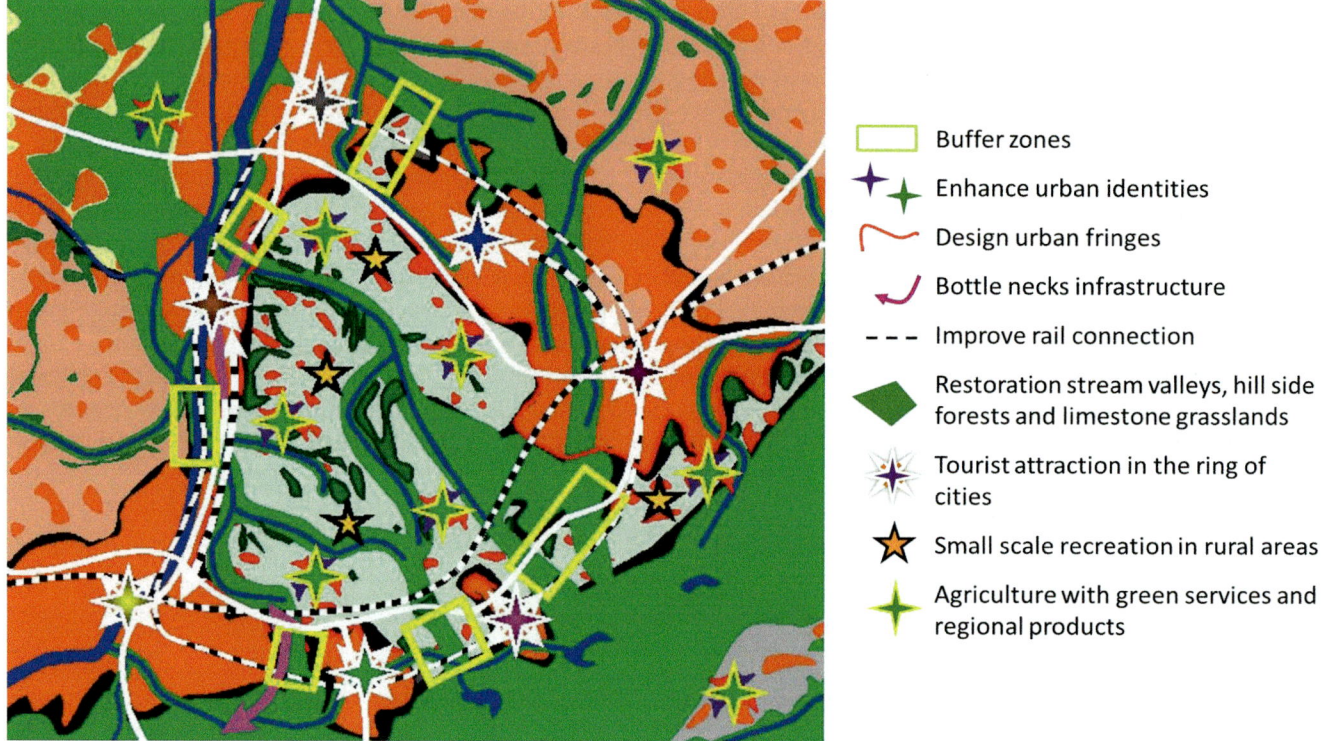

Fig. 5.3 Development perspective for the Three Countries Park, from Projectgroep Drielandenpark (2003)

5.3.2 Influencing the Spatial Planning Process

Besides its influence on spatial planning aims, regional designing can have an effect on spatial planning processes too, by influencing the next steps to be taken as well as supporting decision-making. It often develops and proposes ideas for the structure and organisation of upcoming phases in a spatial development process, as part of a wider strategy, which in turn can influence the manner in which spatial planning processes unfold. For instance, spatial strategies usually define a specific order of activities together with any short- and long-term actions. Furthermore, as regional designs are integrative in nature, they indicate which sectorial developments are interrelated and affect one another, and therefore which ones will require collaboration and reconciliation. Influencing the spatial planning process can indeed be an explicit focus or aim of regional designing (Neuman 2012; Forester et al. 2013; Kempenaar et al. 2016a), alongside the development of a long-term perspective. In such regional design efforts, "tasks, timing and structure of the process are considered first, before elaborating on a spatial solution" (EoWijers-stichting 2012, p. 20). Thus, regional designing has a combined focus on both substantial and procedural issues, recognising the importance of both process and plans in spatial planning.

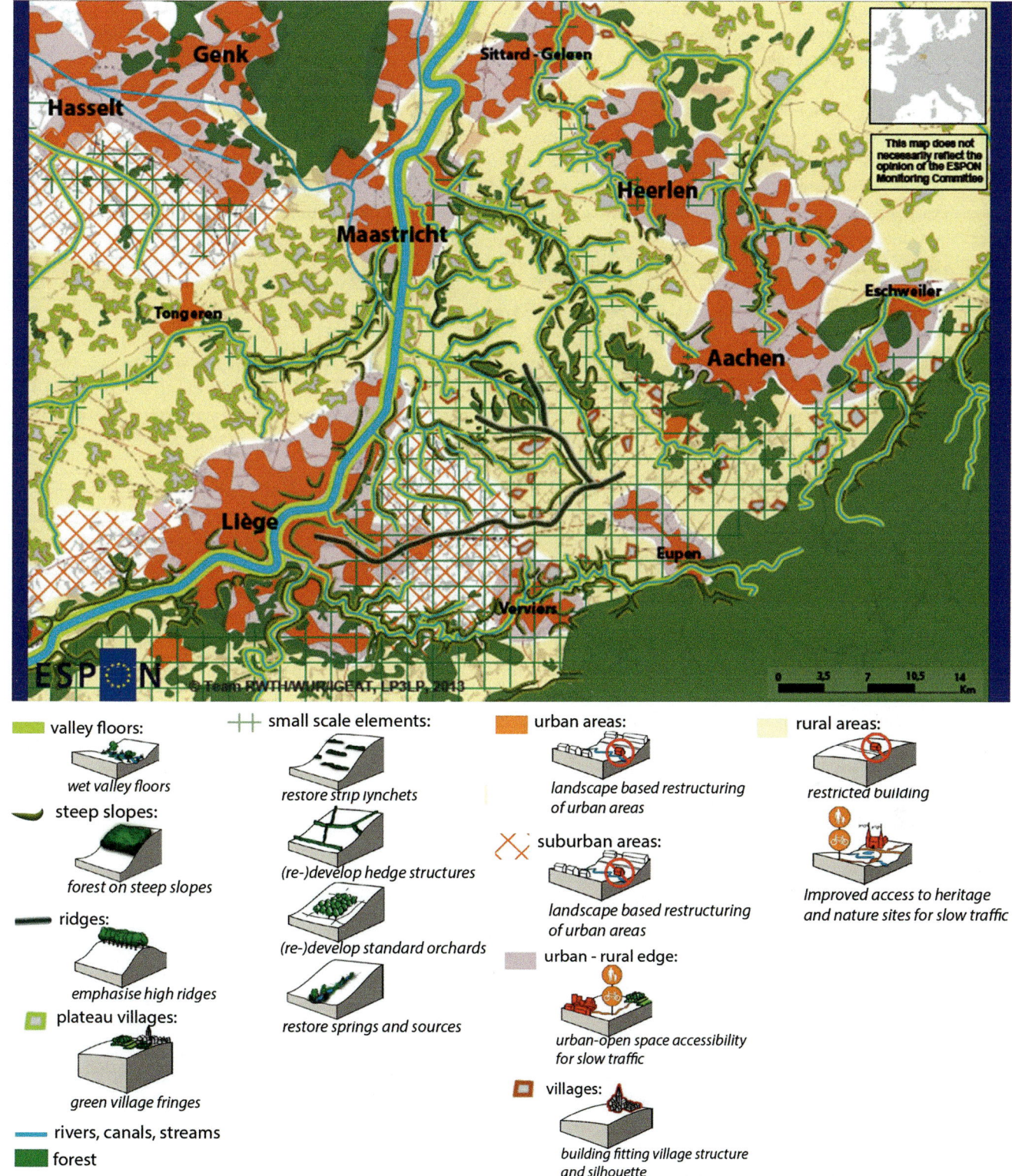

Fig. 5.4 Overall landscape framework for landscape development in the Three Countries Park, from Lohrberg et al. (2014)

The influence of regional designing on decision-making in spatial planning unfolds in multiple ways. Regional designing enables informed decision-making (Van Dijk 2011; Chapman 2011; Kempenaar et al. 2016b) because it often develops different options or scenarios, with each considering all the issues at hand, while at the same time envisioning different outcomes. In certain situations, it is employed to open up public debate and highlight potential problems, which may inform political agendas and lead to their amendment (De Zwart 2015). In other situations, the collaborative regional design process can create consensus on certain issues (Neuman 1998; De Zeeuw et al. 2010; Kempenaar et al. 2016b), often after intense deliberations around opinions, ideas and interests, at times thereby rendering decision-making a mere formality. It is worthy of note that if this consensus is not shared by those not involved in, but affected by, the regional design process, new discussions and debates can arise after the project is finished. In most regional design processes, however, the results indicate consensus on some issues and elaborate the options for decisions on others. As such, regional designing coordinates and aligns different interests, and highlights critical differences based on an integrative (as in non-sectoral) spatial perspective, thus preventing unnecessary discussions or negotiations, and focusing discussions and spatial planning decision-making on the relevant themes and issues.

5.3.3   Influencing the Conditions of Spatial Planning

Regional designing can alter the conditions of spatial planning by affecting the perception of a region and its issues (Neuman 1998; Sieverts 2008; Balz and Zonneveld 2015), as illustrated by the MHAL Region example described in 5.3.1. Furthermore, regional designing can prepare stakeholders for future action and build relationships and networks (Hajer et al. 2006; Forrester et al. 2013; Kempenaar 2017). These influences can be strong assets in spatial planning processes, particularly those that involve structural change and call for collaborative action.

New perspectives on an existing situation, the issues at hand and possible solutions—as produced by regional designing—alter the opinions, views and frames of reference of stakeholders and, therefore, the spatial planning context. The development of a new perspective takes place in a collaborative design process, meaning that stakeholders participate in this development and have a say in it. They share opinions, ideas and interests, which creates insights into their individual positions. Moreover, collective options and possibilities are explored during this collaboration. As a result, the regional design outcomes represent a shared perspective that is supported, or at least understood, by those who were involved in the process. Common and shared ideas, whether they concern the future physical arrangement, the strategy, the organisation or the short- and long-term actions, are a valuable asset for forthcoming stages of the (strategic) spatial planning processes, particularly those situations in which roles and planning responsibilities are in flux.

Many stakeholders involved in regional designing are potential future actors in the discussion and implementation of ideas and strategies. This concerns both the adaptation of the regional design in formal plans, programmes and planning procedures, and the elaboration of spatial adjustments and the execution of (building) plans. During the involvement of future actors as stakeholders, they develop a sense of ownership over the new ideas. This builds support and engagement, prepares them for future action (Simonson and Robertson 2013; Kempenaar et al 2016b) and, as such, alters the conditions for spatial planning.

In addition, regional designing can bond people and build communities (Sutton and Kemp 2006; Meijsmans and Beelen 2010). The interactive design process changes the understanding between stakeholders and can improve their relationships. Regional designing reduces risks and anxieties, potentially unites different groups of people, creates situations in which rivalries can be set aside and, as such, creates conditions that encourage collaboration (Madanipour 2006; Von Seggern et al. 2008; Forester et al. 2013). The cross-border network and relationships that were developed while drawing up the MHAL Spatial Development Perspective in the early 1990s (see 5.3.1), for instance, instigated joint projects and further cross-border collaboration in the following decades (Kempenaar et al. 2017). This illustrates that partnerships and collaboration developed during regional designing can last over a long period of time. Partnerships though are also reported to fall apart due to design proposals (Balz and Zonneveld 2015), implying that regional designing cannot be relied upon to improve networks and relationships. It further indicates that not every regional design process is equally successful or influential.

5.4   The Specifics of an Influential Regional Design Process

The actual influence of regional designing depends on many things. The aims, the stakeholders involved, the stage of the strategic planning process, previous experiences with regional designing and the context of the design process are some of the factors that act upon regional designing and its effects. Although the efforts of the designer(s) and others involved will generally focus on creating successful and influential regional design outcomes, their actual success and influence cannot be controlled. Regional designing, being part of strategic spatial planning, generally has an informal character and takes place in soft planning spaces. This means it has little formal power. The advantage of this is that stakeholders can take a relatively free position towards their direct interests and obligations and engage in an honest dialogue with each other (De Jonge 2009). The informal status also implies it can only propose ideas and suggestions for new situations. Decision-making, both substantive and procedural, takes place in other formal spatial planning arenas. In those arenas, many perspectives, influences and powers are in play, making the actual outcome uncertain and dependant on many issues.

The 'soft power' through which regional designing aims to shape, affect and influence other spatial planning arenas can have significant effects, however (De Jonge 2009; Neuman 2012; De Zwart 2015). It can even lead to the development of new organisations and institutions (Neuman 2012). In order to become influential, not only the regional design but also the design process is critical (Kempenaar 2017), a factor that is within the span of control of those involved in regional designing. Three elements of the design process that determine its future use and value are: the expertise of the designer or design team, interaction with stakeholders and the context in which regional designing is set.

The expertise of designer(s) is critical for achieving quality in both the regional design process and the outcome(s). Designers reframe situations and integrate different kinds of knowledge and information into technically sound, comprehensive regional designs that fit their planning situation, and which they test on a small scale (De Jonge 2009; Kempenaar and Van de Brink 2017). Furthermore, designers visualise information, ideas and options as well as the final regional design. This visualisation plays an important role in triggering and structuring stakeholder interactions and making future situations foreseeable (Weller 2008; Von Seggeren et al. 2008; Meijsmans and Beelen 2010). Finally, designers structure, organise and facilitate the interactive design process with stakeholders and must be able to manage these processes appropriately (De Jonge 2009; Kempenaar and Van den Brink 2018). All these factors make the expertise and skills of the designer critical for the (future) influence of regional designing.

Interaction with stakeholders is the second critical element in the design process (De Jonge 2009; Meijsmans and Beelen 2010; Kempenaar 2017). Stakeholders' knowledge is indispensable for drawing up an appropriate regional design. Secondly, in order for those designs to be taken up and used, the stakeholders' sense of ownership over the ideas that emerges from the collaboration is pivotal because it creates support and engagement and motivates future actions. What the stakeholders' focus should be, as well as who should participate, depends on the subject and aim of the regional design endeavour (De Jonge 2009). For example, for the development of a comprehensive, integrated regional plan it is essential to include representatives of future actors and users, whereas a regional design process that aims to inform and fuel the public debate on a specific issue (for instance, the transition to renewable energy sources) would best focus on engaging a broad range of professionals concerned with such a topic.

The participation of stakeholders in regional designing generally takes place through a series of half-, one- or two-day workshops and interactive events (Kempenaar and Van den Brink 2018). Participating groups can range in size from 10 to 80 people. These interactive events, although they are prepared carefully, almost never unfold as anticipated, calling for on-the-spot responses from the designer(s) who facilitate the events. In order for regional designing to be influential, it is critical to create a genuine level of participation (e.g. Arnstein 1969; Simonson and Robertson 2013), that is to give stakeholders a real say in the conversation and share power over the outcome of the process. When such a level of participation cannot be reached, it can become an act of tokenism and stakeholders are less likely to become co-owners of the regional design ideas.

The context in which the regional design process is embedded is the third critical element for its (future) use and influence, since that is where regional designing predominantly tends to have an effect. The longitudinal case study on the MHAL Region (Kempenaar et al. 2017) revealed that a regional design competition held for the region did not have any impact in the region itself because it was not well embedded in its regional planning context. The competition did influence the professional discourse on regional planning and design in the Netherlands though. This is explained by the fact that it was organised by Dutch professionals, and the majority of participants were part of professional planning and design communities in the Netherlands. However, other episodes of regional designing for the MHAL Region (see 5.3.1) were all properly embedded in the regional context and therefore did influence regional spatial planning. This example illustrates the need to embed regional designing in the appropriate context.

In addition to these critical elements, other factors in the design process also determine the effect of regional designing on spatial planning. The absence of a dominant stakeholder, sufficient time and the avoidance of strong controversies can increase the influence of regional designing (Kempenaar et al. 2017). In addition, timing is an important factor in the effect regional designing can have (Hajer et al. 2006; De Jonge 2009; Kempenaar and Van den Brink 2018). In some situations, regional designs need 'time to ripen' before they are picked up by others. They can lose momentum and become redundant, waiting for a new window of opportunity to arise. Designers and planners involved in regional designing often actively try to affect these kinds of factors in order to improve the uptake and influence of regional designs.

Notwithstanding the expertise of the designer, the participation of stakeholders in the design process, the context in which regional designing is embedded and additional enhancing factors, the actual influence depends on more than the design process alone. When regional designing is employed in situations where a design approach is not appropriate, for example when there is no need for change, or when the outcome is already defined, it can be expected to have little effect (De Jonge 2009). In addition, regional designing acts upon the interrelated and complex web of actions in spatial planning in which a regional design is just one of the perspectives and interests at work. Numerous actions, events and situations determine what actually happens and how planning processes and actual spatial developments unfold. However, if a regional design transfers to formal planning arenas and is given a formal status, or attached to funding programs, the use and influence of that design improve, enabling it to direct actions towards the uncertain future.

Spatial planning situations involve many uncertainties (Zandvoort 2017). They evolve and change due to ongoing developments, foreseen and unforeseen changes, as well as unexpected events and shifts in opinions. Regional designing is a particular method used within strategic spatial planning processes to develop long-term plans and perspectives to navigate through these uncertainties and changes. However, regional designing is more than just a plan-making method, it also alters spatial planning situations. It affects the aims of planning, influences the next steps in the planning process and changes the conditions for spatial planning. As such, regional designing can create strong contributions to governance rescaling processes, in which co-operation among plan actors changes, planning responsibilities are redistributed, and roles and capacities develop. Although guarantees cannot be given in advance, regional designing can instigate and reinforce relationships and networks, create ownership among future actors and develop mutual understanding and shared concepts. These are strong assets in spatial planning situations where roles, responsibilities and collaborations are in flux.

References

Albrechts L, Balducci A (2013) Practicing strategic planning: in search of critical features to explain the strategic character of plans. DISP 49 (3):16–27

Arnstein SR (1969) A ladder of citizen participation. J Am Inst Plann 35(4):216–224

Balz VE, Zonneveld WAM (2015) Regional design in the context of fragmented territorial governance: South Wing studio. Eur Plan Stud 23 (5):871–891

Brand N, Kersten I, Pot R, Warmerdam M (2014) Research by design on the Dutch coastline: bridging flood control and spatial quality. Built Environ 40(2):265–280

Brandt E, Binder T, Sanders EBN (2013) Tools and techniques: ways to engage telling, making and enacting. In: Simonsen J, Robertson T (eds) Routledge international handbook of participatory design. Routledge, New York, pp 145–181

Carmona M, Sieh L (2008) Performance measurement in planning—towards a holistic view. Environ Plann C: Govern Policy 26(2):428–454

Chapman D (2011) Engaging places: localizing urban design and development planning. J Urban Des 16(4):511–530

Cross N (2006) Designerly ways of knowing. Springer-Verlag, London

De Jonge J (2009) Landscape architecture between politics and science: an integrative perspective on landscape planning and design in the network society. Dissertation, Wageningen University

De Roo G, Hillier J (2016) Complexity and planning: systems, assemblages and simulations. Routledge, New York

De Roo G, Silva EA (2010) A planner's encounter with complexity, new directions in planning theory. Ashgate, Farnham

De Zeeuw F, Franzen A, Aalbers K, Van Hal A, Dulski B (2010) Designing the future. Sustainability 2(4):902–918

De Zwart B (2015) Republiek van Beelden, De Politieke Werkingen van het Ontwerp in Regionale Planvorming. Dissertation, TU Eindhoven

Dorst K, Cross N (2001) Creativity in the design process: co-evolution of problem-solution. Des Stud 22(5):425–437

EoWijers-stichting (2012) Eo wijers-prijsvraag 2011–2012 Nieuwe energie voor de Veenkoloniën, op zoek naar regionale comfortzones Juryrapport. Eo Wijers-stichting, Deventer

Forester J, Balducci A, Madanipour A, Kunzmann KR, Banerjee T, Talen E, Richardson R (2013) Design confronts politics, and both thrive!/ Creativity in the face of urban design conflict: a profile of Ric Richardson/From mediation to the creation of a "trading zone"/Conflict and creativity in Albuquerque/Reflecting on a mediation narrative from Albuquerque, New Mexico/From mediation to charrette/Physical clarity and necessary interruption/Ric Richardson responds. Plann Theor Pract 14(2):251–276

Hajer M, Sijmons D, Feddes F (2006) Een plan dat werkt: ontwerp en politiek in de regionale planvorming. NAi Uitgevers, Rotterdam

Healey P (2006) Collaborative planning: shaping places in fragmented societies, planning environment cities, 2nd edn. MacMillan, Hampshire

Innes JE, Booher DE (2010) Planning with complexity: an introduction to collaborative rationality for public policy. Routledge, London

Internationale Coordinatiecommissie (1993) MHAL Ruimtelijk Ontwikkelingsperspectief Ontwerp

Internationale Coordinatiecommissie (1996) Doorwerking Ruimtelijk Ontwikkelingsperspectief MHAL Maastricht/Heerlen-Hasselt/ Genk-Aken-Luik, stand van zaken en resultaten

Keating M (2004) Regions and regionalism in Europe. Edward Elgar

Kempenaar A (2017) Design in the planning arena. Dissertation, Wageningen University

Kempenaar A, Van den Brink A (2018) Regional designing: a strategic design approach in landscape architecture. Des Stud 54:80–95

Kempenaar A, Brinkhuijsen M, Van den Brink A (2017) The impact of regional designing: new perspectives for the Maastricht/Heerlen, Hasselt/Genk, Aachen and Liège (MHAL) Region. Environment and planning B: urban analytics and city science, online first

Kempenaar A, Van Lierop M, Westerink J, Van der Valk A, Van den Brink A (2016a) Change of thought: findings on planning for shrinkage from a regional design competition. Plann Pract Res 31(1):23–40

Kempenaar A, Westerink J, Van Lierop M, Brinkhuijsen M, Van den Brink A (2016b) "Design makes you understand"-mapping the contributions of designing to regional planning and development. Landscape Urban Plann 149:20–30

Knieling J, Othengrafen F (2009) Planning cultures in Europe: decoding cultural phenomena in urban and regional planning. Ashgate, Farnham

Kunzmann KR (2013) Strategic planning: a chance for spatial innovation and creativity. DISP 49(3):28–31

Langner S (2014) Navigating urban landscapes—adaptive and specific design approach for the 'Landschafszug' in Dessau. J Landscape Archit 9(2):16–27

Lawson B (2005) How designers think. Architectural Press, London

Lenzholzer S, Duchhart I, Van den Brink A (2017) The relationship between research and design. In: Van den Brink A, Bruns D, Tobi H, Bell S (eds) Research in landscape architecture, methods and methodology. Routledge, New York, pp 54–64

Lohrberg F, Wirth TM, Brüll A, Nielsen M, Coppens A, Godart MF, Kempenaar A, Brinkhuijsen M (2014) LP3LP Landscape Policy for the Three Countries Park, Atlas of Maps

Madanipour A (2006) Roles and challenges of urban design. J Urban Des 11(2):173–193

Meijsmans N, Beelen K (2010) Designing for a region. SUN, Amsterdam

Neuman M (1998) Does planning need the plan? J Am Plann Assoc 64(2):208–220

Neuman M (2000) Regional design: recovering a great landscape architecture and urban planning tradition. Landscape Urban Plann 47(3–4): 115–128

Neuman M (2012) The image of institution. J Am Plann Assoc 78(2):139–156

Projectgroep Drielandenpark (2003) Ontwikkelingsperspectief Drielandenpark

Limburg Provincie (2012) Ruimtelijk Structuurplan Provincie Limburg, gecoördineerde versie, kaarten. Provincie Limburg, Hasselt

Limburg Provincie (2014) Voor de kwaliteit van Limburg, POL 2014. Provincie Limburg, Maastricht

Rauws W, Van Dijk T (2013) A design approach to forge visions that amplify paths of peri-urban development. Environ Plan 40(2):254–270

Rittel HWJ, Webber MM (1973) Dilemmas in a general theory of planning. Policy Sci 4(2):155–169

Rydin Y (2007) Re-examining the role of knowledge within planning theory. Plann Theor 6(1):52–68

Salewski C, Paine S (2012) Dutch new worlds: scenarios in physical planning and design in the Netherlands 1970–2000. 010 publishers, Rotterdam

Sanyal B (2005) Comparative planning cultures. Routledge, New York

Sartorio FS (2005) Strategic spatial planning. DISP 162(3):26–40

Schatz L (2010) What helps or hinders the adoption of "good planning" principles in shrinking cities? A comparison of recent planning exercises in Sudbury, Ontario and Youngstown. Dissertation, University of Waterloo

Schön DA (1983) The reflective practitioner: how professionals think in action. Basic Books, New York

Simonson J, Robertson T (2013) Routledge international handbook of participatory design. Routledge, New York

Stein U (2005) Planning with all your senses learning to cooperate on a regional scale. DISP 162(3):62–69

Stremke S (2010) Designing sustainable energy landscapes: concepts, principles and procedures. Dissertation, Wageningen University

Stremke S, Van Kann F, Koh J (2012) Integrated visions (part I): methodological framework for long-term regional design. Eur Plan Stud 20(2):305–319

Sutton SE, Kemp SP (2006) Integrating social science and design inquiry through interdisciplinary design charrettes: an approach to participatory community problem solving. Am J Community Psychol 38(1–2):305–319

Van Assche K, Beunen R, Duineveld M, De Jong H (2013) Co-evolution of planning and design: risks and benefits of design perspectives in planning systems. Plann Theor 12(2):177–198

Van Dijk T (2011) Imagining future places: How designs co-constitute what is, and thus influence what will be. Plann Theor 10(2):124–143

Von Seggern H, Werner J, Grosse-Bächle L (2008) Creating knowledge, innovation strategies for urban landscapes. Jovis, Berlin

Waggonner D, Dolman N, Hoeferlin D, Meyer H, Schengenga P, Thomaesz S, Van Den Bout J, Van der Salm J, Van der Zwet C (2014) New Orleans after Katrina: Building America's water city. Built Environ 40(2):281–299

Zandvoort, M (2017) Planning amid uncertainty. Dissertation, Wageningen University

Constrained Governance Rescaling and the Development of a New Spatial Framework for Greater Manchester

6

Graham Haughton

Abstract

This chapter examines the evolution of city-regional planning for Greater Manchester in England. Manchester is central to the current English debates on devolution, emerging as a pioneer for new forms of city-regional governance, becoming the first city-region outside London, for instance, to be granted planning powers. The creation of a new scale of planning has not been plain sailing however, with the publication of a draft plan leading to large-scale local protests, in particular about plans for new housing. This chapter focuses on what these debates tell us about the politics involved in the rescaling of planning.

Keywords

Spatial planning · Governance rescaling · Planning system · Municipal reform · Strategic spatial selectivity

6.1 Introduction: The Remaking of City-Regional Planning

Introducing and empowering a new scale of governance are sometimes treated as a largely technical exercise, announced after little or no local public consultation, typically happening where non-elected governance mechanisms are created. Alternatively, it can be a more public-facing exercise, involving public consultation or even ballots as a precursor to the creation of new institutions. More typical, perhaps, is a range of in-between positions where new governance scales are largely imposed by elite actors and then, once up and running, these bodies find themselves having to spend time and money attempting to win over the public. As part of this process, those introducing a new scale of governance, for instance city-regional planning, will set out two sets of parallel claims, one about the failings of previous devolution settlements and one about the promise of the new settlement, and in particular the new scale of planning. In the case of creating new scales of planning, each time a new set of reforms is introduced which involve a redistribution of powers across scales, such as creating regional planning, and it tends to reflect political thinking at the time about how best to conduct relations between central and local government, and in particular about how much devolution of power central governments are willing to entertain (Allmendinger and Haughton 2013; Haughton et al. 2013).

When the rescaling of planning involves an attempt to create a new higher-tier authority, for a city-region for instance, it typically requires creating a clear message about how future-looking strategies will help to improve prospects for the whole of the new area, presenting the case in ways that capture the collective imagination. In order to convince the public of the merits of the institutional arrangements, considerable effort is put into forging new or stronger spatial imaginaries in an attempt to increase public awareness and acceptance (Haughton and Allmendinger 2015; Hincks et al. 2017). The general public are used to thinking in terms of their neighbourhood or local government area, but when a new scale of policy comes along this presents challenges, as the sense of shared identity, belonging or mutuality tend to be weaker—it is more difficult to get people involved in consultations about regional plans than local plans for instance. This can be a particular issue when the new governance space is conceived of as a soft space, that is one which creates a new geography whose boundaries do not coincide with those of an

G. Haughton (✉)
Urban and Environmental Planning, School of Environment, Education and Development, University of Manchester, Manchester, England
e-mail: graham.haughton@manchester.ac.uk

© Springer Nature Switzerland AG 2020
V. Lingua and V. Balz (eds.), *Shaping Regional Futures*,
https://doi.org/10.1007/978-3-030-23573-4_6

elected tier of sub-national government (Allmendinger and Haughton 2009; Allmendinger et al. 2015; Haughton et al. 2010). Soft spaces can have the advantage of promoting new forms of thinking without being locked into the rigidities of existing administrative arrangements, but suffer in terms of transparency, accountability and therefore public acceptance. To help overcome such obstacles, it can help if there is a strong narrative about future prospects, presented by strong leadership, alongside a powerful vision forged around a new optimistic strategy for the future, involving some kind of visual statement that helps capture the spirit of the proposals and brings people together in a sense of common endeavour, whether based on older cultural affiliations or new possibilities being opened up, for instance by new communication infrastructure.

It is in this context that this chapter examines recent attempts to create a new city-regional spatial strategy for Greater Manchester. The Greater Manchester experience with metropolitan planning is important because of the city-region's prominent role in English devolution debates since 2010, widely held up as an exemplar for what other local authority groups might aspire to (Jenkins 2015; Haughton et al. 2016). Greater Manchester's ten local authorities (see Fig. 6.1) had achieved this prominence because they were able to demonstrate many years of informal but effective city-regional working through the Association of Greater Manchester Authorities (AGMA), built around strong, united local leadership and a pragmatic approach to dealing with central government (Hincks et al. 2017). Part of the success of this work was in presenting the message of Greater Manchester, not Birmingham, being the country's second city, whilst also building internal coherence and buy-in, not least by building an expanding tram network. In 2011, the Greater Manchester Combined Authority (GMCA) became the first formally designated, statutory city-region authority since the Greater London reforms in 1998.[1] The GMCA's initial devolution deal focused on transport, economic development and local welfare reforms.

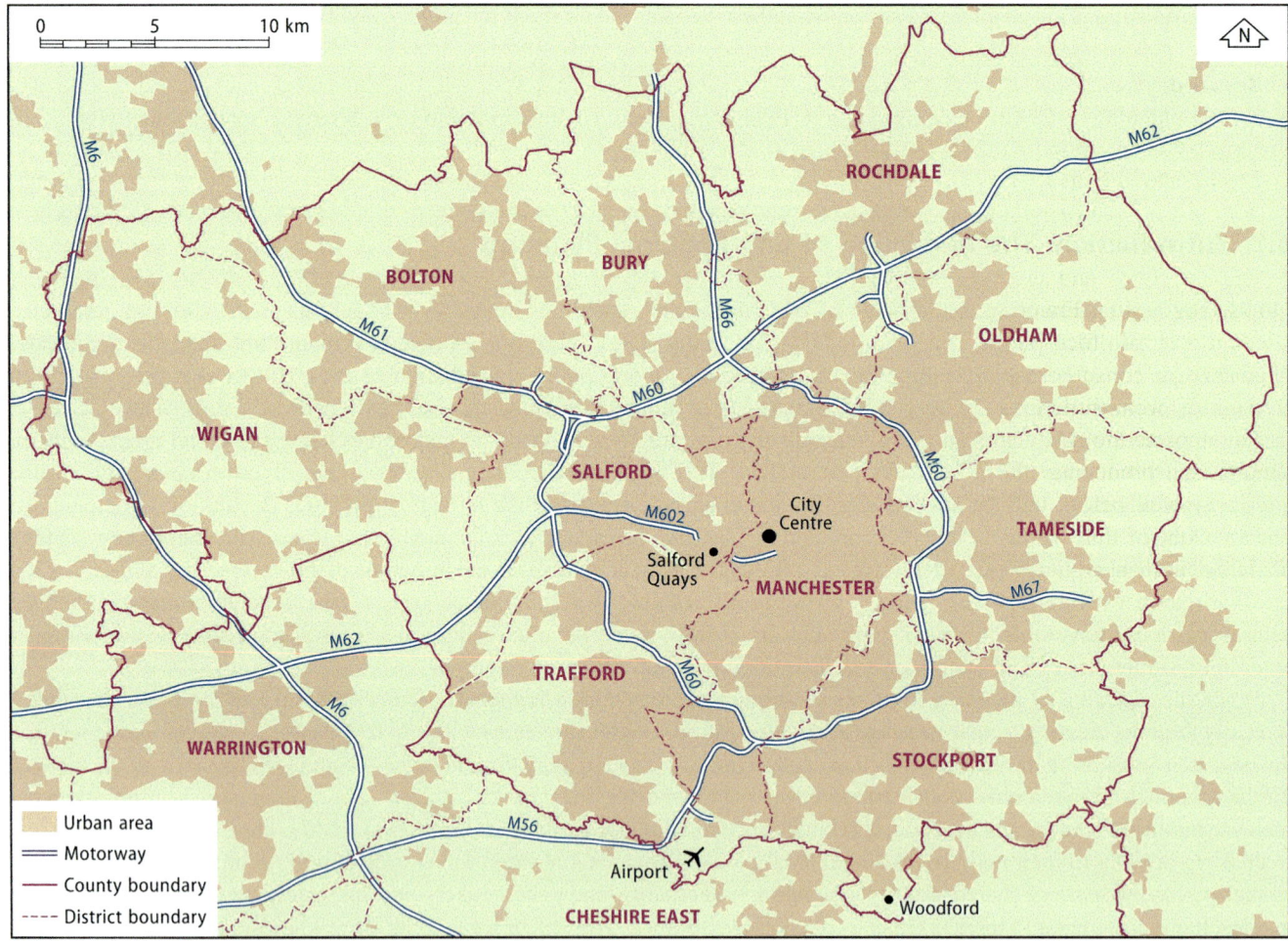

Fig. 6.1 Greater Manchester's ten metropolitan councils

---

[1]This paper deals mainly with metropolitan reforms outside Greater London in the period since 2010. A Greater London tier of government was reintroduced in 1998 with the creation of an elected mayor (with planning powers) and the Greater London Assembly (with scrutiny powers).

Subsequently, in 2014, a further deal was brokered to devolve additional areas of responsibility, including strategic planning. Crucially, as a condition for devolving planning powers to the city-region scale, central government insisted that local authority leaders agree to the principle of an elected mayor for Greater Manchester, to strengthen leadership, transparency and accountability for city-region policies. This agreement allowed the mayor to produce a statutory spatial strategy, adopt compulsory purchase powers and create mayoral development corporations to facilitate development. The spatial framework could only be adopted with the unanimous consent of the mayor and the leaders of all ten local authorities. With this pioneering agreement, Greater Manchester opened up new possibilities for metropolitan planning across England, an act carefully scrutinised by others.

This chapter argues that whilst central government has sought to portray devolution and planning reforms as returning power back to local people, the reality has proven more complex, involving constrained governance rescaling (Sects. 6.2 and 6.3) and competing models for future growth across a divided city-region (Sect. 6.4). Crucially, the devolution and planning reforms introduced by the Coalition (2010–2015) and Conservative governments (2015-present) have come in a period of politically imposed austerity measures, with reduced government funding to develop and implement plans.

The research involved interviews during 2017 with twenty key actors in debates around devolution, planning and the environment in Greater Manchester, covering a range of perspectives including protest groups, politicians, planners, developers and planning consultants. Discussions were all recorded, with informed consent given, then transcribed, coded and analysed over multiple readings, from which key themes emerged. A wide range of secondary documentation was also examined, notably the official supporting documentation for the plan as well as the position statements of the leading actors in the debate.

6.2 The Unravelling of the Initial Draft Greater Manchester Spatial Framework

The history of metropolitan-scale planning for Greater Manchester is far from a linear path towards the current model. The first stage saw the creation of the Greater Manchester Metropolitan County Council, as part of national reforms of local government (1974–1986). This produced a strategic plan in 1984, only for the county council to be abolished in 1986. For the next twenty-five years (1986–2011), the ten local authorities continued to work together voluntarily on planning related issues. The third and current stage (2011–2019) has involved the GMCA commencing work on a statutory Greater Manchester Spatial Framework (GMSF). An initial draft GMSF was released for consultation in late 2016, and it is this which is the main focus of the early sections of this chapter. Responding to the criticisms raised, a revised draft GMSF was published for consultation in January 2019: this is discussed in the final two sections. In effect then, planning in Greater Manchester went from a statutory basis to a softer more voluntaristic basis, before returning to a statutory footing in 2017–18, all the time though with the same 'hard' territorial boundaries that reflected the ten constituent local government areas.

Work on producing the initial draft GMSF combined both statutory and voluntary elements, with preparatory work underway well before the creation of the GMCA, principally in the guise of infrastructure planning. However, no plan emerged out of this work, reflecting the lack of clarity of the legal status of any joint planning work, confirmed when independent legal advice was obtained to this effect. All this changed with the announcement of the intention to put in place new legislation which included the power to develop a statutory mayor's spatial strategy. The subsequent draft GMSF was prepared as a twenty-year vision, comprising two parts. The first was the strategic section, which it was hoped would in due course evolve into the mayor's spatial strategy. The second part was, in formal terms, a separate joint plan of the ten local authorities, produced under existing legislation (Allmendinger et al. 2016). This joint plan section contained a series of detailed proposals for the specific releasing and developing of greenbelt sites.

The decision to include a joint plan section was largely driven by concerns that some of the local authorities were running late in preparing an up-to-date local plan in line with the post-2011 planning legislation, at a time when central government was making it clear that this could lead to sanctions, a subject returned to below. In this context, developing the draft GMSF was intended to address external pressures from national government and developers to plan for more housing, plus internal pressures to develop a plan that would support the city-region leaders' ambitious growth agenda, by allocating new employment and housing sites. It is important to emphasise that this work was prepared under tight financial, staffing and time constraints.

The publication of a draft GMSF in October 2016 proved immediately controversial, attracting over 27,000 public responses, with concern focusing on proposed incursions into the greenbelt for new housing and employment sites. These greenbelt proposals generated a series of demonstrations around the region. Crucially for what was to follow, a decision had been made that despite most of the new development being proposed for brownfield sites, designating these would be left to local plans. This in effect left a vacuum in the document and meant that relatively little was said about proposed development in the urban cores, where most brownfield land was located. More than this, the plan contained no clear commitments on new infrastructure investment, just generalised statements of intent. Whilst important strategic sections were contained outlining broad social and environmental conditions and strategies to address these issues, these somehow failed to capture the imagination of readers, perhaps because the wording of the proposals was suggestive of incremental change rather than radical improvements. The key diagram (Fig. 6.2) did not help in this respect as it did not provide a powerful articulation of the economic, environmental and social aspirations contained in the strategic sections. Instead, the draft GMSF became hobbled by its failure to demonstrate how it would deal with the tensions contained in its proposals, not least between concentrating growth and ensuring areas were not left behind, and between addressing the acknowledged need for more affordable housing and concerns that the greenbelt incursions would be mainly for executive-style housing developments.

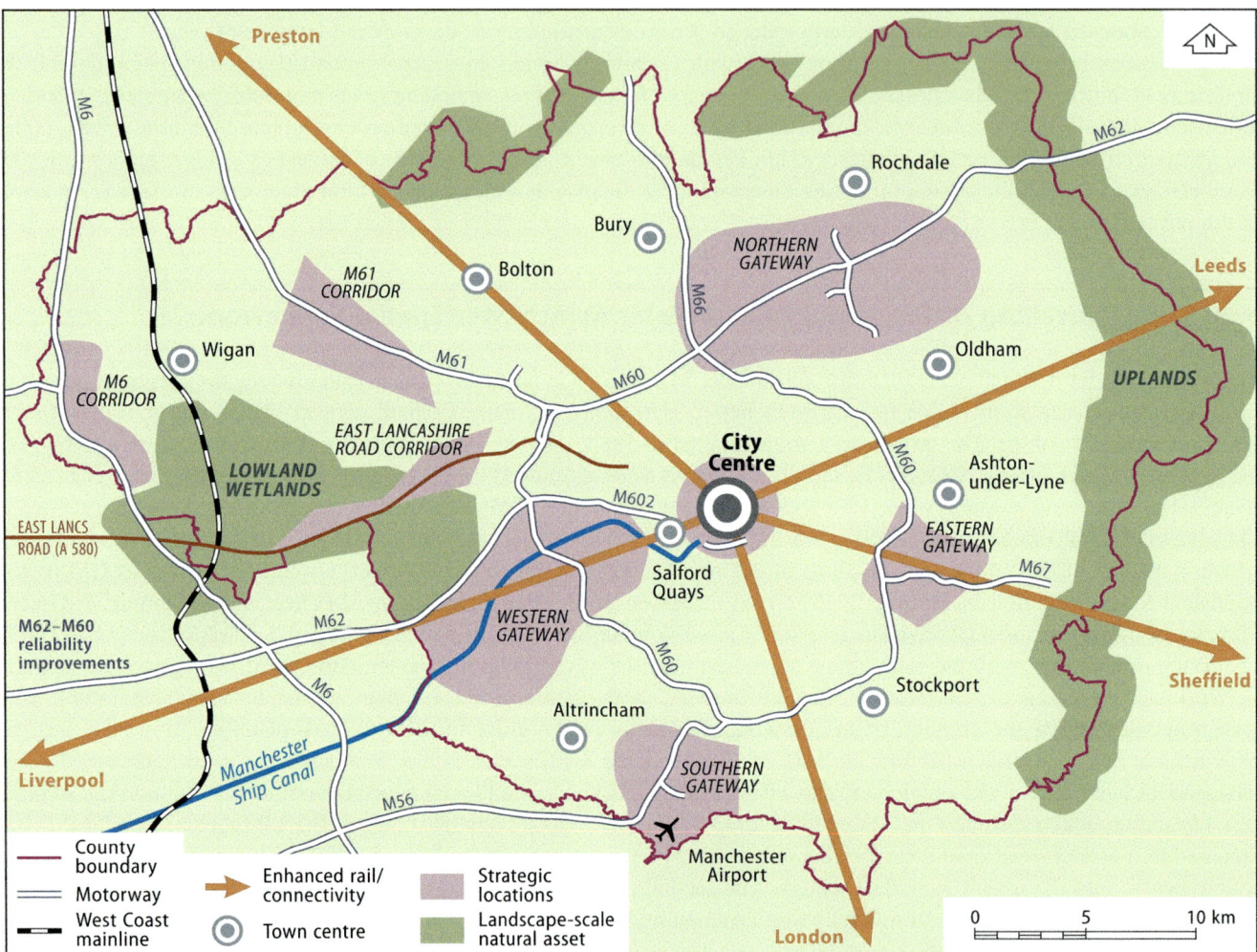

Fig. 6.2 Key diagram in the draft Greater Manchester Spatial Framework (GMSF). Adapted from GMCA (2016, p. 13)

One consequence of an unbalanced plan was an unbalanced consultation response, focused primarily on greenbelt issues. The greenbelt protestors achieved considerable media coverage, to the extent that they were prominent throughout the campaign to elect Greater Manchester's first mayor. The person eventually elected as mayor in May 2017, Labour's Andy Burnham, had been one of those calling for fundamental changes to the GMSF and immediately on taking office he made good on his promise by ordering a redrafted GMSF which would do more to protect the greenbelt, promote affordable housing and develop the potential of the outlying towns across the metropolitan region.

This signalled a potentially seismic shift in Greater Manchester politics, since the first draft GMSF in many ways reflected the ideas of the long-standing political and bureaucratic elite of Greater Manchester, which for almost a decade had been promoting policies based on a 'big is better' skewed reading of agglomeration economics (Haughton et al. 2014, 2016). This model of growth led city-region leaders to focus on policies for enhancing the economic potential of the region's core growth areas in the hope that this would in turn help Greater Manchester's poorer areas. In practice, Greater Manchester has remained a divided city, with concentrations of job growth in the city centre, Trafford, the airport and Salford Quays, whilst many outlying towns struggled, especially in north and east Manchester. Partly as a response to growing concern about the shortcomings of this narrowly constructed, elite-driven growth agenda, from 2016 a parallel discourse began to emerge around 'inclusive growth', drawing on the work of the newly created Inclusive Growth Analysis Unit at the University of Manchester (Lupton and Hughes 2016; Lupton 2017). The 'inclusive growth' agenda involved identifying new models for addressing the needs of the poorest in the region and was quickly embraced by leading members of the political and bureaucratic elite of the city-region, albeit without publicly acknowledging the contradictions involved in remaining committed to an agglomerationist model.

The draft GMSF tried but failed to negotiate a coherent intellectual position around these contrasting visions for the future of Greater Manchester, whilst also addressing aspirations to be seen as a leader in promoting environmental policies such as green infrastructure. Planning has always struggled with balancing economic, social and environmental aspirations, but in Greater Manchester there was no coherent intellectual thinking that brought these together, an issue elaborated on below (Sect. 6.4). The 2016 draft GMSF did not articulate clearly enough how it would deliver on its own agenda to promote areas with growth potential, with even less to offer on aspirations to deliver social justice, climate change and environmental improvements. The proposals failed to win over much of the public because they appeared to promise pain (loss of greenbelt) with little gain, except for developers. This is not what the planners and politicians thought they were offering, but it was what many came to perceive. Support for the draft GMSF quickly unravelled both during the consultation period and afterwards, during the mayoral elections. The problems exposed by the draft GMSF then were partly related to delusional national thinking about letting go of planning powers (Sect. 6.3) plus delusional local thinking about an agglomerationist economic model that was inherently divisive (Sect. 6.4).

6.3 Constrained Governance Rescaling: Planning, Devolution and the Limits of Central Government 'Letting Go'

This section uses the creation of a city-region spatial strategy for Greater Manchester to expose the tensions involved when central government claims to be letting go of some of its powers in order to empower local leaders, whilst still imposing its will on them. Indeed, the process of creating a new metropolitan plan for Greater Manchester tells us much about the unravelling of central government's localism agenda, aiming to move the planning system from being a top-down, hierarchical system with limited flexibility, towards a more bottom-up and flexible approach, led by local actors.

In the past, planning reforms in England tended to be rolled out nationally to a model that would be applied more or less uniformly, for instance metropolitan county council planning in the 1970s and regional planning between 1998 and 2010. However, the coalition government elected in 2010 rejected such strong central prescription, preferring instead to set up arrangements that allowed local actors to come together to decide how they wanted to respond to the general direction of government reforms, a vision first set out in a Conservative Party's Green Paper, Open Source Planning, and subsequently in the 2011 Localism Act (Allmendinger and Haughton 2013; Haughton et al. 2013). It was in this spirit that central government adopted the principle of leaving it to those local authorities who wanted to work jointly towards a devolution deal to come together voluntarily and agree their own boundaries for a new combined authority. Decisions over what powers would then be devolved would be hammered out through bespoke deals, which might or might not involve planning.

The post-2011 reforms were intended to 'free up' and speed up planning processes in various ways: scaling back national planning guidance, most notably by reducing previous detailed, voluminous guidance for local authorities to the 64-page National Planning Policy Framework (NPPF) in 2012; abolishing the regional tier of government in 2010–11, including Regional Spatial Strategies (RSSs); consolidating the role of the local plan as the bedrock of the sub-national planning system; and giving new powers for local people to develop neighbourhood plans. Taken together, these were intended to shift the balance of power away from central government towards elected local councils. In practice, these good intentions soon faltered as central government felt the need to strengthen its hand to ensure local government acted in ways that supported rather than contradicted national government policy.

The issue here was that, beguiled by the exhortations of right-wing think tanks and others to make planning more development-friendly (Haughton and Allmendinger 2016), the government had allowed itself to believe that a combination of reducing the regulatory burden of planning and financially incentivising local authorities and local communities to allow development would produce the much-desired boost to house-building rates. What the ideologically driven reformers failed to take into account was the combination of local democratic pressures and the fact that some local communities would not easily be 'bribed' into accepting more new housing in their area through schemes such as the New Homes Bonus. Local councillors are elected to represent their constituents' views, and if most constituents opposed new development, then quite often so would their elected councillors. The government quickly discovered that it would need to become more directive than it had originally anticipated and instituted new reforms and introduced stringent penalties to put pressure on local authorities to support more housing.

The political justification for reducing the amount of detailed national planning guidance had been that it would make planning less complex and much clearer to the public. Ultimately, however, in order to ensure local authorities moved in the direction they wanted, the government ended up replacing existing technical planning requirements with new ones that would also prove to be unclear and lead to delays, whilst adding in a layer of punitive sanctions for local authorities not doing as they were told. Central direction remained a defining characteristic of government planning policy.

To help situate the emergence of the GMSF as part of the broader rescaling of planning powers, Fig. 6.3 provides a schematic overview of the evolution of the statutory scales of planning and whether they were rolled out nationally or unevenly. Summarising the rescaling aspects of planning since 2010, national planning was to become less prescriptive; regional planning was abolished, and up-to-date local plans were required in all areas; loose-fit, joint working arrangements allowed local authorities to collaborate on issues such as evidence collection; finally, neighbourhood plans could be proposed and developed by local communities themselves if they wanted to (Allmendinger et al. 2016). The upside of this approach was the aspiration of supporting bespoke local solutions to planning issues. The downside was that a complex tier of national regulations was being replaced by an even more difficult-to-navigate set of variegated, sub-national approaches to planning regulation, further confusing and alienating the public.

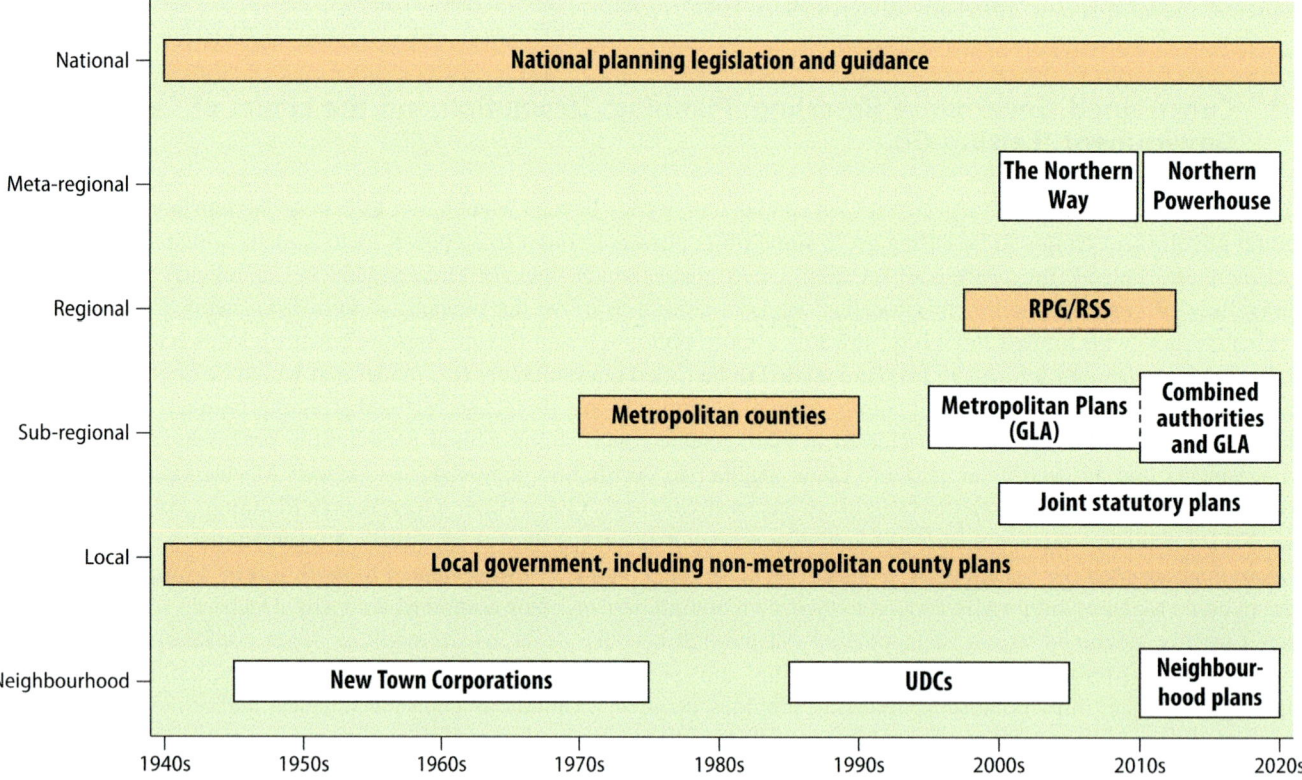

Fig. 6.3 Main statutory tiers of planning in England

Shaded boxes indicate where a standard model provided national geographical coverage, or in one case coverage of all metropolitan county councils. Unshaded boxes are where national geographical coverage is partial or different planning models allowed.

At first glance, this process was entirely in line with a government committed philosophically to allowing local actors to become more engaged in shaping their own planning system, without conforming to a centrally imposed blueprint. Interviews with key actors in Greater Manchester, however, quickly revealed the limits that were imposed on local discretion. In particular, the much vaunted reduction of central planning guidance for local authorities and abolition of the regional tier of planning, because it was supposedly Stalinistic and top-down, was said to have resulted in the paradoxical situation in which central direction had become:

> far more Stalinistic and top down… the paradox being that the government has now more control to intervene over local plans. (Developer 1)

Another interviewee came to a not dissimilar conclusion that the new slimline national planning guidance required planning authorities to demonstrate a five-year housing land supply pipeline:

> NPPF is the work of an evil genius… it is clever because at first you think, well, that's fair enough, you need to plan for five years, I absolutely agree with all of this. But, then in practice a five-year supply is too easily undermined, and the penalties for not having one so severe that then you realise the NPPF is not at all fair. (National campaign group 1)

The draft GMSF provides a good illustration of some of the ways in which central government sought to exert control over local planning policy, notably by altering the balance of power in favour of developers looking to develop on greenfield sites and away from local authorities and communities seeking to resist such pressures. Interviewees pointed to several connected reforms which had encouraged developers and local planners to focus more on whether to allow new housing on greenbelt land, including the abolition of targets for developing new housing on brownfield sites. Most important was the terminology adopted in the NPPF, which allowed the government to claim it was maintaining its support for greenbelts, but then adding that greenbelt protection could be reviewed in exceptional circumstances. For local planners and politicians, the effect of this wording was simple, passing the buck for an unpopular policy from central to local government:

> One exceptional circumstance is if you don't have any other land. And this is quite relevant to GMSF… government can then say, "Well we're not making that decision. We didn't pass that planning application. We didn't allocate that site in the greenbelt. It's that local council." But they're doing it because that's what government requires. (Politician 2)

The new planning rules also required that all local authorities produce an up-to-date local plan, with those failing to do so facing the prospect of local planning decisions being made by national planning inspectors, solely against NPPF with its often vague or permissive phrasing, and not against the local plan. Equally worrying for local authorities was the prospect of losing their New Homes Bonus entitlement if plans were not up to date. Putting this in context, one local planner in interview said their authority would lose an estimated £2 m a year if the sanction was applied. Paragraph 49 of NPPF was important here as it said that for a local plan to be considered as up to date, local authorities must be able to demonstrate that they had in place a five-year supply line for new development sites, based on a calculation known as Objectively Assessed Numbers (OANs). Crucially, national government at this stage refused to provide guidance on how OANs could be calculated. This decision proved disastrous, as it encouraged developers to commission their own experts to develop alternative OAN methodologies which could be used to challenge the figures used by local planners. The winners were the planning consultants and the planning lawyers, as planning decisions continued to be bogged down in technocratic debates around methodologies for OANs.[2]

Almost all interviewees noted the pressure these reforms placed on local planners to bring forward the draft GMSF quickly, in particular the housing allocations, in the hope of avoiding moving into a process known widely as 'planning by appeal', a costly and slow process which meant sites were no longer being judged against an agreed local plan. As a consequence, whilst most interviewees found the draft GMSF problematic for one reason or another, nonetheless all wanted to see a Greater Manchester plan adopted:

> We want a spatial framework, we want development to be guided because we think it's the best way for development to come forward. You're going to get your least harmful sites getting developed in terms of biodiversity… So we want a plan… because we have seen when plans don't exist developers get to build wherever they like. (National campaign group 1)

With some Greater Manchester local authorities still struggling to produce an up-to-date local plan, local politicians recognised that the act of coming together on the draft GMSF sent out important signals that they were addressing the issue:

---

[2]By 2017, the government had realised the scale of the problem and proposed a new standardised methodology for OANs in the hope it would put an end to the planning conflicts and delays created by the previous system.

> Because we're in the GMSF process, I believe we have that protection to say to government, "We're taking this seriously, we're sorting this out." So if we pull out of this strategy, what I'm trying to say to people who want to protect the greenbelt is – and I've used this phrase publicly – that developers will circle us immediately, like vultures, so how do you withstand their deep pockets? We can't outspend them. We don't have deep pockets. (Politician 2)

In the face of national government directives and sanctions, working jointly together was perceived as an effective strategy for local authorities across the city-region.

The rescaling of planning also brought about tensions at the neighbourhood level. Woodford is a prosperous village close to the border with Cheshire East, which has experienced development pressures over a long period, mostly related to a former aerodrome and industrial site. Whilst not resistant to all development, the local community did not want to see large-scale developments dominated by housing that would be unaffordable to the children of local people. A visiting government minister advised locals that they should set up a neighbourhood plan process, which they proceeded to do in 2013. Neighbourhood plans had been launched with great political fanfare as a way in which local communities could take control over the types of development in their area. For the residents of Woodford, such lofty aspirations were soon quashed when the local authority, which had to approve the plan's geographical extent, excluded the main development site, presumably fearing a neighbourhood plan covering the larger area could be used to thwart its future housing ambitions. In this instance at least, neighbourhood planning, far from liberating local communities to help shape local planning, was constrained to the role of supporting the authority's ambitions rather than challenging them:

> Haughton: "So what's your opinion of the Localism Act and the neighbourhood plans, having been at the sharp end?"
>   Protest group 1: "It's, I'm afraid it seems to be a bit of a damp squib…. It's almost as if you can't win. It's a case of someone there has decided this is the way they want to go and then manipulating it to make it happen."

A similar view of planning reforms was held by two of the national campaign groups working in the region, namely that as soon as a community found a way of protesting effectively against development, national government would change the rules:

> It's almost like you every time you win a particular battle, this particular government goes, "Well let's shut that away." (National campaign group 2)

This ran parallel to a more general grievance that removing aspects of the previous system of detailed guidance was leading to reliance on vaguely worded guidance which could be manipulated to favour developer interests over others.

The vision of a rescaling of planning to allow a cascading downwards of power proved to be an illusion, conjured up at the stage of proposing major legislative reforms but subsequently replaced by a vision in which local people were free to do what they were told by the tier of government above them. In practice, planning power was redistributed not so much downwards as in favour of developers and landowners.

6.4   Trying to Reconcile Environmental, Social and Economic Goals

The dominant intellectual framing for the Greater Manchester devolution project has been carefully curated by a narrow technocratic cadre of officers and politicians who have bought into a particular version of agglomeration economics (Haughton et al. 2014, 2016). In this vision, the traditional argument for redistributing growth or tax income from more prosperous parts of the country to the less prosperous is framed as outmoded, unrealistic and unsuccessful. Instead, it is argued, the strategy of Greater Manchester should be to move away from such inter- and intra-regional, cross-subsidy arrangements and focus on improving local productivity, with supportive government investment targeted to areas of proven potential. Policymakers are warned of the dangers of 'spreading the jam too thinly' for fear of generating lower economic returns on public investment (Overman 2013). Agglomeration economics points to the benefits that size can bring to larger cities, for instance larger labour markets and stronger cultural institutions, but that these need to be balanced against 'negative externalities', such as congestion and air pollution. The Manchester model has much to say about the positive aspects of agglomeration but very little to say about any negative environmental and social effects.

The team preparing the draft GMSF was located in the epicentre of such agglomerationist thinking, first AMGA and then the GMCA, supported by the self-styled think tank for Manchester, New Economy, with its much-lauded (or in some quarters much derided; Haughton et al. 2016) Manchester Independent Economic Review (MIER), produced in 2009. Translated into planning thinking, this approach suggested the planners should do everything possible to support growth in the existing economic hotspots of the region, mainly Manchester city centre, the airport, Salford Quays and parts of Trafford, resisting any temptation to use planning powers to redirect growth to other, more 'needy' areas:

> You'd never, I don't think, see it as Manchester or Trafford losing some growth, to be able to spread it, because I don't think that's the prevailing view of how economics works in Greater Manchester. It's not a case of trying to spread the jam more evenly, it's a case of looking at what the assets and opportunities are in the right areas, and being brave enough to say we will try and make the most of that then. (Planner 1)

The 'bootstraps' solution offered to other areas was largely that they should be looking to build on their existing strengths. This said, there was some political pressure to think about growth potential in other areas, leading to the designation of a new economic growth 'gateway' in the north-east of the city-region along the M60/M62, an area which would suit logistics industries in particular. This generated some interesting responses from some of the environmental and greenbelt groups, which saw the proposed growth area as problematic on various counts, not least that it would see a lot of land released but lead to relatively few job opportunities and an increase in road traffic. This was seen to be symptomatic of a wider failing in the draft GMCF, which it was claimed relied on:

> Very outdated thinking in terms of where you're going to put your jobs and your warehouses, your big sheds, and where you are going to build your housing. The spatial framework had next to nothing to say about low-carbon or zero-carbon housing standards, it failed on air quality almost completely… And we have a spatial framework that basically seems to be making it worse. Locating housing and sheds where there's no public transport, next to the major road network, people are going to drive. (National campaign group 2)

Most interviewees also highlighted the limited solutions offered in the draft GMSF for some of the social issues around Greater Manchester. For those preparing the plan, these concerns had coalesced around a concern to promote an inclusive growth agenda, in particular the search for a model which would see the benefits of growth felt more widely across the city-region:

> One of the big phrases we use in GMSF is 'inclusive growth.' And clearly we've got a Greater Manchester economy which is not at all balanced really. There's been a big, big success story around the city centre, and the whole area around the city centre, around the airport… But, if you look at the northeastern side of Greater Manchester, we've got a real issue, we've got a massive concentration of deprived wards. (Planner 2)

Concerns about the geographical imbalances in well-being across Greater Manchester were said to have been prominent in discussions among the politicians responsible for overseeing the production of the draft GMSF. Given the anticipated public reaction against greenbelt release, a particular concern was in justifying the selected areas for releasing greenbelt to support housing or employment sites as representing the fairest outcome overall, protecting greenbelt in areas where there was least open space. Despite such concerns, for reasons outlined earlier, it was the proposed releases of greenbelt land for new housing which most animated debate around the draft GMSF.

An interesting aspect of how events unfolded was the rescaling of institutional capacity in order to respond to the new metropolitan scale of planning. As part of the 'joint plan' section of the GMSF, as is usual in local plans, a call was put out for site allocations. This exercise largely passed the public by, but for landowners and the development industry it was seen as an important opportunity to propose sites which they hoped would be allocated for new housing. It was at this early stage that a group of housing developers came together with the Home Builders Federation (HBF) to create a lobbying body, Housing the Powerhouse. This forum was intended to present a strong and coherent pro-development voice to those responsible for writing the GMSF. The use of the word 'powerhouse' reflected the influence of the Northern Powerhouse agenda, which had been set initially by the Treasury and the then Chancellor of the Exchequer, George Osborne. The Northern Powerhouse is strongly supported by Greater Manchester's political leaders, who helped ensure a strong congruence with their own model of agglomeration economics, aspiring to help the north of England close its productivity gap in ways that did not threaten London's primacy (Haughton et al. 2016).

The aspirational high targets for job growth developed by Greater Manchester leaders were used by Housing the Powerhouse to argue that planners should be equally ambitious in their targets for new housing. Whilst happy to see continuing development of high-density apartments on brownfield sites around the conurbation, and in particular around the centre of Manchester, this was felt to be insufficient of itself. As an aspiring economic powerhouse, more 'aspirational housing' was said to be needed, a shorthand for large detached houses, requiring a relaxation of the greenbelt. The resulting construction boom would add to the powerhouse effect, it was claimed, creating new jobs.

The draft GMCA published in October 2016 went some way towards such ambitions, calling for 227,000 new houses to be built over 20 years, 28% of them on greenbelt land, requiring the release of 8% of Greater Manchester's greenbelt. In response, whilst generally welcoming the proposals, Housing the Powerhouse called for a more aspirational target of 332,860 new homes and more greenbelt release. The problem such ambitious targets posed was twofold. Firstly, it treated the city-region's aspirational job targets as if they were fact, rather than heavily reliant on as yet unknown government spending decisions and potential external factors such as Brexit. Secondly, the proposed level of house building was, to some in the industry, simply unachievable:

I think one of the problems GMSF threw up, was that there was a tension between the economic aspirations of the GM area, and the housing numbers... I think to offer a growth plus agenda, which is more the HBF and Housing the Powerhouse agenda...I think you've got to say, well hold on, prove it can be delivered. ... prove that number can get delivered, otherwise why would you say it? Why has it got credence? Now, never in the past however many years, no one's even got near to the number that GMSF are proposing. ...So, there's a credibility gap. (Planning consultant 2)

The rescaling of institutional capacity was mirrored in other quarters too following the publication of draft GMSF in 2016. This saw an incredibly quick building of community group capability at the local level, with a coordinating group, Save Greater Manchester's Greenbelt, set up to help the groups learn from each other and to develop stronger capacity for responding to the proposals. These groups were conscious of the negative connotations of being labelled 'NIMBYs' and so consciously set out to move beyond stereotypical self-interested protectionist protests, arguing for more affordable homes for instance or for developing more smaller sites. The result was a more powerful discourse mobilised around both environmental and social issues, whilst also challenging some of the practical issues of a plan which proposed releasing large sites requiring new infrastructure, rather than smaller infill sites, whether on brownfield or greenfield sites. Upset by the potential loss of a large green site in the heart of Flixton, one group raised sufficient funds to hire a planning consultant to identify smaller sites in the area, which, they hoped, would collectively support as many houses as the proposed large site.

The Campaign to Protect Rural England (CPRE) also became heavily involved in contesting the draft spatial framework. It commissioned a demographer to challenge some of the population growth projections in the consultation document, using this work to argue that release of the greenbelt land was unnecessary for various reasons, including the availability of brownfield land within the region, and over-predictions of future housing demand. According to CPRE, only 199,885 new homes needed to be built over the twenty-year period, 29,315 less than the target set in draft GMSF.

This has left GMCA planners trying to reconcile strongly divergent views about how many new homes would be needed in future. It may have been some consolation to find that whilst Housing the Powerhouse was writing to leaders criticising them for not being ambitious enough, CPRE was criticising them for being overambitious:

Sometimes it is helpful to have those alternative world views... If we're annoying those two extremes, we must be doing it right. (Planner 1)

Nonetheless, the planners and politicians interviewed acknowledged that the consultation and debates around the draft GMSF had been helpful in many respects, not least of which was the need to look again at the greenbelt proposals and to think again about the reliance on large sites and the potential for smaller sites, the need for more information about infrastructure plans, and more detailed discussion of brownfield site development and how this would be supported. There was a sense, too, that the plan needed a more coherent intellectual argument to justify the proposals and that a stronger visual message would help in getting across the main aspirations contained in the plan.

Responding to the various critiques of the initial draft GMSF and the political promise of a radical rewrite, in January 2019 a revised draft spatial framework was published for public consultation (GMCA 2019), which was considerably more detailed and better illustrated, with more maps, including a conceptual framework (Fig. 6.4) and a new key diagram (Fig. 6.5). Crucially, by this time the elected mayor for Greater Manchester had been in office for some time and became the figurehead for promoting the revised strategy, and also provided the clear democratic link which was previously missing. Interestingly, however, in his speech launching the revised draft GMSF[3] the mayor combined claims about how the devolution settlement had provided the basis for bolder actions in the new strategy with comments about how central government rules had excluded some of the policies they had wanted to pursue. Constrained governance rescaling remained an issue then.

Several other important changes stand out. First, the foregrounding of concerns about achieving inclusive growth, with a clear statement that without intervention the imbalance of growth between the north and the south could be expected to continue, justifying a much stronger emphasis on achieving balanced growth across the whole city-region, which represents a move away from the former core-first arguments. Second, the proposed incursions onto greenbelt land are dramatically cut back and new greenbelt additions proposed. As part of this, stronger commitments are made to build more housing on previously developed land along with clearer commitments to provide the necessary supportive infrastructure to deliver this. Third, and related to the first two issues, proposals are put forward to use the spatial framework to begin to rethink the role of the many other struggling town centres around the city-region, such as Rochdale, Oldham and Hyde, which have been experiencing job losses and a hollowing out of their retail offer, proposing they be reimagined as offering opportunities for residential and associated lifestyle developments. This would be supported by better communication infrastructure, particularly public transport, and walking and cycling networks.

---

[3]https://www.greatermanchester-ca.gov.uk/news/the-future-of-greater-manchester-speech-text/ accessed 22.1.2019.

The new conceptual and key diagrams attempt to capture these changes, reflecting criticisms in some quarters that the illustrative parts of the previous draft GMSF had been underwhelming. Taken together, they represent a serious attempt to create a new spatial imaginary for Greater Manchester, one which respected the hard territorial boundaries of the city-region but created new soft space imaginaries within it. What the new diagrams provide is a visualisation of the commitment to actively promote a more balanced city-regional strategy, one that acknowledged the different pressures and possibilities faced in the northern towns as opposed to Manchester city centre and the more buoyant areas in the south of the conurbation.

SPATIAL STRATEGY

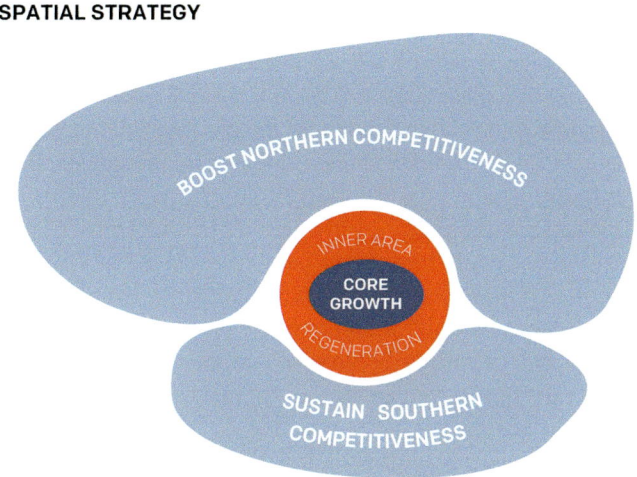

Fig. 6.4 Conceptual diagram in the revised draft GMSF 2019, from GMCA (2019)

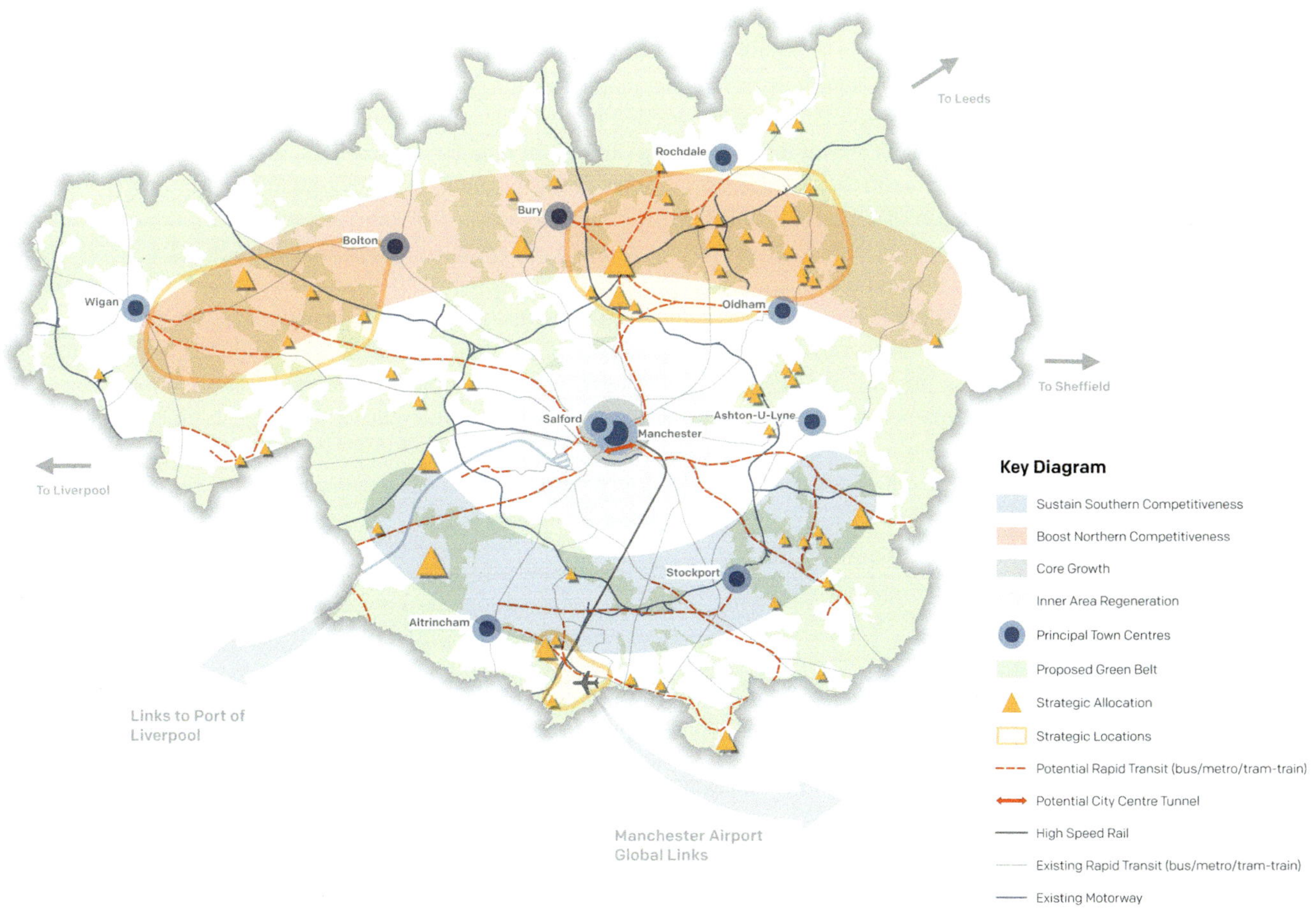

Fig. 6.5 Key diagram in the revised draft GMSF 2019, from GMCA (2019)

6.5 Conclusion

Greater Manchester has occupied a prominent role in recent English debates for devolving powers outside Westminster, including new metropolitan planning powers. The supporters of the devolution project in Greater Manchester argue that it has been an inspirational tale of local leadership working well together and able to work well with central government, resulting in a pioneering devolution package, including England's first statutory city-region authority outside London (Haughton et al. 2016). However, this chapter reveals that the reality is more complex, involving constrained governance rescaling and competing models for future growth across a divided city-region.

The reforms ushered in since the Localism Act were promoted as an invitation to local planning authorities to be bolder in imagining what it was they could do—what scale of plan, what subjects to cover, what stories to tell about how planning might be used to improve the well-being of a place. But at least in Greater Manchester, this liberating potential proved to be notional, with planners instead struggling to ensure the plan met the requirements of national government, working to tight deadlines, and with little public money to help implement any more imaginative ideas. But more than this, perhaps, the first attempts at drafting a Greater Manchester Spatial Framework (GMSF) during 2016–2017 were hampered by an inability to create a coherent and convincing vision for the future of the area that would provide a narrative not just for why it was necessary and desirable, but also for how it could be seen as fair and balanced in weighing up how any costs and benefits would be shared across the city-region. Tellingly perhaps, this was against the backdrop of considerable work being done to develop and promote a Greater Manchester economic vision over the previous decade, a vision that though well received in many quarters was in fact increasingly under question because of its failure to demonstrate whether and how the success of the city centre in particular had helped other areas or address the acknowledged need for more affordable housing. In February 2018, an article in the Manchester Evening News revealed that the major boom in high-rise apartment building in Manchester city centre over recent years had not created a single new affordable home in the area, despite the official commitment to securing 20% affordable housing in all new developments in Manchester (Williams 2018). This gave fuel to those who had become increasingly vocal in the very basis of Manchester's claims to be both economically successful and socially progressive. The so-called Manchester model was simultaneously a success and a failure in creating a new city-regional imaginary, leaving the GMSF drafters stranded between the two.

The Greater Manchester experience also presents important challenges for theory, revealing the need to give greater acknowledgement to the agency of local actors in producing major planning and devolution reforms. Whilst the research revealed the constraints involved, it is important to acknowledge that the rescaling of planning powers was not simply the imposition of a top-down model. But nor was it the idealised planning nirvana envisaged by some conservative thinkers, in which local actors would come together to create their own market-friendly solutions to long-standing, seemingly intractable problems. With the 2019 publication of a revised draft GMSF under the auspices of an elected mayor, a much bolder and clearer spatial vision for the city-region emerged, proposing a new conceptual diagram that introduced new soft spatial imaginaries to the local debate in an attempt to acknowledge and address some of the social and geographical inequalities within Greater Manchester. What is particularly interesting here is that whilst the early soft spaces literature drew attention to claims that they could help release innovative thinking by virtue of not being locked into democratic structures (Allmendinger and Haughton 2009), in the case of Greater Manchester by contrast it appears that the creation of more formalised accountability and democratic structures helped to create the conditions for more creative thinking to emerge.

Acknowledgements Many thanks to Caglar Koksal and the book editors for helpful comments on an earlier draft of this chapter. Thanks to Nick Scarle for drawing the maps and figures.

References

Allmendinger P, Haughton G (2009) Soft spaces, fuzzy boundaries and metagovernance: the new spatial planning in the Thames Gateway. Environ Plann A 41:617–633

Allmendinger P, Haughton G (2013) The evolution and trajectories of English Neoliberal spatial governance: 'neoliberal' episodes in planning. Plann Pract Res 28(1):6–26

Allmendinger P, Haughton G, Knieling J, Othengrafen F (eds) (2015) Soft Spaces in Europe: re-negotiating governance, boundaries and borders. Routledge, London

Allmendinger P, Haughton G, Sheppard E (2016) Where is planning to be found? Material practices and the multiple spaces of planning. Environ Plann C 34:38–51

GMCA (2016) Draft Greater Manchester Spatial Framework, October 2016. GMCA, Manchester

GMCA (2019) GMCA (greater manchester combined authority) greater manchester's plan for homes, jobs and the environment Greater Manchester Spatial Framework—revised draft—January 2019. GMCA, Manchester

Haughton G, Allmendinger P (2015) Fluid Spatial Imaginaries: evolving estuarial city-region spaces. Int J Urban Reg Res 39(5):857–873

Haughton G, Allmendinger P (2016) Think tanks and the pressures for planning reform in England. Environ Plann C 34(8):1676–1692

Haughton G, Allmendinger P, Counsell D, Vigar G (2010) The new spatial planning: soft spaces, fuzzy boundaries and territorial management. Routledge, London

Haughton G, Allmendinger P, Oosterlynck S (2013) Spaces of neoliberal experimentation: soft spaces, postpolitics and neoliberal governmentality. Environ Plann A 45(1):217–234

Haughton G, Deas I, Hincks S (2014) Making an impact: when agglomeration boosterism meets antiplanning rhetoric. Environ Plann A 46 (2):265–270

Haughton G, Deas I, Hincks S, Ward K (2016) Mythic Manchester: Devo Manc, the Northern powerhouse and rebalancing the English economy. Cambridge Journal of Regions, Economy and Society 9(2):355–370

Hincks S, Deas I, Haughton G (2017) Real geographies, real economies and soft spatial imaginaries: creating a 'more than Manchester' region. Int J Urban Reg Res 41(4):642–657

Jenkins S (2015) The secret negotiations to restore Manchester to greatness. The Guardian, 12.2.2015. http://www.theguardian.com/uk-news/2015/feb/12/secretnegotiations-restore-manchester-greatness?CMP=share_btn_tw. Accessed 12 Feb 2015

Lupton R, Hughes C (2016) Inclusive growth: a collective endeavour, 13 Oct. http://blog.policy.manchester.ac.uk/posts/2016/10/inclusive-growth-a-collective-endeavour/

Lupton R (2017) Inclusive Growth: what should be on the new greater Manchester's mayor's agenda? 29 Mar. http://blog.policy.manchester.ac.uk/posts/2017/03/inclusive-growth-what-should-be-on-the-new-greater-manchester-mayors-agenda/

Overman H (2013) The economic future of cities. CentrePiece. Available online at http://cep.lse.ac.uk/pubs/download/cp389.pdf. Accessed 22 Dec 2017

Williams J (2018) No affordable housing is being built in Manchester city centre… so what's going on? Manchester Evening News, 26 Feb. https://www.manchestereveningnews.co.uk/news/greater-manchester-news/no-affordable-housing-being-built-14332101

Administrative Organisation and Spatial Planning in Portugal: A Push Towards Soft Planning Spaces in Europe?

7

Cristina Cavaco and João Pedro Costa

Abstract

In the last decade, soft spaces and soft planning have emerged as new spatial planning and governance concepts, calling for a fresh approach to planning. The European Union has been partly responsible, not only by acting as a driver of soft planning, but also by encouraging the convergence and harmonisation of planning styles into a common European planning culture. However, soft planning does not replace statutory frameworks. Planning deals with both hard (mandatory and regulatory) and soft (non-statutory and non-binding) spaces, although this coexistence is not free of contention. Deviances and mismatches give rise to a number of ambiguities, inconsistencies and contradictions. This chapter examines the meeting ground between hard and soft planning, i.e. how EU-led, soft planning policy initiatives are accommodated and managed within statutory national planning systems, using the Portuguese system as a reference. The Portuguese administrative organisation and spatial planning system provide the background for the analysis, while the study focuses on soft planning initiatives endorsed by EU Cohesion Policy, namely in the last EU programming cycle of 2014–2020. The conclusions point to the tensions and detachments that emerge from the coexistence of EU-led soft planning and statutory spatial planning tools, despite the increasing convergence of the Portuguese system with European spatial planning rationale.

Keywords

Soft planning • Spatial planning • Portugal • European cohesion policy • European structural funds

7.1 Introduction

In the last decade, soft spaces and soft planning have emerged as new spatial planning and governance concepts calling for a fresh approach to planning (Allmendinger and Haughton 2009; Haughton et al. 2010; Faludi 2013; Stead 2014; Allmendinger et al. 2015). Compared with mainstream planning, soft planning challenges the use of hard statutory spaces and binding planning tools. It acts in complex, non-statutory institutional settings, breaking with established government structures, fixed administrative boundaries and rigid organisational frameworks. Unlike traditional statutory planning, soft planning acts in an informal non-binding environment, with an emphasis on:

(i) The coordination and integration of scales, policy sectors and territorial actors around a shared place-based vision, calling for integrated strategies rather than physical regulatory planning approaches (CEC 1997; Albrechts 2004; Nadin 2007; Galland 2012);

C. Cavaco (✉) · J. P. Costa
Universidade de Lisboa, Lisbon School of Architecture, CIAUD, Lisbon, Portugal
e-mail: ccavaco@fa.ulisboa.pt

J. P. Costa
e-mail: jpc@fa.ulisboa.pt

© Springer Nature Switzerland AG 2020
V. Lingua and V. Balz (eds.), *Shaping Regional Futures*,
https://doi.org/10.1007/978-3-030-23573-4_7

(ii) The spatial rescaling of powers, tasks and responsibilities between the different tiers of government, including the development of new planning scales (at a supra- or sub-national level) and the devolution of powers in a multidirectional movement upwards, downwards, sideways or outwards, thereby making room for alternative, non-traditional regional and local planning spaces (Macleod and Goodwin 1999; Swygedoun 2000; Haughton and Counsell 2004; Keating 2008; Roodbol-Mekkes and Brink 2015; Galland and Elinbaum 2015).

(iii) Multi-level and multi-scalar governance based on new institutional arrangements between public and private stakeholders, statutory and non-statutory organisations and making use of flexible, networked and multidimensional delivery mechanisms (e.g. partnerships) over traditional top-down hierarchies (Macleod and Goodwin 1999; Haughton and Counsell 2004; Tasan-Kok and Vranken 2011; ESPON TANGO 2013; Mourato et al. 2015).

Overall, soft spaces and soft planning are part of a major paradigm shift within planning, one where land-use planning has given rise to spatial planning, government has left room for governance, and the nation state has been hollowed out by devolution and spatial rescaling. Together, these mechanisms create new conditions within planning, breaking the ties that previously bound planning to statutory administrative and governmental frameworks.

Soft planning does not replace statutory frameworks, however. Hard (mandatory and regulatory) and soft (non-statutory and non-binding) forms of planning coexist and complement one another (Stead 2014; Purkarthofer 2016). While soft planning provides the statutory framework with a "*form of lubrication (…), acting outside of the frictions of formalised processes*", hard spaces and tools continue to provide a mechanism for the formal delivery of goals (Haughton and Allmendinger 2007: 306). Nevertheless, this coexistence is not free from contention. Deviances and mismatches emerge, giving rise to a number of ambiguities, inconsistencies and contradictions that need clarifying.

The European Union (EU) has had its share of responsibility in this paradigm shift, not only by acting as a driver of soft planning—chiefly by means of its mainstream EU Cohesion Policy (ECP) as well as the provision of Structural Funds (Luukkonen and Moilanen 2012; Purkarthofer 2016)—but also by encouraging the convergence and harmonisation of disparate national planning styles into a common European planning culture and discourse (Knieling and Othengrafen 2015). However, more than strategic discourses, EU Structural Funds are at the core of contentions between EU soft planning initiatives and statutory national planning. At national level, convergence barely goes beyond rhetoric as long as inner political and administrative cultures remain a matrix foundation. At European level, EU policy initiatives and tools become somehow distorted once filtered by national structures and adopted in partnership agreements.

Using the Portuguese planning system as a reference, this chapter examines the meeting ground between hard and soft planning, i.e. how EU-led, soft planning initiatives are accommodated and managed within statutory national planning systems. At what level do EU lesson-drawing processes influence national planning systems? What tensions and incongruences arise from the coexistence of hard, national and soft EU initiatives? What impact do the different approaches have in understanding the role of planning in dealing with a territory's emerging trends and needs? How does this meeting between European and statutory national planning affect the relationship between spatial planning and regional development policies?

In methodological terms, the Portuguese administrative organisation and spatial planning system provide the background for this analysis, while soft planning initiatives endorsed in the last EU 2014–2020 programming cycle, under the banner of EU Structural Funds (ITI, CLLD and Article 7 of the ERDF), are the target of the study. The analysis examines this entangled framework of soft versus statutory planning, first evaluating the rigidity, inertia and lack of effectiveness of national statutory planning, and second, either the benefits or the distortions and shortcomings brought about by the inclusion of soft EU planning spaces in the formal planning system.

The chapter has three different sections. The first addresses how the EU has encouraged soft spaces and planning, namely through ECP and European Structural Funds, promoting soft over hard national planning. The second looks at Portuguese spatial planning vis-à-vis the national administrative organisation, especially policy changes and developments resulting from the effect of mainstream EU spatial planning. The last section discusses the emergence of soft planning in Portugal. It focuses on integrated territorial approaches during the 2014–2020 programming cycle, particularly the tensions and ambiguities between statutory planning and operational programming with regard to convergence between EU-led soft planning policy initiatives and the national statutory system.

7.2 Soft Planning Spaces and the EU's Crusade

EU discourses on spatial development and territorial cohesion (in particular embodied in its Cohesion Policy—ECP) have provided fertile ground on which soft spaces and soft planning can flourish. Although there is not much literature explicitly exploring the influence of the EU's policies on the formation of soft spaces and soft planning practices, the impacts have been recognised by scholars (Luukkonen and Moilanen 2012; Stead 2014; Purkarthofer 2016).

There are two main trends that sustained it. The first was a shift towards a spatial approach to regional development; the second was a shift towards a relational approach to planning and place-making. The EU played a key role in bringing such changes about under the process of Europeanisation (Bhome and Waterhout 2008; Faludi 2014).

Over recent decades, the notion of "territory" has made its way into mainstream EU policy. In the late 1980s, Structural Funds were launched and European policies were targeted at regional level. The territorial dimension was formally added to the ECP, alongside the social and economic dimensions, with the Lisbon Treaty of 2009. Territorial cohesion became one of the main objectives of the EU, confirming the need to nurture regional development from a spatial-thinking perspective (Thoidou 2011). Regional planning (focused on the organisation and physical spatial structure of a region) and regional policy (focused on the disparities between regions in terms of economic development and employment) were thus brought closer together, widening the notion of development and conveying socio-economic disparities through a geographical perspective (Dühr et al. 2007). In the most recent programming cycles, the territorial dimension has gained even more ground within the ECP. Besides being an investment tool oriented towards economic growth, ECP has become an important vehicle to promote soft planning practices, namely through cross-border cooperation, place-based integrated strategies and multi-level governance (Medeiros 2016).

Moreover, planning itself has undergone deep reforms. Together with territorial cohesion, other concepts such as spatial planning and territorial governance have reinforced the aim of treating space in terms of relations and networks, freeing it from Euclidian approaches (Amin 2002; Luukkonen and Moilanen 2012) and Weberian concepts of state (Dusza 1989). There was also an increased awareness of how spatial development and territorial cohesion goals are rarely achieved when set within nested territorial units and framed within traditional governmental settings. While formal planning tools became increasingly criticised for their complexity, inertia and lack of joined-up thinking and detachment from real geographies, new spatially fluid and functional planning spaces cropped up across administrative boundaries, introducing innovative working patterns (that are much more flexible, networked and collaborative) among formal processes.

To convey these underlying trends, the EU employed three types of "catalysts" or policy mechanisms (Bhome and Waterhout 2008; Purkarthofer 2016):

(i) Rules, i.e. EU regulations and directives, coercive and legally binding for member states, but with variable spatial relevance in terms of territorial impacts depending on the nature of the policy measures.
(ii) Ideas, i.e. non-binding documents with a doctrinal and discursive strategic nature but a powerful capacity to influence domestic planning systems through socialisation and lesson-drawing processes (inspiration, imitation and emulation).
(iii) Resources, i.e. EU funds and subsidies to foster economic development in regions that lag behind, which are neither compulsory nor discretionary but have a compelling aptitude to foster the transfer and adoption of EU policy goals and principles at national and sub-national levels.

Since spatial planning was left out as a formal competency of the EU, strategic papers and funding tools stand out as the main "catalysts" in the Europeanisation of spatial planning. Even under European Structural Funds, whose institutional framework is rather formal and constrained by binding rules, the EU has a soft rather than hard approach to spatial planning. The Europeanisation of planning predominantly occurs "in-between", that is across sectors, across government levels and across administrative boundaries (*cf.* Dühr et al. 2007: 302). Indeed, the EU welcomed soft spaces and planning with open arms, and they became an important tool in its crusade to foster territorial cohesion.

The push of EU policies towards soft planning spaces was focused in particular on cross-border territorial cooperation. Territorial cooperation programs, such as ESPON and INTERREG, became vehicles through which to explore Europeanisation trends (Bhome and Waterhout 2008; Dühr et al. 2007; Dühr and Nadin 2007). A number of significant studies gather evidence on cross-border planning and transnational cooperation (Gualini 2003; Perkmann 2007; Sousa 2013; Luukkonen and Moilanen 2012; Stead 2014). However, very little has been said about how Structural Funds, the EU's main regional policy instrument, have been indirectly (though explicitly) fostering rescaling at sub-national and supra-municipal levels and encouraging soft planning spaces within the domestic spheres of planning systems.

In the latest community programming cycles, under the banner of EU Structural Funds, the European Commission (EC) launched a number of policy tools geared towards integrated territorial approaches (ITAs) that can be labelled as soft planning initiatives. This became particularly evident in the 2014–2020 period which has seen ITAs strengthened. Three policy tools—Integrated Territorial Investments (ITIs),[1] Community-Led Local Development (CLLD)[2] and Article 7 of the ERDF Regulation for Integrated Sustainable Urban Development (ISUD[3])—were made available in order to: push the emergence of new territorial spaces acting as drivers for spatial rescaling; assist multi-level governance and promote cooperation and coordination between the different levels of government, with a view to the implementation of common visions and shared solutions; stimulate multidimensional and cross-sectoral interventions; carry out tailor-made and place- or area-based development strategies focused on the specific needs of geographical areas rather than on abstract administrative constructs; and promote the capacity building of institutions and territorial actors, as well as the empowerment, involvement and participation of local authorities, local communities and the civil society (European Commission 2014a, b, c; 2016).

While ITIs represent an inaugural policy initiative of the 2014–2020 period, explicitly calling for the establishment of non-statutory planning spaces, CLLD and urban development initiatives are essentially a redraft of previous community policies (e.g. LEADER, Community Initiatives URBAN I and II, EQUAL). In any case, there is a clear reinforcement of ITAs (e.g. new tools, increased flexibility in the use of funds and combined investments, increased budget specifically geared towards integrated approaches) through which the EU promotes soft planning over hard national planning.

Although there is no enforced compliance with EU-led initiatives, member states are somehow lured by Structural Funds to adopt EU tools and guidelines. Soft planning tools, in parallel with statutory tools, have been often employed to secure the allocation of European funds, even though organisation and coordination between the two are far from satisfactory. Funds and subsidies are much more responsible for underlying tensions between European and national planning, hard and soft planning, and spatial planning and operational programming than strategic papers. EU Structural Funds, over their short-term seven-year programming cycles, compel member states to adopt tools, processes and strategies that are often in competition with long-term binding statutory plans. This introduces a risk of disruption and ambiguity into the planning system and also raises issues of legality and democratic representativeness, which has been already considered a "form of neo-liberalism" or a "shortcut to democracy" (*cf.* Stead 2014: 682).

Compared with statutory planning, which is usually condemned for its complexity, rigidity, slowness and lack of effectiveness, soft planning introduces informality, flexibility, expeditiousness and, last but not least, financial conditions that support implementation interventions. While statutory tools have often failed to accommodate territorial dynamics and deliver development demands successfully, soft planning initiatives supported by Structural Funds potentially increase the effectiveness of plans for spatial transformation.

---

[1]Although the concept of soft planning is not mentioned, the factsheet on ITIs provided by the EC is clear on the purposes that lay behind the creation of such a tool: "*This approach is multi-dimensional, tailored to place-specific features and outcomes, which may mean going beyond traditional administrative boundaries, and may require greater willingness from different levels of government to co-operate and co-ordinate actions in order to achieve shared goals. (…) Any geographical area with particular territorial features can be the subject of an ITI, ranging from specific urban neighbourhoods with multiple deprivations to the urban, metropolitan, urban-rural, sub-regional, or inter-regional levels. An ITI can also deliver integrated actions in detached geo-graphical units with similar characteristics within a region (e.g. a network of small or medium-sized cities). It is not compulsory for an ITI to cover the whole territory of an administrative unit*" European Commission (2014a).

[2]The policy initiative of CLLD is also a way to push forward the creation of soft planning spaces. According to the factsheet on CLLDs provided by the EC, CLLD falls upon "*specific sub-regional areas*" to be "*carried out through integrated and multi-sectoral area-based local development strategies, designed taking into consideration local needs and potential, (…) networking and, where appropriate, co-operation*" European Commission (2014b).

[3]ISUD is fostering soft spaces and soft planning in several ways: covering urban areas that "*range from neighbourhood or district level to functional areas such as city-regions or metropolitan areas*" set up according to the "*specific needs of geographical areas*" and "*to target areas with specific urban challenges*"; strengthening the delivery of integrated actions; fostering multi-level governance namely with "*the development of strong partnerships involving local citizens, civil society, the local economy and the various levels of government is an indispensable element*"; pressing the devolution of powers to the lower tiers of government, namely by requiring the delegation of tasks to urban authorities, without explicitly mentioning who urban authorities are or at which level of government they perform ("*Member states are required (…) to put in place arrangements to delegate a number of tasks (at least project selection) to urban authorities related to implementation of sustainable urban development strategies*") European Commission (2014c).

7.3 The Europeanisation of Spatial Planning in Portugal

Despite the fact that spatial planning is not a formal European remit, and no legally binding EU rules have been directly established at this level, the "effect of Europe" (Ferrão 2011) has influenced national spatial planning systems all over Europe. Portugal is no exception. In the last twenty years, a paradigm shift within the national planning system, driven by European rhetoric on spatial planning, has been acknowledged.

In Portugal, spatial planning was set up in 1998 as an autonomous policy branch providing for an integrated hierarchical planning system (Campos and Ferrão 2015). An inaugural framework act was published (Law 48/98, 11 August) establishing the legal foundations for urbanism, land-use and spatial planning policy. Its aim was to produce an integrated and sustainable development framework for the whole country, including its regions and urban settlements. To this end, a set of principles was set up, demonstrating a change of mindset within Portuguese planning. These ranged from the horizontal coordination of sectorial policies to the vertical coordination of government levels under the principle of subsidiarity, the concertation of public and private initiatives and the participation of the civil society. A multi-scalar articulated system of planning tools (at national, regional and local levels) was also settled for the first time, distinguishing strategic, development-oriented spatial plans from regulatory, land-use plans with a zoning-oriented nature (LD 380/99, 22 September).

The shift of Portuguese planning towards the more strategic discourse of spatial planning and territorial governance was not detached from the influence of the growing European spatial planning culture. With Portugal's entry into the European Economic Community in 1986, the "effect of Europe" became more decisive in shaping domestic policies at doctrinal, legal and programmatic levels (Campos and Ferrão 2015: 36).

The first signs of the direct impact of mainstream European policy on Portuguese planning became evident prior to 1998. The first Community Support Framework (CSF I, 1989-1993) of the ECP was actually the prime mover. During the 1990s, a political reform was implemented that made the Municipal Master Plan (PDM) mandatory for every municipality (Law Decree 69/90, 2 March). Sanctions were announced for defaulting municipalities. These were prevented from applying for European Structural Funds or executing compulsory purchases in the public interest if no effective PDM was in force. Such measures have had a significant impact on national planning. Within a decade, Portugal was overrun with municipal level plans, reversing the former scenario of ad hoc planning. Nevertheless, strategic planning remained a mirage. A blueprint regulatory planning style was adopted by the first generation PDMs, encouraging the government to launch a second planning campaign—PROSIURB[4] (CSF II, 1994–1999)—"*to stimulate the preparation of non-statutory strategic spatial plans*" (Rosa Pires 2005: 240). Although less successful than the PDM campaign, PROSIURB introduced a number of innovative approaches including strategic planning, multi-level governance, integrated urban development and soft planning spaces largely aimed at the city region (Cavaco 2018), thus becoming an embryo for spatial planning in Portugal (Fig. 7.1).

In the late 1990s, following the publication of the European Spatial Development Perspective (ESDP 1999), greater doctrinal emphasis was placed on spatial planning. According to Mourato and Rosa Pires (2007: 36), the ESDP is "one of the most paradoxical dimensions of the European project". It represents the informal setting up of a non-binding planning territorial vision and agenda for the EU, aiming to foster territorial governance in the whole European space and to influence national planning environments within each member state at a discursive level.

Despite the slowness and controversial discussion on how and whether indeed the ESDP has played a significant role in changing planning practices in Portugal (cf. Rosa Pires 2005; Giannakourou 2005; Mourato and Rosa Pires 2007; Campos and Ferrão 2015), the turn of the millennium brought meaningful reforms to the Portuguese planning system and greater convergence with the European rhetoric on spatial planning.

Following the approval of the new legal regime of 1998/1999, the accomplishment of the spatial planning system and its strategic tools at a national (PNPOT) and regional level (PROT) was a clear sign of the underlying changes. The National Spatial Development Policy Programme (PNPOT 2007) was actually a benchmark for such a paradigm shift. It not only introduced into the national context a number of policy guidelines embedded in the ESDP (e.g. the strengthening of a balanced and polycentric spatial development model structured upon cities; the preservation and enhancement of natural and cultural heritage as a development asset; coordination between land-use planning, spatial development, transport, and infrastructure policies, etc.), but it was also delivered as a strategic development-oriented tool. Its aim was to guide both

---

[4]PROSIURB—Programme for the consolidation of the national urban system and to support the execution of the PDM—MPAT. Ministério do Planeamento e da Administração do Território. (1994). Despacho nº 6/94 e Despacho nº 7/94, Diário da República II Série, nº 21, de 26 de janeiro de 1994.

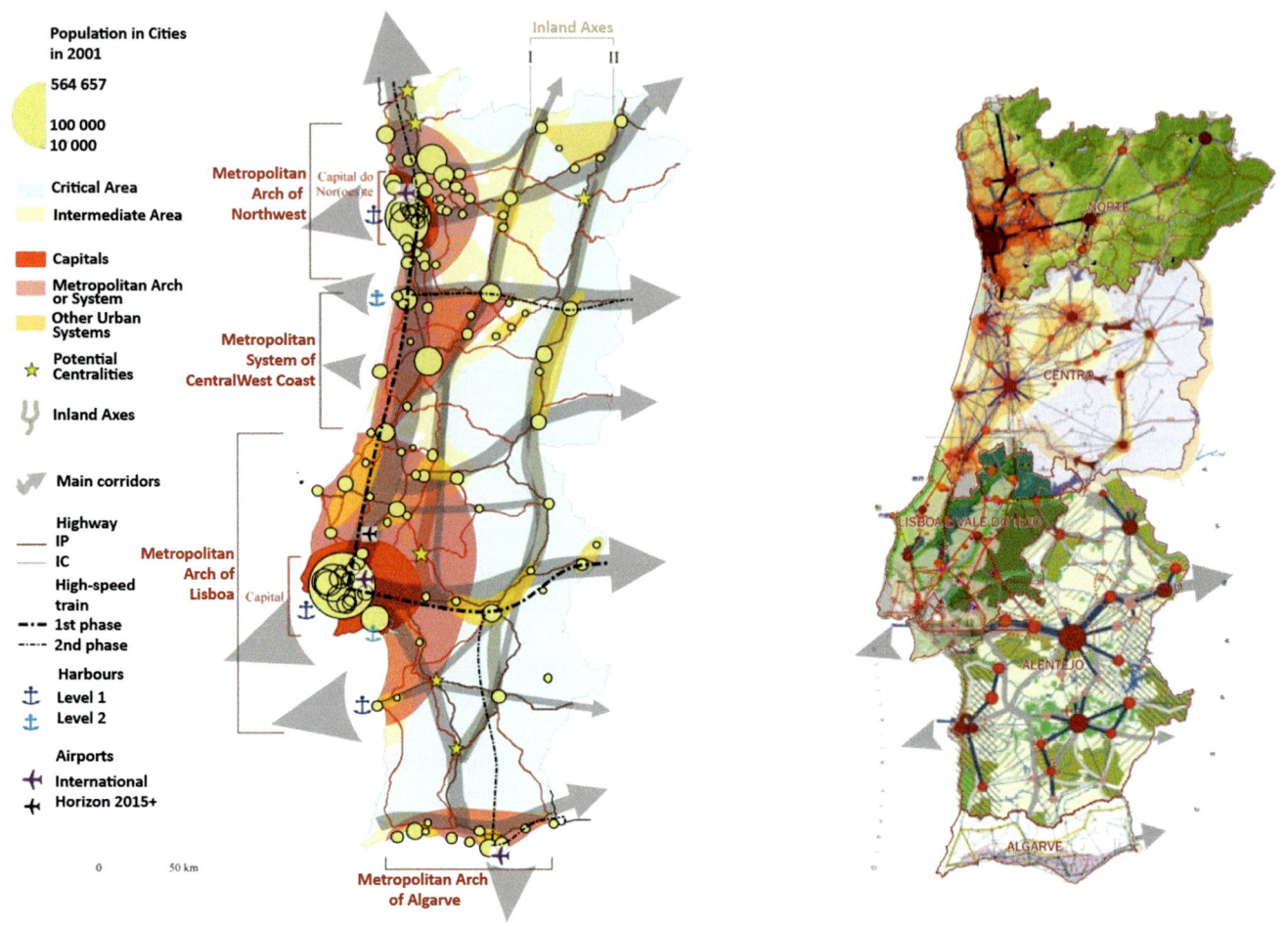

PNPOT - NATIONAL SPATIAL DEVELOPMENT PROGRAMME   **PROT - REGIONAL SPATIAL DEVELOPMENT PLANS**

Fig. 7.1 Territorial models of the National Spatial Development Policy Programme (PNPOT) (left) and the five Regional Spatial Development Plans (PROTs) (right) (Published in PNPOT Law 58/2007, 4 September (left); Territorial models of the five PROTs produced by the Directorate General for Territorial Development (right).)

transnational cooperation in regard to spatial development policies and domestic planning practices at the lower tiers of administration (PNPOT 2007; Cavaco [coord.] et al. 2014: 53–54). The subsequent development of the Regional Spatial Development Plans (PROT), under the umbrella of the PNPOT, was also an important step towards the materialisation of planning in cascade-like hierarchies as well as the pursuit of European rationales at regional level.

Nevertheless, if changes were evident from a doctrinal and legal point of view, in practical terms the process suffered from great inertia. The shift towards spatial planning and territorial governance entails different maturation rates (Mourato and Rosa Pires 2007). Planning practices and institutional cultures do not necessarily change at the pace of discursive trends, for instance. After seven years in force, an assessment (Cavaco [coord.] et al. 2014) of PNPOT revealed that a number of political, institutional and technical constraints were at the heart of its implementation, thereby jeopardising the attainment of its highest goals, which were to foster territorial governance and coordinate place-based, sector-wide policies. Contrary to its initial aims, a sectorial matrix ended up prevailing over integrated place-based approaches,[5] while the institutional and instrumental support basis for the programming, contracting and implementation of integrated territorial approaches proved to be very poor, as was the accountability and commitment of territorial actors and institutions (Cavaco [coord.] et al. 2014; Cavaco and Magalhães 2015).

---

[5]Instead of making use of integrated territorial approaches and place-based policy measures, the PNPOT was settled in a sectorial matrix, i.e. the policy programme is somehow the collection of a set of sectorial policy measures, many of them coming from other existing sectorial programmes and plans, without placing particular emphasis on its place-based integration.

At regional and municipal levels, significant advances were seen, although the panorama was not entirely free from obstacles and shortcomings. In regard to the PROT, the merits achieved during the development process, a result of enthusiastic debate and participation, were shaken by regional asymmetries during the approval and follow-up phases. Two of the five PROTs laid out until 2010 did not come into force due to political reasons, with consequences for the reliability and assimilation of the PROT as a strategic reference for municipal planning.

At the local tier of government, a new generation of PDMs was created, bringing with it stronger technical capacity and greater strategic guidance, in line with national and regional guidelines (Cavaco [coord.] 2016). Yet entrenched inertia and inefficiency still undermine the functioning of the system. Revision procedures require extended periods of time,[6] regional asymmetries persist showing an uneven distribution of planning dynamics,[7] and land-use regulation remains the major target of PDM procedures, in detriment to strategic and governance goals (Costa and Cavaco 2017).

Based on a two-tier administration (central and local) for the mainland,[8] Portugal has always balanced a strong degree of centralisation (strengthened by decades of dictatorship) with a firm municipal tradition which weakened intermediary government levels and intermediate territorial planning units. In 1969, five planning regions were established for the Portuguese mainland, to support regional development.[9] However, they did not gain administrative autonomy. In 1998, the same year a new spatial planning rationale was introduced into the statutory system, a public referendum rejected regionalisation with regard to the institutionalisation of administrative regions as foreseen in the Constitutional Law. The Constitutional Law of 2005 raised awareness about territory and territorial policies, yet the absence of administrative regions persists which restrains the execution of spatial planning policies in line with the European rationale (cf. Ferrão 2016).[10] Since the referendum, other administrative reforms have taken place,[11] but the criss-crossing of territorial divisions and planning levels at sub-national and supra-municipal levels (e.g. planning regions/NUTS II; inter-municipal entities/NUTS III), under only two tiers of administration (central government and municipalities), has always generated friction in regard to constitutional powers and democratic representativeness. That notwithstanding, NUTS II regions were progressively used as the point of reference, not only for regional planning but also for the regional management of de-concentrated, sector-wide policies and EU Structural Funds under the control of de-concentrated central government services (CCDR—Regional Coordination and Development Commissions)[12] (Fig. 7.2).

In 2014/2015 a second wave of reforms took place. Among other objectives, they were aimed at: improving the efficiency, effectiveness and accountability of the planning system; updating the land-use policy in the face of past, speculative behaviours and challenges left by the global financial crisis; and reinforcing inter-municipal cooperation by strengthening sub-regional planning at inter-municipal level. A new framework act (Law 31/2014, 30 May) and legal regime for planning tools (Law Decree 80/2015, 14 May) came into force, clearly distinguishing between territorial programs and territorial plans. The former were strategic and endorsed by the central administration, while the latter were regulatory and the exclusive domain of the local authorities, as they were the only planning tools enforceable for individuals. While a new sub-regional planning level was created, encouraging municipalities to cooperate in defining coordinated development options, the PDM was strengthened as the central vessel of the planning system, having the twofold prerogative of establishing a strategic vision for municipal or inter-municipal territories and also consolidating all the rules and restrictions regarding land-use regulation.

---

[6]More than ten years on average, which explains why in 2016 only 54% of the municipalities had their new PDM in force (Costa and Cavaco 2017).

[7]In the North Region, which does not have an effective PROT in force, 82% of the PDM has been already revised, in the Lisbon and Algarve regions revision rates fell to 21 and 6%, respectively (Costa and Cavaco 2017).

[8]In Portugal, regional autonomy is especially consigned to the Autonomous Regions of Azores and Madeira, while in Portugal's mainland there are only two tiers of government.

[9]Under the 3rd National Development Plan (1968–1973).

[10]According to João Ferrão, "*The current Constitutional Law, in spite of some shortcomings, does not hinder the formulation of a new generation of territorial policies, more efficient, democratic and equal. However, the current political and administrative organization restrains the participation of several public entities in the design and implementation of such policies*" (2016: 123).

[11]E.g.: the amalgamation of parishes from 4259 to 3091, in 2013 (Law 22/2012, 30 May); the reorganisation of inter-municipal entities (Law 75/2013, 12 September) and the revision of NUTS III accordingly (EU Regulation 868/2014, 8 August) which came into force on 1 January 2015.

[12]Most recently, NUTS III have gradually emerged as the preferred scale for contracting between central government and local authorities.

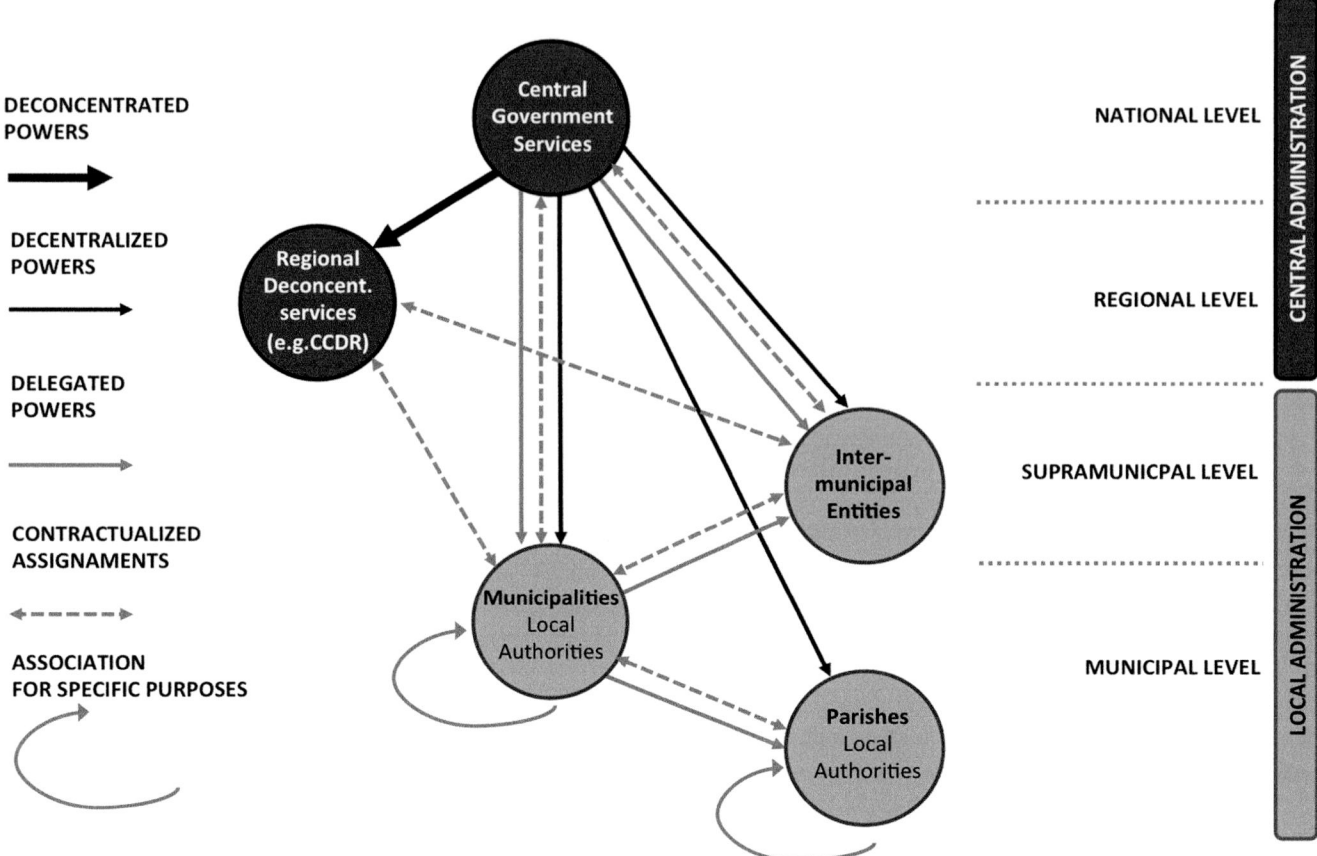

Fig. 7.2 Redistribution of power between institutions and government levels, adapted by authors from a non-published scheme of the Directorate General for Territorial Development

This last wave of planning reforms was also underpinned by significant legal changes for local authorities and inter-municipal entities (Law 75/2013, 12 September; Law Decree 30/2015, 12 February). The reforms reinforced the devolution of powers from the state to local government (following previous decentralisation measures[13]), as well as the transfer of competences away from municipalities, upwards to the inter-municipal bodies and downwards to the parishes (Cavaco [coord.] 2016: 77–79).

Despite all this, inconsistencies and shortcomings persisted that somehow drove out the underlying shift towards the European rhetoric on spatial planning. One of these is the lack of attention paid to territorial governance, the coordination of sectorial policies and the policy mechanisms to endorse place-based integrated actions. Indeed, the existing Territorial Action Programmes (PAT)—especially created to frame the coordination of territorial activities, particularly the programming and contracting of complex territorial developments between the different government bodies and stakeholders, both public and private—were abolished in the legal reform of 2014.

Nonetheless, in the aftermath of the last twenty years, the balance has been quite positive: a strategic benchmark for spatial development is now available, strategic consistency between planning levels has increased, the capacity for territorial management and governance has been improved, local authorities have been empowered, and rescaling movements have contributed to a more balanced distribution of tasks and powers. The pathway towards a new spatial planning culture, however, has not been straightforward. The clash between EU doctrines and domestic planning is inseparable from entrenched organisational patterns and inner administrative cultures, which have traditionally functioned as a tight-knit filter resisting outside forces that might threaten or undermine the established political and administrative order.

---

[13]Law 159/99, 14 September, which foresaw the transfer of a set of competences to the municipalities; Law 169/99, 18 September, which approved the competences framework and legal regime of local authorities; Law 2/2007, 15 January, which established the new financial regime for the municipalities and parishes, strengthening the decentralisation and autonomy of local power.

The Portuguese planning system is anchored in a complex and abstract system of legally binding norms (Newman and Thorney 1996; Nadin and Stead 2008), which has been increasingly weighed down by complexity in spite of efforts made to streamline it. This causes resistance when it comes to complying with European rationales. According to Giannakourou (2005), the European spatial planning culture is mainly a construct of north-west European countries, while southern Mediterranean countries have shown increased difficulties in the "'digesting' and 'metabolising' of EU spatial planning" (320). Two main reasons are given: (i) their urban planning tradition, embedded with an architectural and urban design mentality geared towards building control (see also CEE 1997) and (ii) the so-called Mediterranean Syndrome of government (320) which tends to endorse a rigid, statutory and regulatory planning style.

7.4 Soft Planning in Portugal: Tensions and Ambiguities Between Statutory Planning and Operational Programming

In Portugal, awareness of soft spaces and governance rescaling is scarce. Nevertheless, soft planning practices exist. They have been associated with the development of "integrated territorial approaches" (ITAs) which, in the last few decades, have been specifically encouraged by EU-led initiatives and regulations and also supported by European Structural Funds. ITAs target the specific needs and assets of a certain territory by bringing together spatially sensitive policies and sector-wide interventions in order to support cohesive economic, social and environmental change. Place-based policy, multi-level governance and contracting[14] are the fundamental mechanisms behind ITAs.

ITAs received particular emphasis in the current 2014–2020 programming cycle. New tools and outfits were made available in the Partnership Agreement (Portugal 2020), clearly enhancing the territorial dimension of the ECP at sub-national and supra-municipal levels. Similar approaches have been tested in previous programming cycles, but in a more restricted and experimental way (CSF I 1989–1993; CSF II 1994–99; CSF III 2000–2006). At first, multi-level contracts were pursued as pilot experiments limited to specific associations of municipalities, only being extended to the whole territory in the latest programming cycle (National Strategic Reference Framework—QREN, 2007–2013). In the 2014–2020 programming cycle, ITAs were significantly enhanced in terms of tools and management options.

However, the global framework supporting ITAs in the 2014–2020 period is quite complex. It not only attests the lack of coordination between spatial planning policies and operational programming, it also illustrates how the EU operates on hard national planning in a soft manner (Figs. 7.3 and 7.4).

NUTS III level was adopted as the preferred scale for the application of the ITI, which took the shape of a partnership agreement (PDCT—Partnerships for Territorial Development and Cohesion), i.e. a contract between the central government (by means of the de-concentrated services of CCDR/NUTS II), inter-municipal entities (associations of municipalities/NUTS III) and other non-governmental organisations and private stakeholders. Portugal 2020 did not prevent the application of the ITI to other geographies or the aggregation of contiguous NUTS III; nevertheless, in practice it did not happen. PCDTs were endorsed by each of the inter-municipal entities, becoming the intermediary bodies responsible for the management and selection of territorial investments. The definition of supra-municipal strategies to anchor territorial partnerships (Integrated Strategies for Territorial Development—EIDT) was also made mandatory by regulations. Twenty-three EIDTs, comprising the 21 inter-municipal communities and the two metropolitan areas of Lisbon and Oporto, were therefore established outside the statutory planning system, regardless of the inclusion of strategic inter-municipal planning tools in the hierarchical architecture of the spatial planning system in 2014. Although some references to the existing territorial models of the PROT and the PNPOT are made, most of the EIDT is completely disconnected from the strategic place-based options contained within the statutory tools.

Additionally, other ITAs were approved, mainly focusing on community-led local developments (CLLD—whether they be rural, coastal or urban) and integrated sustainable urban development actions (ISUD). While CLLDs were established as bottom-up approaches raised by local action groups (the requirements for the delimitation of target territories follows population thresholds instead of administrative criteria), ISUDs were addressed to the municipal level and were the direct responsibility of the municipalities (local authorities). Still, further strategic documents were demanded to embrace each of

---

[14]Different types of proceedings can be put in place, ranging from contracts, covenants or partnership agreements. They often comprise contracts and agreements established between different government levels (central and local governments) and between the public administration and private stakeholders.

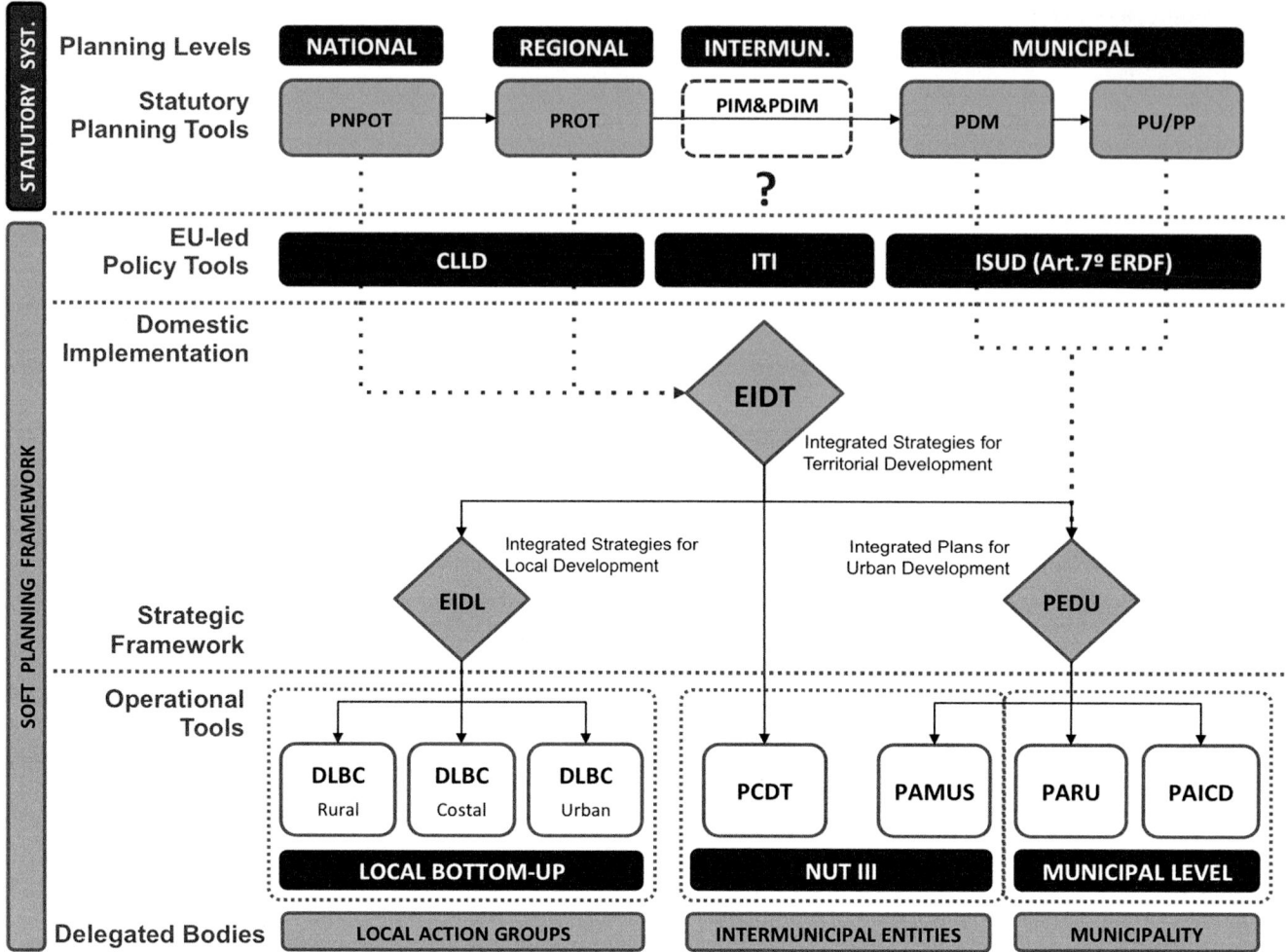

Fig. 7.3 Integrated territorial approaches (ITA) in the 2014–2020 programming cycle: strategies and tools

the territorial approaches: Integrated Strategies for Local Development (EIDL) whenever CLLD is involved and Integrated Plans for Urban Development (PEDU) to frame urban-oriented investments.

With regard to ISUDs, the decision was taken not to include urban development operations within the ITI. Alternatively, ISUDs were addressed to an autonomous arm of the Regional Operational Programmes (POR), one in which the central government (by means of the CCDR as managing authorities) retains the right to veto approval of urban operations. Under the umbrella of the PEDU, three other operational tools cropped up (PAMUS, PARU and PAICD) to guarantee, respectively, alignment with the three selected operational priorities: promoting low-carbon strategies and sustainable urban development (PAMUS—Action Plan for Sustainable Urban Mobility); improving the urban environment (PARU—Action Plan for Urban Regeneration); and regenerating deprived urban areas (PAICD—Integrated Action Plan for Deprived Communities). Municipalities were therefore confronted with the predicament of looking into the long-term spatial development strategies of their PDM, while also developing parallel strategic frameworks (PEDU) focused on EU objectives and priorities in order to finance local investments.

Against the background of the territorial organisation of the state and the statutory planning system, the pursuit of ITAs was controversial. Tensions and ambiguities emerged from the matching (or mismatching) of soft planning initiatives with the statutory planning tools.

On the one hand, ITAs have been a major driver of governance rescaling processes. They have pushed the establishment of policy approaches at regional (NUTS II) and sub-regional (NUTS III) scales, encouraging the extension of planning powers from the central government and local authorities to other intermediary, although non-elected, institutional bodies. To give an example, Regional Coordination and Development Commissions—CCDRs, act over a specific planning region

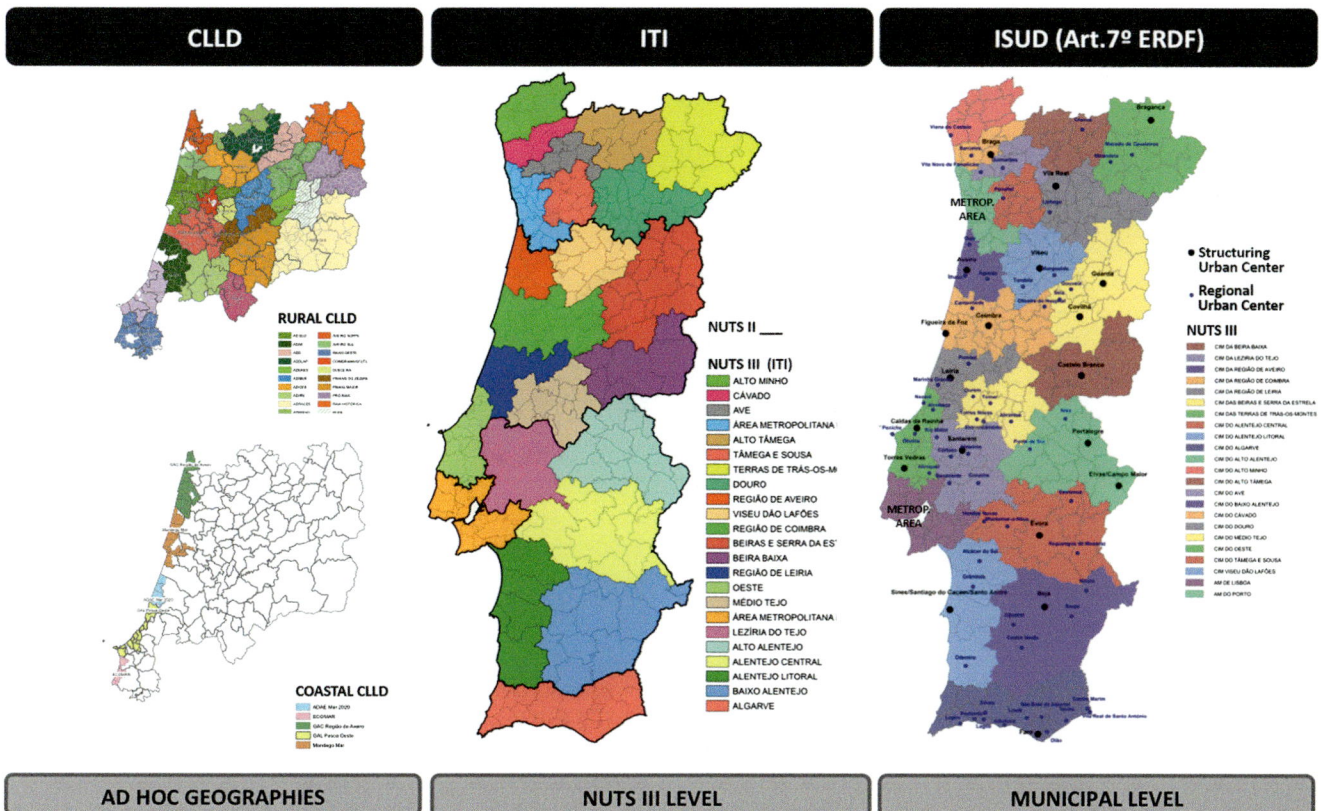

Fig. 7.4 Integrated territorial approaches (ITA)—geographies and administrative levels (NUTSIII according to Law 75/2013—CAOP (Official Administrative Map of Portugal), 2016 (produced on 09-09-2016 by Directorate General for Territorial Development) (left); Structuring Urban Centres and Regional Urban Centres as adopted in the Partnership Agreement (produced on 22-01-2015), SNIT (National System for Territorial Information), Directorate General for Territorial Development (right).)

by de-concentrating central government powers, and inter-municipal entities or associations of municipalities proceed through the transfer or delegation of powers from municipalities.

On the other hand, ITAs have brought new strategic documents and non-binding planning tools into play that somehow duplicate and compete with legally binding tools. A strategic framework is usually required by EU regulations to frame the submission and implementation of territorial approaches, especially at supra-municipal level. However, existing planning tools are not considered to offer such pedigree and are hardly recognised as relevant and updated development-oriented references for convergence purposes. At local level, opinions suggest that PDMs are not acknowledged due to their obsolescence, lack of flexibility, poor development-oriented strategy and inconsistency with neighbouring municipalities (Vitorino 2010). At national and regional level, the PNPOT and the PROT are usually remarked upon. However, appointed synergies barely go beyond rhetorical references, while territorial models and place-based options are often set aside in a surreptitious but deliberate way due to political and economic agendas (Figs. 7.5 and 7.6).

Although there is general consensus about the need to provide an interface between the territorial models of statutory tools and the non-binding strategic frameworks, in practice there is a clear boundary between the two. Spatial planning policies and regional development policies (particularly those framed under EU Structural Funds) act as if they are two separate and autonomous realms (Vitorino 2010; Cavaco [coord.] et al. 2014). This separation begins within the government itself, since spatial planning and regional policy are the remit of different ministries. While, however, there were times where these two policy areas were covered by the same ministry in the past (1980–90; 2005–2009), the last twenty years have brought stronger demarcation, with spatial planning falling under the umbrella of environment and regional development moving closer to economics via the Council of Ministers. Attempts at joining them have been made at regional level, chiefly by means of CCDRs, which cover both areas. Nevertheless, convergence is not straightforward. Coordination is often forced, barely touching the strategic sphere, while the accountability of public agencies and the interactions with stakeholders highlight numerous weaknesses. In the end, regional development, influenced by the impetus of Structural Funds, usually triumphs over spatial planning which has already been labelled a "weak policy" (Ferrão 2011). Nevertheless, while

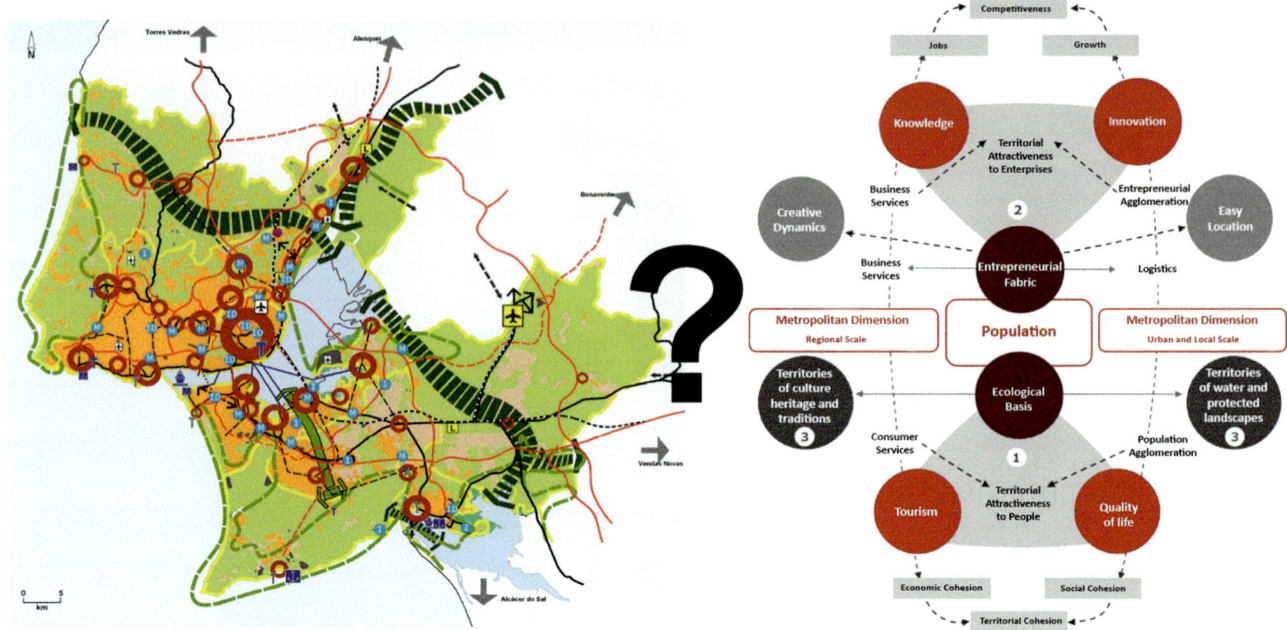

METROPOLITAN AREA OF LISBON SPATIAL DEVELOPMENT PLAN, 2010 (DRAFT)

INTEGRATED STRATEGY OF TERRITORIAL DEVELOPMENT (EIDT) FOR NUT III LISBON METROPOLITAN AREA, 2015

Fig. 7.5 Regional Spatial Development Plans (PROT) versus Integrated Strategies for Territorial Development (EIDT) for the Metropolitan Area of Lisbon (From (left) Metropolitan Area of Lisbon's Spatial Development Plan, draft, 2010, by Coordination Commission for Regional Development of Lisbon and Tagus Valley Region—CCDR-LVT and (right) Vision for the Metropolitan Area of Lisbon in 2020, Integrated Strategy of Territorial Development of the Metropolitan Area of Lisbon, Fig. 50, p. 153. by Coordination Commission for Regional Development of Lisbon and Tagus Valley Region—CCDR-LVT.)

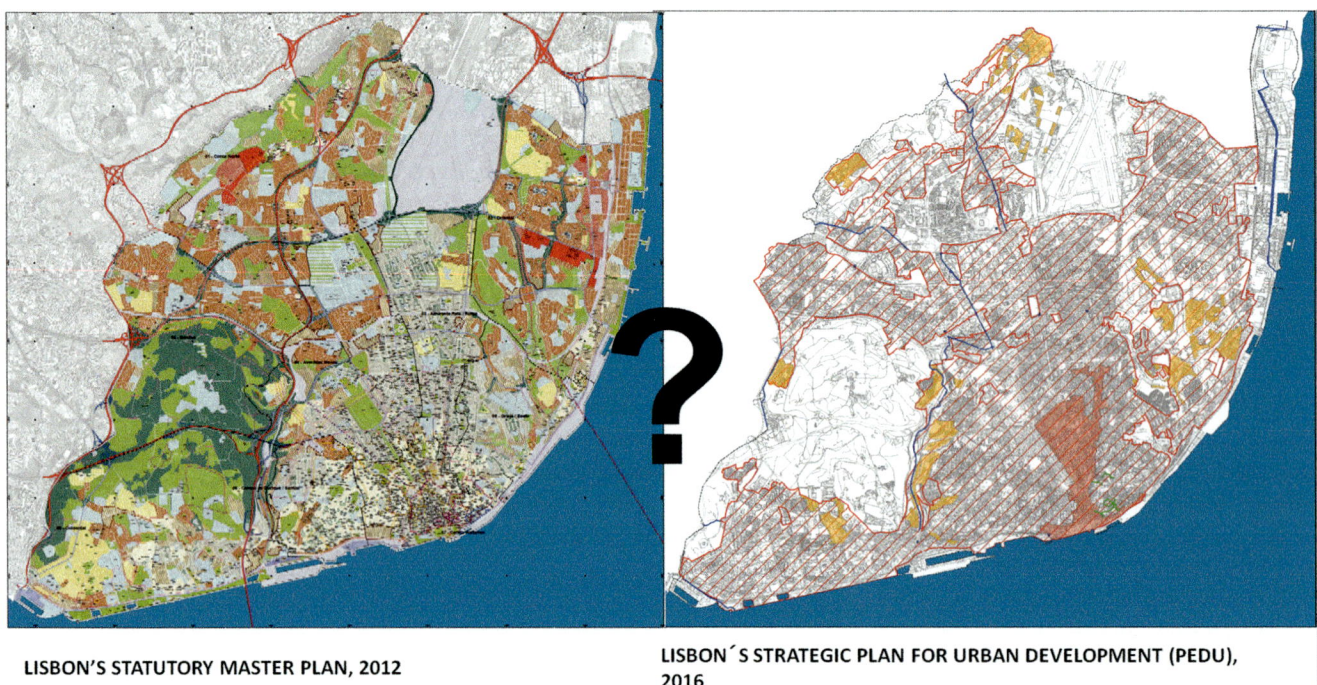

LISBON'S STATUTORY MASTER PLAN, 2012

LISBON´S STRATEGIC PLAN FOR URBAN DEVELOPMENT (PEDU), 2016

Fig. 7.6 Municipal Master Plan (PDM) versus Integrated Plans for Urban Development (PEDU) for the municipality of Lisbon (From (left) Planning Chart, qualification of the urban space, Lisbon's Municipal Master Plan (PDM), City of Lisbon, August 2012, Notice no. 11622/2012, published in the Official Gazette of the Republic of Portugal, 2nd series, no. 168, 30 August (left) and (right) Plan with the location/delimitation of the interventions areas of the PAMUS (Action Plan for Sustainable Urban Mobility), PARU (Action Plan for Urban regeneration) and PAICD (Integrated Action Plan for Deprived Communities), Strategic Plan for the Urban Development of Lisbon, City of Lisbon, December 2015.)

spatial planning tools may have the force of the law behind them, and while they may respect democratic participation and the reconciliation of interests with public consultation, strategic documents on the scope of operational programming do not guarantee any such formal democratic proceedings.

If the ECP and Structural Funds have had the capacity to influence traditional governmental practices, introducing innovative processes and tools oriented towards territorial governance, they must be weighed against internal administrative and political patterns that have curbed the underlying dynamics of governance rescaling. The scarcity of strategic planning tools suited to ad hoc geographical units at supra-municipal scale ("functional regions", Ferrão et al. 2013) and the systematic assignment of ITA to the institutional levels (e.g. NUTS III) clearly demonstrate how the statutory system has seized on EU soft planning processes all the same.

According to Ferrão et al. (2013), a number of issues explain the difficulties with the adoption of soft spaces (non-administrative planning units) as target areas for place-based strategies and policies: (i) the lack of adequate information; (ii) the inexistence of institutionalised spaces for cooperation and decision-making; (iii) the lack of political legitimacy and accountability; (iv) the awkwardness of promoting interaction between non-institutional soft spaces and political, administrative statutory spaces; (v) the different agendas of institutional and organisational cultures; and (vi) the requirement for complex governance structures.

Supported by European Structural Funds and framed under the partnership agreements between the government and the EU, ITAs have mainly resulted from top-down decisions instead of growing from territory-focused, voluntary approaches. To some degree, this explains the absorption of soft initiatives by statutory territorial organisation. However, the use of administrative units to host ITAs often reveals inadequacies in regard to territorial dynamics.

7.5 Conclusions

Over the last few decades, the Portuguese planning system has shown increasing convergence with European spatial planning rationale. A new move towards spatial planning and territorial governance has emerged, making room for soft planning practices.

This paradigm shift has happened in two different ways:

(i) Through the revision and adaptation of the statutory system in line with the principles and doctrines of EU spatial planning;

(ii) Under the allocation of EU Structural Funds and the direct incorporation of ECP tools and EU-led initiatives, geared towards the promotion of soft planning spaces, at domestic level.

However, the meeting of these two apparently confluent pathways has not led to convergence. On the contrary, a number of tensions and mismatches arise from the coexistence of the statutory planning system and the soft planning tools raised by community programming cycles for regional development purposes. On the one hand, instead of looking for common synergies, namely at strategic level, it led to the duplication of strategies and planning tools with temporal and territorial overlaps, thereby creating inefficiency and inconsistency. On the other hand, instead of fostering a connection between strategic planning tools and operational instruments, it gave rise to a separation between the formal legally binding planning system and the means to finance and promote effective spatial development and transformation. While the statutory planning system suffers from inertia, obsolescence and a lack of effectiveness, the operational tools do not provide for democratic representativeness with regard to participation and cooperation procedures.

At the same time, EU doctrines point towards closer ties between spatial planning and regional development, but in practice, there is no such lining up. Spatial planning and regional policies remain two separate realms whose integration is far from satisfactory. Apart from responding to political trends, which fluctuate with national and electoral cycles, this detachment is also a result of institutional and governance culture. As long as the civic culture surrounding spatial planning and territorial governance shows limited development, institutions will suffer from an unchanging governance culture, settled organisational patterns and habits.

By exploring the connections between spatial planning and operational programming within the Portuguese context, this paper aims to contribute not only to a better understanding of the impacts of EU-led policies in the domestic sphere on national policies but also to enrich the debates on the meeting between hard and versus soft planning spaces, and formal and versus informal planning.

Acknowledgments This article is funded by national funds by means of FCT—Fundação para a Ciência e a Tecnologia, under the scope of the research project SOFTPLAN Ref. n°PTDC/GES-URB/29170/2017.

References

Albrechts L (2004) Strategic (spatial) planning re-examined. Environ Plan B: Plan Des 31:743–758. https://doi.org/10.1068/b3065

Allmendinger P, Haughton G (2009) Soft spaces, fuzzy boundaries, and metagovernance: the new spatial planning in the Thames Gateway. Environ Plan A 41:617–633

Allmendinger P, Haughton G, Knieling J, Othengrafen F (2015) Soft spaces of governance in Europe: a comparative perspective. Routledge, London

Amin A (2002) Spatialities of globalisation. Environ Plan A 34:385–399. https://doi.org/10.1068/a3439

Bhome K, Waterhout B (2008) The Europeanisation of planning. In: Faludi A (ed) European spatial research and planning. Lincoln Institute of Land Policy, Cambridge, MA, pp 225–248

Campos V, Ferrão J (2015) O Ordenamento do Território em Portugal: uma Perspetiva Genealógica, ICS Working Papers, Lisboa: Instituto de Ciências Sociais. http://www.ics.ul.pt/flipping/wp2015_1/index.html#

Cavaco C (coord.) et al (2014) Avaliação do Programa de Ação 2007–2013 do Programa Nacional da Política de Ordenamento do Território. Direção-Geral do Território, Lisboa

Cavaco C (coord.) et al (2016) Habitat III—National Report Portugal. Direção-Geral do Território, Lisboa

Cavaco C (2018) Urbanismo como política pública: que mudanças de azimute? Território, Planeamento e Urbanismo. Teoria e prática 1:78–104. http://revistas.ua.pt/index.php/tpu/issue/view/398. ISSN: 2184-1802

Cavaco C, Magalhães M (2015) Avaliação do Programa de Ação do PNPOT. Territorialização, Governança e Inteligência Territorial. In: Julião R P (coord.) (2015). Informação Geográfica, Cadastro e Gestão Territorial. Experiências e boas práticas luso-brasileiras. Ed. CICS.NOVA.FCSH, Lisboa, pp 33–56

CEC (Commission of the European Communities) (1997) The EU Compendium of spatial planning systems and policies. European Commission: Office for Official Publications of the European Communities, Luxembourg

Costa JP, Cavaco C (2017) A revisão dos PDM's de primeira geração. In: Costa JP (ed) Pensar a Cidade, 2005–2015. A crítica da crítica. Caleidoscópio, Lisboa, pp 94–95

Dühr S, Nadin V (2007) Europeanisation through transnational territorial cooperation? The case of INTERREG IIIB North-West Europe. Plan Pract Res 22(3):373–394. https://doi.org/10.1080/02697450701666738

Dühr S, Stead D, Zonneveld W (2007) The Europeanisation of spatial planning through territorial cooperation. Plan Pract Res 22(3):291–307. https://doi.org/10.1080/02697450701688245

Dusza K (1989) Max Weber's Conception of the State. Int J Polit., Cult Soc 3(1):71–105

ESPON TANGO (2013) Territorial approaches for new governance. Final Report, ESPON Coordination Unit, Luxembourg

Estratégia Integrada de Desenvolvimento Territorial da Área Metropolitana de Lisboa, 2014–2020 (2015) Área Metropolitana de Lisboa, Augusto Mateus & Associados, Lisboa. Online: http://www.am-lisboa.pt/documentos/1518970305A2fNI7cy4Ku53CX9.pdf

European Commission (2014a) Integrated Territorial Investments Europa, 2014. Online: http://ec.europa.eu/regional_policy/sources/docgener/informat/2014/iti_en.pdf. Accessed 4 Nov 2017. https://doi.org/10.2776/56347

European Commission (2014b) Community-Led Local Development—Europa, 2014. Online: http://ec.europa.eu/regional_policy/sources/docgener/informat/2014/community_en.pdf. Accessed 4 Nov 2017. https://doi.org/10.2776/2575

European Commission (2014c) Integrated Sustainable Urban Development—Europa, 2014. Online: http://ec.europa.eu/regional_policy/sources/docgener/informat/2014/urban_en.pdf. Accessed 5 Nov 2017. https://doi.org/10.2776/47320

European Commission (2016) Guidance for Member States on Integrated Sustainable Urban Development—Europa, 2016 Online: http://ec.europa.eu/regional_policy/sources/docgener/informat/2014/guidance_sustainable_urban_development_en.pdf. Accessed 5 Nov 2017

Faludi A (2013) Territorial cohesion, territorialism, territoriality, and soft planning: a critical review. Environ Plan A 45:1302–1317

Faludi A (2014) EUropeanisation or Europeanisation of spatial planning? Plan Theory Pract 15(2):155–169

Ferrão J (2011) Ordenamento do Território como Política Pública. Fundação Calouste Gulbenkian, Lisboa, 1st Edition (2011), 2nd Edition (2014)

Ferrão J (2016) O Território na Constituição da República Portuguesa (1976–2005). Dos preceitos fundadores às políticas de território do futuro. Sociologia, problemas e práticas, número especial: 123–134. https://doi.org/10.7458/spp2016ne10353

Ferrão J, Mourato JM, Balula L, Bina O (2013) Functional Regions, Urban-Rural Relations and Post 2013 Cohesion Policy. OBSERVA – Observatório de Ambiente e Sociedade, Estudo 29. Instituto de Ciências Sociais, Lisboa

Galland D (2012) Understanding the reorientations and roles of spatial planning: the case of National Planning Policy in Denmark. Eur Plan Stud 20(8):1359–1392

Galland D, Elinbaum P (2015) Redefining territorial scales and the strategic role of spatial planning. Evidence from Denmark and Catalonia. disP—The Plan Rev 51(4):66–85. https://doi.org/10.1080/02513625.2015.1134963

Giannakourou G (2005) Transforming spatial planning policy in Mediterranean countries: Europeanization and domestic change. Eur Plan Stud 13(2):320–331. https://doi.org/10.1080/0365431042000321857

Gualini E (2003) Cross-border governance: inventing regions in a trans-national multi-level polity. disP—The Plan Rev 39(152): 43–52. https://doi.org/10.1080/02513625.2003.10556833

Haughton G, Allmendinger P (2007) Soft spaces. Plan Town Ctry Plan 76(9):306–308

Haughton G, Counsell D (2004) Regions and sustainable development: regional planning matters. The Geogr J 170(2):135–145

Haughton G, Allmendinger P, Counsell D, Vigar G (2010) The new spatial planning. Territorial management with soft spaces and fuzzy boundaries. Routledge

Keating M (2008) A quarter century of the Europe of the Regions. Reg Federal Stud 18(5):629–635. https://doi.org/10.1080/13597560802351630

Knieling J, Othengrafen F (2015) Planning culture—a concept to explain the evolution of planning policies and processes in Europe? Eur Plan Stud 23(11):2133–2147. https://doi.org/10.1080/09654313.2015.1018404

Luukkonen J, Moilanen H (2012) Territoriality in the strategies and practices of the territorial cohesion policy of the European Union: territorial challenges in implementing "soft planning". Eur Plan Stud 20(3):481–500

Macleod G, Goodwin M (1999) Space, scale and state strategy: rethinking urban and regional governance. Prog Hum Geogr 23(4):503–527

Medeiros E (2016) Is there a rise of the territorial dimension in the EU Cohesion Policy? Finisterra, LI 103:89–112. https://doi.org/10.18055/Finis7940

Mourato J, Rosa Pires A (2007) Portugal e a perspectiva de desenvolvimento do espaço Europeu: o EDEC como institucionalização de um discruso de mudança. In Sociedade e Território. Revista de Estudos Urbanos e Regionais 40:34–43

Mourato J, Vasconcelos L, Farrall H (2015) Building governance: conflict as a driver for policy learning in Portugal. In: Gualini E, Mourato J, Allegra M (eds) Conflict in the city. Contested Urban Spaces and Local Democracy. Jovis Verlag GmbH, pp 266–281

Nadin V (2007) The emergence of the spatial planning approach in England. Plan, Pract Res 22(1):43–62. https://doi.org/10.1080/02697450701455934

Nadin V, Stead D (2008) European spatial planning systems, social models and learning. disP—The Plan Rev 44(172):35–47. https://doi.org/10.1080/02513625.2008.10557001

Newman P, Thorney A (1996) Urban planning in Europe. International competition, national systems and planning projects. Routledge, London and New York

PEDU – Plano Estratégico de Desenvolvimento Urbano do Município de Lisboa (2015) Câmara Municipal de Lisboa, Lisboa. Online: http://www.cm-lisboa.pt/viver/urbanismo/plano-estrategico-de-desenvolvimento-urbano/pedu-documentacao

Perkmann M (2007) Construction of new territorial scales: a framework and case study of the EUREGIO Cross-border Region. Reg Stud 41(2):253–266. https://doi.org/10.1080/00343400600990517

Plano Diretor Municipal de Lisboa (2012) Câmara Municipal de Lisboa, Lisboa. Online: http://www.cm-lisboa.pt/viver/urbanismo/planeamento-urbano/plano-diretor-municipal

Programa Nacional da Política de Ordenamento do Território (2007) Diário da República, Lei nº58/2007, de 4 de setembro de 2007

Purkarthofer E (2016) When soft planning and hard planning meet: conceptualising the encounter of European, national and sub-national planning. Eur J Spat Dev 61

Roodbol-Mekkes P, Brink A (2015) Rescaling spatial planning: spatial planning reforms in Denmark, England, and the Netherlands. Environ Plan C: Gov Policy 33:184–198. https://doi.org/10.1068/c12134

Rosa Pires A (2005) The Fragile Foundations of European Spatial Planning in Portugal. Eur Plan Stud 13(2):237–252. https://doi.org/10.1080/0965431042000321802

Sousa L (2013) Understanding European cross-border cooperation: a framework for analysis. J Eur Integr 35(6):669–687. https://doi.org/10.1080/07036337.2012.711827

Stead D (2014) European integration and spatial rescaling in the Baltic Region: soft spaces, soft planning and soft security. Eur Plan Stud 22(4):680–693

Swygedoun E (2000) Authoritarian governance, power, and the politics of rescaling. Environ Plan D: Soc Space 18:63–76. https://doi.org/10.1068/d9s

Tasan-Kok T, Vranken J (2011) Multilevel urban governance. Handbook: theory and practice. European Urban Knowledge Network, Amsterdam

Thoidou E (2011) The territorial approach to EU Cohesion Policy: current issues and evidence from Greece. SPATIUM Int Rev 25:7–13. https://doi.org/10.2298/SPAT1125007T

Vitorino A (2010) Abordagens Integradas de Base Territorial. Relatório Final, Observatório do QREN

Governance Rescaling in Danish Spatial Planning: State Spaces Between Fixity and Fluidity

8

Daniel Galland

Abstract

This chapter examines governance rescaling processes in the context of Danish spatial planning over the past decade. It contends that the spatial planning system in Denmark has the capacity to redefine and reinterpret conventional territorial scales through the parallel adoption and articulation of legal planning instruments and spatial planning strategies. The recent evolution of spatial planning in this Nordic perspective is indicative of planning systems that have moved away from hierarchical approaches to structuring territory, towards a multifaceted, iterative and more open understanding of planning as an evolving political process. In this context, strategic spatial planning assumes a key role in linking an increasingly fragmented legal framework. Strategic spatial planning transcends former generic and static planning scales, generating new spaces of engagement. The appraisal of legal planning instruments and spatial strategies, as well as the evolving redefinition of territorial scales in Denmark, suggests that the conventional, hierarchical and cascade-style ideal of policy implementation has been superseded. However, the Danish case is also illustrative of spatial planning systems retaining the vertical spatial anchor, as a means of ensuring the stability and permanence that the previous hierarchical power structures offered.

Keywords

Spatial planning • Governance rescaling • Planning system • Municipal reform • Strategic spatial selectivity

8.1 Introduction

The past two decades have witnessed several fluctuations in how well spatial planning systems shape spatial development processes. In Europe, most planning systems have traditionally involved discrete, permanent and fixed scales, conventionally depicted as nested hierarchies, which conflict with spatial transformation processes. Ongoing territorial integration, however, demands reconsideration of spatial mismatches between the boundaries of administrative jurisdictions and the rather fluid territories of functional regions. To understand the implications of governance rescaling, as well as the increasing differentiation of spatial planning roles across administrative levels and spatial scales, the reasons for the evolving concepts of scale as well as representations of space in spatial plans and strategies in Western European nation states require constant review. In this respect, it is worth delving into how fixed, cascade-style spatial planning systems evoking a capillary form of power (Foucault 1975) can be reinterpreted to cope with current territorial dynamics. This approach evolves from the premise that hierarchical planning systems rely on conventional territorial scales which, through routine and bureaucracy, turn into relatively enduring and hegemonic structures for certain periods of time (Foucault 2004). However, recognising that territorial scales are actually fluid, it is worth exploring the relationship between spatial planning strategies, land-use planning instruments and regulatory planning tools.

D. Galland (✉)
Department of Urban and Regional Planning, Norwegian University of Life Sciences, 1430 Ås, Norway
e-mail: daniel.galland@nmbu.no

© Springer Nature Switzerland AG 2020
V. Lingua and V. Balz (eds.), *Shaping Regional Futures*,
https://doi.org/10.1007/978-3-030-23573-4_8

In Denmark, spatial planning and governance have undergone significant reorientations over the course of the past two decades (Galland 2012a, b; Grange 2012, 2014; Olesen and Richardson 2012; Galland and Enemark 2015). Danish spatial planning historically held a comprehensive-integrated character (Commission of the European Communities 1997), an appeal generally attributed to mature planning systems seeking to achieve institutional harmonisation and territorial synchrony (Hajer 2003). In 2007, however, a liberal-conservative coalition government implemented a local government reform which transformed the political geography of Denmark and its existing intergovernmental arrangements. The reform merged 275 municipalities into 98 larger units, abolished a total of 14 counties and created five administrative regions. Just as this implied a considerable redistribution of responsibilities between three levels of government, it similarly changed the comprehensive-integrated rationale associated with the Danish planning system. The latter consequently underwent a series of radical shifts, most notably reflected in governance rescaling processes, and triggered by the changing roles of policy institutions and policy instruments in catering for growth and development. In synthesis, these reorientations comprised: (i) the downward rescaling (from regional to municipal levels) of most spatial planning tasks and responsibilities; (ii) the upward rescaling (from regional to national level) of spatial planning functions associated with the Greater Copenhagen Region; and (iii) the revocation of regional planning as well as the abolition of the Metropolitan Council of Copenhagen.

In contributing to ongoing debates about contemporary governance rescaling, this chapter contends that Danish spatial planning has a tendency to redefine and reinterpret conventional territorial scales through the dual adoption and articulation of legal instruments and spatial strategies. In so doing, it examines the role of each level of planning while also revealing how territorial scales get redefined as a result of changing political objectives and spatial relationships between planning levels. This assessment of legal instruments and spatial strategies, as well as the consequent redefinition of territorial scales in Denmark, suggests that the principle of framework control, which is reminiscent of a hierarchical approach to policy implementation, has been displaced. While the Danish spatial planning system might partly converge with other European counterparts, the spatial implications stemming from governance rescaling show that despite a dilution at regional level, the vertical spatial anchor associated with planning systems is retained by government for the stability and permanence of power structures.

The chapter is structured as follows. Firstly, it presents a theoretical overview that addresses the treatment of scale and the fluctuating roles of spatial planning. This is based on the transition from physical, land-use planning to strategic spatial planning. Secondly, it provides an overview of the recent reorientations of the Danish planning system, addressing its legal tradition, principles and objectives, policies, plans and spatial scales. Thirdly, it examines the roles of legal planning instruments and spatial strategies, as well as their linkage across different levels of government. Finally, based on this assessment, it offers an interpretation of the redefined territorial scales, highlighting a series of planning implications.

8.2 Theoretical Contexts to Understand Governance Rescaling in Spatial Planning

8.2.1 Scalar Structuration

Geographical scales are constantly subject to scalar structuration processes of state spatiality (Brenner 2001). The (re) structuration of territorial scales occurs whenever specific socio-spatial processes (e.g. state regulation) become differentiated into a vertical hierarchy of interdependent geographical scales (i.e. spatial units) (ibid., p. 604). Such processes, as Herod (2011, pp. xv–xvi) puts it, '...*often crystallise into fairly long-standing 'scalar fixes' [therefore] scales are always in a process of becoming and there is always tension between tendencies towards stabilisation and those towards destabilisation*'. While in practice scalar arrangements are intrinsically fluid, they are also constantly standardised into apparently stable organisational structures for certain periods of time. By their own transitory nature, scalar configurations are continually reproduced through political processes such as spatial planning (Marston et al. 2005), a policy domain where roles and capacities are set to fluctuate during the shaping and reshaping of spatial development (e.g. Galland and Enemark 2015). In doing so, the nested hierarchies (i.e. urban, municipal, regional and national) which embody discrete, permanent and fixed scales upon which conventional spatial planning systems are conceived, relentlessly contradict the inevitable processes of scalar restructuration. Territorial management strategies thereby continually demand a reassessment of the spatial mismatches that persistently arise between the fixed, demarcated boundaries of nation states' administrative jurisdictions and the rather fluid, dynamic and functional territories that transcend these categorical borders (e.g. Keating 2009).

Swyngedouw (2004, p. 26) argues that scalar configurations emerge as outcomes of '... *socio-spatial processes that regulate or organise social power relations, (...) such as the process of state devolution or decentralisation*'. In spatial planning, the original concept of scale is tied to the idea that national territories require territorial synchrony to provide functional unity, spatial coordination and structural coherence (Hajer 2003), given that public policies are intrinsically flawed and inconsistent. This hierarchical version of scale in spatial planning is aligned with the dominant notion of scale that Marston et al. (2005, pp. 416–17) defined as '*…a nested hierarchy of differentially sized and bounded spaces.*'

This positivist and rigid notion of scale, along with its assumed degree of permanence, have become challenged by a relational, more temporary concept of scale. Scale per se is relationally conceived as a geographical area within which certain socio-spatial processes become temporarily fixed at any given time. In this sense, according to Swyngedouw (2004, p. 33) scalar configurations would refer to either regulatory orders or networks, '*…an outcome of the perpetual movement of the flux of socio-spatial dynamics*'. This condition implies constant tension between the two types of scalar configurations: institutionalised territorial compromises versus de-territorialisation and re-territorialisation processes (ibid.).

Forms of territorial organisation are created through a scale division of politics and expressed in terms of spatial qualifiers (i.e. local, regional, national) (Cox 1998, p. 20). Governance rescaling relates to the social construction of political scales, for '*…it is geographical scale that defines the boundaries and bounds the identities around which control is exerted and contested*' (Smith 1992, p. 66). The complexity of these political forces can be perceived via 'scale jumping' processes (Smith 1984), whereby political claims established at one geographical scale are expanded to another.

8.2.2 State Spatial Selectivity

State spatial selectivity occurs both vertically and horizontally. When governments act through spatial planning levels, not only do they exclude or jump specific scales but they also tend to disregard actors within those levels. This is particularly evident at subnational levels, where discontinuous maps of political affiliations are superimposed onto existing municipal and regional jurisdictions. Such erratic maps bind the different administrative levels while enabling the transference of vertical directives. The power-asymmetrical nature of nested scalar relations is clearly conceived vertically (Leitner and Miller 2007), yet it can also manifest horizontally, for example in city-regions where urban municipalities attempt to include neighbouring (rural) municipalities in the process of redefining their own territorial structure.

Through an examination of governance rescaling in Danish spatial planning, this chapter will reveal how vertical and hierarchical spatial planning systems conceal entry points into politics, and how national governments tend to use such systems in privileged ways. While it is acknowledged that nested scales associated with spatial planning systems delimit agency as a result of their structure (Marston et al. 2005), this chapter will not consider a flat ontology in relation to scales. Instead, it will refer to conventional scales as spatial qualifiers of the state's territorial organisation, for the purpose of clarifying how spatial selectivity operates in the planning arena. Considering the vertical structure of institutional planning levels, the chapter will further argue that policies are also implemented horizontally, in a discretionary manner within the indeterminate spaces of law and policy.

From the administrative perspective of Danish spatial planning, four territorial scales have historically existed, as shown by the content and scope of ad hoc types of plans. The first of these, national spatial planning strategies, defines the character of national policies and is often centred on the need to attain territorial balance. Since the 1990s, national planning has addressed a range of sectoral issues, often related to European planning directives, including for instance water resources plans, climate plans, transport plans and Natura 2000. From inception until recently regional plans (the second scale) were binding land-use-based instruments that comprised the means to implement national planning objectives. They did this by integrating spatial development policy issues, such as the definition of urban hierarchical patterns with respect to service provision and infrastructure development, public transport, siting of conflicting activities, location of large retail areas and so forth. Regional plans were also a conciliatory tool to balance sectoral considerations. Municipal plans (the third scale) have a binding character and specify the action framework for guiding urban and rural transformation. The municipal plan is the main political instrument for development control and serves as a strategy for social and economic development as well as environmental improvement. Finally, local plans address zoning schemes and the classification of different urban areas in terms of land uses and building types and regulations.

To understand rescaling implications, as well as the increasing differentiation of spatial planning roles across administrative levels and spatial scales, there is a continued need to review the drivers behind the evolving concepts of scale and space used in spatial plans and strategies. In the Danish context, the key issue is how a hierarchical and fixed spatial planning system, which in principle conceives territorial scales rather statically, can be reinterpreted to cope with current territorial dynamics, using spatial strategies. This leads to the question of how territorial scales can be redefined when the spatial planning policies and practices across different levels of planning administration are themselves in flux.

8.2.3 Spatial Planning Reorientations and Strategic Spatial Selectivity: The Co-existence of Land-Use Planning and Strategic Spatial Planning

A canon of literature has long established that spatial planning, as a policy and organisational field, has been subject to continuous reorientation. The most general claim is that spatial planning has moved away from its regulatory and land-use oriented focus towards a more strategic role (Healey et al. 1997; Salet and Faludi 2000; Albrechts et al. 2003; Albrechts 2004, 2006). Until the late 1980s, spatial plans prepared at different levels of planning administration centred on Euclidean concepts (Friedmann 1993) such as central-place hierarchies, urban settlement patterns, physical proximity or commuting patterns between cities. As argued by Healey (2004), this positivist view of space as a primary social ordering principle (Graham and Healey 1999) has been challenged. With the emergence of relational concepts, endorsed by the spatial relations between territories through strategic spatial planning episodes (Healey 2006, 2007; Davoudi and Strange 2009), strategic spatial plans are prepared based on spatial concepts (Priemus and Zonneveld 2003; e.g. van Duinen 2004; Zonneveld 2005) which treat territorial scales more fluidly. As argued by Davoudi (2012), the conception of a spatial and scalar order moves away from the positivist tradition that seeks to '...*tame space and create order*' (p. 432), towards an interpretive tradition where both scale and space are regarded '...*as socially constructed with contingent boundaries which are constantly territorialised and open to political contestation*' (pp. 432–433).

The revival of strategic spatial planning (Salet and Faludi 2000) during the 1990s, and its evolution in Europe to date, requires that the planning domain augments its focus on projects and land-use regulation (Albrechts 2001) with an emphasis on place-making based on relational decision-making processes (Healey 2007). Despite the rigid, cascade-like hierarchy of spatial planning systems, the renewed attention on place highlights the formation of horizontal networks of actors as an important means to influence territorial transformations (ibid.). While this reorientation of governance has been most evident in fostering competitive cities and city-regions, particularly in settings where territorial relationships are characterised by complex urban and regional dynamics, it has a wide reach extending from local to national levels of planning administration.

One implication arising from this is that strategic spatial planning has become discretionary, in that its aim is to link (strategic) objectives with spatial policies. With planning playing a strategic role, national governments enable themselves to move freely within spatial planning systems in pursuit of their own particular interests (e.g. accelerating ad hoc spatial development processes). In this respect, strategic spatial planning interventions emphasise the principle of subsidiarity within spatial planning. At the same time, strategic spatial planning does not deal with particular land-use content in the way that comprehensive-integrated spatial planning systems do. In contrast with forms of regulatory and master planning, strategic spatial planning is negotiated by multiple actors attempting to shape spatial development. Scales thereby shift from being 'hard-edged' containers into rather flexible and less-defined spaces. In complementing 'hard', regulatory spaces of planning, 'soft spaces' emerge as arenas that bring different policy actors together to rework 'the real geographies of development' (Allmendinger and Haughton 2009). So-called soft spaces hence result from the need to attain effective policy delivery and policy integration (ibid.).

In synthesis, what is then strategic about spatial planning and how does this relate to the steering role of nation states? As Jessop (1990) contends, instead of losing their capacities as a result of their 'hollowing out' evolution, nation states maintain a fixed steering role implemented through strategic selectivity (p. 260). In this way, the state retains an inherent capacity to decide which specific actors or institutional arrangements to favour in terms of devolving powers and allocating resources. The power-laden nature of strategic selectivity can also encompass aspects of spatiality. As such, spatial selectivity would then refer to the scales, locations and spaces that the state may or may not favour in local state restructuring (Jones 1997). It is precisely through spatiality that the selectivity debate turns out to be most relevant when analysing the changing character of spatial planning. As Jones (ibid., p. 831) puts it, '*[s]patial selectivity implies that the state has a tendency to privilege certain places through accumulation strategies, state projects, and hegemonic projects*'.

Building on the notions of strategic selectivity and spatial selectivity, Brenner (2004) advances the idea of 'state spatial selectivity'. Reorientations in the institutional setup of spatial planning can thus be understood in terms of state spatial projects and strategies as 'selectivities', that is, spaces supported by spatial strategies and urban regulation: '...*(state spatial) selectivities emerge and are continually modified as inherited formations of state spatial organization interact with emergent political strategies oriented towards the creation of new geographies of state policy and political economic life*' (Brenner 2004, p. 456).

By applying a strategic-relational approach to state spatiality, Brenner (2003) contends that state spatial projects are characterised by initiatives aimed at providing functional unity, operational coordination and organisational coherence. Such projects may include programmes to modify the geographical structure of intergovernmental arrangements (e.g. changing administrative boundaries) or reconfigure their rules of operation (via processes of centralisation and decentralisation). On the other hand, state spatial strategies are mobilised through diverse policy instruments, including economic development initiatives, industry policies, infrastructure investments, spatial planning programmes, labour market policies, regional policies and so forth. In line with Brenner's theory (2003, 2004), state spatial projects have evolved since the time of Keynesian welfarism, from being centralised and administratively uniform towards decentralised and administratively customised. Similarly, state spatial strategies have evolved from being implemented by a single scale promoting socio-economic activities across national territories, towards being executed by multiple scales concentrating socio-economic development at specific locations. Brenner argues that territorialisation (i.e. the re-configuration and rescaling of forms of territorial organisation such as cities and states) constitutes an intrinsic moment of the current round of globalisation (Brenner 1999, p. 442).

The rest of this chapter explores the recent evolution of spatial planning in Denmark in the context of governance rescaling as outlined in this section.

8.3 Danish Spatial Planning in the Context of Governance Rescaling

8.3.1 Scalar Restructuration: Downward and Upward Rescaling of Spatial Planning Tasks and Responsibilities

Historically, Denmark belonged to the 'comprehensive-integrated' tradition of spatial planning and policies, which explicitly sought to deliver a degree of horizontal coordination and vertical integration of spatial policies, across sectors and jurisdictions, respectively (Commission of the European Communities 1997). The rationale behind this tradition is illustrated by a hierarchy of plans put forward by nested levels of planning administration, from national to local. Plans at lower levels cannot transgress the objectives pursued by plans at higher levels (the principle of framework control). This tradition in Denmark originated in response to the significant socio-spatial challenges prompted by industrial development and the rapid economic growth of the post-Second World War era. A first municipal reform, implemented during the early 1970s, essentially reorganised the territory in pursuit of tackling spatial inequality and demographic imbalance. The aim of this state spatial project was to attain territorial synchrony while providing functional unity, spatial coordination and coherence across the whole national territory. This hierarchical logic combined with the spatial planning system at the time boded well for the welfarist, social-democratic pursuit of socio-spatial equality.

In 1992, however, the Danish Planning Act merged several planning laws adopted during the 1970s, marking a significant reorientation in Danish spatial planning. The first section of the act substituted the fundamental objective of spatial planning, namely to attain equal development throughout the whole territory, with the rather imprecise pursuit to accomplish '... *appropriate development in the whole country and in the individual counties and municipalities, based on overall planning and economic considerations*' (Ministry of the Environment 1992). The development-led focus of Danish spatial planning had already begun to shift in the late 1980s prompted by liberal political ideology. In 1989, a national planning report titled '*The Danish regional picture now and in the future*' stressed the need to attain more geographical differentiation (Ministry of the Environment 1989), which implied the localisation of economic growth. Selectively mobilised via state spatial strategies and development initiatives during the 1990s, this perceived demand was localised in the form of large infrastructure investments implemented in Copenhagen (Ministry of the Environment 1992; Ministry of the Environment and Energy 1997, 2000a, b). In this light, the Danish government responded to globalisation demands with strategies promoting economic recentralisation and spatial differentiation (ibid.). The promotion of Greater Copenhagen as an international metropolis and gateway to Scandinavia was similarly portrayed by commentators as a shift towards neo-elitist, market-driven city entrepreneurism (Andersen and Pløger 2007).

In 2007, a liberal-conservative coalition government implemented a new state spatial project which transformed the political geography of Denmark and its existing intergovernmental arrangements (Fig. 8.1). This project broke away from the comprehensive-integrated logic associated with Danish spatial planning, most notably resulting in governance rescaling outcomes such as changed roles of policy institutions and the creation of new policy instruments. Driven by economies of scale in pursuit of greater efficiency and managerial effectiveness, the territorial and administrative restructuration simultaneously prompted the downward and upward rescaling of spatial planning tasks and responsibilities to municipal and national levels, respectively. The reform altered the Danish planning system from its traditional multi-tier configuration to a double-tier structure. This rescaling of planning tasks as responsibilities could even be regarded as a 'centralised-decentralisation' or a recentralisation of government (Andersen 2008). Firstly, the decentralisation aspect entailed giving privileges to municipalities through the downward rescaling of spatial planning tasks and responsibilities. In doing so, the reform repealed regional land-use planning provisions and conceded to the municipal level the right to undertake, and decide upon, land-use

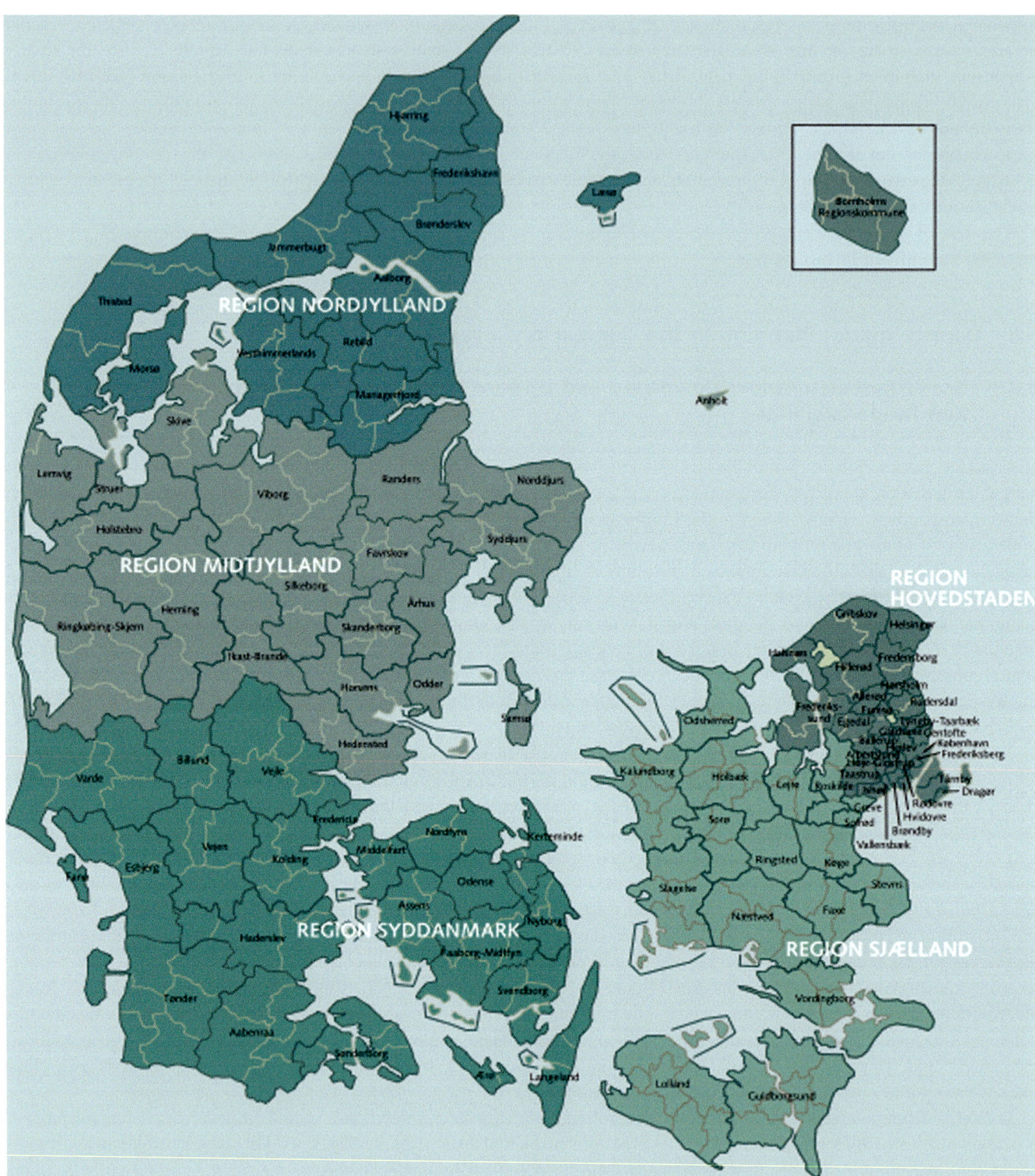

Fig. 8.1 The Map of Denmark displaying political administrative divisions since the implementation of the 2007 structural reform, which yielded a total of 98 new municipalities (grey borders) and 5 administrative regions (black borders). Local Government Denmark, Danish Regions and Ministry of the Interior and Social Affairs (2009)

planning in urban and rural areas. The Planning Act thereby provided municipalities with the autonomy to designate urban zones, locate transport facilities and manage aspects concerned with agriculture, cultural and historical heritage. Secondly, the centralisation aspect entailed assigning new planning controls to the national level (e.g. the right to veto municipal planning proposals and projects of national/regional relevance) as well as upwardly rescaling the land-use planning tasks and responsibilities of the 34 municipalities that comprise the Greater Copenhagen Region.

The abolition of the county level was 'filled-in' by the formation of five administrative regions, which were mainly created for healthcare management and, to a lesser extent, to cater to regional development rather than doing regional planning per se (Galland 2012a). Regional statutory land-use plans had formerly been imperative, not only as a binding instrument for municipal plans, but also as a conciliatory tool to balance sectoral considerations (e.g. traffic services, i.e. harbours, railways and roads; the siting of large-scale facilities, i.e. solid-waste treatment plants, sewage disposal sites, windmill parks). This series of institutional and policy shifts are a clear indication of the relaxation of the principle of framework control, a model with decreased harmonisation and coherence between plans and policies at different administrative levels of planning (Galland and Enemark 2013, 2015). The overall implications concerning the restructuration of Danish spatial planning were to affect the role that each level of planning administration would eventually come to play, but also how territorial scales have been redefined (Galland and Elinbaum 2015). These implications are described further below.

8.3.2 The Evolution of Spatial Strategies and Legal Instruments

The transition away from a comprehensive-integrated system before and after the reform gradually resulted in a combination of spatial strategies and legally binding policy instruments prepared at different planning levels. While all three planning levels prepare strategies that differ in scope, land-use planning instruments are only used by national and municipal levels (see Tables 8.1 and 8.2). National planning reports set out overall spatial policies and objectives after each government

Table 8.1 The Danish spatial planning framework

Policy institutions		Policy instruments		
Level	Planning authority	Type of instrument	Description	Legal effect
National (Planning Act)	Ministry of Business (Danish Business Authority)	National planning report	National visions for (strategic) spatial development	Indicative guidelines and recommendations
		Overview of national interests on municipal planning	National interests from legislation, sector plans and agreements between national authorities	Binding for local authorities. Right to veto municipal plan proposals when contradicting national interests
		National planning directives	Legal provisions (i.e. coastal zone planning; retail planning; siting for wind turbines; location of natural gas pipelines and transmission lines)	Binding for local authorities
		Sectoral plans	Water resource plans and Natura 2000 Plans	Binding for local authorities
Regional (Business Development Act)	Administrative Regions	RGDSs—Regional growth and development strategies	Strategic planning for the (economic) development of each administrative region	Indicative strategies
		Regional Raw Materials Plans		Binding for local authorities
Metropolitan (Finger Plan Directive)	Ministry of Business (Danish Business Authority)	Greater Copenhagen Finger Plan Directive	Spatial development framework of the metropolitan region according to spatial principles and land-use concepts	Binding for 34 local authorities that form the metropolitan area
Local (Planning Act)	Municipal Councils	Municipal (strategic) plans	Strategic development policies	Indicative spatial plans
		Municipal (land-use) plans	Land-use regulations	Binding for local authorities
		Local (land-use) plans	Detailed legal land-use regulations	Binding for landowners

Table 8.2 Redefinition of territorial scales in Denmark

Territorial scales	Scope (redefinition)
National	Between hierarchical and relational conceptions – From rational positivist to relational spatial logics – From hierarchical central places to strategic spatial concepts exhibiting a relational character
Regional	Between hard bounded and soft spaces – From regional land-use planning to the promotion of growth-oriented initiatives to stimulate bottom-up governance arrangements in pursuit of business development
Metropolitan	– Return to a rational positivist logic based on the re-enforcement of physical planning principles (proximity-to-station principle and principle of green wedges)
Municipal	– From central places to territorial network dynamics where medium and small-sized cities and towns play different roles within the larger (merged) municipalities – The 'urban' scale is also redefined and broadened from local to (city) regional

election and focus on providing advisory guidance and recommendations to lower levels, often through the use of varying spatial concepts. The developments associated with these reports have historically entailed different treatments of scale, implying that national planning adopts distinctive roles in fostering spatial development (Galland 2012b; Galland and Enemark 2015). During the 1990s and early 2000s, such reports were influenced by spatial concepts drawn from the European Spatial Development Perspective (ESDP) (Committee for Spatial Development 1999), among them *polycentricity*, *balanced spatial structure*, *urban networks* and *dynamic zones of integration*. These yielded different interpretations of the national scale (see next section). Altogether, several political and economic driving forces accounted for the shift towards strategic spatial planning at the time, including the government's competitiveness agenda, the widening of economic relations and the restructuring of production relations (taking into account the need for Danish cities to acquire new tasks in the international division of labour). At the same time, the discourses of a trans-European spatial planning policy community evidently influenced Denmark, not only in terms of spatial restructuring within the country, but also outwardly in connection to neighbouring geographical regions.

In terms of legal planning tools, the Ministry of the Environment introduced an *Overview of National Interests on Municipal Planning* after the reform, which is nowadays the domain of the Ministry of Industry, Business and Financial Affairs (see Danish Business Authority 2018). This tool outlines government aims and requirements with respect to municipal planning, and municipalities are expected to abide by it in order to avoid a veto of their plans. Following the upward rescaling of metropolitan planning after the reform, a binding planning directive for Greater Copenhagen, first enacted in 2007 and currently in its third version (Fingerplan 2017, Fig. 8.6), established the spatial framework for the whole metropolitan region by securing future urban development in accordance with the so-called proximity-to-station principle (Danish Business Authority 2017). In contrast with other European nation states, Denmark displays a top-heaviness exerted by its metropolitan capital, Copenhagen, with circa 2 million inhabitants representing over one-third of the total population of Denmark. Planning for Greater Copenhagen has historically entailed different institutional experiments but metropolitan plans had always been indicative until the reform. In contrast with its forerunners, the binding character of the Finger Plan was to steer urban development in phases to achieve a balance between land availability, building supply and expected demand in the medium term.

As a binding directive, the Finger Plan regulates land use in the 34 municipalities that comprise Greater Copenhagen by delimiting areas for urban development, green areas, transport corridors, noise impact areas and technical installations. Accordingly, the plan divides Greater Copenhagen into four geographical zones, namely the core urban region (the palm of the hand), the peripheral urban region (the fingers), the green wedges (located between and across the urban fingers) and the rest of the urban region, where urban development is only allowed in connection with municipal centres. The Finger Plan limits municipal development ambitions but also allows municipalities to prioritise development objectives. Due to the phasing element, only certain areas will be developed over the 12-year time frame of municipal plans and, in several cases, only if political agreements are reached with respect to siting ad hoc infrastructure such as railway stations (Elinbaum and Galland 2016).

At regional level, regional spatial development plans (RSDPs) were originally advanced by the five administrative regions after the second reform. Aimed primarily at fostering economic growth in close connection with business development, the RSDPs lacked visual imagery in a strategic spatial sense. RSDPs evidently differed from the repealed regional plans and their scope did not pursue a strategic spatial orientation capable of directing spatial change. Instead, they focused on potential regional strengths, within a number of targeted sectorial areas, and were meant to ensure cohesion with sectorial plans and strategies, namely business development, employment, Local Agenda 21, and education and culture. These unprecedented plans were hindered by coalitions of actors operating beyond the scope of the formal planning system (Galland 2012a). RSDPs were revoked from the Planning Act in early 2014 and substituted by Regional Growth and Development Strategies (RGDSs) under the Business Development Act. The RGDSs primarily foster economic growth, development and employment through the alignment of stakeholders within the administrative regions.

At municipal level, the municipal plans are the main political instrument for development control and serve as a strategy for social and economic development and environmental improvement. Municipal plans integrate political development objectives, land-use guidelines and a framework for the contents of local plans for individual parts of municipal jurisdictions. They provide the linkage between national planning interests and the detailed local plans that provide land-use regulations and are drawn up for every development project. Municipal plans cannot conflict with national planning directives, including water resource plans and European directives and, in the case of the Greater Copenhagen Region, municipal plans cannot conflict with the Finger Plan directive. The more urban municipalities outside of Greater Copenhagen, such as Aarhus and Aalborg, also advance spatial development strategies often based on spatial imagery. Beyond the classical land-use planning functions and regulations, municipal strategies also cover aspects such as urban regeneration, waterfront redevelopment and strategic spatial planning for suburban areas.

8.4 Territorial Scales Redefined: State Spaces Between Fixity and Fluidity?

The national scale in Denmark has been redefined in accordance with both positivist and relational spatial logics, as well as through spatial concepts influenced by internal and external political agendas. Before the 1990s, the national scale was conceived as a space of hierarchical central places defined by urban settlement patterns. Such positivist logic contrasts with the relational logic introduced via the national planning reports prepared during the 1990s. The 1992 national planning report was the first to showcase a strategic spatial rationale through the positioning of Copenhagen and the Øresund as the leading Nordic urban region (Ministry of the Environment 1992, Fig. 8.2). This undertaking not only implied the concentration of economic capacities, infrastructure and urban development in this region, but also produced a new way of conceiving the spatial relations in the country, both inwardly and outwardly, by emphasising the comparative advantage of city networks within a competitive Europe. Subsequent national planning reports redefined the national scale according to the European Spatial Development Perspective (ESDP) concept of polycentric development to promote the development of concentric urban networks and to potentiate the existing national centres in attaining balanced development throughout the country (Ministry of the Environment and Energy 1997, 2000a, b, Fig. 8.3).

The 2006 national planning report emphasised the need to renew spatial planning as a prerequisite for strengthening Denmark's competitiveness in a global economy (Ministry of the Environment 2006). Accordingly, the national scale was strategically redefined, in line with a balanced spatial structure, and focused on promoting two metropolitan regions and a commuting region, also drawing on the ESDP's concepts. Greater Copenhagen and the Øresund Region were together portrayed as a dynamic, integrated zone in conjunction with the region of Zealand, which was depicted as a commuting hinterland with a well-functioning urban structure (Fig. 8.4). At the same time, Eastern Jutland was depicted as a growth corridor representing a functional conurbation defined by a well-connected urban structure and a coherent labour market, which altogether contributed to achieve the desired, nationally balanced spatial structure. The 2013 national planning report (Figs. 8.5 and 8.6) abandoned these notions and concentrated on promoting city-regions located along the national highway system (Ministry of the Environment 2013a, b), thereby aligning itself with the growth-oriented policy agendas pursued by other ministries. Since then, the national scale role has thus been demarcated less strategically given that neither spatial concepts nor specific spatial strategies are used to define it.

The regional scale was originally perceived in relation to the administrative level of the county, and planned accordingly in terms of land-use since the late 1970s until the mid-2000s. With the downward rescaling of regional (land-use) planning responsibilities after the second reform, regional spatial planning attempts took place in new governance spaces characterised by a fragmented landscape. Different 'filling in' processes entailed the creation of these spaces when the Ministry of the Environment advanced a series of initiatives to create partnership projects between municipal councils, regional councils and the state regarding the future development of the two metropolitan regions conceived in the national planning report (see Fig. 8.4). The intention behind promoting such plans was mainly to integrate transport challenges and urban development within the contours of these suggested functional conurbations. At the same time, promoting these initiatives also revealed the ministry's lack of faith in the new administrative regions as the suitable level at which spatial planning strategies should be formulated. Instead, new spaces of governance were advocated to stimulate bottom-up initiatives to work across policy sectors and different administrative levels.

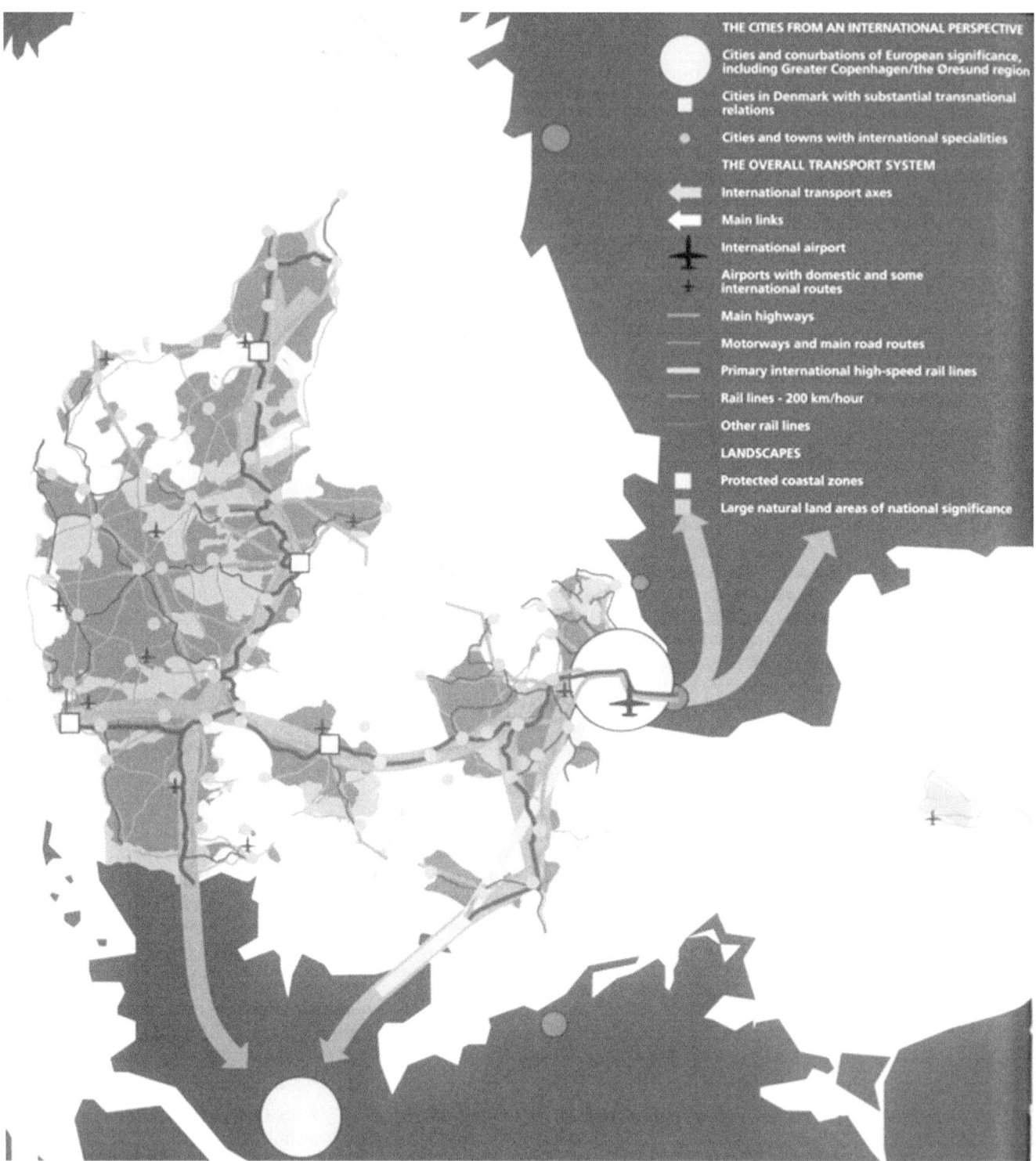

Fig. 8.2 Spatial development perspective in the 1992 national planning report 'Denmark towards the year 2018', from the Ministry of the Environment (1992)

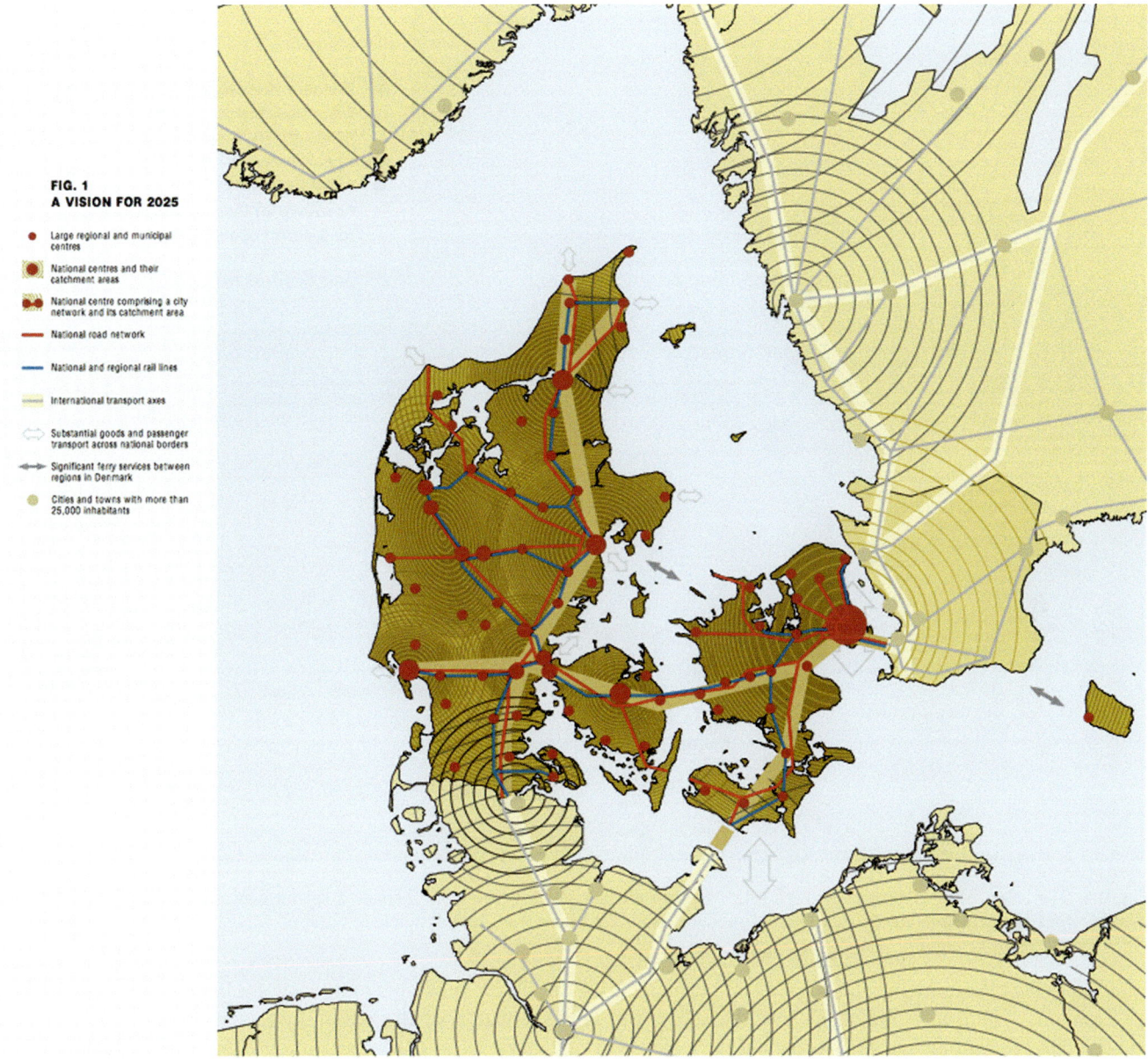

Fig. 8.3 The Map of Denmark representing European spatial agendas and discourses, from the Ministry of the Environment and Energy (2000a, b)

Administrative lightness at the scale of metropolitan regions often generates governance spaces suitable for supra-local planning. In accordance with Cox's (1998) concept of spaces of engagement, this intermediate scale introduces local actors to a new territorial regime and vision. However, the abolition of the Metropolitan Council of Greater Copenhagen (*Hovedstadens Udviklingsråd*) in 2005 and the upward rescaling of its functions and competences to the Ministry of Environment (and later the Ministry of Industry, Business and Financial Affairs) enabled national authorities to create a binding directive. Its aim was to establish a metropolitan spatial development framework, based on the enforcement of national spatial principles and concepts rooted in former positivist spatial logics (Danish Business Authority 2017). The two structural reforms in Denmark, which could be conceived as state spatial projects, have prompted the emergence, decline and even the resurgence of particular city-region planning policies and governance structures in the Greater Copenhagen Region. In view of this, the years following the first structural reform of the 1970s witnessed the creation of a metropolitan planning authority that aimed to coherently orchestrate spatial planning in times of rapid urban growth. The latest structural reform favoured a top-down strategy as a measure to regulate spatial development in Greater Copenhagen. In this latter case, the implementation of the Finger Plan directive should be understood as an upward rescaling or recentralisation, reminiscent of a

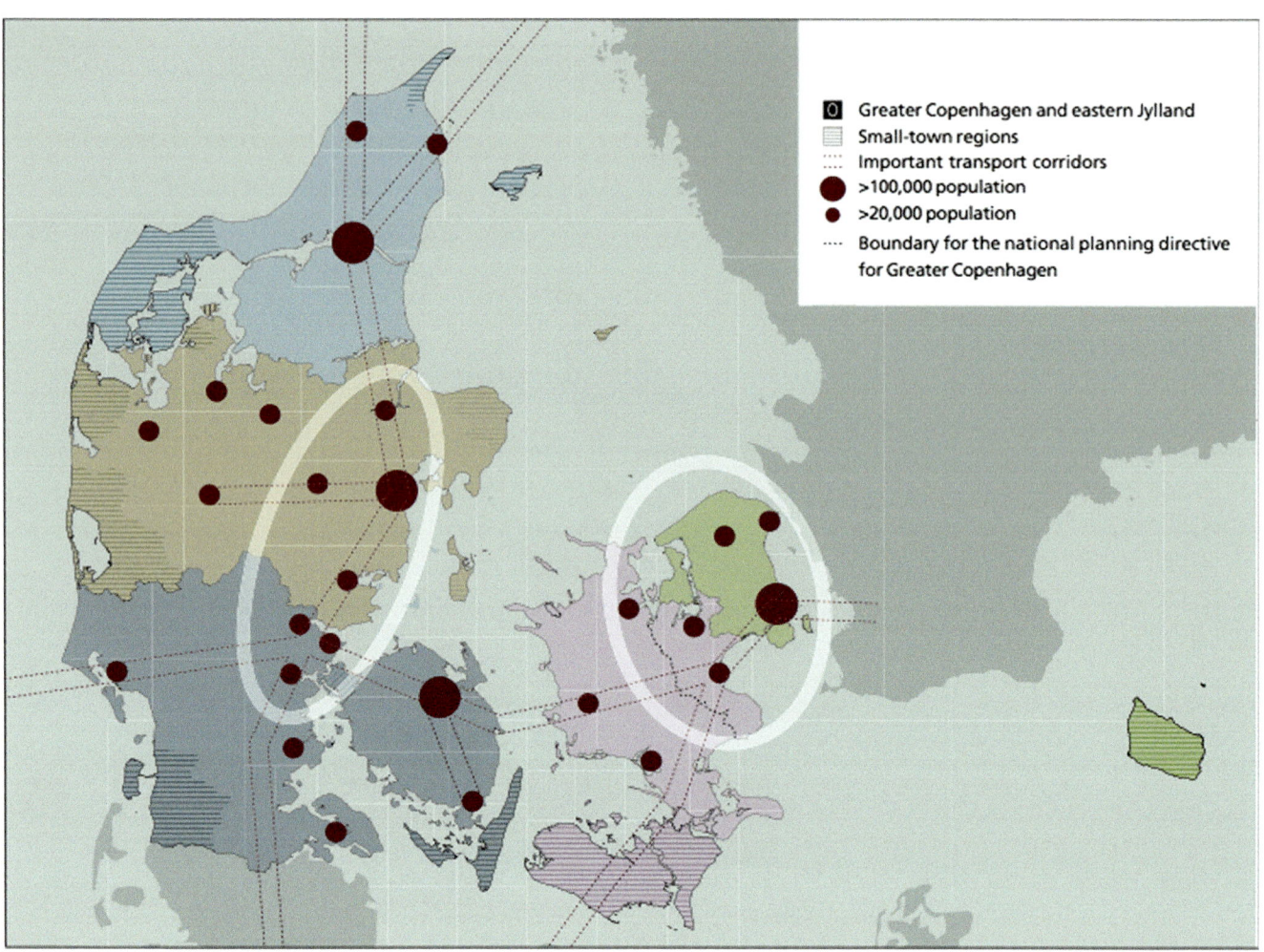

Fig. 8.4 The 'New Map of Denmark' displaying two metropolitan regions based on alternative spatial concepts, namely growth corridor, dynamic zone of integration and balanced spatial structure, from the Ministry of the Environment (2006)

solution to the classic fragmentation problem generated by a multilayer structure comprised of a large number of municipal governments within a metropolitan area. Similarly, the implementation of the proximity-to-station principle potentially implies that central municipalities benefit at the expense of peripheral ones. This scenario represents a new challenge to the future of metropolitan planning in Denmark.

Finally, the municipal scale has always been historically and geographically variable. The treatment of the urban scale in this context is relevant because of its fluctuating relationship to other scales at different times and places. Until the latest structural reform, the municipal scale in Denmark was understood in terms of a single town and its hinterland (i.e. one town —one municipality), as put forward in the 1970s. This understanding related to Christaller's central places settlement pattern, whereby the largest town in a given municipality took a central position to provide towns and villages, both within and beyond the municipality itself, with access to basic and more specialised services (Christaller 1966). As a result of structural reforms and other recent economies of scale, former municipalities in other European countries have been merged into larger administrative units. This represents a radical shift away from the idea of service provision, and the logic of hierarchical territorial positioning, towards redefining the municipal scale in terms of networked territorial dynamics whereby urban phenomena are reinterpreted based on the roles that medium and small-sized cities and towns play in municipal spatial development. In some second-tier cases, such as Aalborg and Aarhus, the interrelation between scales allows the concept of the city to be rethought, taking into consideration the current territorial dynamics whereby spatial planning enables the urban scale to be a local as well as regional concern.

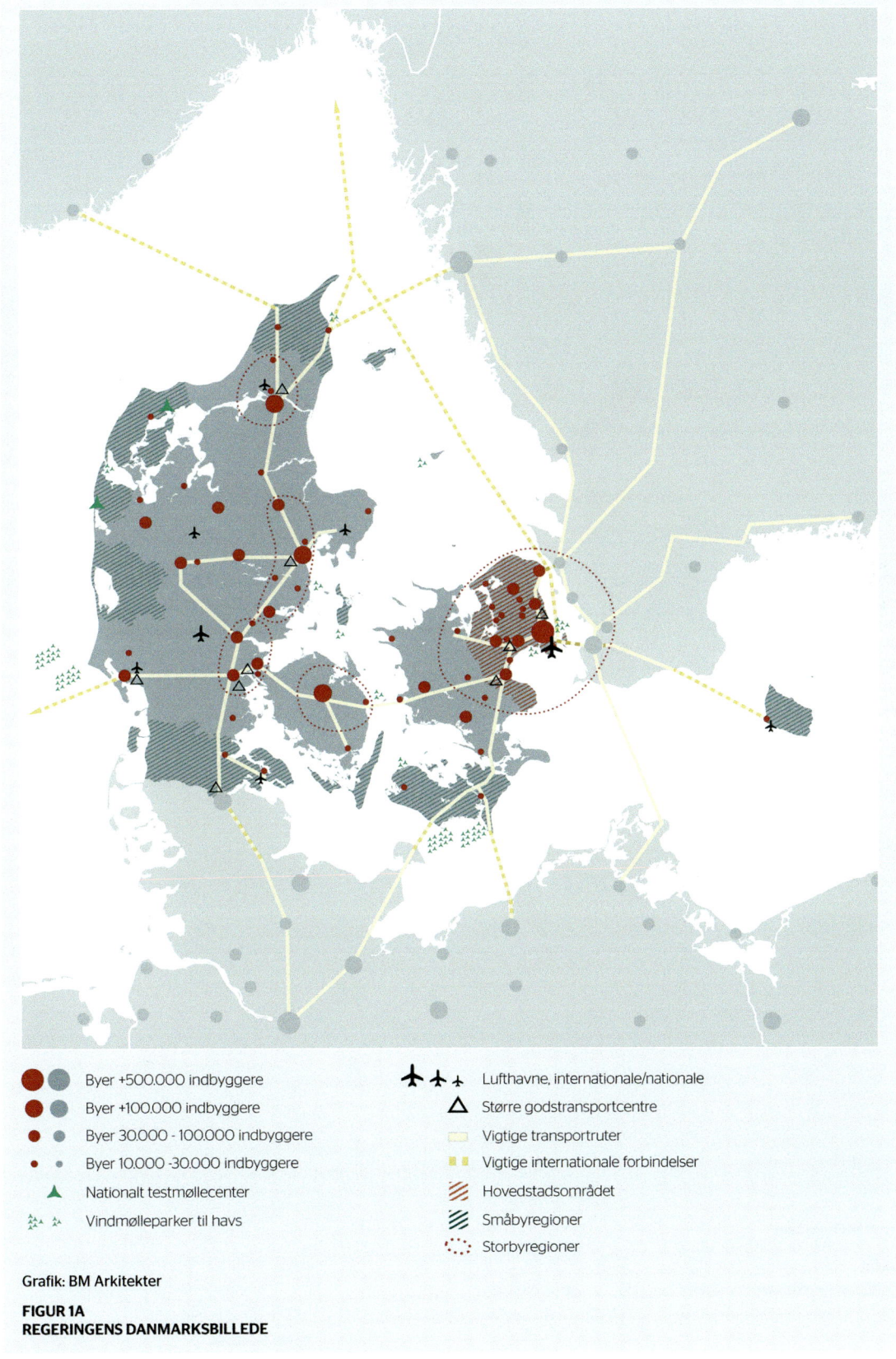

Byer +500.000 indbyggere

Byer +100.000 indbyggere

Byer 30.000 - 100.000 indbyggere

Byer 10.000 -30.000 indbyggere

Nationalt testmøllecenter

Vindmølleparker til havs

Lufthavne, internationale/nationale

Større godstransportcentre

Vigtige transportruter

Vigtige internationale forbindelser

Hovedstadsområdet

Småbyregioner

Storbyregioner

Grafik: BM Arkitekter

FIGUR 1A
REGERINGENS DANMARKSBILLEDE

Fig. 8.5 The Government's Map of Denmark, from the Ministry of the Environment (2013a, b)

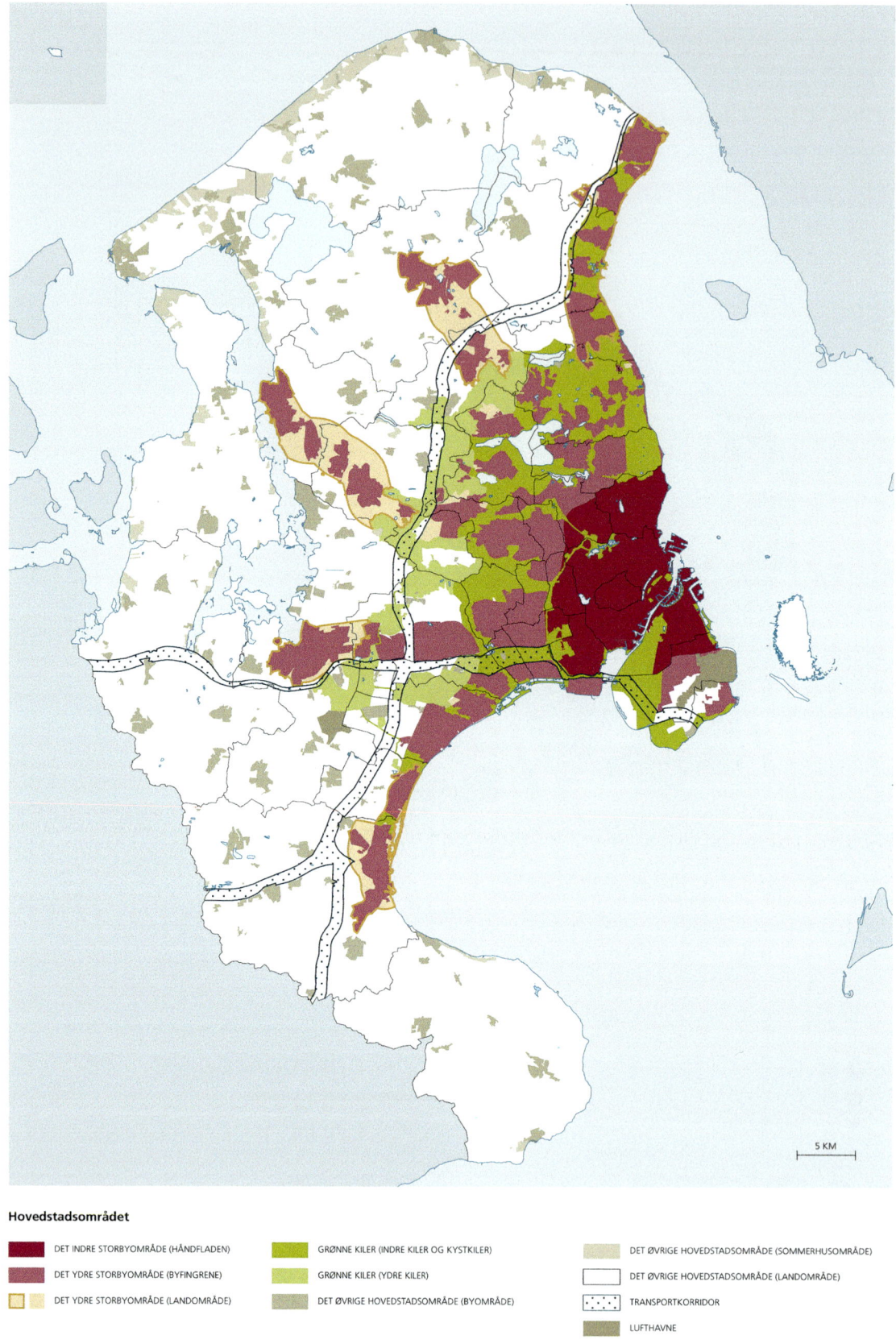

Hovedstadsområdet

■	DET INDRE STORBYOMRÅDE (HÅNDFLADEN)
■	DET YDRE STORBYOMRÅDE (BYFINGRENE)
■	DET YDRE STORBYOMRÅDE (LANDOMRÅDE)
■	GRØNNE KILER (INDRE KILER OG KYSTKILER)
■	GRØNNE KILER (YDRE KILER)
■	DET ØVRIGE HOVEDSTADSOMRÅDE (BYOMRÅDE)
■	DET ØVRIGE HOVEDSTADSOMRÅDE (SOMMERHUSOMRÅDE)
☐	DET ØVRIGE HOVEDSTADSOMRÅDE (LANDOMRÅDE)
⠿	TRANSPORTKORRIDOR
■	LUFTHAVNE

Fig. 8.6 The Greater Copenhagen Region, Finger Plan Directive 2019, from the Ministry of Industry, Business and Financial Affairs (2019)

8.5 Conclusion

This analysis of spatial planning instruments in the context of governance rescaling in Denmark, as well as the redefinition of territorial scales, proposes that the conventional ideal of integrated policy implementation has been superseded. This happens even though the Danish spatial planning system is based on a legislative relationship between different levels. During a 20-year period, strategic spatial planning contributed to clarify the role and relationship between the different planning levels and territorial scales. Furthermore, the analysis shows that the planning system is more than just an incremental sequence of plans that structure the territory. Rather, spatial planning is multifaceted and complex (i.e. iterative, open, co-evolutionary, technocratic) since it also constitutes a steady and evolving political process. In this context, strategic spatial planning plays a key role in linking a fragmented legal framework because strategic spatial plans have attempted to transcend static planning levels through the generation of new spaces of engagement where planning is needed.

The transition from positivist towards relational spatial logics at national level entailed moving away from a national spatial structure, founded on a central-place hierarchy, towards a configuration based on polycentric development and balanced spatial structures. These promote concentric urban networks, growth corridors and city-regions, respectively. The open and flexible character of Danish national planning policy intrinsically relates to the rise of strategic spatial planning at municipal level. This is coupled with the downward rescaling of spatial planning tasks and responsibilities from regional to municipal levels after the structural reform. Both forms of strategic selectivity are indicative of the fact that the cascade-style ideal of the Danish planning system is a mere façade.

Furthermore, the strategic nature of the regional scale becomes evident once land-use regulation is replaced with policy that fosters new spaces of governance which promote economic growth while also encouraging bottom-up development initiatives. The regional scale thereby only occurs intermittently: it tends to appear or disappear when municipalities or administrative regions are reorganised, and also when both municipal and regional functions are matched to acknowledge both the territorial uniqueness of city-regions and the interests of various coalitions of municipal actors. Moreover, the restructuring of the local level occurs through the merging of municipalities, where the new municipal administrations (resulting from the fusion of former municipalities) redefine the scale of urban development, allowing medium-sized cities and small towns to play specialised roles. At the same time, it can also relate to the rather functional implementation of plans for managing conurbations, which dilutes the idea of a city as being linked to municipal idiosyncrasy. Increasingly, cities are being considered not only urban but also regional entities.

Maintaining the planning cascade intact has proven both functional and convenient for both left- and right-wing governments over time. The Danish case alludes to the fact that the conservative nature of the vertical spatial anchor is a reassuring reference for the stability and permanence of power structures. In practice, this is attained through the adoption of top-down binding instruments such as the Finger Plan directive of Greater Copenhagen. From the perspective of public policy implementation, it seems more efficient for the Danish government to maintain a formal and stable structure as a façade, and to act within regulatory gaps to consolidate horizontal alliances when appropriate. This supports Foucault's (1975) argument that national governments normally benefit more from a capillary power structure.

References

Albrechts L (2001) From traditional land use planning to strategic spatial planning: the case of Flanders. In: Albrechts L, Alden J, da Rosa Pires A (eds) The changing institutional landscape of planning. Ashgate, Aldershot, p 275

Albrechts L (2004) Strategic (spatial) planning reexamined. Environ Plan B: Plan Des 31(5):743–758

Albrechts L (2006) Bridge the gap: from spatial planning to strategic projects. Eur Plan Stud 14(10):1487–1500

Albrechts L, Healey P, Kunzmann K (2003) Strategic spatial planning and regional governance in Europe. J Am Plan Assoc 69(2):113–129

Allmendinger P, Haughton G (2009) Soft spaces, fuzzy boundaries, and metagovernance: the new spatial planning in the Thames Gateway. Environ Plan A 41(3):617–633

Andersen HT (2008) The emerging Danish government reform—centralised decentralisation. Urban Res Pract 1(1):3–17. https://doi.org/10.1080/17535060701795298

Andersen J, Pløger J (2007) The dualism of urban governance in Denmark. Eur Plan Stud 15(10):1349–1367

Brenner N (1999) Globalisation as reterritorialisation: the se-scaling of urban governance in the European Union. Urban Stud 36(3):431–451

Brenner N (2001) The limits to scale? Methodological reflections on scalar structuration. Prog Hum Geogr 25(4):591–614

Brenner N (2003) Glocalization' as a state spatial strategy: urban entrepreneurialism and the new politics of uneven development in Western Europe. In: Peck J, Yeung H (eds) Remaking the global economy: economic-geographical perspectives. Sage, London, Thousand Oaks, pp 197–215

Brenner N (2004) New state spaces. Urban governance and the rescaling of statehood. Oxford University Press, Oxford

Christaller W (1966) Central places in Southern Germany (Die Zentralen Orte in Süddeutschland). Prentice-Hall, Englewood Cliffs, NJ

Commission of the European Communities (1997) The EU compendium of spatial planning systems and policies. Office for Official Publications of the European Communities, Luxembourg

Committee for Spatial Development (1999) ESDP European spatial development perspective. European Spatial Towards Balanced and Sustainable of the European Union, Luxembourg

Cox KR (1998) Spaces of dependence, spaces of engagement and the politics of scale, or: looking for local politics. Polit Geogr 17(1):1–23

Danish Business Authority (2017) Fingerplan 2017. Landsplandirektiv for hovedstadsområdets planlægning, Copenhagen

Danish Business Authority (2018) Oversigt over nationale interesser i kommuneplanlægning. Copenhagen

Davoudi S (2012) The legacy of positivism and the emergence of interpretive tradition in spatial planning. Reg Stud 46(4):429–441

Davoudi S, Strange I (eds) (2009) Conceptions of space and place in strategic spatial planning. Routledge, London

Elinbaum P, Galland D (2016) Analysing contemporary metropolitan spatial plans in Europe through their institutional context, instrumental content and planning process. Eur Plan Stud 24(1):181–206

Foucault M (1975) Surveiller et Punir: Naissance de la Prison. Gallimard, Paris

Foucault M (2004) Sécurité, Territoire, Population: Cours au Collège de France (1977–1978). Gallimard, Paris

Friedmann J (1993) Toward a non-euclidian mode of planning. J Am Plan Assoc 59(4):482–485

Galland D (2012a) Is regional planning dead or just coping? The transformation of a state sociospatial project into growth-oriented strategies. Environ Plan C: Gov Policy 30(3):536–552

Galland D (2012b) Understanding the reorientations and roles of spatial planning: the case of national planning policy in Denmark. Eur Plan Stud 20(8):1359–1392

Galland D, Elinbaum P (2015) Redefining territorial scales and the strategic role of spatial planning: evidence from Denmark and Catalonia. disP—The Plan Rev 51(4):66–85

Galland D, Enemark S (2013) Impact of structural reforms on planning systems and policies: loss of spatial consciousness? Eur J Spat Dev 52:1–23

Galland D, Enemark S (2015) The Danish national spatial planning framework: fluctuating capacities of planning policies and institutions. In: Knapp GJ, Nedovic-Budic Z, Carbonell A (eds) Planning for states and nation-states in the US and Europe. Lincoln Institute of Land Policy, Cambridge, MA, USA, pp 339–380

Graham S, Healey P (1999) Relational concepts of space and place: issues for planning theory and practice. Eur Plan Stud 7(5):623–646

Grange K (2012) Shaping acting space: in search of a new political awareness among local authority planners. Plan Theory 12(3):225–243

Grange K (2014) In search of radical democracy: the ideological character of current political advocacies for culture change in planning. Environ Plan A 46:2670–2685

Hajer M (2003) Policy without polity? Policy analysis and the institutional void. Policy Sci 36(2):175–195

Healey P et al (1997) Making strategic spatial plans: innovation in Europe. UCL Press, London

Healey P (2004) The treatment of space and place in the new strategic spatial planning in Europe. Int J Urban Reg Res 28(1):45–67

Healey P (2006) Relational complexity and the imaginative power of strategic spatial planning. Eur Plan Stud 14(4):525–546

Healey P (2007) Urban complexity and spatial strategies: towards a relational planning for our times. Routledge, London

Herod A (2011) Scale. Routledge, New York

Jessop B (1990) State theory: putting the capitalist state in its place. Polity Press, Cambridge

Jones MR (1997) Spatial selectivity of the state? The regulationist enigma and local struggles over economic governance. Environ Plan A 29 (5):831–864

Keating M (2009) Rescaling Europe. Perspect Eur Polit Soc 10(1):34–50

Leitner H, Miller B (2007) Scale and the limitations of ontological debate: a commentary on Marston, Jones and Woodward. Trans Inst Br Geogr 32(1):116–125

Local Government Denmark, Danish Regions and Ministry of the Interior and Social Affairs (2009) Status for the implementation of the local government reform—2009. Copenhagen

Marston SA, Jones JP III, Woodward K (2005) Human geography without scale. Trans Inst Br Geogr 30(4):416–432

Ministry of Industry, Business and Financial Affairs (2019) Proposal for Finger Plan 2019—National Planning Directive for Planning in the Greater Copenhagen Area [Forslag til Fingerplan 2019 Landsplandirektiv for hovedstadsområdets planlægning]. Ministry of the Environment, Copenhagen, Denmark

Ministry of the Environment (1989) Landsplanredegørelse 1989 fra Miljøministeren—Det Regionale Danmarks- billede—nu og i fremtiden. Denmark, Copenhagen

Ministry of the Environment (1992) Denmark towards the year 2018. National Planning Report for Denmark from the Minister for the Environment, Copenhagen, Denmark

Ministry of the Environment and Energy (2000a) Local identity and new challenges. National Planning Report for Denmark from the Minister for Environment and Energy. Ministry of the Environment and Energy, Copenhagen

Ministry of the Environment and Energy (2000b) Local identity and new challenges. National Planning Report for Denmark from the Minister for Environment and Energy. Copenhagen

Ministry of the Environment (2006) The new map of Denmark—spatial planning under new conditions. Copenhagen

Ministry of the Environment (2013a) Grøn Omstilling - Nye Muligheder for Hele Danmark. Copenhagen

Ministry of the Environment (2013b) National Planning Report 2013—Green reconversion—new possibilities for the whole Denmark [Landsplanredegørelse 2013—Grøn Omstilling - Nye Muligheder for Hele Danmark]. Ministry of the Environment, Copenhagen

Ministry of the Environment and Energy (1997) Denmark and European spatial planning policy. National Planning Report for Denmark from the Minister for Environment and Energy. Copenhagen, Denmark

Olesen K, Richardson T (2012) Strategic planning in transition: contested rationalities and spatial logics in twenty-first century Danish planning experiments. Eur Plan Stud 20(10):1689–1706

Priemus H, Zonneveld W (2003) What are corridors and what are the issues? Introduction to special issue: the governance of corridors. J Transp Geogr 11(3):167–177

Salet W, Faludi A (eds) (2000) The revival of strategic spatial planning. Koninklijke Nederlandse Akademie van Wetenschappen, Amsterdam

Smith N (1984) Uneven development. Nature, capital and the production of space. Blackwell, Oxford

Smith N (1992) Contours of a spatialized politics: homeless vehicles and the production of geographical scale. Social Text 33:55–81

Swyngedouw E (2004) Globalisation or "glocalisation"? Networks, territories and rescaling. Camb Rev Int Aff 17(1):25–48

van Duinen L (2004) Planning imagery. The emergence and development of new planning concepts in Dutch National Spatial Policy. University of Amsterdam

Zonneveld W (2005) In search of conceptual modernization: the new Dutch "national spatial strategy". J Housing Built Environ 20(4):425–443

Governance Rescaling and Regional Planning in France: Is Big Really Beautiful?

9

Xavier Desjardins and Anna Geppert

Abstract

In recent years, France has undergone a series of administrative reforms. In 2015, two successive laws modified the boundaries of France's mainland administrative regions, reducing them from 22 to 13 in number, whilst also devolving new competencies to them. The promoters of these laws argued that 'large regions' are levers of power and attractiveness, while changing the boundaries of the regions would demonstrate a real capacity to reform France's existing political–administrative organisation, which has been widely criticised for being cumbersome and costly. In short, the 2015 reform has been touted both as a mechanism for adapting to new economic situations as well as a means for modernising public action. In view of all that, what has actually happened? What are France's regional authorities really capable of today? How does the change in scale allow public action to be transformed? In line with the general perspective of this book, this chapter provides some answers to these vast questions by analysing specifically how the 'large' regions address development policies. The chapter begins by presenting the reform and the new competencies that regions have gained in regional planning. It then looks at the transformations that this renewal of regional planning has brought about.

Keywords

Regional planning • Devolution • Governance rescaling • France • Administrative reform

9.1 Introduction

Powerful, scale-changing modifications are affecting local governments in Europe and across the world. In France, successive reforms of local institutions have taken place since the beginning of the millennium. Recently, their pace has accelerated (2003, 2010, 2014, 2015, 2016, etc.) indicating the difficulties of finding political consensus. Altering the scale of local authorities has become a near-constant activity by 'national reformers' (Desjardins 2014a, b). In 2015, two successive laws modified the boundaries of France's mainland administrative regions, reducing them from 22 to 13 in number, whilst also devolving new competencies to them. Promoters of these laws seemed to reconcile that 'large regions' are seen as levers of power and attractiveness with the fact that changing the regions' boundaries would demonstrate a real capacity to reform France's existing political–administrative organisation, which has been widely criticised for being cumbersome and costly.

What has actually happened? What are France's regional authorities really capable of today? How does the change in scale allow public action to be transformed? How do the 'large' regions address regional and spatial development policies?[1]

---

[1] The French term *aménagement du territoire* may be variously translated as spatial development planning or regional development planning. Here we use the former for national policies and the latter for policies conducted within the regions.

X. Desjardins · A. Geppert (✉)
Sorbonne Université, Paris, France
e-mail: anna.geppert@sorbonne-universite.fr

X. Desjardins
e-mail: xavier.desjardins@sorbonne-universite.fr

© Springer Nature Switzerland AG 2020
V. Lingua and V. Balz (eds.), *Shaping Regional Futures*,
https://doi.org/10.1007/978-3-030-23573-4_9

Care needs to be taken in identifying the actual role played by the regions in terms of spatial development planning. The regions are now responsible for drawing up regional schemes for spatial planning, sustainable development and also territorial equality (*Schémas Régionaux d'Aménagement Durable, de Développement et d'Egalité des Territoires* or SRADDETs). Unlike the previous schemes (*le Schema Regional d'Aménagement, de Développement Durable du Territoire* or SRADDT), the SRADDETs must include accurate mapping (at a scale of 1:150,000) and they are binding for lower-level documents. This new exercise in regional planning has devolved great decision-making powers to the regions. The 2015 law has potentially made regions the new cornerstone of planning, the interface between major national policies and local urban planning decisions. Conversely, the means and attributions of these new regions remain limited by the power of the national government and the recently empowered major cities.

How can this frenzy for scale change be explained? Two types of interpretation stand out in the field of urban studies. From a neo-Marxist perspective, represented especially by Brenner (2004), scale change is quite simply an adaptation of the public action system to the new regime of capital accumulation. The Fordist economy, based on the Keynesian compromise, has given way to a globalised and flexible economy. Central governments have taken note of this reality, reducing their competencies as the national scale has become less important. They have transferred the responsibility for attracting capital to local government levels and especially to metropolitan areas, the so-called winning territories where there is a concentration of higher value-added economic activities. These are also now responsible for maintaining social cohesion, as much as they can. From the second type of interpretation, drawing more on political and administrative sociology (e.g. Offner 2006), the change in scale is not so much an aim as a means, a way of carrying out reforms more quietly by obliging actors to behave differently. Changing the boundaries of a local authority shakes up habits and questions organisational charts, challenging the usual administrative segmentations, etc.

Another rationale stems from the field of European spatial planning: it sees regionalisation as a means for transforming the 'Europe of the nations' into a somewhat more federal 'Europe of the regions' (Keating 1998). Visions conceived during the elaboration and following the adoption of the ESDP (1999) have been promoting cross-border and transnational approaches, suggesting a progressive erosion of national 'straightjackets'. Since the failed referendum of 2005 on the 'Constitutional Treaty', it has become clear that European citizens do not wish to abandon the sovereignty of their nations, and many consultations, including Brexit, have confirmed this fact. In this context, European Spatial Planning has lost momentum as a visioning exercise, and increasingly focuses on the growth-and-jobs agenda. Hence, cities and regions are now seen as drivers of competitiveness, and their 'good governance' as a condition to fulfil this role (European Commission 2011). The cohesion policy focuses on competitiveness and innovation, and the reduction of regional disparities and cross-border issues receive less attention (European Commission 2017).

To address the aforementioned issues, we start by presenting the rationales of the reform, seen from a national and European perspective. For these sections, the timeframe is the last 30 years, since the 1980s and we will see to what extent French regionalisation follows common patterns with neighbouring countries and to what extent it is driven by national objectives and has its own specificities. This leads to the presentation of the place of the new regions in the reformed French planning system. In a second step, we introduce the new competencies which regions have gained in regional development planning. We then look at how this renewal has transformed regional planning since 2015 and the first steps of its implementation. Ultimately, the true scope of this reform will depend on how it is implemented by actors at all levels. The stated ambitions of legislators contrast with what is really being put in place through the design of the SRADDETs. These documents may not be published until 2019, so it is too early to reach any definitive conclusions. However, initial outlines are available and the interaction between actors is already visible. This chapter draws on selected French and international texts, as well as our own involvement as experts providing advice to the regions.[2]

---

[2]Xavier Desjardins is a member of ACADIE. He is involved in supporting regional councils (*conseils régionaux*) responsible for designing the SRADDETs in the Bourgogne-Franche-Comté and Occitanie regions. He is also participating in a mission for the Ministry of Urban Planning, organising a network of locally based central government actors responsible for follow-up planning documents. Anna Geppert was strongly involved in debates on regional development planning when inter-regional contracts were established for the Paris Basin during the 1990s, as well as in the restructuring of France's planning system in the 2000s and collaborative projects between metropolitan areas in the mid-2000s. She has also worked on the role of regions in the redeployment of European Union cohesion policies between 2007–2013 and 2014–2020.

9.2   The Rationales of the Reform

9.2.1   French Regionalisation Does not Follow European Trends

"France needed strong and centralised power to make itself. Today it needs strong and decentralised power not to unmake itself", President François Mitterrand stated in 1981. For more than 30 years, France has been engaged in a resolute shift to decentralise the power that has modernised our country. This shift has continued to deepen in successive steps and is not complete. A complementary and ambitious phase was needed to modernise our territorial organisation in depth, to arm the country to resist shocks better and confirm France's capacity to be a leading developed nation, to support progress, to guarantee cohesion between people and between territories'.

Explanatory memorandum, Law No. 2015-991, 7 August 2015, on the New Territorial Organisation of the Republic (*Nouvelle organisation territoriale de la République: Notre*).

The Notre Law was presented as the completion of the decentralisation/devolution process which France has been engaged in since 1982.[3] This shift is consistent with the regionalisation observed in Europe. In the 1970s, in Italy and Spain, a median route between the centralised French model and the federal German model emerged. They developed a regionalised model with regions being more or less autonomous with strengthened powers. This was seen as having several virtues. From a political point of view, the proximity of elected officials would strengthen democracy. Economically, private actors would more easily be involved in local economies, while from cultural perspective populations and territories would benefit from the respect of historical identities.

Regionalisation took great strides in Europe between the 1980s and the banking crisis of 2008. While it did not affect federal member states (Germany, Austria and Belgium) or very small countries, those member states that were traditionally centralised went ahead with regionalisation. In 1976, Portugal granted regional autonomy status to Madeira and the Azores. In 1982 France gave its regions the status of local government, and in 1998 the United Kingdom implemented devolution for Scotland, Wales and Northern Ireland. Some commentators now speak about a 'Europe of the regions" when observing the diversity of regional changes making up this trend (Labasse 1991). Others view it as a threat to nation states (Keating 1998).

European integration supports this process. Since the presidency of Jacques Delors (1985–95), the regional policy has gained momentum and the regions have become the framework for its application.[4] The Nomenclature of Territorial Units for Statistics (NUTS), set up by the Statistical Office of the European Communities (Eurostat) in the 1970s, has become direct support for public policies. The NUTS 2 level is used to assess the eligibility of the territories for Structural Funds. NUTS 2 territories are purely statistical units of 800,000 to 3,000,000 inhabitants. Depending on the member state, they may correspond either to a level of local government or to a simple administrative or statistical division. However, the development of regional policy and the Committee of the Regions have supported the dynamics of regionalisation (the Committee is an advisory, albeit consultative, body representing local authorities, created in 1992 by the Maastricht Treaty). At the start of the EU enlargements to Central Europe in 2004 and 2007, the effects of regionalisation were visible in the regional reforms of the candidate countries (Poland in 2000 and Hungary in 2002). The regionalised model, which is widely acclaimed, is considered virtuous in terms of public management (more efficient and more economical) and local democracy. The idea that regionalisation is a vector of modernisation, expressed in the explanatory memorandum of Notre Law, is now widely shared across Europe, old and new, east and west.

As of 2008, however, these trends have been reversed. The financial crisis imposed austerity measures to meet the objectives set out in Stability and Growth Pact (1997). In 2012, the Treaty on Stability, Coordination and Governance required signatory member states to set out a multi-annual path to return to a balanced budget. This objective applies to the consolidated public finances of member states covering all public administrations, both centrally and locally. Achieving fiscal consolidation also entails controlling local government spending: in France an objective to evolve local spending (*objectif d'évolution des dépenses locales*, or ODEDEL) was set from 2014 to 2019. In this context, several countries have resorted to a strategy to lighten local government organisation, by merging municipalities (Denmark, Ireland, Greece, etc.) or strengthening cooperation (France). In France, there have also been plans to abolish the departments, though these have not been implemented. Modernisation is no longer taking place through the reform of administrative regions and regional

---

[3]The French word décentralisation involves the devolution of political authority to the regions, departments and the municipalities. We use the terms decentralisation and devolution synonymously here.

[4]When the ERDF was created in 1975, funding was minimal. Resources were attributed by the State, and their use was almost discretionary.

governments, but rather through the emergence of collaborations across local governments in metropolitan areas, via reforms which are in various stages of completion (France, 2010–15; Poland, 2011; Italy, 2014).

In Europe, the trend for regionalisation, understood as an increase in the autonomy of regional governments, is also declining under pressure from regional political movements. These are not new, but the economic crisis has strengthened independence movements in richer regions. National governments are increasingly preoccupied with demands such as those seen in the Basque country, Lombardy and Scotland, or even by open crises such as Flanders and Catalonia. Moves towards recentralisation can be identified, including in states that were traditionally regionalised such as Italy and Spain. The institutions of the European Union, which remains an interstate construction and not a superstate, support national governments to the extent that some commentators are asking whether the 'Europe of the regions' is over (Pasquier 2012). Thus, the effects of the financial crisis have reminded anyone who may have forgotten that states continue to be masters of the game and the 'great architects' of territorial constructions (Geppert 2017). In France, in 2015, two laws organised a new change in scale, creating larger regions with enhanced powers. This shift seems to be out of step with changes elsewhere in Europe, and reflects a very French quarrel between traditionalists and modernisers.

9.2.2 Regions at the Centre of a Quarrel Between Traditionalists and Modernisers

In France in 1982, decentralisation established three levels of local government: municipalities (communes), departments and regions. The cooperation between municipalities is highly institutionalised, in effect adding a fourth quasi-level, the groupings of municipalities. The French planning system has become multi-level (Alvergne and Taulelle 2002). There are redundancies between regions and departments on the one hand, and between municipalities and groupings on the other. For instance, regions are responsible for economic development, but departments intervene in this field. With regard to land use, groupings of municipalities develop the overarching document specifying general orientations (SCOT), while municipalities draw up detailed land-use plans (PLU); however, the latter may also be prepared by groupings of municipalities (PLUi). Should all these levels be retained? This debate has agitated France for nearly four decades. It has had high points, notably during the major debates about spatial planning in 1993–94 (Geppert 1995) and, a decade later, during 'Act II of the decentralisation' process (Geppert 2003). It has taken centre stage again since 2010. The debate is rather confused, crystallising several oppositions: conservatives versus reformers, sovereignists versus pro-Europeans, rural versus urban inhabitants, and supporters of risk-averse management styles versus supporters of project management.

The traditionalists promote long-entrenched government levels. These are the communes which are heirs to mediaeval parishes and provide a level of proximity, allowing citizens to approach elected officials personally and see the results of policy directly. They also include the departments, which were created in 1789 by France's revolutionary government as a new form of administrative partition, a framework for implementing top-down policies from the central government, represented by prefects who receive their instructions from the Ministry of the Interior.

Their opponents consider these levels of government outdated and archaic. They point out the fragmentation and high management costs of France's 36,000 municipalities, and criticise the sociology of elected rural officials. They ridicule the shape of the departments, which were fixed in 1790 so that every citizen could get to the administrative centre within a day's horse ride. They highlight the overrepresentation of rural territories and ageing men in departmental councils, and elected representatives of both levels are depicted as parochial, an image which obviously suffers from stereotyping.

The modernisers promote larger scales of governance. These are the groupings of municipalities which overcome parochial quarrels to develop agglomeration strategies, especially in terms of transport and housing. At the next level, regions are praised for their light, efficient administrations, considered capable of pursuing strategic approaches.

This debate, which has never been clearly settled, does not follow the traditional political lines of division. In 2010, the right-wing government enacted a reform which sent the ball back into the court of the local authorities, where departments and regions would be administered by the same elected representatives and could merge if they wished. In 2012, a socialist government was elected before these measures could produce any tangible results. After dithering over territorial questions for two years, it announced that it would reinforce regional power, without suppressing the departments. Over the last 10 years, the latter have been paralysed financially by their social welfare obligations. The rising importance of this responsibility has led departments to act more and more like 'agencies' implementing national, social-solidarity policies, leaving them with no means to carry out their own strategies. At local level, the right-wing government set up mechanisms that allowed the national government to redesign groupings of municipalities directly. The next government used this mechanism to modify their boundaries in a rough-shod manner (Geppert 2017).

At the end of the day, the modernists appear to be the main beneficiaries of the reform, yet without the traditionalists losing out entirely. The equilibrium that had emerged over several decades, however, has greatly changed. From 2010 to 2014, groupings of municipalities, in particular at the metropolitan level, were enlarged and strengthened. In 2015, the Notre Law established the new regions and redistributed their competencies with the aim of achieving a 'structural reform that reinforces the effectiveness of local government actions' (the Notre Law, Explanatory memorandum). The regional level was strengthened 'by clarifying the competencies of the regions, but also by giving the latter a critical size in geographical, demographic and economic terms' (Explanatory memorandum, Draft Law No. 2015-29, 16 January 2015, relating to the delimitation of regions, regional and departmental elections, and modifying the electoral calendar). These enhanced regions have the potential to play a new, stronger role in the French planning system.

9.2.3 The French Planning System Comes Closer to the 'Comprehensive Integrated' Approach of the EU Compendium of European Spatial Planning Systems and Policies

Although French regionalisation is out of synch with the European trend of increasing the autonomy of regional governments in general, the reform does impact the design of the French spatial planning system and, by giving more weight to the regional level, makes it more similar to the *model* of France's northern neighbouring countries. At the end of the 1990s, the European Commission funded major comparative research to obtain a better understanding of planning systems across Europe. The *European Compendium of Spatial Planning and Policies* which drew on this work identified four 'ideal types' which could be found in the EU15 of the time (European Commission 1997). Within this classification, France embodied the 'regional economic' model, characterised by strong economic action led by the state with the aim of correcting development disparities[5] across regions. Indeed, during the long post-war boom, the national government, via the famous DATAR,[5] would set aside funds to support the modernisation and relocation of industries in less developed regions. As Faludi (2004) recalls, this became a model for the EEC's regional policy through the influence of Jacques Delors and the French staff of the DG Region (then called DG XVI). With the 1982 decentralisation, the regions inherited competencies for spatial planning and the management of regional aid for economic purposes. This was accompanied by changes which faced little opposition, namely the end of regional planning through direct state intervention to correct regional development disparities. Thus, it is now possible to challenge France's inclusion in the 'regional economic' model, even if it is not easy to assign it to another of the Compendium's ideal types (Geppert 2014).

The 1982 decentralisation set up multi-level governance with no hierarchy between local and regional authorities. This equality is reflected in a 'general competency clause', in other words each level of government may intervene in any business concerning its territory, above and beyond the competencies which are explicitly attributed to it by law. At the same time, regional plans that guide the policies and investments of the regions have no binding effect on the local urban planning documents which regulate land-use. This represents a major discontinuity between regional and urban spatial planning.

In 1993–94, a major debate on spatial planning revealed the insufficiency of this cumbersome structure. In 1995, a reform of the planning system sought to create a national spatial development plan (*Schéma National d'Aménagement et de Développement du Territoire*, or SNADT) and set up a continuous hierarchy among statutory plans, from national to the local level. However, by 1997, when France's parliamentary majority changed, the stillborn national plan was abandoned in favour of sectoral schemes, and the regional plans lost their binding nature (Geppert 2001). French multi-level governance thus continues to be a 'layer cake' full of duplicates.

The 2015 reform was another attempt to clarify and prioritise roles. The 'general competency clause' was scrapped for departments and regions, making the region solely responsible for regional planning and economic development. On the other hand, regional plans (Schéma Régional d'Aménagement et de Développement Durable et d'Egalité des Territoires, SRADDET) were made binding. This completed the formal hierarchy of planning documents and abolished the structural break between regional planning and urban planning. Lastly, regional schemes became more comprehensive: regional

[5]This acronym refers to France's previous, national Delegation for Spatial Planning and Regional Development (Délégation à l'aménagement du territoire et à l'action régionale) which was an administrative unit of central government created in 1963 under De Gaulle and disbanded in 2014.

planning had to take economic development into account as well as environment and transport, which used to be dealt with separately. This all called for better coordination and integration of public policies (Fig. 9.1).

This evolution brought France closer to the so-called comprehensive integrated model which has existed in Germany and the Netherlands in particular. This model features a strong integration of public policies, both vertical and horizontal, favoured by the systematic hierarchy of plans at national and local levels. In the reformed planning system, a formal hierarchy was installed between the regional plan and the local plans, which did not exist until 2015. However, the hierarchy has been discontinued at national level: neither spatial development perspective nor strategic plan has been prepared (Geppert 2015). In such a configuration, regions should be expected to take the lead in terms of spatial planning, developing shared visions, coordinating public policies and imposing land-use guidelines. However, the next section will show the limitations of this exercise.

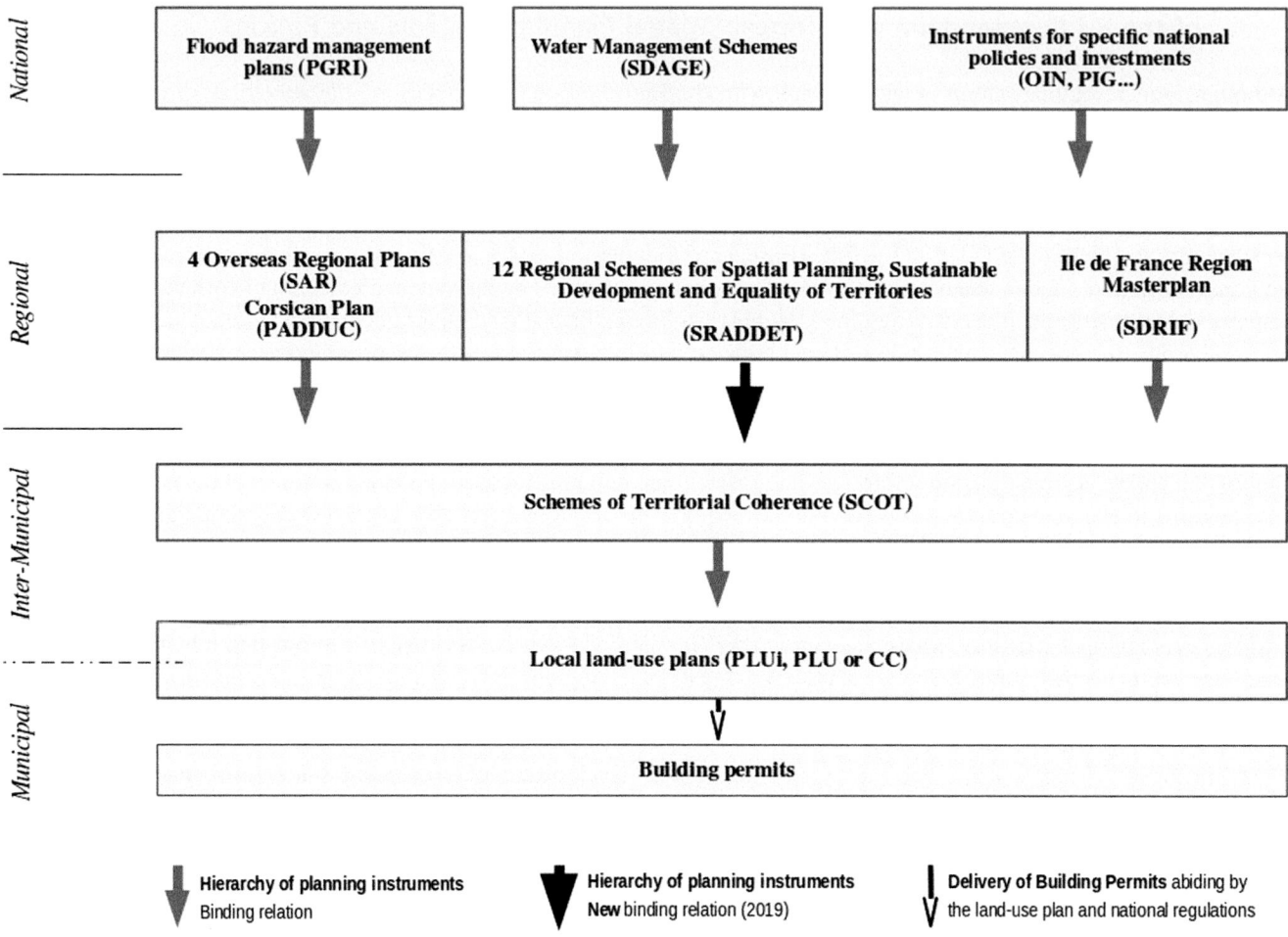

Fig. 9.1 The renewed French planning system as in 2019 (simplified)

9.3   The New Regions: Leaders or Followers in the Renewed Planning System?

9.3.1   In the Long Run, the French Regions Have Gained Power

As the jurist Gérard Marcou recalled, 'France's departments and then regions were created to meet the needs of the national administration, in contrast to the communes. They are characterised as divisions of the national territory, which is not the case for communes' (2015). This observation fits in with France's Jacobin tradition of centralisation. The state—i.e. the central government—is the guarantor of equality between territories and individuals, and has the trusteeship of local government. While communes have had an elected mayor heading their executive, France's departments and regions were directly administered by a representative of the state. The 1982 decentralisation remedied this situation and there have been local and decentralised administrations at both these levels since.

Prior to being local authorities, regions were administrative divisions of France's national territory, established for economic development and spatial planning purposes. The first regional bodies were created in 1915. They were consultative committees for economic activities, responsible for coordinating 'the economic forces of the nation' during World War I. In 1917, the Minister of Commerce, Etienne Clémentel, set up 'economic regions' on the basis of grouping departments together. These were areas for coordinating the economic activities of chambers of commerce, and they concerned transport, social works, technical education and cooperative banking (Chatriot 2002).

In 1960, 21 constituencies of regional action were created to implement 'regional action programmes', the spatial component of France's economic planning. These constituencies were transformed into regional public establishments (*établissements publics régionaux*) with limited responsibilities, mainly centred on regional development (1972). France's decentralisation laws of 1982 and 1983 transformed the regions into local governments with wide-ranging functions: it was a status they took on fully, following the first regional elections in 1986. The competencies attributed to the regions gave great importance to spatial planning and economic development, alongside vocational training and the management of high schools.

Regions have decision-making autonomy, as do departments and communes. In reality, this autonomy is quite relative, it operates within a strong legal framework and France remains a unitary state. On the other hand, it is limited by the modest resources attributed to the regions. For example, in 2017, revenues collected by the regions only amounted to 12.4% of all local government income, compared to 31.8% for departments and 55.8% for all communes (DGCL 2018). Lastly, there is no hierarchy among local governments, which means that regions must, therefore, find their place among the major state-led national policies and local government projects, of cities in particular.

Due to their competencies, regions are a level of local government strongly geared towards public investment. One of the rationales invoked is that this enhances the role of the regions in economic development (Jouen 2015). However, they do not, in fact, have the financial resources to tackle this challenge. In 2017, the regions used 31.9% of their spending for investment, although this only amounted to €9 billion. As a result, France's regions are not able to lead major investments by themselves but need co-financing for their projects. Every six years, the drafting of State-Region Planning Contracts (*Contrats de Plan Etat-Regions*, or CPER) sets out joint investment programmes which also involve other levels of local government. These are also occasions for carrying out 'multi-level governance', allowing existing powers and forces to be measured. In principle, the regions' role is central; however, in reality, it is actually modest. They continue to serve as relays for major state policies, while at the same time attempting to foster projects and strategies that are shared with other local actors. A significant issue with France's territorial reform has been to clarify this governance structure, and the laws adopted in 2010 and 2015 have simultaneously addressed different levels of local government.

The assertion of regional power draws on the attribution of new planning competencies to regional councils. The regions were granted responsibility for all inter-urban public transport, ending the surprising separation of responsibilities which existed between inter-urban rail transport (for which the regions have been responsible since 2000) and inter-urban road transport, previously organised by the General Councils of the Departments (Desjardins 2014b). At the same time, the regions must now design planning schemes that are binding for local urbanisation documents.

It remains to be seen whether France's new regions, enlarged and with enhanced regulatory powers relating to spatial development planning, will become truly independent actors or whether they will continue to be cogs in national government policies. The first decision for the new regions was to choose their new name. Some refer to themselves as a part of France (Grand Est, Hauts-de-France), whereas others use a reinvented historical or cultural name (Nouvelle Aquitaine, Occitanie, Normandie). This may mirror two distinct views of their role. Some regions appear to consider themselves as divisions of the state, stressing the governmental nature of the region in organising public actions and services. This expresses a form of complementarity and subsidiarity or even competition with the 'large state'. Others seek to be a 'small nation', emphasising their cultural and political singularity vis-à-vis the 'large nation'. The relation to the French state differs across regions.

9.3.2 The Diversity of the Regions May Be Understood by Referring to Three Ideal Types

The relationship between the state and territories is different across three categories of French regions. In the Capital-Region around Paris, the territory corresponds to a functional reality and the state continues to be a major actor. In contrast, France's overseas territories have for a long time benefitted from a certain degree of autonomy and the issues they face are more to do with their relationship with the French nation as a whole. In France's other regions, the key question concerns the coherence of the regional territory.

With Paris as its centre, Ile-de-France has a very specific situation given its status as the Capital-Region. The devolution of regional planning was late (1995) and only partial, the state is still very influential. 'State operators' carry out strategic functions in transport (RATP, SNCF), as major landowners (Paris hospitals, the universities, the army, Paris airports) or even in the head offices of companies closely linked to the State (especially in defence industries). To draft its regional plan, this region has an Institute for Spatial Planning and Urbanisation (*Institut d'Aménagement et d'Urbanisme*) which employs about 100 urban planners. Its plan (*Schéma Directeur de la Région Ile-de-France*, SDRIF) is mapped out at a scale of 1:150,000 and very precisely frames local urban planning documents. Moreover, even though it is drafted by the region, the SDRIF is actually enacted by the national government. This is a tool for achieving coherence across major, structural investments which are mainly financed by the state, as well as decisions on land use by communes. Thus, the Ile-de-France region remains, to a certain extent, a state affair even though it benefits from geographic coherence (an urban area strongly structured by its centre-city), demographic weight (11 million inhabitants) and a budget of €5 billion. Although the functional urban area exceeds the region's limits, its boundary was not changed by the 2015 reform, partly perhaps so as not to further augment France's most powerful region.

France's overseas territories draft 'regional planning schemes' (SARs), which have a similar status to the regional sustainable-development plan for Corsica (*plan d'aménagement et de développement durable de la Corse*, PADDUC). As with Ile-de-France, these schemes are legally enforceable with respect to local urban planning documents. Furthermore, they may set out specific measures to be respected in coastal and mountain zones. These territories are very specific, highly maritime or islands, and much poorer than mainland French regions. The regional schemes have to be adapted to these particular contexts with regard to national rules, whilst at the same time facilitating the implementation of concerted strategies for local development. The boundaries of these regions were not altered by the reform, and the major issue they face is their relationship to the French nation: on the one hand, some want independence, but on the other, they receive substantial funding from mainland France.

In France's mainland provinces, regional plans are primarily a tool for piloting public policies. Prior to 2015, the regions drafted their regional plans (*Schéma Régional d'Aménagement et de Développement Durable du Territoire*, SRADDT,) as a spatial development perspective which oriented the planning policies of the region. In addition, future SRADDETs have the power to bind strategic urban planning documents and local regulations (Fig. 9.1). Moreover, the SRADDETs will integrate a set of schemes that have so far been dispersed and relate to biodiversity, energy, climate and transport. In theory, SRADDET is a powerful, integrative and prescriptive planning instrument. In practice, however, it requires the geography of the region to make sense, which is not always the case, neither in terms of urban settlement, as in Ile-de-France, nor in terms of identity, as overseas.

The 2015 modification of boundaries was a missed opportunity to improve the regions' geographic relevance. It occurred after a confusing and highly publicised debate, the ins and outs of which have been well documented (Torre and Bourdin 2015). The breakdown that was finally adopted kept the old boundaries for four regions and created seven new regions by merging two or three existing regions together. Albeit the smallest regions were merged, yet the size of the new regions varies from 2.5 to 12.2 million inhabitants, a variance factor of 4.75. Moreover, before the reform, the 22 regions already included some of Europe's largest regions, such as Ile-de-France or Provence-Alpes-Côte d'Azur. The "critical scale" argument thus lacks consistency. Likewise, the new boundaries do not reflect the shape of the urban systems (Fig. 9.2).

In terms of regional identity, several choices contravened the wishes of the inhabitants: Brittany was not merged with the Pays de Loire department, which would have led to a large Breton region. Alsace, which is a small region yet with a specific historical identity, the preservation of which was a condition for its integration into France after World War I, was diluted into an immense grouping of three former regions. This policy reflects the apprehension of secessionist movements spreading across Europe over the last decade (Jouen 2015). Be that as it may, however, these new actors have to embrace the renewed regional planning.

Urban systems in France
without Paris Region

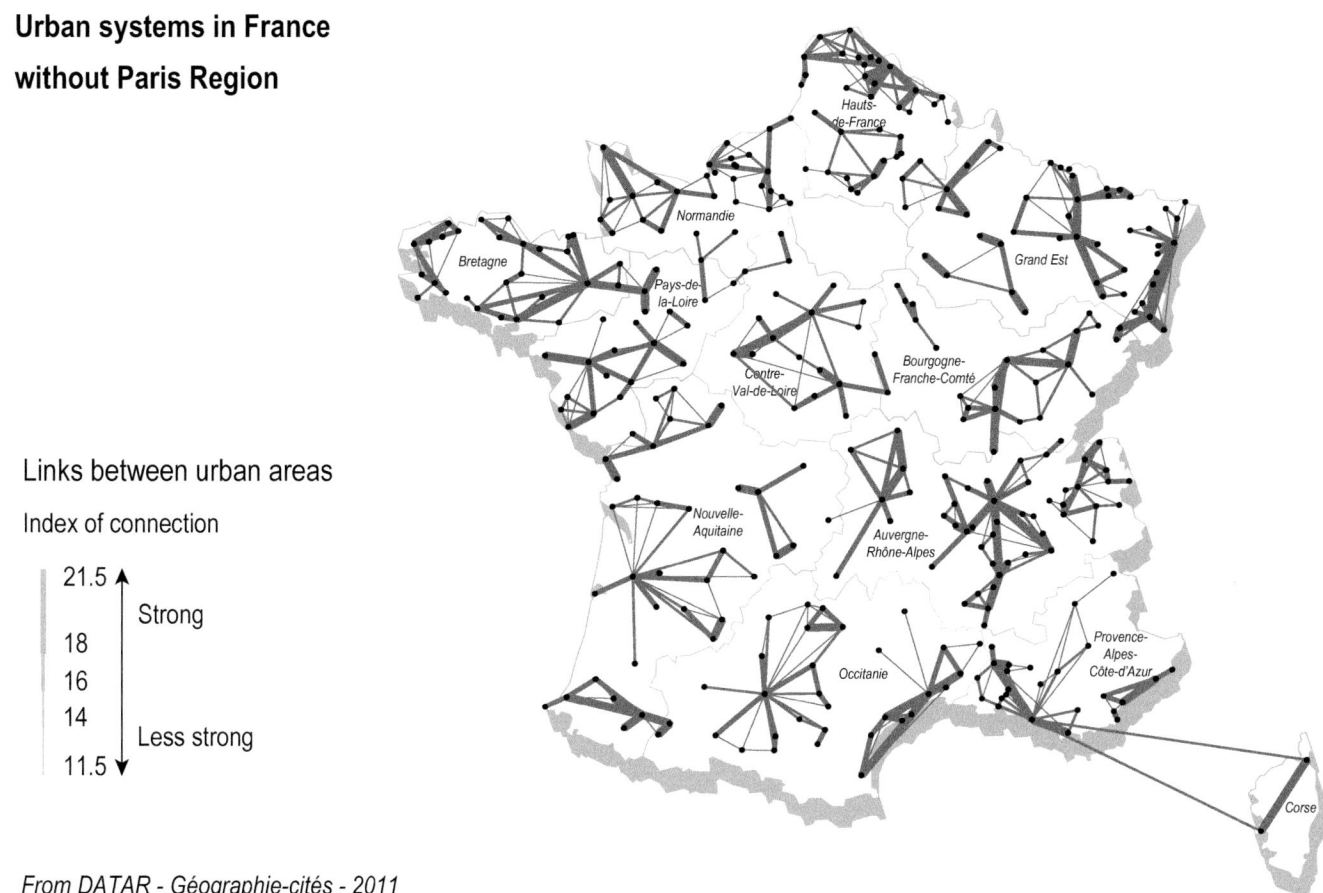

Links between urban areas

Index of connection

21.5
  Strong
18
16
14
  Less strong
11.5

From DATAR - Géographie-cités - 2011

Fig. 9.2 New regions and urban systems, from Berroir et al. (2012)

9.4   Regional Planning Announces High Expectations but Its Achievements Are Modest

The new large regions have much visibility and political weight. With the 2015 regional elections, politicians from the national arena took the presidency of the largest regions: Laurent Wauquiez (Auvergne-Rhône-Alpes, former minister of Higher Education), Christian Estrosi (Provence-Alpes-Côte d'Azur, former minister of Industry), Xavier Bertrand (Hauts-de-France, former minister of Health), Valérie Pécresse (Ile-de-France, former minister of Higher Education), and so on. At the same time, regional development planning bodies of some regions adopted the name "DATAR" informally, or even formally, as in Nouvelle Aquitaine. This clearly suggests a desire to revive the 'heyday' of spatial development planning, albeit at a regional level. However, the reality appears somewhat disappointing.

9.4.1   Regional Planning Is Expected to Combine Visioning, Technical Expertise and Political Negotiation

In the French tradition of regional and spatial planning, the DATAR used to embody both forecasting and visioning. In 1971, Jérôme Monod highlighted the risks of unbalanced development in the country with his 'Scenario of the Unacceptable' (*Scénario de l'inacceptable*). In 1993, the DATAR's vision of the most suitable future of French cities and regions, expressed both in text and maps, was discussed in a national consultation (DATAR 1993; Geppert 2015). In 2000, the DATAR showed a series of alternative scenarios depicting various possible futures, ending in a plea for a 'polycentric scenario'. Both maps and texts were used to support the reflection. Since the 2000s, spatial representations have disappeared from the DATAR forecasting programs, *Territoires* 2030 (2004–2008) and *Territoires* 2040 (2009–2012) (DATAR 2012).

According to the association of municipal groupings, the rich French tradition of *aménagement du territoire* has been a laboratory for many innovations. Today, many local representatives feel that the state has no national strategy, or at least that the momentum is lost. This reflects the change of attitude of a national government that no longer considers itself responsible for elaborating a vision of France's spatial development at the national level, leaving this task to the regions. Will the SRADDET develop visioning at regional level? It seems unlikely, for both technical and political reasons.

Technically speaking, regional plans are cumbersome and complex in their implementation. The SRADDETs are meant to gather together, in one document, former regional schemes for ecological coherence and regional schemes for climate, air, energy, intermodal transportation as well as new regional plans for waste management. The SRADDETs are thus meant to replace various existing schemes and plans. The technical work is therefore highly significant. Meanwhile, legislative and regulatory texts are mute about how to link the various sectoral policies: the state has left it to the regions which are responsible for linking the different decrees it has juxtaposed.

To do so, regions have limited means, especially in terms of personnel. Unlike Ile-de-France, other regions have modest staff and very small planning departments. The requirement that SRADDETs use indicative maps on a scale of 1:150,000 (the scale used in Ile-de-France) is symbolic of the gap between the high expectations stated by the law and the real capacity of the regions (Vanier 2018). Regional presidents might be tempted to set aside schemes that are complex, technocratic and hence hard to promote. However, by law, the SRADDETs must be approved by 2019. In order to grapple with these schemes, locally elected officials may be tempted to use them as part of their political platforms.

Politically, regions are facing the power of metropolitan areas, which have their own development projects (Cremaschi et al. 2015). Hence, regions are tempted to focus their efforts 'out-of-town', while their competencies—innovation, regional rail transport, etc.—relate strongly to large agglomerations. For example, the president of Bourgogne-Franche-Comté promises that, in the contract with local authorities, there is "one euro for rural = one euro for the urban[6]", even if the urban areas hold more than 75% of the inhabitants of the region. Having little capacity to put forward new development discourses that are also acceptable to metropolitan territories, many regions risk reducing the spatial development discourse to mere wishes to "compensate" non-metropolitan areas, re-echoing a discourse about peripheral France that is much in fashion at present (Behar 2016). This discourse contrasts two Frances: the metropolitan areas, well-integrated into economic globalisation, and the rural and peri-urban areas, considered to be the victims of this economic mutation. Such reasoning may overlook an important planning objective, namely to make the best of the complementary territories especially in respect of spreading favourable economic dynamics. In practical terms, regions have small budgets and so have no scope to redistribute monies across territories.

9.4.2 The New SRADDET Are Expected to Integrate Better Regional and Local Planning Endeavours

The ambition of turning the regions into a new and leading planning platform ran head-on into the geopolitical, financial and technical realities of regional councils. Yet it is interesting to outline how the new planning schemes change public policies.

Spatial planning combines three objectives: to provide a shared spatial vision of the future, organise public investment programs and govern land use (Demazière and Desjardins 2016). Until now, regional development schemes sought principally to define a vision and allocate a small share of regional budgets through contracts. With the integration of sectoral schemes, the SRADDETs have to address investment policies for infrastructures (mainly in transport). Tackling the green infrastructure, they have gained legitimacy in defining land-use rights. Bringing together different sectoral policies in a single scheme creates new opportunities. Investments in rail transport may be conditioned by urban planning regulations in the vicinity of stations. Contracts may also be used to work with communes on projects to manage fragile environmental areas, etc. It may in future be possible to move from an approach based on interlocking 'vision', 'programs' and 'rules', which has been the planning method used so far, to a more hybrid approach connecting stages and functions.

Regional planning also appears to be a possible catalyst for local planning policies. Since the early 2000s, strategic spatial planning has made a notable and relatively unexpected return to the local level. The inter-municipal Schemes of Territorial Coherence (SCOTs) have emerged as a new instrument (Faure and Vanier 2016). France has gradually been covered with SCOTs, of variable quality. In urban areas, they tend to be comprehensive, including very precise guidelines for local land-use plans. In rural areas, they are drivers for collaboration rather than real planning instruments. While regional planning exercises are unlikely to formulate very precise planning recommendations at the local level, they will certainly

---

[6]Conseil Régional de Bourgogne Franche-Comté, *Ma Région, Le Magazine*, no. 4, April 2018.

address territorial issues and question local actors. Regional plans could nurture more assertive local leadership on local planning issues, fostering the development of more effective strategic spatial planning in rural and suburban areas. In retail planning, given the superabundance of real estate, regional rules might reduce competition between neighbouring municipalities (Desjardins and Loisel 2018).

9.5 Conclusion: A Pyrrhic Victory?

In the introduction, we presented two types of interpretation of current reforms, one of Marxist inspiration, the other more related to political sociology. The neo-Marxist interpretation is only partially verified: the greater region is at the service of competitiveness, but the political reality strongly reduces its capacity for action. The sociological interpretation also seems partly relevant: the change of scale alters the stakeholders and their relationships; yet, it is not proven that public action has become more effective or better synchronised. Much will depend on the implementation of the reform in the coming years. For the time being, provisional conclusions may be proposed.

First, politics matter. A strongly publicised ambition of these reforms has been to create (very) large regional actors, bringing together the expertise necessary to handle international competition between territories. However, a first glance at the new regions qualifies this perspective, since the evolving realities are heterogeneous. Some regions were expanded whilst others remained within their existing boundaries. The size and real power of France's new regions, therefore, vary significantly, and the new breakdown of the regions cannot be explained only in territorial or functional terms. The political game has strongly influenced the design of France's new regional map.

Second, the new regions are neither very strong nor very consistent. The stated ambitions of legislators contrast with what is really being put in place through the design of the SRADDETs. As a matter of fact, the victory of the regions may be only apparent. Often, their large boundaries delineate spaces with little historical, geographical, cultural, social and economic relevance. The binding powers and comprehensive nature of regional plans contrast with the insufficient political and financial strength of the regions. At the end of the day, in terms of spatial planning and economic development, the regions seem to be clutched between powerful players. From above, regions are still bound to implement or adapt national and EU policies, at least to obtain funds. Downwards, they may at best play the role of negotiators and catalysts for agglomeration and metropolitan authorities. Of course, situations vary according to the capacity of the region—the Paris Region is an exception—as well as its internal structure, which may be more or less coherent, and the relations with its partners and/or competitors.

In this context, for many regions, and in particular those with enlarged perimeters, the ongoing planning exercise provides an opportunity for them to get to know themselves, to test their internal geographical and political balance, and to develop and examine narratives adapted to their new boundaries. Whether this will lead to a new understanding of regional planning remains to be seen. So far, here and there, some ideas are being discussed in terms of transport, retail planning, the development of rural areas and support for small and middle-sized cities. At local level, the ongoing re-composition of municipal groupings, often entailing the elaboration of new SCOTs, brings a certain instability for which the new regions might welcome success in elaborating strategic, long-term visions. The coming years will reveal the outcome of these parallel evolutions.

References

Alvergne C, Taulelle F (2002) Du local à l'Europe: Les Nouvelles Politiques d'aménagement du territoire. Presses Universitaires de France, Paris

Behar D (2016) Inégalités territoriales: aggravation ou changement de nature? The Conversation

Berroir S, Cattan N, Guérois M, Paulus F, Vacchiani-Marcuzzo C (2012) Les systèmes urbains français et leur métropolisation.DATAR

Brenner N (2004) New state spaces, urban governance and the rescaling of the statehood. Oxford University Press, Oxford

Chatriot A (2002) Les "Régions économiques" d'une guerre à l'autre: aménagement du territoire, discours, projets et pratiques. In: Caro P, Dard O, Daumas J-C (eds) La politique d'aménagement du territoire, Racines, Logiques et Résultats. Presses Universitaires de Rennes, Rennes, pp 53–64

Cremaschi M, Delpirou A, Rivière D, Salone C (eds) (2015) Métropoles et régions entre concurrences et complémentarités: Regards croisés France / Italie. Planum Publisher, Roma Milan

DATAR (1993) Débat National pour l'aménagement du territoire - Document Introductif. La Documentation Française, p 124

DATAR (2012) Les démarches de prospective: du Scénario de l'inacceptable à Territoires 2040. Territoires en mouvement 11:14–16

Demazière C, Desjardins X (2016) La planification territoriale stratégique: une illusion nécessaire. Revue internationale d'urbanisme 2. Available http://riurba.net/Revue/la-planification-territoriale-strategique-une-illusion-necessaire/ Accessed 30 July 2018

Desjardins X (2014a) La réforme par le changement d'échelle : retour sur une ambition déçue de la coopération intercommunale. Géographie, Economie, Société 16:147–153

Desjardins X (2014b) Mobilité, démocratie et échelles de l'action publique locale. In: Flonneau M, Laborie L, Passalacqua A (eds) Les transports de la démocratie. Presses universitaires de Rennes, Rennes, pp 83–100

Desjardins X, Loisel M (2018) Repenser la planification commerciale à l'heure d'Amazon. Urbanisme 408:46–49

DGCL (2018) Les collectivités locales en chiffres 2018. Direction Générale des Collectivités Locales, Paris. Available https://www.collectivites-locales.gouv.fr/collectivites-locales-chiffres-2018-0. Accessed 30 July 2018

European Commission (1997) The EU compendium of spatial planning systems and policies. Office for Official Publications of the European Communities, Luxemburg

European Commission (2011) Cities of tomorrow. Challenges, visions, ways forward. Publications Office of the European Union, Luxemburg

European Commission (2017) My region, my Europe, our future. Seventh Report on economic, social and territorial cohesion. Publications Office of the European Union, Luxemburg

Faludi A (2004) Territorial cohesion: old (French) wine in new bottles? Urban Stud 41:1349–1365

Faure A, Vanier M (eds) (2016) Scot et territoires: quels acquis? Quelles perspectives? Available https://enigmes.hypotheses.org/files/2016/05/SCoT-et-territoires.pdf. Accessed 30 July 2018

Geppert A (1995) Spatial planning in France—a new deal? In: Proceedings of the VIII AESOP congress, 24–27 Aug 1994. Yıldız Technical University Press, Istanbul, 2:298–311

Geppert A (2001) Schémas de service collectifs: objectif cohérence. Pouvoirs locaux 50:22–24

Geppert A (2003) Clarifier les rôles et les financements. Pouvoirs locaux 59:83–86

Geppert A (2014) France, drifting away from the 'regional economic' approach. In: Reimer M, Getimis P, Blotevogel H (eds) Spatial planning systems and practices in Europe. A comparative perspective on continuity and changes. Routledge, London, pp p109–p126

Geppert A (2015) Planning without a spatial development perspective? The French case. In: Knapp G, Nedovic-Budic Z, Carbonell A (eds) Planning for states and nation/states: a TransAtlantic exploration. Lincoln Institute of Land Policy, Cambridge, Massachusetts, pp 381–410

Geppert A (2017) Vae Victis! Spatial planning in the rescaled Metropolitan Governance in France. Raumforsch Raumordn 75:225–241. https://doi.org/10.1007/s13147-017-0492-1

Jouen M (2015) The new French Regions, from a European standpoint. Policy paper 150, Notre Europe Jacques Delors Institute. Available https://institutdelors.eu/wp-content/uploads/2018/01/pp146-frenchRegionsfromeujouenjdinov2015.pdf. Accessed 18 June 2018

Keating M (1998) The New regionalism in Western Europe: territorial restructuring and political change. Edward Elgar, London

Labasse J (1991) L'Europe des régions. Flammarion, Paris

Marcou G (2015) L'État, la décentralisation et les régions. Revue française d'administration publique (4/2015) 156:887-906

Offner J-M (2006) Les territoires de l'action publique locale. Revue française de science politique 56:27–47

Pasquier R (2012) Le pouvoir régional. Mobilisations, décentralisation et gouvernance en France. Presses de Sciences Po, Paris

Torre A, Bourdin S (eds) (2015) Big bang territorial. La réforme des régions en débat, Armand Colin, Paris

Vanier M (2018) Le SRADDET, la carte et le territoire. Urbanisme 408:65

Strategic Planning in Russia: From National to Local Government Approaches

10

Leonid Limonov and Artur Batchaev

Abstract

This chapter provides information on the origin, establishment and development of strategic planning in the Russian Federation (Russia). St. Petersburg was the first city in Russia to adopt a strategic plan, in 1997, after which strategic planning found its way to other Russian cities and regions. Strategic planning was first initiated at the grassroots level rather than at the top levels of public authority. It was only in 2014 that strategic planning processes were standardised and formalised in Russian legislation. In Russia, strategic planning has become an important tool of state and municipal governance. Not only public authorities, but also scientific, community-based and political organisations, as well as the business community and civic activists all, contribute to the development and implementation of strategic planning documents. Strategic planning involves coordinating the interests of the key stakeholders in the development territory and it has a number of complex problems. These are largely due to lack of consistency, firstly between strategic planning documents adopted at different levels of public authority, and secondly between the provisions and parameters of documents relating to different types of planning. The final part of the chapter presents the main findings regarding the improvement of approaches to strategic planning in Russia.

Keywords

Territorial strategic planning in Russia • System of planning documents in Russia • Metropolitan areas in Russia • Territorial development scheme • Intermunicipal and interregional cooperation in planning

10.1 Introduction

The purpose of this chapter is to comprehensively assess the strategic planning system in Russia and make proposals to improve it. Strategic planning is understood as target setting, forecasting, planning and programming in regard to the social and economic development of Russia, its regions, municipal entities, sectors of the economy, public and municipal governance as well as national security. When compared to other forms of planning in Russia, it is distinct in its aspiration to integrate planning activities by different levels of government, different governmental sectors and private entities to achieve long-term goals. It is aimed at solving sustainable social and economic development issues and at ensuring the national security of Russia. Strategic planning in Russia is accommodated in legal terms. The federal law "On Strategic Planning in the Russian Federation" applies to all three levels of public authority in Russia: federal, regional and local. A similar approach is used in the fields of spatial (territorial) and financial planning. However, other than spatial and financial

L. Limonov (✉) · A. Batchaev
International Centre for Social and Economic Research "Leontief Centre", 7th Krasnoarmeyskaya Str, 25, 190005 St. Petersburg, Russia
e-mail: limonov@leontief.ru

A. Batchaev
e-mail: artur@leontief.ru

© Springer Nature Switzerland AG 2020
V. Lingua and V. Balz (eds.), *Shaping Regional Futures*,
https://doi.org/10.1007/978-3-030-23573-4_10

planning, strategic planning is more oriented towards setting goals for social and economic development in the long term and defining the measures to be taken to achieve these goals.

Research for this chapter involved collecting, systemising and analysing a large amount of data, information and knowledge on strategic planning processes, both on the national and subnational levels of public authority in Russia, in the period from the early 1990s to date. A special focus was placed on checking consistency between strategic and other types of planning documents (spatial, social and economic, financial and budgetary). In addition, due consideration was given to consistency between planning documents developed at the three levels of public authority and in the corporate sector. Important aspects of this work include an assessment of the degree of public contribution to the preparation of planning documents and the availability of resources for their implementation. On the grounds of this comprehensive analysis, we identified the most challenging issues facing strategic planning in Russia and make proposals to solve them. For the latter, we draw on both Russian and international practices.

Below we first review the emergence of strategic planning in Russia (Sect. 10.2). We then explain how strategic planning is embedded in the administrative structure of Russia (Sect. 10.3) and what its current main principles are (Sect. 10.4). In Sect. 10.5, we identify the main problems of Russian strategic planning. In our concluding Sect. 10.6, we argue for approaches to resolve these problems.

10.2 Initial Experience of Strategic Planning in Russia

Several types of planning are currently employed for state and municipal governance, the most common of which are strategic, socio-economic, spatial and financial planning. When focusing on the relationship between the subject and object of planning, they can be further classified as 'self-planning', 'collective planning', 'planning on instruction' and 'directive planning' (Tambovtsev 2017). Strategic planning is the newest type of planning to be used in state and municipal governance in Russia. It has been actively taken up by its cities and regions since the second half of the 1990s.

St. Petersburg was the first city in Russia to develop, adopt and implement a strategic plan. The Strategic Plan of St. Petersburg was adopted in December 1997. It was never ratified in law and was essentially an agreement on social accord, with a declaration signed by 143 representatives including the Governor of St. Petersburg, several deputies of the city and federal parliaments, senior managers of the largest city enterprises, as well as cultural, educational and scientific organisations and other key stakeholders. The development of the St. Petersburg plan was inspired by the transformative approach of the 1990 Strategic Plan of Barcelona.[1] Its developers aptly noted that "in response to the ever-increasing speed of changes in the economy and society and to the intensification of competition in all spheres, strategic planning is becoming an essential component of governance" (Zhikharevich and Limonov 2003, p. 9).

The first years of the St. Petersburg plan saw the development and testing of a scientific, methodological framework and procedures for strategic planning. In this context, strategic planning was understood as the "independent defining of goals and main areas of social and economic development by a local community in a dynamic competitive environment" (Zhikharevich and Limonov 2003, p. 10). The key point is that a local community was seen as the main actor of planning: a plan was to consider contributions from all stakeholders relevant to the development of a territory, rather than being "handed down" from a higher level of public authority, as was the case before.

Annual discussion forums on strategic planning have been held in St. Petersburg since 2002 and have quickly acquired an all-Russian status. They became an open arena for exchanging experiences of strategic planning methods and practices. The International Centre for Social and Economic Research, or 'Leontief Centre', has been responsible for organisational and methodological support for the development and monitoring of the implementation of the St. Petersburg plan and, in 2003, it established the Resource Centre for Strategic Planning.

---

[1]The first Strategic Plan of Barcelona was adopted in 1990. It was aimed at supporting structural, socio-economic transformations, preparations for the 1992 Summer Olympic Games, and integration into the European Union. The second Strategic Plan of Barcelona was adopted in November 1994 and encompassed the Barcelona Metropolitan Area. The latest Strategic Plan of Barcelona, 'Vision-2020', was adopted in 2010.

The Strategic Plan of St. Petersburg was operative from 1997 to 2004. During this period, the majority of its measures and objectives were implemented.[2] The positive experience of St. Petersburg was then reproduced in other Russian cities and regions, including Yekaterinburg, Novosibirsk, Omsk, Kazan and many others. Subsequently, the practice of strategic planning spread to municipal and federal districts, individual metropolitan areas and physiographic regions, for instance, the Arctic Zone of Russia, the Far East, the Baikal Region and some others. In addition to these different subnational entities, strategies have also begun to be developed for certain industries, economic complexes, sectors of the economy and areas of development, in particular at the federal level (housing and utilities, transport, forestry, tourism, etc.).

Thus, the initiative, methodology and practices of strategic planning in Russia originated and were first established at the regional level.[3] Once tested in St. Petersburg, strategic planning spread out to other levels and public authorities.

10.3 The Administrative and Territorial Structure of Russia in the Context of Strategic Planning

Russia is a federation. Its legislative system is based on the principles of the continental (Roman-German) legal system and the main source of law is enacted laws. Russia has three operative levels of public authority—federal, regional and local.[4] Each level has its own powers and those powers can be divided into four groups: the first group includes powers of the Russian Federation (federal powers); the second includes powers of concurrent jurisdiction of the Russian Federation and constituent entities (federal districts) of the Russian Federation; the third includes powers of constituent entities (regions) of the Russian Federation; and the fourth represents powers of municipal entities.

Russia's administrative and territorial structure consists of eight federal districts encompassing 85 regions (the constituent entities of the Russian Federation). All regions have equal rights in their relations with the federal centre and each other. Russia is a multinational state. Fifty-nine of the Russian regions are formed geographically, the other 26 regions being defined by ethnic criteria, i.e. by the boundaries of areas densely inhabited by one, two or more ethnicities. Most of these regions are republics.[5]

Each region consists of a number of municipal entities. The Republic of Tatarstan has the largest number of municipal entities (956) and Magadan Oblast the fewest (9) as of the beginning of 2017. In recent years, the number of municipal entities in Russia has tended to decrease, from 23,304 on 1 January 2011 to 22,327 by 1 January 2017, largely as a result of municipal entities merging together, with smaller rural and urban settlements being included within larger cities or municipal districts. Data on the administrative and territorial structure of Russia are given in Table 10.1.[6]

In addition to federal districts, regions and municipal entities, Russia has a number of other territorial and administrative entities. These include large physiographic regions (the Arctic Zone of Russia, Siberia, the Urals, the Far East, etc.), basin districts (the basic unit of management with respect to water bodies in Russia), eco-resort regions (such as the Caucasian Mineral Waters Region), protected natural areas, economic zones, gambling zones, territories of advanced social and economic development, closed administrative-territorial entities, metropolitan areas and also urban territories. These territorial or administrative entities are established for different purposes. In some cases, the economic development of territory requires preferential conditions for business and governmental funding of industrial infrastructure. In other cases, the critical

---

[2]The Strategic Plan ceased to be effective in March 2004 due to the approval of the Regulation on Administration of Executive Authorities for National Planning in St. Petersburg (Decree of the Government of St. Petersburg No. 402, 16 March 2004). According to the Regulation, a Strategic Plan was understood as a system of legal regulations including the following: the Main Areas of Activities of Executive Authorities, the Master Plan, and the Register of State Functions. The Regulation ceased to be in force on 14 August 2007. In 2007–2013, St. Petersburg had a Long-term Concept of Social and Economic Development instead of a Strategic Plan. In 2014, the Strategy of Economic and Social Development of St. Petersburg Until 2030 was approved (Decree of the Government of St. Petersburg No. 355, 13 May 2014), which is still in effect.

[3]St. Petersburg is a city of federal importance—an entity of the Russian Federation equal to the region.

[4]The federal level of public authority corresponds to the national level, the regional level corresponds to the subnational level and the local level is represented by two levels (settlement and district) of municipal self-government.

[5]The Russian Federation has six types of region: republic, krai, oblast, city of federal importance, autonomous okrug and autonomous oblast. The type of region reflects its historical development (for example, Krasnodar Krai, Smolensk Oblast), role (for example, the City of Federal Importance Moscow), the ethnic composition of its population and the availability of a region-forming ethnicity (for example, the Republic of Buryatia, the Nenets Autonomous Okrug).

[6]In Russia, there are seven types of municipal entities. The criteria for classifying municipal entities include the following: area, settlement type, population, and scope of functions performed. Entities with significant population numbers that function as a city have the status of an urban district. Administrative-territorial entities with large areas have the status of a municipal district.

Table 10.1 Administrative and territorial structure of the Russian Federation

Federal (national) level	Regional (subnational) level	Local level
Federal districts—8	Constituent entities of the Russian Federation (regions)—85	Municipal entities—22,327
North-West Central Southern North Caucasian Volga Ural Siberian Far Eastern	Including (by type): Republics—22 Krais—9 Oblasts—46 Cities of federal importance—3 Autonomous okrugs—4 Autonomous oblast—1	Including (by type): Urban settlements—1589 Rural settlements—18,101 Municipal districts—1784 Urban districts—564 Urban districts with intra-urban division—3 Intra-urban districts (an intra-urban municipal entity which is part of an Urban district with intra-urban division)—19 Intra-urban territories of cities of federal importance—267

Sources The Constitution of the Russian Federation; Decree of the President of the Russian Federation No. 849, 13 May 2000, "On Plenipotentiary of the President of the Russian Federation in a Federal District"; Regions of Russia. Social and Economic Indicators. 2017: Collection of Statistics. Rosstat–Moscow: 2017, p. 34

factor might be environmental protection or the management of natural sites, and some territorial entities are even self-formed due to intrinsic processes, especially metropolitan areas.

In 2014, the Federal Law "On Strategic Planning in the Russian Federation" (No. 172-FZ, 28 June 2014) introduced a new territorial entity known as a 'macroregion'. This is a territory encompassing two or more regions where the social and economic conditions require that certain social and economic development goals, objectives, priorities and areas be set for the purposes of developing strategic planning documents. Russia's scientific community has no unified concept of a 'macroregion'. Some scholars see them as large physiographic regions, such as, for instance, the Arctic Zone of Russia, Siberia, the Far East or the Baikal Region (Leksin and Porfiriev 2016). Others believe a macroregion is the same as a federal district, yet a federal district may include sub-macroregions (Ivanovsky et al. 2016).

Macroregions are new territorial entities with a strategic planning component. They are supposed to be listed in the 'Strategy of Spatial Development of Russia' (see Table 10.3); however, at the time of writing this strategy is still being developed. A 'strategy of social and economic development' should also be developed and implemented for each macroregion. The 'Decree of the Government of the Russian Federation No. 822', dated 8 August 2015, approved regulations for how a 'strategy of social and economic development' for a macroregion should be developed and adjusted, with a focus on its content and procedures.

Russia is not alone in having no unified concept of a 'macroregion' and indeed the sixth Central European Conference in Regional Science highlighted that:

Academic literature suggests many definitions of the macroregion, which indicates its ambiguity and multidimensionality differently perceived in various scientific disciplines. (Studzieniecki and Przybylowski 2017, p. 487)

To give an example, in Europe macroregions are defined around large-scale geographical features such as seas, rivers or mountains. The large European macroregions, for instance, include the Alpine Region, Baltic Sea Region and Danube Region, to name a few. Specific strategies and planning documents are developed in respect of each of these macroregions, for example the European Union Strategy for the Alpine region (2015), the European Union Strategy for the Baltic Sea Region (2009) and the European Union Strategy for the Danube Region (2010).

Russia is characterised by strong centralisation of power, with the most important powers being held by the federal centre. Federal law governs most important activities in Russia and a number of federal agencies have territorial divisions operating in Russian cities. Due to the strong centralisation of power, the legal and methodological basis for strategic planning has to be developed at the federal level. Furthermore, given the administrative and territorial structure and power of the federal centre, the system of planning in Russia has to have a strictly hierarchical design. General planning documents set out on the federal level apply to the country as a whole. Regions, however, develop their own plans too, based on the basic provisions of federal planning. These plans should be region-specific, elaborating on provisions from the federal plans. From 2000 onwards, when a new administrative and territorial subdivision was introduced in Russia, regional plans also had to take into account the provisions of the federal districts' strategies. At the lowest, municipal level of planning, plans have to take into account the provisions of planning documents from all three levels of governance—federal, federal district and regional.

The obligation to integrate multi-level and multi-sector plans calls for a strategic planning approach. However, throughout the 1990s, the federal authorities did not show much interest in strategic planning. This was due to the following factors. First, the term 'planning' became discredited in the last years of the USSR. Large-scale directive planning (where a plan had the force of law and production of all, even the most minor products, works and services, was planned) used in the USSR was one of the reasons for the collapse of the socialist economy. Back then, many liberal Russian economists argued for the minimisation of state intervention in the economy and did not see any prospects for planned regulation. Second, in the context of the deep social and economic crisis that hit all aspects of life of Russian society in the early 1990s, strategic planning was not an issue of priority or urgency. In many respects, this applied not only to strategic planning, but to planning in general.

Scholars concluded that "until recently, the majority of modern researchers saw planning as a mildly relevant phenomenon at the periphery of theories and practices of the modern economy which is a market economy by definition and considers only few market 'failures'" (Buzgalin and Kolganov 2016, pp. 8–9). In the absence of common methodological approaches to planning at the national level, the preparation of municipal and regional planning documents was not insignificantly influenced either by the old Soviet traditions or by foreign experience. In this context, it was noted that "the development of methodological tools for territorial strategic planning in Russia was driven by foreign experience which was superimposed on the strong traditions of the Soviet planning system" (Zhikharevich 2004, p. 56).

The preparation and implementation of conceptual, programme, planning and forecasting documents have long been regulated by the provisions of the Federal Law "On State Forecasting and Programs for Social and Economic Development of the Russian Federation", adopted in 1995 (No. 115-FZ dated 20 July 1995).[7] The contents of this law provide clear evidence that planning played a minor role in Russian public governance at that time. For example, the term 'planning' is only used once in this law, in the title of Chap. 5 "State Forecasting and Short-term Planning of Social and Economic Development of the Russian Federation". Furthermore, the law provided no interpretation of the terms 'planning' and 'plan,' in contrast to the concepts of 'state forecasting', 'concept' and 'programme for social and economic development'.

This was mainly due to the generally unstable situation in the country and the search for the most relevant model of regulating social and economic processes. One of the recognised researchers of strategic planning commented on this as follows: "Everyone was aware of the defects of the centralised system of governance administered in the collapsed USSR, which became particularly evident during the last decades of this superpower. Post-Soviet Russia had rejected the political and economic system of the USSR and began to build a new system for managing the economy and society. However, this was done by trial and error and could hardly be a success in the context of a deep economic and political crisis of the 1990s" (Seliverstov 2016, pp. 7–8).

The lack of a federally established legal framework for socio-economic and strategic planning was not an obstacle to the legislative regularisation of other types of national planning (such as spatial (territorial), and financial planning). These were all provided with well-designed legal frameworks. The legal framework for spatial (territorial) planning was laid down in the Town Planning Code (the Code of the Russian Federation No. 190-FZ dated 29 December 2004) and that for financial planning was defined by the provisions of the Budgetary Code (the Code of the Russian Federation No. 145-FZ 31 July 1998). The provisions of the above codes set forth quite detailed procedures for the development, coordination, approval and implementation of documents on spatial (territorial), and financial planning.

10.4 The Main Principles and Documents of Strategic Planning in Russia in the Current Period

A legal framework for strategic planning in Russia was established only in 2014, with the enactment of the federal law "On Strategic Planning in the Russian Federation" (No. 172-FZ, 28 June 2014). Notably, this law appeared more than sixteen years after the adoption of the Strategic Plan of St. Petersburg. The revival of interest in planning at the national level was driven, on one hand, by positive experiences of planning in a number of leading countries such as France, Germany and Japan, for instance. On the other hand, Russia continued to search for its own optimal development models that best fit its historical and cultural traditions. In this connection, the following analysis well describes the current dynamics in Russia: "the search for new models of economic development which intensified after the global economic and financial downturn, as well as the search for mechanisms for modernisation of the Russian economy in the framework of a non-resource-based model of development—all this has made researchers return to their discussion of the importance of planning in the modern market economy…" (Buzgalin and Kolganov 2016, p. 9).

The strategic planning system in Russia operates on the basis of the principles listed and outlined in Table 10.2.

---

[7]Federal Law No. 115-FZ dated 20 July 1995 ceased to be in force on 11 July 2014 in accordance with Federal Law No. 172-FZ dated 28 June 2014.

Table 10.2 Basic principles of strategic planning in the Russian Federation

Strategic planning principles	Brief description of strategic planning principles
Unity and integrity	Consistency of principles and methodology for management and function of the strategic planning system; consistency of the procedure for strategic planning and reporting on the implementation of planning documents
Division of powers	Participants of the strategic planning process set the goals and objectives and define ways to achieve them within the scope of their respective powers
Succession and continuity	Participants of the strategic planning process develop and implement planning documents on a successive basis, taking into account the outcomes of implementation of any previous planning documents and their implementation stages
Balance, efficiency and effectiveness	Consistency and balance between planning documents in terms of priorities, goals, objectives, activities, targets, resources and implementation timing. Methods and ways of achieving goals should be selected based on the need to achieve the required results while minimising resources
Responsibility of participants	Participants of the strategic planning process are responsible for the timely and quality development and adjustment of planning of documents, achieving goals and the effective and efficient accomplishment of objectives
Transparency (openness)	Planning documents must be published officially, excluding any documents or partial documents that contain information treated as state, trade, official or other protected secrets
Realism and availability of resources	Goals and objectives should be defined based on their achievability within the set timeframes given limitations on resources and risks When developing and approving planning documents, resources to support activities should be identified
Measurability of targets and consistency between measures and objectives	It should be possible to measure the outcome of goals using quantitative and/or qualitative targets, or other assessment criteria used in strategic planning. Measures used in planning documents should be consistent with objectives
Management by objectives	Defining priorities and objectives; developing interrelated national, regional and municipal programs in terms of objectives and timing; defining amounts and sources of finance

Source Federal Law "On Strategic Planning in the Russian Federation"

The strategic planning system in Russia is quite democratic, in general. Representatives of the business community, scientific and community-based organisations and individuals all contribute to the development, coordination and implementation of most strategic planning documents. Draft planning documents are subject to public review and debate, with all proposals and observations, if possible, taken into account when redrafting the documents. This transparency is only limited where a document, or any part of it, contains state, trade or official secrets.

According to the federal law "On Strategic Planning in the Russian Federation" (hereinafter referred to as "Federal Law No. 172"), strategic planning involves four types of activities: target setting, planning, forecasting and programming. This law further defines the types of strategic planning documents to be developed within each of those disciplines as well as at each level of public authority. Table 10.3 lists the strategic planning documents developed within each of the four disciplines and at each level of public authority.

Table 10.3 Types of strategic planning documents in Russia

Strategic planning activity	Strategic planning documents		
	Federal level	Regional (subnational) level	Local level
Target setting	The Annual Presidential Address to the Federal Assembly	Strategy of social and economic development of region	Strategy of social and economic development
	The Strategy of Social and Economic Development of Russia		
	The Strategy of National Security of Russia, the Basic Principles of State Policy, doctrines and other instruments in the field of national security		
	The Strategy of Scientific and Technological Development of Russia		
	Industry-specific documents on strategy planning		
	The Strategy of Spatial Development of Russia		
	Strategies of social and economic development of macroregions		
Planning	Main areas of activities of the Government of Russia	Plan of action for the implementation of the strategy of social and economic development	Plan of action for the implementation of the strategy of social and economic development
	Spatial planning schemes of Russia	Spatial planning scheme (master plan for cities of federal importance)	
	Activity plans of federal executive bodies		
Forecasting	Forecasts of scientific and technological development	Medium and long-term forecasts of social and economic development	Medium and long-term forecasts of social and economic development
	Strategic forecast	Long-term budget forecast	Long-term budget forecast
	Medium and long-term forecasts of social and economic development		
	Long-term budget forecast		
Programming	State programmes	State programmes	Municipal programmes
	The State Armament Programme		

Source Federal Law "On Strategic Planning in the Russian Federation"

Although over three years have passed since the adoption of Federal Law No. 172, by no means all of the above documents have been developed and approved. For example, as of March 2018, even an important document such as the Long-term Strategy of Social and Economic Development of Russia—which is due to replace the 2008 Concept of Long-term Social and Economic Development of Russia Until 2020 (approved by the Executive Order of the Government of Russia No. 1662-r dated 17 November 2008)—has not been adopted.

At the regional level of governance, almost all-Russian regions currently have the full set of required documents in place (Table 10.3). Regions have years of experience in developing and implementing strategies and other strategic planning documents, dating back to the late 1990s. The preparation of a 'long-term forecast of social and economic development' was traditionally part of the work of strategic planning, thus providing the rationale for a new 'spatial planning scheme', ensuring synchronisation and a consistent approach to defining target values and other key components. 'State programmes' and 'medium-term forecasts of social and economic development' are used to support a draft budget for a financial year (for one or three years). The 'spatial planning scheme' defines the possible uses of a region's territory. The 'budget forecast' and 'plan of action for the implementation of the strategy of social and economic development' are new documents required from the regions, in accordance with Federal Law No. 172, yet at this level of governance there are no apparent or significant difficulties with their development and preparation.

In contrast to the federal and regional levels, municipal entities are not strictly required by Federal Law No. 172 to have the full set of strategic planning documents. This is because in Russia, as in many other countries of the world, laws provide local government with a degree of independence and autonomy. In Russia, local government is a separate level of public authority, the lowest one and the one closest to people. In 1996, Russia signed the European Charter of Local Self-Government, which was ratified in 1998. As an international treaty, this Charter takes precedence over Russian law.

Federal Law No. 172-FZ stipulates that municipal districts and urban districts may, by agreement of local government bodies, develop, approve and implement 'strategies of social and economic development', as well as a plan of action to implement them. However it contains no provisions regarding the other types of local strategic planning documents. At the same time, according to the Budget Code (the Code of the Russian Federation No. 145-FZ, 31 July 1998), in order to provide a rationale for a draft local budget municipal entities need to have a 'medium-term forecast of social and economic development' and 'municipal programmes'. Thus, Russian law requires municipal entities to have only two out of the six types of strategic planning documents. The expediency of "the development of other strategic planning documents, including a strategy, is decided by local government bodies" (Batchaev 2017, p. 167). Despite this legal looseness, most municipal entities have 'strategies of social and economic development' in place and are implementing them.

In contrast to the federal and regional levels, the strategic planning documents required for municipalities do not include spatial planning schemes. This is perhaps a flawed approach because it does nothing to help achieve consistency between strategic and spatial planning documents.[8] Furthermore, Russian municipalities have significant powers with respect to spatial planning—they regulate the use of territory and urban development. Municipal districts also prepare, approve and implement spatial planning schemes, and settlements and urban districts have master plans. Spatial planning schemes and master plans determine the purpose of use within territories based on a set of social, economic, environmental and other factors. Their aim is to ensure sustainable development, expand the capacity of utilities, transport and social infrastructures, and to make sure that the interests of individuals and associations are taken into account. Spatial planning documents take into account the resource requirements of both the economy and the population within the territory.

Spatial planning in municipalities involves the development of a number of documents that define specific aspects of urban development. These include land use and development regulations as well as town planning standards and regulations. The provisions and parameters set within these documents are extremely important for the development of municipalities because they set the bar for providing favourable living conditions for the whole population. For example, town planning standards are a set of estimated rates for the minimum allowable level of territorial improvement as regards the availability of utilities, transport infrastructure, social facilities and amenities and their accessibility to the public.

10.5 The Main Problems in Strategic Planning in Russia

A new strategic planning system has been in operation in Russia since 2014. However, it has not yet solved all the existing problems in this sphere, problems that impact both the national and subnational levels. Some of the current issues in this field are as follows.

1. *Plan preparation*: At the federal level, the 'Strategy for the Spatial Development of Russia' has not been prepared, approved or adopted. The present 'Concept of Long-term Social and Economic Development of Russia Until 2020' was approved in the heat of the global financial and economic crisis, in the autumn of 2008. It has since become obsolete in many respects, failing to reflect the entire range of current problems. The absence of nationally adopted goals, priorities, objectives and mechanisms for achieving them creates serious problems for strategic planning at the subnational level.
2. *Consistency between plans at levels*: Strategic planning documents of different levels are not properly synchronised with each other and lack consistency. In Russia, it is quite common that regional strategies are not fully consistent with industry-specific, federal strategies or development strategies of the federal district to which a region belongs. Municipal strategies, in turn, often fail to be consistent with development strategies for their own region. At subnational level, strategic planning documents have differing implementation time spans. In some regions, municipal strategies are planned until 2020, in others until 2025, 2030 or even 2035.

---

[8]In Russia, spatial planning is one of the types of planning in the public authority system. Spatial planning documents are spatial planning schemes and master plans.

3. *Methodological framework*: The development of a methodological framework for strategic planning (e.g. methods, instructions, etc.) is substantially delayed. It is only with respect to federal-level documents that a framework for strategic planning is fully in place. At the regional level, a framework exists for almost the full range of matters. At the municipal level, there are significant gaps. The laws require that a methodological framework for strategic planning be uniform for all entities operating at a particular level of public authority. For example, when developing and updating their strategies of 'social and economic development' and implementation plans, all the 85 Russian regions should adhere to the provisions of the Methodological Guidelines approved by the Order of the Ministry of Economic Development of Russia No. 132 dated 23 March 2017.

4. *Consistency with sector plans*: Strategic planning documents are often uncorrelated and inconsistent with socio-economic, spatial and financial planning documents. This problem has been prevalent for quite a long time. In order to solve it, measures were taken to make regional spatial planning documents part of strategic planning documents. At the federal level, the 'Strategy of Spatial Development of Russia' is the main strategic planning document and it aims to ensure a connection between all spatial planning documents. Strategic and financial planning are linked with each other by fulfilling the requirement of the Budget Code—that the documents to support a draft budget for a financial period must include a 'medium-term forecast of social and economic development' and 'state (or municipal) programmes.' However, despite the measures taken, it is not uncommon to find inconsistencies and conflicts between strategic and other types of planning documents.

5. *Planning resources*: Some strategic planning documents are not supported by adequate resources. For example, the targets set out in a strategy are not always properly backed up with resources. Often, when justifying resourcing at regional and municipal levels, only funds available from budgets are taken into account, while other types of resources, such as land, labour, fuel and power resources, as well as funds from private companies, are not given proper consideration. Due to the inadequate justification of resources, many regional and municipal strategies are clearly declarative in nature. State and municipal mid-term programmes are more easily justified by the available resources, with the funding provisions for such programmes reflecting the budget liabilities of the relevant governmental authorities and local government bodies.

6. *Implementation*: Mechanisms for implementing strategic planning documents can be far from adequately addressed. For example, a review of a strategy may not provide a clear understanding of how it will be implemented. Usually, a strategy will be implemented on the basis of an accompanying action plan, as well as by way of implementing corresponding state (municipal) programmes. At the same time, effective mechanisms such as public–private partnerships (municipal–private partnerships), intermunicipal cooperation, implementation of strategic investment projects and social responsibility of businesses, are often overlooked.

7. *Level of detail*: Strategies and other key strategic planning documents at the regional level are very detailed. Regional strategies are often set out in documents of 100–150 A4 pages or more. They describe in detail all the finer points of the strategy and contain a large number of indicators and other parameters that are extremely difficult to predict for the long term. Planning begins to acquire directive features, as was the case in the time of the administrative-command system. For example, at the subnational level, strategies and state and municipal programmes are approved by regional laws (decisions of a representative local government body) or by decisions of the supreme executive authority (top official) and must be complied with.

8. *Relation with private planning initiatives*: Strategic planning documents are not usually properly linked with strategies, plans and projects implemented at the corporate level by large public and private companies. In Russia, strategic planning is carried out not only at the level of public and municipal governance but also by top corporations. Companies, such as Gazprom, Lukoil, Sberbank, Russian Railways, VTB Group and many other major Russian companies have their own development strategies. At the same time, many regional and municipal strategies do not take corporate planning strategies into account to the extent needed within a territory.

9. *Environmental aspects*: Most strategic planning documents do not adequately address the environmental aspects of territorial development. Despite the fact that the main purpose of the majority of regional and municipal strategies in Russia is to improve the quality of life of the population, environmental issues are not regarded as a main priority. Sustainable development goals cannot be reached without addressing environmental issues,[9] which involves "a balanced development of economic, social and environmental components" (Bobylev and Solovyova 2017, p. 26). Quality of life cannot be expected to improve without providing a favourable environmental climate within a territory. In this

---

[9]The Sustainable Development Goals for all countries of the world in 2016–2030 were approved by the UN Conference in September 2015.

respect, regional and municipal strategies in Russia are very different from those in other leading countries of the world. In these countries, environmental issues are necessarily taken into account in both national and supranational planning documents. For example, one of the priorities in the European Union development strategy up to 2020, "EUROPE 2020: A strategy for smart, sustainable and inclusive growth", is sustainable growth, defined as promoting a more resource efficient, greener and more competitive economy.[10]

10. *Interregional and intermunicipal cooperation*: Russia has no practice of preparing strategic planning documents with respect to the neighbouring regions or municipal entities. Urban agglomerations (metropolitan areas), suburban city areas or urbanised territories are not considered as objects of planning. In Russia, strategic planning is limited to areas within the existing administrative boundaries. Many of these areas have no legal status and therefore are not seen as objects of management. Yet the coordination and pooling of resources, in order to solve common problems, are very relevant issues for many neighbouring regions and municipalities in Russia. In response to this, some measures have been taken to better coordinate development efforts across neighbouring regions and cities in Russia in recent years, resulting in the establishment of joint commissions and working groups, execution and implementation agreements and development of spatial planning schemes for agglomerations. One such example is the Concept of Joint Urban Development of St. Petersburg and Territories of the Leningrad Region (Agglomeration) in the Period Until 2030 with a Perspective Until 2050. However, such activities are still only fragmentary and are not yet widespread in Russia.

11. *Governance*: Furthermore, it is worth noting that strategic planning is part of the overall system of public and municipal governance in Russia. Therefore deficiencies in the governance system itself have a corresponding impact on strategic planning. In this respect, the practice of making and implementing strategic management decisions is one of the most significant factors: "strategic blunders in the development of the state in a number of key areas have an equally strong negative impact on the current situation in the country related to defects in public administration… This concerns the strategic decision-making system, while the key features of strategic decisions are that they have a strong influence on the most important aspects of the social and economic development of the country, such influence is long-term in nature, and there is a strong dependence on the changing conditions of the external environment and a need to adapt to them" (Seliverstov 2016, p. 9).

10.6 Conclusion: Main Findings

This chapter has identified multiple issues and trends in the development of the strategic planning system in Russia. Based on our comprehensive assessment, we have come to the following conclusions.

Due to positive experiences and inspired by international examples, strategic planning has become an important tool and an integral part of supra-local public and municipal governance in Russia. Strategic planning involves coordinating the interests of the key stakeholders in the development of the territory. Not only federal and regional public authorities and local government bodies, but also scientific, community-based and political organisations, the business community and individuals with proactive attitudes (so-called 'civic activists') contribute to the development and implementation of strategic planning documents. These documents provide extensive information not only for short-term managerial decision-making of public authorities. They also contain data on how a territory, industry, sphere or area of activity should be developed in the long run.

The fact that strategic planning in Russia is predominantly democratic in nature makes it possible to argue that the gradual transition from state or municipal government to coordinated civil society–state (or civil society–municipal) governance is a realistic outlook. Such a transition will not be possible without the implementation of communicative planning approaches. As stated in an article by a Russian scholar, "planning activities should be focused on inter-subject reasoning, which is necessary to understand the interests of participants" (Tambovtsev 2017, p. 30).

---

[10]The two other priorities of the EU's Strategy are smart growth (developing an economy based on knowledge and innovation) and inclusive growth (fostering a high-employment economy delivering social and territorial cohesion).

Regardless of the open nature of planning activities in Russia and the broad adoption of foreign practices, Russian strategic planning documents differ significantly from their international counterparts. A particular difference is in the way how planning agendas are set out. When comparing Russia with the European Union, for example, it shows that "there are two competing principles in designing priorities for development: 'sectoral' and 'integral', as well as significant differences in approaches to the development and structuring of priorities" (Klimanov and Chernyshova 2017, p. 31). In addition, federal-level strategic planning documents in Russia contain an important national security objective.

Our assessment indicates that there is a need for strategic planning beyond predefined boundaries in Russia. Where planning goes beyond the limits of administrative boundaries, international best practice is poorly relied upon. This is the case with interregional and intermunicipal cooperation, and the planning of urban agglomerations, metropolitan areas, large urbanised zones and the territories of labour markets. Scholars note that "the search for new sources of economic growth makes us look for them in many spheres of life, including the development of interregional and intermunicipal cooperation" (Batchaev et al. 2012, p. 8). In this respect, Russia should use the positive examples of the USA, France, Germany, Japan and other countries. For example, in Germany, cooperative planning is carried out between Berlin and the neighbouring federal state Brandenburg, with plans for the development of agglomerations being developed and implemented. The Plan for the Development of the Rhine-Ruhr Agglomeration Until 2030 provides for the implementation of about 400 projects with investments totalling about six billion Euros (Stroev and Reshetnikov 2016).

An important area in the improvement of strategic planning documents in Russia should be an increased consideration of sustainable development principles. More emphasis should be made on the development of a society that allows for satisfying the growing needs of current generations without compromising the opportunities for the development of future generations. Sustainable development implies a harmonious state of the economy, social sphere, population and environment and their transformation for the better. In this regard, Russian strategic planning documents should pay much more attention to environmental issues. This is relevant for metropolitan and industrial cities, as well as regions and municipal districts where the extraction of natural resources takes place. Strategic planning documents should be aimed at meeting the principles of sustainable development to a greater extent than is currently the case.

Last not least does our analysis of problems show that strategic planning in Russia is at a 'crossroad' at the moment. When taking one direction, its future development may involve the enhancement of prescriptive principles, an increased level of detail, hierarchical structuring of documents and bureaucratic control over their implementation. This would lead to an increase in the contradictions between the public and open nature of the process of developing and agreeing on strategic planning documents and the often formal manner of their implementation by public authorities. When taking another direction, future improvements may come from the expansion of democratic elements of the process and the preservation of the predominantly indicative nature of planning documents. In this approach, regional and municipal strategies may be considered as plans adopted by the entire local community—agreements on a social accord in effect. It is then important to understand that strategic planning not just produces "an outcome document, but (is) also a mechanism and process of its development and updating as an essential tool for accumulating knowledge, identifying ideas and initiatives, and reaching social accord" (Zhikharevich et al. 2004, p. 20).

References

Batchaev A (2017) On methodological approaches to the development of strategies of social and economic Development of a Municipal Entity. Regional Economy and Development of Territories. Ed. by L.P. Sovershayeva. (in Russian: Батчаев А (2017) О методических подходах к разработке стратегии социально-экономического развития муниципального образования. Региональная экономика и развитие территорий Под ред. Л.П. Совершаевой.) GUAP, St. Petersburg 1(11):167–169

Batchaev A, Zhikharevich B, Lebedeva N (2012) International experience in managing the development of Urban Agglomerations. (in Russian: Батчаев А., Жихаревич Б., Лебедева Н. (2012) Международный опыт управления развитием городских агломераций). Izvestiya Russkogo Geograficheskogo Obschestva [News of the Russian Geographical Society] 144(4):1–10

Bobylev S, Solovyova S (2017) Goals of sustainable development for the future of Russia (in Russian: Бобылев С., Соловьева С. (2017) Цели устойчивого развития для будущего России). Problemy Prognozirovaniya 2:26–32

Buzgalin A, Kolganov A (2016) Revival of planning: lessons from history (political and economic discourse) (in Russian: Бузгалин А, Колганов А (2016) Возрождение планирования: уроки истории (политико-экономический дискурс)). Problemy Teorii i Praktiki Upravleniya [Problems of Theory and Practice of Management] 7:8–20

Federal Law "On Strategic Planning of the Russian Federation" (No. 172-FZ dated 28 June 2014)

Ivanovsky L, Khodachek A, Viktorov A et al (2016) Strategy of social and economic development of the North-West Federal District for the period until 2020 (updated). Draft. St. Petersburg

Klimanov V, Chernyshova N (2017) Priorities for the development of the state in strategic planning documents in Europe and Russia. (in Russian: Климанов В, Чернышова Н (2017) Приоритеты развития государства в документах стратегического планирования стран Европы и России.) Problemy Teorii i Praktiki Upravleniya [Problems of Theory and Practice of Management] 3:19–32

Leksin V, Porfiriev B (2016) Organization of statistical research and systematic monitoring of the development of Macroregions. (in Russian: Лексин В, Порфирьев Б (2016) Организация статистических исследований и системного мониторинга развития макрорегионов.) Region: Economika and Sotsiologiya [Region: Economy and Sociology] 3(91):3–27

Seliverstov V (2016) Strategic planning and strategic blunders: Russian realities and trends. (in Russian: Селиверстов В (2016) Стратегическое планирование и стратегические просчеты: российские реалии и тенденции.) Region: Ekonomika and Sotsiologiya [Region: Economy and Sociology] 4(92):6–46

Stroev P, Reshetnikov S (2016) Planning of the spatial development of Germany. Ekonomika Severo-Zapada: Problemy i Perspektivy Razvitiya [The Economy of the North West: Problems and Prospects for Development] 2–3(51-52):110–120

Studzieniecki T, Przybylowski A (2017) Multilevel governance issues in EU Macroregions. 6th Central European Conference in Regional Science —CERS, 2017:486–494

Tambovtsev V (2017) Planning and opportunism. Voprosy Economiki 1:22–39

The Budget Code (the Code of the Russian Federation No. 145-FZ dated 31 July 1998)

The Concept of Long-term Social and Economic Development of Russia Until 2020 (approved by the Executive Order of the Government of Russia No. 1662-r dated 17 November 2008)

The Town Planning Code (the Code of the Russian Federation No. 190-FZ dated 29 December 2004)

Zhikharevich B (ed) (2004) Territorial economic strategic planning: 35 years of Canadian experience. Leontief Centre, St. Petersburg

Zhikharevich B, Limonov L (2003) Territorial strategic planning in the transition to a market economy: experience of Russian Cities. Ed. by S. Vasiliev. (in Russian: Жихаревич Б, Лимонов Л (2003) Территориальное стратегическое планирование при переходе к рыночной экономике: опыт городов России Под ред. С. Васильева). Leontief Centre, St. Petersburg

Belgian Design Laboratories of Post-sprawl Urbanisation

Michiel Dehaene

Abstract

What makes urban projects urban and what does it take to urbanise deliberately? This is a highly pertinent question in the Flemish context, where the regional design agenda is driven by the collective challenge to move away from the notoriously anti-urban legacy of sprawl that has shaped the Flemish Region. The argument of this chapter seeks to answer the question: what does it mean to design for the urban at the regional scale? In order to answer this question, this chapter attempts to gather clues from design research laboratories and collective efforts to deal with regional design in Flanders and Brussels. This analysis produces an inverse way of looking at the relationship between design and governance rescaling within the regional context. Designing for the urban involves articulating the various scales at which urbanisation processes play out, in order to define concrete settings within which variously scaled dynamics can be made the object of concrete and locally supported actions. It also means identifying local actions that enable communities to convert the collective burden of urbanisation into collectively shared opportunities.

Keywords

Urbanisation • Design research • Post-suburban development • Flemish urban renewal programme • Horizontal metropolis

11.1 Introduction

In studying the relationship between regional design and governance rescaling, this chapter begins with a reflection on the urbanisation dynamics that influence both governance and design dynamics. Design enters into this reflection, not directly as a practice promoted by rescaled tiers of government, but as part of wayfinding exercises (Ingold 2011) in which designers are asked to scale urban problems in order to make them available as the subjects of planning and urban governance. The recent renewal of regional design practices is not just a call for design to address the regional scale, but may also be looked at as the effort to address, through design, multi-scalar dynamics that shape a region undergoing transition.

More specifically, this chapter looks at how the Flemish Region is entering a post-suburban development phase (Phelps et al. 2010), confronting a new geography that breaks away from that spatial planning logic which actively encouraged development throughout the entire territory and enacted social redistribution and equal opportunities through spatial dispersion and support for equal standards everywhere. As Flanders enters a process of re-urbanisation, this chapter calls for a deeper reflection on what it takes to design for the creation of urban conditions.

M. Dehaene (✉)

Department of Architecture & Urban Planning, University of Gent, Ghent, Belgium

e-mail: michiel.dehaene@ugent.be

© Springer Nature Switzerland AG 2020

V. Lingua and V. Balz (eds.), *Shaping Regional Futures*,

https://doi.org/10.1007/978-3-030-23573-4_11

The chapter also outlines current efforts to break away from a long history of anti-urban planning policies. In the 1990s, these efforts produced new design methodologies that saw the return of people and investment to the cities. In that same period, the Flemish Region officially adopted the urban project working model, which was subsequently introduced into regional planning practices in Flanders. The urban project represents the coming together of project-driven investment and urban design, thus brokering context-specific, sectorially integrated, public–private urban development schemes.

The project-driven urban renewal policies of the nineties were quickly followed by attempts to consolidate urban agglomeration dynamics at the regional scale. These efforts to introduce design at the regional level explicitly borrowed from the urban project tradition, albeit without much reflection on the implications of the change of context, including the specific nature of regional-scale issues. This chapter engages in this reflection by discussing five recent design explorations that seek to get to grips with new urban questions within emerging metropolitan regions of Flanders. It also seeks to demonstrate how design can address urban questions at the regional scale by fashioning itself as a scaling practice that articulates urban questions so that they can become the object of local coalition building and practical action. In constructing this argument, the paper draws on insights from both urban theory (and the interpretation of urbanisation) as well as urban design theory and the role specific urbanisms may play in structuring the urban condition.

11.2   Urbanising Flemish Regional Design?

The political responsibility for spatial planning was transferred from the level of the Belgian nation-state to the Flemish, Brussels and Walloon regions, as part of the second constitutional reform (1980–1988). This led to the adoption of the Flemish Spatial Structure plan in 1997, which tried to produce a double break with the past. First, it introduced an ambitious form of planning in a country that had generally used statutory planning to facilitate development rather than to guide it. Second, it explicitly aimed to put an end to the anti-urban nature of planning and housing policies in Belgium. In contrast to the long history of sprawl (De Meulder 1999; Grosjean 2009; De Block and Polasky 2011) the plan tried to introduce a compact city policy. On the macro-scale, the plan concentrated economic development within the core region identified at the time as the Flemish diamond (Fig. 11.1). On the meso-scale, the plan introduced urban growth boundaries around the central cities.

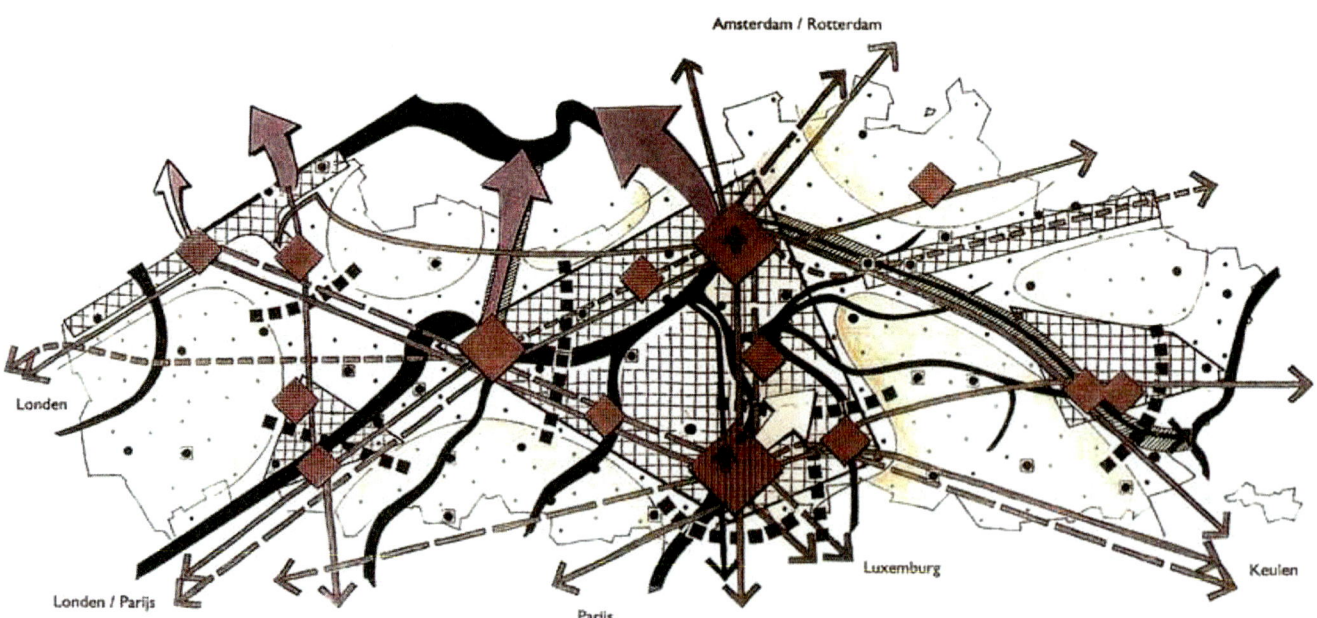

Fig. 11.1 Synthetic representation of the guiding principles of the Flemish Structure Plan 1997. The Flemish Diamond at the centre of the drawing encircles the cities of Ghent, Antwerp, Louvain and Brussels, by Studiegroep Omgeving

Since 2013 as yet inconclusive preparations for a new plan have been underway. Starting from an evaluation of the weaknesses and strengths of the previous plan, the Flemish planning administration has given up the label 'structure planning' and requalified its approach to planning as 'policy planning'. Policy planning has the explicit aim of overcoming the implementation gap within the previous plan. The draft policy plan proceeds from a more empirically grounded assessment of urbanisation dynamics within the Flemish territory. It has dropped the notion of the Flemish Diamond and seeks to come to terms with the difference between agglomeration dynamics in the corridor between Brussels and Antwerp, as opposed to the secondary agglomeration effects measured around cities like Ghent, Bruges and the bipolar constellation of Hasselt–Genk (Van Meeteren et al. 2016).

These exercises highlight the relative autonomy of these agglomeration dynamics and bring to the foreground marked territorial differences that have crystallised even within a territory that was deeply affected by the politics of sprawl. While the policy plan and its supporting studies reveal a new interpretation of urbanisation, the policy plan on the whole produces few concrete suggestions regarding the appropriate scales and territorial delimitations within which the sustainable (re) urbanisation of a region like Flanders can be organised. The policy plan, like the structure plan it will replace, continues to operate in the absence of a proper system of metropolitan governance. The possibility of addressing urban questions remains suspended between local (municipal) levels of government and the Flemish Region. In the absence of a proper system of metropolitan governance, Flanders has produced a long and arguably rich tradition of developing urban agglomerations through various forms of ad hoc cooperation between local authorities (Broes and Dehaene 2017). The current ambition to re-urbanise urban fringes of the metropolitan area is producing a new wave of such exercises.

While the policy plan is awaiting its definitive approval and practical implementation, various tiers of government have been engaged in design research aimed at rendering what the sustainable reconversion of urban sprawl in Flanders might look like specifically. These joint efforts seek to define new planning methodologies at the supra-local level, experimenting with area-based, cross-sectorial and integrated forms of planning. While the areas studied do not necessarily look particularly urban, and may indeed have been shaped by anti-urban ambitions, the problems they are confronted with today can be understood as urban. More than a century of efforts to spread development geographically and avoid urban questions have lead, in certain places, to forms of accumulation and produced local challenges and feedback loops that can be interpreted as urban questions. The reason to read them as urban questions is programmatic because it shifts the attention from the logic that produced the conditions to the consequences and possibilities shaped over time. It draws attention to new possibilities of taking action that have opened up over time, and which can be seized as people begin to explore alternative ways of inhabiting these historical conditions, using the existing, semi-urbanised landscapes against the grain, thus ascribing new meaning to existing settings.

In imagining an urban future for the legacy of sprawl, which is geographically unevenly distributed, the main challenge is to structure that unevenness and to imagine a process of 'urbanising in place'. This would intensify interdependency in one place, yet in others try to take the radical consequence of functioning off-grid outside of the structured arrangements for collective consumption. This work of spatial differentiation begins to read urbanisation as a process of territorial specialisation producing multi-scalar, territorial geometries but also diverging social dynamics. Urbanising in place, in that sense, means mobilising imaginaries that show the extent to which specific places and social settings within the urbanised landscape are ready to move towards more urban and collective ways of functioning (Fig. 11.2). Urbanising in place is a plea to attach investment in a region to those places that exist on the threshold of a more integrated and urban way of functioning, i.e. places where the consequences of urbanisation can already be felt—places where essential amenities, public spaces and a level of public transport may still be missing, for instance, but spaces that, through targeted investment, could be pushed over that threshold and moved into a new, more urban state of aggregation.

Fig. 11.2 For the 'Collective Housing' pilot project of the Flemish State Architect, Bovenbouw Architecten produced a series of images demonstrating various ways in which collective housing constellations could be used to occupy positions in the suburban fringe (around Antwerp) that offer alternatives to historical track development. The work of Bovenbouw imagines a different relationship with the landscape, trading the progressive consumption of open space for a way of building that produces new collective landscapes. Bovenbouw chose to represent this position through 'picturesque frames', through a low, embodied perspective that speaks directly to future and current inhabitants of this still suburban context

These threshold conditions should not only be understood in physical or infrastructural terms, they also need to be defined in terms of a particular sociopolitical dynamic to determine whether or not places are ready to change. They apply to those places where groups and individuals begin to realise that they have been subjected to urbanisation and are ready to shape their own urban history. This might be by virtue of the fact that they are simply tired of being stuck in traffic and no longer feel liberated by individual forms of mobility, or it might be because they are confronted with the disadvantages of suburban living when having to run their family as a single parent, or it might even be because they are questioning the health consequences of living next to the ring road and the exposure to high concentrations of particle matter in the air they breathe. These people and the places they occupy define the particular settings within which a new political deal, shaped around new collective ways of structuring the urban condition, may be shaped.

The task of designing urbanisation might then be about designing this new deal, and in particular, the spatial differentiation needed as well as how it can be positioned, localised and scaled. The question of governance rescaling and its relation to design then becomes a matter of moving competences between various levels of governance, and may also be thought of as the hard work of (re)qualifying the process of urbanisation itself, caught in-between the logic of socio-economic exchange and efforts to fix this logic within dedicated regional territorial boundaries. This may require not only specific institutional arrangements but also the identification of those specific localised assignments around which emerging urban communities may come together.

11.3 Urbanisation as a Scaling Process

Urbanisation intensifies the ways in which people live together. When subjected to urbanisation, people's lives become increasingly entangled and interdependent. Urbanisation is first encountered as misery: as traffic jams, noisy neighbours, smells from a factory or dirt in the street. Only when properly organised and when investments are made, in what Manuel Castells calls 'collective consumption', may urban conditions deliver the benefits that render cities attractive places of choice and opportunity. Living under urban conditions requires a form of governance as well as a physical infrastructure capable of living up to this heightened sense of interdependence, with mutual attachment to a given place where problems need resolving (Castells 1972; Saunders 1984; Merrifield 2014).

Urban questions pinpoint those moments in the urbanisation process in which the group(s) affected by urbanisation are confronted with a collective crisis due to the lack of organisation necessary to live together in an urban way. When such arrangements are in place, people can enjoy urban benefits to a greater or lesser extent and are in a position to rely on shared infrastructure. They can have access to adequate housing, may benefit from the use of urban utilities, can enjoy amenities, have access to public space and find a job, etc. They also find themselves in a new social context, defined by neighbours and fellow citizens who are at the mercy of the very same conditions. This new situation in which people are de facto implicated in each other's lives requires new forms of solidarity not shaped around traditional relationships of kin, shared background, race or religion, etc. but rather around place-based solidarities (Corrijn 2012).

Urbanisation perpetually shifts the balance with respect to this state of relative interdependence. Where the additional organisation is needed, where urban questions arise, but also where it is possible to mobilise around urban questions and collective solutions, all these questions manifest themselves within perpetually changing geographies. The anti-urban nature of dispersion policies deliberately circumvents the possibility of coming together around urban questions. Sprawl defines a counter-geography that literally deactivates collective organisation. Sprawl, one could say, depoliticises urban questions, moves them away from those places where the latent urban crisis calls for urgent action and where communities can be mobilised due to shared predicaments. Sprawl geographically allocates the consequences of urbanisation elsewhere and rearranges relationships of dependence between old centres and new peripheries within non-urban geometries. It also leads to a rescaling over time, shifting the consequences of a certain lifestyle to future generations. This is clear when we look at the environmental impact of sprawl, the consequences of soil sealing, the increasing frequency of flooding and the loss of biodiversity, etc.

Urban planning typically differs from spatial planning in that it tries to consolidate the collective benefits of urban living. Whereas planning in general is primarily motivated by reducing the negative externality and inefficiency of living together, urban planning typically acts to increase positive externality (Dehaene 2013; Sternberg 2000) by imagining the public spaces, infrastructures, utilities, as well as spatial and aesthetic qualities necessary to shape and share the surplus value of urban accumulation as a non-dividable, collectively produced asset (Remy 1966). While urbanisation is to a large extent a self-organising process, positive urban conditions do not come about by default. Today, investing in urban collective arrangements is more of a choice. While in the old industrial metropolis, investing in sanitation, public space and housing was still a matter of survival and a necessary precondition for social reproduction, today the possibilities of avoiding urban miseries have multiplied, and so have the options of economically strong groups to pick their place within uneven urban geographies.

Choosing for the urban is a scalar choice. Opting for the creation of urban conditions entails siding with the value and the positive external effects that can be derived from proximity and the collective sharing of assets. The urban cultivates social interdependency and attempts to derive mutual benefits, rendering spatial specialisation into a mechanism that can generate difference and choice. It entails the pooling of resources to enable choice and variety and requires strategies to render these choices accessible in a socially inclusive manner. By contrast, sprawl promises a state of independence, but by the same token it also installs a state of collective deprivation as regards the benefits that could be derived from urban forms of collective organisation. Designing sustainable post-sprawl options requires identifying the scales and places where conditions may be shaped to reengage mutual attachment to the local context and enable investment for services and programming. Post-sprawl design leaves behind a social contract, based on the same and distributed treatment of the territory everywhere and the temporary illusion of independence, and radically opts for spatial differentiation, selectively introducing urban forms of organisation within the de facto urbanised landscapes produced by urban sprawl.

11.4 Urban Design as a Scaling Practice

While urban design is the subject of degree programmes offered in universities and colleges around the world, the link between the urban and design is anything but obvious. The urban is not simply the object of design. Cities are not simply designed the way a car or a piece of furniture is. The ethos of urban designers differs from that of many other design disciplines, in the sense that it is permeated by a strong awareness that there is a limit to the extent to which society, and cities for that matter, can be engineered. The return of design to the fields of urban and spatial planning, in the eighties and nineties, went hand in hand with a critique of top-down, blueprint planning and the notion that one can plan or design for an end state. The critique of planning drew inspiration from new design theories and vice versa. The first generation of critics identified planning as a particular type of knowledge practice, requiring other forms of rationality and a new understanding of the planning process. Planning was not to be understood as a hard science but a science of muddling through (Lindblom 1959). It was praised as reflective practice (Schön 1982) and planning problems were identified as wicked problems (Rittel and Webber 1973). In a second phase, these theoretical works came with an acknowledgement of the need for design (Cross 1982; Broadbent 1973) and design thinking (Rowe 1987) in city making. Today, urban design is still tempered by the tension between the relative autonomy of design intervention and the heteronomy of urban form as the exponent of complex, socially embedded urbanisation processes (Dehaene 2015).

The critique of comprehensive end-state planning not only criticised the anti-urban nature of much planning discourse, but it also enabled a more historical and evolutionary take on change agency, moving away from a technocratic, functionalist and instrumentalist understanding of the role of planning and design. In the 90s this culminated in what was identified by authors such as Manuel De Solà-Morales as the tradition of the urban project. De Solà-Morales described the return of designerly and project-driven forms of city making. The origins of such ways of working belong, he explained, to 'another modern tradition' rooted in the process of building the modern metropolis in the 1920s and 1930s. In contrast to the tradition of the CIAM movement that had replaced the hard work of design at an intermediate scale with ideological principles and universal models, this other modern tradition of the urban project grew out of a direct commitment to the particular, to context and to process. In his text, De Solà-Morales summarises the working proposition of the urban project in five points: (1) impact outside the contours of the project, (2) mixed use, (3) intermediate scale (to be understood also in terms of an intermediate time horizon), (4) voluntary use of urban architecture, and (5) the strategic input of public means (De Solà-Morales 1987).

The practice of design in the context of the urban project is not just a technique, a method or a particularly effective way of working. The design tradition of the urban project makes a statement for the particular rather than the universal, celebrating the historical contingent in contrast to the seemingly necessary. Design in this context is part of a general critique of modernity, and is backed up with theoretical positions that draw on the simultaneous cultural, spatial and urban turn. Design wanted to bring back the hard work of transforming cities in particular situations, at defined scales, answering localised problems through concrete interventions that could be definitively imagined. In discussions, Bernardo Secchi often insisted on the fact that making the effort to design literally kept planners and designers from colossal mistakes because they took it upon themselves to test concrete solutions, in concrete, and concretely scaled settings.

In the Belgian context, the urban project was promoted as a fully fledged paradigm based on a commitment to both design and the urban condition. It was officially adopted as a way of shaping urban renewal processes in the Flemish urban renewal policy programme (Vervloesem et al. 2012) and to a certain extent in the Brussels Neighbourhood Contracts (Degros 2014). The techniques of the urban project produced a specific design ethos, yet at the same time tried to get to grips with the constraints of emerging public–private development logic, and the consequences of a neo-liberal urban development landscape (Oosterlynck et al. 2010). The full assessment of whether or not the working hypothesis behind the urban project was successful in its implementation within the Flemish Urban Renewal Programme goes beyond the scope of this paper. In retrospect, however, both in its development as a practice and the conceptual elaboration of the paradigm, most attention went into thinking about the role of design and also of design as a facilitating tool. Design was celebrated for its capacity to help deliver effective solutions in building vital coalitions, in enabling participative processes as well as in shaping more integrated transdisciplinary solutions and working processes, etc. While reflection on the urban condition and urbanity created the conditions in which a new role for design could be imagined, in practice particular attention to the urban quickly receded into the background in favour of investing energy into the strategic importance of proceeding through design-based and project-driven forms of governance. It is important to remind ourselves that the urban project, as defined by De Solà-Morales and others, was not just a pragmatic choice for the procedural benefits of design in city making. It was an explicit commitment to urbanisation as a cumulative process in which layers of meaning can be stored, multiplicity and diversity can be celebrated, inherent contradictions can be staged and overlapping logic can be articulated.

The qualification 'urban' frames projects in cultural terms. Urban can only be interpreted by acknowledging what it means to live in a particular and historical context. Adopting such a cultural, interpretative perspective produces a specific concept of change. The change affected by a project is not simply understood as a physical transformation but is also informed by changes in the meaning attached to a particular condition and the way in which people relate to their environment. Change in such a perspective not only requires changes in spatial configuration, but also changes in the use and practices of re-appropriation, both in the practical and symbolic sense of the word. Places become urban not merely by virtue of an increase in built density or because of the increase in the number of people living in the same place. They become urban because of the way people interact, renegotiate their positions and acknowledge their mutual interdependence.

What is interesting about such a particular, interpretative and localised understanding of the urban is that it is not simply scalable. It shares characteristics of non-scalability with ecological and other relational conditions (Tsing 2015). Relations that are reproduced locally can be embodied locally; relations that are embedded in a context cannot be imagined at other scales. Think of how place-based solidarities and identification with a particular context depend on actual people functioning within a given context. Many of the ecological problems the post-sprawl situations are facing stem from the denial of that interdependence. They have broken the link between localised forms of resource stewardship, local feedback loops and forms of local knowledge and continue to generate consequences that escape urban control, both in the sense that they generate negative external effects elsewhere, but also due to the collective inability to socially reproduce the positive external effects that traditionally define the urban and the benefits of living in cities. The hard work that is needed, then, is to identify settings in which the larger environmental challenges can be related to specific conditions and specific arrangements in which people can act and begin to mobilise as a moving force their strong sense of interdependence and attachment to a specific place.

The remainder of this paper looks at a series of design experiments that try to redefine the regional planning context in Flanders. Many of these experiments draw inspiration from the relative success of the urban renewal projects from the past 20 years. Each is discussed below in terms of its effort to translate an urban reflection in a regional design context.

11.5 Design Laboratories of Urban Scaling?

The following five practices represent some of the more prominent design exercises taking place at the regional scale in Flanders. Part of the material is drawn from a study conducted within the context of the spatial policy research centre. In that context, these experiments were conceptualised as collective learning practices.[1] In the context of this chapter, however, the cases are discussed in the light of the distinctive contribution made to formulating an urban regional agenda (Kuhk et al. 2016). Most of these exercises explore geographies and geometries within which metropolisation is taking place in Flanders/Belgium, around Brussels, Antwerp, Ghent and along the coastline.

11.5.1 Labo XX—Choosing the Twentieth-Century Belt

Labo XX is an umbrella term for a series of design investigations that explore the prospect of accommodating the future growth of Antwerp within the so-called twentieth-century belt, i.e. the older suburbs within the municipal boundary situated outside the urban motorway (Verhaert et al. 2014). In 2012, when Labo XX was set up by former city architect Kristiaan Borret, the general aim was still very much focused on answering the question, which part of the predicted population growth could best be housed within the municipal boundaries of Antwerp? Today, the discussion has shifted more towards a general reflection on how urban densification can be used as an investment process from which the city can benefit. Within Labo XX, densification is not looked upon as a goal, but as a reality to be accommodated in such a manner that it leads to the balanced growth and development of urban agglomeration. The first round of design work, conducted by four different design firms, was explicitly organised as a test of the urbanisation perspective. The offices explored complementary themes that linked the question of densification to urban assignments. BUUR focused on mobility issues. Maat-Possad explored the link between densification and the improvement in amenities and urban services. Palmbout-De Nijl-Blauwdruk looked at the balance between density and public, open-space provision. 51N4E–Connect&Transform looked at financial mechanisms that could help accelerate redevelopment, in a setting where land is typically in private hands and property structures are highly fragmented.

The teams were not asked to answer the question where to densify and where not, but rather to ask which ways of densifying were preferential and where those could be best accommodated? Which areas were more suitable for implementing specific principles? What form would densification take if mobility were leading? What if services were the key? What about open spaces? What about the possibility to redevelop? Each of these exercises presented different visions on how to urbanise further. The teams developed samples and tentative maps indicating spaces that, given some additional investment, could intensify the current state of urbanisation.

Perhaps most illustrative of this approach is the work of BUUR. At first sight, their work may read as a classic implementation of transit-oriented development principles. But upon closer inspection, the office presented a clever reading of how the existing tram network could be shaped in line with a densification strategy. BUUR moved the focus from current discussions about how the radial lines should be extended further into the suburbs, to the incremental development of a circle line. This line, which they named the 'Rocade', is designed to serve the existing centres of the fringe as well as the larger amenities and public services (sports clusters, hospitals, the university and the airport). The Rocade creates new nodes in the tram network and makes secondary locations along the main radial corridors accessible. The main effect is a leap from singular radial lines offering new stops to the creation of extra nodes. BUUR shifts the criterion for densification from 'the simple presence of a tram stop' to proximity to true nodes which allow residents to access a broad range of amenities and make use of multiple lines and modes of transport. The tram is no longer an excuse to pave over the last greenfield location at the end of the line, but a tool to make the leap from suburb to city (Fig. 11.3).

---

[1]https://www.ruimtelijkeordening.be/SteunpuntenBeleidsrelevantOnderzoek/SteunpuntRuimte/Toekomstverkenningen.

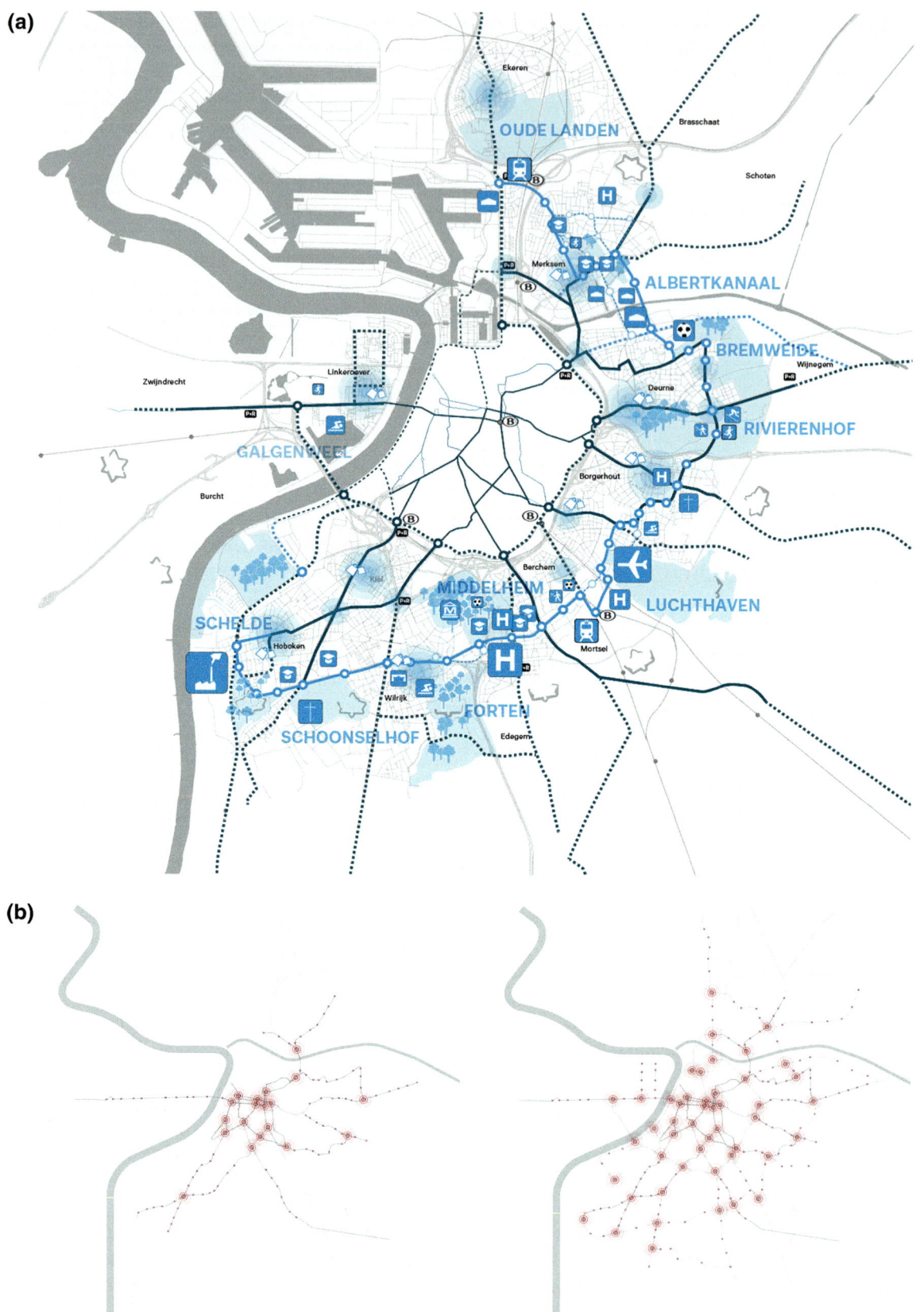

Fig. 11.3 Team BUUR. **a** The trace of the Rocade designed to service both residential districts and the regional functions of the university, hospital, airport and sports campuses. **b** From stop to hub. The further expansion of the tram network is modelled as a qualitative leap in service level

11.5.2 Metropolitan Coastal Landscape Laboratories: The Urban Coastal System

Over the past seven years, the Flemish spatial planning department and the Flemish State Architect sponsored a series of design explorations that looked at the relationship between climate change, coastal defences and the possible development of the urbanised area along with the Belgian coast. Part of this design research was conducted in the form of exploratory scenarios depicting extreme alternatives: raising dikes versus letting water in. When the public presentation of these scenarios met strong resistance from local political actors, the Flemish government put the exercise temporarily on hold. In 2015, the planning department commissioned a new study from a consortium formed by Tractebel, FABRICations and H + N + S. The consortium was asked to explore, together with local actors, concrete possibilities of re-organising the coastal urban system. In an effort to rebuild the legitimacy of this long regional design trajectory, 18 municipalities were included, both the coastal municipalities and the neighbouring municipalities more inland.

This setting created a context in which there was a direct confrontation between the status quo of municipal autonomy on one hand, and the quest for a well-structured, climate-robust coastal system on the other. Historically, municipal autonomy has contributed to sprawl and non-selective forms of urban growth. Letting each municipality decide for itself has led to the pursuit of similar development plans everywhere. In an effort to counteract this effect, the design exercise chose to actively translate urban challenges by highlighting differences. One of the evident spatial consequences of urbanisation is, after all, spatial differentiation and spatial specialisation. This is typically manifest in the development of central spaces, but also in residential districts, arrival spaces and commercial districts, etc. Urban sprawl begins by breaking with a tradition of uniformity.

This quest for the difference was undertaken by the consortium in a process that organised design workshops in four different municipalities. Each was selected because of the markedly different dynamic present in that locale. Oostende is the centre of the urban system with a concentration of supra-local functions. Blankenberge holds a place within the periphery of the coastal system, facing changes in the nature of the city as a popular coastal resort. Zevekote (a small polder village in the municipality of Gistel) hardly grows and is facing vacancies within the historical centre (Fig. 11.4). De Panne is part of a larger piece of coastal landscape with great ecological and recreational value. The design workshops tried to imagine mechanisms of redevelopment that could valorise local potential and shift the focus from the progressive consumption of open space to the production of more resilient urban infrastructures. This took the form of redevelopment schemes for the suburban fringe of Blankenberge. Efforts to cancel new residential allotments in favour of the redevelopment of vacant public buildings were made in Zevekote. Exercises rethought the infrastructure of housing estates built in the Dunes of De Panne. Design schemes imagined new combinations of housing and productive functions within the port of Oostende, etc.

The design work in this study steered a precarious course between the demands of local authorities and the development of a regional agenda. By focusing on different dynamics, the workshops made clear that a regional urban agenda should be negotiated around different issues within different sections of the territory and at different scales. The design work was successful in identifying local actions that could contribute to a territorial differentiation strategy.

11.5.3 Brussels 2040—The Horizontal Metropolis

Brussels 2040 was a very open consultation regarding the future of the wider agglomeration of Brussels, exploring a territorial area that covers both the jurisdiction of the Brussels Capital Region (the authority commissioning the study) and a large section of Flanders (Dejemeppe and Périlleux 2012). The Brussels Agglomeration is the only metropolitan area that has an integrated public body that can implement some form of metropolitan governance. The territory governed by the Brussels Capital Region is significantly smaller than the functional urban area and is surrounded by Flemish municipalities that historically have tried to resist the expansion of Brussels on their turf. The Brussels Capital Region invited three design teams to present a vision for the shape that metropolitan growth could take: a team revolving around the office of Bernardo Secchi and Paola Viganò (including Karbon), a collaboration between L'AUC and 51N4E and finally KCAP.

In particular, the Secchi–Viganò team worked at the intersection of regional design and urbanisation. They looked at the direction urban growth has historically taken, asking the broader community of the urban agglomeration to temporarily suspend highly charged and contentious discussions. Secchi–Viganò presented the provocative vision of Brussels as a horizontal metropolis, rethinking the legacy of sprawl against the background of a discussion on the *longue durée* of metropolisation. [See also the text by Paola Viganò on the horizontal metropolis in this volume.]

The horizontal metropolis presents a vision of the wider metropolis as structured by two sets of three valleys: three valleys inside the urban core (the Zenne and the tributaries of the Molenbeek and Maalbeek) and three river valleys within the agglomeration (the Dender, Zenne and Dijle). This produces reflections on the role the biophysical system may play in structuring further urbanisation of the region. The metaphor of the horizontal metropolis also serves as an alternative reading for

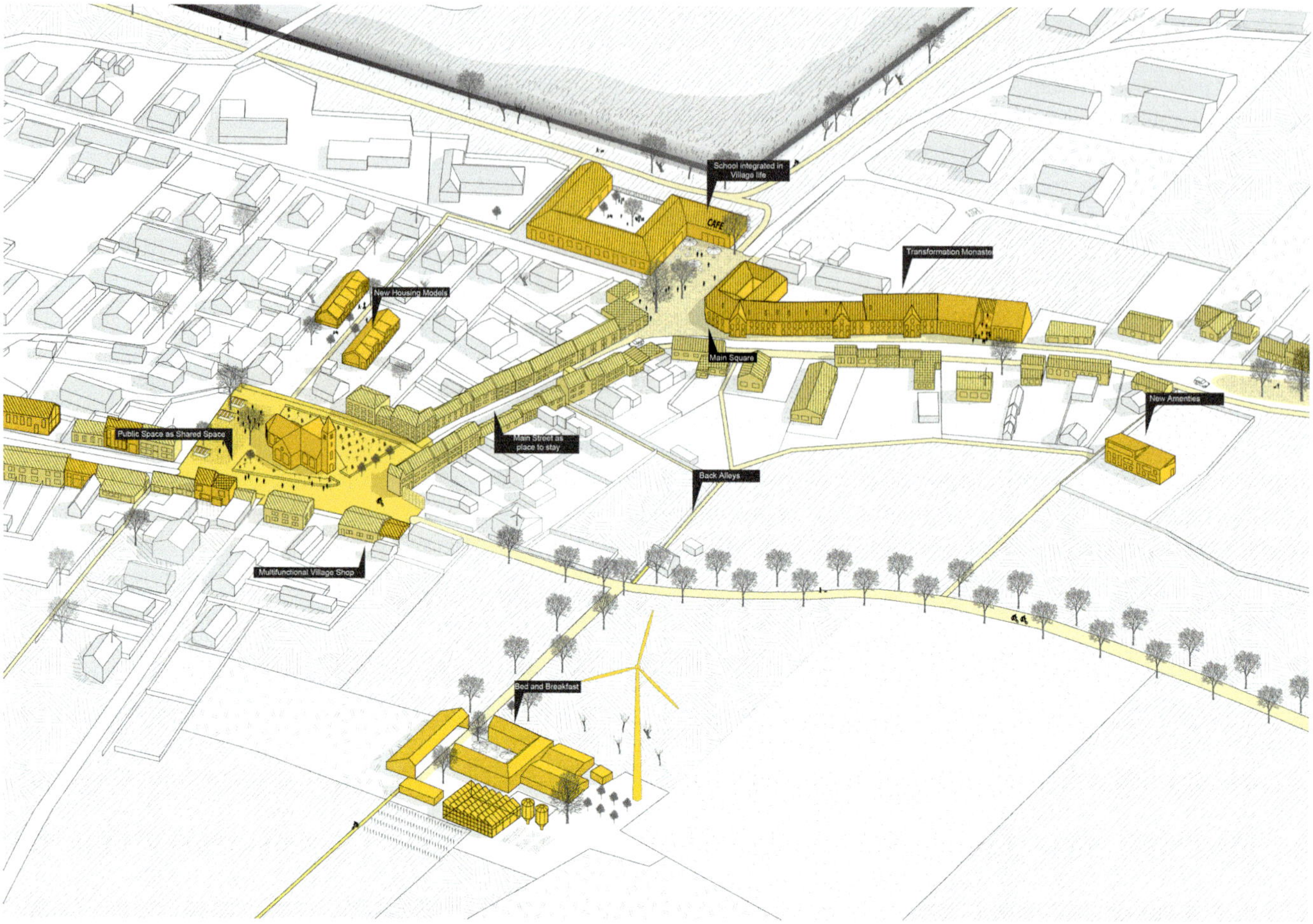

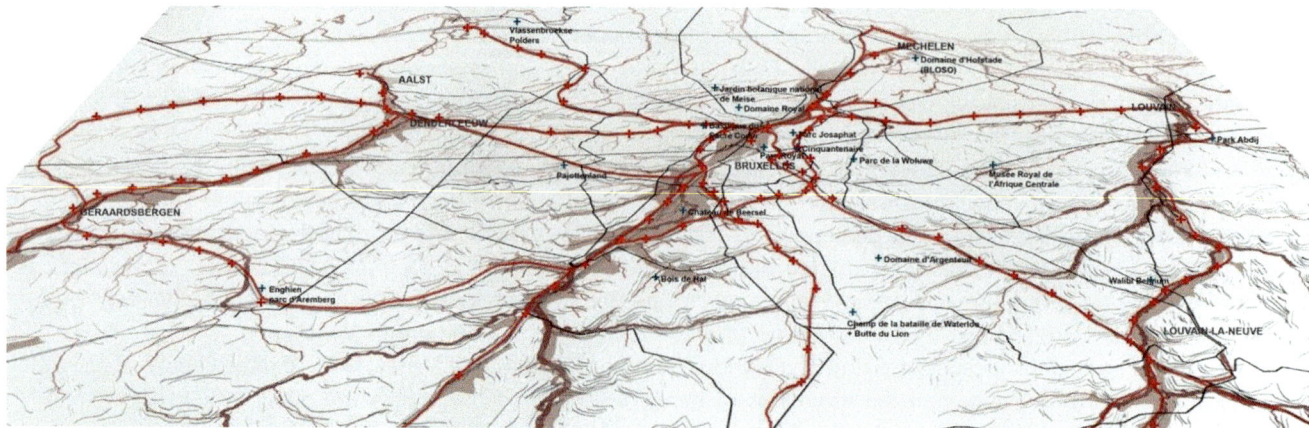

Fig. 11.4 Synthetic representation of the design workshop in Zevekote, by Fabric and Tractebel. Zevekote is barely growing. The cloister and the village school are empty. Rather than discussing where the next residential allotment should go, the workshop proposed reprogramming the old core of the village, including the possible reuse of the empty buildings there

a development model that plays off the centre against the periphery. It shows a metropolitan area with a long history of urbanisation in which benefits were shared and distributed within open geography. The study shows how the metropolitan region incorporated finely grained and diversified geography of old settlement patterns that reflect local circumstances and mark subtle differences between contrasting hydrographic and soil conditions. This valley system was later reinforced by the introduction of an elaborate railway system that, in its morphology, echoed the structure of the valleys. It produced a distributed development pattern that translated equity into distributed geographies, combining the benefits of generalised mobility with the relatively cheap availability of land (Fig. 11.5).

Fig. 11.5 Metropolitan region around Brussels, structured as a horizontal metropolis grafted onto three river valleys, by Studio 012 Secchi–Viganò

This structural work is combined with the investigation of concrete samples, in which speculative scenarios are combined with concrete representations of the new urban spaces that could follow from these proposed alternative development pathways. The no-car scenario, for example, leads to efforts to renegotiate the use of public space between new users, new mobilities and new parking policies, for instance. The horizontal metropolis presents a vision in which regional dynamics are translated into local practices that may gradually change the conditions of living together in the city. While the direct impact of the study may have been limited, the representations were well-suited for the exhibition that resulted from this design consultation. The design experiments focusing on the renegotiation of public space speak directly to the grassroots struggles that seek to restrict the use of cars within the centre of the city, including the successful movement 'picknicking the streets' and more recently the design activism of 'bye bye petite ceinture' (Byebyepetiteceinture 2018). These exercises explicitly mobilise how urbanisation is negotiated through the direct conditions that specific communities are subjected to, and they produce alternative imaginaries as the intellectual support and inspiration for these communities in their struggle to break the status quo (Fig. 11.6).

Fig. 11.6 Speculative models representing the alternative use of public space in a no-car scenario, by Studio 012 Secchi–Viganò

11.5.4 Atelier Brussels: A Good City Has Industry

Atelier Brussels was a design atelier taking place at the 2016 Rotterdam Biennale, funded by the Brussels Capital Region, the Flemish waste management company and the Flemish Spatial Planning department (AWB 2016). The exercise focused on the conflict between industrial production and urbanisation, trying to amend the logic surrounding urban renewal and densification which fuelled the systematic replacement of former manufacturing areas with housing and office development. Premium real estate projects not only produce gentrification but also push out activities that have economic value, but they do not reflect high(er) land values.

Within the context of this exercise, three architects' offices were invited to conduct design research on how the manufacturing industry can be preserved within the urban mix of functions or proactively incorporated into new developments. The design explorations took two main approaches. How could production space be created by combining it with functions that can pay for the land? Other investigations looked at complementary programmes creating value within the mix of functions, creating urban milieus that value the positive external effects produced by the presence of productive functions, from the use of residual heat to shared services.

The design research reaffirms that the urban is first of all a use value and that it can only be reproduced if we install mechanisms that protect accumulated urban (use) value against land speculation.

Here too, the results were presented within an exhibition and in a series of well-attended accompanying debates. Both the exhibition and the debates were structured around ten principles that translated the findings of the design research into possible action points. Perhaps more interestingly, the design research in turn served as material to engage in discussions about these broader principles, the relative success of which led to the consolidation of Atelier Brussels. The theme of the productive city is being explored further at the 2018 Architecture Biennale, Rotterdam (Fig. 11.7).

Fig. 11.7 Plus Office explored different configurations in the Brussels Canal zone, combining productive and residential typologies. The industrial footprint defines residential morphology rather than the other way around

11.5.5   IABR 2018 the Missing Link: Atelier Central Urban Core East Flanders

This project atelier is part of the 2018 and 2020 International Architecture Biennale, Rotterdam. The atelier focuses on demographic growth in the metropolitan area of Ghent and explores how investment in the area may also facilitate a transition towards more sustainable urbanisation. The work within this atelier has only just started. What is interesting is the specific methodology proposed under the title of 'the missing link' (Alkemade et al. 2017). The missing link points to the gap between the broad sustainability goals that have been defined on the one hand (climate goals, halting land consumption, ambitious modal split), and particular projects and experiments set up as part of operational efforts to meet some of these goals. What is missing are the specific political pathways that could describe how projects would be scaled or accelerated to meet these strategic goals.

Aware of the limitations of resorting to direct impact through projects, this atelier has launched an alternative methodology. Rather than trying to design possible futures at the regional scale, the atelier put out a call for actors to mobilise partners in the region to come together around a set of common/recurrent problems. It will then run design workshops with groups of partners working around similar issues that they themselves have identified as worthwhile. Design is deployed as a way of articulating the actions of many, and to set up a process of collective learning (AWB 2017).

11.6   Conclusion

This chapter has looked at concrete design work that seeks to renew the Flemish regional planning practice as it attempts to come to terms with the legacy of sprawl. It presents the argument that rather than looking at these experiments as efforts to explore the role of design at the regional scale, we might better understand their merit as an effort to introduce urban considerations and properly organised urban collective arrangements in a landscape that has historically been deprived of them. In doing so, the questions of scale figures differently, and design appears as a practice introducing scales at which urban considerations may be articulated, rather than as a practice aimed at scaling up (or down).

In this effort to negotiate the dynamics of urbanisation, designers mobilise skills that have been deployed regularly in a context of more traditional urban projects. The model of the urban project has been hailed because of its capacity to steer complex urban transformation, using design skills to bring parties together around a set of common goals that can be placed under a form of project management. In Flanders, over the past 15 years, consistent efforts have been made to introduce project-driven logic at the regional scale. This has been translated though efforts to scale up and produce area-based, integrated projects.

By placing the emphasis on the urban rather than the project, this chapter seeks to position the agency of design differently. Design is not just a facilitator of project-driven logic, but it plays an important role in scaling urban questions in such a manner that they can be the subject of concrete, localised, concerted action. In the context of a regional planning agenda that attempts to confront the anti-urban legacy of sprawl and distributed development patterns, this framing is pertinent. This interpretation opens up an understanding of design processes that do not simply produce regional equivalents of actions previously tried at larger scales. The designing of the urban condition is understood as part of the crafting relations of place-based solidarity and the valorisation of relations of proximity that cannot be simply scaled. The design efforts show a process in which regional challenges are rescaled to be structured as urban questions around which newly shaped urban coalitions and local communities can be rallied.

References

Alkemade F, Declerck J, Van Broeck L (2017) The missing link. Online: https://iabr.nl/en/curator/curator-statement_iabr2018-2020. Last consulted 15 May 2018

AWB (2016) A good city has industry. Online: http://www.architectureworkroom.eu/documents/ABXL_Bozar_GUIDE_ENG_DEF_webres.pdf. Last consulted 15 May 2018

AWB (2017) Regionale Oproep IABR—OVK. Online: https://iabr.nl/en/projectatelier/ovk_regionaleoproep. Last consulted 15 May 2018

Broadbent G (1973) Design in architecture: architecture and the human sciences. Wiley, London

Broes T, Dehaene M (2017) Mastering the urbanisation process: the urban questions of engineer August Mennes in the Antwerp agglomeration. Plann Perspect 32(4):503–531

Byebyepetiteceinture (2018). Online: http://byebye.petiteceinture.be/. Last consulted 15 May 2018

Castells M (1972) La question urbaine. Paris, François Maspero

Corrijn E (2012) Breuklijnen in de Vlaamse stedelijkheid. In: Holemans D (ed) Mensen maken de Stad. Antwerpen, Epo, pp 98–116

Cross N (1982) Designerly ways of knowing. Des Stud 3(4):221–227

Dehaene M (2013) Gardening in the urban field. A&S/Books, Gent

Dehaene M (2015) Stedenbouw als verstedelijkingskunde. In: Schram A, Colenbrander B, Doevendans K, De Meulder B (eds) Stadsperspectieven: Europese Tradities in de stedenbouw. Nijmegen, Vantilt, pp 296–312

Dejemeppe P, Périlleux B (2012) Brussel 2040. Drie visies voor een metropool, Brussel: Brussels Hoofdstedelijk Gewest

De Meulder B, Schreurs J, Cock A, Notteboom B (1999) Patching up the Belgian urban landscape. OASE 52:78–113

De Block G, Polasky J (2011) Light railways and the rural-urban continuum: technology, space and society in late nineteenth-century Belgium. J Hist Geogr 37(3):312–328

Degros A (2014) Bruxels, [Re]discovering its space. Public spaces in the Sustainable Neighbourhood Contracts, Brussels: Brussels Capital Region

De Solà-Morales M (1987) Another modern tradition Urbanismo-Revista 5:21–27

Grosjean B (2010) Urbanisation sans Urbanisme. Une histoire de la «ville diffuse». Mardaga, Bruxelles

Ingold T (2011) The Perception of the environment. Routledge, London/New York

Kuhk A, Dehaene M, Dumont M, Schreurs J (2016) Toekomstverkenning als collectief leren. Ruimte Vlaanderen, Brussels. Online: https://www.ruimtelijkeordening.be/Portals/108/docs/Onderzoek/Steunpunt_Ruimte_3_Toekomst_3.2.pdf

Lindblom CE (1959) The science of "muddling through". Public Adm Rev 19(2):79–88

Merrifield A (2014) The new urban question. Pluto Press, London

Oosterlynck S et al (eds) (2010) Strategic spatial projects: catalysts for change. Routledge, London

Phelps NA, Wood AM, Valler DC (2010) A postsuburban world? An outline of a research agenda. Environ Plann A Econ Space 42(2):366–383

Remy J (1966) La ville, phénomène économique. Vie Ouvrière, Brussels

Rittel HWJ, Webber MM (1973) Dilemmas in a general theory of planning. Policy Sci 4(2):155–169

Rowe P (1987) Design thinking. MIT Press, Cambridge, MA

Saunders P (1984) Social theory and the urban question. Routledge, London

Schön DA (1982) Some of what a planner knows: a case study of knowing-in-practice. J Am Plann Assoc 48(3):351–364

Tsing A (2015) The mushroom at the end of the world: on the possibility of life in capitalist ruins. Princeton University Press, Princeton

Sternberg E (2000) An integrative theory of urban design. J Am Plann Assoc 66(3):265–278

Van Meeteren M, Boussauw K, Derudder B, Witlox F (2016) Flemish diamond or ABC axis? The spatial structure of the Belgian metropolitan area. Eur Plan Stud 24(5):974–995

Verhaert I, Vanobbergen T, Dehaene M et al (2014) Lab XX: opting for the twentieth-century belt. City of Antwerp, Antwerp

Vervloesem E, De Meulder B, Loeckx A (eds) (2012) Urban renewal in Flanders 2002–2011. A particular practice in Europe. ASP Editions, Brussels

Metaphors, Figures of Space and the Horizontal Metropolis

12

Paola Viganò

Abstract

This text addresses the need for an investigation into the metaphors we use when we design, interpret and reflect on contemporary cities and their future. Based on a series of concrete experiences where a set of conceptual metaphors have been proposed as powerful constructive tools, this paper opens up a wide reframing of the future city and metropolitan project and the construction of its narrative.

Keywords

Urban metaphors • Spatial figures • Horizontal relations • Metropolis

12.1 Conceptual Metaphors: Between the Modern and the Contemporary City

On a map of Europe, it is possible to identify a series of metaphors which have been used to describe, interpret and evoke the deep change the urban space has undergone over the last decades (Fig. 12.1). A few of them, to be more precise, are more than a century old, some were introduced during the big expansion following reconstruction after the Second World War, and others followed in a concentrated group between the 1980s and 1990s, when the form and constitution of the city started to be recognised as irremediably different from the past.

Each of these metaphorical concepts mentions and contains a feature of the place that inspired it, its economic and social history and the conditions under which it was formulated. As a whole, they represent the many facets of a pervasive phenomenon that not only has changed our judgment on urban transformations, but has slowly led to new definitions of positions, theories and projects for the contemporary city. These lie at the root of a potentially long-term genealogy of the contemporary project (Viganò 2017; Barcelloni Corte and Viganò forthcoming). Each of them highlights a difficulty that the metaphor helps to overcome, the issues that characterise the change and its cultural specificities.

However, this paper will not address genealogy on this occasion; rather, it will explore the use of metaphors by urbanists and then propose some reflections on the relevance of particular metaphors which, in the last decades, have allowed us to speak about what obscure aspects we were incapable of knowing much about. This may, for example, have influenced the future of some large metropolitan areas, allowing, via the use of conceptual metaphors, assumptions and strategies to be built that have enabled the exploration of new design images for their territories.

In its brief conclusions, this paper will clarify the need for this work, moving between different levels of abstraction that do not exclude, but rather build, relations whose meaning would otherwise be impossible or too distant to grasp.

Metaphors are rhetorical figures that feed the discourses of urbanists as well as our everyday life; indeed, most of the concepts we use are metaphorical in nature (Lakoff and Johnsen 2003). Metaphors are able to structure not only our

P. Viganò (✉)
Ecole Polytechnique Fédérale de Lausanne (EPFL), Lausanne, Switzerland
e-mail: paola.vigano@epfl.ch; ; paola.vigano@iuav.it

P. Viganò
Università IUAV, Venice, Italy

© Springer Nature Switzerland AG 2020
V. Lingua and V. Balz (eds.), *Shaping Regional Futures*,
https://doi.org/10.1007/978-3-030-23573-4_12

Fig. 12.1 Provisional and incomplete portrait of the European City-Territory, from Viganò, Sega (2013)

discourses, but also our thinking. In this sense, they are rhetorical figures capable of connecting heterogeneous materials (Genette 1966, 1972) and are particularly useful when we are in the difficult position of interpreting something which we do not really know or understand, phenomena which we are unable to describe.

Metaphors have structured urbanists' discourses (Secchi 2000, 2013) and the construction of their knowledge, mediated through a relationship with reality enabled by the use of metaphors—tools that involve the translation of one object into another that is capable, in some way, of representing the same. The history of the city and regional projects is full of metaphors that span time and are endowed with great inertia, while at the same time being capable of marking a specific period, a specific narrative or account (Secchi 1984). Reflecting on the metaphorical devices used to narrow the gap between the available theories, interpretations and concrete urban phenomena—the newly emerging urban forms and types—highlight the questions and the difficulties perceived and revealed each time. Reconceptualising the city has meant developing different readings, focusing on different aspects connected to specific geographic and cultural contexts and also tackling the various difficulties encountered there through the invention of new metaphors.

In the transition phase between the modern and contemporary city, three distinct groups of themes can be distinguished that reveal the main preoccupations and the challenges perceived as crucial in the transformation of urban spaces (Viganò 2016).

Between the end of the nineteenth and the early years of the twentieth century, the first theme concerned the new scale and form of the city. The second concerned the materials used to design the metropolitan and regional scale, in particular the "void" as a material to be reconceptualised, as in the *ville-paysage*. The city had changed its nature, and the inversion of the traditional relationship between built and open space durably marked its landscape and the very characteristics of the same (Viganò 1999). The third theme is metaphors that concern new spatial and procedural structures which are imagined to be consistent and coherent within the concrete conditions of the production of space. It is important to reconsider these themes because they touch upon the difficulties we still encounter in our experiences, interpretations and design explorations. The problem of the new city scale and its shape has expanded to the theme of planetary urbanisation, suggested in the form of a hypothesis by Lefevbre (1970) and more recently taken up by other scholars (Brenner 2014). The theme of the design of the urban and territorial materials able to represent and make the new space work at the different scales would require much more ingenious and courageous experiments than are those currently possible to us. The role of open space in the new spatial configuration is, despite the efforts made between the late nineteenth and early decades of the twentieth century, still uncertain and seeking its own justification, for instance, in terms of a productive landscape or the ability to offer ecosystem services useful for conurbations that contain these spaces.

The question becomes particularly complex when we touch on the theme of spatial or procedural structures capable of acting as a reference and guiding the transformation of the fragmented space of cities, metropolitan areas and regions over time. Some spatial structures that do not belong to the great designs of modernity, capable of influencing the course of history, rather have the potential of "weak structures" (Vattimo 1985). Without considering them representative of the post-modern era alone, these terms are useful for grasping the issues and potential of designing contemporary spaces. Once again, the use of metaphors—such as that of weak structure to talk about the role that, for example, a minor watercourse could play in a territorial project—highlights the rigidity of the structures typical of victorious modernity, rigid compared to the grounds, contexts and territories, yet able to bend and reform in places and then impinged upon by agents stronger than they are or by a widespread set of acts of resistance. These reveal the almost infinite capabilities of adaptation that the contexts develop, independently of the "vocations" that we claim to have read in their "genetic code"—metaphors that are not always useful, even misleading, and that illuminate claimed teleological paths, inscribed in an unchangeable destiny.

12.1.1 A Lung for the City. A Twenty-Four-Hour Workshop Where All Can Extend Their Knowledge and Delight in Learning[1]

Taking a step back, we can introduce the metaphor used by Cedric Price, an eccentric and acute mind, to speak about his project for the Villette park competition in Paris in 1982. Not much is known about his participation, and the proposed design and representations have been almost forgotten, despite the fact that they still appear extremely rich and contemporary after more than thirty years. The park is a special metaphorical object, and the city has often been imagined through the lens of a park, notwithstanding the difference in scale and matter of imagining cities as parks and designed as such.

The Villette park competition, at the beginning of the 1980s, was a melting pot for new urban ideas. However, Cedric Price's starting point was a very traditional metaphor: the park as a lung for the city. In this, Price reconnects to the hygienist project and its arsenal of metaphors, almost always organic, such as that of the park-lung that allows the city to breathe. However, after the tribute to modern urban planning, he almost immediately departs from it, heading off in another direction by opening, via another metaphor, a different path in our imagination: a park as a twenty-four-hour workshop (Fig. 12.2a). The park becomes a productive and functioning workspace, day and night, a place of elaboration and production that anticipates contemporary debate on the productive city. In the park, visitors will be able to "extend their knowledge and delight in learning" (Price 1982). The space project defines the framework, the support for the activities which are manifold and include the production of research and agriculture. The park is its infrastructure. Through this metaphor, the park-workshop is designed to enable (Fig. 12.2b): it is both the support and the lever that amplifies actions, imagination and knowledge of the world, a theme at the centre of every reflection on space.

The metaphor not only allows us to deal with aspects that are unclear, but also, via its ability to make the unknown imaginable, allows us to pass from the metaphorical field to that of the projective imagination and the prototypical field, to the construction of space prototypes, starting from the metaphor. Cedric Price's park is one such spatial prototype that we can access through the images that accompany the project report. The prototype is anticipated by a metaphorical conceptualisation that helps to bridge the lack of images and structured references. At the same time, the two metaphors used—the lung and the workshop—refer to a plurality of coherent images because they are structured by both metaphors, upon which spaces and discourses are articulated.

---

[1]Cedric Price, Park de La villette Competition 1982—Report, 1982 CCA Archives, Cedric Price: 156 Parc 1.3.3 Report concours parc de la Villette.

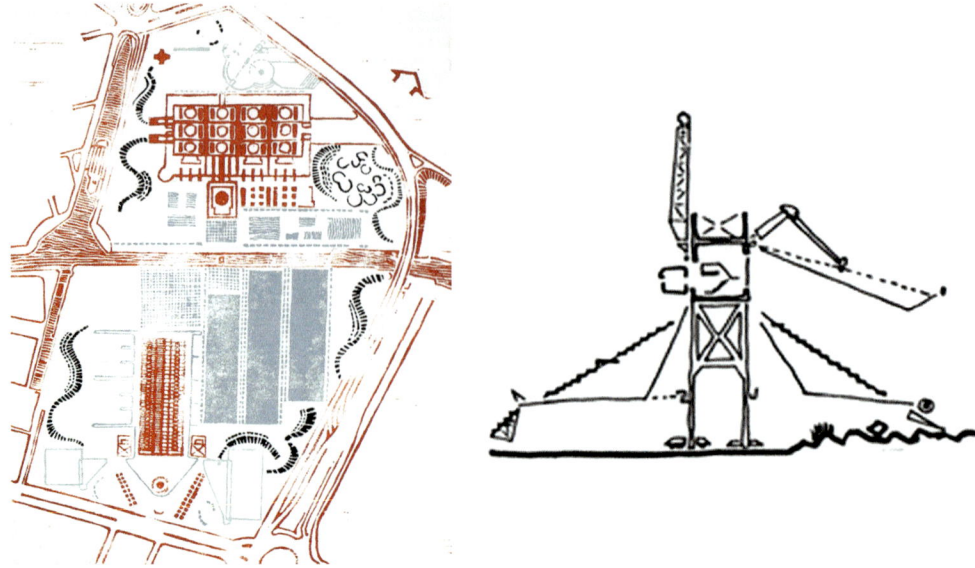

Fig. 12.2 Cedric Price's park de la Villette proposal, from Price (1982)

The resulting tale or account does not end with the project presented by Price but remains open to everyone's imagination, to both individual and collective interpretations of a lung and a workshop park that can perform in different ways. This is, of course, also true for the territorial metaphors and prototypes/models that germinate from them, illuminating the projective character that they contain and which we often cannot fully grasp.

12.2 The Horizontal Metropolis

One of our prototypes has been the "Horizontal Metropolis", an oxymoron that was introduced to set a vision for the Brussels region at the 2040 horizon (Secchi and Viganò 2012). It is an attempt to define a metropolitan space with characteristics that are far from the traditional image of the metropolis with its centralised organisation, hierarchy and peripheries. It also blends and merges the interpretation of a concrete space (the metropolitan region of Brussels) with a projective gaze (Fig. 12.3a, b), a vision for a region where the main city has never been the centre and that only today, with a renewed and reinforced international role is slowly becoming more attractive, thereby demanding a reconsideration of the complex relations with its intense, productive and diffuse territory (Van Meeteren et al. 2016). Close complementary, competitive and synergistic relations between city and countryside have shaped the organisation of this territory where generalised accessibility has been possible thanks to great investment in mobility infrastructures and throughout the territory. This space is not homogeneous, but marked by its geography—the three valleys—and the metropolitan figures that play a role in structuring and orienting the self-same space. By defining this space as a Horizontal Metropolis, we are not only outlining its social and physical features, but also abstracting its imperfect horizontal characteristics—its latent potential towards horizontal territorial and urban relations—so that they can be reframed within a project-based idea: the design of a Horizontal Metropolis in Brussels for the 2040 horizon.

Prototypes are precise investigations which run the risk of failing through concrete experimentation. In our field, the experimentation space is mainly public and inspires collective debate, through which hypotheses are subjected to a process of verification or falsification. This experimentation is made possible and supported by images that try to give the future a real colour, as if we could enter it and understand its possibilities or, on the contrary, its shortcomings, especially those that would be the undesirable outcome of a sum of good intentions. The hyper-realistic representations we used contain many details of a daily future: this is the case with the vision for the "Western Garden" in the most fertile part of the metropolitan area. It shows how, starting from the theme of training and education, new spaces for schools, sports facilities and services can be imagined along with new urban agriculture, a public transport mesh and, finally, areas that reduce the flood risk along

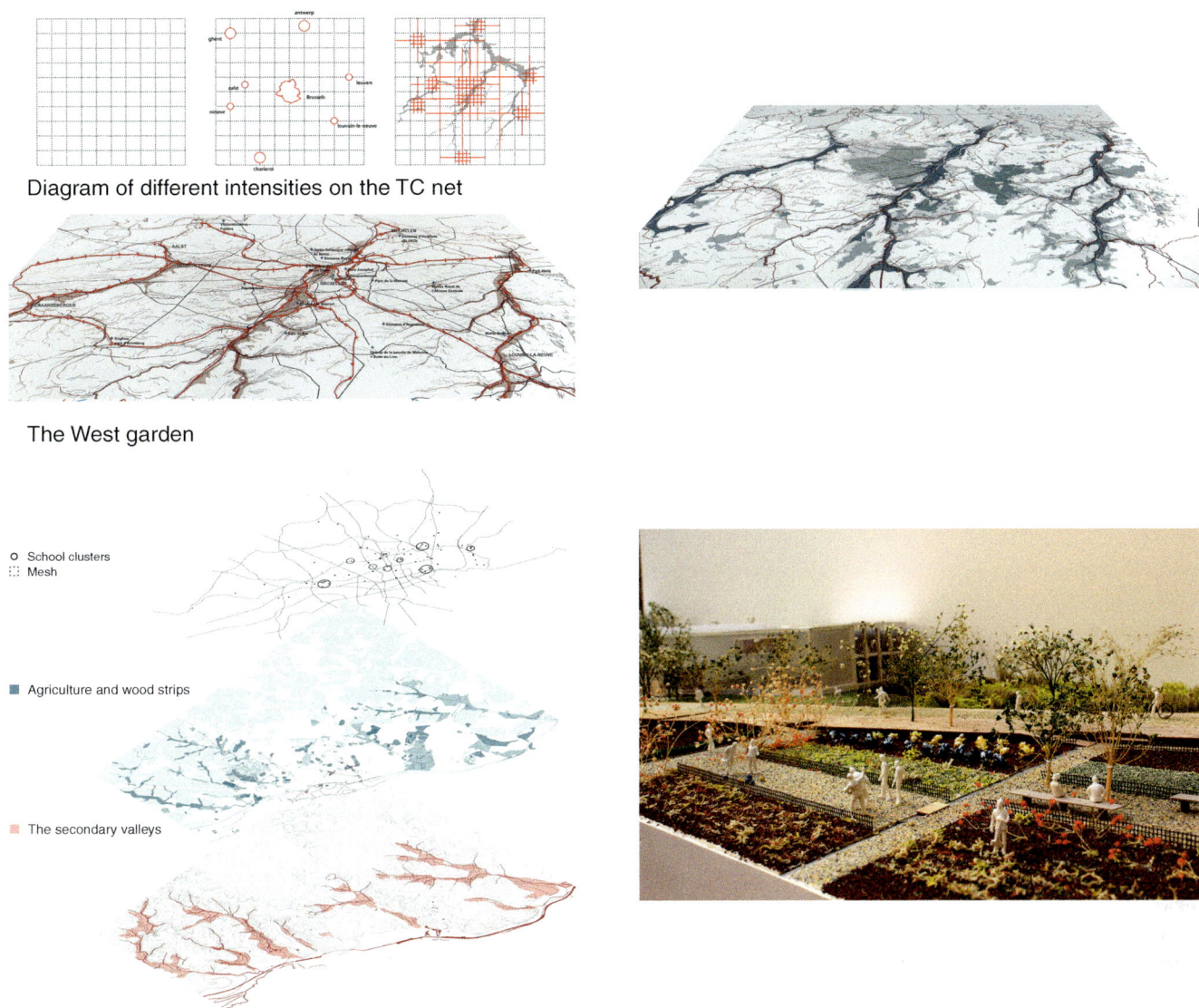

Diagram of different intensities on the TC net

The West garden

○ School clusters
∷ Mesh

■ Agriculture and wood strips

■ The secondary valleys

Fig. 12.3 Bruxelles 2040: la Métropole horizontale 2010–2012 from Secchi and Viganò (2012)

the Senne tributaries, together with a new biodiversity (Fig. 12.3c, d) and the requalification of entire neighbourhoods. As a whole, the Western Garden is a device for improving the western suburbs of Brussels, at one and the same time a space of emancipation and an ecological space that reinforces its ties with both the denser areas of the city, through the strengthening of ecological and social continuity along the water courses and waterfronts, as well as with the great inhabited countryside of Pajottenland.

12.2.1   Horizontality

The question of horizontality is crucial, although it is by no means new. In the writings and diagrams of Gloeden (1923), Berlin is reconceptualised and projected into a model of metropolitan horizontality. The unbuilt ground becomes a connective space of cells without hierarchy, complementary to each other like the cells of an organism, yet when compounded they form a green belt—a powerful metaphor that urbanism and urban planning have not yet surpassed which includes them all within the great metropolis. It is not a polycentric space, but rather an a-centric space, that has no centre. Territorial

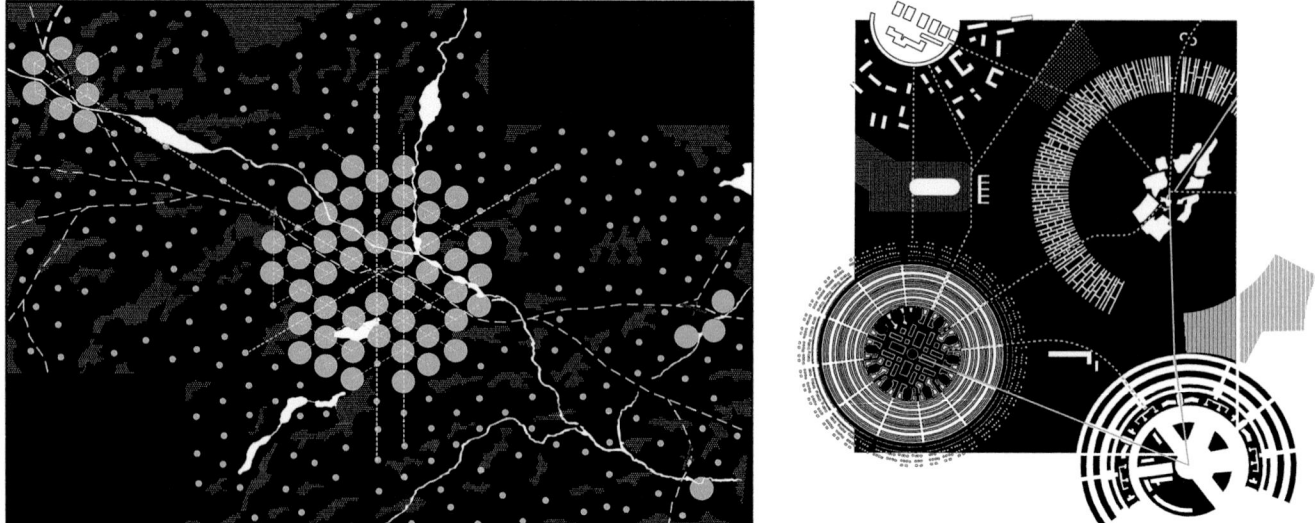

Fig. 12.4 Interpretative redesign of the Gloeden Inflation der Grosstädte diagram, from Viganò (2016)

rationalities shape and organise the great railway infrastructure that follows the valley, while an abstract geometric pattern organises measures and distances between densely inhabited cells, as well as their mutual relations, in addition to the tram network that connects them and stops in the middle of the green belt, the only element capable of providing continuity and legibility to the metropolitan space (Fig. 12.4a, b). It is only from the green belt that the city with its landscapes can be seen and its novelty understood compared to the city of the past. Thus, it is a metaphor that on all scales, from the territorial project to the city area, has exerted an enormous influence on our ability to imagine the urban space of the future. This case also enables us to understand the inertia of metaphors that become entangled in our discourses and block our thoughts. For if we imagine the city of the future, yet continue to structure our reflections around ancient metaphors or—in the case of metaphors proposed by modern urbanism—those that are at least a century old, using and reusing them, we will not notice the wear and tear on, nor the stability and accumulation of experiences bound up in, the tale or vision that the metaphor includes.

At the same time, metaphors are often not fully understood, or else they are trivialised. This is still the case of the green belt which, in the reinterpretation of Gloeden's diagrams, reveals its nature as a connective surface and not just as a green margin. Its role facilitates the space of the metropolis; it contains much more than just parks and gardens, but also public transport and facilities, i.e. the fundamental infrastructure of the entire metropolitan space. Gloeden's diagrams, as shown in *Territories of Urbanism*, (Vigano 2016) reappear in many subsequent reflections. For instance, in the Grand Paris, they form an a-centric composition of high-density cells within the SDRIF (*schéma d'organization de la région parisienne*), designed between 1963 and 1966 by Paul Maymont, who radically deconstructs the centrality of the Parisian compact core (Fig. 12.5). They also underpin the description of the green lagoon that contains fragments of Unger's Berlin, islands that are "cities in the city" (Ungers 1978).

12.2.2 Figures of Space

Research on the Horizontal Metropolis continued well beyond the metropolitan area of Brussels, tackling different territories in North America, Europe and China. This occurred through a series of experiences bound by a common research protocol,[2] with the construction of an atlas for every situation and with the realisation of tables and models on the scale of the Broadacre City model (created in 1935 by Frank Lloyd Wright and Taliesin's students), to explore the deep and non-selective metamorphosis of the urban space implicit in each economic, demographic and ecological transition aiming for

---

[2]The research was exhibited as a side event of the Venice Architecture Biennale in 2016 (curated by P. Viganò with Chiara Cavalieri and Martina Barcelloni Corte) and in 2018 at the BOZAR in Brussels with the addition of three new case studies (Flanders, Brussels Capital Region and Wallonia) to the previous five.

Fig. 12.5 Paul Maymont, 1963–1966, schéma d'organisation de la région Parisienne

higher sustainability. The meaning of this work is not to replicate Wright's decentralised vision, but to allow one to emerge from the places we already inhabit—a stretch of alpine valley furrowed by heavy infrastructure, an aged commercial strip in the metropolitan area of Boston or on the outskirts of the Leman Alpine metropolis, in the diffuse cities built by water in southern China and in the Venetian hinterland. Their durability through diffuse but overall adaptations enhances their space and their social capital.

Figures of space are meant to design and structure the Horizontal Metropolis, to reinforce and reestablish horizontal relations, connectivity and the balanced distribution of opportunities in the urban-territorial space. They rely on the material construction of the territory, on the organising power of territorial rationalisation and infrastructures, affirming the *long durée* in functional/ecological terms, but also investigating the need to upgrade and adapt the existing spatial capital. Figures that are relevant for regional design are not only those derived from the main infrastructures, but those that can multiply their role or the reinterpretation of natural or artificial patterns (the fine hydrographic network or the patterns of agriculture) which have been severely manipulated in the roaring age of modernity.

The models of the Horizontal Metropolis have been constructed deeply reflecting on which spatial elements would be able to structure the metamorphosis and to construct, as rhetoric figures, a new discourse on the project of the contemporary city-territory project (Fig. 12.6). For example, with the Boston Horizontal Metropolis, a new image of the traditional commercial strip stemmed out of a union of strategies related to run-off from impervious surfaces, buffer areas, water body qualities and accessibility, as well as new golf courses reusing overly generous parking spaces, or the densification of old wooden prefabricated houses and the reinstatement of tramway lines. In such cases, a new public space that is absent today appears, one that can finally structure a transformation of the American sprawl at urban and regional scale (Figs. 12.7, 12.8, 12.9 and 12.10).

Weak structures are not the "levees" (another metaphor) sketched by Benton MacKaye in *The New Exploration* (MacKaye 1928)—those were envisioned to stop metropolitan growth—but rather they are organising devices which are thought to cross and intersect all possible opportunities to recycle and reconfigure the North American sprawl.

Fig. 12.6 Horizontal
Metropolis, a radical project.
Images from the Valais
case-study, from Cavalieri,
Viganò, eds. (2019)

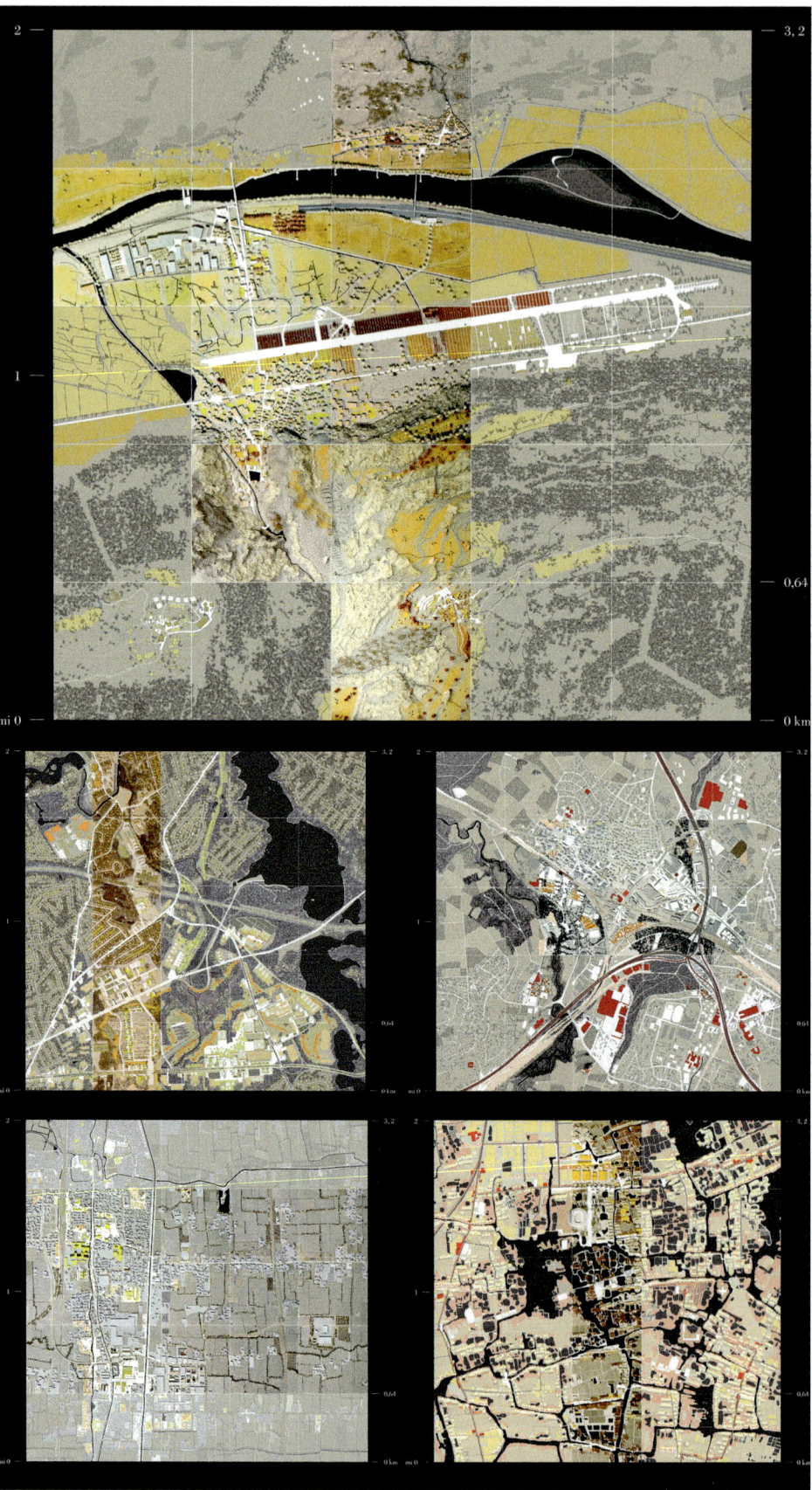

Fig. 12.7 Horizontal Metropolis in Boston. The metamorphosis of the "middle ground", from Cavalieri, Viganò, eds. (2019)

It is through both research and concrete experiences that conceptual metaphors can reveal their powerful constructive role at different scales, able to reframe a narrative and discourse about the city and its projects. The metaphors we use, and on which we might carry out quantitative and qualitative analyses, mark all our difficulties and are among the most sensitive instruments we have available to elaborate our thoughts. This research work and these project experiences are necessary to foster a concrete awareness of the epochal transition involving all territories, which will irrevocably transform them.

Fig. 12.8 Work by John Frey in the Territorialism Laboratory at Harvard GSD, from Viganò (2014)

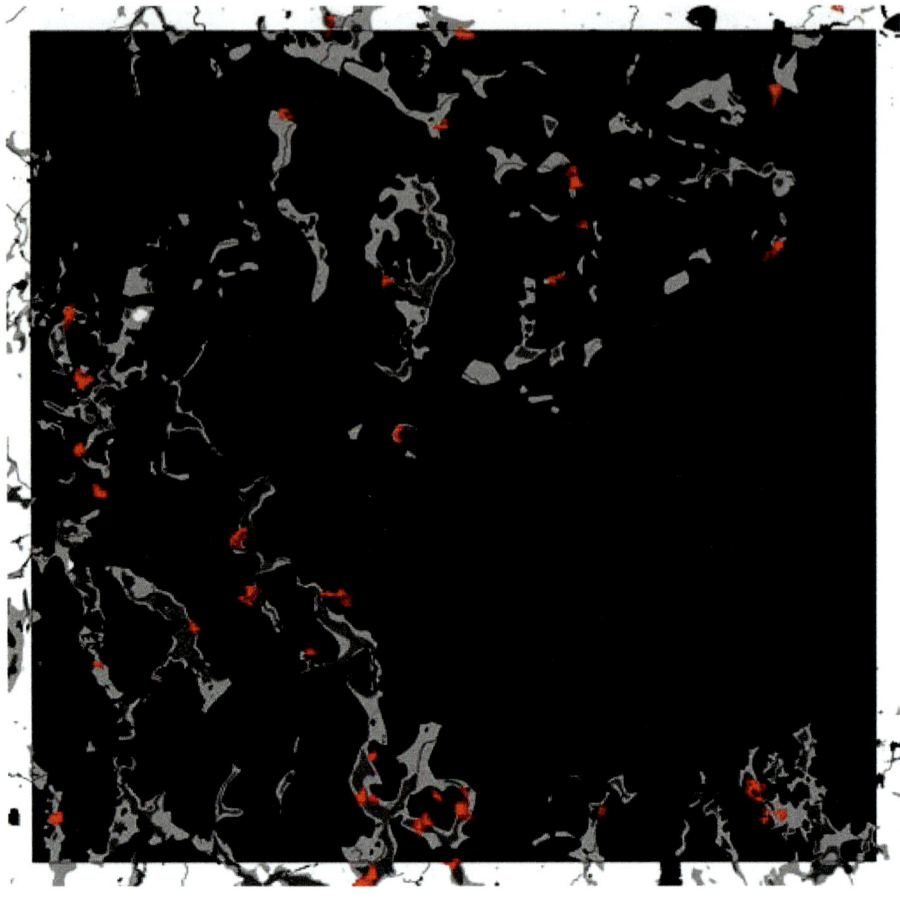

Fig. 12.9 Work by Omar Davis in the Territorialism Laboratory at Harvard GSD, from Viganò (2014)

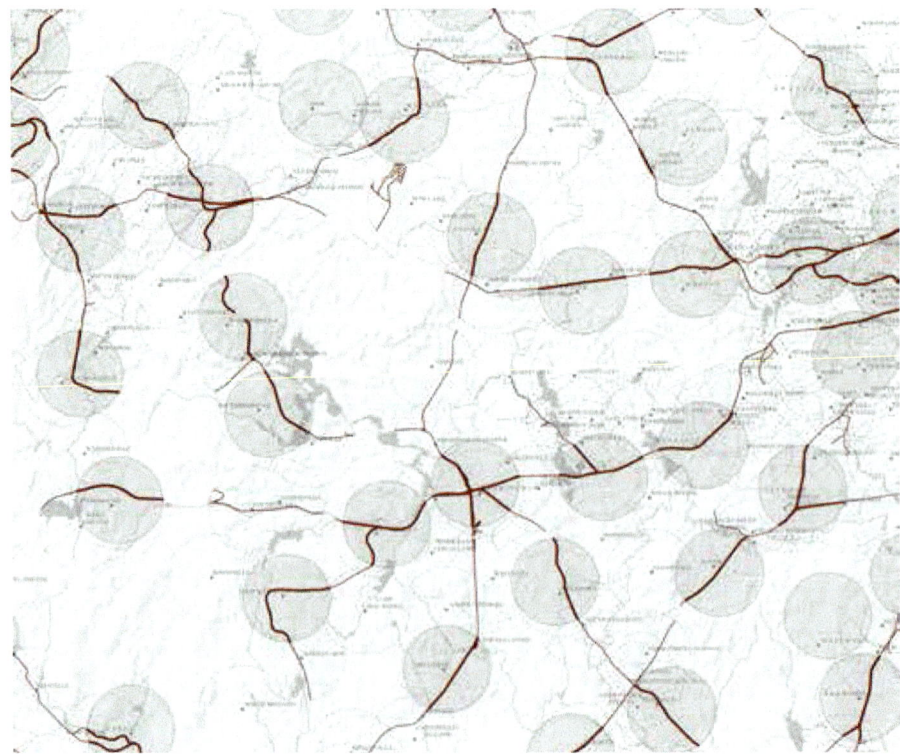

Fig. 12.10 Work by Phoebe White in the Territorialism Laboratory at Harvard GSD, from Viganò (2014)

References

Barcelloni Corte M, Viganò P (eds) (forthcoming) The horizontal metropolis. An anthology. Springer

Brenner N (ed) (2014) Implosions/explosions—towards a study of planetary urbanization. Jovis, Berlin

Cavalieri C, Viganò P (eds) (2019) The horizontal metropolis a radical project. Park Books, Zürich

Genette G (1966) Proust Palimpseste. In. Figures I. Editions du Seuil, Paris

Genette G (1972) Discours du récit. Essai de méthode. In. Figures III. Editions du Seuil, Paris

Gloeden E (1923) Inflation der Grosstädte. Der Zirkel Architecktur Verlag, Berlin

Lakoff G, Johnsen M (2003) Metaphors we live by. The University of Chicago Press, Chicago (Originally published 1980)

Lefevbre H (1970) La révolution urbaine. Gallimard, Paris

MacKaye B (1928) The new exploration: A philosophy of regional planning. Harcourt Brace & Co, New York

Price C (1982) Concours International Parc de la Villette—Report, 1982 CCA Archives, Cedric Price: 156 Parc 1.3.3 Report concours parc de la Villette

Secchi B (1984) Il racconto urbanistico. Einaudi, Torino

Secchi B (2000) Prima lezione di urbanistica. Laterza, Bari

Secchi B (2013) A new urban question 3: when, why and how some fundamental metaphors were used. In: Gerber A, Patterson B (eds) Metaphors in architecture and urbanism. An introduction. Transcript Verlag, Bielefeld

Secchi B, Viganò P (with Creat, Egis Mobilité, G Hausladen-TU München, IDEA Consult, Karbon') (2012) Bruxelles et Ses Territoires, Plan Régional de Développement Durable. Elaboration D'une Vision Territoriale Métropolitaine À L'horizon 2040 Pour Bruxelles. Report

Ungers OM (1978) Die Stadt in der Stadt. Berlin Das Grüne Stadtarchipel. With Riemann P, Kollhoff H, Ovaska AA, Koolhaas R. Lotus International 19

Van Meeteren M, Boussauw K, Derudder B, Witlox F (2016) Flemish diamond or ABC-axis? The spatial structure of the Belgian metropolitan area. Eur Plan Stud 24(5):974–995. https://doi.org/10.1080/09654313.2016.1139058

Vattimo G (1985) La fine della modernità. Garzanti, Milano

Viganò P (1999) La città elementare. Skira, Milano, Genève

Viganò P (2014) Territorialism. Harvard GSD Press, Boston

Viganò P (2016) Territories of urbanism—the project as knowledge producer. Routledge-EPFL Press (Originally published in Italian 2010)

Viganò P (2017) The Horizontal Metropolis: "deux ou trois choses que je sais d'elle". In: Lorenzo Degli Esposti (ed) Milan Capital of the Modern, ACTAR

Open and Closed Figures in Dutch Spatial Planning

13

Carlo Pisano and Veronica Saddi

Abstract

Thanks to their strong evocative power, figures of speech—rhetorical expression that uses language in a nonliteral way—have always been part of the urban vocabulary, facilitating visions and urban projects. This chapter addresses the reasons for, and methods of using figures of speech in urban planning, using the Netherlands as a case study. The reading of the various rhetorical devices will be based on the proposed distinction—one of the many possible—between closed and open figures, that is between those figures based on the definition of shape or structure and those that instead express an open structure and a relational scheme. The figures will be described in terms of their specific characteristics, contexts and fields of action. This analysis recognises different historical tendencies in the use of figures in urban planning, strictly related to the specific need to manage or drive territorial transformations. Among the specifically Dutch-born figures, the *patchwork* metaphor will be analysed in depth, especially as proposed by Willem Jan Neutelings in his 1989 Patchwork Metropolis project, and further investigated in terms of the abstract model and its implicit meanings, related to a certain way of living and transforming the urban territory.

Keywords

Dutch spatial planning • Urban metaphors • Rhetoric figures • Urban concepts • Regional design

13.1 The Role of Figures of Speech in Urban Studies

The rise of the metropolitan influence over recent decades has sparked the need to conceptualise vast urbanised territories and to develop a structured way of envisioning metropolitan complexities. This has given rise to a variety of theories and interpretations of how urban dynamics exhibit new dimensional and qualitative features compared to the traditional, compact city.

On the one hand, there is a tendency, especially with institutions and administrations, to classify the current urban setting according to measurable criteria and an almost deterministic approach that is built on a recombination of familiar tools and consolidated concepts. As an example, the European Union, in collaboration with the Organisation for Economic Co-operation and Development, developed specific studies designed to recognise and define the urban configurations of European metropolitan and regional systems, paying particular attention to functional urban regions defined as Metropolitan (metro) Regions (Dijkstra and Poelman 2011). The report 'The State of EU Cities' (European Commission 2016) proposed, for instance, a hybrid definition that considers both administrative and demographic dimensions, dividing the metropolitan

C. Pisano (✉)
Department of Architecture, Regional Design Laboratory, University of Florence, Florence, Italy
e-mail: carlo.pisano@unifi.it

V. Saddi
Ministry of Cultural Heritage and Activities, Florence, Italy
e-mail: veronica.saddi@gmail.com

© Springer Nature Switzerland AG 2020
V. Lingua and V. Balz (eds.), *Shaping Regional Futures*,
https://doi.org/10.1007/978-3-030-23573-4_13

regions—proposed as urban areas with more than 250,000 inhabitants or NUTS3—into three typologies[1] depending on whether or not they include the capital city, or other internationally renowned cities.

On the other hand, several urban analyses have considered metropolitan areas not just as a collection of enlarged cities and villages but as a complete new form of city. This alternative interpretation—pursued by many prominent researchers ranging from Soja (1989) to Sieverts (2003) and from Viganò et al. (2018) and Secchi (2011) to Allen (1999)—does not follow quantitative analyses based on demographics or administrative configurations but is based instead on the explorative and mediatory capacity of the design approach. This different point of view is grounded in the ability of design to gather knowledge, to envision and contextualise, as well as to connect and organise plans and processes (Meijsmans and de Zwart 2009). This approach is often based on the use of figures of speech that are employed to select and manage complex and specific territorial conditions such as urban dispersion or morphological features. Among these, *rurbanisation, diffuse city* (Indovina 1990), *city of cities* (Hertweck and Marot 2013), *horizontal metropolis* (Viganò et al. 2018), *fractal city*, *metropolitan archipelago* (Indovina 2003) and *zwischenstadt* (Sieverts 2003) are just few examples.

However, this is not an innovative approach. From organic figures such as Copenhagen's *five fingers* or Chandigarh's circulatory system *7 V concept*, to environmental metaphors such as the Helsinky *archipelago* or Boston's *pearl necklace*, the history of urbanism is populated by all sorts of rhetorical devices. Despite the differences between these urban traditions, in times of dramatic transformation, when an old order is broken and a new one takes its place—when social and economic regimes or governance scale change, for example, or when it is necessary to manage or guide complex conditions such as extreme ecological transformations or economic crises—the planning machine has often taken refuge behind figures of speech, both to describe a new and unknown condition as well to propose long-lasting visions. Indeed, herein lies the main significance of rhetorical figures—they serve to make sense of what we can't fully grasp, somehow enveloping the complexity of the situation within a unifying logic (Viganò 2010). The use of figures in the urban field also forces us to distinguish certain characteristics and dynamics of a given city or territory through a comparison with more or less similar elements, or rules, that are evident in the chosen figure of speech in their purest form.

Furthermore, similar to what Genette (1997: 91–92) postulates in his essay on second-degree literature, the imitation of a metaphor—or its application—can only occur indirectly. Whilst the metaphor is neat, defined and immutable, it necessarily becomes ambiguous, out of focus, flexible and transitory when applied to a specific case because it implies a series of choices, simplifications and hypotheses that can differ from case to case. This is also extremely relevant for urban strategies where the specific context becomes the surface on which the pure figure is mirrored, giving us a much deeper image loaded with meanings concerning the issues pertaining to the territory.

As in the literature, the different figures used in urban planning are devices meant to propose specific interpretations of phenomena and issues that would otherwise be hard to explain, whilst at the same time, they preserve a rich ambiguity. By means of *analogy,* two concepts can be combined together, thus providing an explicit key to understanding an otherwise overly general concept (for instance, the city archipelago of Ungers or the Dutch Randstad). A *synecdoche* defines an object or place by describing a part of it that is intertwined in a causal or spatial relationship, thus highlighting the primary aspects of a complex condition (Sieverts' Zwischenstadt); through *oxymorons,* two opposite terms are associated, creating original and meaningful contrasts (for instance, the Diffuse City of Indovina or Horizontal Metropolis of Viganò and Secchi), whilst a *metaphor* associates the qualities of one concept with another, without an explicit logical connection to clarify their relationship (Sprawl or the Dutch Green Heart), thus leaving the field wide open for interpretation.

The use of figures of speech in urbanism can be also convenient at several stages of the planning process. As a research device, figures of speech help to describe what is unknown, or too complex, in terms of something familiar and they provide a way to criticise particular phenomena such as the dispersion or fragmented condition of the contemporary city. As an act of imagination (Viganò 2010), analogies and metaphors prove essential in proposing future visions (Guida 2011), and as an instrument of communication, they also guide design choices more effectively (Secchi 2011). The representation of the territory through figures of speech, in fact, 'besides describing certain realities of today or certain socio-cultural transformation processes, is what fosters one policy rather than another' (Dematteis 1995, 71).

The aim of this chapter is thus to explore the benefits brought by a conscious rather than superficial use of figures of speech in urban and strategic planning and to highlight how these instruments have evolved and adapted to changing needs

---

[1]The three types of metro-regions are: 1. capital city regions; 2. second-tier metro-regions; and 3. smaller metro-regions. The capital city region is a metro-region which includes the national capital. The second-tier metro-region is the group of largest cities in the country excluding the capital.

in this field. The next section discusses the transition from closed to open figures, analysing the Dutch context where specific territorial, economic and political conditions have produced a flourishing interaction between the use of figures of speech and their implementation in urban planning.

13.2 Open and Closed Figures

Beyond its evocative power, a figure of speech can be considered as a concept built on several levels, where each term is carefully chosen and underlies a series of more implicit meanings that refer to each other, thereby building a much more complex story. A figure encompasses a whole series of considerations, axioms and beliefs that inevitably concern not only the city itself but also social, economic and ecological aspects as well as how they are related and can evolve.

Therefore, figures of speech used in urbanism—at different times and more or less universally known and agreed—can be classified in different ways according to their particular intention or aim. Secchi (2010), for example, proposes a distinction between *associative* metaphors that describe the city in terms of some other sphere related to our physical or mental experience (for instance, the city as a forest, human body part or machine) and *conceptual* metaphors which define the city in terms of abstract concepts (such as continuity, order, process or balance, for instance).

Here, we propose a further distinction, based on a figure's ability to maintain its own identity despite certain variables being altered. Hence, the proposed classification distinguishes between *closed* and *open* figures, according to a figure's level of adaptability in the face of complexity, whilst at the same time remaining coherent with its explicit rationality.

The term 'closed figure' describes those figures of speech that are fundamentally based on a formal approach to the city. As such, they are mainly concerned with the definition of shape or structure. *Randstad*, *ladder* and *five fingers*, for instance, are all devices with limited flexibility and are characterised by a strong statement, i.e. a stance that clearly sets out a distinction between what is good and bad or what is acceptable and what it is not. Altering even one single variable, therefore, drastically transforms the figure or its operational effectiveness. For instance, a heart cannot survive after being split into three parts any more than a hand with six fingers can be considered an acceptable norm.

On the contrary, figures of speech that populate the second group are characterised by an open structure and a relational scheme (Davoudi and Strange 2008) that allows and guides transformations. Without aspiring to a specific output or outcome, 'open figures' rather set out basic rules that must be respected in their formation. As such, they are process-oriented rather than focused on achieving a specific form: for example, changing the colour swatch of a tile does not invalidate a *mosaic* metaphor. However, open figures are more generic and less mandatory and confined to a particular spatial situation, so they are often accompanied by a specification that better qualifies their aim and scope, for example, the *green* mosaic or the *porous urban carpet*.

Of course, this differentiation does not involve a neat separation between inherently open/closed, formal/informal, spatially confined/undefined or flexible/inflexible figures. The same figure, depending on how it is loaded with meaning, can in fact be used in different ways according to a specific aim or context. This was indeed the case with the *archipelago* metaphor. In 1977, it was used by O. M. Ungers as a 'closed' figure, to emphasise a specific possible configuration of the then-shrinking city of Berlin, and later reinterpreted by the Italian philosopher Massimo Cacciari in 1997 as an 'open' figure, representing the intense relationships and complementarities on which the different European states should build their union.

It is also possible to recognise different historical tendencies in the use of figures in urban planning. Whilst the heroic period of modernism was mainly guided by closed metaphors meant to govern the morphology of urbanisation across open territories, in more recent times, more relational and open figures have proliferated, intended as flexible devices for the transformation of already-urbanised territories. Thus, at the beginning of the twentieth century, the linear and garden city were common urban models, whereas at the approach of the new millennium, urban models such as the green matrix, patchwork, eco and smart city started to emerge.[2]

---

[2]Note how Davoudi and Strange (2008) also highlighted a similar tendency by describing a shift towards a more relational understanding of space through the redefined planning process.

13.3 The Netherlands Through Figures

The Dutch case offers a way to better understand the reasons behind this classification, being particularly emblematic in terms of the clarity and frequency of its urban metaphors. From a general perspective, as already mentioned, the use of figures of speech in urban planning has always been connected with the need to govern dramatic transformations (such as population growth, shrinking phenomena or the need to address the effects of climate change) and guide rapid innovation, especially as it relates to technological improvements in transportation. It is no coincidence that a country such as the Netherlands—characterised by high density in terms of population and services, a dynamic economy and severe flood risks—has, many times during its history, turned to rhetorical figures to help interpret and plan the evolution of its complex territorial configuration.

In particular, the aspiration to balance population distribution and activities throughout the country has inspired many new terms in the search for equilibrium between two extremes, two 'fears', so to speak: on the one hand, the fear of a widespread dispersion over many small centres—whose underlying pattern actually dates back to the middle ages—because it would lead to a destruction of the countryside, unnecessary car-based mobility and undermine the vitality of cities and towns. On the other hand, the concentration scenario is feared as much as its opposite, for the 'metropolis' would lead to a deeply uneven development across the country—a prosperous centre and a poor periphery.

During the twentieth century, many planning schemes and policies tried to mediate between extreme dispersion and extreme concentration. Indeed, from the national Randstad/Green Heart policies of the 1960s, 1970s and 1980s (see Faludi and van der Valk 1994), to the compact city policies of the 1990s and early 2000s, Dutch planning seems rooted in figures of speech.

One of the most famous figures in Dutch urbanisation is the *Randstad* analogy. It was allegedly first introduced in the 1930s by Mr Pleasman (director of KLM[3]) who, during an aerial reconnaissance to find the best location for a new airport, described the Western Dutch territory as an urbanised territory around a green heart, coining for the first time the Randstad/Green Heart dichotomy.

Then, immediately after World War II, the Dutch central government took greater control over the national territory through a series of subsidies and regulations to create a central, modern welfare. Since the 'First National Spatial Planning Act' of 1958, the urban model based on opposition to Randstad/Green Heart has become the founding and winning idea of Dutch politics, to the point that in 1966 Peter Hall stated: 'There seems little doubt that for most of the still-growing world cities of the present time, the Dutch solution is the right model'.

The 'Second National Spatial Planning Report' of 1966 represented the beginning of one of the most influential planning concepts developed in the Netherlands, the *concentrated deconcentration* model. This oxymoron was meant to propose a balance between metropolitan concentration on the one hand and radical deconcentration on the other hand. It became the catchphrase to promote the creation of green, medium-sized living environments, that is, housing in moderately dense neighbourhoods with towns and villages which are characteristic of large parts of the Netherlands (Wandl et al. 2014, 50–63). Later on, this model was renamed the 'segmented city' (Fig. 13.1).

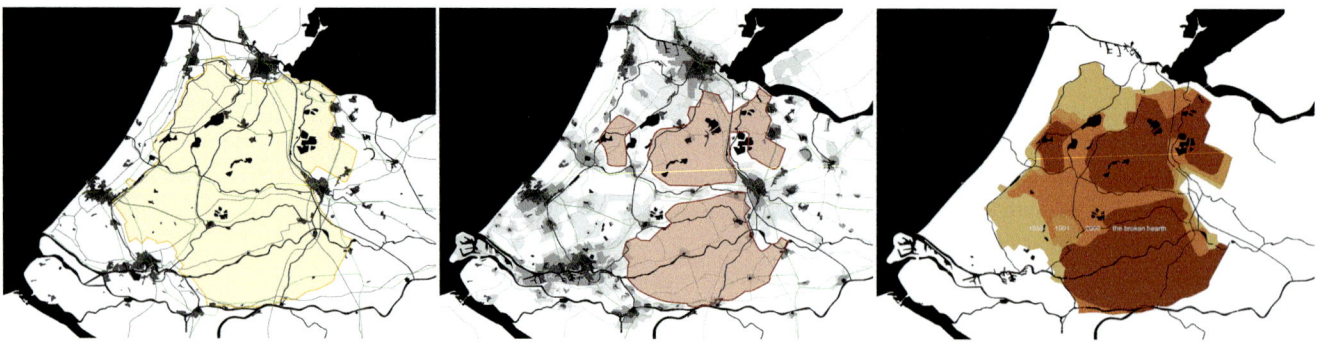

Fig. 13.1 The broken heart: evolution of the Randstad/Green Heart figure between 1939 and 2008, derived from the superposition of urban areas over time, Pisano (2018a)

---

[3]The Royal Dutch Airlines (Koninklijke Luchtvaart Maatschappij, KLM).

During the 1960s and 1970s, opposition to the Randstad/Green Heart led the planning discussion. The definition of such a neat closed figure—and the conviction to put it into practice—fostered its implementation through political and planning initiatives intended to create a clear separation between a large, albeit controlled, metropolis and a paradisiac arcadia. But from the 1980s onwards, this dream was progressively demolished. The shift was undoubtedly connected with political and economic changes that affected the Netherlands from approximately the late 1970s and the second oil crisis. At that time, in fact, the country started to face a general reorganisation with the beginning of the neoliberalisation movement (Waterhout et al. 2012). This is still reflected in the current planning system, in which the national government struck off about three-quarters of the planning agenda and dismantled some major organisations, including the ministry bearing spatial planning in its name (Zonneveld and Evers 2014).

The reaction to this changing political landscape and the consequences for urban planning came firstly from the design and research sector, through a series of radical visions and urban concepts which started to question prevailing interpretations of the urban form. Where previously such interpretations had been coined in a dichotomy intrinsically related to the Randstad concept—'red' and 'green', or 'built' and 'open', for instance—new ones started to explore the potential of design at regional scale (Banz and Zonneveld 2015), embracing international discussions and spatial concepts. Organisations such as 'Architecture in Rotterdam' (AIR), the 'Eo Wijers Foundation' or the ensemble of academics and professionals behind the 'The Netherlands Now As Design' project (NNAO) aimed to visualise ideas and frame problems (Sutton and Kemp 2006) by defining appropriate fields of action (Neuman 1998; Sieverts 2008; Balz 2017) using novel approaches for planning policy (Van Dijk 2011). Many urban designers started to take a different approach altogether, interpreting political and economic changes and proposing novel and prospective projects that were far more realistic and in tune with socio-spatial trends (Pisano 2017), thus playing an influential role in transforming closed figures into open ones.

Among them, three architects in particular focused on the area between Rotterdam and The Hague,[4] interpreting its peculiar decentralised configuration as a 'new' metropolis spread out over an entire region and in the form of a field— Palmboom (1987) with the 'Urbanised Landscape'; OMA, Alkemade (2002) with the 'Field Metropolis' of the Deltametropool project; and Neutelings (1989) with the 'Patchwork Metropolis'. Contrary to the Randstad analogy—which despite some remnants was effectively dismantled when urbanisation started to saturate not only the space in between the cities, but also the very central, supposed green, heart—this new series of figures of speech focused more on the relations between parts, with a general layout that could be flexibly transformed within certain rules.

For example, in his study, Palmboom (1997) showed how the founding agricultural structure of the territory has in fact conditioned even the most recent urbanisation, limiting it to the simple possibility of superimposing new urban plans on top of an invariable original structure, subdivided into polders.

Recognising the fragmentary condition of the Randstad was actually the starting point for the development of the *field metropolis* concept, developed by the OMA team during a 1998 research project by the Deltametropool foundation, coordinated by Dirk Frieling. Its aim was to study the Randstad as a unique metropolitan region of 2800 km^2 and almost 7 million inhabitants that was able to compete with the world's largest metropolis.[5] The lack of a centre or 'hollow core'—in contrast to familiar metropolitan regions like London, Paris and New York—represented for OMA the very identity of the territory between Rotterdam and The Hague and seemed worthy of investigation: 'whilst the north is continuing to develop from the core city Amsterdam, as a classical concentric metropolis, the south occupies a far less coherent urban area. However, the south offers much potential. The question is how urban architectural intervention and administrative alteration in the economically stumbling South Wing[6] can produce a metropolis that will act as a single unit'.[7]

By laying a straight grid over the area between The Hague and Rotterdam and designating it as 'city', OMA's team created the logic for further development that could incorporate into this new 'field, grid or pixel city' not only the main cities of The Hague and Rotterdam, but also the minor villages, parks and agricultural polders.

The *field metropolis*—visualised by OMA through a large backlit model composed of square, coloured blocks—illustrates the potential of this enlarged territory to work exactly like a metropolis and to be designed as such: 'the South Wing has plenty of opportunities for expansion; with the enormous port, the government centre, Rotterdam airport, research and knowledge centres of world renown such as TNO, the University of Technology in Delft and the Erasmus Medical Centre.

---

[4]This happened to be an ideal, strategically placed test area explicitly showing the potential of the changes taking place, which raised the interest of the public, national and local administrations.

[5]Within this think tank in 2002, the Rijksbouwmeester launched a design competition in which Floris Alkemade (OMA), Dirk Sijmons (H+N+S), Teun Koolhaas (TKA) and Luigi Snozzi took part.

[6]The South Wing is the Dutch province that includes Rotterdam and The Hague as its main urban centres.

[7]OMA website: <http://oma.eu/projects/delta-metropool> seen 12-01-2015.

The area has a great deal to offer its residents. The number of theatres, museums and dance clubs is comparable to the Amsterdam region. The open spaces can still be developed into attractive natural areas. Based on targeted investment in for example the infrastructure, the South Wing could operate more effectively as a unit'.

Finally, the Patchwork Metropolis project was developed by the young Dutch architect W. J. Neutelings[8] after the Department of Housing Development of the City of The Hague commissioned him to study the feasibility of a new urban district between the centres of The Hague and Delft. This area, called *Zuidrand*, is part of a much larger conurbation which extends from Rotterdam to The Hague: a specific portion of the territory that clearly exhibits the effects of the explosive post-war growth of urban and suburban areas, leading to a gradual blurring of the distinction between town and countryside. This enlarged study area, called 'De Tapijtmetropool' or the 'Patchwork Metropolis', is therefore described as a continuous field of patches that extend from the North Sea to the Nieuwe Maas river in the south (Fig. 13.2).

Fig. 13.2 Open figures in the Zuidrand (from left to right): 'Patchwork Metropolis' by Willem Jan Neutelings (1991), 'Urbanised Landscape' by Frits Palmboom (1997), 'Deltametropool' by OMA and Floris Alkemade (http://oma.eu, 2015), all figures adapted by the authors

13.4 The Patchwork Metropolis

For our purposes, of the above-mentioned figures of speech, it is the *patchwork* metaphor that most fully represents the potential of the open figures as a flexible instrument. The Patchwork Metropolis project was published in 1991 in a small monograph that the publisher, 010, dedicated to the winner of the biennial Maaskant Prize for the most promising young Dutch architect. The project was introduced by a brief but intense text in which Neutelings clearly defined the premise of his research: «The absurd notion of a romantic polarity between a paradisiacal Arcadia and a megalomaniac metropolis, a sprawling red stain in an endless expanse of green […] has long been inadequate for interpreting the reality of the situation.» (Neutelings 1991: 40)

Although it was only published in a six-page article, the Patchwork Metropolis soon became an influential metaphor for that generation of young architects, urban planners and civil servants persuaded to—or at least conditioned to—interpret the Dutch urban morphology as a system of dense urban centres placed in a pristine rural setting.

Neutelings was one of the first to see the complex condition of the Dutch territory and to try to dismantle the prevailing doctrine that had been based on a distinction between urban and rural. 'If you look closer at the city, like a biologist, you would clearly see that inside this red spot there are many green areas and inside the green a lot of red spots'.[9] The patchwork figure challenges traditional interpretations of the urban form that are based on a dichotomy between 'built' and 'open' spaces, usually referred to as 'red' or 'green' on a map. The territory was then considered as a whole, characterised by the

---

[8]Born in 1959, he was only 30 years old when he was commissioned for the 1989 project.
[9]Extract from an interview with W. J. Neutelings' author (21 June 2011) included in Pisano 2018a, b.

presence of functions, activities and flows that, albeit with different intensity and meanings, did not exclude any area from the metropolitan dynamics.

More specifically, the *patchwork* metaphor is a composition of entities arranged together, in which a superior unity or comprehensive plan is missing. It does not contemplate any explicit syntax[10] but just a vocabulary of patches. The *parataxis*[11] technique in the literature, the 'note by note' organisation of pieces of musical syntax and the *collages* of the Dadaists and Robert Rauschenberg's art therefore appear as a prolific field of analysis and comparable with the patchwork metaphor in urbanism.

The *patchwork* metaphor, which synthesises Neutelings' understanding and interpretation of the area between Rotterdam and The Hague, is also the leading principle of the design proposal for the *Zuidrand*. Through the compilation of a catalogue of new patches, Neutelings clarifies the scale and conditions of the area's future development: for instance, new commercial boulevards arranged along a motorway, socio-bungalows with a wide range of accessories, a linear park crowned by duplexes and roof-garden dwellings, a square for events arranged below a motorway spaghetti junction, dwellings for retirees close to a golf course. These all form a vocabulary of new patches, carefully inserted into the existing patchwork according to parameters of proximity and accessibility.

Therefore, the *patchwork* figure is not simply an analytical instrument to describe the specific Dutch territorial configuration in 1989—a sort of site-specific manifesto that draws from the territory its most characteristic traits and rationalities—but it is also a radical, abstract model built on a few precise principles that are able to govern its transformations. This abstraction involved a deep analysis not only of the physicality of the territory and its discontinuities, proportions, distances and shortcuts but also of how urban dwellers move and live within it and of the existence of different rhythms of transformation and qualities that only emerge at a specific scale.

Neutelings does not propose the *patchwork* as an optimal model but as the only feasible one, in fact anticipating how the Dutch territory would be transformed shortly thereafter.

Indeed, the supplement of the fourth spatial planning policy, released in 1991, proposed new housing developments under a mother policy called 'Vinex'. These new neighbourhoods, planned close to the main dense centres, were meant to strengthen the position and economy of the main cities and were developed in the form of new patches isolated within the infrastructure network. However, due to decentralisation, many responsibilities moved for the first time to local governments which, unable to deal with them, usually started long-term contracts with developers. Consequently, these Vinex sites fell prey to the private sector, both in terms of investors and real estate developers who unexpectedly (for the government) started buying up all the available land where such sites could potentially be designated and of the public–private partnerships that formed to develop these sites (Waterhout et al. 2012). This process produced more than 800,000 new dwellings over a decade and filled in, at least partially, the area between the main cities of the Randstad with a system of infrastructures that connected the new districts to the existing urban fabric, whilst at the same time separating them from their immediate surroundings.

As a territorial project, the Patchwork Metropolis was able to anticipate the construction process of the new portions of the Dutch cities, especially around its edges or in between important infrastructure systems. By describing a segmented metropolis built on patches variously aggregated and crossed by different urban dwellers, Neutelings highlighted in an enthusiastic and disenchanted way many aspects of the contemporary city, proposing a formative figure that still endures in some planners' minds. The impact of the Patchwork Metropolis manifesto has still not worn off, even after quarter of a century. Indeed, one of the design studies related to the 2014 International Architectural Biennale of Rotterdam was entitled '*Tapijtmetropool*', which quoted and explicitly referred to the 1989 project.[12]

---

[10]Quite explicitly, Neutelings stated 'Holland is, to be sure, made up of individual chunks of city, but there's virtually no network, all told only one railway and one motorway stitch the fragments together. 'Corridor'—another official concept suggesting cohesion—is a misleading word if ever there was one. All it boils down to here is a succession of enclaves along a motorway slip road that will never develop into true urban axes' (Neutelings 2000).

[11]The parataxis (from Greek for 'act of placing side by side') is a literary technique that favours short sentences with the use of coordinating rather than subordinating conjunctions (Fish 2012).

[12]This is the 'Project Atelier [Design Studio] BrabantStad', set up in 2013 by the IABR in alliance with the Province of North Brabant. The combined municipalities of Hertogenbosch, Eindhoven, Tilburg, Breda and Helmond (together called Brabant City in English) and the water boards of North Brabant were keen to search for opportunities that lie hidden in Brabant's urban tapestry. The design research was carried out by Architecture Workroom Brussels, Floris Alkemade Architect and LOLA Landscape Architects. See: Dacier et al. (2014).

13.5 Conclusion

In summary, the Dutch spatial planning case is emblematic in emphasising the difference between closed and open figures. It has been explained how in the Netherlands, both institutions and designers have historically repeatedly turned to figures of speech in order to interpret and plan the evolution of its territorial configuration. Moreover, a shift in their use it has been recognised connected with the political and economic changes that affected the Netherlands from roughly the late Seventies and the second oil crisis. At that time, in fact, whilst the country started facing a general rearrangement, welcoming the beginning of the neoliberalisation process, the *Randstad/Green Heart* opposition, here intended as a closed figure, was progressively demolished, paving the way for a brand new series of more flexible and relational urban concepts supported by the use of open figures.

Unlike the *Randstad/Green Heart* model, the *patchwork* metaphor seems to exhibit a greater adaptability to change—fitting better with the neoliberal regime—whilst remaining coherent with its own explicit rationality. As a spatial planning metaphor, the *patchwork* is in fact able to produce either a completely random system of diffuse urban settlements, coherently arranged in the most topical locations of the Randstad, or a system of a few compact and highly dense cities surrounded by a differentiated agricultural and ecological land pattern. In this lies the power as well as the ambiguity of open figures, for they propose a simple framework that can only be guided by accepting certain rules.

Whilst it is true that relation-oriented open figures enable higher transformation levels than closed ones, based on physical and geometric qualities, this does not mean that they can bear any transformation. The limit depends on both the intrinsic qualities of the figure itself, which must be deeply investigated, and how the specific territory adheres, even potentially, to those characteristics. A precise and careful analysis of a term and its secondary meanings (Genette 1997) can disclose, by means of comparison, the characteristics of a territory that is consistent with it.

In the case of the Dutch *patchwork*, the admissibility of a transformation is related to certain innate characteristics of the figure itself. The comparable dimension between patches juxtaposed to each other, for example, is one of the most interesting features of the Dutch territory; it has never witnessed the emergence of huge neighbourhoods yet, at the same time, it has always avoided scattered urbanisation. Another inalienable aspect is that of being a 'multi-coloured' territory, not imposing any dominant hue or reference pattern, and Neutelings' description of variety as a contemporary life experience sums it up perfectly. Sticking to the figure therefore offers a choice of policies as well as design guidelines that allow a respectful evolution of these characters, whilst leaving a blank canvas for the choice of 'colours' and 'textures'.

On a more general level, the analyses of different figures of speech in spatial planning, their primary and secondary meanings (Genette 1997), as well as the different allures and cross-references nestled behind each term, demonstrate the importance of sharing, within the urban discipline, an appropriate vocabulary of figures which hitherto have often been used indifferently. To clarify if a given urban part is a 'centre', then a 'piece', 'patch' or 'finger' serves to encourage a comparison using a precise and quite complete idea of the city—of its relations with the territory, the society that inhabits it and its characteristics in terms of mobility, ecology, etc.—all without losing that evocative power that finds its most prolific and fertile value in the unspoken.

References

Allen S (1999) Points + lines: diagrams and projects for the city. Princeton Architectural Press, New York

Balz VE, Zonneveld WAM (2015) Regional design in the context of fragmented territorial governance: South Wing studio. Eur Plan Stud 23 (5):871–891. https://doi.org/10.1080/09654313.2014.889662

Balz VE (2017) Regional design: discretionary approaches to regional planning in The Netherlands. Plann Theor, 1473095217721280

Cacciari M (1997) L'arcipelago. Adelphi, Milano

Dacier E, Declerck J, Francke M, Naudts N (eds) (2014) Reweaving the urban carpet. IABR, Rotterdam

Davoudi S, Strange I (eds) (2008) Conceptions of space and place in strategic spatial planning. Routledge, London and New York

Dematteis G (1995) Progetto implicito. Il contributo della geografia umana alle scienze del territorio. Franco Angeli, Milano

Dijkstra L, Poelman H (2011) Regional typologies: a compilation. European Union Regional Policy 01/2011

European Commission (2016) The State of European cities 2016. Cities leading the way to a better future. European Unione, UN-Habitat

Faludi A, van der Valk A (1994) Rule and order: Dutch planning doctrine in the twentieth century. Kluwer Academic Publishers, Dordrecht/Boston/London

Fish S (2012) How to write a sentence: And how to read one. Harpercollins, New York

Genette G (1997) Palinsesti: la letteratura di secondo grado. Einaudi, Torino

Guida G (2011) Immaginare città: metafore e immagini per la dispersione insediativa. Franco Angeli, Milano

Hall P (1966) The world cities. World University Library, London

Hertweck F, Marot S (2013) The city in the city: Berlin: a green archipelago. Lars Muller, Ennetbaden

Infovina F (ed) (1990) La città diffusa. Quaderno Daest 1, IUAV, Venezia

Indovina F (2003) La Metropolizzazione del territorio. Nuove gerarchie territoriali. Economia e Società regionale – Oltre il ponte 3–4

Meijsmans N, de Zwart B (2009) Towards a culture of regional design exploration of a practice in the making. Oase 80:108–125

Neuman M (1998) Does planning need the plan? J Am Plann Assoc 64(2):208–220. https://doi.org/10.1080/01944369808975976

Neutelings WJ (1991) Willem Jan Neutelings Architect. Uitgeverij 010, Rotterdam

Neutelings WJ (2000) Our Lack of highways. Archis 3:79–80

Palmboom F (1997) Policentrismo e paesaggio urbanizzato in Olanda. Zodiac 18:64–85

Pisano C (2017) The segmented metropolis. The Tussengebied according to Neutelings, Palmboom and Alkemade. MONU Magazine 26:52–57

Pisano C (2018a) Patchwork metropolis. Progetto di città contemporanea. Lettera Ventidue, Siracusa

Pisano C (2018b) The patchwork metropolis: between patches, fragments and situations. In: Viganò P, Cavalieri C, Bacelloni Corte M (eds) The horizontal metropolis between urbanism and urbanization. Springer Verlag, Berlino, Germania, pp 93–100, ISBN: 978-3319759746, https://doi.org/10.1007/978-3-319-75975-3_9

Secchi B (2010) Il futuro si costruisce giorno per giorno. Territorio 53:8–18

Secchi B (2011) Isotropy versus hierarchy. In: Ferrario A, Sampieri A, Viganò P (eds) Landscape of urbanism. Officina, Rome, pp 168–171

Sutton SE, Kemp SP (2006) Integrating social science and design inquiry through interdisciplinary design charrettes: an approach to participatory community problem solving. Am J Community Psychol 38(1–2):125–139. https://doi.org/10.1007/s10464-006-9065-0

Sieverts T (2003) Cities without cities: an interpretation of the Zwischenstadt. Routledge, London

Sieverts T (2008) Improving the quality of fragmented urban landscapes—a global challenge. In: von Seggern HJ, Werner L, Grosse-Bächle (eds) Creating knowledge, innovation strategies for designing urban landscapes. Jovis, Berlin, pp 253–264

Soja E (1989) Postmodern geographies: the reassertion of space. In: Critical social theory. Verso Press, London

Van Dijk T (2011) Imagining future places: how designs co-constitute what is, and thus influence what will be. Plann Theor 10(2):124–143. https://doi.org/10.1177/1473095210386656

Viganò P (2010) I territory dell'urbanistica. Il progetto come produttore di conoscenza. Officina Ed., Rome

Viganò P, Cavalieri C, Barcelloni Corte M (eds) (2018) The horizontal metropolis between urbanism and urbanization. Springer International Publishing

Waterhout B, Othengrafen F, Sykes O (2012) Neo-liberalization processes and spatial planning in France, Germany, and The Netherlands: an exploration. Plann Pract Res 28(1):141–159

Wandl A, Nadin V, Rooij R (2014) Beyond urban–rural classifications: characterizing and mapping territories-in-between across Europe. Landscape Urban Plann 130:50–63. https://doi.org/10.1016/j.landurbplan.2014.06.010

Zonneveld W, Evers D (2014) Dutch national spatial planning at the end of an era. In: Reimer M, Getimis P, Blotevogel H (eds) Spatial planning systems and practices in Europe; A comparative perspective on continuity and changes. Routledge, New York/Oxon, pp 61–82

Concepts of Landscapes: Informing Local Plans in Albania

14

Roberto Mascarucci

Abstract

The innovative evolution of urban planning in Albania (as elsewhere) is attempting to replace the traditional approach with a new strategic one. The most important innovation in a strategic approach is the notion that the quality of a planning outcome mainly relates to interdependence among its constituent variables and decisions taken at different scales. Accordingly, this chapter examines strategic planning in three cities surrounding Tirana, the capital of Albania. Planners in charge of the local spatial plans there have recognised five different types of landscape (coastal area, agricultural plain, infrastructure corridor, foothill settlements, mountain area), which are usually considered as specialised strips of territory arranged parallel to the coast. However, the planners believe it is necessary to join them up in order to facilitate integration between different assets and create synergy between local communities. The overall strategy, therefore, is based on the functional integration of the five landscapes, through environmental corridors formed by the river courses, in order to achieve: (i) ecological integration between the coast and the mountain; (ii) complementary integration between urban functions of the historic settlement system and the productive functions localised behind the new infrastructure system; (iii) synergy between environmental protection areas and their possible use for economic purposes, through integrated forms of environmental tourism.

Keywords

Spatial planning • Albania • General local plan

14.1 Introduction

The experience of simultaneously developing three General Local Plans (GLPs) for the municipalities of Kruja, Kurbin and Lezhë is part of a process, strongly supported by Prime Minister Edi Rama's government that redefines the entire system of urban planning in Albania.

As a part of recent urban planning reforms (Law 107/2014), the Albanian parliament reorganised the entire system of territorial governance, instituting the Territory National Council (known by the Albanian acronym KKT). The KKT establishes actions and approves plans from the National Agency of Territorial Planning (AKPT), offering technical assistance and monitoring urban planning legislation and coherence between different plans. In the administrative reform of 2015, the Albanian parliament reduced 308 rural communities and 65 urban municipalities to a mere 61 new municipalities, following a trend that is moving towards the streamlining and efficiency of local governing bodies.

In terms of spatial planning, this innovation in territorial government policy in Albania has led (contextually) to the development of the General National Plan (Plani i Pergjithshem Kombetar), the Integrated Inter-Sectorial Plan for the Coast (Plani i Integruar Ndersektorial Bregdeti) and the Integrated Inter-Sectorial Plan for Tirana-Durrës (Plani i Integruar

R. Mascarucci (✉)
Department of Architecture, University of Chieti-Pescara, Chieti, Italy
e-mail: roberto.mascarucci@gmail.com

© Springer Nature Switzerland AG 2020
V. Lingua and V. Balz (eds.), *Shaping Regional Futures*,
https://doi.org/10.1007/978-3-030-23573-4_14

Ndersektorial Tirane-Durrës). It has also brought incentives and financing for the development of local plans at the scale of the new municipalities.

During the initial phase (begun in 2016), funding was provided to develop GLPs for 26 new municipalities, divided into ten lots that were awarded to ten different groups following an international competition: the company UTS-01 of Tirana was awarded Lot n.1, which included the three GLPs of the municipalities of Kruja, Kurbin and Lezha. An interdisciplinary team was created and composed of experts in urban planning, architecture, economy, environment, agriculture, landscape and GIS, and I played the role of team leader.

Consequently, this chapter deals mainly with this context, with particular reference to the concepts of landscape and its management under governance rescaling.

14.2 The Innovative Content of the Reform Process

It is well known that most recent innovations in urban planning tend to replace a traditional structure by introducing a new strategic approach. The characteristic element of these innovations lies in the consideration of the quality of output based on the interdependence of diverse components and their capacity to maximise synergy between decisions at different scales.

The role of strategic visions can be decisive in the construction of territorial policies based on a multi-level governance process. Assuming that development objectives can only be founded on shared objectives and implementation tools, the new role of regional spatial planning becomes the shared construction of general goals and specific, short-term targets (Mascarucci 2008).

In this regard, the reform introduced in Albania is full of novelties: a contextual approach to diverse planning tools, with strong ties between local plans and the strategic indications of higher tier plans, and also the role of the AKPT in developing new plans.

The efficacy of urban planning is, moreover, increasingly related to implementation, focusing on the feasibility of proposals: it is now considered pointless to plan solutions that will never bear fruit. Urban planning now openly confronts the challenges of realistic proposals, the feasibility of interventions and the accurate timing necessary to achieve the objectives. In this respect, the Albanian reform introduces highly innovative elements, such as combined decisions regarding the confirmation of the ground and possible sources of finance for structuring interventions. There is also an obligation to complete plans by providing a project implementation plan (distinguished by priority level) and identify possible sources of financing.

The risk, however, is that in moving towards an urban planning approach that is overly conditioned by the limits of means, planners can lose sight of the many positive aspects of a traditional approach. The strategic structuring of plans and programmes, borrowed from the world of economics, risks relegating the specificity of an urban planning approach to the back burner, to a mere interest in forms, spaces and physical relations in the territory. On the contrary, it is important that priorities be established based directly on the territory itself, its morphological characteristics and the opportunities tied to its resources, such that new synergies are founded on physical links and ties to the actual place.

The sense of place (of any place) is always linked to its functional and strategic location within the networks that structure the territory. When this territorial reference suddenly changes on a vast scale, the role of local areas also changes. The project must define its multifaceted sphere of relation and design modifications linked to the intervention. Essentially, we are speaking of modifying physical space: the territorial project must propose content that relates to how the physical transformation of the territorial order will be governed at different scales. It must also deal with the spatial effects of policy and the conscious modification of plans that derive from the introduction of new elements, both structural and infrastructural (Mascarucci 2003a).

The new intentions behind the GLP in Albania, in truth, allow for greater harmony between urban planning policy and economic drivers, without losing the territory's implicit indications. This largely thanks to the importance that the new planning processes assign to listening to citizens, through presentations and discussion forums at different stages of the planning process. Such processes are able to: (i) govern the transformation of sites based on a coherent objective of economic valorisation, firmly bound to the resources offered by a territory; (ii) guarantee the functionality of individual interventions with respect to more general networks, proposing detailed planning solutions coherent with a more general scheme; (iii) favour the possible location of productive areas, as long as they are aligned with development trends presented by a vast-scale context.

The new structure of Albania's planning processes allows for a transition from the old conformative approach of hierarchically ordered plans to a new performative approach that, being strategic, measures the validity of outputs based on the extent to which they contribute to objectives. This inevitably involves variable territorial areas of reference, necessarily diverse in their pertinence to the issues at hand. If the city remains the most precious lever in the development of the local system, the regional level remains the most suitable arena for identifying the pertinent dimensions of strategic development.

Thus, the task that different-scale planning policies need to address is that of linking local systems with regional networks and making it easier for them to access global networks by constructing territorial visions which ensure that all elements form a coherent and cohesive whole. This territorial vision, however, is different from a traditional plan. In any case, it should not be viewed as the product of a rational agency that imposes choices from a higher level, but rather as a response to local development requests, in accordance with the broader context (Mascarucci 2003b).

In this sense, the recent institutional reforms in Albania impose a new dimension of urban planning, requiring a shift to broader-scale plans where: (i) strategic planning refers to the entire national territory or its possible regional organisation; (ii) territorial spatial planning occurs at municipal scale; (iii) the local plan simultaneously defines urban destinations and intervention projects. In each case (and at different scales), this innovative approach is founded on the simultaneous definition of general strategies and possible interventions. At various planning policy levels, new tools guarantee the logical and operative connection between an overall vision and specific interventions. This is indispensable when it comes to ensuring the coherence of individual interventions with the general framework, in order to permit the gradual and progressive realisation of action programmes imagined as an organic whole. It is also necessary in order to guarantee the overall efficacy of processes and the quality of their results.

The execution of land-use plans through development projects also involves the introduction of content that can bring concrete and immediate opportunities for implementation. In accordance with territorial-scale strategic visions, a plan must provide tactical opportunities to ensure that strategic choices actually do get enforced. In fact, the operative content of the new GLP tends to transform it into a real urban project, capable of ensuring both the implementation of territorial-scale strategies as well as the certainty and rapidity of procedures for implementing development forecasts. In many European situations, particularly in Italy, dialogue between strategic and urban planners is rare. In Albania, however, the intention was to introduce concrete operative interventions within the GLP, through forecasts tied to implementation phasing and linked to the economic-financial programming of municipal budgets.

14.3 Characteristics of the Local Urban Plan

Given its new strategic mission, urban planning can no longer operate just at the municipal scale because it is too narrow to address the design of large conurbations (which extend well beyond municipal borders) or to propose new territorial roles for small-to-medium cities (unable to achieve a critical mass). Above all else, in order to truly implement a strategic development project, we must recognise new patterns of settlement and put in place (in various forms and at different scales) a new institutional structure, without which it is impossible to deliberately construct a development project.

In Albania, this new institutional structure occurred simultaneously as part of the planning reform that reduced municipalities from 373 to 61 and rendered the new GLP mandatory for the new aggregated municipalities. Based on Law 107/2014 (effective as of 1 October 2014) and its related implementation regulation (Decree 671/2015), the GLP is subordinate to regional scale plans (when they exist), the General National Plan (GNP), and ultimately also to National Sector Plans (NSPs) or Detailed Plans for Areas of National Interest (DPANI). GLPs must be prepared at a scale between 1:5,000 and 1:25,000 and implemented through a sector plan and/or detailed plan (Law 107/2014, art. 20), although they may also be implemented through strategic investments, pilot projects and building permits.

In reality, the GLP is a plan with three dimensions that, in other European countries (Italy for example) remain separate: the strategic dimension of spatial planning on a vast scale, the regulatory dimension of local urban planning and the operative dimension of project feasibility. This multi-dimensionality may bring new local development opportunities, though to achieve this the implementation agenda must be constructed from suggestions offered by the territory, in its twofold definition as a system of spaces and actors.

The GLP studies and interprets local realities using five systems: settlement, environment, agriculture, water and infrastructure. These five systems are each defined in law, with their overlaps defining a complete framework for an interpretative reading of the territory. Thus, they are the fundamental components of successful projects. The position of the diverse parts of the territory within one or more of the five systems determines not only its strategic destination but also its legal framework.

One of the most appreciable characteristics of the new GLP (as reformulated by the 2014 law) is that of being able to develop into a project. Steps to define the desired spatial configuration and identify the required actions to achieve it are not always part of the same planning instrument. The relationship between a project and a plan is defined at diverse scales, for instance, a plan can lead to projects at scales other than those it was developed for, just as a project can provoke effects at scales where it plays no direct role. For example, there is a tendency to underestimate the reciprocal influence between the organisation of local spaces and global socioeconomic dynamics. Economic development policies are still overly disconnected from policies governing the transformation of territorial and urban space. The functional relationship between the design of settlements and development strategies is instead strong and biunivocal: spatial choices made at territorial and urban scales can influence the economic dynamics of a context, to the same degree that the strategic choices of a system can provide new opportunities for urban development.

Strategic planning, which includes the redesign of infrastructure networks, can transform urban voids into new development opportunities. An urban plan for a city can be a determinant in creating the conditions to make that city more attractive to people and investors. The spatial configuration of an infrastructure node may provide the essential conditions to turn a simple intermodal connection into a complex interconnection capable of bringing about new socioeconomic development dynamics. An informed consideration of relations at different scales permits a correct conceptualisation of a particular area, with its many internal and external spatial relations, thereby overcoming recurrent difficulties in translating network complexities into an equally complex design.

The GLP has several clear advantages: (i) governing land transformations in coherence with economic valorisation objectives through the close relationship between zoning indications and the determination of financial requirements; (ii) guaranteeing the functionality of individual interventions with respect to the more general system of networks, owing to performance verification using the AKPT during the development and approval of local plans; (iii) favouring possible locations for production facilities capable of attracting foreign investment, a combined effect of zoning and forecast structural interventions.

14.4 The Territorial Strategy at the Inter-municipal Level

The opportunity given to the UTS-01 group of simultaneously planning three municipalities (Kruja, Kurbin and Lezhë) offered the chance to reflect on a common, territorial strategy that would serve as the foundation for successive planning decisions for different urban contexts.

The overall territory of the three municipalities occupies more than 1000 square kilometres, includes 20 historic towns and is home to 171,738 inhabitants (2011 data). In reality, it embraces the entire territorial system from the northern border of Tirana to the southern edge of Scutari.

This vast territory can be conceptually interpreted through five possible landscapes (intended as territorial units characterised by homogenous geographic and morphological-spatial conditions, anthropic layers and primary land uses, together with forecast programmes and the governance of transformations):

1. the coastal area, including the variety of different conditions along the shoreline, characterised by lagoons and vast marshlands alternating with short sections of beach, in all cases with notable environmental qualities and landscapes, and thus subject to varying degrees of protection and conservation;
2. the agricultural plain, characterised by a flat morphology and the historical network of drainage and irrigation channels that make for a fertile terrain, now affected in some areas by urban sprawl phenomena;
3. the infrastructure corridor, which crosses the agricultural plain longitudinally and contains the principal high-speed road infrastructure, an attractive option for the location of new industrial and commercial settlements;
4. the anthropic system in the foothills, consisting of a succession of urban centres variably arranged along the old national road (also connected by the railway), the result of the historic approach to anthropic settlement when the plane was unsuitable for habitation;
5. the coastal and internal mountains, which include both the western mountainside dropping down towards the plain, as well as the more internal valleys that, together, represent an important reservoir of natural conditions and ethnocultural traditions to be defended and eventually exploited for tourism compatible with the conservation of the environment and landscape.

The succession of the five landscapes unfolds without any interrelation. Each landscape (each environmental system) appears to be self-referential and there is no dialogue with the others, hindering the development of synergies that could instead easily evolve through a profitable complementary relationship. This interpretation of the territory in functional bands running parallel to the coast does not value the vast possibilities that would come through functional integration between the diverse bands.

The unified strategy underlying the three GLPs is, by contrast, founded on the concept of diversity through homogeneity. It is based on two essential issues: first, the opportunity to consider the homogeneity of the territory between Tirana and Lezhë as having value, despite the diversity of functional solutions to be proposed; second, the need to design a new model for this territory that establishes a relationship between the five different landscapes and considers possible synergies between the different landscape bands as the true resource of integrated and synergetic development.

The spatial vision for this vast area is thus based on functional integration between the five landscapes to obtain the following advantages: possible ecological integration between the coastal territory and the mountains, by establishing environmental corridors structured by watercourses; opportune and complementary integration between the urban functions of historic settlements (foothill road) and productive functions located, or to be located, near to the new infrastructure system (high-speed road); possible synergy between protected environments (along the coast and in the mountains) and their possible economic use, through integrated forms of natural tourism (organised use of natural resources); a different role for diverse parts of the system, without overlaps or duplications but with forms of complementary specialisation; the possibility of assigning diverse, specialised, territorial functions to different sites based on the logic of respective integration tied to a project with complementary functions (Fig. 14.1).

There are many factors supporting this vision. First of all, the need to establish a relationship between the natural environments of the coast and mountains by creating ecological corridors that foster biological exchanges (via the system of rivers). Then, in such a case, access to the coast must be envisioned in the form of penetrating axes ending in cul de sacs, given that the marshy nature of the coast does not permit movement along the coastline. Furthermore, the division of the territory via a series of axes running perpendicular to the coast permits discretisation, namely access to the road infrastructure at just a few points, which is necessary to transform the current high-speed road into a proper motorway. Finally, the functional relationship between the sea and the mountains allows the development of forms of integrated tourism that benefit from the full complement of resources offered by the territory. The system of local centralities must also regain a role and function, especially in relation to the creation of new productive and functional poles situated along transport axes (the motorway and railway).

The idea of promoting a strategy for transversal reconnection between the five landscapes is substantiated through the identification of infrastructural connections with the specific role of: (i) favouring tangible and intangible exchanges between different environments; (ii) facilitating the synergies linked to the complementary nature of uses and functions; (iii) implementing a wide range of relations between diverse environments.

It is evident that this proposal requires precise identification of transversal elements capable of ensuring both the possibilities and advantages of the synergetic relationship between the diverse specialised bands. In some cases, these transversal conditions are evident, in others they must be created so that they can set the rhythm of a new functional organisation within the territory.

As part of this vision, there are two types of transversal reconnections:

- the first (orange corridor) is structured primarily by road infrastructures and motorised travel;
- the second (green corridor) is inspired by softer movements (ecological corridors, bicycle and pedestrian paths, slow mobility).

In keeping with the diverse strategic nature of these two types of transversal connections the two axes, or corridors, identified play different roles as they traverse the five landscapes:

	Orange corridor	Green corridor
A. (coast)	Seaside tourism	Environmental tourism
B. (plain)	Services for agriculture	Farm stays
C. (infrastructure)	Discretised accesses (interchanges)	Overpass/underpass
D. (foothills)	Services for manufacturing	Services for tourism
E. (mountains)	Access to inner areas	Alpine tourism

The orange corridor is a system of strategic reconnection between the five landscapes that: (i) permits easy road connections between the coast and the internal mountains, also favouring inverse motorised accessibility from inland areas

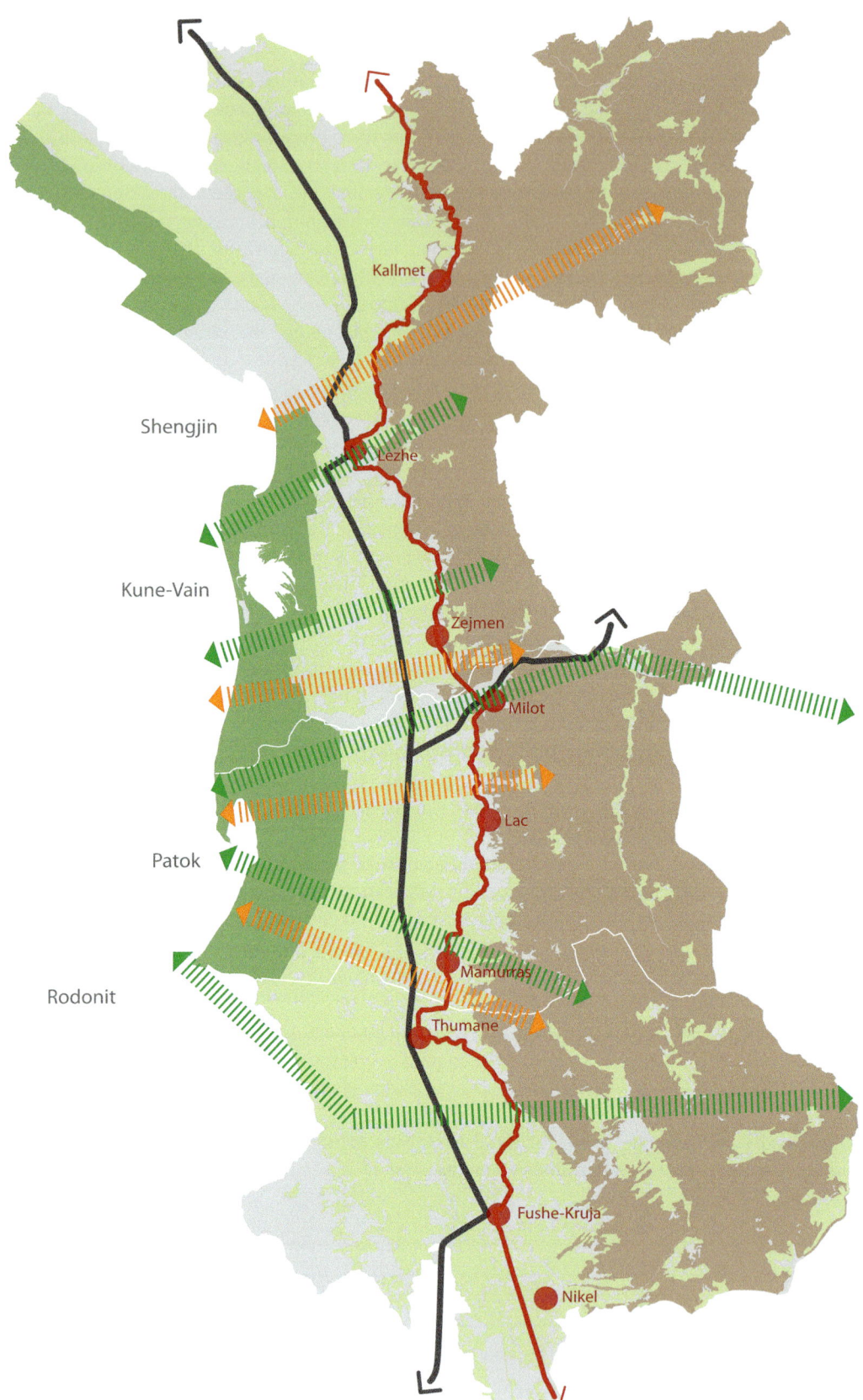

Fig. 14.1 Overall strategy for the Tirana region, elaborated by the author

out towards the coast; (ii) in reference to the mountain landscape, indicates the development axis for the road connection towards inland areas; (iii) in reference to the foothill settlements, favours the location of new facilities for productive systems; (iv) in reference to the infrastructural corridor, identifies the location of the main interchanges for motorway access; (v) in reference to the agricultural plain, favours the location of structures and facilities for agriculture; (vi) in reference to the coastal area, identifies a centre of development for tourism and bathing, with the necessary services.

The green corridor is, by contrast, a lighter system for reconnecting the five landscapes that: (i) permits ecological reconnections between the coast and internal mountain as well as a functional connection based on slow mobility; (ii) in reference to the mountain landscape, identifies possible starting points for hiking excursions, with the necessary services; (iii) in reference to the foothill settlements, favours the location of new tourism facilities and alternative forms of hospitality; (iv) in reference to the infrastructural corridor, resolves the problem of crossing the motorway by introducing underpasses and overpasses; (v) in reference to the agricultural plain, favours the location of structures and facilities for the development of farm stays and rural tourism; (vi) in reference to the coastal area, identifies a centre for environmental tourism, with a low impact on the landscape based on ecologically compatible solutions (Fig. 14.2).

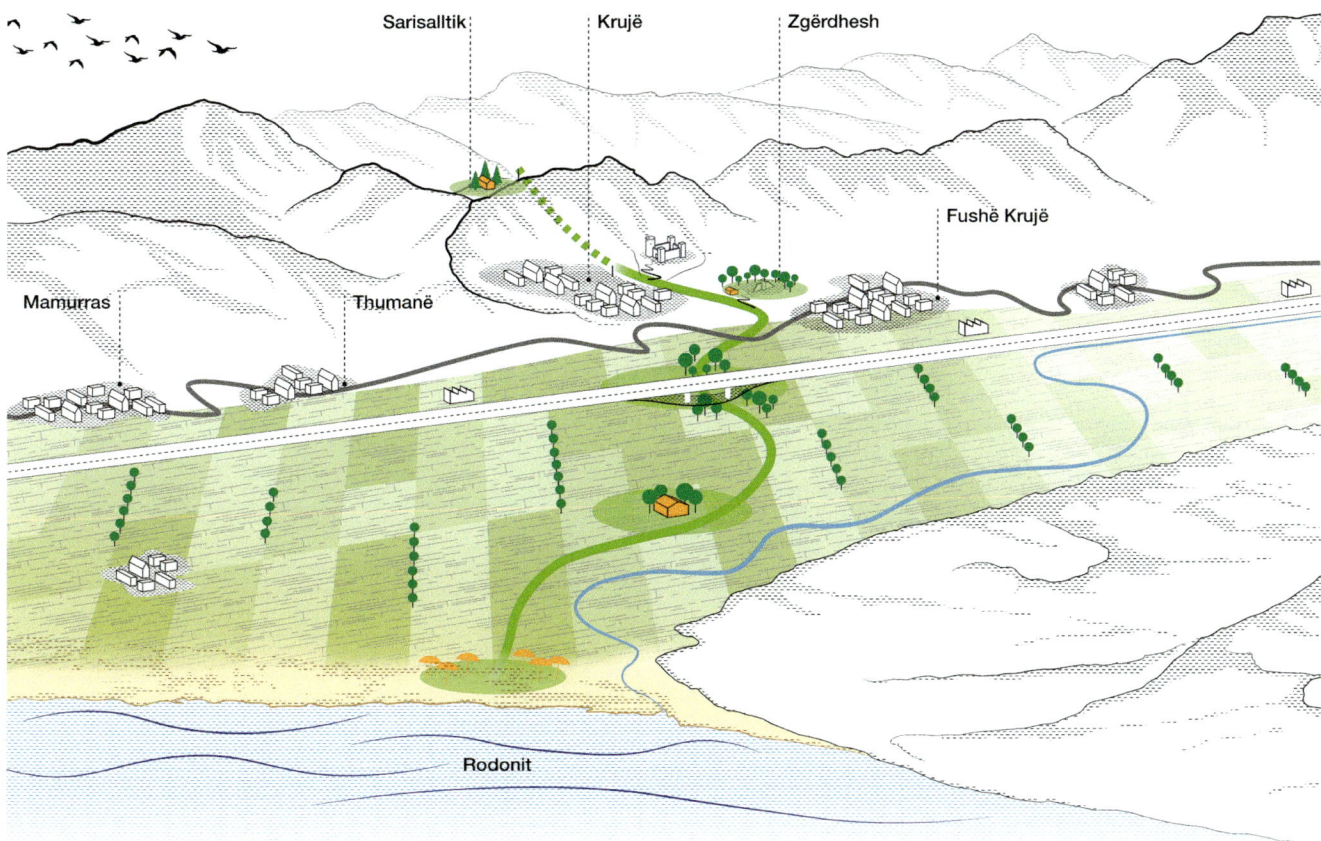

Fig. 14.2 Perspective view of a green corridor in the Tirana region, elaborated by the author

14.5 Defining a Strategy for the Territory of the Three Municipalities

In the territory of Kruja, the five landscapes identified in the spatial vision at the inter-municipal scale assume a particular definition, owing to the morphological diversity and influence of nearby Tirana. If we consider only the municipal territory, the coast does not exist. In fact, access to the sea for the inhabitants of Kruja (and Tirana) occurs at the mouth of the Ishëm

River (Rodon Bay). The agricultural plain is limited to the small area of Bubq and Thumanë which suffers from the problems of flooding and overlapping functions. The municipal territory of Kruja presents a few specific issues. The problem of the continuous location of production activities along the edge of the road (the wood industry in Nikël) has been overcome by planning a new high-speed road from Thumanë to Tirana. The foothill settlements have developed along the old national road (which is in poor conditions) and include the towns of Nikël, Fushë-Krujë, Borizanë and Thumanë. The mountain is characterised by the important presence of Kruja and its castle. However, further inland we find other important resources, including the religious and panoramic area of Sari Saltik, Qafë-Shtamë National Park and the mountain villages of Cudhi.

In the territory of Kurbin, the five landscapes are highly recognisable, without particular local definitions. Kurbin is a typical territory in which integration of the five landscapes may offer notable advantages tied to the complementary synergy between functions. The coastal area includes the typical area of the lagoon (Patok) and the beach (the area of Adriatik). The agricultural plain presents the typical problems faced in this area, with a sparse canal system and the risk of uncontrolled, settlement sprawl. The infrastructural corridor is particularly affected by the location of production activities along the high-speed road, which constitutes a problem when it comes to upgrading the road into a motorway. The proposed solution is thus to facilitate access to the production areas by creating slip roads for the necessary motorway access. The foothill settlements have developed at the base of the mountain and include the important towns of Mamurras, Lac and Milot. The mountain introduces the theme of the coastline with its coastal slope and internal valley. Both environments are home to important natural and cultural resources which need to be conserved and promoted through eco-tourism and trekking (Figs. 14.3 and 14.4).

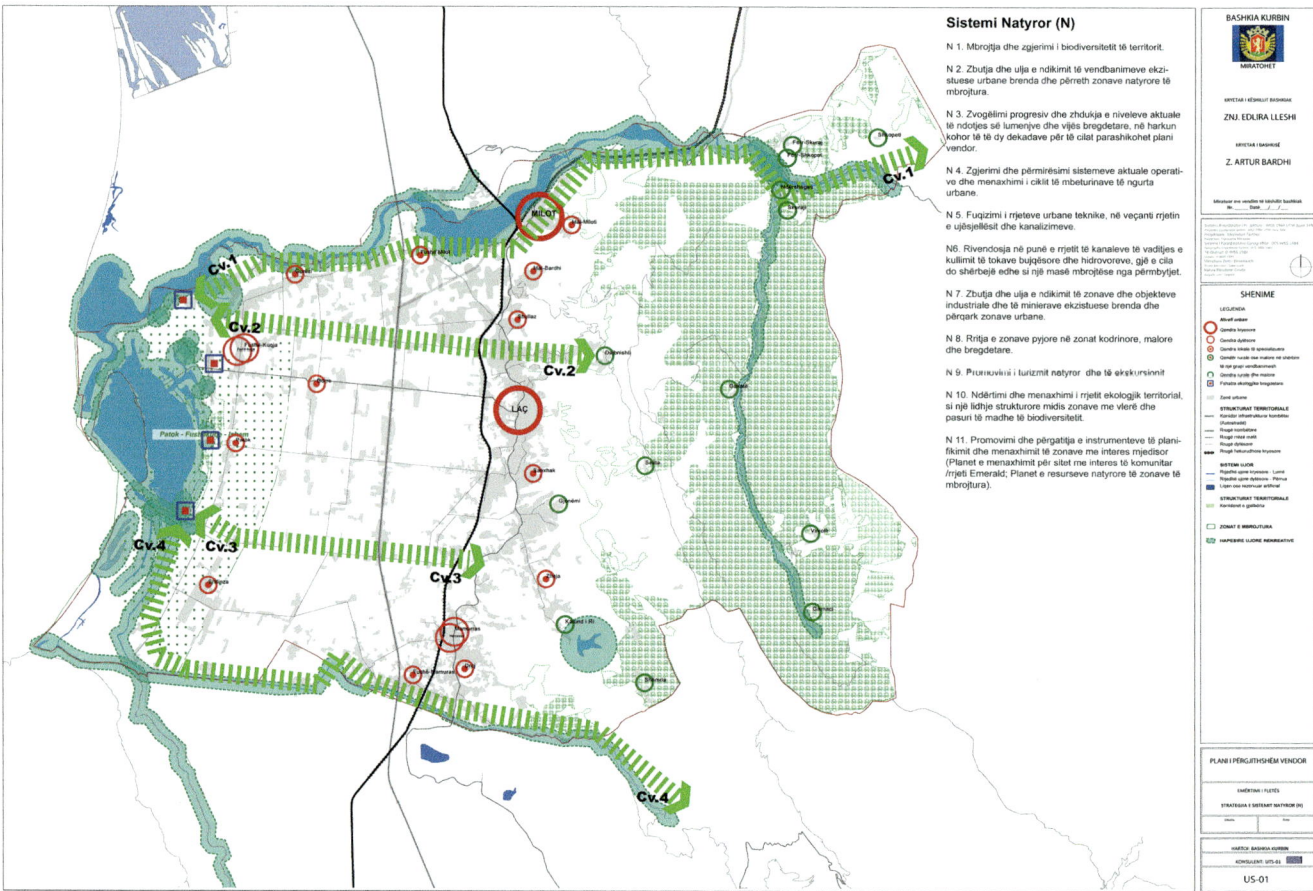

Fig. 14.3 Environmental system in the General Local Plan (GLP) for the Kurbin Municipality, adapted by author

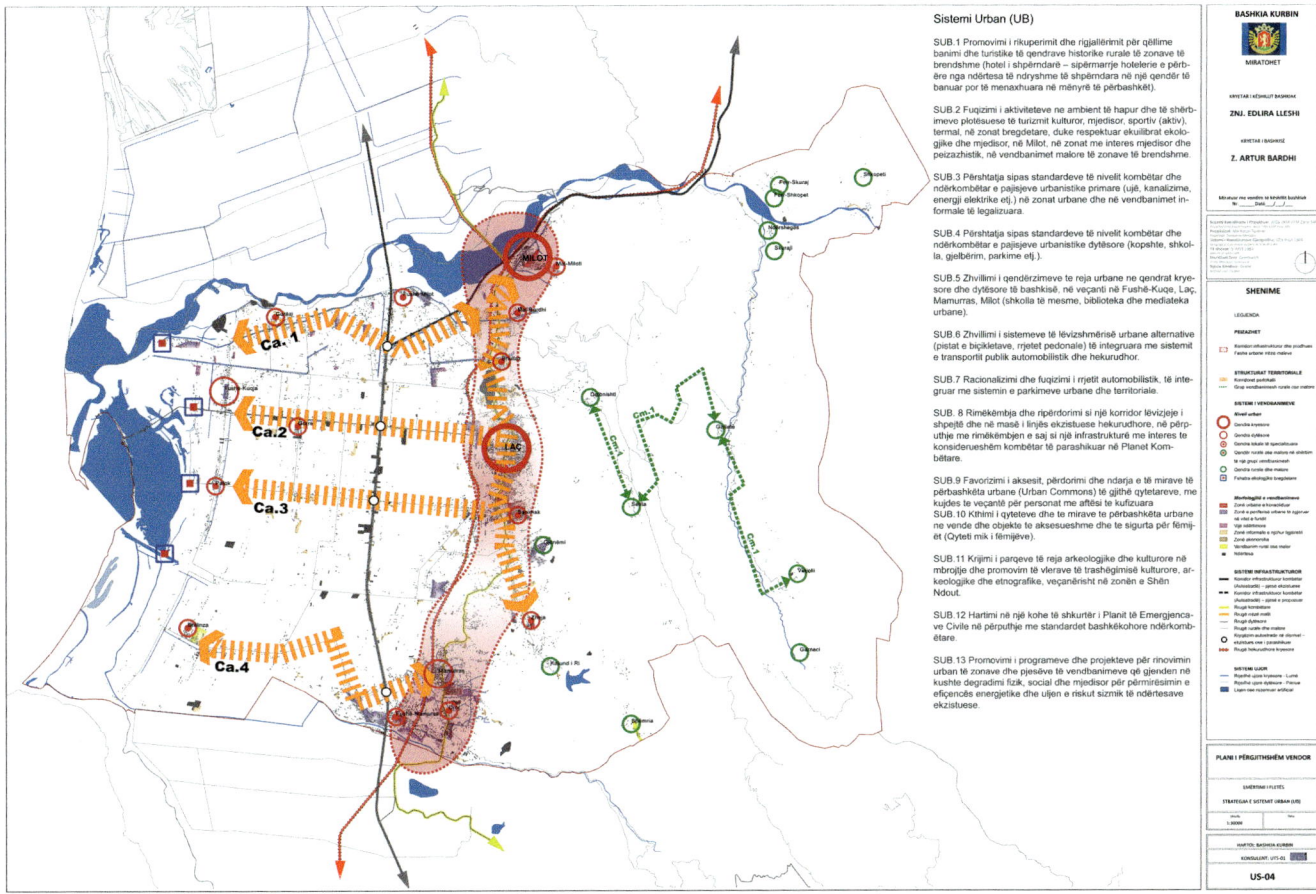

Fig. 14.4 Urban system in the General Local Plan (GLP) for the Kurbin Municipality, adapted by author

In the territory of Lezhë, the five landscapes are once again immediately recognisable, even if the local topography determines a number of specific conditions (though without contradicting the general framework). The coastal area again consists of typical lagoon areas (Kunë-Vain), as well as tourist bathing establishments (Shëngjin) and beaches (Rana, Hedhun and Tale Beach). The fragility of the natural coastal environment and the legislation that safeguards it (at a higher level) demands careful evaluation when it comes to development projects, in order to avoid growth hypotheses that conflict with the maintenance of the very resources supporting them. The agricultural plain is a highly prominent area (Shënkoll) and demonstrates the typical themes of this agricultural landscape (the need to restore canals, the promotion of local products, the informal settlement of Barbullojë, etc.). In this territory, the theme of the infrastructural corridor is defined in a very specific manner, given the need to bypass the city with ringroad connections to both the west and east of Lezhë. The foothill settlements reach the edge of Lezhë, along the old national road that runs from Milot across the base of the mountain, east of the railway. The mountain area is comprised of diverse sub-environments, each with specific local characteristics. These include the valley of Balldre, the area of Kallmet i Medh, the large internal complex of Ungrej, the natural reserve at Berzan and the mountain attraction of Maja and Veles.

14.6 From Strategy to Urban Plan

With more specifically urban aims in mind, the identification of the five landscapes also provides indications that are useful for intervention strategies. It is in fact already evident that the current and planned specificity of the diverse landscapes may provide useful indications for a differentiated treatment of urban areas.

The area defined as urban (Decision no. 5 dated 29 December 2014) by the Territory National Council (KKT) can be further broken down, recognising specific types of urban morphology which may be the object of opportune intervention policies, differentiated by the landscape in which they are located. In other words, overlapping different urban typologies with the five landscapes makes it possible to articulate policies for governing transformations in different sites.

The following section defines the urban morphological types in order to apply diverse urban-transformation strategies to the territory, and also in relation to the different types of landscapes in which they are situated.

Consolidated Urban Area

The consolidated urban area includes the most central parts of settlements of a certain importance: it combines, in a single morphological type, historical areas (eventually recognised as a sub-group) as well as more recent ones (the effect of an idea of the city consolidated through practice or explicit planning).

Suburban Area of Expansion

The suburban area of expansion recognises in one single category all the diverse forms of the recent expansion of the built environment: new peripheral neighbourhoods, suburban sprawl, sparse construction of a certain consistency, informal and legally unrecognised expansion.

Strand-Like Settlement

The strand-like settlement consists of more or less continuous constructions along road edges, which cannot be recognised as a primarily urban area.

Informal Settlement

Legally recognised informal settlements are defined following specific decisions issued by the National Council of Territory Regulation (KRRTRSH).

Productive Settlement

Productive settlements are represented by a collection of buildings for production use (industrial, craft, commercial, tertiary), erected in proximity to elements of territorial aggregation (road, rail, etc.).

Rural Village

The rural village encompasses situations where a concentration of suburban constructions, for historical or functional reasons, has the effect of a compact settlement.

The overlap between diverse types of landscapes and urban morphologies determines the strategic indications for governing urban transformations:

URB/01
Recognition of an urban centre, the possibility of building on included lots, the modernisation of technological networks, the retrofit and development of a higher level of urban services.
URB/02
Recognition of the urban periphery, the possibility of urban renewal, the modernisation of technological networks and basic urban services.
RUR/01
Recognition of a decentralised settlement condition, possibility of building renovations, the modernisation of technological networks and neighbourhood services.
RUR/02
Recognition of an existing settlement, incompatibility with the need to protect the environment and landscape, modernisation of technological networks and freezing of current conditions.
IND/01
Recognition of the existing production settlement, modernisation of infrastructural networks and planning interventions involving streamlining and organisation.

An innovative approach to urban planning, focused on obtaining higher quality results, is based on the simultaneous preparation of a general strategy as well as specific projects. Projects for each site are designed at the same time and coherent with the underlying strategic vision, in order to maximise the synergy between development dynamics and the spatial qualities of places. This close connection between strategic planning and the design of specific interventions is the basic condition for guaranteeing the efficacy of processes and the quality of their results. For this reason, the GLP, in addition to the general framework of coherence, must also contain the design of places of strategic interest. Their design should be emblematic and exemplary of possible best practices in urban regeneration and territorial development, with the ability to become guidelines for future interventions.

Strategic projects can be of different types. Whilst they all focus on the general development of the territory, they may each contribute in different ways to the achievement of strategic objectives.

To summarise, it is possible to classify strategic projects within the following categories:

- design of systems;
- development projects;
- pilot projects.

The design of systems (or, in other words, underlying projects) is indispensable in ensuring that local systems have the necessary prerequisites for development. Systems permit the achievement of the essential pre-conditions for the start-up of any development programme, guaranteeing the minimum base efficiency without which it is impossible to imagine the successful functioning of the whole territorial system. Examples include the functional efficiency of the settlement system, the environmental sustainability of the mobility system, the liveability of the urban system and so on. The content of system-design projects is generally not strategic, by definition, and often has to do with the normal services of a territory. In territories with a serious lack of basic services, it may be correct (if not essential) to assign a strategic quality to projects that aim to resolve these shortcomings. In the specific case of the urban systems examined here, attaining a minimum level of functionality for the territory is without doubt a necessary pre-condition for any development programme.

Development projects, on the other hand, are true strategic projects. In other words, they have a master plan with the role of triggering virtuous processes of territorial and socioeconomic development. In general, these projects present a few basic characteristics: (i) they are susceptible to the context of the master plan; (ii) they are highly relevant and strong drivers; (iii) we expect them to deliver a strong impact on development processes. They represent the operative response to the plan's aims (or intentions) in a given territory: they mitigate development risks identified in a local context. This makes them important projects, with a notable influence on both the economic resources required and development expectations. Given their specific nature, they are generally few in number within a territory: the idea is that for each municipal context the plan identifies from one to three development projects.

Pilot projects are also tied to the identification of the most consonant lines of development for the territory in question; whilst smaller in scale, they nonetheless have a powerful impact in terms of communication. As part of a strategic plan, pilot projects have the role of demonstrating, with hard facts, the development potential of a given territory. The principal characteristic of these projects is that they can be realised immediately and with limited economic resources: they are, for the most part, demonstrative actions that do not require significant investments, although it is important, instead, that they are able to start quickly and demonstrate the positive nature of the plan's development actions within a short period of time.

An initial evaluation of the technical priorities tied to different projects involved the classification of all development projects into three feasibility phases: short term, medium term and long term. The short term refers to a period of one to five years, the medium term refers to a period of six to ten years, and the long term extends beyond ten years.

The following criteria were used to classify projects in the short-term category: (i) the possibility of immediate intervention; (ii) the possibility of acquiring financial resources rapidly; (iii) the absence of opposition or the easy establishment of consensus.

Short-term development projects can also be entrusted with the role of being pilot projects (other than being a priority). This makes them projects designed to showcase and spread the idea of development and demonstrate its virtuous effects in a communicable and convincing way.

14.7 Conclusions

In operative terms, the overlap between the different landscapes identified, the diverse characteristics of the corridors, the specific morphologies of settlements discovered in the territory and the possible range of interventions, identifies a variety of synergetic and complementary actions that contribute to the land-use plan through development projects. These include defining the urban settlement rules (there are more than 1,500 charts of rules for interventions for an equal number of elementary urban units, for each plan), the evaluation of project feasibility in the short/medium term (for priority strategic projects and pilot projects).

The innovative capacity of an urban plan proposed as a development project lies in its ability to implement a strategy through rules for managing urban planning and also through interventions with known cost estimates, possible sources of financing, confirmed procedures and schedules.

A plan can become a project regardless of the scale of its application. Defining a desired spatial configuration and jointly identifying the actions required is an operation that can be undertaken at any scale, whether it is to regenerate a city or create a territory-wide, distributed system of services and facilities, or an organised network for managing the flow of goods or people.

Innovation in settlement structure means reorganising the physical, social, institutional and political structure of territorial systems to be competitive. Urban planners are responsible for spatial regeneration. We are confident we are doing the right thing when we state the existence of a biunivocal relationship between socioeconomic dynamics and the form of the settlement space. Urban planning choices can affect the evolution of the socioeconomic system: not only do important economic phenomena condition the configuration of the city, but opportune decisions about spatial planning at the urban level may also help trigger new socioeconomic development processes.

The most relevant innovation lies entirely in the logical connection between the process of implementing an urban plan and the economic-financial programme of municipal budgets. Recent trends towards the reorganisation of local entities, both in terms of functional aggregation and managerial capacity, enable and demand a perspective that introduces the theme of the economic-financial stability of development programmes into the mechanisms of urban planning, thereby also eventually bringing new methods of consultation and new forms that actively involve municipal governments in public–private partnerships.

References

General Local Plan, Municipality of Kruja, approved by the City Council with Decision no. 75 of 6 January 2017 and by the National Territorial Council with Decision no. 5 of 8 February 2017

General Local Plan, Municipality of Kurbin, approved by the City Council with Decision no. 98 of 27 January 2017 and by the National Territorial Council with Decision no. 6 of 8 February 2017

General Local Plan, Municipality of Lezha, approved by the City Council with Decision no. 194 of 25 September 2017 and by the National Territorial Council with Decision no. 6 of 16 October 2017

Mascarucci R (2008) Goal Congruence. Il ruolo del territorio nelle visioni strategiche. Meltemi, Rome

Mascarucci R (2003a) Project for sensitive territories and resources. Planum, Milan

Mascarucci R (2003b) Regional development and transnational spatial vision. In: Congress proceedings AESOP-ACSP, Leuven

Integrating Experiences: Palermo Mediterranean Gateway City. Identity and Innovation

15

Daniele Ronsivalle

Abstract

Metropolitan transformations of the Palermo as a Mediterranean city, guided by envisioning it as a 'fluid' gateway city, have been seen as an example for the planning of other such cities in Italy and Europe. The 2025 strategic vision for Palermo was inspired by three key components: (i) the relevance of Palermo as 'hub territory' in European level concerns in territorial and infrastructure development policies; (ii) the urban and regional experience with the concept 'fluid city' (envisioning the city as a portal and place of interaction and exchanges, not just in terms of goods and people); and (iii) new metropolitan vision produced by new regional and national legislation on metropolitan areas. This chapter develops an understanding of how the strategic spatial plan, approved by the City Council in 2016, selected these issues and connected them in one coherent vision, both at urban and metropolitan levels. The first sections trace the emergence of the plan. One concluding section reflects on the relevance of an innovative approach to the 'smart city' for Palermo's urban strategies. Main conclusions summarise development and emphasise on a need for conceptual integration.

Keywords

Palermo Mediterranean capital city • Fluid city paradigm • Palermo meta-politan system • Strategic territorial platforms and meridian multimodal corridor • Human smart city

15.1 Regional Design and Visioning for Palermo: The Fluid City as a Paradigm for the Mediterranean City

This chapter presents a case study of a medium-sized metropolis, Palermo, which has seen considerable growth through urbanisation over the last 50 years and a radical change in population distribution over the last 20 years. The provision of metropolitan, city-centre services over this long period has not kept pace with the increase in city users, creating overcrowded conditions. Master plans designed by the municipality have paid attention to housing issues at the expense of infrastructure and urban services, which have long remained in the background. At the regional level, meantime, provincial and regional administrations have not been able to initiate spatial restructuring policies or redistribute infrastructures and services. In the last ten years, both due to the reversal of urbanisation and the need to integrate national and Mediterranean infrastructures, the municipality has started a new process to revise the city's development strategies. In this, it has relied on new interpretations of the city.

The above-described failure of localisation policies highlights a great weakness in the present planning system: its lack of capacity to capture urbanisation as dynamic process. Failure calls not just for a revision of policies but for a new identity to be found. It is argued here that this identity arises from the eponymous nature of the city. Palermo is an ancient Phoenician port. The port acts as an access portal, or gateway, to the territory beyond, thus generating Mediterranean relations.

D. Ronsivalle (✉)
Department of Architecture, University of Palermo, Palermo, Italy
e-mail: daniele.ronsivalle@unipa.it

© Springer Nature Switzerland AG 2020
V. Lingua and V. Balz (eds.), *Shaping Regional Futures*,
https://doi.org/10.1007/978-3-030-23573-4_15

Port systems not only reflect an interface between land and water but inevitably also influence the life of the city. This influence is captured in the concept of 'fluidity'.

The 'fluidity' concept has taken on a strategic significance in waterfront regeneration, as outlined in the Fluid City Paradigm (Carta 2016). It calls for waterfront regeneration taking into account a wider and deeper vision that addresses the interface between sea and land, no longer just as a coastline but as a territory with its own influence and identity. The 'fluid city' is made up of traffic connections that generate new products and new ideas: a fluid city, therefore, is a city that creates culture. It is able to activate a new urban metabolism by regenerating architectures and producing new landscapes (Clément and De Pieri 2005). It can generate a powerful relational network through the permanent flow of urban culture. Just as a waterfront is not merely a line, but rather a complex set of historical, formal, spatial, and social relationships, so waterfront cities have strong historical, formal, spatial, social, and functional relationships, both within themselves and with other waterfront cities. They often have a high territorial rank because of their great ability to perform the functions required of an urban hub through two-tier networks composed of both waterfront and inner cities in metropolitan and sub-regional contexts. Thus, the waterfront city acts as an intelligent hub because it has the ability to distribute flows (goods, people, know-how, services and public utilities) and disseminate functional loads between the various territorial subjects and centres that together make up the urban structure. In historic cities, this ability is manifest in the distribution of urban powers (for instance, royal, civil, religious and commercial), and functional connections between the inner territories and the metropolis.

One of the inevitable consequences of the tightly woven relationships between cities, ports and inland coastal areas is that intervention tools used for the regeneration of urban waterfronts must be capable of intercepting, interpreting and transforming the entire city and not just the coastline. The urban waterfront is a 'spark of urban regeneration' (Carta 2013), and it demands targeted efforts to create the feeling of a waterfront that encompasses more than a physical location but rather a fluid sense of the whole city, hence the 'Fluid City' identity (Carta 2013). This recognition has been applied in Palermo. It started with the acknowledgement of its historic identity (now in crisis due to the absence of development strategies distinct from the urban development plans often financed by the mafia). Acknowledgement led to new questions. What new strategy could the city adopt? How could it create a new metropolitan and regional role, setting aside the stigma of traditional models?

The very shape and origin of the city were found to provide an answer. When the Municipality of Palermo started to focus on an urban strategy in 2004, during the Venice Architecture Biennale, it rethought the conceptual and cultural boundaries of the waterfront. In Palermo, the road axis from the sea represents the way in which the urban space of the waterfront city turns into the space of the metropolis, the mother city, connected both to its gateway (the port) and the interior lands that contribute to its development. So, the waterfront border in Palermo is represented by the Cathedral of Monreale, which no longer faces the sea but the Benedictine manors that extend from Monreale towards the southern coast of Sicily (see Fig. 15.1).

Below, it is discussed how the understanding of Palermo as a "fluid city" has informed and was reflected in strategic spatial planning frameworks for the city of Palermo. Section 15.2 explains how the concept first was reflected in the concept 'platform territories' (a response of the Italian government to EU infrastructural policies) and how it was then taken up in a 'meta-politan' vision for the city of Palermo. Section 15.3 reflects on how it relates to current attempts to profile Palermo as a 'smart city'. In conclusions, impact and outlooks are summarised. The importance of consistently inspiring the spatial plan of Palermo with the wider concept of 'fluidity' is emphasised.[1]

---

[1]In the same years, before financial crisis of 2008, many other cities around Europe provided some solutions in order to integrate ports and urban contexts.

These cities worked in reason of their rank and their position: the large port-cities, the cities in which the relationship between city and harbour is producing a new way to live the sea; the riverfront cities in which the commercial port has modified its hierarchy; the city builds a new identity based on a kick-off event (Ronsivalle 2016).

As in Ronsivalle (2016), these cities are divided in three groups: the large port-cities, the cities in which the relationship between city and harbour is producing a new way to live the sea, the riverfront cities in which the commercial port has modified its hierarchy and the city builds a new identity based on a kick-off event.

The first group is composed, for example, by cities as Rotterdam and Hamburg: the relevance of the port and the weakness of the city are harmonized in a strong change of urban and portal policy.

The second group is composed by cities like Amsterdam, Barcelona, Lisboa, Genova, Marseille, Trieste, Valencia: the split between city and harbour is now solved by integration policies and strategic actions on urban regeneration.

The third group is composed by Bilbao, Bordeaux, Liverpool, Lyon, Newcastle upon Tyne, Sevilla: they were riverfront cities with a commercial or industrial harbour, nowadays they are cities that radically changed the general development strategy. In all these cities, however, waterfront policies start from the reticular context they generate: they are not only wonderful places with sea-side pedestrian streets or museums.

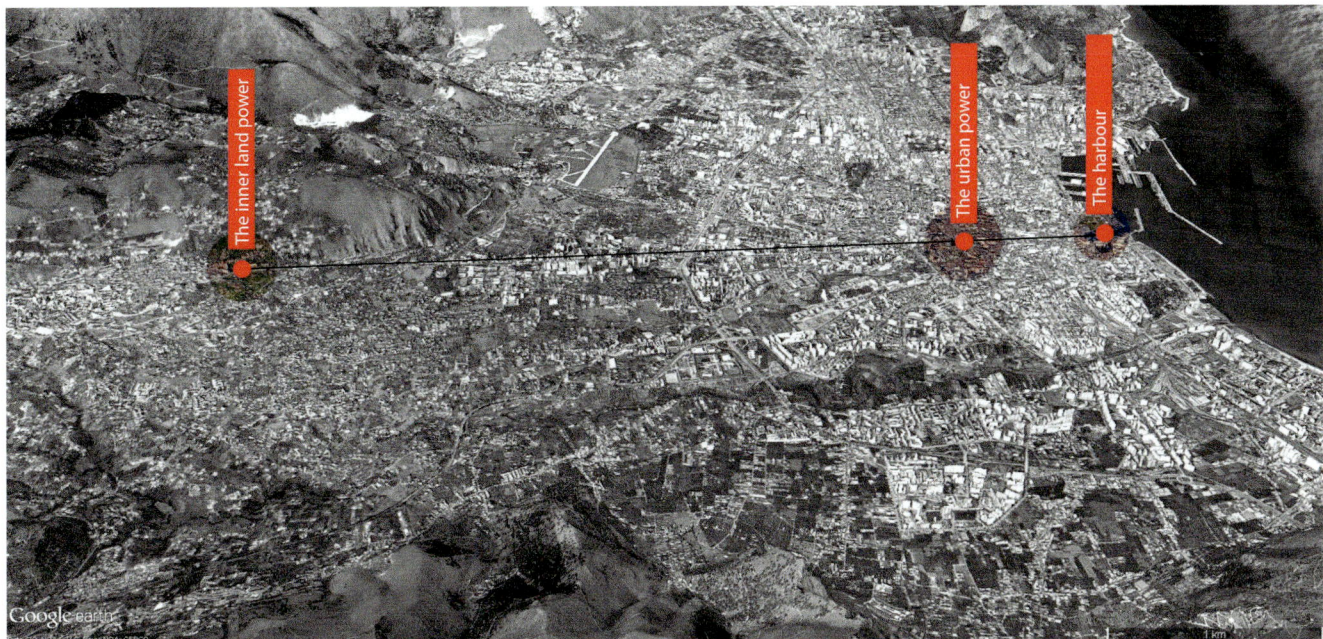

Fig. 15.1 Palermo's historic waterfront showing relations between the harbour as gateway to the city, and Monreale as a gateway to the inner areas (elaborated by the author)

15.2   Key Drivers and Challenges: Palermo, Gateway City in a Euro-Mediterranean Vision

15.2.1   Meridian Corridor Policy and Territorial Platforms: A National Strategic Framework

In 2003, the Italian Ministry of Infrastructures (MIITT) supported the study for a reticular model in the Mediterranean, based on the idea of a 'Meridian Corridor'. The Ministry was searching for a new way to intercept east–west flows in the Trans European Network for Transport (TEN-T) by then. At the same time, the Ministry, supported by the Italian Scientific Society of Urban Planners (SIU), proposed a minor Copernican revolution by founding the concept 'platform territory'. The concept responded to two points of view regarding the relationship between cities and infrastructures, as follows:

1. an infrastructure axis, a sea route, road or railway line is no longer a mere vector joining point A to point B, but a territorial band connected to territorial contexts. Such territorial bands, therefore, can change the interaction with the infrastructure and create added value to goods moving along the infrastructure;
2. cities and interconnected hub territories create selective interdependencies (Carta et al. 2007) between cities and territories, both in public development policies and the economies generated by local relations or trans-scalar ones.

The 'Platform Territory' as a concept, according to SIU & MIITT research, produces a new vision in which cities, infrastructures, production sites and natural and cultural resources interact by providing occasions for trans-scalar interactions (Carta et al. 2017). In particular, regions in Sicily turn out to have a special condition, when seen as such platform territories. Due to their position on the east–west flows of the Meridian Corridor, as two analyses by MIITT show, the concept is more relevant in Sicily than in other regions (see Fig. 15.2). The hub territories of Catania, Syracuse and Augusta in the east, together with Palermo, Trapani and Termini Imerese in the west, represent clearly recognisable nodes of urban concentrations of the platform territories. In effect, they are two unconsolidated metropolitan systems, a sort of meta-politan system (as explained in the next section) that is not bound by NUTS 3 administrative boundaries but connected at an appropriate functional level: they are a sort of proto-metropolis, with all the components of functional metropolitan systems, but without such systems logic currently.

The final strategic synthesis for these hub territories can be found in the Selective Interdependencies Scenario (SIU-MIITT 2006). Fuelled by a process that considered multi-scalar and multi-actor points of view, this scenario proposed a

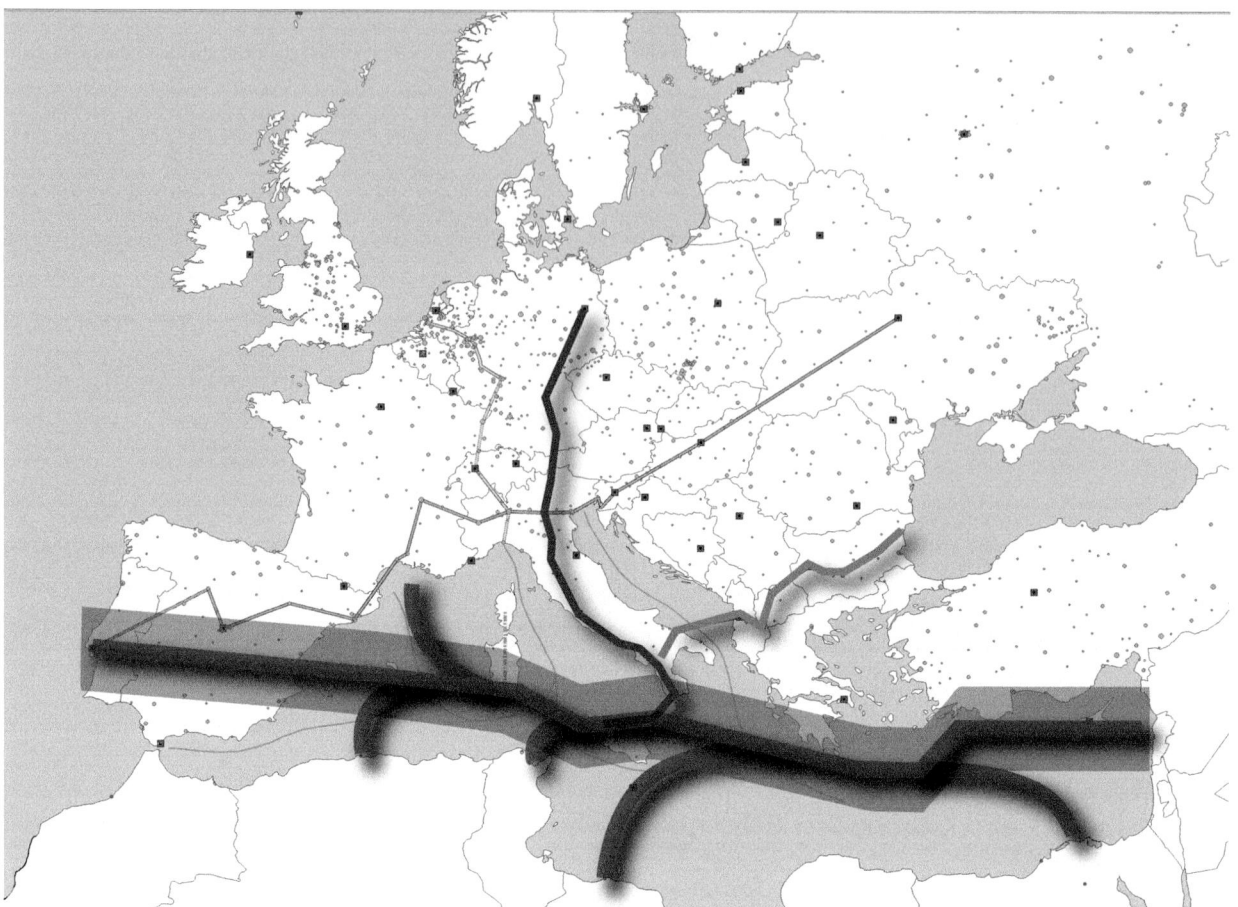

Fig. 15.2 Meridian Corridor as a framework for connecting and commutating the flows in the Mediterranean system, from Carta (2009, p. 233)

framework for actively designing complex metropolitan development strategies, responding to the above issues. It aimed at identifying the below-listed needs:

- **synergies** between infrastructure networks and territorial systems, in terms of existing and programmed infrastructure as well as territorial specialisations for production platforms;
- **dynamism** of development, in terms of overall competitiveness and, above all, the development of research, innovation and internationalisation;
- administrative **vitality**, in terms of design skills and management of complex programs;
- **connectivity** and **polycentrism** in terms of capacity to establish systems between the ninth-level nodes of pan-European networks and local systems referred to as the 'power generators' of the top-level nodes.

Consequently, as part of drafting the National Strategic Framework for 2020, in 2005, the Italian Ministry of Infrastructures accelerated territorial development of the infrastructure network in southern Italy as a way of increasing national competitiveness through improvement in urban nodes and network connectivity. The Ministry proposals were fuelled by a vision (see Fig. 15.3) in which the creation of productive and innovative clusters, platform connectivity, and re-urbanisation drives the redevelopment of nodes and the provision of collective services. Above all, it envisioned the redefinition of metropolitan functions: the node city in this vision is a territory that enables the management and distribution of the flows of goods, traffic and people moving in the Mediterranean system; in short, the city is both a gateway and a router. Its effects are:

- more capability in gateway relations among cities in a local context;
- more advanced opportunities for urban regeneration and territorial competitiveness;

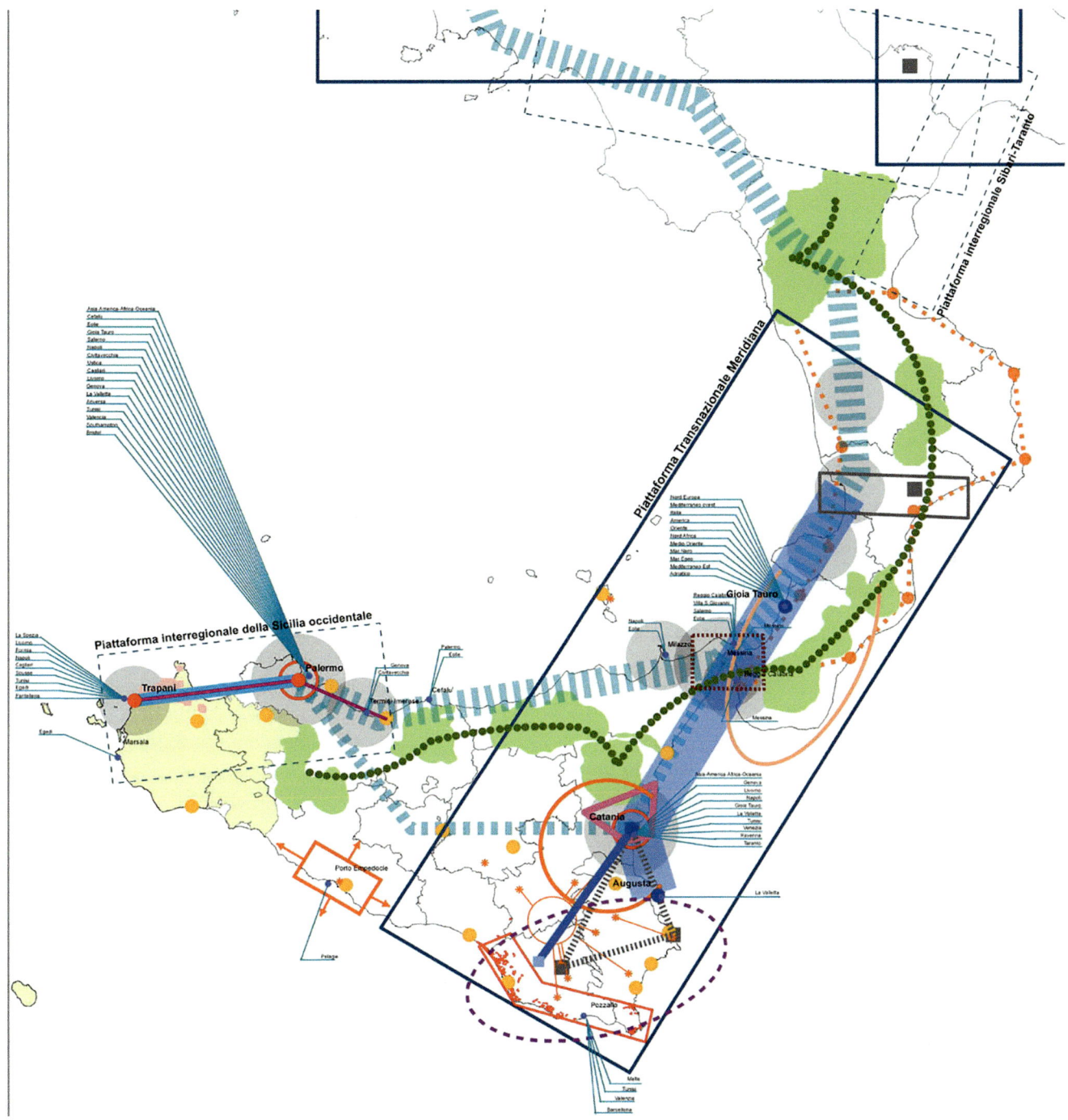

Fig. 15.3 Strategic territorial platforms in Sicily: the selective interdependencies scenario (SIU) by the Ministry of Infrastructures, from Carta et al. (2007, p. 232)

- more capability for adding value, not only economic, as a catalyst for the flow of goods and resources that cross the mobility armatures in the Mediterranean area.

The vision produced in the SIU-MIITT research (SIU-MIITT 2006) evolved in an extensive and complex decision-making context in which network and multi-scalar policies, locally and nationally, imposed actions (made more distinct by the Sicilian regional autonomy) were co-ordinated and co-exist. Each new, strategic urban and metropolitan planning season is an opportunity to infuse new polycentric and reticular development. Each one can provide new impetus for reinforcing connections between large infrastructure networks, city systems and the long-range connectivity of territorial frameworks. This vision has evolved into the strategic plans of the platform territories, coming to fruition in the implementation of development policies for Sicily's metropolitan cities. Since Palermo, Catania and Messina (the three highest-ranking metropolitan cities in Sicily) are also waterfront cities, they base their development strategies on interface and gateway capabilities.

15.2.2   Strategic Plan for the Capital City of Palermo: A Meta-Politan Vision

In 2009, after drawing up national policies with the Ministry of Infrastructures, the Municipality of Palermo finally drafted its first strategic territorial plan, including a vision for the metropolitan city. As early as 1986, the Sicilian Region identified by law a metropolitan area around Palermo, but there was no regional authority to strategically follow-up the proposed rescaling. Only the structural plan of Palermo province had anticipated on it, however, only through some methodological reflections on the topic in 2002. Consequently, it was not until 2009 that a plan and program for the metropolitan city was actually drafted. Palermo used to be seen as a monocentric and gravitational metropolis, in the earlier rather impromptu planning approaches. The aims of the new strategic draft were to define a functionally integrated polycentric city, both in terms of a physical distribution of high-ranking services, and in terms of a new thematic distinction of places. Aims were combined within a new reticular framework called the 'nine cities'. Nine future development directions were embodied in graphic representations, each of them a key visions in the strategic plan (see Fig. 15.4). Each 'city' was placed into the polycentric, reticular urban framework, thus avoiding the dispersion of resources and enabling the necessary investment multiplier that a strategic plan requires (Carta 2014, p. 200).

The "nine cities" (in fact eight thematic + one overarching one) and their aims were:

- the **connecting city**, focused on the development of slow mobility, a tram system, an intermodal rail system, and fast broadband internet connections;
- the **tourism city**, focused on building a recognisable brand in the context of international tourism, by means of select public and private actions and projects;
- the **worldwide city**, focused on internationalisation and foreign policies as a stage for actions at EU level;
- the **culture city**, focused on the development of the historic centre of Palermo;
- the **productive city**, focused on connecting two Urban Enterprise Zones promoted by Italian policies on Urban Free Tax Zones;
- the **welfare city**, focused on the development of leisure and places that support well-being;
- the **creative city**, focused on stimulating innovation and creativity in the humanistic and scientific fields; creating places for education and research;
- the **inclusive city**, for social cohesion and community integration, localised primarily in a first residential area ring around the centre of Palermo;
- the **metropolitan city**, with the intention to modify the boundaries of the earlier metropolitan area (defined under a 1986 regional law) and with the aim to coordinate upcoming development.

The 'nine-cities' strategy was used by the Municipality of Palermo until 2012. In 2012, a new mayor decided to update it, in anticipation of new regional laws for metropolitan cities. The Municipality of Palermo had confirmed the strategic reticular model even prior to the instatement of the regional law 15/2015 (see Carta 2017). On own initiative, it had decided to not limit itself to being a mere service provider for citizens and businesses of a larger area thus avoiding the reproduction of gravitational models that research has indicated to be obsolete.[2] Also in 2012, it chose to continue a path that had earlier been started by the Ministry of Infrastructures: by re-interpreting the nine-cities strategic vision, it continued the metropolitanization of the territorial system by perceiving it as a territory of hubs.

One result of re-interpretation (described in Carta 2017) was the decision by the Mayor of Palermo to act according to a *meta-politan* strategic scenario, formulated in 2015. This scenario, accomplished by Maurizio Carta, Stefano Stanghellini and Creta srl (see Carta et al. 2017), was not merely metropolitan, i.e. it not only included the belt municipalities around Palermo and the former province. It considered a broader regional area stretching from Cefalù (no more than 75 km to the

---

[2]See data and evaluations from Urban@it (2016).

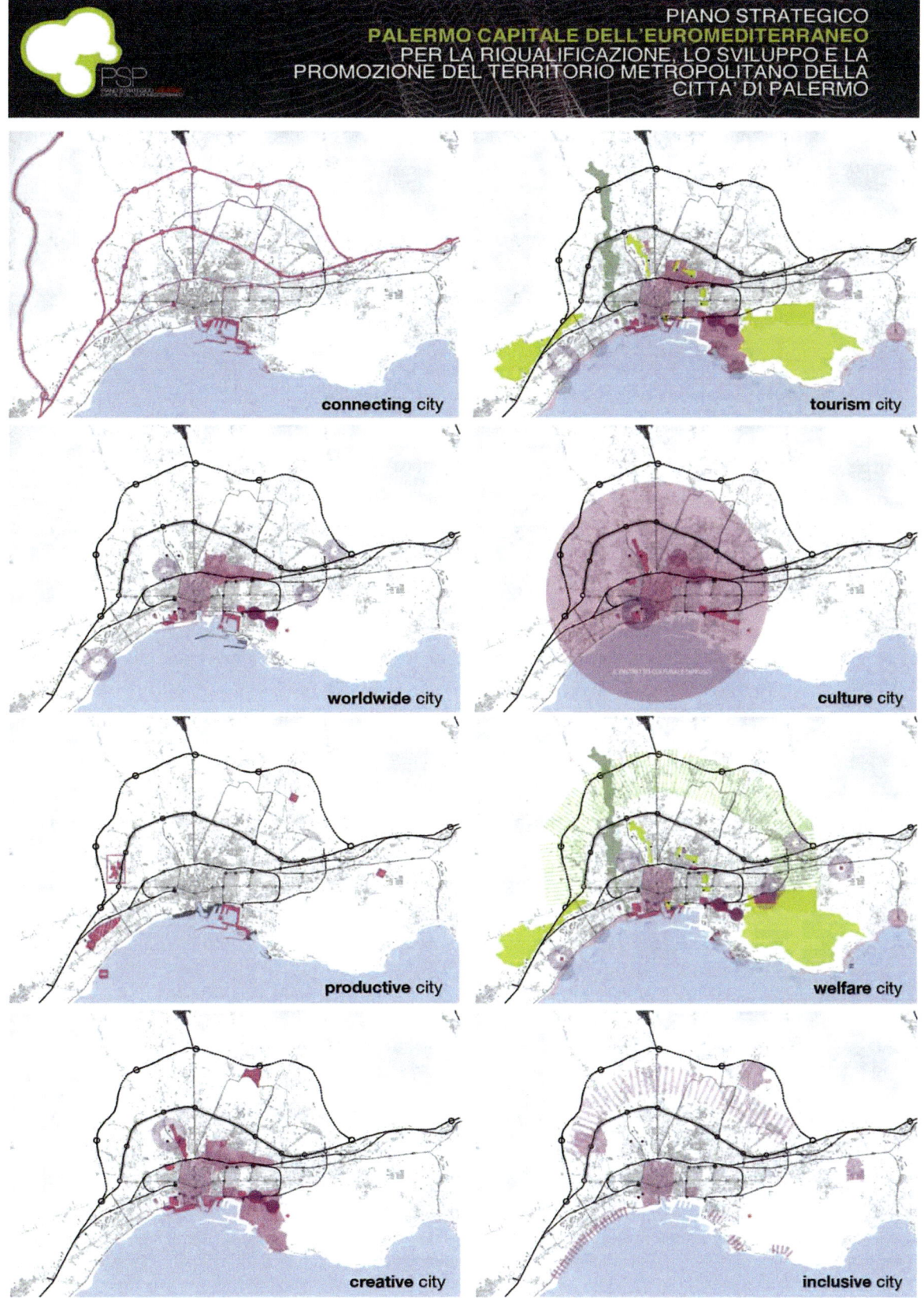

Fig. 15.4   Palermo Capital City: nine (eight plus one) strategies, from Carta (2014, p. 203)

east) to Marsala (no more than 130 km to the west from Palermo). The aim of the scenario was to inform an updated strategic vision for Palermo Capital City (following the advice of Carta, Stanghellini and Creta srl). It was meant to give orientation and guidance for broader and therefore more coherent territorial transformations. The mayor's decision meant that the new Palermo strategic plan ascribed to the spatial and infrastructural dimensions of the 'Territorial Platform' concept. Palermo came to be seen as a catalyst in western Sicily, because of its importance in the European and Mediterranean context. It gained a role as an activator of competitive factors and provider of social, economic and cultural policies and mobility systems (see the feasibility studies of the Ministry of Infrastructure and Transport on the Western-Tyrrhenian Platform and the Hub-Territory deriving from SIU-MIITT 2006, partially published in Carta 2014).

The competitiveness, sustainability and cohesion agendas embodied in the scenario required policies linked to new, smart, creative, resilient, sustainable and solid development paradigms. They also required respecting the capacities of the metropolitan city and other municipal administrations and therefore a context of innovative decision-making, permanent evaluation of results, co-ordination of choices and co-planning. After the 2012 change of political agenda for the new municipal and metropolitan administration, in 2015, the Mayor of Palermo began the last phase of the strategic plan which embodied the latter requirement: the *Feasibility Study of the Action Plan for the Strategic Plan for Palermo Capital City* (advised by Maurizio Carta, Stefano Stanghellini and Creta srl). Its goal was to define the role of Palermo in the Euro-Mediterranean context in more detail (including its competitive forces) and, more importantly, to identify the concrete actions required for physical, social, economic and cultural requalification. As Carta et al. (2017) have noted, the study strongly benefitted from the shared orientation, address and consistency of how territorial transformations were taken up in a 2025 city vision.

This feasibility study enacted the strategic plan proposed to all stakeholders, institutional and otherwise. It facilitated a process capable to simultaneously consider operational decisions on the inner city and intermediate territorial levels (the urban region), while also respecting connections to the meta-politan area of the western Sicily Territorial Platform (see SIU-MIITT 2006). The process was applied to both urban as well as metropolitan and regional dimensions, identifying the strategies best-suited to each scale. It included activating the relevant inter-sectorial policies, drawing up executive regeneration projects, and identifying the resulting rules that would enable strategies and projects to be implemented. Last but not least, it ensured the most effective decisions, through employing consideration of timing and procedures.

Through this non-hierarchical process, planning, decision-making and implementation together fostered an understanding of areas as cultural hubs. Already accomplished designs by the municipal administration were fed back into the feasibility study and used to generate an urban identity. Redevelopment and transformation projects with a wide array of cultural themes proved to be the way to reposition Palermo strategically within Italy and Europe. Indeed, Palermo's nomination as 2017 EU Culture Capital and 2018 Italian Culture Capital demonstrates how effective the strategy[3] has been.

15.2.3 The Palermo Metropolis 2025 Keywords

The last phase of metropolitan planning in Palermo concerned the meta-politan city (Ascher 2009), in which boundaries were defined according to functional identities and quality-of-life goals (Carta 2017). Carta (2017) defines Palermo Metropolis 2025 as a metropolis of cities, or 'hyper-metropolis',[4] which is not just a group of cities in the physical sense—i.e. the municipalities it comprises and those with which specific agreements have been signed—but also in the social, economic and cultural sense. In his perception, specific downtowns, services, public utilities and networks all adapt to a thematic development of the 'hyper-metropolis (Fig. 15.5).' The concept suggests the idea of interconnected places and functions in which every node of the urban network has potentialities for accommodating flows, e.g. can connect to another function, in the same place or a different one. In synthesis, the Palermo hyper-metropolis is a metropolis of neighbourhoods, small- and medium-sized towns, farmland and production areas, habitats and cultures, which together are capable of guiding people and

[3]The culture policy for Palermo is viewed from the perspective of integration and multiculturalism. The 'Palermo Charter on International Human Mobility' was approved in 2015 by the city to overcome barriers to international human mobility. The Palermo Charter is not just an international document or poster of which the city is a promoter, but it is the vision of the city of the future. It is the key through which Palermo builds its ever-evolving identity and opens up a new horizon for the Mediterranean, in the centre of which is Palermo, the capital.

[4]The term 'hyper-metropolis' is like the strategic concept of HyperCatalunya. The study called HyperCatalunya promoted by Generalitat de Catalunya, Institut Català del Sòl in 2003, sought to identify the potential of Catalonia as city. The project was undertaken in conjunction with specialists in the different strata of information that configure the territory (nodes, networks and environments) with the aim of discovering new categories of projects with which to address the habitability of a territory in the process of urbanisation. See also Gausa (2009). Multi-Barcelona/Hiper-Catalunya. Hacia un nuevo abordaje de la ciudad y el territorio contemporaneos. List, Barcelona.

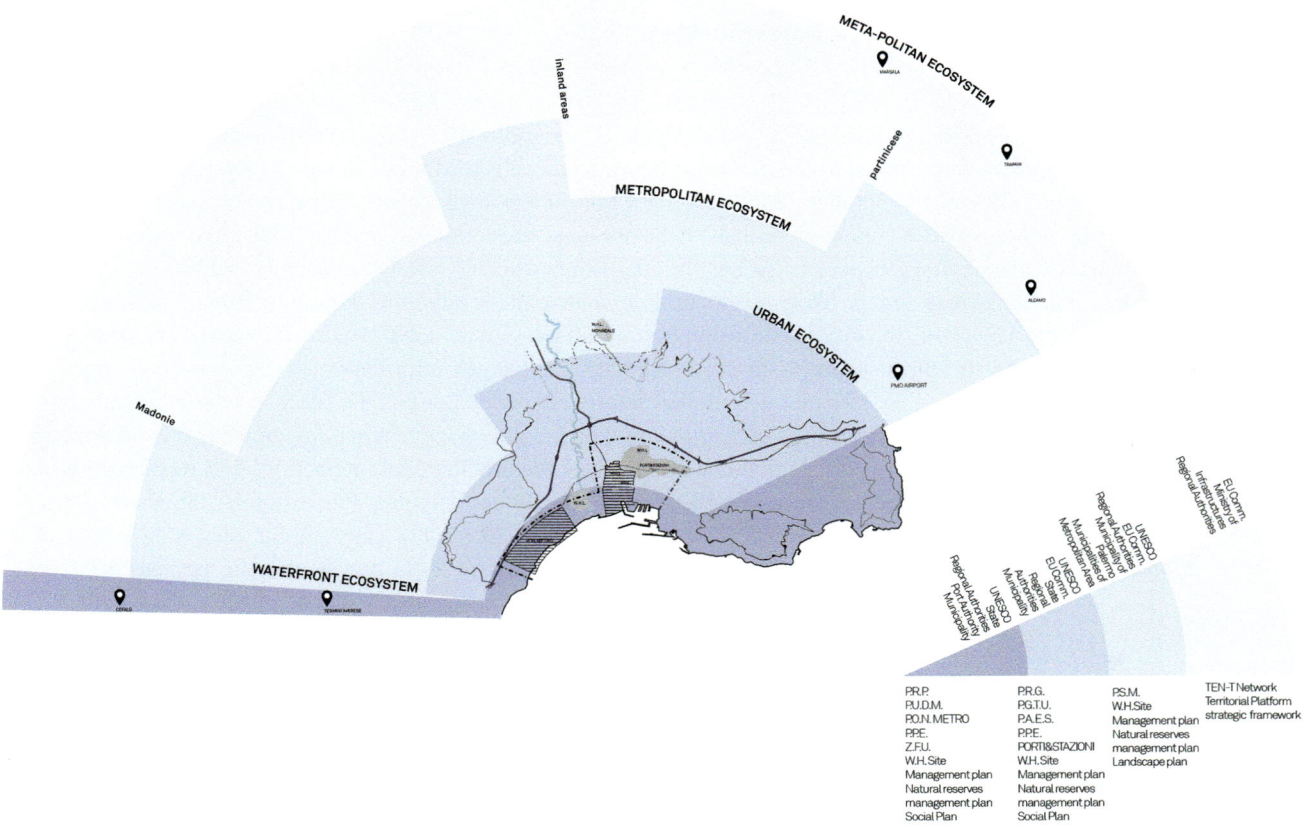

Fig. 15.5 The rationale of the Palermo meta-politan system: the variable perimeters adapt to specific strategies within a single direction, governed by the city of Palermo and by the thematic networks designed into the meta-polis governance model. *Source* Adapted by the author from Carta (2017, p. 72)

territories towards circular development, within the scope of renewed integral ecology and contributing to care for the common home.

The research and design project used a set of keywords to describe the make-up of this hyper-metropolis, as follows:

- **metabolic city** describes a new hyper-metropolitan concept, one which is fuelled by the reconstruction of closed life cycles through the launch of urban redevelopment projects geared to functional integration and the emergence of energy processes involving the quality of open spaces, energy production and urban mobility;
- **city of culture** denotes a city that is not only a place of events and cultural events, but also an educational city for its citizens and visitors. Moreover, the strategic plan itself takes on a 'pedagogical' function as it is capable of extracting potential for transformation from the human and urban identity resources;
- **city that welcomes** encapsulates the rights of citizenship and freedom of movement. Palermo 2025 recomposes the fabric of the city to include diversity, combine functions and enrich the metropolitan experience with the other municipalities with which it shares its vision;
- **city** describes a place which adapts to the **changing climatic conditions** and hydrogeological sensitivities of the territory, modelling positive relationships within it. It opens up physical, territorial transformations as new landscape projects, with resilience as a key driver for the urban project.

The keywords define the strategic design at urban and metropolitan levels, localising functions, infrastructures and facilities.

15.3 A New Governance and Planning Factor for the Palermo Hyper-Metropolis: The Human Smart City as a Tool for the Palermo Meta-Polis

Talking about the 'hyper-metropolis', Carta et al. (2017) introduce the relevance of ICT in shaping it. They argue that new ICT developments have changed our perception of the city, in particular a metropolis with a high level of functional integration and a large population. Developments have transformed perception through an enhanced mode in which physical and virtual space and sites undergo mutually dependent alteration, thus crushing a one-dimensional reality. Contemporary landscapes are born from the creative relationships between communities that, on the one hand, are composed by people who live at local places and, and on the other hand, by people in a global city that has shrunk its dimensions (Oswalt and Rieniets 2006).

Nowadays, the 'smart city' concept is likely to become an untouchable taboo (Townsend 2013), indifferent to the transformation of the city. However, the city, aside from gaining a new 'smart' label, has in fact never changed over the millennia. It continues to be the place where man seeks security, exchanges information, builds new components and develops shared messages. By doing so, like into a compiled informatic code, a city is the place in which humans increase their access to a set of inalienable rights, inscribed in the value of life and philosophy. When the pre-ordered and widespread urban information starts to come together and agglomerate, it changes the gravitational interactions and relationships. What is 'city' becomes more and more dense and recognisable compared to what it is not. For example, the Royal Palace in Palermo on the early peninsula, known as *piede fenicio*, for example, is like a big cartographic placeholder because its symbolic reference generates relations, between territorial security and central royal power, that are beyond the physical

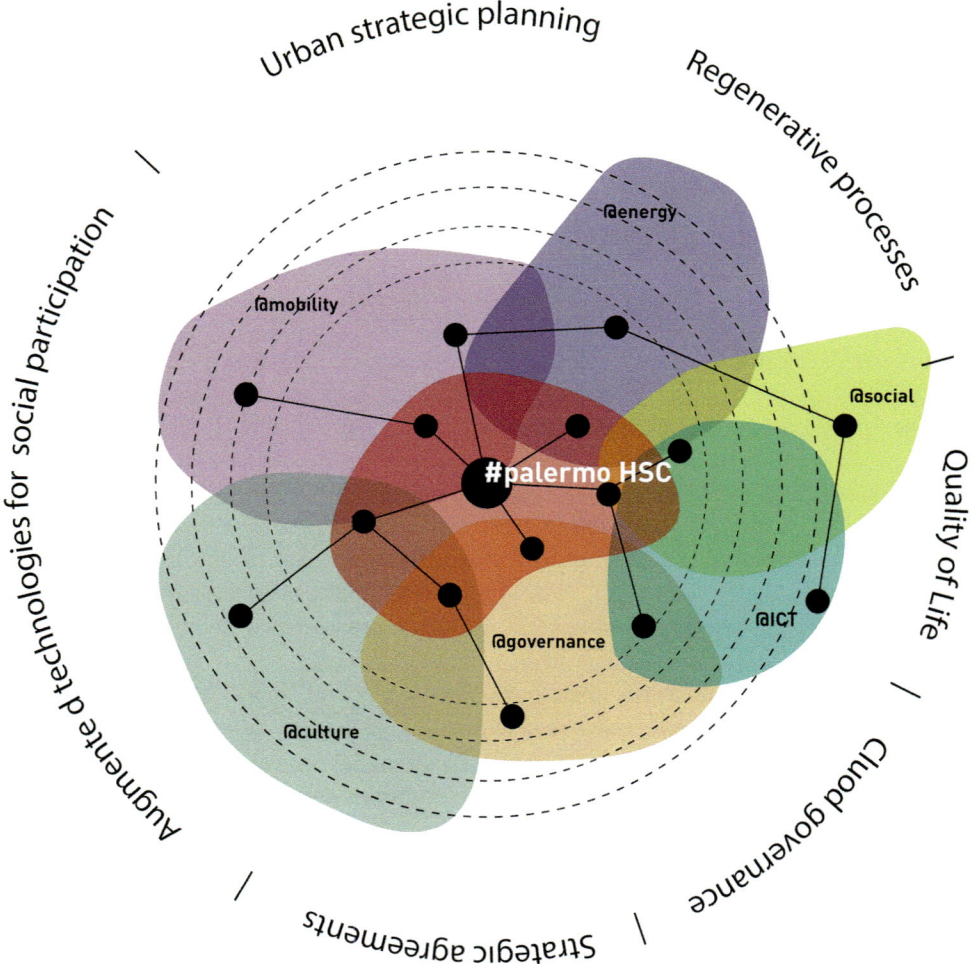

Fig. 15.6 Human Smart City Nebula. The classic hexagonal smart city model has taken on a new structure to integrate the choices for urban regeneration. It has become a cloud of interactions, within which it is possible to retrace the routing function of the laboratory and the interlacing of research functions and applicative goals. The nodes in the gravitational field of the Human Smart City model (#HSC) are connected on the issues of the smart city framework, but the #HSC model discovers new interactions, elaborated by the author, also in Carta et al. (2017, p. 184)

security needs of its inhabitants. The monolithic volumes of the Pisan Tower, with two rampant lions and its interior mosaic decorations, are the persistent urban information of urban royal power.

The basal processes of urban life and its functions remain fundamentally unchanged even when settlement systems change to have more complex, distributed, interactive, reactive and metabolic grids. The city sets itself up as a dynamic and complex system, a network of networks ranked by the major node functions that support the new urban economies. Nowadays, the amount of information has increased: Palermo produces increasingly large data and information clusters that are made up of sensors and actuators and are enriched by cultural and business intelligence. However, ICT cannot be an 'urban prosthesis'. Rather it must be coupled with enablers of social innovation. Palermo, as a 'Smart City', obliges us to return to a holistic and metabolic view of the city. The Palermo Metropolitan Strategy for 2025 focuses therefore on the smart 'human city'—a city made by humans—which requires a new analytical and planning approach to govern its evolution. Schuler (2016), for example, states that smartness is shown in the urban context when the following ingredients are present:

- knowledge;
- an attitude and a common aspiration understood as civic intelligence;
- urban organisational capital;
- relational capital which includes reputation, social networks, trust and opportunities;
- economic and financial resources.

The concept of 'the smartest person is the room', as in Weinberger (2011), is an important element for understanding what the Palermo human smart city could really be, and how planners can approach its growth and transformation in a strategic urban vision fit for a metropolis like Palermo.

When the Strategic Plan for Palermo Capital City 2025 applies a new relationship between city places, functions and inhabitants (see the hyper-metropolis, Sect. 15.2.2)—as between room and inhabitants in 'intelligent room' concept—knowledge places are perceived to be more specialised than each citizen, and to be more widespread. Knowledge is no longer in those who produce or receive it only. It is also a component of the physicality of the places themselves—widespread and devoid of a truthfulness validated a priori, such that false information can become true. The 'intelligent room', therefore, is not a decisive and positive place in itself, but it needs criteria and clear assessment tools to prevent false data deliberately becoming the true need of urban communities. The commitment to the human smart city is most closely aligned with Palermo strategic planning when the innovative tools for communication, production and management of services are used to develop integrated and strategic planning protocols. These protocols seek to accelerate the development of urban intelligence and enable creativity and culture-based values that are rich in social intelligence and resilient to climate change. The Palermo Strategic Plan 2025 explores urban transformation trends through up-to-date scientific studies—theoretical, methodological and experimental—as well as smart urban projects that in fact belong to a field of technological spatial hybridisation. The logic of the connections between the human Smart City and Palermo strategies suggests a smart city model like a nebula (see Carta et al. 2017, pp. 176–187), where the strategic plan is used to solve critical conditions of traditional smart city projects. These are summarised in:

- **Coaxiality**: urban technologies co-exist with the physical reality. However, spaces are often adjuvants only, and not carrier of technologies.
- **Predominance** of digital over physical transformation: technological innovation does not consider how it affects transformations in the city.
- **Indifference**: designers in the technology field do not deal with the real effects of urban transformations.

The 'nebula' model, as a rethinking of the smart city model, contributes to solutions that are co-generated: innovative technological components contribute to the generation of new urban transformations and urban transformations are an engine that enables technology (Fig. 15.6). Strategic planning integrates processes and finds solutions capable of intersecting all the urban regeneration activities, from urban renewal to social participation in physical events and digital solutions. The Palermo Human Smart City (#PalermoHSC in Fig. 15.6) is the digital shape of the hyper-metropolis, because it integrates technology and society and, as in the nineteenth-century city, the new technologies produce new features and designs in the urban regeneration process. In Palermo, urban strategies and cultural functions are most important because of their ability to weave hypertextual relations amongst inhabitants, users and cities. In poor economic conditions, Palermo's urban strategies identify information as a new asset of the urban economy, and as in other metropolitan areas, the plan aims to produce, process and transfer data in increasing quantities. Many new urban solutions are connected to the production of big data. However, as pointed out, the city has always been an information production system; the new challenge for the government and the sustainable development of the urban system is inherent in selection and data interpretation strategies. In synthesis, the need to adopt a new interpretive paradigm that capitalises, in real time, on the changes taking place is now imperative. It must define actions able to keep the evolution of the urban system within sustainable negentropic trajectories and construct a new technical-disciplinary planning vision, connecting places, resources and the community in real, digital ways.

15.4 Conclusions and Outlook: Performance of the Palermo Gateway City Towards 2025

The outcomes of the strategic planning process from 'Palermo Gateway City' to 'Palermo Metropolis 2025' are measured on four levels:

- improvement of governance in reorganising regional and large-area planning;
- integration with the Land Use Plan of Palermo, especially since the master plan defines the intervention priorities, quantifies the spaces necessary for the realisation of metropolitan-rank services and designs the urban ecological network;
- the definition of a political framework (so-called mayor's plan) to guarantee finance for the interventions while also providing safe funding opportunities for investors and the public;
- the relevance of digital transformation to Palermo 2025s urban integrated policies, out of the rhetoric of the smart city, but integrated with social innovation and community participation.

Regarding the improvement of interscalar governance, the Strategic Plan for Palermo integrates urban, metropolitan and regional level contents. The nature of the 'Platform Territory' (as described in Sect. 15.2.1), which the strategic plan

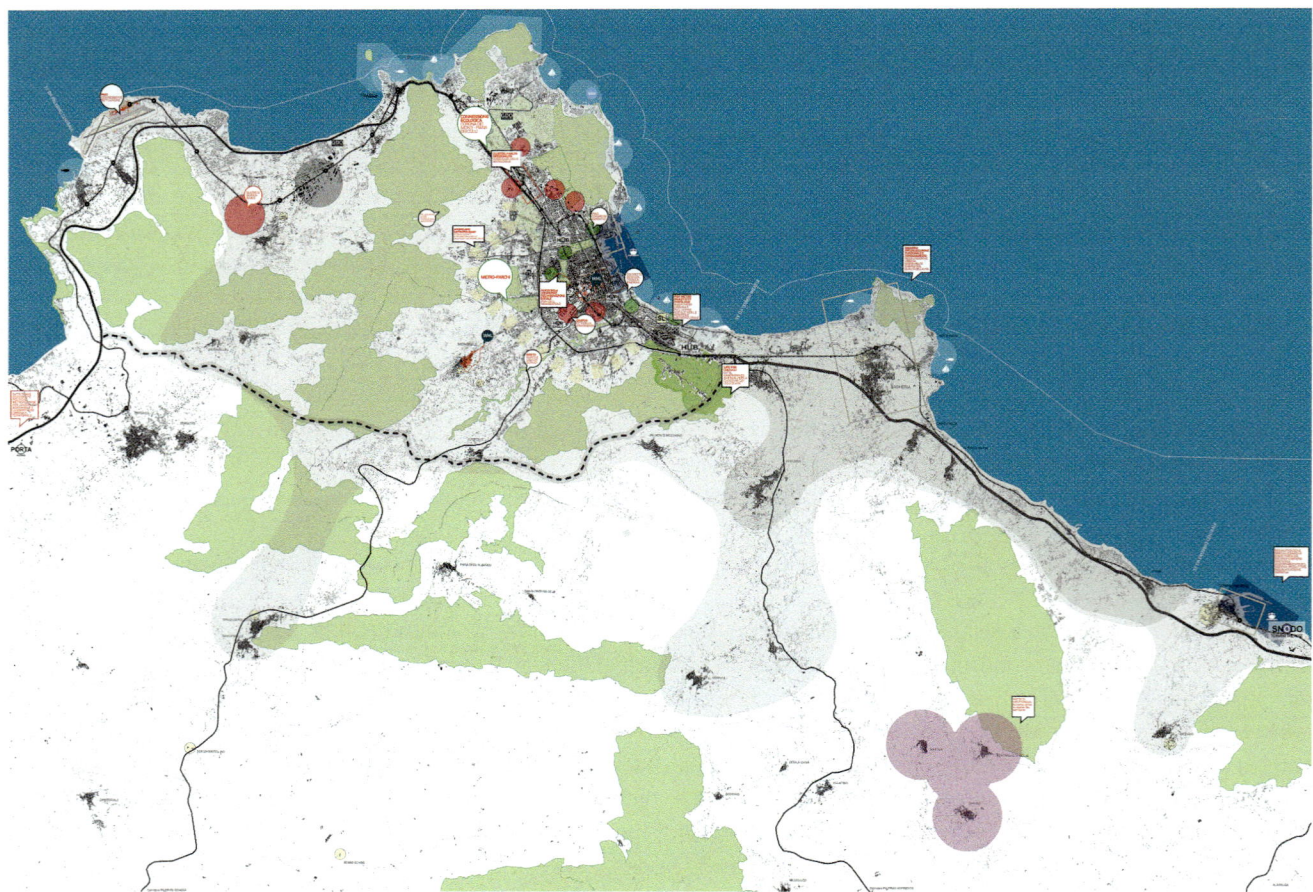

Fig. 15.7 Hyper-metropolitan level of the Palermo Strategic Plan, from Carta (2017, p. 89)

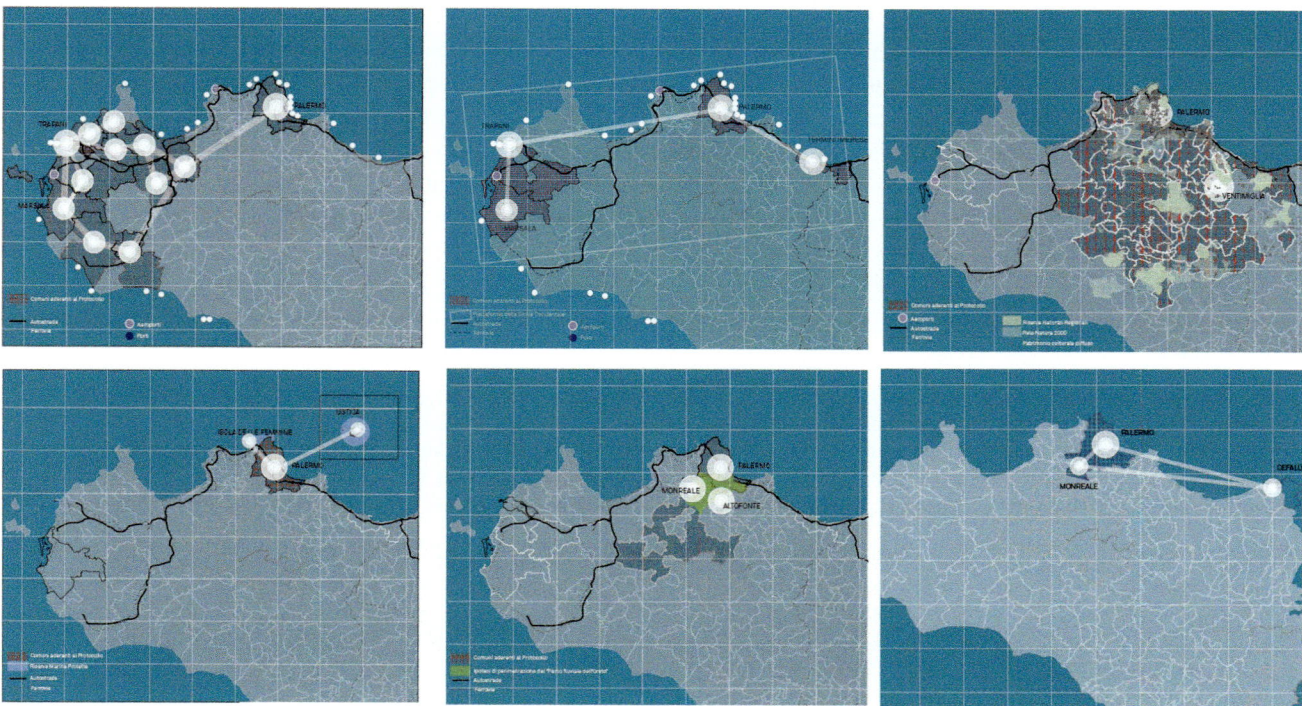

Fig. 15.8 Variable geometry of agreement for strategic actions in the metropolitan area of Palermo. From left, above, to right, bottom: sustainable mobility, infrastructures, green tourism, island policies, ecological sustainability and culture

affects, facilitates the definition of how metropolitan-rank functions sited within the metropolitan territory are able to serve the whole reference system and, therefore, at what functional level they are placed.

The map of metropolitan-level strategies selects and orients the regional functions and shows them in relation to the metropolitan territories of reference.

The polycentric reticular view that characterises urban regeneration strategies finds greater relevance and specificity in the metropolitan dimension, since it helps to substantiate the passage from an obsolete, gravitation metropolitan model to a super-organism model. All urban nodes perform functions and connections, akin to a server for the urban clients (see Fig. 15.7).

The variable geometry is the baseline for management of the strategic metropolitan level.

The multilevel system of governance for the metropolitan area of Palermo is composed of functional relations, represented in a systemic vision that aligns planning tools with various contexts and scales, and identifies the subjects who exercise their powers in relation to spheres of influence. Metropolitan governance, therefore, acts within a flexible and scalable system of tools and powers, regulating a metropolitan ecosystem in which each component interacts with the others through various instrumental interfaces (see Fig. 15.8).

Regarding integration with the master plan, the city administration uses strategic plan policies on ecological networks to define timely activities and coordinate private subjects in the development and refurbishment of neighbourhoods in peri-urban settlements, in order to preserve natural values and ecological connections. The details of many public spaces, utilities and infrastructures are designed according to both the strategic and master plan.[5] For instance, the municipality of Palermo will design two new schools, the greenway Palermo-Monreale as well as new tramlines, all by way of public competitions, with design ideas being delivered to designers to apply them.[6]

Regarding the mayor's plan, activities, events and challenges are proposed by the local administration and supported by the strategic plan. The UNESCO site management plan, Palermo Italian Cultural Capital 2018, Manifesta 12, Palermo Capital for Youth 2017 and also entry to the European Cultural Capital 2019, are all the result of the new synergy between urban and metropolitan politics with cultural and other sectorial strategies.

---

[5]The existence of an active relationship between urban strategies and land use might seem obvious, but in Palermo the lack of synchrony in the planning of the various types of planning has often made it impossible to integrate.

[6]The technical and economic feasibility of these ideas were covered in the last phase of the Strategic Plan.

Regarding digital transformation, the municipal administration has launched community participation activities, with greater responsibility for local districts, a widespread application of digital participation for citizens (ParteciPA IT platform) and of the digitalisation of inter-institutional relations for project evaluation (adoption of the IT platform ConcorriMI).

Basically, the metropolitan policies for the city of Palermo have evolved very much since the beginning of the process: a strong increase in the integration of choices and the awareness of one's own urban identity are the most relevant effects. The strategic plan has never become a law or an unchangeable document on which voters or researchers can assess the performance of public administrations but has become a shared image of the city on which the transformation projects are confronted and have found a framework of coherence that renews the city.

References

Ascher F (2009) L'âge des métapoles. Editon de l'Aube, Paris

Carta M (2009) Governare l'evoluzione. Principi, metodi e progetti per una urbanistica in azione. FrancoAngeli, Milano, pp 228–248

Carta M (2013) Il "Teorema del Waterfront": un approccio progettuale integrato e creativo. In: Carta M (ed) L'Atlante dei Waterfront. Visioni, paradigmi, politiche e progetti per i waterfront siciliani e maltesi. Edizioni del Dipartimento di Architettura, Università degli Studi di Palermo, Palermo, pp 35–46

Carta M (2014) Reimagining urbanism. Creative, smart and green cities for the changing times. ListLab, Trento

Carta M (2016) The fluid city paradigm: a deeper innovation. In: Carta M, Ronsivalle D (eds) The fluid city paradigm: waterfront regeneration as an urban renewal strategy. Springer International Publishing, Cham, pp 1–10. https://doi.org/10.1007/978-3-319-28004-2_1

Carta M (2017) Hyper-metropolitan Palermo. Unconventional strategies and mapping for circular metropolitan scenarios. In: Carta M, Lino B, Ronsivalle D (eds) Re-cyclical urbanism. Visions, paradigms and projects for the circular metamorphosis. ListLab, Trento, pp 70–91

Carta M, Lino B, Ronsivalle D (2017) Re-cyclical urbanism. Visions, paradigms and projects for the circular metamorphosis. ListLab, Trento

Carta M, Gagliano D, Ronsivalle D (2007) Piattaforma Meridiana, in Ministero delle Infrastrutture, Dicoter (ed), Reti e territori al futuro. Materiali per una visione. Edizioni del Ministero delle Infrastrutture, Roma, pp 220–233

Clément G, De Pieri F (2005) Manifesto del Terzo paesaggio. Quodlibet, Macerata

Gausa M (2009) Multi-Barcelona/Hiper-Catalunya. Hacia un nuevo abordaje de la ciudad y el territorio contemporaneos. List, Barcelona.

Oswalt P, Rieniets T (2006) Atlas Der Schrumpfenden Städte. Distributed Art Pub Incorporated

Ronsivalle D (2016) The fluid city experience: an update. In: Carta M, Ronsivalle D (eds) The fluid city paradigm. Springer International, Cham, pp 99–163. https://doi.org/10.1007/978-3-319-28004-2_10

Schuler D (2016) Smart cities + smart citizens = civic intelligence? In: Human smart cities, urban and landscape perspectives. Springer International Publishing, Cham, pp 41–60. https://doi.org/10.1007/978-3-319-33024-2_3

Townsend AM (2013) Smart cities: big data, civic hackers, and the quest for a New Utopia. W. W. Norton, New York

Urban@it (2016) Rapporto sulle città. Metropoli attraverso la crisi. Il Mulino, Bologna

Weinberger D (2011) Too big to know: rethinking knowledge now that the facts aren't the facts, experts are everywhere, and the smartest person in the room is the room. Basic Books, New York

Regional Design: S, M, L. A Multi-level Perspective on Designing a Region

16

Agnes Förster

Abstract

The concept of regional design has often been discussed in the context of the emergence of design competitions and temporary design studios as informal regional arrangements that aim to foster joint strategy-making and coordinated action at a regional scale. This chapter highlights the importance of understanding effective design interventions in metropolitan regions. To assist in this, it presents and discusses a set of interrelated levels for spatial transformation: 'S' denoting lifestyles, 'M' denoting neighbourhoods and 'L' networks. All three levels take effect in existing environments and thereby operate as agents of change. They can be conceived as categories for regional projects that bring the region's 'producers' and 'users' into productive interaction. In such projects, regional design has both a product and a process dimension. Concrete projects add to longer-term processes of cooperation and co-production among regional actors. The skilful combination of all three levels of intervention may create effective leverage for a functional, habitable region.

Keywords

Regional design • Multi-level perspective • Regional interventions • Regional transformation • S-M-L approach

16.1 Introduction

Metropolitan regions are a man-made reality for millions of inhabitants who experience day-to-day life beyond municipal borders. They derive their vibrancy from living, working, education, shopping, leisure time and culture, all woven together by mobility. From the perspective of residents, employees and other users, the functionality and quality of living available round the clock are key issues at a regional scale. As a consequence, there are a multitude of agreement, coordination and network demands for spatial planning. Coordinated development requires an enormous effort on the part of municipalities, encompassing regional associations, supra-regional districts crossed with out-of-district public transport agencies, location initiatives and special purpose associations. The level of the metropolitan region has been further defined. Originally it was an analytic-functional approach (Hall and Pain 2006), which in Germany was then normatively configured (BBR 2000) and finally implemented at the national level through organisational reforms, business offices, goals and measures (Initiativkreis Europäische Metropolregionen in Deutschland IKM 2018).

However, although Germany's institutionally defined metropolitan regions function on the meta-level of manifold regional organisation, they are mostly toothless tigers for coordinated spatial development. They lack competence and authority in key areas such as mobility, infrastructure, housing and open space, as well as a mandate for land-use planning and management. Hence, the focus of these institutions is mostly on exchange and networking within the metropolitan region, and on transparency and lobbying external partners.

Against this background of institutional weakness at regional and metropolitan levels, and missing incentives for supra-municipal cooperation and coordination at federal and national levels, we observe the emergence of new

A. Förster (✉)

Planning Theory and Urban Development, RWTH Aachen University, Aachen, Germany

e-mail: foerster@pt.rwth-aachen.de

© Springer Nature Switzerland AG 2020

V. Lingua and V. Balz (eds.), *Shaping Regional Futures*,

https://doi.org/10.1007/978-3-030-23573-4_16

design-oriented communication processes at a regional level. The term 'regional design' can be understood as a heuristic to better understand recent activities such as the international competitions Greater Helsinki Vision 2050, Le Grand Paris and Metropole Ruhr, or the workshop for Metrobild Zürich and the collaborative planning process for an agglomeration in the Cologne-Bonn region. In all of these cases, interdisciplinary design teams developed regional images, strategies and suggestions for governance and communication structures. The desired effects of these design endeavours operate at several levels: the mobilisation of regional resources, the creation of a joint, regional frame of reference and strengthening joint fields of action and projects. However, these effects are not immediate. The process starts with various learning curves of communication, analysis, design and vivid visualisation. It is expected that when regions are assembled into one image they will contribute to a growing regional consciousness, improved coordination structures and jointly developed goals. The concept of 'regional design' is therefore described as a circular process that involves regional actors and their specific regional setting in learning processes that are fuelled by strong visual skills and spatial imagination at regional level. Its effects can be measured against the enhancement of communication and cooperation structures among regional actors and institutions and their subsequent learning steps (Förster et al. 2016).

This chapter aims to complement the notion of 'regional design' as it relates to process-oriented regional design plans as regional frames of reference. To this end, it conceptualises relevant dimensions of designing a region, starting from a systemic understanding of spatial change within an existing region. Design as a product may lead to better regional space, including morphology, functionality and processes (Boesch 1989). On the other hand, design as a process may trigger communication and interaction by the use of spatial–visual techniques that take effect in relation to particular people. As such, regional design can, therefore, be conceived from two different entry points: the 'users' and the 'producers' of regions and their respective interplay. Firstly, regional design can be regarded from its goal to enhance day-to-day life within the region. This means applying a user-centred view of residents, employees, commuters, visitors and other communities. Secondly, the regional design is part of a communicative practice that addresses regional actors and stakeholders in order to encourage and enable joint action that produces and enhances functionality and quality of life within a region.

The chapter draws on the author's experience from recent design and consultancy assignments in Germany and has been published, in excerpts, in the book 'Living the Region—Rhine-Main. The Redesign of a Metropolitan Region' (Förster 2018). Public clients at municipal up to regional level demand design approaches that link planning content at the interface of applied research and strategy-making for the careful management of communication processes. Experience with different planning issues and spatial scales is coupled with a multi-level perspective on designing a region. As such, the chapter shall be understood as an intellectual experiment that explores different facets of effectively intervening in regional processes as well as their possible combinations.

16.2 Designing and Negotiating Effective Regional Interventions

This chapter focuses on a range of design activities that enhance people's lives in metropolitan regions. It proposes three interrelated levels of spatial intervention, negotiation and actor interaction: 'S' denotes lifestyles and addresses the small scale of the individual, 'M' denotes neighbourhoods and points to a medium scale of intervening in the built and unbuilt environment, and 'L,' networks, embraces large-scale regional infrastructure, open space and actor networks. Each level draws attention to different aspects of the built environment, with different participants and processes resulting from it. The three tiers can be conceived in two ways. First, the three levels address the dimensions of a region as perceived and experienced by inhabitants and users. Second, the three levels point to different types of intervention that take effect in existing environments and operate as agents of change within a region.

Although the trial of S, M, L refers to different entry points for regional change with correspondence to different spatial scales, they do not correlate to administrative levels within a region. Instead, the tiers of intervention refer to projects that are negotiated, designed and implemented with high relevance for metropolitan regions. Projects are capable of focused, subject-oriented cooperation, from which longer-term processes of cooperation and co-production among regional actors can develop. As a consequence, the institutional setting within a region may further develop, intensify or clarify.

The relationship between selective interventions—S, M or L—and their intentional or unintentional, direct or indirect and regional impacts demands careful case-by-case negotiation and assessment. The skilful combination of all three levels may create effective leverage for functional and habitable regions. Consequently, alignment between activities at the S-M-L levels is a crucial regional design task. The following sections outline the proposed three levels of designing a region, always combining both product and process dimensions.

16.2.1 S—Lifestyles: Transforming Regional Patterns of Use

The S-level addresses interventions that influence individual behaviour and add up to spatial patterns of use at the regional scale. Processes of co-creation as well as digital technologies that go hand-in-hand with newly available regional data stimulate changing roles and learning cycles among the 'users' and 'producers' of a region. The following paragraphs discuss 'S' from the perspectives of space, participants, process and effect.

Space: Where and what? Cities are marked by a variety of ways of life, interests and milieus. At the regional and metropolitan scales, this variety increases substantially. Living, work, leisure time, provisioning and care are day-to-day activities with inter-municipal patterns of use. The interactions of supply and demand become manifest in individual lifestyles, the availability of choices and decisions. These add up to functional and spatial patterns and development trends, on a regional scale.

Participants: Who does what with whom? Residents, employees, students, tourists and others all make use of a region's spatial distribution and its related functions and services, while at the same time more and more people participate in its design. On the one hand, major triggers are the social and cultural trends of collaboration, do-it-yourself, individual composition and personalisation. These are complemented by the effects of digitalisation, which has opened up new possibilities for communication, networking and design. Digitalisation supports new links and interrelations between users with their mobile devices and applications, related processes of data collection and synchronisation, as well as regional spaces and patterns. Whether the individual opportunities and forces of spatial design in a region actually gain in strength depends on the participants in the background? Who has the data? Who can process it? Who has the start-up capital to develop new applications and disseminate them (Schüller and Förster 2017)?

Process: How and when? Until now, change processes that take place among users, machines, space, providers and operators have not been subject to government planning and control. Such processes, which occur rapidly to very rapidly, are usually below the radar of spatial planning's normal temporal horizon. Due to the high speed of feedback, the system is constantly developing and learning quickly. 'Regulating behaviour' is a level at which spatial planning instruments could be deployed (Jung 2008). In the course of individualisation and digitalisation, such control levels gain significant importance. For instance, 'nudging' goes beyond bans, commandments or financial incentives. Nudging is a behavioural economics method to provoke, guide and shape human behaviour (Thaler und Sunstein 2008). The method operates on a subconscious level through the placement and formulation of offers to support the desired behavioural goal in a targeted fashion. Urban planning has rediscovered temporary implementations, laboratories and experiments as formats to initiate and support complex cooperation and reconciliation processes, rebuilding and upgrading plans as well as long-term planning projects. Future spatial qualities and user opportunities should be recognised and registered earlier, in order to test them and check for expected perceptions and behavioural patterns.

Effect: What is going on and unfolding? The change in individual behaviour and lifestyles is a significant level of negotiation for fundamentally transforming energy, urbanisation and land use in the sense of a 'Great Transformation' (WBGU 2011). This becomes especially evident in growing metropolitan regions. For example, challenges in the area of mobility cannot be solved by extending and expanding the transportation network alone. Changing mobility behaviour is, therefore, key to stabilising the system and guaranteeing access to the metropolitan region. The spatial transformation potential of changing lifestyles is shown clearly in the relationship between stationary and online trade, in the location behaviour of those looking for housing in urban, suburban and re-urbanised regions, and also in the changed open-space culture or new multi-local work worlds.

Example: 'Navigator and service' The orientation and accessibility of the metropolitan region can become a spatial design subject through media, apps, signage and hot spots etc. Existing offers and spaces should become more noticeable and accessible and the management of regional building stock improved. Regional maps and media are important instruments in the dialogue of the tri-national cooperation of the 'International Building Exhibition' (IBA) Basel 2020. A unified tariff system and electronic run-around tickets, such as in the Netherlands, can promote barrier-free movement in the public transportation network. Measures like these also increase the awareness of a networked region on a daily basis.

Example: 'Experiments and actions' A free public transportation day pass, strolls in regional green corridors, driving 1000 e-bikes for 24 h, a Long Night of the Museums or Music, mobile planning workshops and on-site questionnaires are all possibilities that can temporarily influence space and spatial relationships. The IBA Basel 2020 initiated 'IBA-Kit',an information container as a location for dialogue in and about the region and the art event 'Spiegelkugel', both of which tour the metropolitan area in the tri-national Basel conurbation (IBA Basel 2020).

Example: 'Dynamics of the housing market' The interplay between individual lifestyles and preferences and the availability of locations within a region is particularly significant in apartment searches. In growing municipalities and cities, apartment searches often take on a regional scope, following an evaluation and decision-making process with opposing criteria such as costs, accessibility, dwelling type, design and living space and attractiveness of the neighbourhood. Searches follow different temporal and spatial stages. At the end, the successful seeker of an apartment can offer a full search history, during the course of which he discovered and reappraised new housing supply and locations within the region. With the spread of online portals for searches, regional data on search history is generally available. Accordingly, a productive communication and learning process could be initiated that puts the revealed preferences and latent demand of different target groups on the map of municipal and regional strategies and projects (Thierstein et al. 2015, 2016; Schüller et al. 2018) (Fig. 16.1).

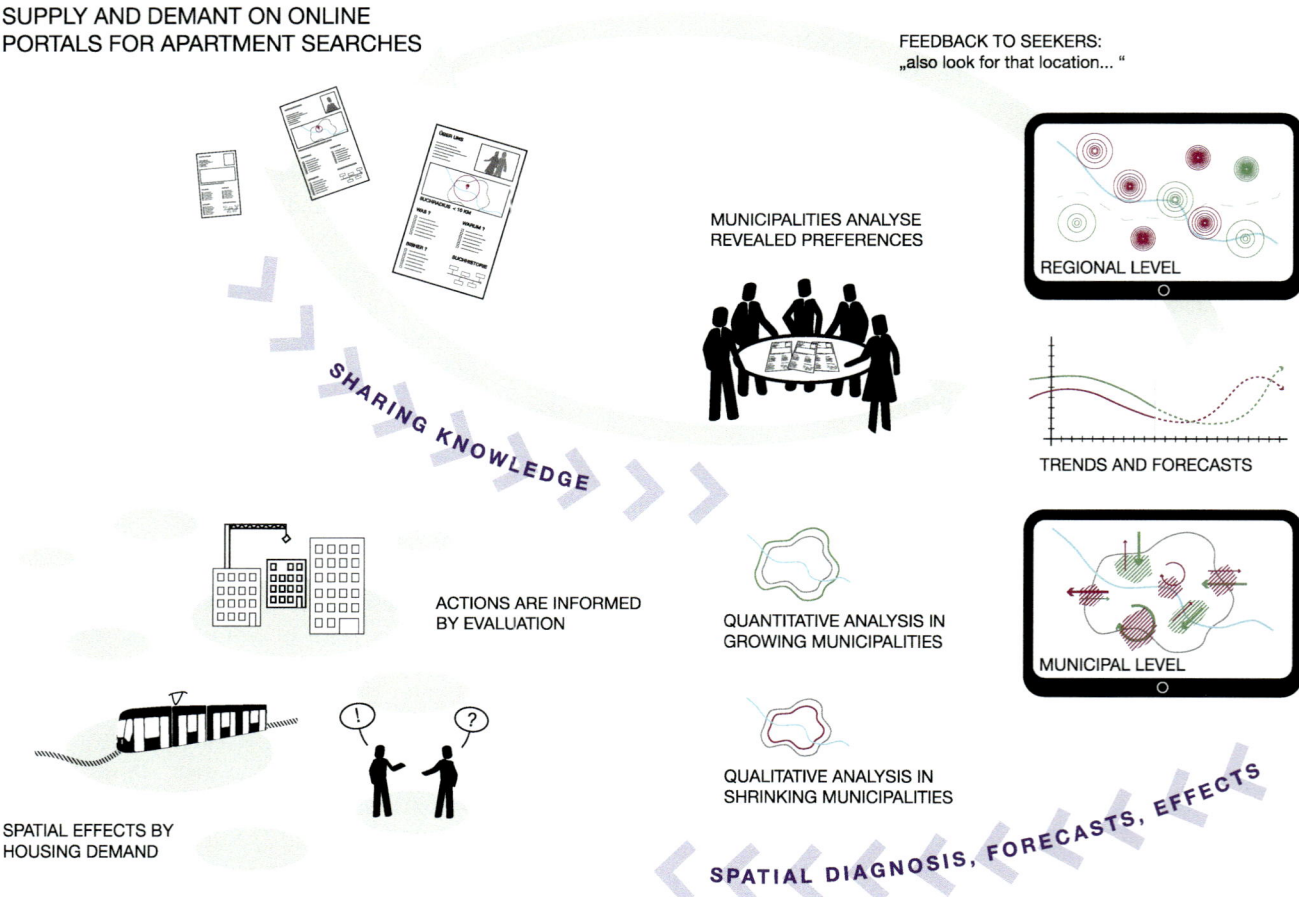

Fig. 16.1 A schematic manual for using online portals for apartment searches, designed to better link the preferences of different target groups with a region, and part of broader municipal and regional strategies to meet latent housing demands, design by Stephanie Wenzel and Agnes Förster (STUDIO | STADT | REGION, 2017)

16.2.2   M—Neighbourhoods: Stepping Stones of Regional Change

Viable neighbourhoods within a region may serve as catalysts for regional change. Immediate perception and experience at the manageable level of an urban quarter, local community, workplace or educational location provide a good starting point for the redesign of the mix of uses and services, daily and weekly patterns of mobility as well as material flows. Successful pioneer projects are ready for dissemination within the region.

Space: Where and what? Metropolitan regions include cities and municipalities of all different sizes, locations and functionality, all of which exercise their planning authority. Contiguous areas and neighbourhoods comprise a level of control below municipalities. If we mentally divide the region into such areas, a new picture emerges. The affiliation with a particular municipality is much less significant than the spaces, functions, services and connectivity it provides. At neighbourhood or district level, living, working and mobility can be negotiated and designed locally. The critical mass of offers and users and the minimum functional complexity are fertile grounds for creating an interaction of spatial, social, organisational and technical innovations. The neighbourhood level is an important starting point for organising regional change because it is malleable and perceptible on the ground, while simultaneously operating as an effective component within a larger regional portfolio and network of locations. In downtown areas, city outskirts, urban landscapes or more rural areas, all neighbourhoods are facing the challenges of living together, creating short distances between multiple options, furnishing a basis of existence that takes account of the future, and bundling resources as well as local and regional synergies.

Participants: Who is doing what with whom? Neighbourhoods are designed by landowners, current and future inhabitants and long-term operators in conjunction with municipality planners. In addition to designated transformation and expansion areas designed by one body, many are characterised by complex multi-actor constellations. Successful developments bring the participants in the conception and planning phases together with the operators such as housing companies, property managers and future users of the district, thereby enabling feedback mechanisms and learning processes.

Process: How and when? While spatial negotiations at regional level are often full of wishful thinking, these negotiations are already being conducted in neighbourhoods today. Location initiatives, development societies, associations, consortia and co-ops all ensure the creation of interfaces and synergies between buildings, open spaces, accesses and connections, through the use of proposals and target groups. The neighbourhoods level is a suitable laboratory for negotiating these basics and testing them out in real-life contexts.

Effect: What happens and what is created? Neighbourhoods are spaces of transformation, and they function as spatial intermediaries in the region. Some of their important aspects are: the connection between different land uses, target groups, daily rhythms, the increase of area efficiency and husbanding resources, usable and enjoyable local open spaces, or the linking of different transport modes with improved incentives for inter-modality. A habitable region features a well-balanced portfolio of different settlement models and use offers as spaces for development, provisioning and a home for different target groups. Neighbourhoods as laboratories radiate outwards, providing impulses and finding their imitators, influencing the planning and building culture in the region. Districts thus transform the region as particular uses and target groups take over, incorporating and making new locations visible.

Example: 'Community living' The Zurich cooperative 'Kraftwerk1' chose, for its third housing project, a location in the agglomeration of Zurich, within the municipality of Dübendorf. The building site, on a former industrial area right beside two heavily used roads, initially appeared to be unsuitable for housing. However, following the conception of a new district, the cooperative achieved the redevelopment of the area with diverse housing typologies, living concepts, small businesses, social infrastructure, community space and high-quality open space. Residents that had initially looked for apartments in inner-city locations met with providers from Dübendorf and adjacent municipalities. Together, these new cooperative members transformed the area spatially, socially and culturally. The opportunity to participate actively during the planning and construction process supported the arrival and appropriation of the new residents into their neighbourhood (Bau- und Wohngenossenschaft Kraftwerk1 2019) (Fig. 16.2).

Fig. 16.2 Zwicky Süd' as a new district for community living in the agglomeration of Zurich, design by STUDIO | STADT | REGION, 2018

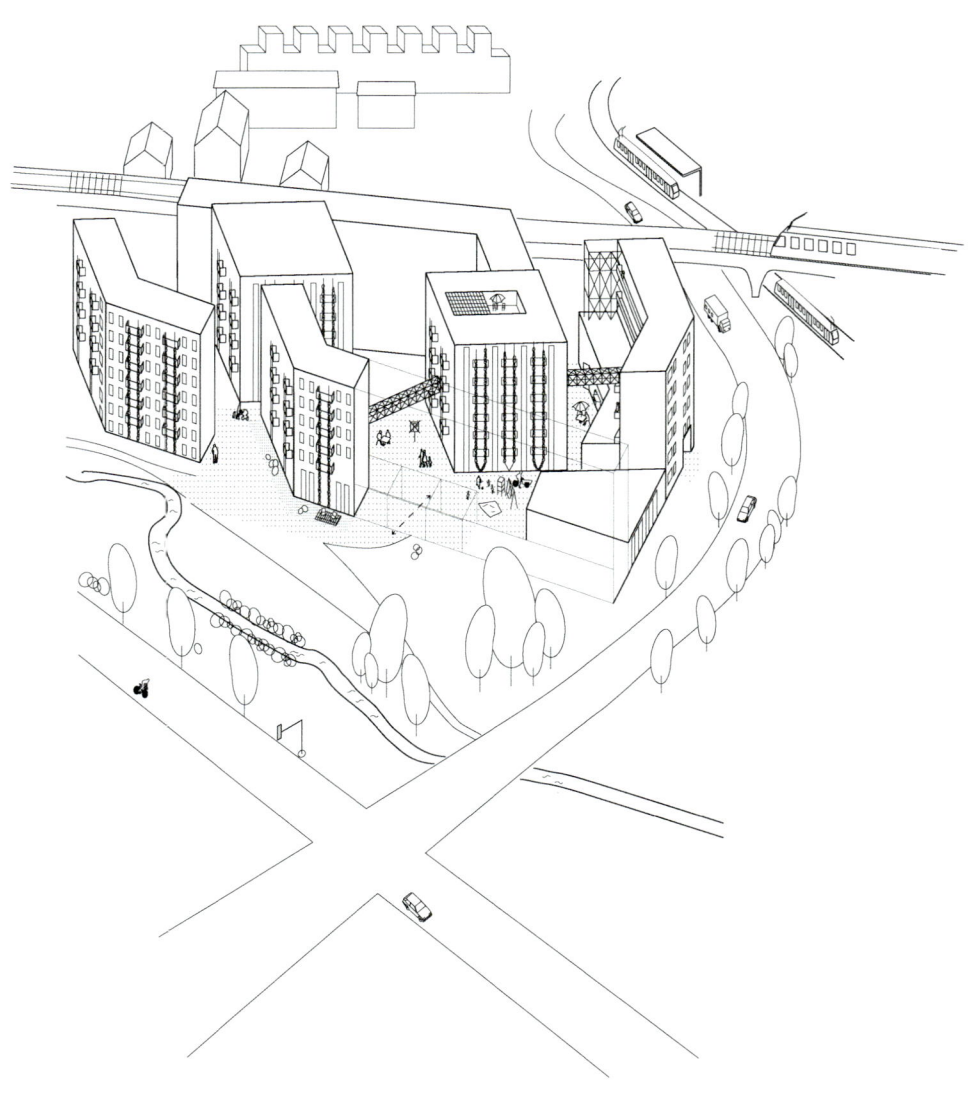

Example: 'Active Rail Stations' Within the IBA Basel 2020 process, the project group active rail stations is bringing together ten municipalities surrounding the tri-national rail network, each addressing their rail stations in the context of adjoining areas and functions as well as their connections to important local and regional residential, work and leisure destinations. Its aim is to organise a portfolio of attractive rail stations as anchor points for the inner development of the respective municipalities and, moreover, to organise public space and life from a multi-level perspective, linking local urban space to tri-national movement, from slow to high speed. Ultimately, the upgrading of the rail stations to safe, usable urban environments enhances the overall attractiveness of the tri-national public transport network. As a first step, the project group jointly defined basic functions that had high relevance for every station. In addition, shared talents are being developed, through which the different rail stations will be able to connect internal development with building culture, civil society with culture, and identity with perception in project families (Fig. 16.3). The process should be understood a bottom-up networking, joint lobbying and branding endeavour, for which the instrument of the IBA provides incentives. At the same time, the IBA Basel office introduces planning know-how and joint communication and perception platform (Förster et al. 2017a).

Example: 'Commerce and the city'
The city of Munich and three municipalities from the region are in the process of discussing the challenges of six selected commercial locations, jointly showing development perspectives. This planning and advisory project combine the overall research from European case studies and the deduction of a joint toolbox for area development within the Munich metropolitan region, with its application in the selected commercial locations (Fig. 16.4). It is the embodiment of an urban and regional portfolio approach. The analysis of the European case studies provides innovative impulses which, combined into eleven tools, are then distributed among four mega-topics of 'added value', 'surface and space', 'connection and inclusion' and 'control'. The toolbox works on three levels: knowledge transfer of innovative practice projects outside and inside the Munich metropolitan region, strategy development support for specific areas with a proactive municipal role, as well as a process understanding of the development and quality assurance. The latter is required for the joint marketing of high-quality commercial sites in the urban-regional dialogue and also to encourage their imitation (Förster et al. 2017b).

16.2.3 L—Networks: Connecting and Expanding Regional Lifelines

The L-level investigates the region from the perspective of its network quality. Transport infrastructure, water and energy supply as well as waste disposal provide for the viability of a region. Economic value chains have a spatial dimension that is deeply rooted in non-physical relationships of information, communication and cooperation. Furthermore, actor–networks create the conditions for the capacity to act at a regional scale.

Space: Where and what? Regional quality of life becomes concrete when the perception of locations is connected when spaces are experienced on the move and daily and weekly routines are organised in multiple locations and scales. Connections and networks spread out relations and movement within space reveal communication and exchange. Networks refer to joint resources such as energy, water, clean air, open space or mobility. At the same time, they can be understood as communication, cooperation and control structures, in which regional participants coordinate their space-related activities. Over a longer period of time, networks have developed in the region and are available in many places. Intelligent extension of the network and its optimisation are significant challenges, rather than new construction.

Participants: Who does what with whom? Considering networks from the viewpoint of conversion and retrofitting means identifying, activating and empowering the relevant participants. In turn, that means exploring the potential for synergies and connections through the regional selection of participants. A selective approach for negotiation can then be derived, bringing together key participants in the context of regional challenges for the first time. Regional partnerships are formed according to goals and effects, connecting decision-makers from different administrative levels with the responsible parties from business and civil society.

Process: How and when? The network level aims at change and management processes. These can start when psychological stress is high, when regional incentives and rewards are available or when a joint idea and vision has been designed and distributed. Selected participants come together in the format of a think tank or a task force in order to work together on the formulation of concrete questions and to carry out tasks. For that to happen, spaces are needed outside of daily business and established bodies, where shared goals and trust can be built up among idea generators, decision-makers and operators. Selectivity in this procedure can be reflected in the processing of focusing on or transforming spaces.

Fig. 16.3 A comprehensive
toolbox, joint homework and
shared talents: the implementation
programme of the project group
active rail stations within IBA
Basel 2020, from Förster et al.
(2017a)

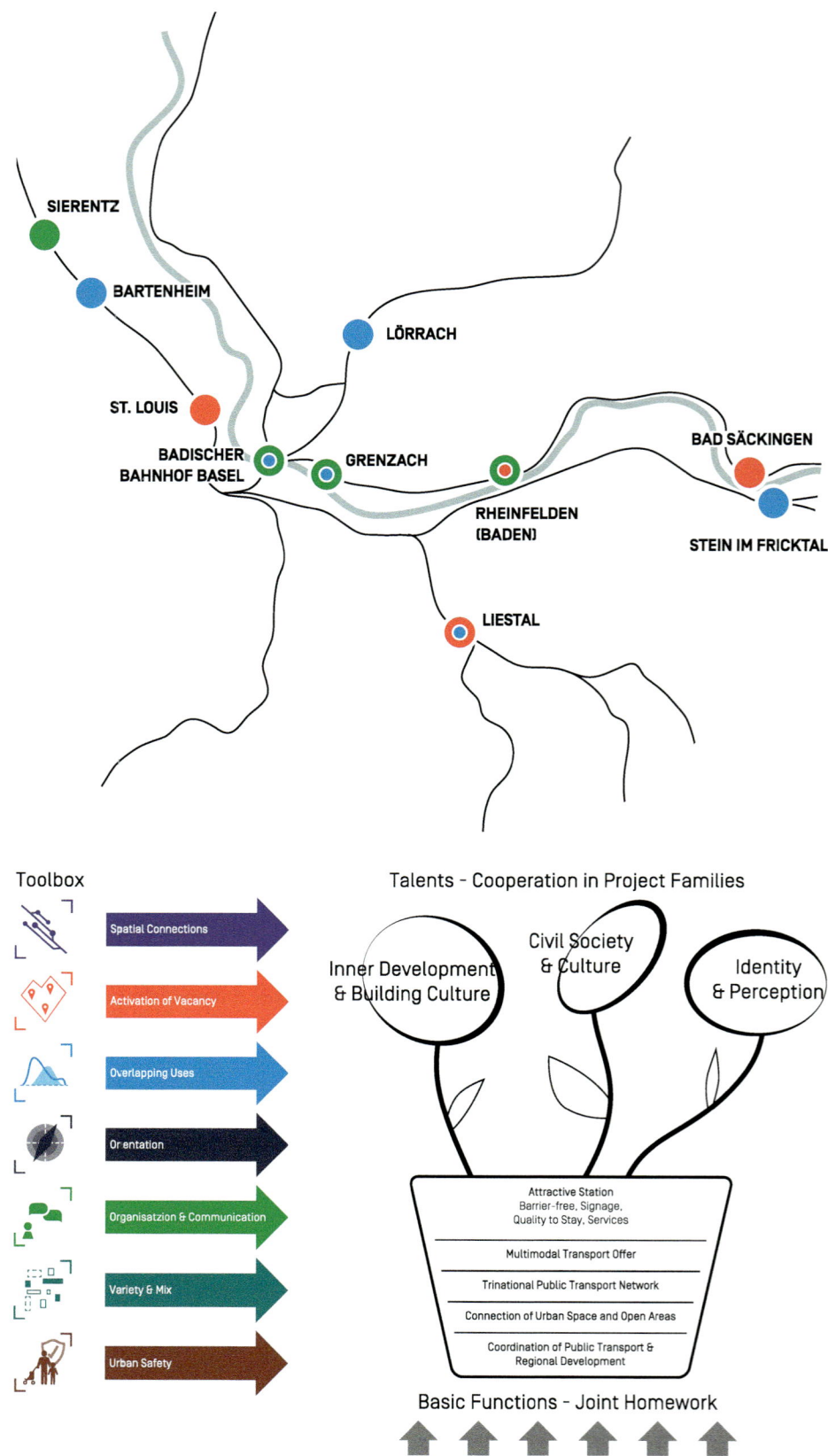

Fig. 16.4 A toolbox designed for the joint strategy development of commercial locations within the Munich metropolitan region, from Förster et al. (2017b)

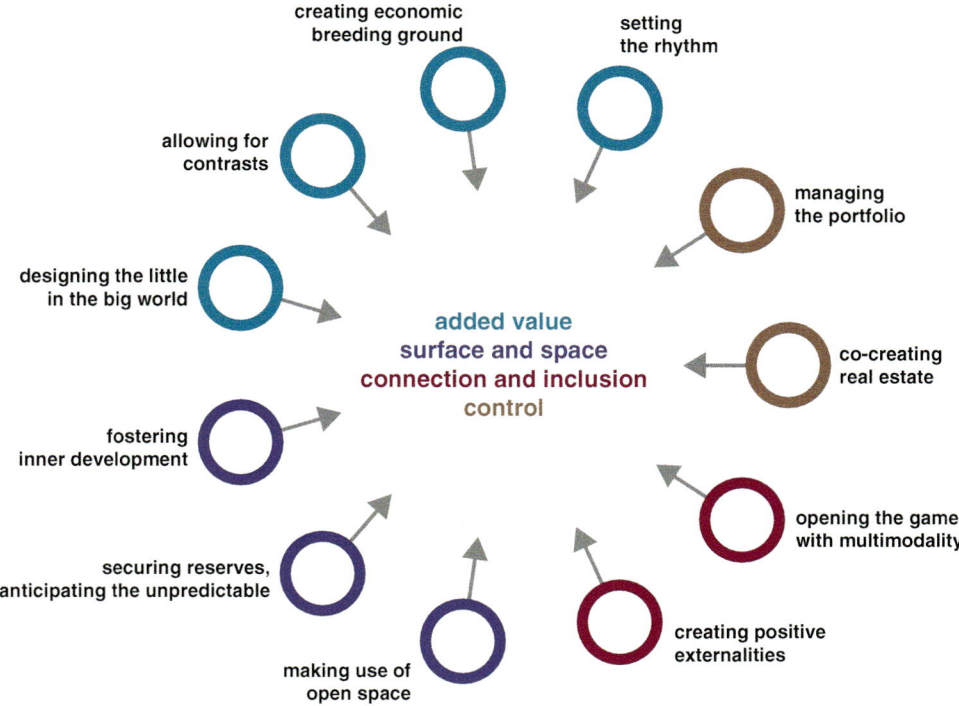

Effect: What happened and what was created? At the level of regional networks, these robust, resilient structures provide more options, freedom of choice and alternative offers. They include more opportunities for interchange, more spaces to stay, multiple and new forms of provisioning as well as dense networks of social, cultural and economic transactions. Networks are closely connected with the regional infrastructure. Extending physical infrastructure very often costs billions and takes decades to complete and, in the best cases, lasts for a century. Targeted interventions and temporary measures can have a catalysing effect in a region and set processes in motion, even before a major project is realised and the overall network has been refurbished.

Example: 'Bridging gaps in the network' Prominent examples of the strategy of supplementing regional networks at neuralgic points, to raise the network quality as a whole while at the same time creating new spaces, functions and perceptions, are the Öresund Bridge, the new connection between the cities of Copenhagen and Malmö and the 'Glattalbahn', a light-rail system that links the city of Zurich with the economically strong municipalities in its north to Zurich Kloten International Airport. In the Munich metropolitan region, rail-based public transport takes a highly monocentric network form. For decades, this has been discussed as the main weakness that hinders the area's transformation to a less car-oriented region. As a result, the administrative district of Munich has started an initiative to identify options for new light-rail connections that will release this monocentric network, using rail-based bypasses and rings (Fig. 16.5). This kind of gap closure demands hand-in-hand strategies that closely link transport offers and services with the development of residential and business locations. Overall, network effects will be negotiated and matched with sub-regional and local settlement and landscape development (Landratsamt München 2017).

Example: 'Open-space perspectives' New perspectives for open common areas are a topic of discussion in many European urban regions. The landscape creates a network of spatial, social, cultural, ecological and climatic effects. As a fundamentally positive influence, the landscape also promotes cooperation. Networks of landscape spaces are merely not obvious but have to be discovered, laid bare, enriched and potentiated. The Glatt Valley is discovering the still unimpressive river bed of the river Glatt, and the superimposed open-space concept 'Fil Bleu' will draw attention to it and make it real again (Grün Stadt Zürich 2017). The urban development in Munich's northeast district brings the state capital into dialogue with the neighbouring municipalities (Fig. 16.6). The discovery of the connecting free space can be used as a common positive force in the dialogue process, creating desirable addresses next to existing village centres (Förster and Wenzel 2018).

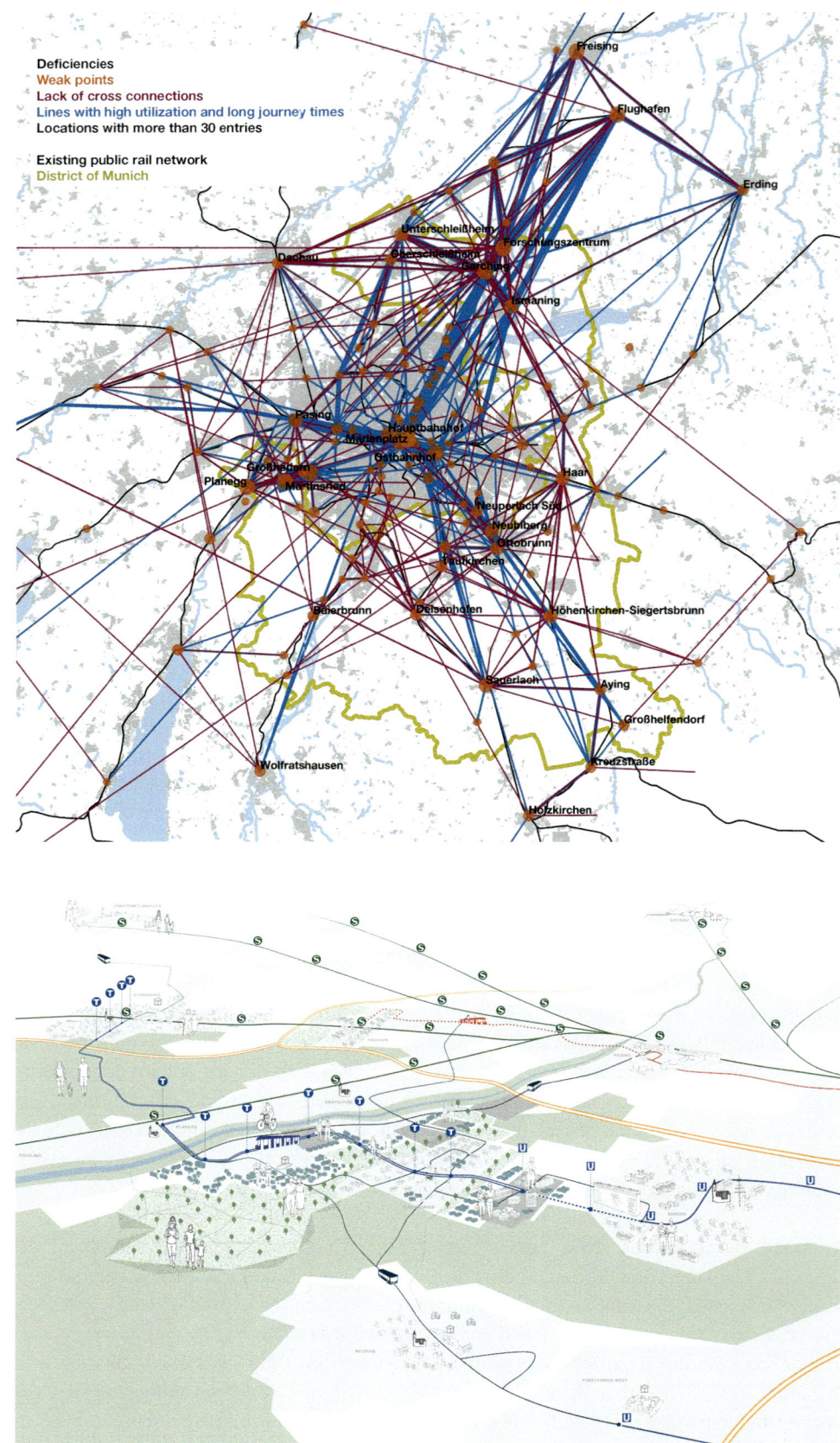

Fig. 16.5 Developing perspectives for rail-based public transport in the Munich metropolitan region: weak-point analysis and concept sketch concerning a new tangent in the southwest of Munich, design by Agnes Förster and Stephanie Wenzel, from Landratsamt München (2017)

Fig. 16.6 Results from a citizen and expert workshop exploring the potential of interconnected vacant spaces in the northeast of Munich, from Förster and Wenzel (2018). *Photo* Christin Büttner/text:bau

Example: 'Added-value landscapes' Regions are productive systems. Economic activities may be understood as spatial innovation systems, whose organisational and spatial cooperative structures can be understood by means of network analysis. The marine economy in north Germany or the automobile industry in locations like Ingolstadt, Munich or Stuttgart is a good example of this. If the reference is not only to the firms' locations, but also includes spatial production factors, the network picture develops into an 'added-value landscape'. Seen from that standpoint, at the regional and metropolitan level the health industry could develop into an important sector. Its attraction derives from a density and breadth of different health offers in connection with a restful landscape, appealing culture, provisioning and restaurant facilities, functional public transportation and barrier-free urban spaces. With an improved connection between universities, business and public authorities the 'Triple Helix Approach' will become a significant driver for innovation for cities and regions (Etzkowitz und Leydesdorff 1995). At the networks level, in the sense of 'added-value landscapes', spaces and cooperation and the facilities that are still missing must be identified: intermediaries have to be strengthened, incubators must be installed or key functions and facilities must be augmented, for example, supra-regional continuing education, an international school or a cultural centre that transcends sectors and target groups. The subjects of regional added-value chains and innovation landscapes were taken up repeatedly in the Metropole Ruhr competition (Regionalverband Ruhr 2014), by the five teams, and conveyed in their regional concepts and designs. 'Added-value landscapes' connect the functional area of negotiation for business, education, culture and social aspects with spatial fields of action, both of which have not yet been sufficiently coupled at the regional level.

16.3 S, M, L—Designing Regional Transformation

The S, M and L negotiating levels outlined here work on different levels within the system. They show that a process can start now, and start small, and that it is important to keep watch on large-scale projects and shape-specific locations in the region. This allows us to introduce a differentiated planning approach with several competent negotiators, various models of regional control and different processes of cooperation and communication. The planning timescales vary correspondingly.

According to many of the examples described above, S-M-L can be considered as an ongoing regional development process in which different activities run in parallel, initiated both by top-down strategies and bottom-up initiatives. Additionally, the deliberate combination of S-M-L may represent an advanced concept for multi-level regional design. One most recent case from the Munich metropolitan region illustrates how institutional capacity-building at the metropolitan scale shall be advanced by well-coordinated interventions. Currently, key players in the metropolitan region are exploring the possibilities of joining forces for a coordinated regional-change process on mobility issues, at metropolitan scale, that makes use of the S-M-L approach.

These key players consider the option of an 'International Building Exhibition' (IBA) as a soft instrument of city and regional planning. Although the genesis of IBA, as an instrument, traces back to the beginning of the twentieth century in Germany, it gained popularity after the end of the IBA 'Emscher Park', in 2000, with its tangible projects fostering structural change in a region that was formerly dominated by the coal and steel industries. Since then, IBA has evolved from a building exhibition to a process-oriented planning instrument that stimulates learning within a ten-year period of exception (IBA Thüringen GmbH 2019). In the Munich case, the current feasibility study proposes 'spaces of mobility' as a pressing issue and guiding theme for an IBA process within the metropolitan region (Fig. 16.7). A change process will be organised that starts from three interrelated perspectives—'I-we-together'—that together form the idea of a regional kinetic sculpture (Fig. 16.8). 'I' represents individual behaviour and the potential of starting small projects or temporary experiments that immediately change the use and perception of means, in the context of transport and communication as well as public space. 'We' looks at the level of the districts and neighbourhoods that organise the interplay between housing, work and mobility, at sub-regional and local scale. 'Together' includes physical networks, such as transport infrastructure, as well as joint regional images and improved cooperation structures that jointly tackle the ongoing rapid growth of jobs and inhabitants within the metropolitan region (Förster und Petrin 2018).

Fig. 16.7 Impressions from the International Building Exhibition (*Internationale Bauaustellung*, IBA) symposium 'Spaces of Mobility,' involving actors in the Munich metropolitan region, design by STUDIO | STADT | REGION, 2018

Based on the proposed concept 'I-we-together', the feasibility study organised a dialogue with political decision-makers as well as experts from public administration and actors from the market and civil society. The aim was to activate mobility issues in the growing region and to show and discuss possibilities for joint action, beginning with specific projects, under the umbrella of an IBA process.

In the Munich 'spaces of mobility' case, the S-M-L approach has two main objectives: first, to push forward and accelerate projects that help to maintain the quality of life within the rapidly growing metropolitan region. This is about fostering decisive action among metropolitan stakeholders. Second, the process aims to coordinate actions from multiple perspectives and multiple scales within the three tiers. Projects shall be kick-started following the swarm intelligence of multilateral metropolitan actors and at the same time be aligned within a regional system perspective. IBA may act as a temporary agency limited to 10 years that provides a test field for an emerging metropolitan governance setting.

Based on this example, regional development can be understood as an open-ended process, which passes through concrete milestones and clearly marked stages of learning. This kind of spiral-shaped development of regional cooperation is encapsulated by the concept of 'Awareness-Products-Processes' (Förster und Thierstein 2008). The creation of a regional consciousness is the prerequisite for tackling concrete projects, which in turn can be stabilised through cooperation structures and coordination processes. The whole process is nonlinear: we should take on S, M and L in parallel, and as urgent needs demand, applying joint activities and measures whilst simultaneously subjecting regional arenas and dialogues to tests and dry runs.

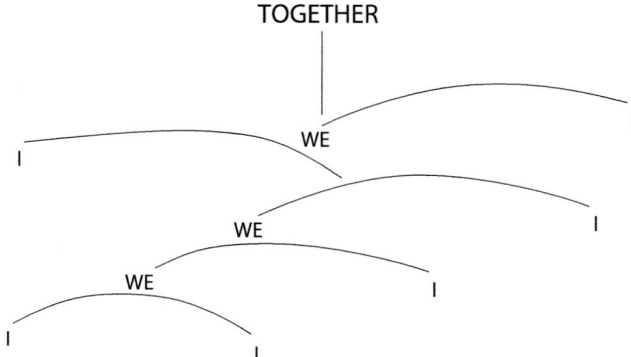

Fig. 16.8 'I-we-together' concept, developed as a guiding theme and organisational structure for the IBA 'Spaces of Mobility' symposium, from Förster and Petrin (2018)

References

Bau- und Wohngenossenschaft Kraftwerk1 (2019) https://www.kraftwerk1.ch. Accessed 10 Dec 2018

BBR Bundesamt für Bauwesen und Raumordnung (2000) Raumordnungsbericht 2000. Berichte Band 7. Selbstverlag des BBR, Bonn

Boesch M (1989) Engagierte Geographie: Zur Rekonstruktion der Raumwissenschaft als Politik-orientierte Geographie. Steiner, Stuttgart

Etzkowitz H, Leydesdorff L (1995) The triple helix—university-industry-government relations: a laboratory for knowledge-based economic development. EASST Rev 14:14–19

Förster A (2018) Region S, M, L. living, working, mobility etc. In: Holl C, Nowak F, Vöckler K et al (eds): Living the region—Rhine-Main. The redesign of a metropolitan region. Wasmuth, Tübingen

Förster A, Petrin J (2018) IBA unterwegs – Räume der Mobilität. Presentation in the expert forum "Regionale Zukunftsstrategien" within the Regional Housing Conference 17 Oct 2018 in Rosenheim. https://wohnungsbaukonferenz.de/wp-content/uploads/2018/10/RWBK-2018-Fachforum1-IBA.pdf. Accessed 10 Dec 2018

Förster A, Thierstein A (2008) Calling for pictures. The need for getting a picture of mega-city regions. In: Thierstein A, Förster A (eds) The image and the region—making mega-city regions visible! Lars Müller Publishers, Baden, pp 9–34

Förster A, Wenzel S (2018) Stadtentwicklung im Münchner Nordosten. Beteiligung der Öffentlichkeit im Frühjahr 2017. München: Landeshauptstadt München, Referat für Stadtplanung und Bauordnung. https://www.muenchen.de/rathaus/dam/jcr:7a5db510-69c9-425b-83d9-5c8673e38d12/Stadtentwicklung%20im%20Münchner%20Nordosten.pdf

Förster A, Balz V, Thierstein A, Zonneveld W (2016) The conference „shaping regional futures: mapping, designing, transforming!" A documentation. München/Delft. https://mediatum.ub.tum.de/node?id=1328668. Accessed 10 Dec 2018

Förster A, Herten L, Wenzel S (2017a) Aktive Bahnhöfe – Das gemeinsame Umsetzungsprogramm. Report on behalf of IBA Basel 2020. http://iba-basel.net/etc3/20180115_abh_bericht_web_dt.pdf. Accessed 10 Dec 2018

Förster A, Wenzel S, Thierstein A, Gilliard L, Scholze L, Brunner B (2017b) Gewerbe & Stadt. Gemeinsam Zukunft gestalten. München. https://mediatum.ub.tum.de/1398132

Grün Stadt Zürich (ed) (2017) Fil Bleu. Überregionales Freiraumkonzept Glattraum. Zürich

Hall P, Pain K (2006) From metropolis to polypolis. In: Hall P, Pain K (eds) The polycentric metropolis. Learning from mega-city regions in Europe. Earthscan, London, pp 3–16

IBA Basel (2020) http://iba-basel.net/de/home. Accessed 10 Dec 2018

IBA Thüringen GmbH (2019) www.open-iba.de. Accessed 10 Jan 2019

Initiativkreis Europäische Metropolregionen in Deutschland IKM (2018) http://www.deutsche-metropolregionen.org. Accessed 10 Dec 2018

Jung W (2008) Instrumente räumlicher Planung. Systematisierung und Wirkung auf die Regimes und Budgets der Adressaten. Dr. Kovac, Hamburg

Landratsamt München (2017) Perspektiven im öffentlichen Personennahverkehr im Landkreis München. Final report, 17 Jan 2017. https://formulare.landkreis-muenchen.de/cdm/cfs/eject/gen?MANDANTID=72&FORMID=6148. Accessed 20 Nov 2017

Regionalverband Ruhr (ed) (2014) Ideenwettbewerb Zukunft Metropole Ruhr. ruhr-impulse. Essen. https://ideenwettbewerb.metropoleruhr.de/fileadmin/user_upload/metropoleruhr.de/Ideenwettbewerb/Konzepte_Planerteams/Buch_MR50_low.pdf. Accessed 10 Dec 2018

Schüller K, Förster A (2017) Digital Literacy für die Stadt. Informationen zur Raumentwicklung 1/2017:108–121

Schüller K, Förster A, Thierstein A, Ottmann M (2018) Gamification, Prognosemärkte, Wikis & Co: Neues Wissen für die Stadt? Assisted by Hindinger C, Grimm K, Busch P, Frisch S, Galeano S, Wenzel S. Bundesinstitut für Bau-, Stadt- und Raumforschung Bonn. https://www.bbsr.bund.de/BBSR/DE/Veroeffentlichungen/Sonderveroeffentlichungen/2018/gamification-wissen-stadt-dl.pdf?__blob=publicationFile&v=2. Accessed 10 Dec 2018

Thaler RH, Sunstein CR (2008) Nudge: improving decisions about health, wealth, and happiness. Yale University Press, New Haven & London

Thierstein A, Förster A, Conventz S, Erhard K, Ottmann M (2015) Kurzfassung – Wohnungsnachfrage im Großraum München. Individuelle Präferenzen, verfügbares Angebot und räumliche Maßstabsebenen. In: Wohnungsmarkt Bayern 2015. Beobachtung und Ausblick. München, Bayerische Landesbodenkreditanstalt. https://bayernlabo.de/fileadmin/dwn/BayernLabo_Wohnungsmarkt-Bayern-2014_Einzelseiten.pdf. Accessed 10 Dec 2018

Thierstein A, Wulfhorst G, Bentlage M, Klug S, Gilliard L, Ji C, Kinigadner J, Steiner H, Sterzer L, Wenner F, Zhao J (2016) WAM Wohnen Arbeiten Mobilität. Veränderungsdynamik und Entwicklungsoptionen für die Metropolregion München. Lehrstuhl für Raumentwicklung und Fachgebiet für Siedlungsstruktur und Verkehrsplanung der Technischen Universität München. https://mediatum.ub.tum.de/1292926. Accessed 10 Dec 2018

Wissenschaftlicher Beirat der Bundesregierung Globale Umweltveränderungen WBGU (2011) Welt im Wandel: Gesellschaftsvertrag für eine Große Transformation. Berlin. http://www.wbgu.de/hauptgutachten/hg-2011-transformation/. Accessed 10 Dec 2018

Anna Schindler

Abstract

The interrelation between regional design and planning is a subject that has been important to the Metropolitan Area of Zurich since the first steps were taken towards founding the "Zurich Metropolitan Conference" in 2005/2006 (https://www.metropolitanraum-zuerich.ch/home.html). It is the first time that the federal planning system in Switzerland has opened up to one of the many activities in the metropolitan area of Zurich, considering the whole region as a functional space. A unique new form of spatial planning tool has been created, merging the structure plans of eight adjacent cantons into one big picture of the metropolitan region, thereby literally shaping the future of the region. The planning system in Switzerland is organised on different levels, and the function of the Zurich Metropolitan Conference and its projects is not part of this formal institutional framework. This is an advantage in many respects because it is possible to transcend the borders between the different levels of Switzerland's federal system more easily, but it also creates difficulties for the implementation of new interdisciplinary ideas in existing political and administrative structures. The competencies in the federal system are clearly regulated and supported by a legal basis that has often been legitimised and reaffirmed through referenda. Any attempt to collaborate across the boundaries of cantons and municipalities presents the system with new challenges. The "Metrobild" Project to create a "picture" of the metropolitan area, introduced by the Metropolitan Conference, illustrates the advantages and disadvantages of involving regional design in (formal) planning. Although not the basis, it was an important source of inspiration for the Metro-ROK ("Raumordnungskonzept", the Spatial Planning Concept of the Metropolitan Area of Zurich). Even though concrete planning at the metropolitan level might not yet be a reality, planning without looking beyond the municipal boundaries is no longer an option today. The following two examples show what regional planning means in concrete terms for a city such as Zurich.

Keywords

Metropolitan Area Zurich • Political system of Switzerland • Regional design • Regional planning

17.1 The Metropolitan Region of Zurich in the Confederational Political System of Switzerland

In order to reflect on the role of regional design in Zurich regional planning, it is important to first understand how the surroundings of Switzerland's core city Zurich are structured. The canton of Zurich is situated in north-eastern Switzerland. It covers an area of 1700 km^2 and is home to 1.5 million inhabitants, which makes it not the biggest canton by size but the most populated canton in Switzerland. Furthermore, one million employees work in the canton—or 21% of the Swiss workforce.

Switzerland's political system operates as a confederation. It consists of three levels: the confederation, 26 cantons and 2294 municipalities. Besides these three levels, the canton of Zurich is further divided into 11 regions, each of which is composed of an association of several municipalities. The planning system is differentiated on these four levels. The confederation develops sectoral plans and strategies, as well as stipulating the Federal Constitution and the Law on Spatial

A. Schindler (✉)
Urban Development of the City of Zurich, Zurich, Switzerland
e-mail: Anna.Schindler@zuerich.ch

© Springer Nature Switzerland AG 2020
V. Lingua and V. Balz (eds.), *Shaping Regional Futures*,
https://doi.org/10.1007/978-3-030-23573-4_17

Planning System of Switzerland

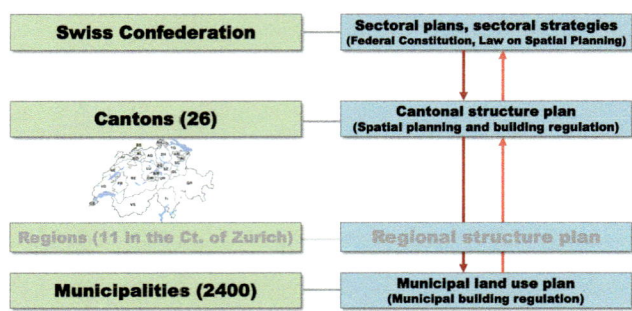

Fig. 17.1 Planning System of Switzerland, from: Building Department of the Canton of Zurich (2015)

Planning. The cantons are obliged to adopt sectoral plans and strategies into their cantonal structure plans as well as into spatial planning and building regulations at the cantonal level. The regions develop regional structure plans which include the conditions dictated by the canton. Finally, municipalities develop land use plans on the municipal level and stipulate municipal building regulations. The city of Zurich is the first and only municipality in Switzerland to develop a structured plan on the communal level—the "Communal Structure Plan of Urban Development." This plan picks up on the themes of the municipal level Regional Structure Plan, going into specifics, fleshing out details and demonstrating how the requirements for qualitative spatial development can be met practically. This plan seeks to guide the urgent need for densification in the existing territory of the city due to anticipated population growth of another 25% in the next 15–20 years. Besides this structure plan, which will be finished and implemented by the end of 2018, the Building and Zoning Ordinance is the city's strongest planning instrument which covers the immediate urban developments. All these institutional planning tools, however, focus on their respective level—cantonal, regional, municipal—and are interdependent within a hierarchical structure. There is a lack of a perspective that goes beyond the boundaries of these respective systems and that takes into account functional space comprising multiple levels (Fig. 17.1).

The Zurich Metropolitan Area includes over 238 municipalities, in eight cantons, with a total population of around three million. With over one million workplaces, the area generates approximately 40% of the Swiss GDP. This makes the Zurich Metropolitan Area the leading economic region of Switzerland. Given the increasing economic, political and social ties in this functional space, and the conviction that the main challenges today can only be solved by looking beyond political–territorial boundaries, these eight cantons and their 65 towns or municipalities joined forces to establish the Zurich Metropolitan Area Society in July 2009. It was the first time in Switzerland that a metropolitan area had organised itself into a political structure, and indeed the way it functions is still unique in this country (Fig. 17.2).

In addition to increased cooperation and a more intensive exchange, the main aims of the Metropolitan Area Society are to promote quality of life and strengthen the Zurich Metropolitan Area as an exceptional national and international business location.

The Zurich Metropolitan Area Society is a purely political organisation, comprising executive representatives from the eight member cantons and (currently) 120 towns and municipalities. Business, enterprises and civil society are not represented. The strategic lead is assigned by the Metropolitan Council, which is composed of two chambers. One chamber has eight members, one from each of the eight cantons; the other eight members are from the 120 towns and municipalities, all elected politicians in their hometown or home canton. Decisions pertaining to political opinions and statements of the Metropolitan Conference, as well as to projects and funds, are made jointly and in mutual agreement by the cantonal and city chambers after preliminary deliberations, and then presented to the members at the annual conferences. The Metropolitan Conference decides the overall budget (Fig. 17.3).

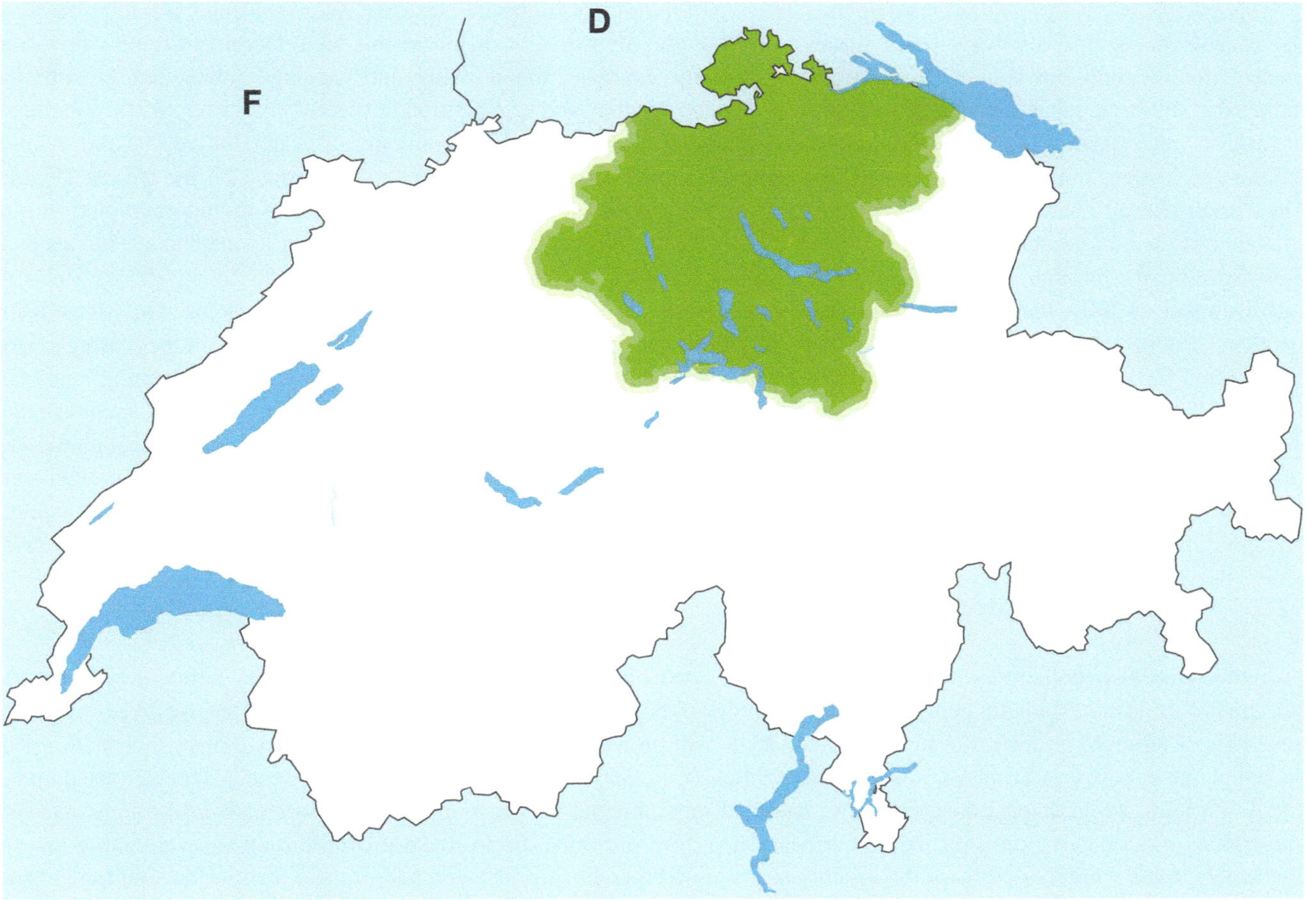

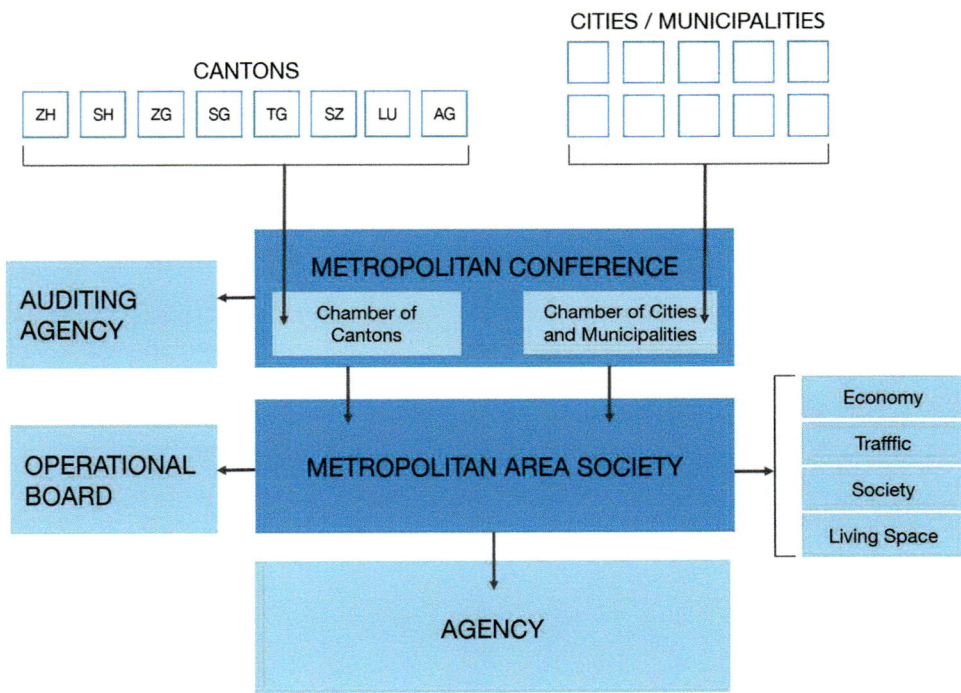

Fig. 17.2 The Zurich Metropolitan Area, from: Zurich Metropolitan Area (2018)

Fig. 17.3 Organisational chart of the Zurich Metropolitan Conference, from: Zurich Metropolitan Conference (2018)

There are different factors that make up the strengths of the Zurich Metropolitan Area. The most important to point out is the great diversity in a relatively small space, as well as the high quality of life in this area. Dominant trends, however, present the metropolitan area with major challenges: for example, the ongoing and expected population growth, the increasing strain on resources or the tension between cooperation and competition. Especially with regard to population growth and the resulting consequences for spatial planning, transport and the economy, it is imperative that the municipalities and cantons in the metropolitan area get together to think about possible solutions and emphasise the area as a whole. The Zurich Metropolitan Conference—organised by an association of the same name—is not only an important platform for exchange at the various state levels; it also has the objective of strengthening cooperation among its members. This happens most specifically through joint projects in four focus areas of business, transport, society and living space. Since its establishment in 2009, the society has carried out more than 25 such projects in these four focus areas. The Metro-ROK (ROK = "Raumordnungskonzept": Spatial Planning Concept) grew out of one of these projects at the beginning of the cooperation for the "Metrobild" project. Other projects deal with a wide range of issues beyond urban planning concerns, yet all of them reference functional space with Zurich as the urban core. They explore current key issues and challenges for the metropolitan area—from the consequences of the immigrant workers in the Zurich metropolitan area for economic and structural growth, to internal densification and added-value equalisation in various smaller centres in the metropolitan area, through to planning-related and political options for reducing morning and evening commuter peaks on public transport.

17.2 Projects and Outcomes

To understand how collaboration in the Metropolitan Area of Zurich is generating results on the different political and administrative levels, without being part of the confederation, it is important to take a look at the tangible successful outcomes of different projects, not just the Metro-ROK. All projects by the Metropolitan Conference place their main focus on cooperation between business, society and politics, specifically the cooperation that transcends the various political levels. Projects are initiated by experts from cantonal or municipal administrations, policy-oriented institutions and also universities, in collaboration with the authorities. Their core aim must be to make a contribution to overcoming current challenges in the whole, or parts, of the functional space, to be practically relevant and to yield practicable solutions for the challenges identified as well as to feature innovative, creative project ideas. Depending on their focus, they are associated with one specific action area—business, transport, society or living space—in which the urban planning issues are explored. The Metropolitan Conference is committed to maintaining and strengthening the diversity and attractiveness of its living space. It has launched various projects to help protect and integrate green areas and local recreational facilities, to coordinate settlement and transport development, to minimise land use and also ensure the careful consumption of energy resources. Given the fact that none of these challenges adhere to political boundaries, a coordinated approach is adopted within the metropolitan area. The members of the association make use of the Metropolitan Conference as a platform for cross-border coordination in spatial planning policy.

The area of spatial planning has a special place at the Metropolitan Conference. It calls for coordination beyond boundaries and a view of the region as a whole. This is reflected in the federal guidelines for spatial planning, for example, in the Spatial Concept for Switzerland, in which ideas and actions in functional spaces are clearly publicised. On the other hand, planning authorities are clearly distributed at lower levels of state, and spatial planning is first and foremost the responsibility of the cantons.

Nevertheless, the Zurich Metropolitan Area Society runs different projects at the intermediate planning level between cantons and municipalities. One is the "Parkland" project, which presented the Zurich Metropolitan Area as a diverse parkland area. The "Added Value through Consolidation" project provides concrete examples of added value in high-density areas. The "Inter-Municipal Financial Equalisation and Spatial Planning" project examines the interplay between the instruments of inter-municipal, financial equalisation and spatial planning (Fig. 17.4).

Fig. 17.4 The "Parkland" project represented the Zurich Metropolitan Area as a diverse parkland area, from: Zurich Metropolitan Area

In the business area, the aim is to support innovation and research in the Metropolitan Area of Zurich in order to strengthen the favourable location factors. The focus was initially on the "Green Region" theme, with an aim to contribute to energy efficiency in the Metropolitan Area of Zurich. In collaboration with the sponsoring organisation "Energiestadt," it was possible to increase the number of Ecological Cities to six by the end of 2014. This means about 45% of the Metro member municipalities today are certified as "Energy Cities."

After the successful implementation of the Energy Cities, the focus turned to more urgent challenges—i.e. the economic strength of the metropolitan area after the difficult Swiss referendum on work immigration in 2014. The project "Strengthening the Metropolitan Area as a Production Location" aimed to counteract the shortage of skilled workers in Switzerland. Current initiatives in the Zurich Metropolitan Area to combat the shortage of skilled labour were identified, evaluated and made available to other players. The aim was to improve the framework, particularly in the manufacturing sector. The federal level shall take a leading part in the elaboration of a national strategy in the fields of labour market, education and institutional framework. Through that self-serving interests will be resolved and synergies can be used. The project was completed in the summer of 2015.

Another important project deals with the huge changes that commerce and retail are going through: online-commerce, delivery on demand, cross-channel commerce, and so on, are all elements of digitisation that are currently revolutionising the retail trade.

In the area of transport, the focus, particularly at the beginning, was on joint lobbying at a national level. For this purpose, key infrastructure projects were defined to extend road and rail. The Metropolitan Area Society achieved a major success when the Swiss government decided, in 2012, to increase the budget for financing and developing the rail infrastructure in Switzerland from CHF 3.5 billion to CHF 6.4 billion, which made it easier to finance key infrastructure projects in the Zurich Metropolitan Area.

Today, the municipalities and cantons are particularly interested in projects where they can take on a pioneering role in current areas of interest. For example, the "User Financing" project deals with how users can be more involved in the financing of infrastructure projects.

The "Reduction of Traffic Peaks" project, completed in November 2017, developed concrete solutions to relieve transport systems at rush hour. The study identified three priorities: the introduction of more flexible working hours and working-from-home schemes, staggering the start and end of school times at larger schools such as colleges and high schools, and a more differentiated tariff system on public transport. The results aimed to support the cantons and munici-palities in developing projects with schools and companies that would reduce traffic peaks.

In the area of society, the challenge from the very beginning has been that it does not clearly fit any one political field but is instead an interdisciplinary area. An important project in this area was "Immigration and Population Growth." Using three migration scenarios for 2030, this project described the key challenges triggered by migration and population growth in the areas of business/labour market, society/integration, space/settlement and governance.

After its first six years of existence and co-working, the Zurich Metropolitan Area Society slightly adjusted its focus and developed a program of focal projects for the years 2017–2020. The program is a guideline for the Metropolitan Council and a frame of reference for new projects. It aims to fulfil the following functions:

- First, to be a frame of reference for project developers (push/pull function).
- Second, to be a basis of decision for or against projects.
- And finally, to be a guideline for the Metropolitan Council.

The three areas of the program are:

1. Developing solutions for actual challenges.
2. Strengthening the identification with the Zurich Metropolitan Area.
3. Supporting cooperation between the members.

As it has done ever since its inception, the Metropolitan Conference also uses the priority program to initiate and support commercial, political and social projects that help tackle the challenges currently facing the Zurich Metropolitan Area, although these have changed since the Metropolitan Conference was founded. Accordingly, from 2017 to 2020, the focus is on the areas of skill shortages, Industry 4.0 and Services 4.0, the provision and financing of public services and the impact of economic and population growth on society, the economy and spatial planning. The circle of possible project initiators and sponsors has also expanded: projects no longer have to be launched from within the administration itself but can also be submitted to the Metropolitan Conference by independent organisations.

The four thematic priorities of the program were developed through a field analysis of the urban environment. Various sources were consulted for this, including legislative planning by the confederation, cantons and municipalities, focus topics from directors' conferences and recent articles by think tanks and organisations. The topics from the field analysis were then reviewed with regard to their potential for the Metropolitan Policy Conference. Important criteria here were the association's capacity for action and impact as well as the need for action determined by the association members. The four main topics all relate to several of the four action areas from Vision 2030. The two different perspectives vary in their timeframes (the Vision applies until 2030, while the priority program relates to the time period 2016–2019) and in their level of detail.

In 2016, the Metropolitan Conference started a call for projects entitled "Impacts of the Economic and Demographic Growth" that seek to develop solutions for current challenges. It was open to universities, colleges, NGOs, think tanks and corporations as well as to individual initiatives. The goal is to achieve additional value for the whole Metropolitan area, strengthen Zurich as a desirable business location and increase its competitiveness through a common and coordinated procedure. Many valuable projects were submitted, ranging from the fields of work and education to clustering and mobility, to planning and waste recycling.

17.3   The "Metrobild"—Three Possible "Pictures" of the Zurich Metropolitan Area

Among these new project ideas are different concepts of spatial planning, for instance, by smart use of mobile phone data or by identifying everyday structures of mobility and implementing new shared transportation systems. However, as with all spatial planning work in the Zurich Metropolitan Area, there was an underlying simple need: there was no tool, no spatial plan for the area as a whole. Therefore, there was no basis of common understanding of the needs and developments of the functional space that was accessible to all planners in the area. This was the motivation behind the "Metrobild" project (meaning "Metro-picture," a snapshot of the Metropolitan Area), which was to lead to a completely new planning tool by the end. The inspiration behind this project came from looking at the structure of the Zurich Metropolitan Area. Its various sub-areas complement each other with regard to their existing structural conditions. However, the metropolitan area is not a space with homogenous interests: its sub-areas compete for different attractive uses. This intensified competition among sub-areas, together with fast-evolving markets and continuing structural change, demands maximum land availability and high flexibility of use at strategically important locations.

Against this backdrop, cantons, towns and municipalities in the metropolitan area should develop a shared awareness for the functional–spatial qualities and their distribution. Three planning teams were invited—two from Switzerland and one from Germany—to "read" the Zurich Metropolitan Area and draw up an innovative picture, based on reality, of the whole area. This had to represent a spatial development vision and answer the question, "What will the Zurich Metropolitan Area look like in 30 years?" It was to be expressed in the form of a "picture" because this stays in the imagination better than complex planning concepts.

With the implementation of the Metrobild workshop process, the association Metropolitan Region Zurich sought to bring about an initial expression of a spatial vision for development in the form of pictures. These pictures were intended as a guideline for the medium- and long-term development of the metropolitan area in both quality and quantity. Furthermore, the pictures would also contribute to a common understanding of the cantons, cities and municipalities for the functional–spatial qualities and their distribution in the Zurich Metropolitan Area.

Development of the "Metrobild" took place in the form of test planning reflected from the outside. This was to ensure a cooperative and discursive process. The whole process took place in three phases ("reading," "developing ideas" and "drawing up a Metrobild"). Each phase was concluded with a discussion among the planning teams and experts drawn from public administration, externally, and two representatives from ETH Zurich (Swiss Federal Institute of Technology in Zurich). The City and Landscape Network at ETH Zurich has, after all, been involved in the development of the Zurich metropolitan region in research and teaching for several years. In the autumn 2010 and spring 2011 semesters, master's students in the architecture department grappled with similar issues to those of the teams involved in the Metrobild workshop process.

To coordinate the activities of the Zurich Metropolitan Conference and ETH Zurich, a cooperation was agreed to facilitate the exchange of information. This was limited to the Metrobild workshop process and ended with the conclusion of this process.

The process resulted[1] in three "Pictures" which all showed a totally different vision of how the metropolitan area could be developed. There was no winning entry. How to apply the Pictures was left open since the results were seen not as a final solution, but more as a foundation for further action. The three Pictures were described in a panel report which formed the basis for a consultation process with all the Metropolitan Conference's members. Around half of the members took part and agreed, to a large extent, on developing a basic spatial concept under cantonal leadership.

The three separate Pictures all pointed out specific elements of the metropolitan area. Planners from Yellow Z, the first team, scanned the metropolitan area and read it as a landscape city that could be purposefully developed. As supporting evidence, Yellow Z referenced two historical planning models: the "Garden City" published by social reformer Ebenezer Howard in 1900, and the "Decentred Concentration" that Swiss architect Armin Meili propagated in the 1940s. According to Yellow Z, both models are present in the Zurich Metropolitan Area.

Yellow Z was of the opinion that growth would offer the region the possibility to position itself as a garden city of the twenty-first century. This should happen according to strict guidelines: expansion had to follow sustainable concepts such as the 2000-Watt Society. The metropolitan area should produce sufficient fruit and vegetables, cover its energy needs with solar and hydro-electric power and offset CO_2 emissions within the area.

The "Metro Garden City" (Yellow Z's Picture) was a thought-provoking proposal for a landscape-based, highly urbanised region which could also be a model for other sustainable metropolitan regions. Its strength lay in thinking of the region on a large scale and strengthening existing qualities, but without considering the metropolitan area as a specific space (Fig. 17.5).

---

[1]https://www.metropolitanraum-zuerich.ch/files/Metro/user_upload/Dokumente/ThemaLebensraum/Metrokonferenz_Metrobild_Jurybericht_4Nov2011pdf.pdf.

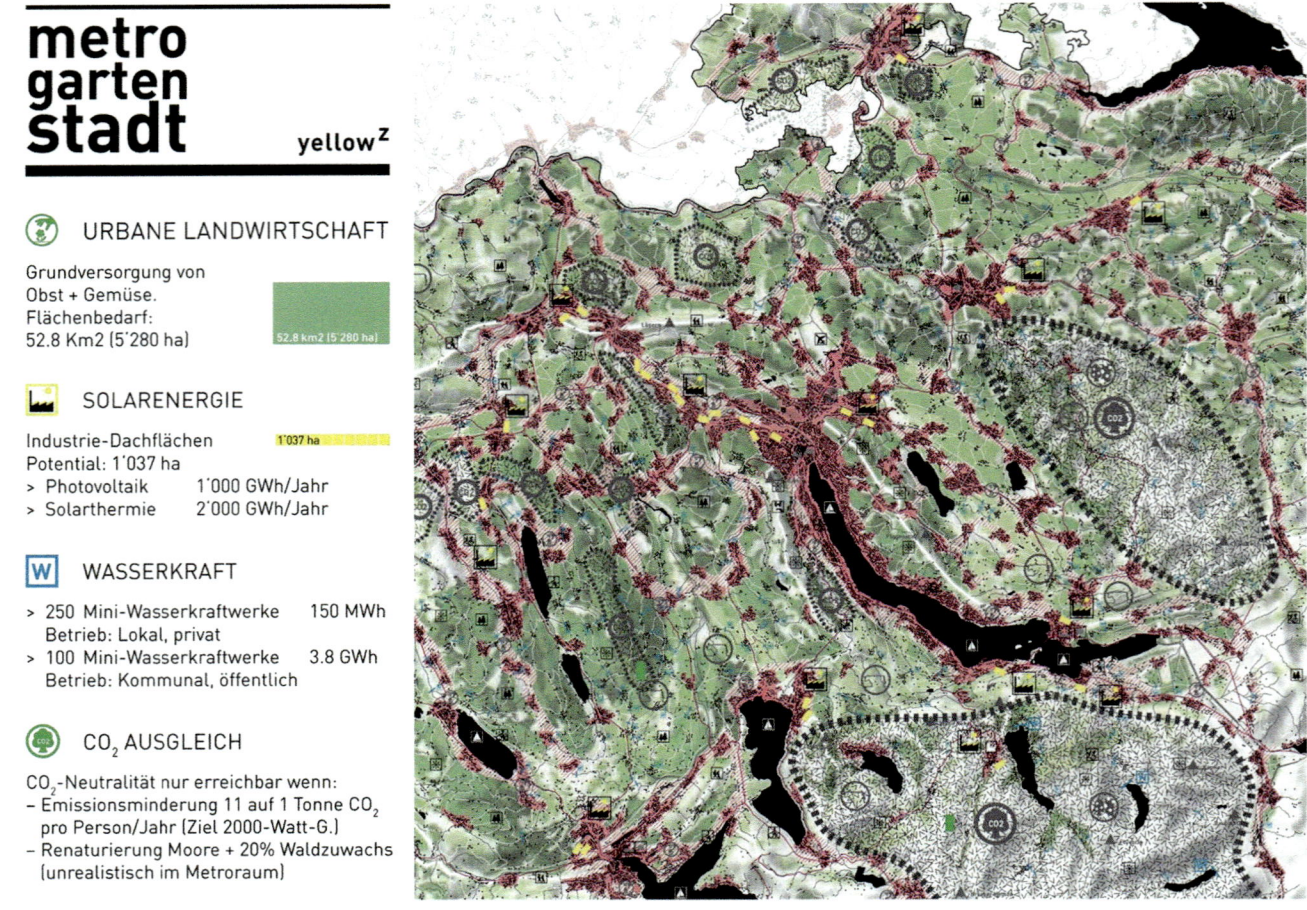

metro garten stadt yellow^z

🌱 URBANE LANDWIRTSCHAFT

Grundversorgung von
Obst + Gemüse.
Flächenbedarf:
52.8 Km2 (5'280 ha)

52,8 km2 (5'280 ha)

☀ SOLARENERGIE

Industrie-Dachflächen
Potential: 1'037 ha   1'037 ha
> Photovoltaik   1'000 GWh/Jahr
> Solarthermie   2'000 GWh/Jahr

W WASSERKRAFT

> 250 Mini-Wasserkraftwerke   150 MWh
  Betrieb: Lokal, privat
> 100 Mini-Wasserkraftwerke   3.8 GWh
  Betrieb: Kommunal, öffentlich

CO₂ AUSGLEICH

CO_2-Neutralität nur erreichbar wenn:
– Emissionsminderung 11 auf 1 Tonne CO_2
  pro Person/Jahr (Ziel 2000-Watt-G.)
– Renaturierung Moore + 20% Waldzuwachs
  (unrealistisch im Metroraum)

Fig. 17.5 "Metro Garden City", from: Yellow Z (2011)

Another approach was chosen by the Hosoya Schaefer team from Zurich. They started by asking themselves how and where the 400,000 population and 200,000 workplaces forecast for the Zurich Metropolitan Area by 2030 could be accommodated. Hosoya Schaefer architects first located scope for growth. Their Picture was titled "Location Mosaic" and illustrated the elasticity and capacity of locations with a colour scale. While the city of Zurich itself does not offer much scope for radical change, there are possibilities for growth in the polycentric urban network. According to Hosoya Schaefer, a "coopetitive" diversity is necessary, i.e. the various locations cooperate and compete at the same time, creating new quality.

From their "Metrobild," Hosoya Schaefer derived strategies for the future of various locations. Some sounded rather familiar: the Glattalstadt region was to become the "Science Valley" and "Logistics Ring" of the city and the Limmattal region the "Start-up Valley." The region around the upper part of Lake Zurich with the historic centre of Rapperswil and the leisure area around Pfäffikon was seen as "Uptown," as an alternative to "Downtown Zurich."

Thus, the conclusion from Hosoya Schaefer was: in the polycentric urban network everything is there already, it only needs to be enhanced, i.e. a more clearly profiled division of labour is necessary among the sub-areas (Fig. 17.6).

Fig. 17.6 "Location Mosaic", from: Hosoya Schaefer Architects (2011)

The creators of the third Picture, a team of three, posed the questions: Which areas and sub-areas make up the Zurich Metropolitan Area? Which features and qualities stand out? Which are evolving and which are threatened? Berchtold Krass, Studio UC and Integral Ruedi Baur—the only team not based in Zurich—subjected the area to a morphological analysis. This served as the basis for a diverse and extremely colourful Picture of the metropolitan area.

The team identified 23 sub-areas within the metropolitan area and gave them detailed profiles. Some of the features are evolving under the existing pattern of economic and building activity while others are threatened (Fig. 17.7).

Fig. 17.7 "Metrobild", from: Berchtold Krass (2011)

In order to recognise the latter, Berchtold Krass proposed a planning "weather map" based on spatial observations: it would act as an early-warning system and indicate where pressure points are building up. According to Berchtold Krass, spatial diversity is one of the outstanding qualities of the metropolitan area and it should be preserved and developed: the sub-areas should be more consciously recognised by each other, complement each other and take on tasks for one another. "Existing together" were the magic words that described more a process than the scope of a regional development (Fig. 17.8).

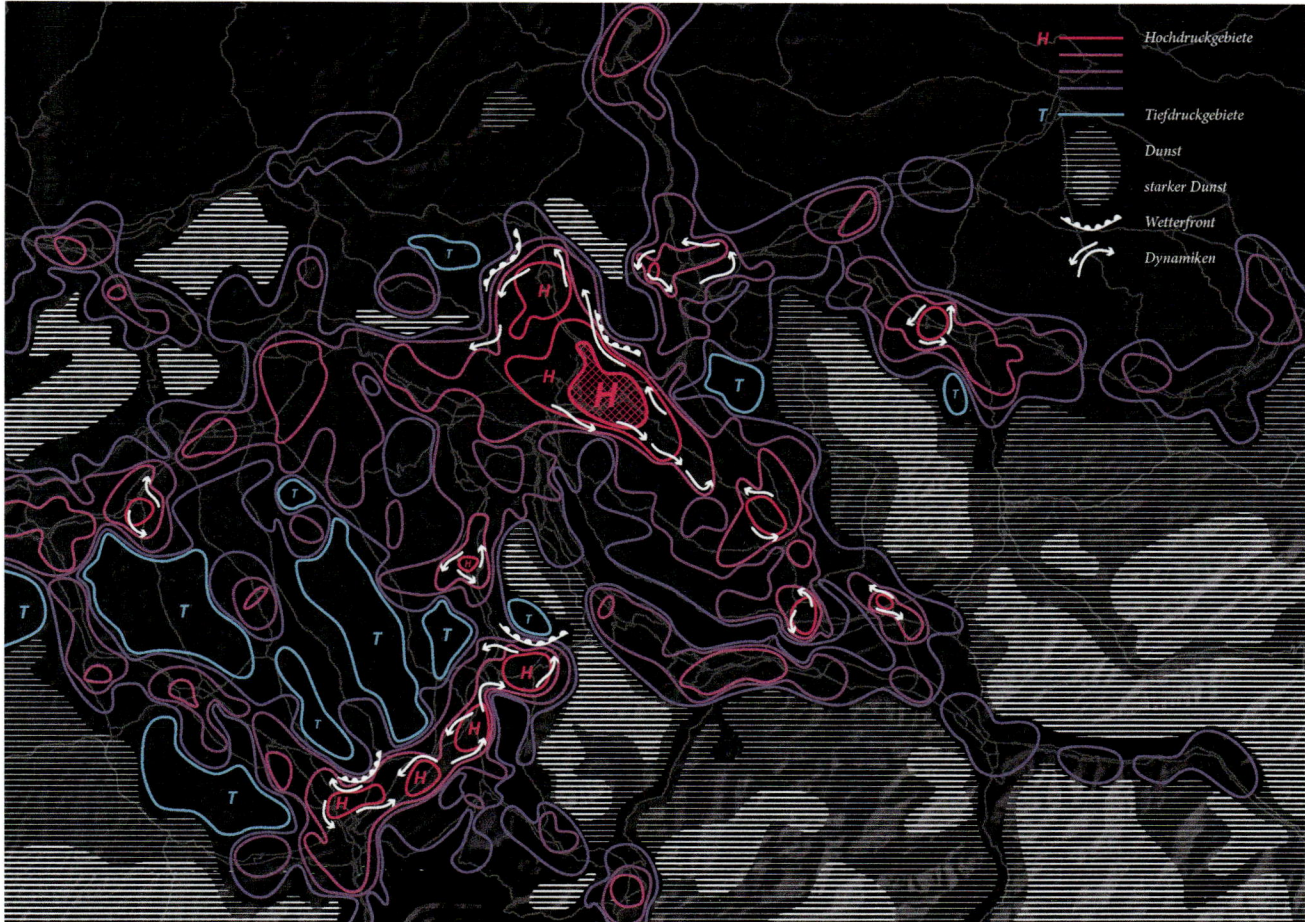

Fig. 17.8 "Weather map", from: Berchtold Krass (2011)

17.4 The "Metro-ROK"—Upscaling the Different "Pictures" to a Structural Plan for the Zurich Metropolitan Area

The workshops in which the three Metro Pictures were discussed were also attended by ETH Zurich, represented by Lukas Küng and Prof. Marc Angélil. Within the framework of the National Research Program NFP 65, "New Urban Quality", the Zurich Metropolitan Area was examined as a key case study. In this interdisciplinary research project led by the "Metrobild" project team and ETH Zurich, an attempt was made to create a synthesis of knowledge gained from the "Metrobild" and "Parkland" pilot projects, also bringing in other principles and documents from the area of transport. The resulting "Quick-ROK" would serve as the possible foundation for an overarching development strategy for the Zurich Metropolitan Area.

An important follow-up to this work was the development of a regional planning concept for the whole metropolitan area.

In parallel to the Metrobild project, cantonal planners from the Zurich Metropolitan Area Society's eight member cantons started their first reflections on a Metro-ROK (Spatial Planning Concept).[2] Published in 2017, the Metro-ROK is not to be seen as a direct product of the "Metrobild" project, but rather as fulfilling the wish clearly expressed by the Metropolitan Conference for a regional planning concept for the whole metropolitan area. The three Metro Pictures and the Quick-ROK definitely served as inspiration for the cantonal planners. The Metro-ROK is not binding on the authorities but provides them with an informal tool and an orientational framework for spatial planning in the Zurich Metropolitan Area. It fulfils the important task of strengthening the understanding of the metropolitan area as a coherent functional space and complies with

---

[2]https://www.zh.ch/internet/de/aktuell/news/medienmitteilungen/2015/metro-rok.html.

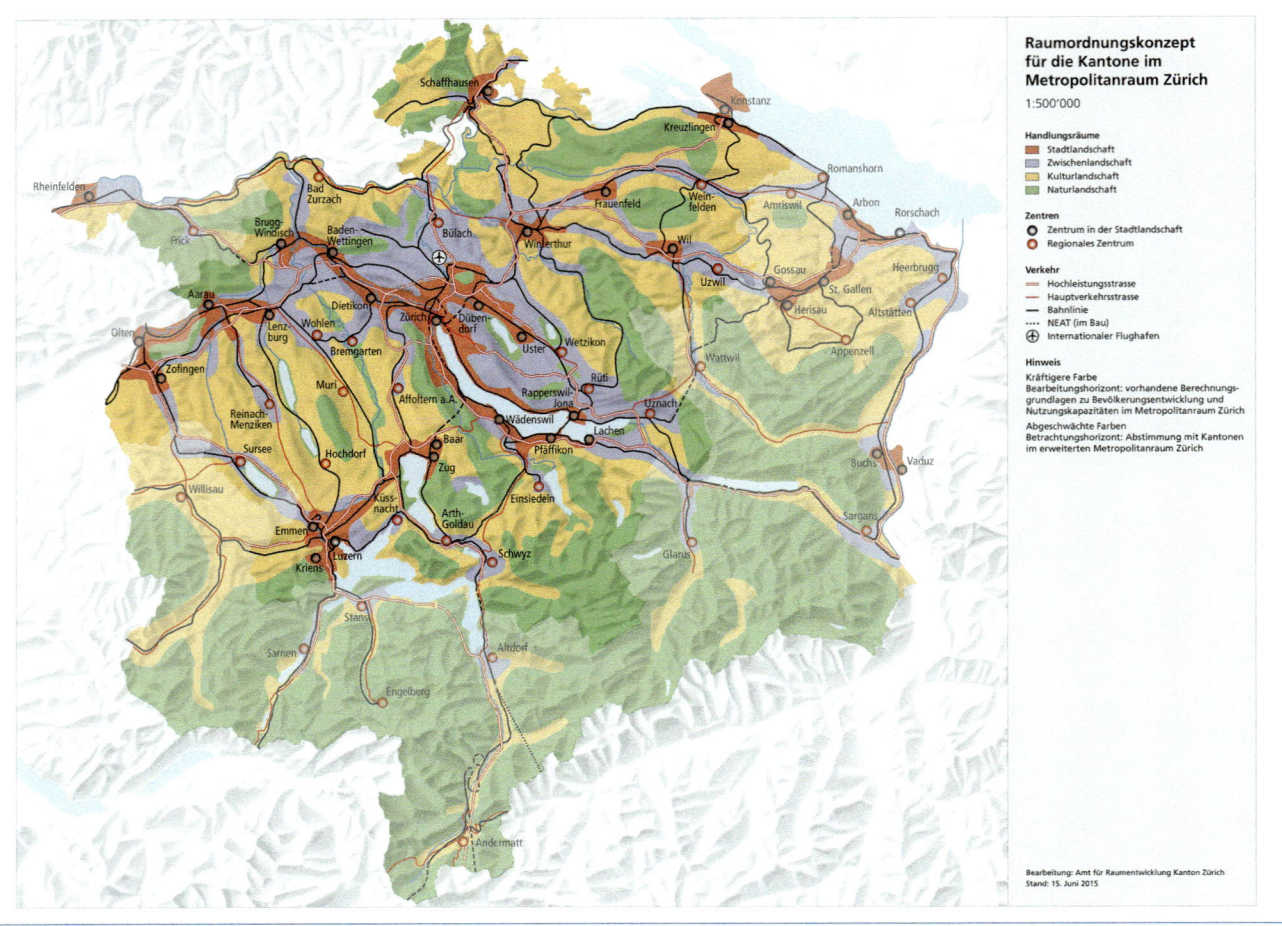

Fig. 17.9 "Metro-ROK" spatial planning concept, office for spatial development of the Canton of Zurich (2015)

the requirements of the spatial concept for Switzerland. In succession, the member cantons identified the common denominators in their development plans. Although this represents progress in terms of cross-border planning, unfortunately, the cities and municipalities were not part of the consensus process. Nevertheless, the cooperation between the cantons flows into several projects in sub-spaces of the metropolitan area, which has a great impact on the municipal level (Fig. 17.9).

In Switzerland, spatial planning is first and foremost the responsibility of the cantons, which draw up cantonal development plans for central planning, as summarised previously. At the municipal level, these land use plans are adapted to the development plans and then incorporated. This gives the municipality control over and responsibility for its area but always within the framework of the requirements of the state and the canton. It is the task of a city or a municipality to coordinate the regional development plan and to steer the utilisation planning process—building and zoning codes, special building specifications and design plans—as well as the district planning process in current building projects. In Zurich, the main planning themes are dealt with in the "Spatial Development Strategy" (RES 2010) (Fig. 17.10).[3]

---

[3]https://www.stadt-zuerich.ch/hbd/de/index/staedtebau_u_planung/planung/raeumliche_entwicklungsstrategie/publikation.html.

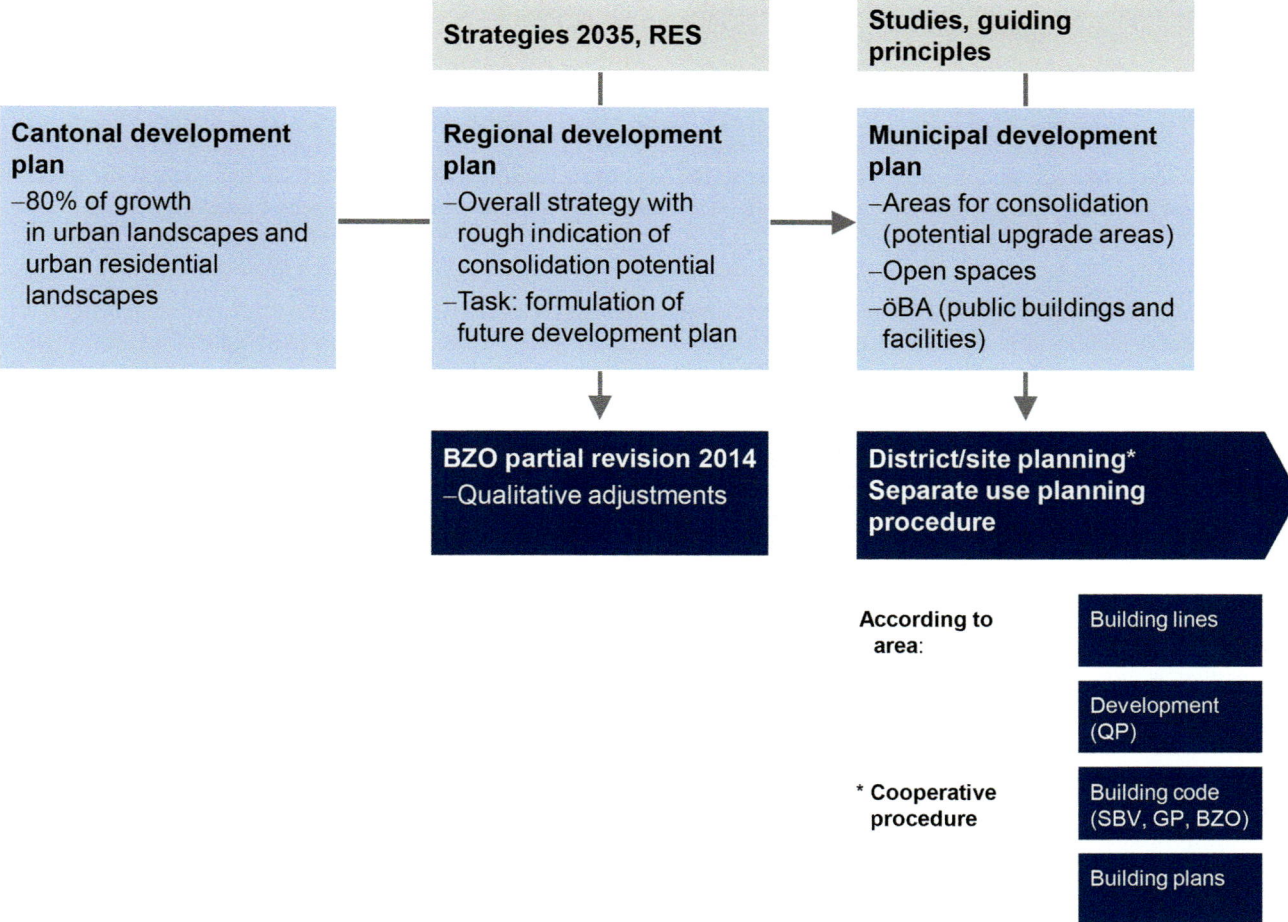

Fig. 17.10 A summary of the interplay among strategies, the development plan and BZO (prepared by the author)

Therefore, although Metrobild has no direct influence on the key tasks of municipal spatial planning, it may still serve as a reference when planning extends beyond the boundaries. It was therefore officially recognised by the councils of the eight cantons in the Zurich Metropolitan Area and adopted as a guideline for cantonal planning, as well as for planning cooperation among their cantons—for the first time in the history of planning in Switzerland, it created a common basis at a high level. Four different fields of action were described: agglomerations with core cities, landscapes between major cities with regional hubs, cultivated landscapes with regional hubs and natural landscapes.

Metro-ROK makes statements about all action areas pertaining to growth distribution and the harmonisation of housing development, traffic and landscape. The urban landscape and transitional landscape play key roles among the four action areas. Spatial development will be promoted most intensely in urban-action area landscapes going forward. The quality of the spatial development will be decided in future in the transitional landscapes, as it is here that the tendency towards a more growth-dominated urban area or towards a cultural landscape characterised by low growth will show itself. This takes into account existing realities, reveals the desired outcome of regional planning and sets out measures for future changes and developments. The Metro-ROK has a time horizon until 2030 and provides an important guideline for coordination and cross-boundary issues in spatial planning. It also provides a good basis for further cooperation in the Zurich Metropolitan Area.

Eighty percent of future growth will take place in the urban landscape, as well as in regional centres in the transitional landscapes and cultural landscapes. The remaining 20% will take place in the transitional and cultural landscapes.

Recommendations for Action from the Metro-ROK

Regarding the individual types of settlements and landscapes, the Metro-ROK formulated various planning-related and political recommendations for future action:

- In the urban landscape as a whole, but especially in the centres of the urban landscape, the cantons set out the planning conditions for the density categories: very high (>300 inhabitants + employees per hectare of construction zone), high (150–300) and medium (100–150).
- In view of the strong densification trend, the quality of urban development is the priority. Urban development solutions need to be tailored to the individual development areas.
- With a dense architectural model, it is important to maintain the diversity of the settlements to avoid ending up with bland uniformity. The use of exterior spaces to create identity will grow in importance. The cantons and municipalities maintain and create sufficient open spaces and green areas.
- The cityscape will be increasingly characterised by its variety of uses. Particular emphasis must be placed on public buildings and facilities with urban appeal.
- Offering a wide range of housing allows all social classes to live in the cityscape.
- Cooperative processes between landowners, investors and communities should be in place to ensure the quality of living space and safeguard public interests.
- The greatest potential for urban development lies in the vicinity of the railway stations; this potential needs to be activated.
- The diverse mosaic of landscape uses and the typical urban nature are to be preserved and fostered. Sufficient space must be made available for "spontaneous" endeavours (e.g. beekeeping on rooftops, allotments as an interim use for unused areas). The various bodies of water and their banks should be preserved as attractive open spaces and recreation areas and, where possible, made accessible to the public. Near-natural sections must be protected.
- The expansion of national motorway connections to cityscapes should be facilitated, all the while controlling individual motorised transport so as to avoid giving any incentive to switch from public to private transport.
- Leisure, day-to-day and commuter traffic are to be managed in such a way as to reduce traffic peaks at rush hour. The local options for recreation are to be safeguarded in this respect.
- In the transitional landscape, any development should take place first and foremost in the regional centres.
- The increasing displacement of lower-yield uses from the urban landscape into the transitional landscape makes it important to safeguard industrial parks there in future, in particular, for local and regional commerce.
- The transitional landscape has tended towards urban sprawl in recent years. Measures must therefore be taken going forward to improve the quality of life in this action area, by safeguarding and upgrading undeveloped green areas, for example.
- Together with the municipalities, the cantons are responsible for deciding whether these areas will develop into urban structures or remain within the traditional framework of lower densities. Structural and utilisation planning measures are in place to create the necessary conditions to be able to absorb the growth and prevent unstructured urban sprawl. In particular, transitions from the edges of the settlements into open countryside and transitions into the urban or cultural landscape should be carefully and actively structured. One option for such an active structuring is provided by cantonal common lands as public assets, for example, and large contiguous areas.
- In the cultural landscape, further growth of settlements in the area is to be prevented. Likewise, the merging of individual settlement conglomerates, which would lead to the emergence of further transitional landscapes, must be prevented. The density and structure of settlements must be adapted to the landscape and the diversity of the cultural landscape must be preserved. The replication of past typical structural patterns or elements of sprawling transitional landscapes should be avoided.
- There should no longer be any quantitative growth in the natural landscape. In this space, the existing qualities are to be strengthened and, if necessary, protected with pertinent measures (e.g. implementation of protection ordinances).

Some of these individual recommendations form the basis of later or current projects by the Metropolitan Policy Conference; others lie in a clearly defined cantonal, municipal or national competency and can only be implemented within existing regulations and using the usual planning tools.

17.5 The Core City of Zurich

As the largest urban centre in Switzerland, the City of Zurich influences the development of the whole Metropolitan Area. Building development is also closely linked with that of the neighbouring towns and municipalities. This is why Zurich attaches importance to cooperative work based on partnership with all neighbours. This occurs in various fields of activity and projects—for example, in the joint planning of projects which extend beyond the city limits. An example of this is the "Fil bleu," a transregional, open-space concept along the river Glatt in the Glattal Valley near Zurich, in which the City of Zurich cooperated with three other towns/municipalities.

An important platform for regional planning adjustment is provided by the planning associations. The City of Zurich is a member of the Regional Planning for Zurich and Surroundings, or RZU, an umbrella organisation under which the City of Zurich and the six adjacent planning regions Furttal, Glattal, Pfannenstil, Zimmerberg, Knonaueramt and Limmattal, as well as the Canton of Zurich, have joined forces. The RZU area has a total population of approximately 970,000 people (2015) (66% of the canton's population on 39% of its area) and a workforce of approximately 760,000. The RZU carries out projects which are in the interest of the whole region and fosters cooperation among its members—as shown with the following two concrete examples, indicating how the City of Zurich contributes to planning projects with a regional dimension.

The first example is the "Limmattal Regional Project Show."[4] This project bears a certain resemblance to the Metropolitan Conference—in its organisation as an association, but also in the three fields of activity in which concrete projects are to be supported and promoted: Society of Tomorrow, Infrastructure of the Future and Agglopark River Park. Obviously, the perimeter of Limmattal is much smaller—it covers "only" the Limmattal area—and the planned tasks are much more concrete and locally based than is the case with the Metropolitan Conference. It is primarily initiatives from private or institutional players that are supported and not those from public authorities. These are gathered in a call for projects, and they then receive initial funding and should start up after five years.

The first step towards the Agglopark was the opening of the Limmat Riverside Pathway in 2014. In October 2016, the Limmattal Project Show took over the Agglopark project. The association will continue the work and proceed with the promotion of projects. The aim is to benchmark the projects in the Agglopark as best-practice examples for cross-boundary planning. The vision for 2025 shows the central axis of the Agglopark, the Limmat River, as a recreational space for the public. The space offers a wide variety of landscapes between Zurich and the city of Baden: the nature of the riverside areas mutates from urban boulevards where people stroll, to quiet retreat areas, swimming spots and species-rich habitats for plants and animals. For the municipalities in the Limmattal, the Agglopark is the central guideline for a common development strategy of open space.

The second project is being carried out by the City of Zurich together with the Regional Planning for Zurich and Surroundings.[5] Its title is "Envisaging and Developing the Metropolitan Area of Zurich with a Common Housing Policy," and it assumes that, as far as housing policy is concerned, the regional level will be very important in the future—more important, in fact, than the municipal level.

In the RZU area, there should be housing available that is adapted to the RZU members' quantitative and qualitative development aims, as well as to the various demands of the housing market—housing for everyone, in effect. With the aid of building and living-environment analyses, social–spatial development, as well as the potential and shortcomings of the available housing, the resulting "Agenda for the Housing Region of Zurich" should be described in concrete terms at regional housing conferences with political and local authority representatives and other key players.

In 2017, the results from the first analyses were consolidated. In 2018, the RZU will promote a wide political debate about the conditions and planning necessities to initiate the "housing and living" location factor in the RZU area. For this purpose, the neighbourhood regions, the RZU member municipalities, the City of Zurich and the Canton of Zurich will be included in the debate and, hopefully, develop common strategies.

Together with the cities of Oslo, Prague, Brno, Lyon, Terrassa, Lille, Brussels, Vienna and Turin, Zurich has been participating in the ESPON-project SPIMA (Spatial Dynamics and Strategic Planning in Metropolitan Areas, 2017/2018). ESPON (European Observation Network for territorial development and cohesion) is a spatial observation network in which Switzerland takes part. It elaborates comparative analyses and scenarios of spatial development dynamics. SPIMA is the follow-up project of the Eurocities Working Group "Metropolitan Areas." ESPON is going to collect and evaluate data in

---

[4]https://regionale2025.ch.
[5]www.rzu.ch.

collaboration with project partners. The data collected should answer the main research question: How does spatial development function at the metropolitan level and in which context, especially in the participating metropolitan areas? Basically, the project wants to investigate how collaboration works between the subordinated political institutions, core cities and surrounding municipalities and regions with regard to metropolitan areas.

In general, the city of Zurich experiences considerable challenges forced upon it by sustained population growth, demographic development and social change, the rising demand for convenience, the need to upgrade built-up areas and the preservation of its high quality of life. Compliance with the requirement of the spatial planning strategy, according to which 80% of the population growth is going to take place within urban spaces, would mean a total increase of around 420,000 people in the "urban landscape" and "urban residential landscape" action spaces by 2040. An increase of around 80,000–100,000 people is expected in the "landscape under pressure," "cultural landscape" and "natural landscape" action spaces. In view of this expected growth, the question arises as to whether the action spaces can accommodate such growth without further measures?

Another key factor for the Zurich Metropolitan Area is the intact landscape. There are not only large connected landscapes but also traditional agricultural landscapes and open spaces in the built-up areas. There is a lot of pressure on these areas caused by population growth. These challenges also led to the Metro-ROK mentioned previously.

Conclusion and Direction for further Projects in Spatial Planning in the Zurich Metropolitan Area

Six years after the Zurich Metropolitan Area Society was founded, there is now an ongoing discussion about the whole organisation. The enthusiasm of the members has dwindled and smaller municipalities have started to leave the association. Here, the challenge is to keep up the strategic discussions about the further development of the metropolitan area, especially in the more difficult processes of integrating the Metro-ROK into cantonal structure plans, and to keep the smaller municipalities involved in the development of the metropolitan area.

In conclusion, the Zurich Metropolitan Area is institutionally well on the way to elaborating tools to guide the future spatial development of the metropolitan area. However, because of the need to develop measures to deal with the challenges —known ones and the new ones that will arise—the Zurich Metropolitan Area is focusing on new fields of action: the smart use of big data for spatial planning, the development of the gas infrastructure and the challenges of logistics in more and more dense cities. For a long time, housing development questions always focused primarily on capacity planning. The objective of the "SmartUse" project is to base housing development more on the actual behaviour of those who use it, and therefore to draw on new data sources to better understand their needs. Daily routines between home, work and leisure activities within the Zurich Metropolitan Area are analysed with a focus on the quality and intensity of use of public spaces, streets and open spaces. A sustainable transformation of urban landscapes can only succeed if spatial development is transformed from "hardware-oriented" capacity planning to "software-oriented" usage management.

Another major issue is the energy infrastructure: gas networks exist in 80% of the Zurich Metropolitan Area's member municipalities. These networks belong almost exclusively to the public sector. Increasing energy consumption from population and economic growth is being offset by decreasing consumption due to energy retrofits and climate change actions. Additionally, there is a climate-policy-driven shift from the consumption of fossil fuels to the use of renewable energy resources. What does this mean for the future of gas networks? The gas infrastructure in the Zurich Metropolitan Area is to be further developed in a future-oriented manner while at the same time preventing bad investments, such as dismantling or expansion.

Last but not least, the issue of logistics in the last mile is likely to become more important over the next few years. Given the current upheavals in the field of logistics, some rapid changes can be expected to take place soon. Not least of all, growing cross-border online trade is exerting enormous pressure on the last mile. For this reason, the dissemination of innovative offers for the last mile of the logistics chain in the Zurich Metropolitan Area should be accelerated by standardising and improving framework conditions.

The Zurich Metropolitan Area is facing up to all these challenges and is developing solutions that suit the region step by step. Coordination and cooperation are more important than ever with regard to these issues, which can never be solved by one entity alone, whether canton or municipality. The model of the Zurich Metropolitan Area shows how the future of spatial development could work—and it would mean a considerable step forward if it could be recognised by the Swiss planning system as a successful way of shaping our regional future.

References

Berchtold Krass space&options (2011) Schlussbericht Metrobild, ein Bild für den Metroraum Zürich

Hosoya Schaefer Architects AG Zurich (2011) Schlussbericht Metrobild

KantonsplanerInnen des Metropolitanraums Zürich (2015) Raumordnungskonzept für die Kantone im Metropolitanraum Zürich. Metro-ROK

Metropolitankonferenz Zürich (2011) Jurybericht zum Workshopverfahren Metrobild

Stadt Zürich, Hochbaudepartement, Amt für Städtebau (2010) RES, Räumliche Entwicklungsstrategie des Stadtrats für die Stadt Zürich

Yellow Z Urbanism Architects (2011) Metrogartenstadt, auf dem Weg zu einer landschaftsbasierten urbanen Region

Enhancing the Perception of Regions: A Vision for the Metropolitan City of Florence

18

Giuseppe De Luca, Valeria Lingua, Fabio Lucchesi, Luca Di Figlia, Raffaella Fucile, and Carlo Pisano

Abstract

This chapter focuses on the definition of a vision for the metropolitan city of Florence required by recent planning reform in Italy. The forms of governance in place and the boundaries they assume are discussed in relation to the historical evolution of settlements and functional trends and their recognition and orientation through joint planning instruments at different levels (from joint inter-municipal studies to the Regional Landscape Plan). The actual strategic planning process that occurred in the metropolitan city of Florence is presented as a vision-making process based on regional design theories, in which different metaphorical narratives and representations are explicitly intended to enhance the strategic planning process by shaping the boundaries of the urban region and conceiving of a shared vision for its future spatial development.

Keywords

Strategic planning • Visioning • Metropolitan city • Metropolitan planning • Functional region

18.1 Introduction

After the revision of the institutional system brought about by Law no. 56 of 7 April 2014, important changes occurred in ten main Italian regional cities which were obliged to form joint metropolitan city governments and engage in strategic planning. Metropolitan cities are now in the early stages of defining their strategic plans, prompting questions about the dimensions and characteristics of the metropolitan area, as well as its image in the metropolitan community and the ambition and vision of a metropolitan city. A great need for visioning practices has emerged, both to build up the urban region (from the administrative border to a collective identity) and to define a shared vision of its territorial development.

The paper focuses on the process of defining the vision for the metropolitan city of Florence within this panorama of governance rescaling. The forms of governance in place and the boundaries they assume are discussed, as well as the

G. De Luca (✉) · V. Lingua · L. Di Figlia · R. Fucile · C. Pisano
Regional Design Lab, Department of Architecture, University of Florence, Florence, Italy
e-mail: giuseppe.deluca@unifi.it

V. Lingua
e-mail: valeria.lingua@unifi.it

L. Di Figlia
e-mail: luca.difiglia@unifi.it

R. Fucile
e-mail: raffaella.fucile@unifi.it

C. Pisano
e-mail: carlo.pisano@unifi.it

F. Lucchesi
Cartography Lab, Department of Architecture, University of Florence, Florence, Italy
e-mail: fabio.lucchesi@unifi.it

© Springer Nature Switzerland AG 2020
V. Lingua and V. Balz (eds.), *Shaping Regional Futures*,
https://doi.org/10.1007/978-3-030-23573-4_18

regional design process which—through the shaping and discussion of targeted visions—leads to the definition of a shared vision.

In the debate on the role of representation and visioning in governance rescaling processes, the case of the strategic plan for the metropolitan city of Florence is presented as a vision-making process based on regional design theories, which led to an approach aimed at considering in a synergistic and integrated way two different design scales (macro and micro), with their projects and practices (stories). These resulted in identity issues among the diverse territories within the metropolitan city (from "Chiantishire" to the Mugello region, passing through the historic centre of Florence, a UNESCO World Heritage Site), integration among city uses and users (inhabitants, tourists, city users and, more recently, migrants) and new forms of housing and living (co-living, co-working). While the macro-stories are derived from statutory, traditional planning scenarios, the micro-stories are related to the tactics field and became a fundamental element for achieving the three strategic visions of the plan, aimed at bringing about a new "metropolitan renaissance".

The aim of this chapter is to contribute to a better understanding of how designing and visioning can enhance the strategic planning process by shaping the boundaries of urban regions and conceiving of a shared vision for their spatial futures. First, a theoretical reflection on the role of representations is provided. It is followed by a review of how attention came to be placed on metropolitan cities in Italian planning and concludes with the current challenges. Within this framework, previous arguments are tested on the core case by exploring how the metropolitan city of Florence has been represented over time, and how a recent design process met the current challenges.

18.2 Making the Region and Its Future Visible: The Role of Representation

This chapter focuses on the process of framing urban regions and envisioning their possible future development. This practice, founded on visioning, is intended both to indicate physical changes and stimulate debate on the sharing of responsibilities and resources (Balz and Zonneveld 2015). Moreover, through the use of spatial representations of the plausible future of urban regions, the visioning process establishes a sense of place and gives it meaning (Ache 2013). Vision-making is deeply engaged with specific spatial environments and their distinct geographies and has territorial implications. It challenges formal spatial planning by leading to the definition and redefinition of issues, boundaries and solutions (Balz 2018). Furthermore, the positioning of the metropolitan city in the global competitiveness system draws major benefits from being rooted in the recognition of local features in a regional dimension. This applies even more so in the case of governance rescaling, whenever a great need emerges to deal with the link between administrative boundaries and the complexity of socio-economic and governance relationships (EMA 2015).

Considering the functional region as an area that people and businesses refer to in carrying out their activities (Friedmann and Weaver 1979) implies referring to regional networks, material and immaterial flows between the centre and the periphery, metropolitan transport networks, and the locational dynamics dominated by these flows (Thierstein and Förster 2008; Glasson and Marshall 2010). These "conglomerates of places and activities," stretching across multiple and multi-scalar administrative boundaries, are shaped by "the rapid decentralization of economic activities; increased mobility due to new transport technologies; multiple travel patterns; fragmented spatial distribution of activities; changes in household structure and lifestyle; and the existence of complex cross-commuting" (Davoudi, 2003: 981). This is why new analytical and planning methods are required when analyzing a region or even a mega-region (Förster et al. 2016).

In this scalar restructuring process, visioning practices, by providing images, scenarios and visions, are expected to contribute to the territorial, symbolic and institutional shaping of a region (Paasi 2009). This process corresponds to the act of creating the orientation that Healey refers to as "strategic framing," i.e. framing and identifying critical actions by recognizing strategies through a process of evocation, visualization, naming and framing (Healey 2007: 188–189) that requires "intense simplification and selectivity" (Healey 2009: 449). In spatial planning, thus, spatial framing asks the planner to engage in a process of "selecting, organizing, interpreting, and making sense of a complex reality to provide guideposts for knowing, analysing, persuading, and acting" (Rein and Schön 1993: 146).

These guideposts come in the form of spatial representation (Faludi 1996; Neuman 1996; Dühr 2007; Zonneveld 2008) providing a visual image of the region and projecting future hypotheses onto the present. In acquiring this purpose of creating meaning, images lose their status of visualization for communication and the transfer of information and turn into spatial representations (Davoudi 2011; Balz 2018).

Spatial representation is a privileged vehicle of urban communication (Mascarucci 2004; Gabellini 2010) and has the capacity to stimulate debate within decision-making processes and to encourage shared projects (Secchi and Viganò 2009).

During planning processes, multiple communication approaches can be identified, which vary according to the intended recipient of the message and the type of content they should deliver.

Where a plurality of languages exists, Gambino (2000) proposes a taxonomy of representations according to the communicative scope: (i) representations with a regulatory function at juridical level, (ii) representations aimed at outlining strategic orientations shared between a plurality of actors and (iii) representations with argumentative and support functions for discussion. This classification was re-framed by Lucchesi (2007) who distinguished between prescriptive, illustrative and exploratory representations of possible futures, paying particular attention to: "[…] implications of effectiveness connected to the different functions [that] can influence the operative modalities of the construction of images" (Lucchesi 2007: 48). Different illustrative techniques and methods are used according to the functions and desired communicative effectiveness.

Focusing on the last kind of representation, concerning the future, different technical and rhetorical constructions can be traced, as Viganò (2009) noted: scenario, visioning and visions. These terms, although theoretically distinguished by a specific and autonomous connotation, are often associated and overlapped.

In Italy, the most known technique to elaborate future development is the scenario technique, which has been investigated by several authors in both research and professional practice (Secchi 2003; Magnaghi 2007; Gabellini 2010). Scenarios can be understood as a series of hypothetical narratives that answer the question: "what would happen if …" (Secchi 2003). The value of this technique in the construction of the territorial project is twofold: it enhances cognitive recognition and planning (Magnaghi 2007). Thus, the term scenario acquires different meanings and is often used as a synonym of "vision" and "image" due to its polysomic nature. According to Gabellini (2010), the terms visioning and vision have greater lexical "ambiguity" and their meaning may change with respect to the reference framework. The term visioning, or community visioning, was widely used in North America in the 1980s in reference to metropolitan areas, where the visioning process was intended to involve the community in the definition of a shared future. In the European context, on the other hand, visioning refers to the elaboration of visions, i.e. complex representations that signify and summarize an image of the future of a regional area as a background and common ground for long-term actions (Zonneveld and Verwest 2005).

In this sense, "A vision is not a plan: it is, at the same time, a great deal less detailed and more complex; it does not define rights and specific duties, or construct executive procedures, but rather delineates a vanishing point, a horizon of meaning for an entire community while specifying the appropriate strategies to reach it. A vision is open and flexible, but endowed with discriminating power: not every action is appropriate within a single vision. It can receive, change or refute not on a juridical basis, but on a logical basis of substantial and formal coherence" (Secchi 2003). This process of thinking about the future by selecting and reasoning lies between the need for spatial representations to both assist the analytical process of co-producing knowledge and, simultaneously, aid policy definitions through their spatial transposition.

In this contribution, we refer to the ability of representations to build up robust argumentative structures and visions of the future in the context of regional design approaches (Thierstein and Förster 2008; Balz and Zonneveld 2015; Lingua 2017). We refer to regional design as a method of argumentation based on the use of spatial representations of future developments or visions, to link the three main logics behind the use of spatial representations: analytical logic, concerning scientific spatial knowledge; normative logic, conveying values and roles for systematising spaces; and organizational logic derived from prevailing territorial control (Balz 2018). As the latter involve political and ethical deliberation, regional design represents the discursive component of planning concepts, i.e. the argumentative connection between the analytical and the normative dimension of planning concepts (Balz and Zonneveld 2015). We assume that, by activating a regional design process, representations can contribute to "an extreme effort of imagination" (Velo and Pace 2018; Lingua 2018) by providing new analytical perspectives of the region, exploring spatial, functional and temporal organization and, in the end, promising a better region (Förster et al. 2016).

This contribution describes how a regional design approach was employed to define the vision for the strategic plan of the metropolitan city of Florence in a governance rescaling context in which metropolitan cities—as government structures operating within pre-defined boundaries—have a duty to produce a strategic plan. In this context, this approach was intentionally used for a twofold purpose: to define the metropolitan region across administrative boundaries and build up the vision and related strategies for a long-term future in 2030 (Lingua 2017) by visualizing the policies and interventions that emerged in the planning process (Thierstein and Förster 2008). The case study is based on the proposition that, within the current Italian institutional and planning system, where a recent reform fostered the use of spatial representation to play a renewed role in the form of scenarios and visions, the regional design approach can contribute by envisioning both the regional dimension of metropolitan cities and their future in the context of strategic metropolitan planning. It is argued that the administrative reorganization following Italian Law 56/2014 and the subsequent establishment of metropolitan cities (De Luca and Moccia 2015, 2017) has led to a renewed propulsion of design-led approaches.

18.3 Italian Metropolitan Regions at Stake: The Paradoxes and Challenges of Institutional Rescaling

The establishment of metropolitan cities has been under discussion since the post-war period in Italy. In the second half of the 1960s, the discussion led to a strategic document by the Ministry of Finance and Economic Programming called "Progetto'80" (MBPE 1970). The document, however, never brought about direct political action and remained a mere indication of strategy but nothing more (Renzoni 2012).

The first real political action to establish metropolitan cities in Italy as an institutional body occurred with Law 142/1990 on local self-government. The task of recognizing the boundaries of the metropolitan areas was given to the regions, but none of them succeeded in institutionalizing them. It was necessary to wait until the constitutional changes that followed the amendment of the 5th title in 2001 when, for the first time, the metropolitan city was constitutionally recognized as an autonomous institution constituting the Italian Republic.

In point of fact, metropolitan cities were only established in 2014 within the framework of the "Delrio law"[1] (Law 56/2014). This law sought to transform all Italian provinces into second-level institutions with non-elected assemblies and to reduce their jurisdiction. Provinces that incorporated major regional capital cities were abolished and replaced with "metropolitan cities". Finally, local authorities in small cities were required to join a "union of municipalities" with a minimum population of up to 5,000 inhabitants. The "Delrio law" was included in a general project of institutional reorganization in Italy that required a further amendment to the 5th title of the Constitution; it concerned the role of local authorities and provided for the definitive abolition of provinces.[2] However, before the constitutional amendment could come into force it was put to a popular referendum on 4 December 2016. The change was rejected by 59.5% of the votes.

After the constitutional referendum, the situation of the metropolitan cities did not change, while that of the old provinces did. In the wait for the new "Delrio law 2.0", one certainty remains for the provinces: metropolitan cities do not change, nor do they need further regulatory steps to function. If anything, they must quickly adopt territorial governance instruments: both the metropolitan strategic plan and the metropolitan territorial plan.

According to the 2014 "Delrio" law, the metropolitan city is defined as a regional institution with the aim of: managing the strategic development of the metropolitan area, promoting and managing the services, infrastructures and communication networks of interest to the metropolitan city in an integrated way, and taking care of institutional relations pertaining to its own level, including those with the cities and metropolitan areas of Europe.

While this institution was defined as early as 1990 with Law no. 142, the "Delrio reform" to create metropolitan cities came to life with an institutional stratagem: it changed the ten main provinces with regional capitals (Turin, Milan, Venice, Genoa, Bologna, Florence, Rome, Bari, Naples and Reggio Calabria) into metropolitan cities without changing the territorial boundaries. Along with these ten newly established metropolitan cities, four metropolitan cities (Palermo, Catania, Messina and Cagliari) were thereafter established with regional laws, enacted by the regions with special status. The new institutional dimension also required the creation of an architecture of strategic and administrative government tasked with predicting and implementing the development and competitiveness of the territory as it pertains to the metropolitan city.

Covering an area of almost 50,000 km^2, equal to 16.5% of the national territory, and with 1,328 municipalities (16.5% of the national total), these 14 metropolitan cities accommodate 22.1 million inhabitants (36.4% of the national population) and 9.6 million families.

The economic, social and cultural forces required to compete in a global setting are concentrated in these cities; hence, they should play a leading role in strengthening the competitiveness of both Italian and European territories. There are however profound differences between them in terms of size (6,827 km^2 in Turin versus 1,171 km^2 in Naples) and number of inhabitants. While Rome has 4.34 million inhabitants, Reggio Calabria has only 557,000. There are also significant differences in the role of the municipalities as capitals: Rome has 2.87 million inhabitants whereas Cagliari has 154,000. The average taxable income per capita in Milan is €17,802; in Catania it is only €7,441. In another five metropolitan cities (in order: Naples, Reggio Calabria, Palermo, Bari and Cagliari) taxable income lies below the Italian average (De Luca and Moccia 2017).

---

[1]Named after the Ministry in charge of the process of power devolution and institutional reorganization.

[2]This amendment was approved, by a simple majority, in Parliament and published in *Official Gazette* no. 88 of 15 April 2016. The revocation of provinces was conceived of together with the overcoming of equal bicameralism (Chamber of Deputies/Chamber of the Senators) and the reduction of the number of parliamentarians, in the name of the "spending review," i.e. the containment of operating costs faced by institutions at all levels.

There are also significant differences in the territorial organization and connections, and the size of the functional urban region. In the major Italian cities, these differences are rooted in their long history: some were city-states, like Genoa, Venice, Florence and Milan; others were capitals of the kingdom, such as Rome, Naples and Turin; others were regional reference hubs, such as Cagliari, Palermo and Bari. An examination of the territorial sphere of influence over which these metropolitan cities developed their relations shows that their extension does not always correspond to that of a metropolis. Only a very limited number of cities play an international role; most are important at interregional level. After all, the institutional stratagem that gave birth to metropolitan cities in Italy has paved the way for a series of paradoxes that are not easy to solve. The most obvious of these paradoxes is the distance between the institutional boundary and the territorial boundary defined by economic dynamics (Fig. 18.1). By making the institutional boundaries of the metropolitan cities coincide with the institutional boundaries of the previous provinces, a paradox has arisen: functional urban areas and institutional borders do not correspond in the metropolitan city. Some cases are very emblematic: such as the Metropolitan city of Bologna, where the territorial system of the metropolitan city is fully incorporated into the former province, but a central, denser part with a population of 650,000 is recognizable: 65% of the entire metropolitan area (Gabellini et al. 2017); or the Metropolitan city of Genoa, where the city has a relatively small urban nucleus and a reticular structure that extends along the coast and along the interior valleys, almost defining a sort of city territory (Bobbio and Lombardini 2017), and finally, the case of the Metropolitan city of Venice, with a small central historic core and a very large territory with low population density (Viganò et al. 2017).

Fig. 18.1 Metropolitan city boundaries (in black) and the extent of their functional urban areas (in grey)

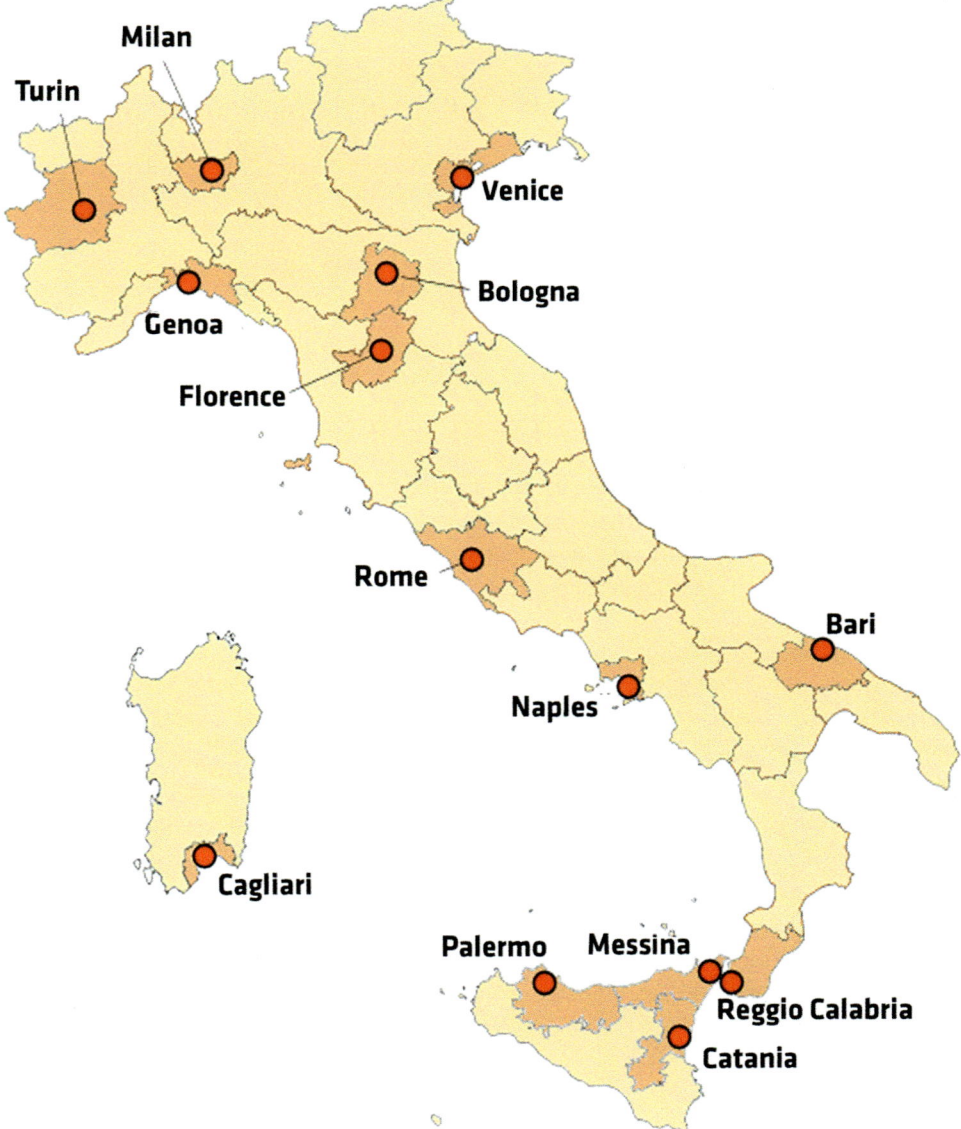

Florence and Bologna are the only cases of bordering metropolitan cities: these two cities are physically contiguous and are connected by high-speed railway, making travel time between them very quick (37′) and frequent (every half an hour): this is why a public/private cooperation table is expected in the near future to develop coordinate and unitary urban and territorial policies.

Above all, the paradigmatic case of the metropolitan city of Florence emerges (De Luca 2016, 2017): the metropolitan city coincides with the former province of Florence, while all economic activity has historically developed along the interprovincial basin (metropolitan area) from Florence to Pistoia (Fig. 18.2).

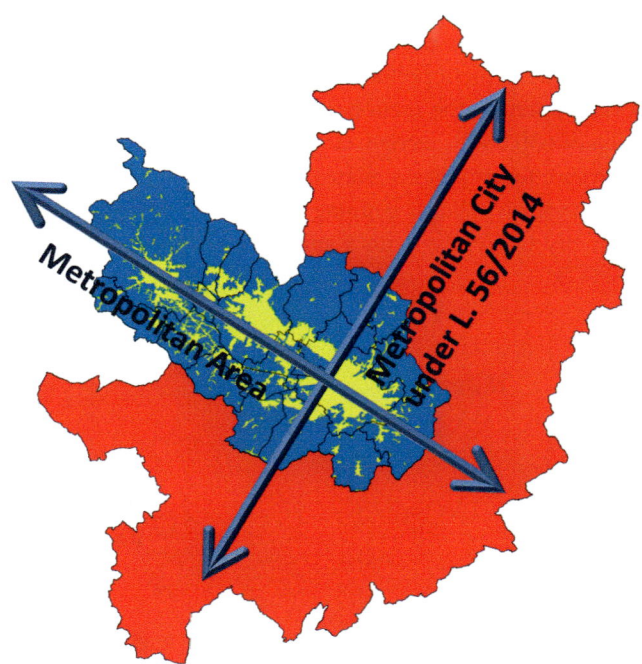

Fig. 18.2 Axis of the metropolitan area of Florence. The blue area indicates the metropolitan area of Florence–Prato–Pistoia, where the "Structural Scheme" was planned. Tuscany Regional Resolution 212/1990. The red area indicates the area of the metropolitan area of Florence. National law 56/2014

Since the nineteenth century, the central part of the inter-provincial basin has gradually developed into a conurbation of metropolitan public transport, supported by long-distance networks. Increasingly, broad supra-municipal services have been established, seeing important activities move from larger cities to smaller towns and a change in the morphology of the land that held everything together. Over time, these processes have created a complex economic-territorial mesh system in a single large metropolitan basin: the plain. Here, planning policies were not implemented by explicit supra-municipal-level coordinated public policies, but by the strength of the mix of public and private investments forced to coexist.

The provinces of Florence, Prato and Pistoia, which cover an area of 4,800 km^2 (one-fifth of the surface area of Tuscany), are home to 40% of the population and enterprises in the region, hence, half the total regional GDP. In 1990, the Tuscany region approved a territorial planning document, known as the structural plan for the Metropolitan Area of Florence–Prato–Pistoia. This is still the most important attempt the region has made to support and guide the development of this crucial area of Tuscany through the prefiguration of a spatial structure arranged around lines and recognizable landmarks.

The intersection of the "historically" recognized metropolitan area—governed by a planning tool such as the structural plan for large areas—and the metropolitan city as identified by Law 56/2014, in just the borders of the province of Florence, unequivocally reveals the orthogonal directions of the two axes and, therefore, of the possible territorial development policies. The perimeter of the metropolitan city becomes an issue of utmost urgency. We cannot have, on the one hand, a leading international city like Florence with a catchment area of influence that only partly overlaps that of metropolitan institutions, and on the other, a metropolitan basin with two medium-sized towns, Prato and Pistoia, going in a completely opposite direction to that of the leading city. Above we have outlined a regional design approach in theoretical terms. Considering the case of the metropolitan city of Florence, a set of research questions arises: How should we interpret this economic and territorial reality? Which approaches and theoretical analysis tools should be used? Can the visioning and representation approach help to show the region and its dynamics in a complex context like the one just described?

In order to answer these research questions, it is certainly of interest to examine the role the long history of territorial transformation has played in building up the current physical image of the large area around the city of Florence, using a cartographic analysis to understand the evolution of the spatial imaginary of the Florentine metropolitan area and its territorial transformations.

18.4 The Definition of the Florentine Metropolitan Dimension: An Historical Overview

In order to understand the evolution of visions presenting spatial solutions to the problems of the Florentine metropolitan area, a critical reading of the cartographic and visual materials produced during the various sub-regional planning attempts over the last decades appears useful. It is based on a reading of the link between spatial policy choices affecting the metropolitan area and spatial representation conveyed by related cartographic documents, based on both the information contained in the map and the visual variables used to define this information. We must however start with a historical consideration: the development of this internal lowland area (the second one in Tuscany after the Valdichiana) and the structures that have taken shape on it are linked to its geographical position: the natural intersection between the fundamental North–South divide of Italy and the main one in Tuscany (the Arno Valley). This has always been the most densely populated area in Tuscany, and it has always been the crossroads of trade and a magnet for public and private investments. To have carved out a "piece" of this long plain to then define it as "metropolitan" constitutes naive violence against the economic and social facts and practices of use together, but also against the urban history of the last sixty years. Seen from the lowlands, it appears as a single immense city delineating an entirely new urban geography. This continuous urban fabric, often compact, has produced both a recognizable environment and a clear landscape.

The most recent image of the flat plain was produced by the landscape plan of the Tuscany region, completed in 2015 (Fig. 18.3). The landscape plan of the Tuscany region explains both the landscape structure and its historical definition through images. In this part of the region, the landscape structure coincides with the plains and the surrounding hills covering the neighbouring provinces of Florence, Prato and Pistoia.

Reflections on the existence of an increasingly integrated and interconnected conurbation arose from the first works to prepare the local town plan of the city of Florence in 1951. The works outlined a first inter-municipal planning scheme based on the hypothesis of a linear "ribbon" development of the city of Florence along the plain. The idea was then developed in the local regulatory plan of 1962, definitively approved in 1966. The plan, among other indications, identifies an "equipped axis" reaching as far as Pistoia as the main element of the road system and the functional organization of the plain, and considering a wider territorial unit it includes not only the interprovincial basin but also part of the valleys that gravitate around it: a real metropolitan area (Fig. 18.4a). These studies led to the first image of the metropolitan area of central Tuscany, the cornerstone of which is the city of Florence (Fig. 18.4b). The desire to have different denotations is evident: the morphological identity of the basin of the plain is clear, represented with powerful chiaroscuro making it stand out against the rendering of the hillside, characteristic of contemporary digital elaborations; the structuring role of the historical centres is emphasized, and the fundamental design vision concerns the definition of an equipped axis extending to Prato and Pistoia and containing building expansion in the northern part of the "Piana". The territory matters in generating metropolitan images.

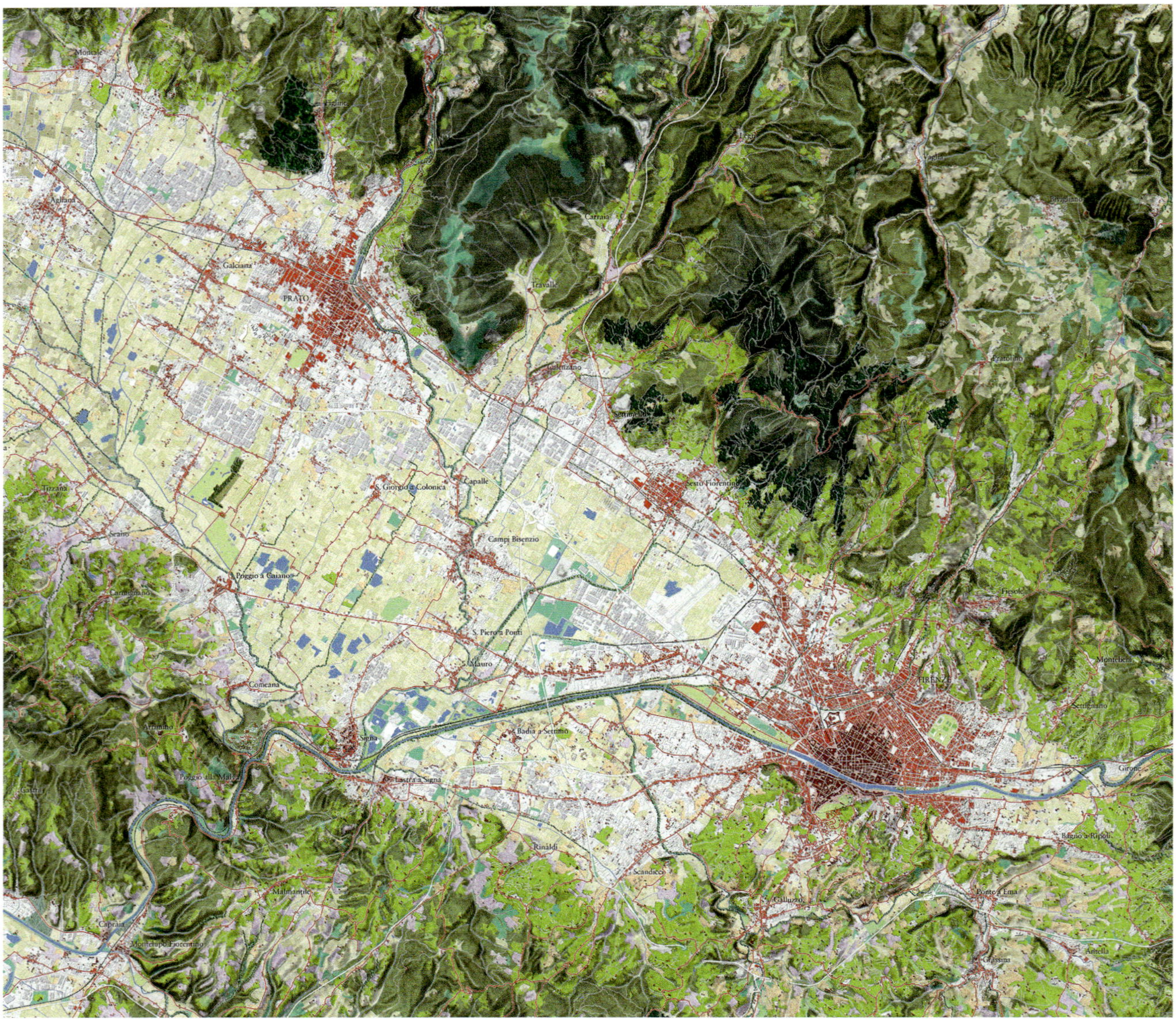

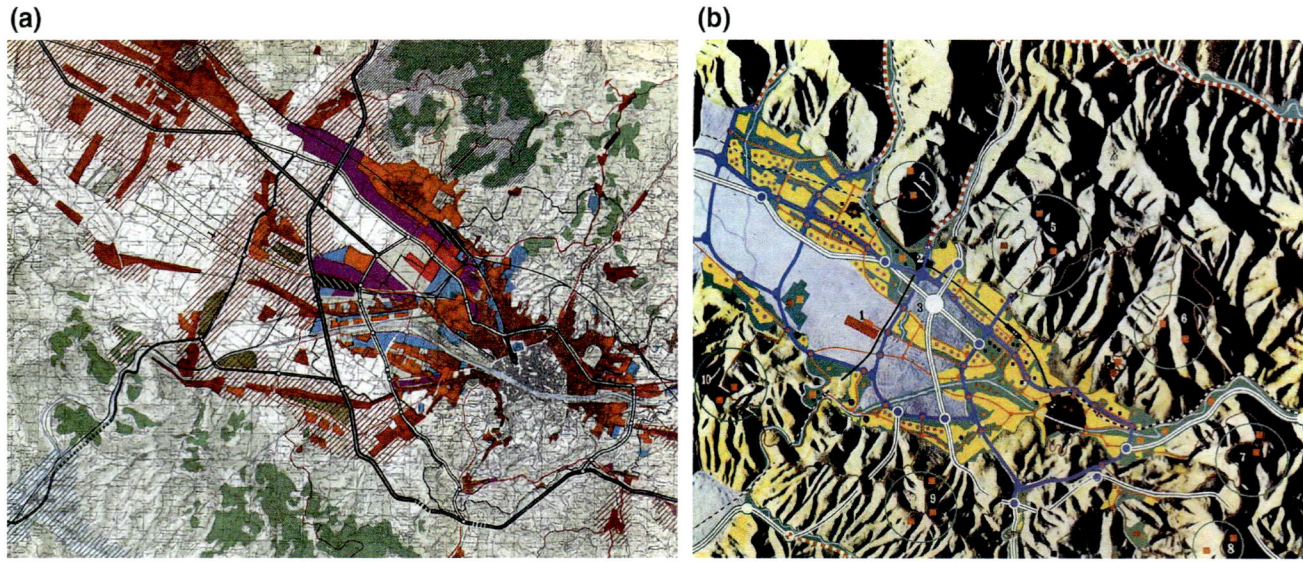

Fig. 18.3 Tuscany region, Landscape plan, Map showing the landscape features 1:50,000, 2015. The Florentine plain

(a)   **(b)**

Fig. 18.4 a Local regulatory plan of Florence with intercommunal planning features, 1962; **b** Guidelines for a scheme of the Inter-Municipal Plan, 1964/1965

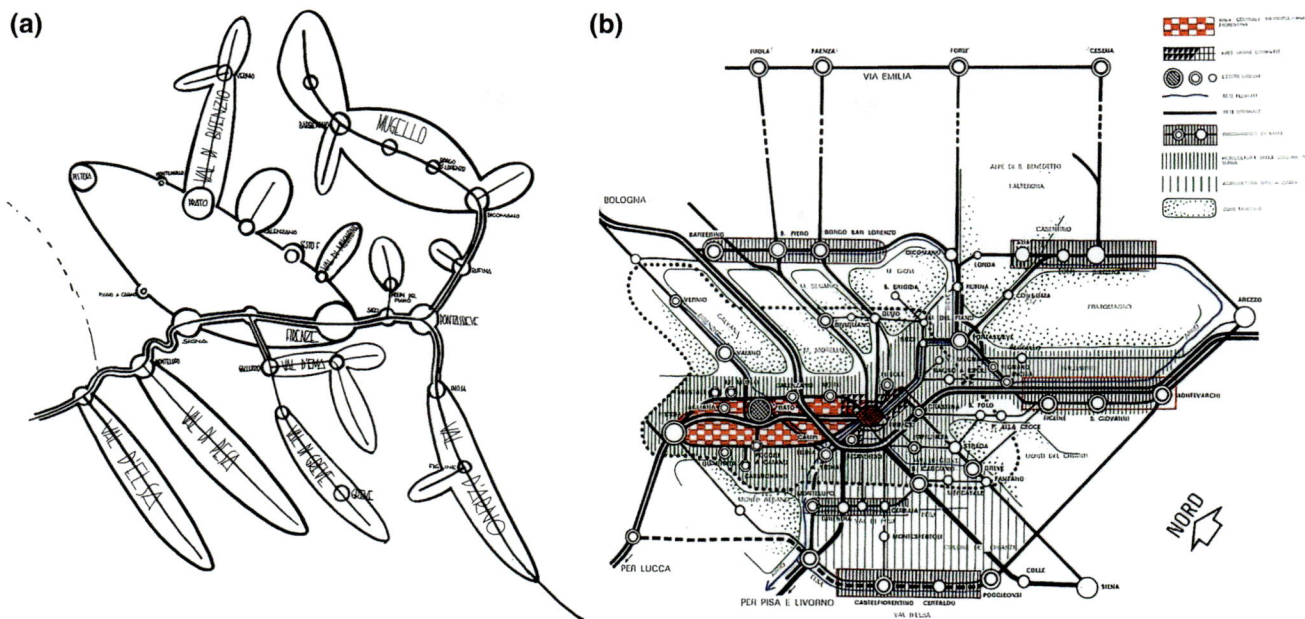

Fig. 18.5 a Studies for the Florentine inter-municipal plan. Urbanization scheme and morphology of the valleys, 1973; **b** Studies for the Florentine inter-municipal plan, Territorial framework, 1973

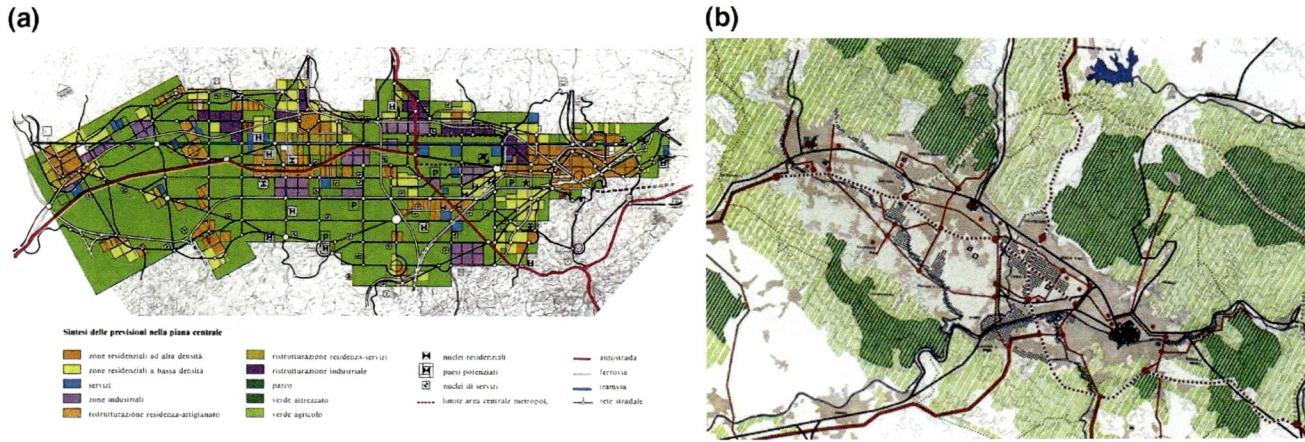

Fig. 18.6 a Florentine inter-municipal plan. Second part of the work, summary of the vision for the central plain, 1978; **b** Tuscany region: Proposal for a Structural Scheme for the Florence–Prato–Pistoia plain, external territorial references, 1990

After this Guideline image (Fig. 18.4b), a second phase of preparatory studies was put in place, albeit with the contribution of an essential graphic highlighting the morphological identity of the Florentine region and the role of the Arno and of the intermountain basins and valleys in the structuring of the settlement's organization (Fig. 18.5a, b). The final ideogrammatic image from 1978 (Fig. 18.6a), produced to describe the vision of a better infrastructural and functional layout of the plain, is substantially isolated from the hilly context and ignores the canonical cartographic orientation, aligning the horizontal plane to denote a polycentric and at the same time unitary structure. This image, although it was never approved by the region or by local and inter-municipal authorities, acted as a guideline for the positioning of enhancement infrastructures such as the railway axes, parks and industrial parks in the cities of Sesto Fiorentino (part of the first belt of Florence) and the city of Prato, along the highway.

Thanks to these great infrastructures, since the 1980s, the Florence–Prato–Pistoia area, viewed from a residential, structural and environmental perspective, constitutes a united geographical area. Nevertheless, it is intersected and fragmented by too many physical and institutional caesuras, from municipal boundaries to transport viability infrastructures and the persistent tendency to aggregate the interventions in a "polar" way around the three main centres, without any overall coordination. Precisely for this reason, in 1988 the Tuscany region implemented a policy of coordination between local institutions in order to achieve a coordinated territorial plan. This gave rise to the Structural Scheme for the metropolitan area of Florence, Prato and Pistoia, under the guidance of a recognized master of Italian urbanism: Giovanni Astengo. The Structural Scheme was approved by the Regional Council in 1990 (Fig. 18.6b), with Regional Act no. 212 (Astengo 1990). It had the double merit of highlighting the metropolitan problem in Tuscany and, at the same time, tracing the territorial features identifying a group of twenty municipalities falling within the Florentine area, concerning the Florence–Prato–Pistoia area.

The idea was to shift the centre of gravity of planning and regional planning—in the absence of explicit national sector laws—towards a conceptual representation of the region coinciding with a problem area. This was achieved by producing a different model predicting a spatial development trend for the interprovincial basin between Florence and Pistoia, which was affected by the relocation of the production system and tertiary sector processes. It was also necessary to tackle the increasingly evident congestion of the infrastructural networks, including the motorway running through the area (De Luca and Summer 1991). For the first time, there was a large metropolitan area that extended over a territory of two provinces and a central heart, the plain from Florence to Pistoia (Fig. 18.6b). This is the economic "heart" of Tuscany with 41% of the population, 46% of employment in services and 47% of the industrial sector. The Tuscany region's political choice immediately clashed with national law no. 142, approved that same year, 1990. This national law on local government on the one hand foresaw the birth of the metropolitan city of Florence and its surrounding area, and on the other established the Province of Prato. The result was that the previous set up of the area as a whole region was lost despite a separate management in charge of three provinces (Firenze, Prato and Pistoia), each institution in charge of a planning instrument. The structural scheme, nevertheless, is still active and was resumed as a policy document for territorial policies until the entry into force of the metropolitan city under Law 56/2014.

This was the context against which the 2015 visioning process evolved.

18.5   A Vision for the Metropolitan City of Florence

Since its operational definition on 1 January 2015, the lack of correspondence between the administrative boundaries of the metropolitan city of Florence—lying within the boundaries of the Province of Florence (42 municipalities) as established by Law 56/2014—and its functional urban area has been evident to administrators, citizens and regional scientists (De Luca and Lingua 2015). The metropolitan city includes some territories with a strict historical and territorial identity, such as Chiantishire in the southeast, the Mugello mountains to the northeast, and an already-in-place union of 11 municipalities in the Elsa Valley (southwest), headed by the municipality of Empoli. Conversely, the socio-economic gravitational area extends in the opposite direction, to the neighbouring provinces of Prato and Pistoia in the Pisa–Florence development system, and has been the focus of previous regional planning instruments and economic programming strategies.

As its functional axis is perpendicular to the institutional one (Fig. 18.3), the case of the metropolitan city of Florence has become a paradigmatic example of the paradoxes of the Italian institutional reorganization. The boundary of the metropolitan city, not seizing on the socio-economic and functional trends that emerge in the densely populated settlements seamlessly joining the three cities of Florence, Prato and Pistoia, includes municipalities from the northeast to the southwest whose territories and settlements have strong historical roots and are perceived to be "outside" and "other" than Florence.

As a matter of fact, citizens, politicians and policy makers have difficulty in conceiving of the metropolitan city as a unitary cooperative institution. The stakeholders' difficulty in defining the metropolitan area and its problems became apparent during the participatory process launched under the slogan "Together for the plan" at the beginning of the planning process in November 2015, after the establishment of a Scientific Committee in charge of guiding and coordinating the strategic planning process.

Aside from these institutions and the mayor of Florence, who is also governor of the metropolitan city, most politicians from the other 41 municipalities involved were hesitant to participate, and citizens only referred to the metropolitan dimension when considering the impact of infrastructures that were already the focus of ongoing conflicts (airport enlargement, incinerator localization and the high-speed railway station). At the beginning of 2016, the strategic plan was conceived of as a "collection" of projects without localization or a spatial dimension. Since then, spatial analyses and regional studies have been conducted to define strategic projects to be implemented, but an ambition and vision for the metropolitan city was lacking (Lingua 2018). In March 2016, conscious of this need, the metropolitan city of Florence signed a Memorandum of Understanding with the *Regional Design Lab* of Florence University's Architecture Department (DIDA), the aim of which was to define the image of the metropolitan city, both today and in the near future (2030), applying a regional design process.

So that the actual image of the city could be defined by identifying diverse scenarios of its current state and trends in the metropolitan area, relying on its historical role and evolution, a large number of regional studies (provided by previous regional and urban plans and programmes, as well as ad hoc spatial analyses and regional studies) were made available (see Sect. 18.4). These analyses were combined with both design-related knowledge expressly produced for the strategic plan by active research organizations and institutions, primarily diverse departments of Florence University, and the results of the participative process "Together for the plan".

The process of defining current scenarios and trends has led to the synergistic and integrated consideration of projects and practices (stories) found at two different design scales: micro and macro. During the participatory process, storytelling about current and evolving projects and practices gave visibility to the "micro-stories" within small areas of the metropolitan territory and community. These concerned thematic actions, for instance, to enhance ancient grain supply chains in the Empoli countryside or the "milk streets" in the Mugello area. They also concerned the activation of solidarity networks in the core cities as well as in small villages, and forms of co-housing and co-living practices. These micro-stories intersected with the "macro-stories" concerned with the supra-local scale, where institutional public projects, as well as semi-public and private projects involving public services, were identified. Macro-stories covered a range of topics such as the metropolitan city's position in global world economics, the strengths and weaknesses of public transport, the promotion of start-ups through incubation and acceleration processes, and the definition of metropolitan agricultural parks.

In the overall framework both types of stories were combined: while the macro-stories derive from statutory, traditional planning, the micro-stories relate to tactics and are conceived of as operational actions (Lingua 2018). The joint consideration of macro- and micro-stories led to the definition of different ways to live inside the metropolitan dimension, to perceive it and to develop socio-economic activities within the metropolitan city. These different perceptions were represented in diagrammatic language through the metaphor of "rhythms" (see Fig. 18.7). In the musical field, this word refers to an ordered succession of sounds that repeat over time according to a certain frequency. This rhetorical device has been adopted to reflect the complexity of territories and to visually translate the relationship between micro- and macro-stories into current dynamics that represent the characteristics and identity of the area. Each area has been associated with a musical tempo (very lively, lively, etc.), which confers substantial diversification but does not assign any value attribution: the adjective "fast/slow" does not express dichotomous readings of positive/negative judgement, nor an evolutionary evaluation. It rather refers to different and distinct ways of living in and perceiving the metropolitan city: fast and slow are not development trends, but lifestyles defining the difference between different development trends (Chiantishire is always linked to slow food and a nature-led countryside life, while the north-west fashion retail area is characterized by fast rhythms linked to innovation dynamics). This is why, in certain cases, the rhythms overlap: this means that in the same area different rhythms can coexist and interact with each other on the same frequencies. In this case, they enter into resonance, and this allows distinct elements to enter into dialogue and build relations. As a result, the metaphor of rhythms enhances both the distinctive features of an area and synergistic relationships, as well as forms of constructive dialogue within the other metropolitan areas.

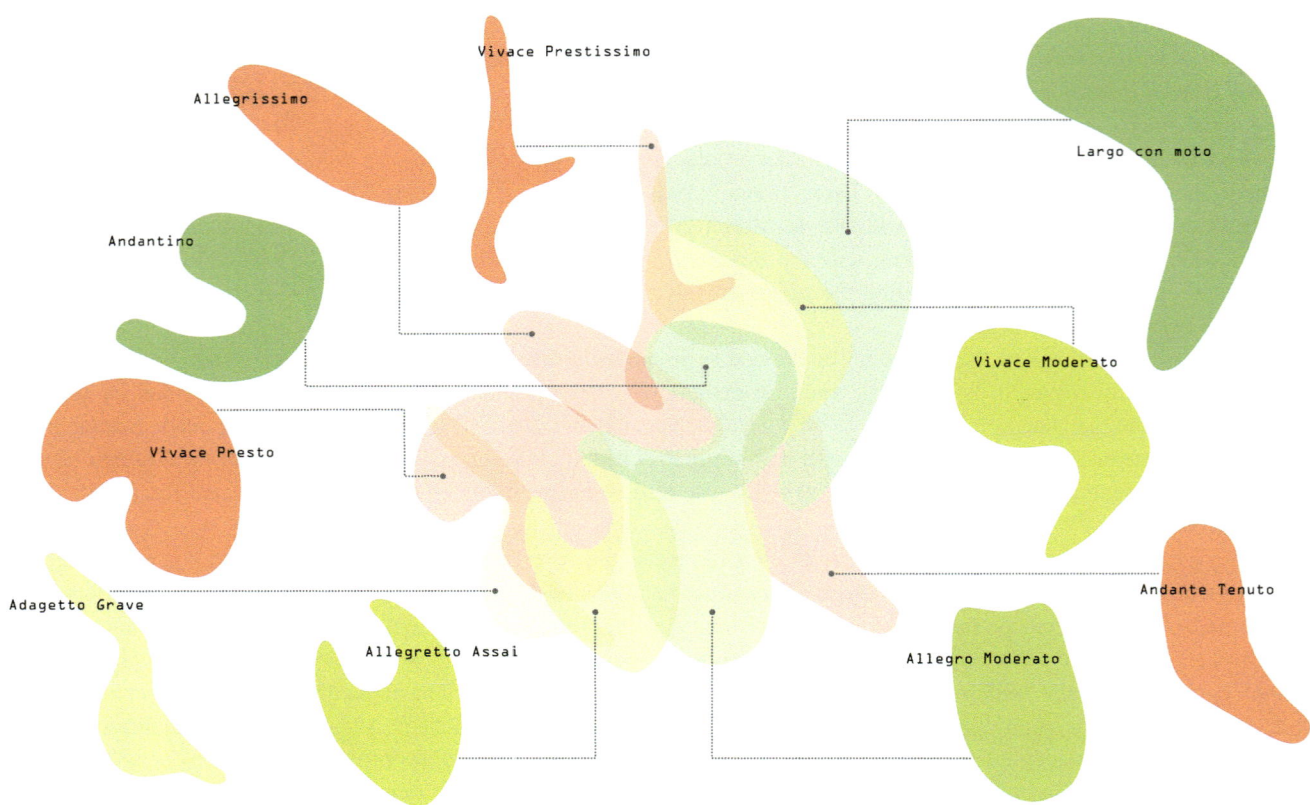

Fig. 18.7 Strategic plan for the metropolitan city of Florence. "Metropolitan Territorial Rhythms" (Città Metropolitana di Firenze 2017b)

From a methodological perspective, metropolitan rhythms are the final result of a proactive reading of the territory intended to join variable geometries coming from both the "paradox" of the institutional reform and functional and socio-economic trends. To avoid the mismatch between the institutional boundaries of the metropolitan city, coinciding with the former province of Florence, and the functional urban area historically developed along the interprovincial basin from Florence to Prato and Pistoia, a 100×100 km^2 area has been used as the ground to define both current trends and future scenarios. This frame covers the entire area defined both by the institutional and functional metropolitan areas. Within this square, rhythms find spatiality through figurative language with a strong symbolic connotation obtained through operations of compositional selection and abstract synthesis of geo-localized elements. Those examined involved four macro-fields of interest: accessibility to the territory, landscape and land use, economic and productive dynamics and urban conditions. The definition of spatial areas with different rhythms derived from a multi-criteria analysis attempting to assimilate and summarize the plurality of physical elements and dynamics of the complex Florentine metropolitan reality, involving natural, anthropic and physical elements of greater relevance, cooperative governance networks and their related soft planning spaces, was combined with indicators concerned with the measurement of "Fair and Sustainable Development". Rhythm represented the ground where ongoing and future projects in different fields (mobility, urban renewal, innovation, etc.) were identified. The weak and overlapping borders of the areas have shifted the discussion from the boundary and possible aggregation of municipalities to projects to be carried out together in order to achieve better livability, both in the specific sub-region and in the whole metropolitan area. As a matter of fact, the issue of accessibility was treated in the participative process in reference to nimby conflicts concerning great infrastructures, such as the enlargement of the airport in a ring city and the localization of the high-speed train station in the core city. The discourse on universal accessibility and "slow" life rhythms in peripheral areas shifted the discussion to the train system and led to the definition of a strategy concerned with the metropolitan use of the actual railway lines. Moreover, the metaphor of different rhythms to achieve harmony has been perceived as the proper way to approach the issue of the cohabitation of diverse historical and territorial identities (Mugello, Chiantishire, Empoli) that do not really feel part of the metropolitan area.

Moreover, the presence of multiple and even overlapping rhythms (polyrhythm) has been presented to the metropolitan council and the stakeholders involved as a qualifying factor for the metropolitan system. The metaphor was made to suggest the need to find harmony within the whole territory through three strategic visions (Universal accessibility, Widespread opportunities, Land of well-being) aimed to bring about a new "Metropolitan Renaissance" evoking the image of a cultural rebirth of the Florentine territory, referred not only to the UNESCO site or the core city but to the entire metropolitan city. Both the strategies and the final mission were represented starting with rhythms and composing them into a sole image of the future of Florence in 2030 (Fig. 18.8a).

The strategic plan was approved by the council of the metropolitan city of Florence in April 2017. Since then the "Metropolitan Renaissance" as a narrative device has started to be cited in political discourses and in diverse stakeholder projects. This emerged in both June and December 2018, respectively, at the presentation of "The General States" of the metropolitan city and when the first monitoring of the implementation of the strategic plan went ahead 18 months after its approval. For this last event, the image of the strategic plan's mission, "Metropolitan Renaissance," was printed on a 4 × 4 m square placed on the ground in front of the metropolitan council, and each mayor of the municipalities included within the metropolitan city was asked to sign it. This was a metaphorical appropriation of the Strategic Plan's mission by the institutions forming part of the metropolitan city. Moreover, the "Metropolitan Renaissance" metaphor was represented on the cover of the planning documents as a "Vitruvian man" opening his legs and arms to embrace the whole metropolitan area (Fig. 18.8): this image circulated on social networks and the news because of its immediate capacity to be understood as an extension of the renaissance to the whole territory of the metropolitan city.

(a)　　　　　　　　　　　　　　　　　　**(b)**

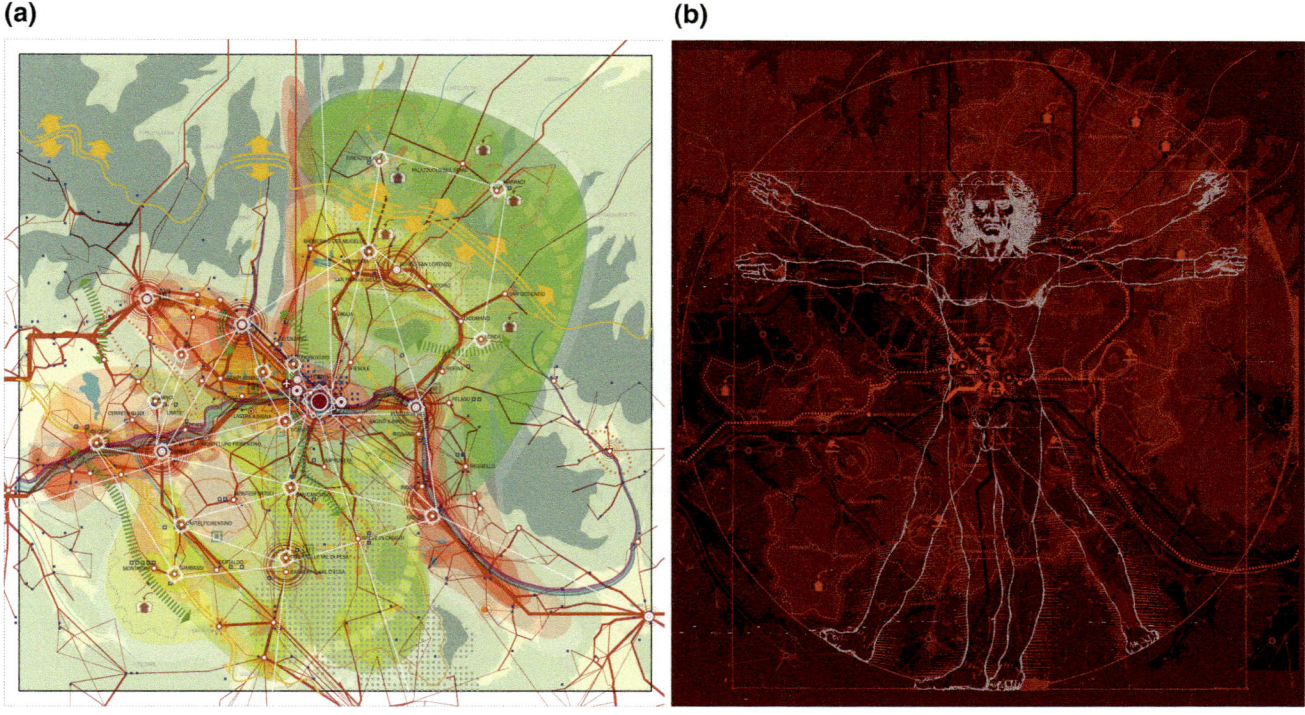

Fig. 18.8 Strategic plan for the metropolitan city of Florence: final vision of the "Metropolitan Renaissance", **a** map and **b** metaphorical image on the cover of the documents (Città Metropolitana di Firenze 2017b)

18.6 Conclusion

The current uncertainty in strategic planning in Italy, brought about by Law 56/2014, is emblematically represented by the case of the strategic plan for the metropolitan city of Florence. The strict correspondence between the metropolitan city as a new second-level institution and previous provincial boundaries, established by this new law, gives rise to the paradoxical mismatch between administrative limits and metropolitan spatial specificities, functional trends and settlements. The national law does not address the functional and collaborative spaces defined by polycentric governance, and they are not even addressed at local level (Cremaschi et al. 2015). Yet this is the crucial point: in order to address the issue of the most appropriate forms of governance for strategic planning across local administrative boundaries, coordinating strategic supra-local policies and actions, the strategic planning process should illustrate how the metropolitan area works, its functions and connected organizational models, as well as their incorporation into the region (Messina 2014).

This was a challenge in a context like the Florentine one, where both the administrators and citizens involved in the participatory process seemed unfamiliar with "metropolitan" thinking and struggled to conceive of the metropolitan city as a unitary institution. In this context, the "administrative" paradox and the lack of a shared perception of the metropolitan city of Florence as one coherent organism was tackled by the group in charge of defining the strategic plan by using regional design as a method to make the metropolitan city visible and legible and to build up institutional capacity through a visioning process. In the strategic plan for the metropolitan city of Florence, regional design was conceived of as a suitable method to approach the definition of the dimension and dynamics of the metropolitan city and to define a shared vision, summarizing in few representations the strategic policies and objectives defined by the metropolitan community. Representations of the actual size and trends of the metropolitan city, as well as its future, assumed an important role in the definition of the strategic plan, the actual results of which can be fully assessed at the end of the current implementation phase in terms of the communicative and argumentative effectiveness of spatial representations and concepts.

The base of the representation, a 100×100 km^2 transcending boundaries dictated by law was capable of matching the administrative limits with an already-existing relational area and of opening a governance relations event up to the neighbouring provinces of Prato and Pistoia. Within this area, from a methodological perspective, the metaphorical device of "metropolitan rhythms" represents a way to display the complexity of the territory and to visually transpose the project elements deriving from different areas with their specificities. It answered the need for spatial representations to assist in the analytical process of co-producing knowledge and, simultaneously, aid policy definitions through their spatial transposition.

Through this device, the partition of the metropolitan area has been approached through a dynamic reading of the territory, based on traditional and new parameters such as the perception of livability, accessibility and the speeds of the metropolitan region. This reading has showed a composite reality in perpetual change that could hardly be fully explained through a fixed and rigid image (descriptive/interpretative dimension).

The narration and communication of actual and future projects through the metaphor of slow vs cheerful rhythms has shifted the debate from the administrative boundary to how to coordinate and make small and large scale projects operative in different areas (discursive dimension).

Finally, the definition, through these projects, of the whole strategic vision for the metropolitan area has moved within the framework of a place-based approach (design dimension). For this purpose, the "realm of the unsaid" (Fini and Pezzoni 2011: 93) was captured in the micro-stories that emerged through the participatory process and were matched with local and supra-local projects. The metaphor of rhythms represented the basis to construct direct dialogue between the plurality of actors involved in the planning process and for its communication to a wider non-expert audience and led to debate on ways to find harmony between the different parts of the metropolitan areas with diverse local and historical identities.

The final visions arrived at through this discussion were represented both as metaphorical and ideogrammatic representations of the future of the whole metropolitan area, drawing on the heritage of images produced historically in the studies carried out in the second half of the last century on an inter-municipal scheme. In this vein, the three strategic visions proposed in the strategic plan extend across the metropolitan city boundaries (concerning the functional area of Prato and Pistoia) and aim to direct attention towards a recognizable and unifying image of the metropolitan city by representing a dynamic territory in which "[…] the strategic metropolitan plan represents the platform for the implementation of shared policies and projects" (Città Metropolitana di Firenze 2017a: 17, author's translation).

The case of the metropolitan city of Florence is not exhaustive of the Italian experience, but it has played a role in recent Italian debates on institutional reform at a time when it was halted by the 2016 referendum and now needs to be reviewed. De Luca and Moccia (2017) argue that this could represent a best practice of strategic planning due to both the method, based on regional design theories and practices, and the results and timing (just one year) to define the whole vision for the metropolitan city and approve the plan. This was the second plan approved in Italy, after the Metropolitan City of Milan. This chapter has defined the elements that turned this experience into a best practice, evidencing that the use of spatial representations in the framework of a regional design approach can respond to two main needs. On the one hand, visioning answers the need to define an overall picture of the metropolitan area, extending out of and crossing institutional boundaries and capable of systematically integrating multiple projects at different scales, with a regional but place-based approach. On the other hand, the visioning process has reduced the complexity of a broad area by continuously shifting between different scales (micro and macro), even though the use of metaphors capable of challenging stakeholders' imaginations and conveying a strategic vision that, while ensuring comprehensive consistency, can be recognized as a common and collective reference.

References

Ache PM (2013) Between Vision and response capacity—configuring metropolitan development. Radboud Universiteit Nijmegen, Nijmegen, 12 June 2013

Astengo G (ed) (1990) Schema strutturale per l'area metropolitana Firenze, Prato, Pistoia. Quaderni di Urbanistica Informazioni 7. INU, Roma

Balz VE (2018) Regional design: discretionary approaches to regional planning in The Netherlands. Plan Theory 17(3):332–354

Balz VE, Zonneveld WAM (2015) Regional design in the context of fragmented territorial governance: south wing studio. Eur Plan Stud 23 (5):871–981

Bobbio R, Lombardini G (2017) La Città metropolitana di Genova. In: De Luca G, Moccia FD (eds) Pianificare le città metropolitane in Italia. INU edizioni, Roma, pp 39–56

Città Metropolitana di Firenze (2017a) Piano strategico metropolitano. Atlante di piano. Mimeo, Firenze

Città Metropolitana di Firenze (2017b) Piano strategico metropolitano. Verso il Piano strategico metropolitano. Mimeo, Firenze

Cremaschi M, Delpirou A, Rivière D, Salone C (2015) Métropoles et régions entre concurrences et complémentarités: Regards croisés France/Italie. Planum Publisher, Roma-Milano

Davoudi S (2003) European Briefing: Polycentricity, in European spatial planning: from an analytical tool to a normative agenda. Eur Plan Stud 11:979–999

Davoudi S (2011) The legacy of positivism and the emergence of interpretive tradition in spatial planning. Reg Stud, 46:429–441

De Luca G (2016) The paradigmatic case of the Metropolitan City of Florence. Procedia. Soc Behav Sci 223:108–112

De Luca G (2017) La Città metropolitana di Firenze. In: De Luca G, Moccia FD (eds) Pianificare le città metropolitane in Italia. INU edizioni, Roma, pp 207–240

De Luca G, Summer M (1991) Lo Schema strutturale per l'area metropolitana Firenze-Prato-Pistoia. In: Indovina F (ed) La ragione del piano. Giovanni Astengo e l'urbanistica italiana. Franco Angeli, Milano, pp 121–144

De Luca G, Lingua V (2015) Programmare o pianificare i territori delle città metropolitane? Il caso di Firenze tra vision spaziali e processi di trasformazione economico-produttiva. In Atti della Conferenza Nazionale SIU. Italia 45-'45, vol 1. Radici, Condizioni, Prospettive, Planum Publisher, Territori dell'economia, Roma-Milano, pp 233–239

De Luca G, Moccia FD (eds) (2015) Immagini di territori metropolitani. INU edizioni, Roma

De Luca G, Moccia FD (eds) (2017) Pianificare le città metropolitane in Italia. Interpretazioni, approcci, prospettive. INU Edizioni, Roma

Dühr S (2007) The visual language of spatial planning. Exploring cartographic representations for spatial planning in Europe. Routledge, Abingdon

EMA (2015) Conclusion del seminari sobre competitivitat territorial I cohesió social de les metròpolis europees. Barcelona. http://www.amb.cat/documents/11696/2235908/CON_EMA_Barcelona2015_CAT+web.pdf/fddee475-c2cd-405e-abc0-a25198c2bc20

Faludi A (1996) Framing with images. Environ Plan 23(1):93–108

Förster A, Balz V, Thierstein A, Zonneveld W (2016) The conference shaping regional futures: mapping, designing, transforming! A documentation. Munich, Delft

Fini G, Pezzoni N (2011) The Antwerp *structure plan*. A new planning language for the twenty-first century city. Urbanistica 148:90–98

Friedmann J, Weaver C (1979) Territory and function: The evolution of regional planning. Edward Arnold, London

Gabellini P (2010) Fare urbanistica. Esperienze, comunicazione, memoria. Carocci, Roma

Gabellini P, Proli S, Tondelli S (2017) La Città metropolitana di Bologna. In: De Luca G, Moccia FD (eds) Pianificare le città metropolitane in Italia. Interpretazioni, approcci, prospettive. INU Edizioni, Roma, pp 159–206

Gambino R (2000) Le rappresentazioni come scelte di valore. In: Marson A (ed) Rappresentanza e rappresentazione nella pianificazione territoriale. Atti del seminario, Venezia 1999. IUAV—D.A.E.S.T. http://www.iuav.it/daest/pubblicazioni/uno2000.html

Glasson J, Marshall T (2010) Regional planning. Routledge, Abingdon

Healey P (2007) Urban complexity and spatial strategies. Towards a relational planning for our times. London, Routledge

Healey P (2009) In Search of the "Strategic" in Spatial Strategy Making, Planning Theory & Practice, 10(4):439-457

Lingua V (2017) Cambiamenti di paradigma: il Regional Design per progettare l'area vasta. In: Atti della XIX Conferenza Nazionale SIU. Cambiamenti. Responsabilità e strumenti per l'urbanistica al servizio del paese, Catania 16–18 giugno 2016, Planum Publisher, Roma-Milano, pp 1891–1898

Lingua V (2018) Regional design for strategic planning: a vision for the metropolitan city of Florence. In: Velo L, Pace M (eds) Utopia and the project for the city and territory. Officina edizioni, Roma, pp 158–164

Lucchesi F (2007) Visualizzazione, pre/visione e scenari: una ipotesi interpretativa. In: Magnaghi A (ed) Scenari strategici. Visioni identitarie per il progetto di territorio. Alinea, Firenze, pp 47–64

Magnaghi A (ed) (2007) Scenari strategici. Visioni identitarie per il progetto di territorio. Alinea, Firenze

Mascarucci R (ed) (2004) Vision. Meltemi, Roma

Messina P (2014) Innovazione del policy making per lo sviluppo locale ed europeizzazione. Il caso del Veneto. In: D'Amico R, De Rubertis S (eds) Istituzioni per lo sviluppo tra Comune e Regione. Unione europea e prove di ente intermedio in Italia. Franco Angeli, Milano

Ministero del Bilancio e della Programmazione Economica - MBPE (1970) Progetto 80. Rapporto preliminare al programma economico nazionale 1971/1975, con introduzione e note a due voci per l'avviamento ad un civile dibattito a cura di Giorgio Ruffolo e Luciano Barca. Sansoni, Firenze

Neuman M (1996) Images as institution builders: metropolitan planning in Madrid. Eur Plan Stud 4(3):293–312

Paasi A (2009) The resurgence of the 'Region' and 'Regional Identity': theoretical perspectives and empirical observations on regional dynamics in Europe. Rev Int Stud 35:121–146

Rein M, Schön D (1993) Reframing policy discourse. In: Fisher F, Forester J (eds) The argumentative turn in policy analysis and planning. UCL press, London, pp 145-166

Renzoni C (2012) Il Progetto'80. Un'idea di Paese nell'Italia degli anni Sessanta. Alinea, Firenze

Secchi B (2003) Progetti, visioni, scenari. Planum. J Urban. http://www.planum.net/topics/secchi-diario.html

Secchi B, Viganò P (2009) Antwerp. Territory of a new modernity. SUN, Amsterdam

Thierstein A, Förster A (eds) (2008) Making mega-city regions visible!. Lars Müller Publishers, Baden

Velo L, Pace M (eds) (2018) Utopia and the project for the city and territory. Officina Edizioni, Roma

Viganò P (2009) Prefazione. In: Costa A, Fabian L, Pellegrini P, Bozzuto P (eds) Storie del futuro. Gli scenari nella progettazione del territorio. Officina Edizioni, Roma

Viganò P, Pellegrini P, Fabian L, Munarin S, Tosi MC (2017) La Città metropolitana di Venezia. In: De Luca G, Moccia FD (eds) Pianificare le città metropolitane in Italia. Interpretazioni, approcci, prospettive. INU Edizioni, Roma, pp 123–157

Zonneveld W (2008) Visioning and visualizing. Experience from the Northwest European mega-city region. In: Thierstein A, Förster A (eds) (2008) Making mega-City Regions Visible! Lars Müller Publishers, Baden

Zonneveld W, Verwest F (2005) Tussen Droom en Retoriek [Between Dreams and Rhetorics]: De conceptualisering van Ruimte in de Nederlandse Planning. NAI Uitgevers, Rotterdam

Conclusion

19

Valeria Lingua and Verena Balz

Abstract

The strategic spatial planning experience led to the uncovering of the typical mechanisms involved in addressing conflicts that emerge as a result of spatial development. The main aim of the book is to identify interrelations between *governance rescaling*—the responsiveness of planning collaboration to the tensions and dilemmas that arise—and *designing and visioning*, i.e. the consideration of spatial imaginaries during planning procedures. The experiences provided in this book prove that these mechanisms enhance each other: design-led approaches influence the formation of governance and enhance hard and soft governance integration; vice versa, governance rescaling is enhanced by visioning and the visualisation of (new) planning spaces through 'travelling images'. Interrelations between them provide a set of interesting propositions for further research. Firstly, the assumption that regional design plays a role in governance models makes interaction between actors central. Modes of co-governance gain relevance in the attempt to understand how regional design performs in governance rescaling and scalar (re)structuration processes. A second proposition concerns the ability of design to bridge gaps between different forms of planning and planning frameworks. Due to its explorative and reflexive nature, it may have the particular ability to contribute to consolidating planning with different degrees of formality, at different levels of scale and/or focused on different planning sectors.

Keywords

Regional design • Governance rescaling • Visioning • Soft governance • Travelling images

19.1 The Spatial Dimension of Governance Rescaling

The strategic spatial planning experience led to the uncovering of the typical mechanisms involved in addressing conflicts that emerge as a result of spatial development. This book seeks to increase our understanding of two of these mechanisms: *governance rescaling*—the responsiveness of planning collaboration to the tensions and dilemmas that arise—and, under the header '*designing and visioning*', the consideration of spatial imaginaries during planning procedures. The main aim of the book is to identify interrelations between governance rescaling, designing and visioning. Its proposition is that these mechanisms enhance each other: that design-led approaches influence the formation of governance and, vice versa, that governance rescaling is enhanced by visioning and the visualisation of (new) planning spaces. As our field of inquiry is not fully established, we took an explorative approach to the composition of this book. We asked scholars and practitioners from the fields of spatial planning, governance, geography and design to investigate our broad proposition by using their particular experience, expertise and knowledge. The contributions in the book are divided into three parts. Part 1 contains reflections on theoretically founded interrelations between spatial planning, governance and design. Part 2 focuses on governance

V. Lingua (✉)
Regional Design Lab, Department of Architecture, University of Florence, via P.A. Micheli 2, 50121 Florence, Italy
e-mail: valeria.lingua@unifi.it

V. Balz
Department of Urbanism, Delft University of Technology, Delft, The Netherlands
e-mail: v.e.balz@tudelft.nl

© Springer Nature Switzerland AG 2020
V. Lingua and V. Balz (eds.), *Shaping Regional Futures*,
https://doi.org/10.1007/978-3-030-23573-4_19

rescaling processes with contributions that investigate the institutional reforms that occurred through shifts in power, competencies and reference scales in Europe, paying particular attention to how these reforms involved notions of specific spatial conditions and development in regions. Part 3 investigates designing and visioning practices and reflects on how these practices relate to ongoing planning and governance processes. Below we summarise the notions supported by a range of authors in all sections of the book. At times, we supplement these shared notions with references to additional literature. In the final section, we briefly reflect on the implications of the notions for further research.

19.1.1 Changing the Motivations Underlying Governance Rescaling Processes

In many European countries, a shift in planning scales and roles has occurred in recent years, taking on different forms and generating a variety of results. The contributions in this book show that a general trend concerns the up-scaling of co-operation, reflected in the enlargement of existing regional territories. This has occurred in France, Denmark and Italy. The purpose of these 'scalar re-structuration' processes (Galland, *ivi*) has changed with respect to previous decades. Before, regionalisation processes and the definition of city regions aimed to achieve the coordinated use of resources and efficient policy implementation, but now it is about competitiveness. This is evident in France, where the highly publicised ambition of the reforms was to create gigantic regional actors capable of handling international competition between territories (Desjardins and Geppert, *ivi*), and in Denmark, where the recentralisation of government and the formation of five administrative regions sought primarily to cater to regional development by fostering economic growth in close connection with business development, rather than regional planning per se (Galland 2012 and ivi).

19.1.2 A Variety of (New) Planning Instruments

Scalar re-structuration processes have generated a need for new or adapted planning instruments at different institutional levels. The contributions in this book indicate a variety of approaches to the implementation of revised territories. In France, new regional spatial plans have become compulsory; a development that seems 'out of synch' (Jouen 2015: 13) in an EU panorama in which regional plans are conceived of as indicative frameworks. However, the binding powers and comprehensive nature of the new regional plans (SRADETT) confirm a trend in Southern Europe. Regional planning also became compulsory in other southern EU countries. In Italy, new regional plans are an instrument for defining the landscape structure of regions, but, as in Portugal, these regional spatial plans are detached from issues such as development and growth (Cavaco and Costa, *ivi*). A different trend can be observed in Northern Europe: the need for regional plans seems to be questioned, as the revoked regional spatial strategies in England and the new growth strategies in Denmark demonstrate. These new planning instruments are associated with bottom-up multi-stakeholder forms of governance at both regional level (perceived as 'fields for partnership creating', as noted by Wilgaard Larsen (2017)) and inter-municipal level. Their main emphasis is on collaboration and partnership. Finally, in England, the revocation of the regional spatial strategies and the introduction of the notion of strategic planning were intended to take into account the co-governance attitudes of municipalities and already-in-place partnerships across local boundaries. In such different panoramas, questions about what has caused these varieties arise.

19.1.3 Matching Scales of Spatial Development and the Territorial Scope of Governance

Governance rescaling processes have brought a set of critical aspects to the fore. One particularly important aspect for this book is the relationship between the newly established territories and spaces where autonomous spatial development evolves. A functional region can be perceived as a regional network shaped by dynamic material and immaterial flows between places (Thierstein and Förster 2008; Glasson and Marshall 2007). Analyses of current rescaling processes indicate that the boundaries established by new regional institutions are often divorced from areas that are defined by such dynamic flows. A set of chapters discuss this missing correspondence in depth. The 2015 definition of French mega-regions is, for instance, discussed as 'a missed opportunity to improve the regions' geographic relevance' (Geppert and Desjardins, *ivi*). The same observation is made about the new Italian metropolitan areas. Here, the 'metropolitan city' was embraced as a great institutional innovation after decades of inertia. However, the correspondence between the ten metropolitan regional capital cities and the previous provincial boundaries created a paradox (De Luca et al., *ivi*): in many cases, administrative boundaries do not correspond to functional dynamics, being too large (Turin), too tiny (Naples) or even completely shifted with respect to the metropolitan urban system and related identities (Florence).

19.2 Political and Economic Implications of Using Geographies

Territorial partitions cannot be explained only in reference to functional relationships or administrative concerns. The cases presented in this book show that the political game matters too. On the one hand, the policy of merging administrative boundaries (municipal territories all over Europe, as well as regions in France and Denmark) reflects the apprehension of secessionist movements spreading across Europe over the last decade (Jouen 2015). On the other hand, these reforms have sought to create powerful regional actors capable of handling national and international competition between territories. In the light of these arguments, a spatial rationale is not enough to explain changes in governance and institutional architecture. The planning culture of each country (Nadin and Stead 2008; Knieling and Othengrafen 2009) and broader political movements seem to be factors too. Neoliberalism is for instance a phenomenon that has evidently affected both the review of statutory planning systems and strategic planning practices (Olesen 2014). As an example, the rhetoric of competitiveness, reflecting a general appreciation of neoliberalisation, characterised the Danish reform in 2007 as well as the revocation of regional spatial strategies in England in 2011. In Denmark, spatial concepts aligned with globalisation agendas have led to the identification of growth corridors and dynamic zones of integration at regional level. At city level, a shift from urban hierarchies to functional settlement areas occurred, triggering new forms of territorial governance. In England, the introduction of a new scale of governance (the city region) has led to two claims concerning, respectively, the failings of previous devolution settlements and the potential of the new planning scale (city-regional planning) and the connected redistribution of powers across scales. These claims tend to reflect the political thinking at the time on both the amount of power that central governments are willing to devolve and—as a consequence—the interrelations between central and local government (Allmendinger and Haughton 2010; Haughton et al. 2013, Haughton, *ivi*).

19.2.1 The Co-existence of (or Tensions Between) Soft and Hard Planning

Some authors in this book use the concept of 'soft planning' to reflect on governance rescaling and on the flexibility—or 'softness'—of spatial planning frameworks and how this likewise fosters governance-led or state spatial selectivity. They discuss how hard and soft planning modes complement and influence one another, e.g. during the formalisation of visions. Cavaco and Costa (*ivi*) note that in Portuguese practice, there is still a clear boundary between the two modes, despite general consensus on the need to provide an interface between statutory tools and territories and non-binding strategic frameworks. This is due to both the division of responsibilities between different administrative levels and sectors and the attitude of planners. Other authors observe that tensions arise when soft planning and visioning practices become institutionalised and compulsory. As reported by Limonov and Batchaev (*ivi*), strategic planning in Russia was first initiated from the bottom-up thanks to the experience of the 1997 St. Petersburg' strategic plan. Since 2014, when strategic planning processes became a formal obligation at all levels in Russian legislation, this innovation has posed problems in terms of consistency between plans at different levels and sectors. The authors envisage two possible ways to resolve these problems. They argue that strategic plans should become more indicative (or soft) or, on the contrary, that they should become more detailed and prescriptive to strengthen their capability to instruct implementation. This contradiction reflects the incongruity between soft strategic and hard planning frameworks. It points to the need to clearly define the status and role of governance-led approaches in a hierarchical formalised planning system. Similar issues are at stake in Italy, where strategic planning became compulsory for 10 major metropolitan cities in 2014 after two decades of experimenting with strategic planning as a voluntarist practice (Servillo and Lingua 2014). This has led to some paradoxes: the 'strategic metropolitan plan' as a new planning instrument overlaps with previous provincial plans and has to find a new role within previous planning at all levels. In the case of the Metropolitan city of Florence, the strategic plan has been made accountable through the use of regional design methodologies (De Luca et al., *ivi*). In both cases, the gap is between the communicative and collaborative nature of a strategic planning process and the need to institutionalise its results, so that it becomes part of formal planning documents to be adopted and implemented by public authorities.

19.3 Regional Design and Visioning in Governance Rescaling

19.3.1 The Common Ground of Practices

A central ambition of strategic spatial planning is to consider the specificities of the built environment in planning decision-making and to coordinate the involvement of actors who appreciate this environment in different ways. Spatial representations are consequently both a core instrument and outcome of design-led approaches to planning and governance. Spatial representations involve 'collective understandings of socio-spatial relations that are performed by, give sense to, make possible and change collective socio-spatial practices. They are produced through political struggles over the conceptions, perceptions and lived experiences of place' (Davoudi 2018: 101). Design is a practice where 'the seeming objectivity of a consensual design world is not a given but an achievement, a product of the work of communicative inquiry' (Schön 1988, p. 183). Many contributions in this book embrace these two notions, in particular by drawing on theories about spatial concepts, metaphors, discourses, narratives and frameworks. This points to a social-constructionist perspective forming the most commonly shared ground upon which interrelations between governance rescaling, designing and visioning evolve.

19.3.2 Spatial Imaginaries in Governance Rescaling

When associated with governance, the instrumental use of spatial representations gains prominence. Depictions of geographies in the form of maps, models and text are then aimed at 'accumulating sufficient allocative, authoritative and imaginative force to shape both the materialities and identities of particular places' (Healey 2006, p. 527). The contributions to this book indicate that the pragmatic use of designs and visions involves a broad variety of conditional factors. The 2010 UK Localism Act gave local planning authorities more freedom to define the scales of strategic spatial planning interventions. In Greater Manchester—referred to as a best practice in this context—new spatial imaginaries emerged only after a compromised framework was formalised due to intense public pressure (Haughton, *ivi*). An analysis of Dutch regional design practices shows that their performances were shaped, in particular, by the actors who were to judge the relevance of design proposals for formal planning decisions (Balz et al., *ivi*). In Italy, Germany and Switzerland design and visioning approaches were deliberately embedded into formally required spatial planning processes, aiming to establish higher-tier authorities and related strategic planning frameworks. The performances of design and visioning practices were strongly confined by the tactical role of representations in these processes (Gilliard et al., *ivi*, Schindler, *ivi*, De Luca et al., *ivi*). Several authors discuss how initially unintentional designs gained organisational meaning after having been placed in a given planning context. They stress that their evocative power evolves against the background of historically rooted territorial conceptions (see, e.g., Pisano et al., *ivi*, Vigano, *ivi*). In conjunction, the contributions show that the performances of designing and visioning practices—aimed at supporting the emergence of new spatial representations—are highly responsive to a given institutional context. Two notions stand out. Firstly, it seems that the degree of 'softness' of prevailing planning frameworks influences the emergence of new imaginaries. A high degree of softness or flexibility thereby does not necessarily result in creativity and new representation. Imaginative thinking in the realm of governance may also be triggered —deliberately or not—by discontent about 'hard' rigid planning. Secondly, it seems that designing and visioning practices perform well in terms of creating new ideas about the built environment when they are closely and explicitly associated with new organisational or institutional imaginations, e.g. new planning instruments, authorities, forms of co-operation, matches between hard and soft planning approaches or, most fundamentally, a change of planning systems. This notion implies that designing, visioning and governance rescaling processes are co-generative processes.

19.3.3 A Process-Perspective on Design

Regional design is presented in this book as a planning practice capable of reconciling a variety of actors' perspectives. Design may lead to the combination of different organisational political and analytical stances, sector interests or disciplinary knowledge. The authors, in particular, stress its ability to synthesise insights into spatial development at different spatial scales, thus positioning the development of local places in the context of regional and supra-regional development (see in particular Dehaene, *ivi*). Its ability to integrate different actors' perspectives leads several authors to conceive of regional design as a methodology that seeks to improve planning processes (in particular Gillard et al., *ivi*, Kempenaar, *ivi*, Förster, *ivi*). A set of procedural qualities are related to this notion. Design-led approaches are perceived to contribute to comprehensive decisions, given their holistic nature. Due to an intense use of visualisations, they are associated with accountability. Because design practices are often collaborative endeavours, they are related to legitimacy. A set of issues arise from perceiving designing and visioning as planning procedures. The perception involves a 'transformative' perspective on spatial development (Gillard et al., *ivi*) and also emphasises the reflexivity of planning procedures. In essence, it implies that demands for governance rescaling are a natural outcome of design-led planning procedures.

19.4 Perspectives: A Research Agenda

What is meant by design and visioning performances in governance rescaling? Which key aspects of governance determine the performance of designing and visioning? The aim of this book was to provide some answers to these questions by making interrelations between designing, visioning and governance rescaling the central focus. The experience, expertise and knowledge presented in this book have advanced the reflection on this relationship. The reflections help to direct further research on the role of regional design in spatial planning and governance rescaling, as well as on the contribution of regional designers as advocates of this form of interstitial planning.

19.4.1 Enhancing Hard and Soft Planning Integration: A Focus on Interaction

Soft planning spaces are defined by collaboration between public and private stakeholders, organisations and institutions. They have different degrees of formality and involve many different formulas and degrees of validation (Torfing et al. 2012). When formally required plans pass through statutory approval procedures, soft planning practices are often expected to affect these procedures: to align plans with particular spatial and organisational circumstances in regions and areas. Multiple interactions between hard and soft forms of planning emerge as a consequence. The analyses presented in this book indicate that the attempts to manage these relationships are ambiguous and incongruent. Soft planning practices are, for instance, made compulsory. Voluntarist and non-formalised soft planning practices are used to tackle institutionalised forms of governance in place, in another instance. In order to explore the resulting changes in governance modes, as well as the associated changes in planning territories and instruments, we propose reading governance rescaling processes through the lens of *interactive governance*. This concept shifts the focus from distinct forms of governance to *interaction* between forms of governance and related institutions. Interactive governance relates to both hierarchic and co-governance modes and refers explicitly to their interconnections, seeking to explain the emergence of new planning strategies by continuous reflexivity between hard and soft planning spaces.

A shift towards interaction opens up interesting perspectives for unravelling the aforementioned challenges. Two propositions come to the fore: firstly, recognition of the relative position of a process and the actors involved provides a better understanding of the interrelations between the different stakeholders and the objectives they pursue. In particular, it helps when looking at the horizontal and vertical interrelations between the different governance modes in order to verify where (even explicit) situations of meta-governance emerge and where and when soft-governance processes manage to influence hierarchical governance and its tools. Secondly, the ways in which soft-governance processes have influenced the formalised planning instruments can be explored by evaluating the performance of interaction. In interaction between hard and soft planning, performance may be reflected in changing decision-making processes, resources and responsibilities, as well as in changing regional frames of reference and fields of action.

19.4.2 Assessing the Role of Images in the Realm of Governance: Travelling Images

A focus on interactive governance opens up a second avenue for further research, concerned with changes in the discourses and narratives that underlie the perception of regions. Based on the contributions in this book, it can be assumed that an understanding of the changing spatial representations used during interactive governance processes allows for a deeper understanding of how different governance and planning processes—soft and hard—influence each other. Observations show that there are a variety of mechanisms at work during the production and use of planning geography. Resulting images point at their transformation during a 'travelling' process: their continuous adaptation to the requirements that result from and enable interaction.

Notions about the scales and facets of regions incorporated into images become appropriated in a context of multiple actors. Moreover, this process of visualisation is often not casual, but is expressly conceived to change actors' minds. Images represent carefully staged suggestions for new approaches to spatiality. 'Travelling metaphors' (Albrechts et al. 2003; Healey 2006; Hyvärinen 2013) are from time to time purposefully used to approach cities, city regions and regions from a different perspective. The concept of travelling images and framing ideas implies a set of suggestive research questions about the performance of images in interaction. A first question concerns how images travel from different planning and institutional levels (from bottom to top and back) and between different planning arenas (from soft to hard and back) and how they change while absorbing the actors' preferences and narratives. A second question regards the role of the planner. A planner is required to demonstrate 'knowledgeability, imaginative skill, courage and ethical sensibility' (Healey 2009: 454), exercise critical yet sensitive judgement and be able to gain trust (Mäntysalo 2013). When perceiving travelling images as instruments through which planners adapt planning and governance approaches, questions concerning good and accountable use in decision-making arise.

19.4.3 Understanding the Role of Regional Design in Governance

Visions and visioning practices are a long-standing ingredient of strategic spatial planning (Albrechts 2004). An understanding of regional design practice seems to have the capacity to complement and deepen existing knowledge on the role and functioning of these spatially expressed normative agendas in decision-making. Compared to visioning, regional design is a more explorative, reflexive process. The authors of this book recognise that such exploration can result in new spatial planning dynamics, including governance rescaling processes. A set of explanations stand out when considering how design causes such dynamics. (1) Design-led approaches make a region visible. Spatial representations of the spatial planning object —the built environment and the social actions that shape this environment—may introduce new analytical knowledge, political values and/or territorial concerns. The contributions make it apparent that representations are in particular connected to strategic framing processes that involve 'intense simplification and selectivity' (Healey 2009: 449). (2) When used in the realm of governance, regional design relates to institutional and organisational capacity (see also Neuman and Zonneveld 2018). While visioning practices rely on built consent, regional design practice embodies a broader, more procedural perspective. Practices recognise that capacity building may involve confrontational political decision-making processes, in particular when territorial implications are at stake. (3) Regional design is a creative practice. The dynamics it causes may come as a surprise at times; they may be due to unforeseen and unplanned associations of spatial imaginaries instead of fully rational argumentation. (4) Regional design performances within the realm of spatial planning are enabled by an existing planning and governance context. Planning instruments, the formality of planning frameworks, hierarchical governance and soft planning spaces are factors that determine the performances of regional design, among others. There is strong recognition that regional design draws on existing reservoirs of meaning. Design theorists note that design is 'a relatively simple set of operations carried out on highly complex structures, which are themselves simplified by 'theories' and modes of representation' (Hillier and Leaman 1974, p. 4).

When combining this perception of design with notions of governance, a set of propositions for further research come to the fore. Firstly, the assumption that regional design plays a role in governance models that make interaction between actors central. Modes of co-governance gain relevance in the attempt to understand how regional design performs in governance rescaling and scalar (re)structuration processes. A second proposition concerns the ability of design to bridge gaps between different forms of planning and planning frameworks. Due to its explorative and reflexive nature, it may have the particular ability to contribute to consolidating planning with different degrees of formality, at different levels of scale and/or focused on different planning sectors.

19.5 Final Remarks

Spatial planning seeks to tackle tensions between spatial and collaborative planning rationales. Governance rescaling processes are linked to changes in horizontal and vertical co-operation, leading to the redistribution of responsibilities, roles and resources among actors and territories. They reside within a collaborative planning rationale. Designing and visioning concern the consideration of geographies in planning and are thus involved in introducing a spatial rationale into planning processes. The contributions in this book demonstrate that both governance rescaling and designing/visioning are intricate and complex mechanisms. Interrelations between them provide a rich field for further investigation. Finally, we would like to point out that engaging with this field requires an open mindset. Design and spatial planning draw on fundamentally different cultures concerning both research and practice. Designers and planners not only draw on different theories, but they also speak different languages, one based on graphic representations and the other text. Moreover, their approaches to the resolution of the problems encountered are substantially different. Designers tend to use solutions to understand the problems; planners build paths from a problem definition to a solution. The authors of this book have engaged in the adventurous endeavour of combining these disciplines. We believe that any new investigations require a similar open mind and adventurous attitude.

References

Albrechts L (2004) Strategic (spatial) planning reexamined. Environ Plan B 31:743–758

Albrechts L, Healey P, Kunzmann K (2003) Strategic spatial planning and regional governance in Europe. J Am Plan Assoc 69(2):113–129

Allmendinger P, Haughton G (2010) Spatial planning, devolution, and new planning spaces. Environ Plan C Gov Policy 28:803–818

Davoudi S (2018) Policy and practice spatial imaginaries: tyrannies or transformations? Town Plan Rev 89(2):97–124

Galland D (2012) Is regional planning dead or just coping? The transformation of a state sociospatial project into growth-oriented strategies. Environ Plan C: Gov Policy 30(3):536–552

Glasson J, Marshall T (2007) Regional planning. Routledge, London

Haughton G, Allmendinger P, Oosterlynck S (2013) Spatial planning and the new localism. Plan Pract Res 28(1):1–5

Healey P (2006) Relational complexity and the imaginative power of strategic spatial planning. Eur Plan Stud 14:525–546

Healey P (2009) In search of the "strategic" in spatial strategy making. Plan Theory Pract 10:439–457

Hillier B, Leaman A (1974) How is design possible? J Arch Plan Res 3(1):4–11

Hyvärinen M (2013) Travelling metaphors, transforming concepts. In: Hatavara M, Hydén LC, Hyvärinen M (eds) The travelling concepts of narrative. Jhon Benjamins, Amsterdam, pp 13–42

Jouen M (2015) The new French Regions, from a European standpoint. Policy paper 150, Notre Europe Jacques Delors Institute. Available https://institutdelors.eu/wp-content/uploads/2018/01/pp146-frenchRegionsfromeujouenjdinov2015.pdf. Accessed 18 June 2018

Knieling J, Othengrafen F (eds) (2009) Planning cultures in Europe. Ashgate, Farnham

Mäntysalo R (2013) Coping with the paradox of strategic spatial planning. disP 49(3):51–52

Nadin V, Stead D (2008) European spatial planning systems, social models and learning. disP 44(172):35–47

Neuman M, Zonneveld W (2018) The resurgence of regional design. Eur Plan Stud 26(7):1297–1311

Olesen K (2014) The neoliberalisation of strategic spatial planning. Plan Theory 13(3):288–303

Schön DA (1988) Designing: rules, types and words. Des Stud 9:181–190

Servillo L, Lingua V (2014) The innovation of the Italian planning system: actors, path dependencies, cultural contradictions and a missing epilogue. Eur Plan Stud 22(2):400–417

Thierstein A, Förster A (eds) (2008) The image and the region. Making mega-city regions visible. Lars Müller Publishers, München

Torfing J, Guy P, Pierre J, Sørensen E (2012) Interactive governance. Advancing the paradigm. Oxford University Press

Wilgaard Larsen P (2017) Delineating partnerships from other forms of collaboration in regional development planning. Int Plan Stud 22(3):242–255